Road Atlas

USA   CANADA   MEXICO

ROAD MAPS *are organized geographically.* United States, Canada, and Mexico road maps are organized in a grid layout, starting in the northwest of each country. To find your way, use either the **Key to Map Pages** inside the front cover, the **Listing of State and City Maps** on page 3, or the **index** in the back of the atlas.

COUNTRY COLORS
Colors represent countries throughout the atlas.
Red → Canada
Green → Mexico
Blue → United States
Purple → United States (Northeast Corridor)

MAP SCALES
Scale bars are shown at a constant length throughout the atlas for quick and easy scale comparison between regions.

DRIVING DISTANCES
Use this chart to check driving distances between major cities within each map. Refer to distance and driving time information at the back of the atlas for travel over greater distances.

LOCATOR MAPS
A quick glance at this miniature map lets you check which states and/or provinces are shown on each page.

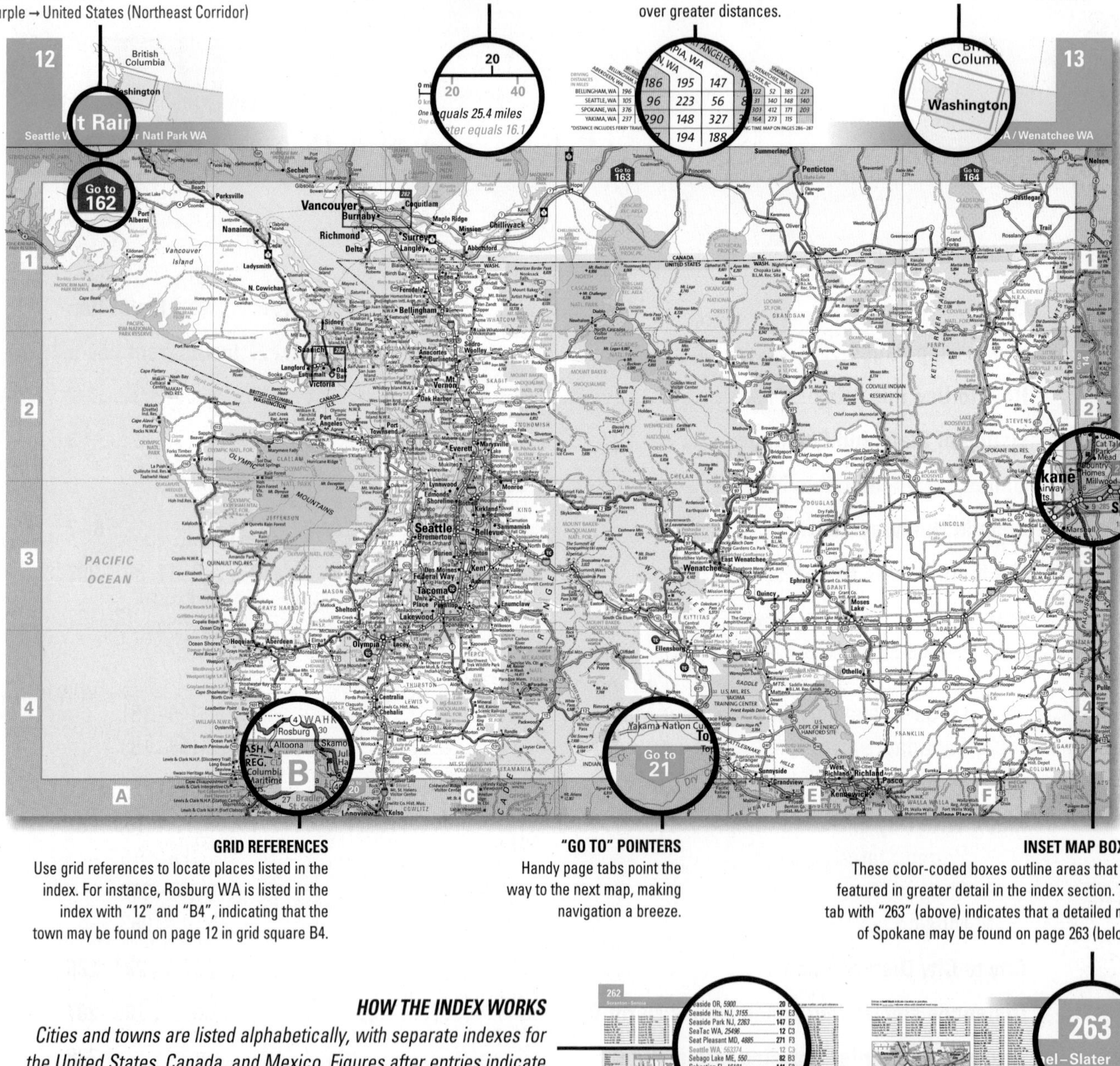

GRID REFERENCES
Use grid references to locate places listed in the index. For instance, Rosburg WA is listed in the index with "12" and "B4", indicating that the town may be found on page 12 in grid square B4.

"GO TO" POINTERS
Handy page tabs point the way to the next map, making navigation a breeze.

INSET MAP BOXES
These color-coded boxes outline areas that are featured in greater detail in the index section. The tab with "263" (above) indicates that a detailed map of Spokane may be found on page 263 (below).

HOW THE INDEX WORKS
Cities and towns are listed alphabetically, with separate indexes for the United States, Canada, and Mexico. Figures after entries indicate population, page number, and grid reference. Entries in bold color indicate cities with detailed inset maps. The U.S. index also includes counties and parishes, which are shown in bold black type.

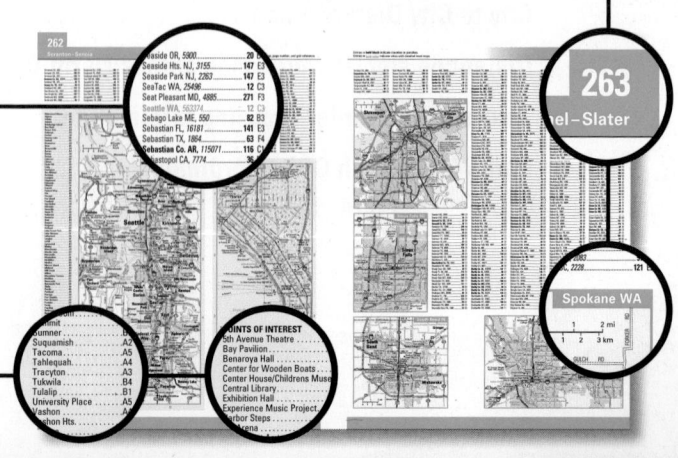

INSET MAP INDEXES
Many inset maps have their own indexes. Metro area inset map indexes list cities and towns; downtown inset map indexes list points of interest.

0 mi   125   250   375
0 km 125 250 375 500
One inch equals 217 miles
One centimeter equals 138 kilometers

Canada Highway Map

0 mi 200 400
0 km 200 400 600

One inch equals 250 miles/Un pouce équivaut à 250 milles
One cm equals 159 km/Un cm équivaut à 159 km

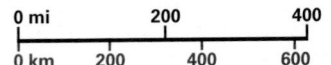

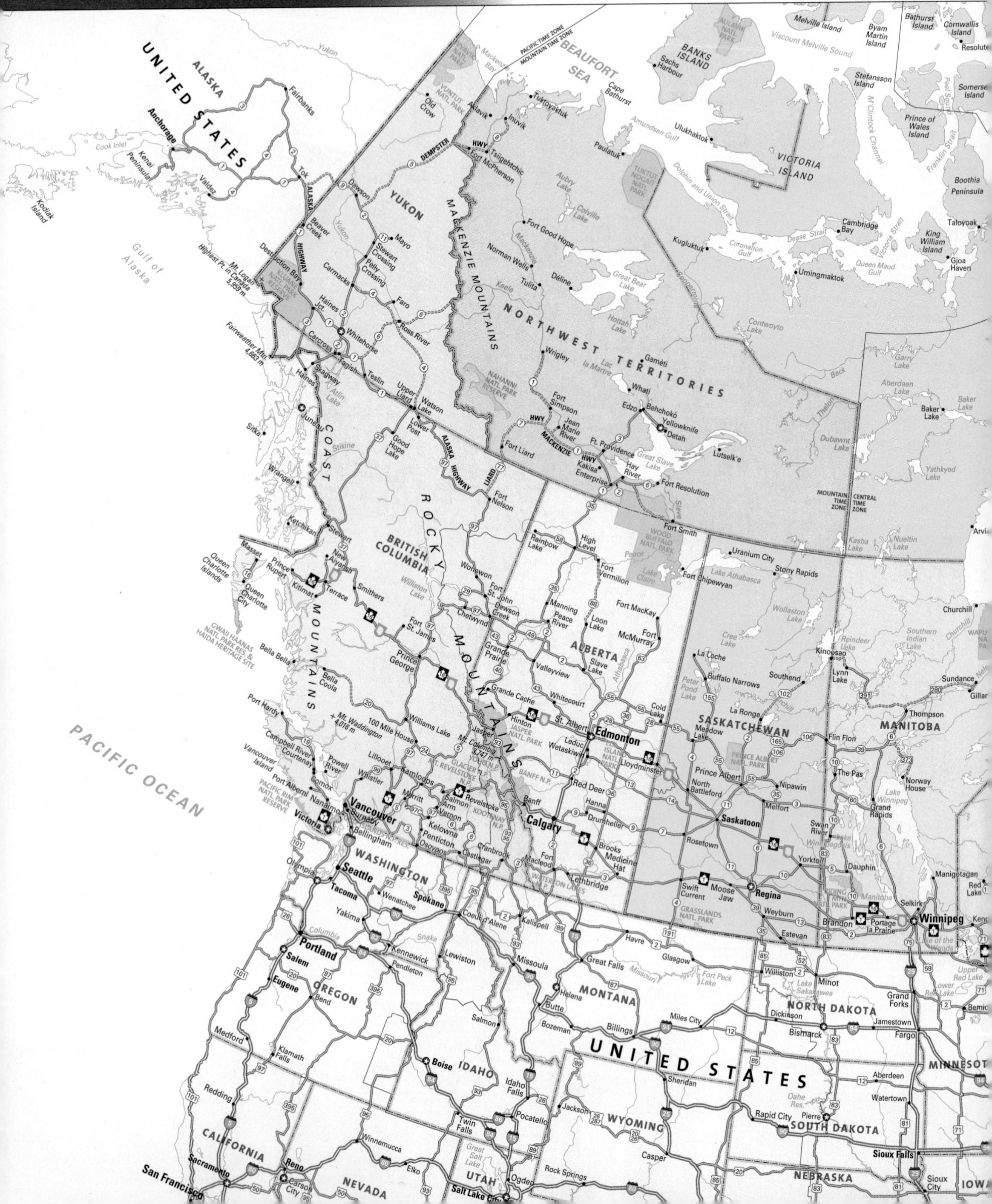

Michelin Scenic Drives

Experience the thrill of the open roads of North America with these great Scenic Drives from Michelin. The famous star ratings highlight natural and cultural attractions along the way.

★★★	Highly recommended
★★	Recommended
★	Interesting

Michelin Scenic Drives are indicated by a green and yellow dashed line (▬▬▬▬) on corresponding atlas maps for easy reference. The following 16 drives are also plotted for your use. The maps are found on the pages listed to the right.

US SCENIC DRIVES

Coastal Carolinas★★	115, 123, 275, 237, 131, 200, 261
Florida's Northeast Coast★★	222, 139, 141, 232
Florida Panhandle★	265, 137, 136, 247
Hill Country★★	192, 61, 60, 257
Litchfield Hills★★	148, 94
Napa Valley/Sonoma★★	36
New Jersey Pine Barrens★	191, 147, (105, 104)
North Coast/Mendocino★★	259, 36
San Juan Country★★	40
Snake River Valley★	221, 23, 22, 196, 30
Southern New Mexico★	211, 56, 226, 48, 49, 57
Willamette Valley★	251, 20, 257, 212

CANADA SCENIC DRIVES

Alberta Badlands★★★	277, 164, 165
Annapolis Valley/Atlantic Shore★★	180, 181, 277
Saint John River Valley★★	277, 180, 178
Thompson Canyon★	282, 163

Note that sections of the routes described, particularly those through high elevations or wilderness areas, may be closed in winter.

🚗 NORTHWEST DRIVING TOURS

ANCHORAGE/FAIRBANKS/DENALI★★★

892 miles/1,436 kilometers   Maps 189, 154, 155

From **Anchorage**★, Alaska's largest city, take Rte. 1 (Glenn Hwy. and Tok Cutoff) N and then E through the

Caribou, Denali National Park

© Andrew Coleman/iStockphoto.com

broad Matanuska Valley to the small town of Tok. The route passes agricultural communities, the Matanuska Glacier and the Wrangell Mountains before heading up the Copper River Basin. From Tok, take the Alaska Hwy. (Rte. 2) NW to **Fairbanks**★, a friendly town with a frontier feel. The road passes the **Trans-Alaska Pipeline** and **Big Delta SHP,** then parallels the Tanana River. From Fairbanks, opt for Rte. 3 W that crosses the river at Nenana, then veers S to **Denali NP**★★★, home of spruce forests, grassy tundra, grizzlies, moose and North America's highest peak, **Mount McKinley** (20,320ft). Return S to Anchorage via Rtes. 3 and 1.

BADLANDS★★

164 miles/264 kilometers   Maps 253, 26

From **Rapid City**★, South Dakota, drive SE on Rte. 44 through Farmingdale and Scenic, then east to Interior. To enter **Badlands NP**★★, take Rte. 377 NE 2mi to Cedar Pass and stop at the park's **Ben Reifel VC**. From there, **Cliff Shelf Nature Trail**★★ (.5mi) is popular for its shady juniper trees, and **Castle Trail**★★★ (5mi) is spectacular in early morning when the moonscape valley and pointed spires get first light. Turn left onto Rte. 240, **Badlands Loop Road**★★★, along the northern rim, where prairie grasslands give way to buttes and hoodoos. **Pinnacles Overlook**★★ is a sweeping

viewpoint to the south. Drive N to I-90, and cross the interstate N to the town of Wall. On Main St. visit **Wall Drug**★, a "drug store" tourist attraction with over 20 shops filled with historical photos, cowboy regalia, wildlife exhibits and Western art displayed in five dining rooms. In the backyard a roaring, 80ft **Tyrannosaurus** sends toddlers running. Leave Wall on I-90, driving W. Take Exit 67 to Ellsworth Air Force Base, where the **South Dakota Air and Space Museum** displays a B-1 bomber and other aircraft. Continue W on I-90 back to Rapid City to conclude the tour.

BLACK HILLS★★

244 miles/393 kilometers   Maps 253, 26, 25

From **Rapid City**★, drive S on US-16, then US-16A S past Keystone. Take Rte. 244 W to **Mount Rushmore NM**★★. Continue W on Rte. 244 to the junction of US-16/385. En route S to Custer, **Crazy Horse Memorial**★★ honors the famous Sioux chief. From Custer, head S on US-385 through Pringle to the junction of Rte. 87. Take Rte. 87 N through **Wind Cave NP**★★ and into **Custer SP**★★. Follow **Wildlife Loop Road**★★ (access S of Blue Bell, across from Rte. 342 junction) E and N to US-16A. Then travel W to join scenic **Needles Highway**★★ (Rte. 87) NW to US-16/385 N. Where US-16 separates, continue N on US-385 to **Deadwood**★★, a former gold camp. Turn left onto US-14A, driving SW through **Lead**★, site of the former **Homestake Gold Mine**★★, to Cheyenne Crossing. Drive N on US-14A to I-90, turning SE back to Rapid City.

COLUMBIA RIVER GORGE★★

83 miles/134 kilometers   Maps 251, 20, 21

From **Portland**★★, Oregon's largest city, take I-84 E to Exit 17 in Troutdale. There, head E on the winding

Abbreviations

N	North	Rte.	Route	NPR	National Park Reserve
E	East	Mi	Miles	NRA	National Recreation Area
S	South	Km	Kilometers	NWR	National Wildlife Refuge
W	West	Sq Ft	Square Feet	PP	Provincial Park
NE	Northeast	NHS	National Historic Site	SHP	State Historical Park
NW	Northwest	NL	National Lakeshore	SHS	State Historic Site
SE	Southeast	NM	National Memorial/	SP	State Park
SW	Southwest		National Monument	SR	State Reserve
Hwy.	Highway	NMP	National Military Park	VC	Visitor Center
Pkwy.	Parkway	NP	National Park		

Historic Columbia River Highway★★ (US-30), which skirts the steep cliffs above the river. For great **views**, stop at **Vista House at Crown Point**★. You'll pass the 620ft **Multnomah Falls**★★ and the sheer stone walls of **Oneonta Gorge**. At Ainsworth State Park (Exit 35), rejoin I-84 and travel E to Mosier (Exit 69), where US-30, with its hairpin turns, begins again. Continue E on US-30, stopping at **Rowena Crest Viewpoint**★★ for grand vistas—and wildflowers. Just past the Western-style town called **The Dalles**, take US-197 N to conclude the tour at **The Dalles Lock and Dam VC**★★.

GRAND TETONS/YELLOWSTONE★★★

224 miles/361 kilometers   *Map 24*

⊚ *Note: parts of this tour are closed in winter.*
From **Jackson**★★, drive N on US-26 to Moose. Turn left onto Teton Park Rd. to access **Grand Teton NP**★★★ and **Jenny Lake Scenic Drive**★★★. From Teton Park Rd., drive N to the junction of US-89/191/287 (**John D. Rockefeller Jr. Memorial Pkwy.**) and follow the parkway N into **Yellowstone NP**★★★ to **West Thumb**. Take Grand Loop Rd. W to **Old Faithful**★★★, the world's most famous geyser. Continue N on the Grand Loop Rd., passing **Norris Geyser Basin**★★ en route to **Mammoth Hot Springs**★★★. Turn E on Grand Loop Rd. to Tower Junction, then S into the **Grand Canyon of the Yellowstone**★★★. Continue S from Canyon Village through **Hayden Valley**★★ to Lake Junction. Head SW, back to West Thumb, to conclude the tour.

PACIFIC COAST/OLYMPIC PENINSULA★★★

419 miles/675 kilometers   *Maps 245, 12*
From the Washington state capital of **Olympia**, drive N on US-101 (Pacific Coast Scenic Byway) to Discovery Bay. Detour on Rte. 20 NE to **Port Townsend**★★, a Victorian seaport. From Discovery Bay, head W on US-101 through **Port Angeles** to the **Heart O' the Hills** park entrance for **Olympic NP**★★★ to see **Hurricane Ridge**★★. Back on US-101, head W, then S to the park entrance leading to **Hoh Rain Forest**★★★. Follow US-101 S, then E after Queets to **Lake Quinault**★, home to bald eagles, trumpeter swans and loons. Continue S on US-101 to Aberdeen, taking Rte. 105 to the coast. At Raymond, return to US-101 S to **Long Beach**. Follow Rte. 103 N past the former cannery town of **Oysterville** to **Leadbetter Point SP**★ on Willapa Bay, where oysters are still harvested. Return S to **Ilwaco** and drive E and S on US-101 to **Astoria**★, Oregon, to end the tour.

THE OREGON COAST★★

368 miles/592 kilometers   *Maps 20, 28*
⊚ *Various construction projects along US-101 may cause driving delays.*

Leave **Astoria**★, Oregon's first settlement, via US-101, heading SW. **Fort Clatsop National Memorial**★★ recalls Lewis and Clark's historic stay. **Cannon Beach**★ boasts a sandy **beach**★ and tall coastal rock. At the farm community of **Tillamook**★, go west on 3rd St. to **Cape Meares** to begin **Three Capes Scenic Drive**★★. Continue S, rejoining US-101 just beyond Pacific City. Drive S on US-101 through **Newport**★, then **Yachats**★, which neighbors **Cape Perpetua Scenic Area**★★. From **Florence** to **Coos Bay**★ stretches **Oregon Dunes National Recreation Area**★★. At Coos Bay, take Cape Arago Hwy. W to see the gardens of **Shore Acres State Park**★. Drive S on Seven Devils Hwy. and Beaver Hill Rd. to rejoin US-101. Pass **Bandon**★, known for its cheese factory, and **Port Orford**, with its fishing fleet. Farther S, **Boardman State Park**★ shelters Sitka spruce, Douglas fir and **Natural Bridge Cove**. End the tour at **Brookings**.

🚗 SOUTHWEST DRIVING TOURS

BIG BEND AREA★★

581 miles/935 kilometers   *Maps 211, 56, 57, 62, 60*
Head S from **El Paso**★ via I-10, then E to Kent. Take Rte. 118 S to Alpine, passing **McDonald Observatory**★★ (telescope tours) and **Fort Davis NHS**★★. Continue S to Study Butte to enter **Big Bend NP**★★★, edged by the Rio Grande River and spanning 1,252sq mi of spectacular canyons, lush bottomlands, sprawling desert and mountain woodlands. The park has more species of migratory and resident birds than any other national park. Travel E on Maverick Dr. to the main VC at **Panther Junction** in the heart of the park (US-385 and Rio Grande Village Dr.). Then take US-385 N to Marathon. Turn E on US-90 to Langtry, site of **Judge Roy Bean VC**★. Continue E to **Seminole Canyon SP**★★, with its 4,000-year-old pictographs. Farther E, **Amistad NRA**★★ is popular for water sports. Continue on US-90 to conclude the tour in Del Rio.

CANYONLANDS OF UTAH★★★

481 miles/774 kilometers   *Maps 39, 40*
From **St. George**★, drive NE on I-15 to Exit 16. Take Rte. 9 E to Springdale, gateway to **Zion NP**★★★, with its sandstone canyon, waterfalls and hanging gardens. Continue E on Rte. 9 to Mt. Carmel Junction, turn left onto US-89 and head N to the junction with Rte. 12. Take Rte. 12 SE to **Bryce Canyon NP**★★★, with its colored rock formations. Continue SE on Rte. 12 to Cannonville, then S on Kodachrome Dr. to **Kodachrome Basin SP**★★, where sandstone chimneys rise from the desert floor. Return to Cannonville, and drive NE on Rte. 12 through

Boulder to Torrey. Take Rte. 24 E through **Capitol Reef NP**★★—with its unpaved roads and trails—then N to I-70. Travel E on I-70 to Exit 182, then S on US-191 to Rte. 313 into **Canyonlands NP**★★★ to **Grand View Point Overlook**. Return to US-191, turning S to access **Arches NP**★★★ — the greatest concentration of natural stone arches in the country. Continue S on US-191 to **Moab**★ to end the tour.

CENTRAL COAST/BIG SUR★★★

118 miles/190 kilometers   *Maps 236, 44*
From **Cannery Row** in **Monterey**, take Prescott Ave. to Rte. 68. Turn right and continue to Pacific Grove Gate (on

Balancing Rock, Big Bend National Park

©Eric Foltz/iStockphoto.com

your left) to begin scenic **17-Mile Drive**★★, a private toll road. Exit at Carmel Gate to reach the upscale artists' colony of **Carmel**★, site of Carmel **Mission**★★★. The town's **Ocean Avenue** meets the turquoise waters of Carmel Bay at **Carmel City Beach**★★. Leave Carmel by Hwy. 1 S. Short, easy trails at **Point Lobos SR**★★ line the shore. Enjoy the wild beauty of the **Big Sur**★★★ coastline en route to San Simeon, where **Hearst Castle**★★★, the magnificent estate of a former newspaper magnate, overlooks the Pacific Ocean. Continue S on Hwy. 1 to **Morro Bay**, where the tour ends.

COLORADO ROCKIES★★★

499 miles/803 kilometers   Maps 209, 41, 33, 40
Note: US-34 (Trail Ridge Rd.) and Rte. 82 S of Leadville to Aspen are closed mid-Oct to Memorial Day due to snow.
From **Golden**★, W of **Denver**★★★, drive W on US-6 through Clear Creek Canyon to Rte. 119, heading N on the **Peak to Peak Highway**★★ to **Nederland**★. Continue N on Rte. 72, then follow Rte. 7 to the town of **Estes Park**★. Take US-36 to enter **Rocky Mountain NP**★★★. Drive **Trail Ridge Road**★★★ (US-34) W and S to the town of **Grand Lake**★. Continue S to Granby, turn left on US-40 to I-70 at Empire. Head W on I-70 past **Georgetown**★★ and through **Eisenhower Tunnel**. You'll pass ski areas **Arapahoe Basin, Keystone Resort**★ and **Breckenridge**★★. At Exit 195 for **Copper Mountain Resort**★, take Rte. 91 S to **Leadville**★★, Colorado's former silver capital. Then travel S on US-24 to Rte. 82 W over **Independence Pass**★★ to **Aspen**★★★. Head NW to I-70, passing **Glenwood Springs**★★ with its **Hot Springs Pool**★★. Drive E on I-70 along **Glenwood Canyon**★★ and the Colorado River to **Vail**★★. Continue E on I-70 to the old mining town of **Idaho Springs** to return to Golden via Rte. 119.

LAKE TAHOE LOOP★★

71 miles/114 kilometers   Map 37
Begin in **Tahoe City** at the intersection of Rtes. 89 and 28. Drive S on Rte. 89. **Ed Z'berg-Sugar Pine Point State Park**★ encompasses a promontory topped by the **Hellman-Ehrman Mansion**★ and other historic buildings. Farther S, **Emerald Bay State Park**★★ surrounds beautiful **Emerald Bay**. At the bay's tip stands **Vikingsholm**★★, a mansion that resembles an ancient Nordic castle. At **Tallac Historic Site**★, preserved summer estates recall Tahoe's turn-of-the-19C opulence. From Tahoe Valley, take Rte. 50 NE. **South Lake Tahoe**, the lake's largest town, offers lodging, dining and shopping. High-rise hotel-casinos characterize neighboring **Stateline** in Nevada. Continue N to Spooner Junction. Then follow Nevada Rte. 28 N to **Sand Harbor**★★ (7mi), where picnic tables and a sandy beach fringe a sheltered cove. Continue through Kings Beach to end the tour at Tahoe City.

MAUI'S HANA HIGHWAY★★

62 miles/100 kilometers   Map 153
Leave **Kahului** on Rte. 36 E toward **Paia,** an old sugar-plantation town. Continue E on Rte. 36, which becomes Rte. 360, the **Hana Highway**★★. The road passes **Ho'okipa Beach Park**, famous for windsurfing, and **Puohokamoa Falls**, a good picnic stop, before arriving in Hana, a little village on an attractive bay. If adventurous, continue S on the Hana Highway to **Ohe'o Gulch**★★ in **Haleakala NP**★★★, where small waterfalls tumble from the SE flank of the dormant volcano Haleakala. Past the gulch the grave of aviator **Charles Lindbergh** can be found in the churchyard at Palapala Hoomau Hawaiian Church. End the tour at Kipahulu.

REDWOOD EMPIRE★★

182 miles/293 kilometers   Maps 36, 28
In **Leggett**, CA, S of the junction of Hwy. 1 and US-101, go N on US-101 to pass through a massive redwood trunk at **Chandelier Drive-Thru Tree Park**. To the N, see breathtaking groves along 31mi **Avenue of the Giants**★★★. At **Humboldt Redwoods SP**★★ explore nature's bounty, including a trail through **Founder's Grove**★★. The trail begins at the Founder's Tree, once considered the world's tallest (364ft before the top 17ft broke off). Also discover **Rockefeller Forest**★★★, the world's largest virgin redwood forest. To the north along US-101, **Eureka**★ preserves a logging camp cookhouse and other historic sites. The sleepy fishing town of **Trinidad**★ overlooks a tranquil turquoise harbor. **Patrick's Point SP**★★ offers dense forests, agate-strewn beaches and clifftop **views**★★. At **Orick**, enter the **Redwood National and State Parks**★★, which protect a 367.8ft-high **tree**★. In addition, the park also contains 33mi of beaches. The tour ends in **Crescent City**.

SANTA FE AREA★★★

267 miles/430 kilometers   Maps 189, 48, 260, 49
From **Albuquerque**★, drive E on I-40 to Exit 175 and take Rte. 14, the **Turquoise Trail**★★, N to **Santa Fe**★★★. This 52mi back road runs along the scenic Sandia Mountains and passes dry washes, arroyos and a series of revived "ghost towns." Continue N on US-84/285, turning NE onto Rte. 76, the **High Road to Taos**★★. East of Vadito, take Rte. 518 N to Rte. 68 N into the rustic Spanish colonial town of **Taos**★★, a center for the arts. Head N on US-64 to the junction of Rte. 522. Continue W on US-64 for an 18mi round-trip detour to see the 1,200ft-long, three-span **Rio Grande Gorge Bridge** over the river. Return to Rte. 522 and take this route, part of the **Enchanted Circle**★★ Scenic Byway, N to **Questa**, starting point for rafting trips on the Rio Grande. Turn onto Rte. 38, heading E to the mining town of **Eagle Nest**. There, detour 23mi E to US-64 to **Cimarron**, a Wild West haunt. Back to Eagle Nest, travel SW on US-64, detouring on Rte. 434 S to the resort town of **Angel Fire**. Return to Taos on US-64 W to end the tour.

SEDONA/GRAND CANYON NP★★★

482 miles/776 kilometers   Maps 249, 54, 47, 213
Drive N from **Phoenix**★ on I-17 to Exit 298 and take Rte. 179 N toward **Sedona**★★ in the heart of **Red Rock Country**★★★. The red-rock formations are best accessed by four-wheel-drive vehicle via 12mi **Schnebly Hill Road**★ (off Rte. 179, across Oak Creek bridge from US-89A "Y" junction), which offers splendid **views**★★★. Then head N on Rte. 89A through Sedona

Pueblo, Taos

©Natalia Bratslavsky/iStockphoto.com

to begin the 14mi drive of **Oak Creek Canyon★★**. Continue N on Rte. 89A and I-17 to **Flagstaff★**, commercial hub for the region. Take US-180 NW to Rte. 64, which leads N to the **South Rim★★★** of **Grand Canyon NP★★★**. Take the shuttle (or drive, if permitted) along **West Rim Drive★★** to **Hermits Rest★**. Then travel **East Rim Drive★★★** (Rte. 64 E) to **Desert View Watchtower★** for **views★★★** of the canyon. Continue to the junction with US-89 at Cameron. Return S to Flagstaff, then S to Phoenix via I-17.

🚗 NORTHEAST DRIVING TOURS

THE BERKSHIRES★★★

57 miles/92 kilometers   *Map 94*

From **Great Barrington** take US-23 E to Monterey, turning left onto Tyringham Rd., which becomes Monterey Rd., to experience scenic **Tyringham Valley★**. Continue N on Main Rd. to Tyringham Rd., leading to **Lee**, famous for its marble. Then go NW on US-20 to **Lenox★**, with its inviting inns and restaurants. Detour on Rte. 183 W to **Tanglewood★**, site of a popular summer music festival. Return to Lenox and drive N on US-7 to **Pittsfield**, the commercial capital of the region. Head W on US-20 to enjoy **Hancock Shaker Village★★★**, a museum village relating the history of a Shaker community established here in 1790. Rte. 41 S passes West Stockbridge, then take Rte. 102 SE to **Stockbridge★★** and its picturesque **Main Street★**. Follow US-7 S to the junction with Rte. 23, passing **Monument Mountain★** en route. Return to Great Barrington.

CAPE COD★★★

164 miles/264 kilometers   *Maps 151, 95*

At US-6 and Rte. 3, cross **Cape Cod Canal** via Sagamore Bridge and turn onto Rte. 6A to tour the Cape's **North Shore★★**. Bear right onto Rte. 130 to reach **Sandwich★**, famous for glass manufacture. Continue on Rte. 6A E to **Orleans**. Take US-6 N along **Cape Cod National Seashore★★★**, with its wooded and marshland trails, to reach **Provincetown★★**, a resort town offering **dune tours★★** and summer theater. Return to Orleans and take Rte. 28 S through **Chatham★**, then W to **Hyannis**, where ferries depart for **Nantucket★★★**. Continue to quaint **Falmouth★**. Take Surf Rd., which becomes Oyster Pond Rd. to nearby **Woods Hole**, a world center for marine research and departure point for ferries to **Martha's Vineyard★★**. Take Woods Hole Rd. N to Rte. 28. Cross the canal via Bourne Bridge and head E on US-6 to end the tour at Rte. 3.

MAINE COAST★★

238 miles/383 kilometers   *Maps 82, 251, 83*

From **Kittery**, drive N on US-1 to **York★**, then along US-1A to see the 18C buildings of **Colonial York★★**. Continue N on coastal US-1A; rejoin US-1 at Cape Neddick and continue N through **Ogunquit★**. Turn right at Rte. 9 and drive to **Kennebunkport★**, with its colorful shops. Take Rte. 9A/35 to **Kennebunk**. Then travel N on US-1 to **Portland★★**, Maine's largest city, where the **Old Port Exchange★★** brims with galleries and boutiques. Take US-1 N through the outlet town of **Freeport**, then on to **Brunswick**, home of **Bowdoin College**. Turn NE through **Bath★**, **Wiscasset**, **Rockland**, **Camden★★**, **Searsport** and **Bucksport**. At Ellsworth, take Rte. 3 S to enter **Acadia NP★★★** on **Mount Desert Island★★★**, where **Park Loop Road★★★** *(closed in winter)* parallels open coast. From the top of **Cadillac Mountain★★★**, the **views★★★** are breathtaking. The tour ends at **Bar Harbor★**, a popular resort village.

HUDSON RIVER VALLEY★★★

125 miles/201 kilometers   *Maps 240, 148, 94*

Begin at **Sunnyside★**, home of author Washington Irving. Continue N on US-9 to Tarrytown to visit neighboring **Lyndhurst★**, a Gothic-Revival mansion. Tree arches and old stone walls line the way to **Philipsburg Manor★** and then on to **Kykuit★★** for **views★** of the river and gardens. **Van Cortlandt Manor★** is another striking estate to visit. Follow Rte. 9D to US-9 to Poughkeepsie, home of **Vassar College**. **Hyde Park** offers the **Home of Franklin D. Roosevelt NHS★★**, the **Eleanor Roosevelt NHS★** and the lavish **Vanderbilt Mansion★**. Further N through Rhinebeck and Staatsburg sits **Staatsburg State Historic Site★**, a 79-room Beaux-Arts Mansion. Return to Poughkeepsie and cross the river to US-9W, along the West Bank, and travel S to the Cornwall Hospital Exit. From Rte. 107, follow Rte. 32 to **Storm King Art Center★**, an outdoor museum of contemporary sculpture. Along Rte. 128, detour to **West Point★★** and then back to US-9W to the **Stony Point Battlefield State Historic Site**. Return to Manhattan along Palisades Interstate Pkwy. for superb **views★★**.

SOUTH SHORE LAKE SUPERIOR★

530 miles/853 kilometers   *Maps 211, 64, 65, 69*

From **Duluth★**, drive SE on I-535/US-53 to the junction of Rte. 13 at Parkland. Follow Rte. 13 E to quaint **Bayfield**, gateway to **Apostle Islands NL★★**, accessible by boat. Head S to the junction of US-2, and E through Ashland, Ironwood and Wakefield. There, turn left onto Rte. 28, heading NE to Bergland, and turning left onto Rte. 64. Drive N to Silver City and take Rte. M-107 W into **Porcupine Mountains Wilderness SP★**.

Apostle Islands National Lakeshore

National Park Service

Return to Rte. 64 and go E to Ontonagon. Take Rte. 38 SE to Greenland, then follow Rte. 26 NE to Houghton. Cross to Hancock on US-41 and continue NE to Phoenix. Turn left onto Rte. 26 to Eagle River and on to Copper Harbor via **Brockway Mountain Drive★★**. Return S to Houghton via US-41, then travel S and E past Marquette, turning left onto Rte. 28. Head E to Munising, then take County Road H-58 E and N through **Pictured Rocks NL★**. End the tour at Grand Marais.

VILLAGES OF SOUTHERN VERMONT★★

118 miles/190 kilometers   *Map 81*

Head N from the resort town of **Manchester★** by Rte. 7A. At Manchester Center, take Rte. 11 E past **Bromley Mountain** ski area, to Londonderry. Detour N on Rte. 100 to **Weston★**. Continue on Rte. 11 to **Chester**, turning right onto Rte. 35 S to reach **Grafton★**, with its **Old Tavern**. Farther S, Rte. 30 S from Townshend leads to **Newfane** and its lovely village **green★**. Return to Townshend, then travel W, following Rte. 30 through West Townshend, passing **Stratton Mountain** en route to Manchester. S of Manchester by Rte. 7A, the crest of Mt. Equinox (3,816ft) is accessible via **Equinox Skyline Drive** (fee). Then continue S on Rte. 7A to end the tour at **Arlington**, known for its trout fishing.

Please turn to page 301 for more Michelin Scenic Drives for USA East and Canada.

British Columbia

Washington

0 mi 20 40
0 km 20 40 60

One inch equals 25.4 miles
One centimeter equals 16.1 kilometers

Map: Seattle WA / Mt Rainier National Park WA — including Vancouver Island, Olympic National Park, Puget Sound, Seattle, Tacoma, Olympia, and surrounding areas.

DRIVING DISTANCES IN MILES	ABERDEEN, WA	BELLINGHAM, WA	MT. RAINIER NP, WA	OKANOGAN, WA	OLYMPIA, WA	PORT ANGELES, WA	SEATTLE, WA	SPOKANE, WA	TACOMA, WA	VANCOUVER, BC	WENATCHEE, WA	YAKIMA, WA
BELLINGHAM, WA	196		186	195	147	127*	88	360	122	52	185	221
SEATTLE, WA	105	88	96	223	56	83*		278	31	140	148	140
SPOKANE, WA	376	360	290	148	327	362*	278		303	412	171	203
YAKIMA, WA	237	221	87	194	188	223*	140	203	164	273	115	

*DISTANCE INCLUDES FERRY TRAVEL   SEE ALSO DISTANCE AND DRIVING TIME MAP ON PAGES 286–287

0 mi   20   40
0 km   20   40   60
One inch equals 25.4 miles
One centimeter equals 16.1 kilometers

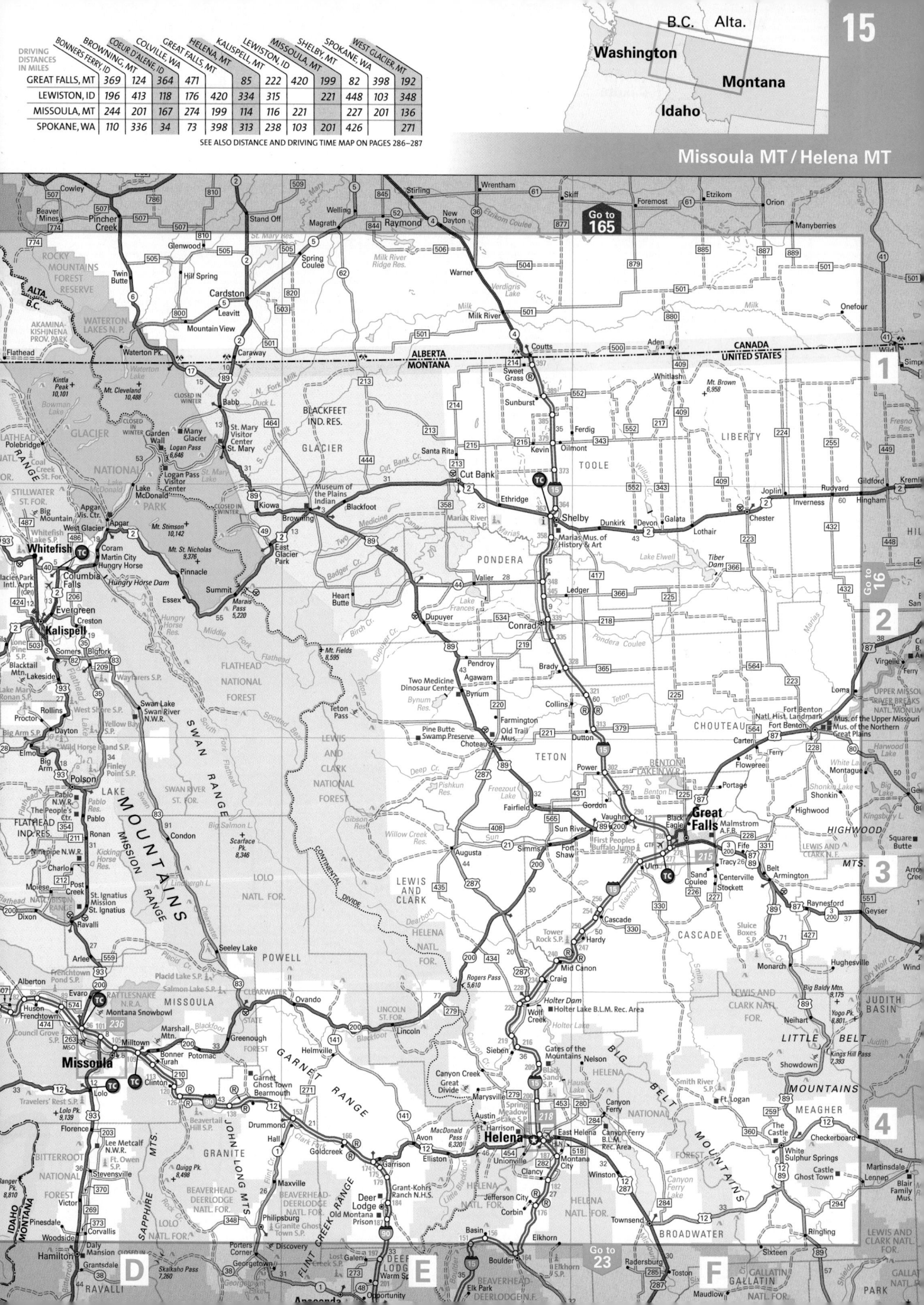

SEE ALSO DISTANCE AND DRIVING TIME MAP ON PAGES 286–287

DRIVING DISTANCES IN MILES	BONNERS FERRY, ID	BROWNING, MT	COEUR D'ALENE, ID	COLVILLE, WA	GREAT FALLS, MT	HELENA, MT	KALISPELL, MT	LEWISTON, ID	MISSOULA, MT	SHELBY, MT	SPOKANE, WA	WEST GLACIER, MT
GREAT FALLS, MT	369	124	364	471		85	222	420	199	82	398	192
LEWISTON, ID	196	413	118	176	420	334	315		221	448	103	348
MISSOULA, MT	244	201	167	274	199	114	116	221		227	201	136
SPOKANE, WA	110	336	34	73	398	313	238	103	201	426		271

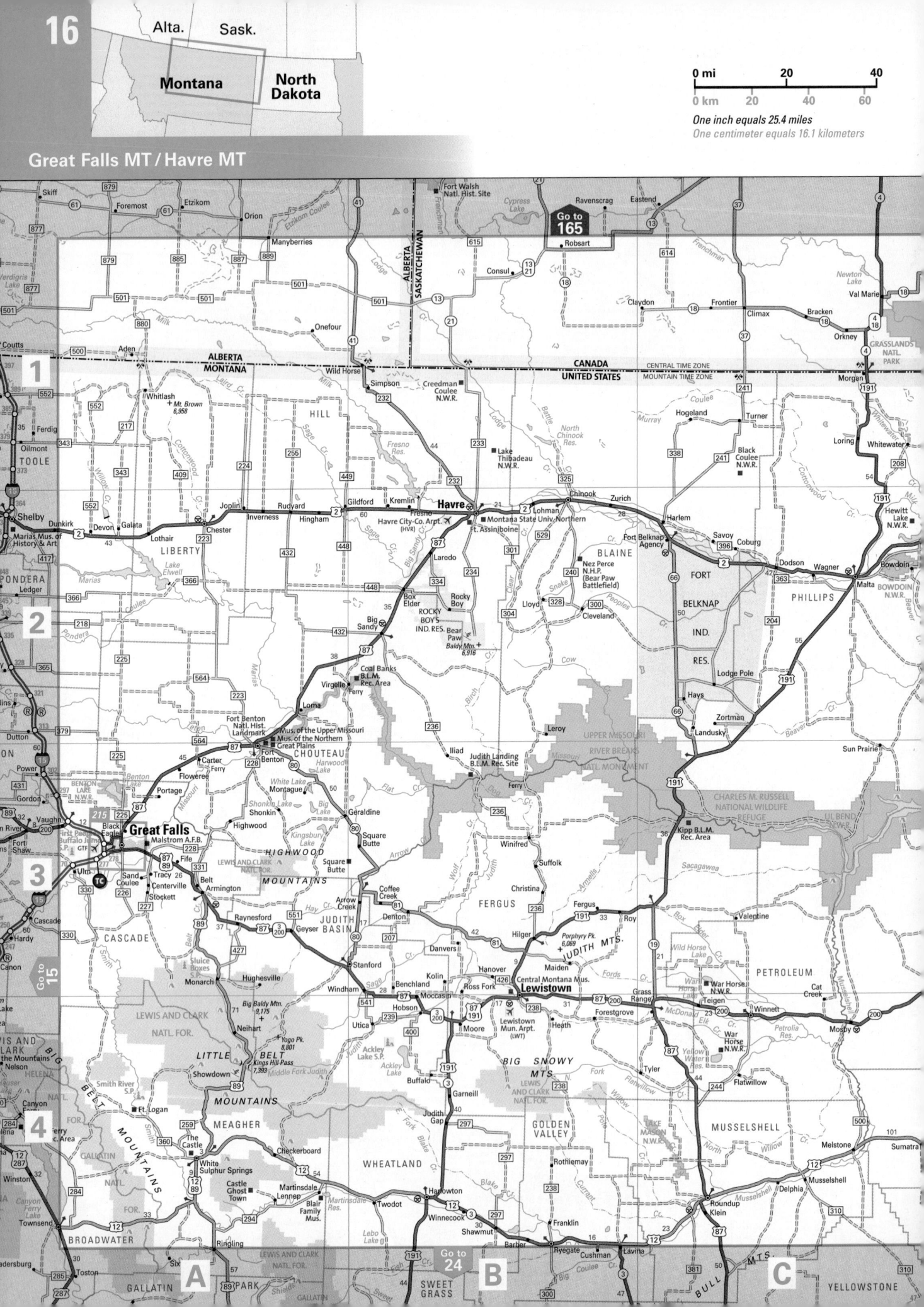

Alta. Sask.

Montana | North Dakota

One inch equals 25.4 miles
One centimeter equals 16.1 kilometers

Go to 165

Go to 15

Go to 24

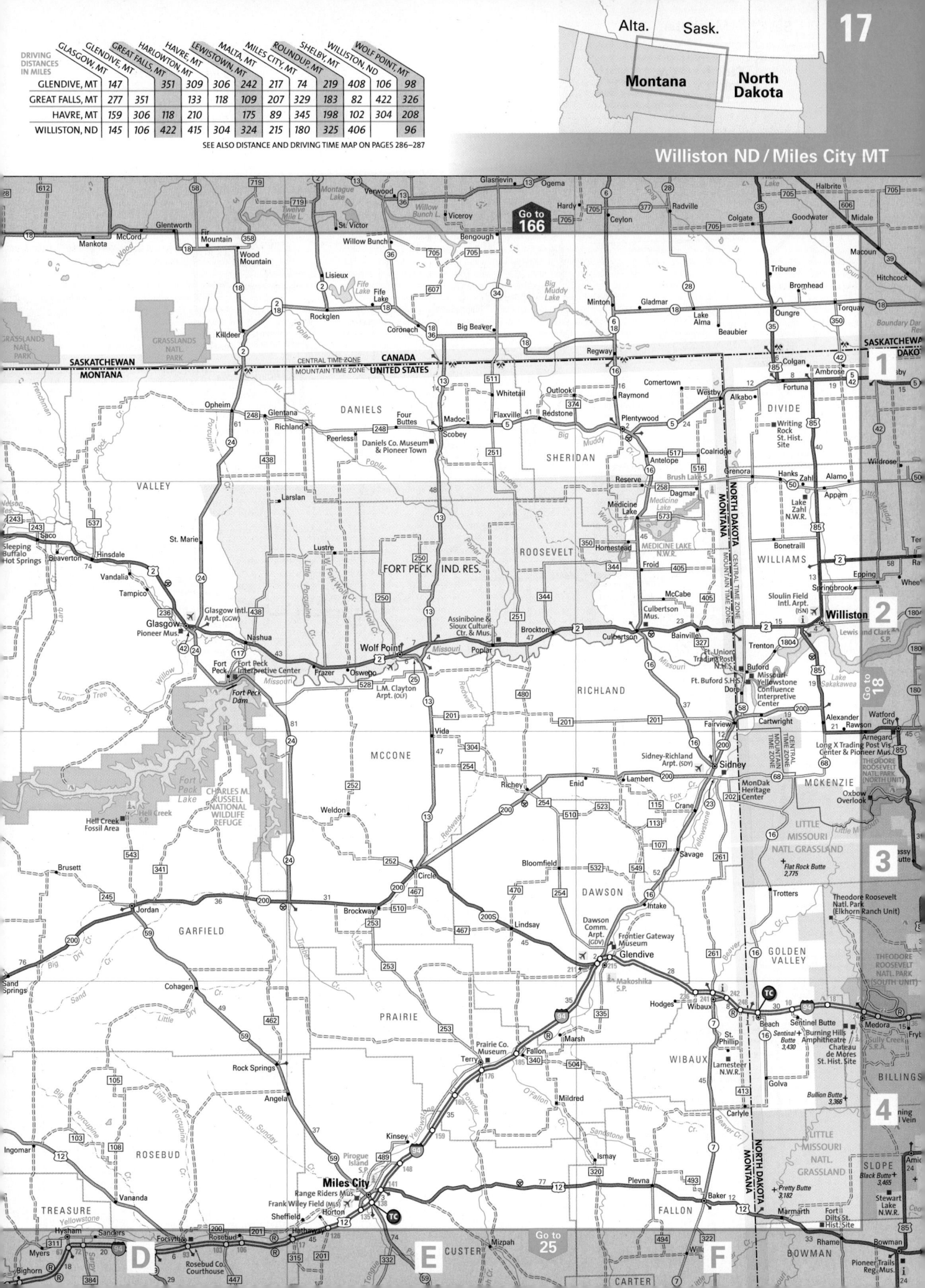

DRIVING DISTANCES IN MILES	GLASGOW, MT	GLENDIVE, MT	GREAT FALLS, MT	HARLOWTON, MT	HAVRE, MT	LEWISTOWN, MT	MALTA, MT	MILES CITY, MT	ROUNDUP, MT	SHELBY, MT	WILLISTON, ND	WOLF POINT, MT
GLENDIVE, MT	147		351	309	306	242	217	74	219	408	106	98
GREAT FALLS, MT	277	351		133	118	109	207	329	183	82	422	326
HAVRE, MT	159	306	118	210		175	89	345	198	102	304	208
WILLISTON, ND	145	106	422	415	304	324	215	180	325	406		96

SEE ALSO DISTANCE AND DRIVING TIME MAP ON PAGES 286–287

Alta.   Sask.

Montana   North Dakota

0 mi   20   40

0 km   20   40   60

One inch equals 25.4 miles
One centimeter equals 16.1 kilometers

DRIVING DISTANCES IN MILES

	BISMARCK, ND	BOTTINEAU, ND	DETROIT LAKES, MN	DICKINSON, ND	FARGO, ND	GRAND FORKS, ND	JAMESTOWN, ND	MINOT, ND	PEMBINA, ND	RUGBY, ND	THIEF RIVER FALLS, MN	WILLISTON, ND
BISMARCK, ND		189	244	97	199	274	105	116	347	153	319	229
FARGO, ND	199	271	45	291		79	97	268	152	221	113	424
GRAND FORKS, ND	274	198	125	367	79		173	212	77	148	61	340
MINOT, ND	116	76	313	178	268	212	171		238	64	276	128

SEE ALSO DISTANCE AND DRIVING TIME MAP ON PAGES 286–287

0 mi · 20 · 40

0 km · 20 · 40 · 60

One inch equals 25.4 miles
One centimeter equals 16.1 kilometers

PACIFIC OCEAN

Go to 12

Go to 28

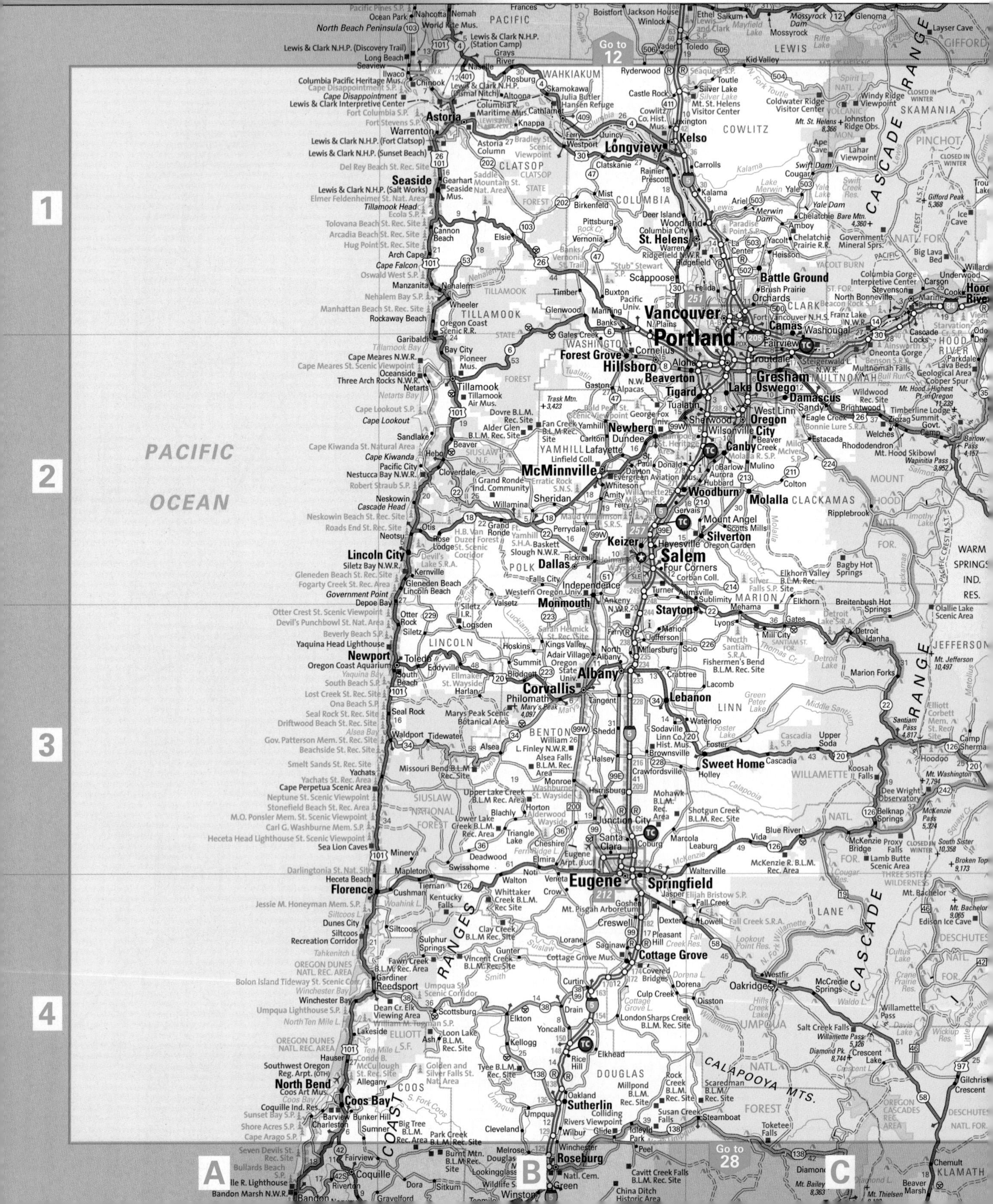

DRIVING DISTANCES IN MILES

	ASTORIA, OR	BEND, OR	BURNS, OR	COOS BAY, OR	EUGENE, OR	KENNEWICK, WA	LA GRANDE, OR	NEWPORT, OR	PORTLAND, OR	SALEM, OR	THE DALLES, OR	WALLA WALLA, WA
BEND, OR	252		142	227	115	245	295	183	158	134	137	276
EUGENE, OR	216	115	257	105		328	377	101	112	65	198	359
KENNEWICK, WA	306	245	256	440	328		111	328	212	264	131	49
PORTLAND, OR	97	158	299	224	112	212	261	116		48	82	243

SEE ALSO DISTANCE AND DRIVING TIME MAP ON PAGES 286–287

Washington
Montana
Oregon
Idaho
Wyoming

0 mi   20   40
0 km   20   40   60

One inch equals 25.4 miles
One centimeter equals 16.1 kilometers

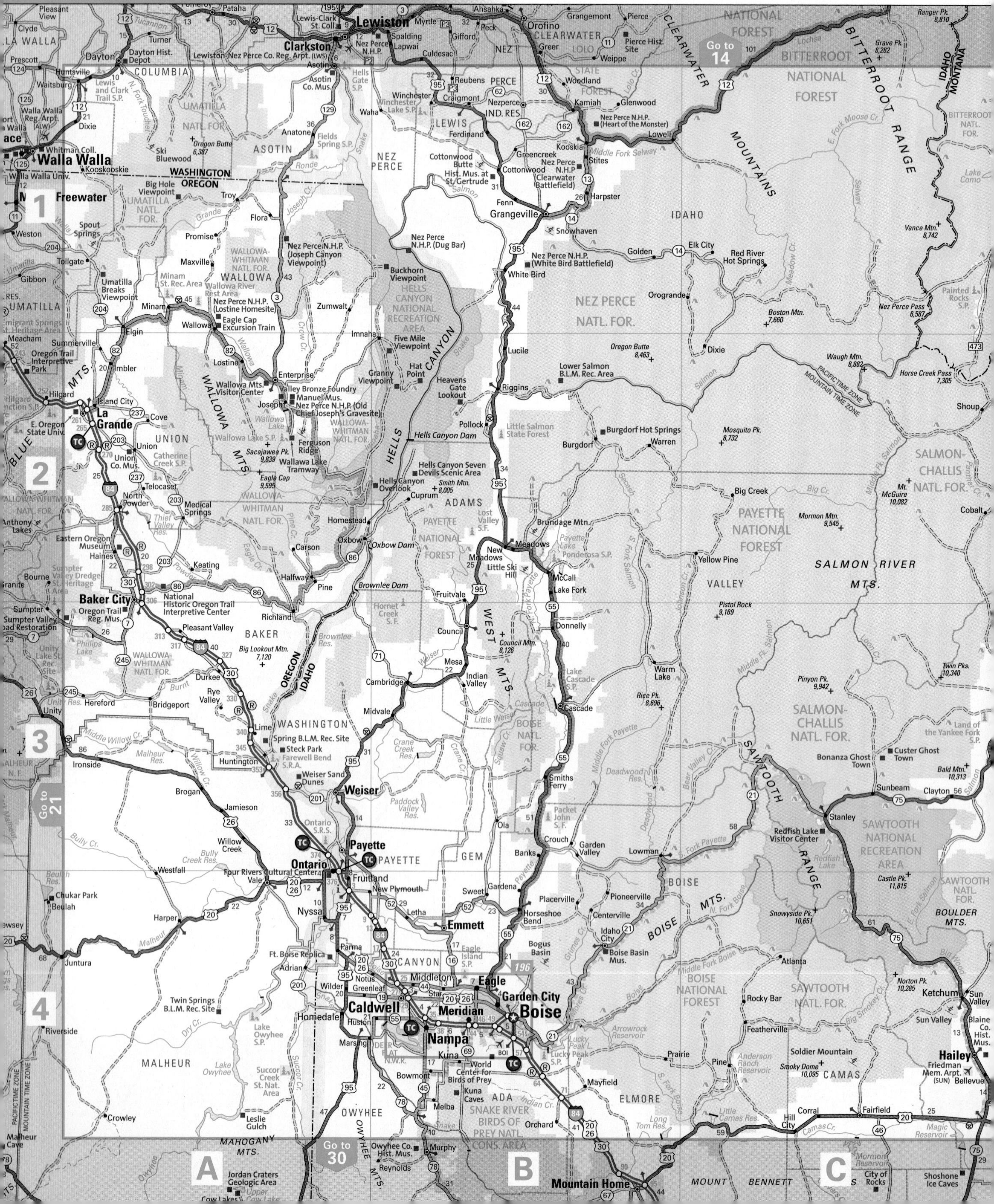

Boise ID / La Grande OR

Go to 14
Go to 21
Go to 30

Washington
Montana
Oregon
Idaho
Wyoming

SEE ALSO DISTANCE AND DRIVING TIME MAP ON PAGES 286–287

Montana
North Dakota
Idaho
South Dakota
Wyoming

0 mi 20 40
0 km 20 40 60
One inch equals 25.4 miles
One centimeter equals 16.1 kilometers

Row 1

BROADWATER · Townsend · Toston · Maudlow · Sixteen · Ringling · MEAGHER · Castle Ghost Town Lennep · Martinsdale · Bair Family Mus. · Martinsdale Res. · Twodot · WHEATLAND · Harlowton · Winnecook · Shawmut · Franklin · Ryegate · Cushman · Lavina · Barber · Go to 16 · Roundup · Klein · Delphia · Musselshell · MUSSELSHELL · TREASURE · Myers · Bighorn · Custer

GALLATIN · GALLATIN NATL. FOR. · LEWIS AND CLARK NATL. FOR. · Wilsall · Clyde Park · Melville · CRAZY MTS. · Conical Pk. 10,731 · Sacagawea Pk. 9,665 · Menard · Loga · Belgrade · Gallatin Field Arpt. (BZN) · Bridger Bowl · BRIDGER RANGE · SWEET GRASS · Big Timber · Springdale · Greycliff · Reed Point · GOLDEN VALLEY · Broadview · Hailstone N.W.R. · Rapelje · Halfbreed Lake N.W.R. · Comanche · Acton · Molt · Shepherd · Huntley · Ballantine · Worden · Pompeys Pillar Natl. Mon. · Pompeys Pillar · YELLOWSTONE · Yellowstone River S.P. · BULL MTS.

Row 2

Bozeman · Montana State Univ. Mus. of the Rockies · Gallatin Gateway · Livingston · Depot Center · McLeod · Greycliff Prairie Dog Town S.P. · STILLWATER · Columbus · Park City · Silesia · Laurel · Billings · ZooMontana · Pictograph Cave S.P. · Huntley Project Mus. · Toluca · Hardin · Big Horn Co. Hist. Mus. · CROW INDIAN RESERVATION · Crow Agency · Little Bighorn Battlefield Natl. Mon. · Custer Battlefield Museums

Pine Creek · PARK · Emigrant · Pray · Chico Hot Springs · Miner · Corwin Springs · Jardine · Gardiner · ABSAROKA · GALLATIN NATL. FOR. · Limestone · Nye · Dean · Fishtail · Roscoe · Absarokee · Cooney S.P. · Joliet · Edgar · Boyd · Pryor · Fromberg · CARBON · Bridger · Old Fort Smith · Fort Smith · Bighorn Lake · Big Horn · Lodge Grass · St. Xavier · Garryowen · Wyola

Big Sky · Gallatin Petrified Forest · Luther · Red Lodge Mountain · Washoe · Bearcreek · Belfry · Red Lodge · Granite Pk. Highest Pt. in Montana 12,799 · Lake Fork Rock Cr. · CUSTER NATL. FOR. · Pryor Mountain Wild Horse Range · Big Ice Caves · BIGHORN CANYON NATL. REC. AREA · Lodge Grass Storage Reservoir · BIGHORN NATL. FOR. · Parkman

Row 3 (Yellowstone area)

Go to 23 · Mammoth Hot Springs · Cooke City · Silver Gate · Tower Jct. · Colter Pass 8,000 · Pilot Pk. 11,708 · Beartooth Pass 10,947 · Vista Point · Clark · MONTANA / WYOMING · Elk Basin · Frannie · Deaver · Cowley · Byron · Mason-Lovell Ranch · Medicine Wheel Natl. Hist. Landmark · Little Mountain Caves · Dayton · Fallen City

Norris Geyser Basin · West Yellowstone · Yellowstone Arpt. (WYS) · Norris · Canyon Village · Mt. Washburn 10,243 · Saddle Mtn. 10,670 · Mt. Holmes 10,336 · ABSAROKA RANGE · Clarks Fork · Crandall · Dead Indian Summit 8,060 · Dead Indian · Heart Mtn. 8,123 · Powell · Ralston · ALT 14 · Willwood · Garland · Lovell · Bighorn Canyon Vis. Ctr. · Kane · CLOSED IN WINTER · Burgess Jct. · Granite Pass 9,033 · Shell Falls · Dome Pk. 10,828 · BIG HORN

Madison · Gibbon · Upper and Lower Falls · Lake Village · Lower Geyser Basin · Upper Geyser Basin · Old Faithful · Craig Pass 8,262 · West Thumb · West Thumb Geyser Basin · Pahaska Tepee · Sylvan Pass 8,530 · Wapiti · SHOSHONE · PARK · Buffalo Bill Hist. Center · Old Trail Town · Buffalo Bill Res. · Cody · Yellowstone Reg. Arpt. (COD) · BIGHORN BASIN · Emblem · Greybull · Greybull Mus. · Shell · Red Gulch Dinosaur Tracksite · Basin · Otto · Medicine Lodge St. Arch. Site

Row 4

Island Park · Upper & Lower Mesa Falls · Shoshone Lake · Lewis Lake · Yellowstone Lake · Mt. Hancock 10,214 · CONTINENTAL DIVIDE · JOHN D. ROCKEFELLER, JR., MEM. PKWY. · Fortress Mtn. 12,085 · Valley · CARTER MTN. · Charles J. Belden Museum · Meeteetse · Pitchfork · Manderson · Hyattville · Medicine Lodge St. Arch. Site

Lamont · Felt · Tetonia · Driggs · Alta · Grand Targhee · TETON RANGE · GRAND TETON NATL. PARK · Jackson Lake · Moran Jct. · Mt. Leidy 10,326 · Grand Teton 13,770 · Jenny Lake · Togwotee Pass 9,658 · WIND RIVER RANGE · Younts Pk. 12,156 · Francs Pk. 13,153 · Sunshine · Duck Swamp Interpretive Area · Washakie Mus. · Worland · Worland Mun. Arpt. (WRL) · Ten Sleep · WASHAKIE · Tensleep Canyon

Grand Targhee · Jackson Hole · Moose · Kelly · Jackson Hole Airport (JAC) · Teton Village · Wilson · NATIONAL ELK REFUGE · Granite Hot Springs · Grand Teton 13,770 · BRIDGER-TETON NATL. FOR. · Union Pass 9,210 · Natl. Bighorn Sheep Interpretive Center · Dubois · ROCKY MTS. · WIND RIVER IND. RES. · HOT SPRINGS · Grass Creek · Legend Rock St. Petroglyph Site · Hamilton Dome · Gebo · Kirby · Lucerne · Winchester · Castle Gardens Scenic Area · Big Trails

Jackson · Snow King · Hoback Junction · GROS VENTRE RANGE · Doubletop Pk. 11,682 · Teton Pass 8,431 · Palisades Pk. 9,780 · SUBLETTE · Burris · Crowheart · WIND RIVER RANGE · Gannett Pk. Highest Point in Wyoming 13,804 · Bear Pk. 10,755 · SHOSHONE NATIONAL FOREST · FREMONT · Thermopolis · Hot Springs S.P. · Hot Sprs. Mus. & Cultural Ctr. · East Thermopolis · Wyoming Dinosaur Center · Wind River Canyon · Guffy Pk. 8,046 · BOYSEN S.P. · COPPER MTN. · Boysen Res. · Bonneville · Lysite · Lost Cabin · Shoshoni · Moneta · Hiland

Alpine · Grand Canyon of the Snake R. · Go to 32 · Pavillion · Morton · Kinnear · Riverton Reg. Arpt. (RIW) · Midvale · LINCOLN · Go to 23

DRIVING DISTANCES IN MILES	BILLINGS, MT	BOZEMAN, MT	BUFFALO, WY	CODY, WY	GILLETTE, WY	JACKSON, WY	MILES CITY, MT	RAPID CITY, SD	SHERIDAN, WY	SPEARFISH, SD	W. YELLOWSTONE, MT	WORLAND WY
BILLINGS, MT		141	165	111	233	287	144	379	131	333	232	161
BUFFALO, WY	165	306		180	70	342	237	216	34	170	396	91
SPEARFISH, SD	333	474	170	350	100	512	186	53	202		564	261
W. YELLOWSTONE, MT	232	90	396	147	464	128	376	610	363	564		236

SEE ALSO DISTANCE AND DRIVING TIME MAP ON PAGES 286–287

North Dakota • Minnesota
South Dakota • Iowa

Rapid City SD / Pierre SD

One inch equals 25.4 miles
One centimeter equals 16.1 kilometers

0 mi   20   40
0 km   20   40   60

DRIVING DISTANCES IN MILES

	ABERDEEN, SD	BROOKINGS, SD	HOT SPRINGS SD	HURON, SD	MITCHELL SD	MOBRIDGE, SD	PIERRE, SD	RAPID CITY, SD	SIOUX FALLS SD	WAHPETON, ND	WALL, SD	WATERTOWN, SD
ABERDEEN, SD		150	412	90	146	99	160	357	204	154	303	98
PIERRE, SD	160	188	247	115	155	107		193	226	301	138	189
RAPID CITY, SD	357	390	56	313	275	243	193		346	543	55	436
SIOUX FALLS, SD	204	57	401	127	73	303	226	346		210	292	103

SEE ALSO DISTANCE AND DRIVING TIME MAP ON PAGES 286–287

Oregon

California   Nevada

0 mi   20   40
0 km   20   40   60
One inch equals 25.4 miles
One centimeter equals 16.1 kilometers

Medford OR / Redding CA

PACIFIC OCEAN

Major towns and features labeled on the map include:

Coos Bay, Coquille, Bandon, Myrtle Point, Port Orford, Gold Beach, Brookings, Crescent City, McKinleyville, Arcata, Eureka, Fortuna, Rio Dell, Scotia

Sutherlin, Oakland, Roseburg, Winston, Myrtle Creek, Canyonville, Glendale, Wolf Creek, Grants Pass, Central Point, Medford, Phoenix, Talent, Ashland, Jacksonville

Yreka, Weed, Mount Shasta, Dunsmuir, Weaverville, Shasta Lake, Redding, Anderson, Red Bluff

Klamath Falls, Altamont, Chiloquin

National Forests and areas: ROGUE RIVER NATL. FOR., SISKIYOU NATL. FOR., KLAMATH NATL. FOR., SIX RIVERS NATL. FOR., SHASTA-TRINITY NATL. FOR., TRINITY NATL. FOR., REDWOOD NATL. PARK, DEL NORTE, CRATER LAKE NATL. PARK, ROGUE RIVER–SISKIYOU NATL. MON.

COAST RANGE, SISKIYOU MTS., KLAMATH MTS., CASCADE RANGE, TRINITY MTS.

Counties: COOS, DOUGLAS, JACKSON, JOSEPHINE, CURRY, KLAMATH, DEL NORTE, SISKIYOU, HUMBOLDT, TRINITY, SHASTA, TEHAMA

OREGON / CALIFORNIA state line

Go to 20
Go to 36

Mt. Shasta 14,162
Mt. Thielsen 9,182
Mt. Bailey 8,363
Mt. McLoughlin 9,495
Boulder Peak 8,299
Pearsoll Peak 5,098

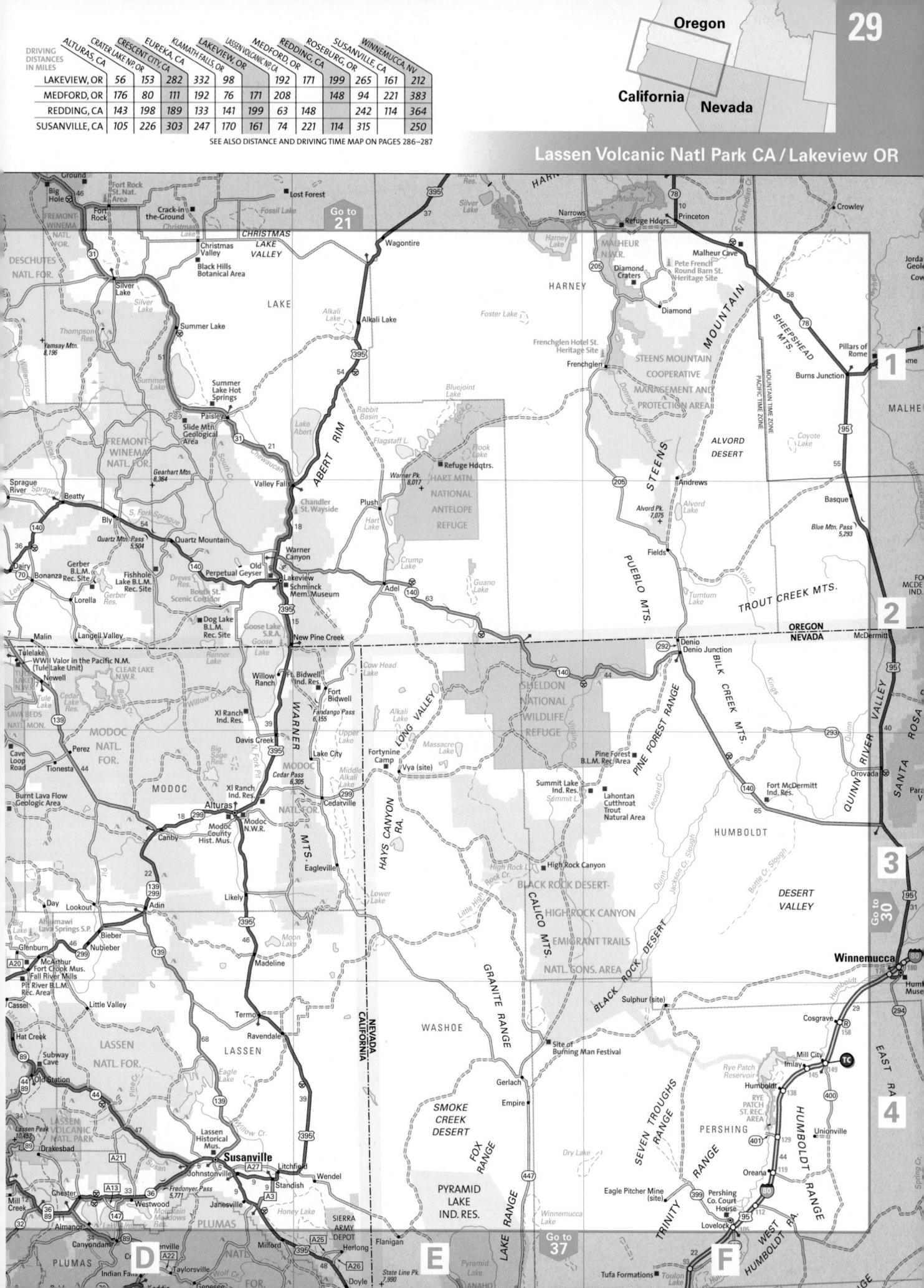

Oregon

California   Nevada

Oregon | Idaho
Wyoming
Nevada | Utah

0 mi 20 40
0 km 20 40 60
One inch equals 25.4 miles
One centimeter equals 16.1 kilometers

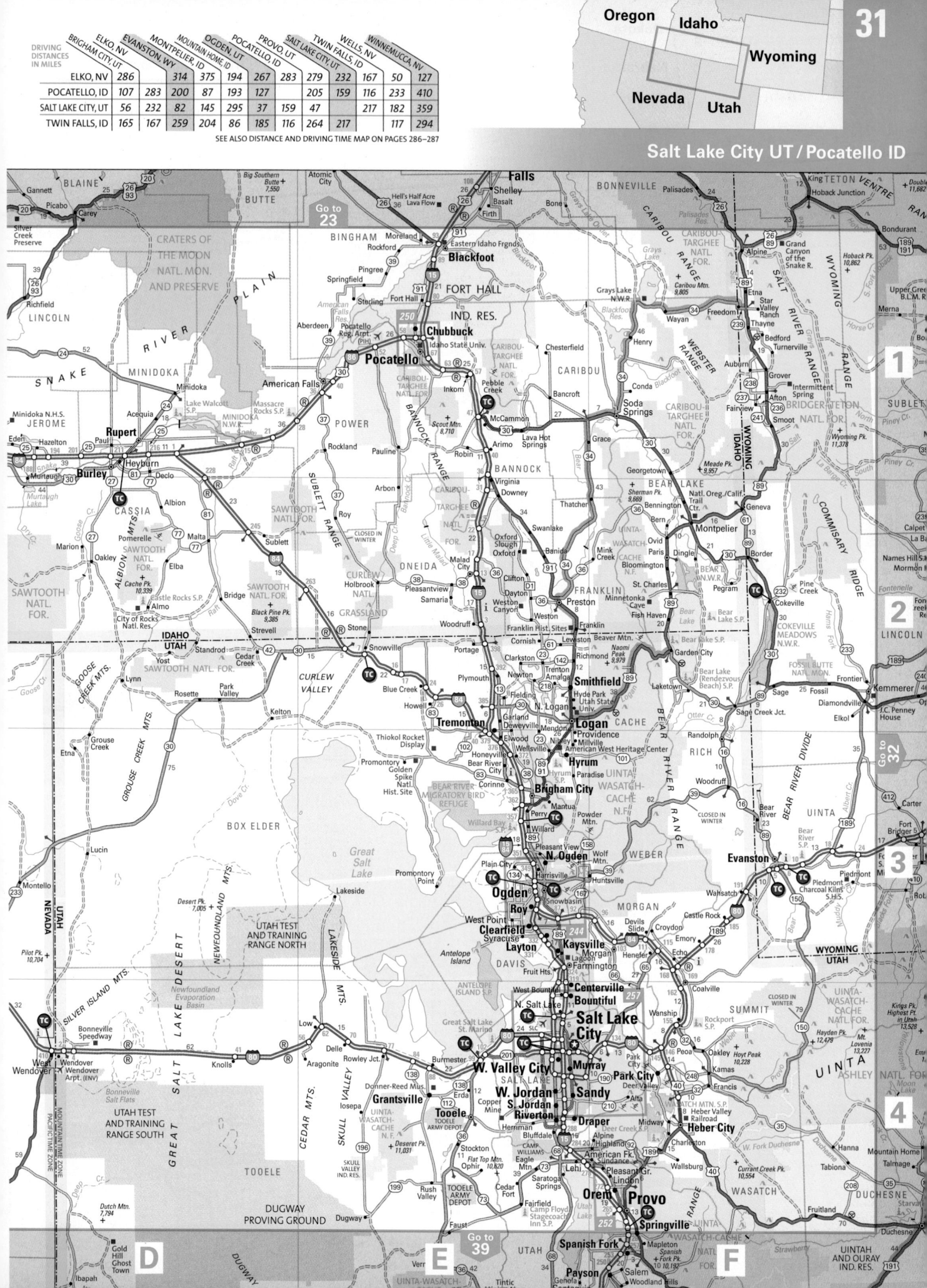

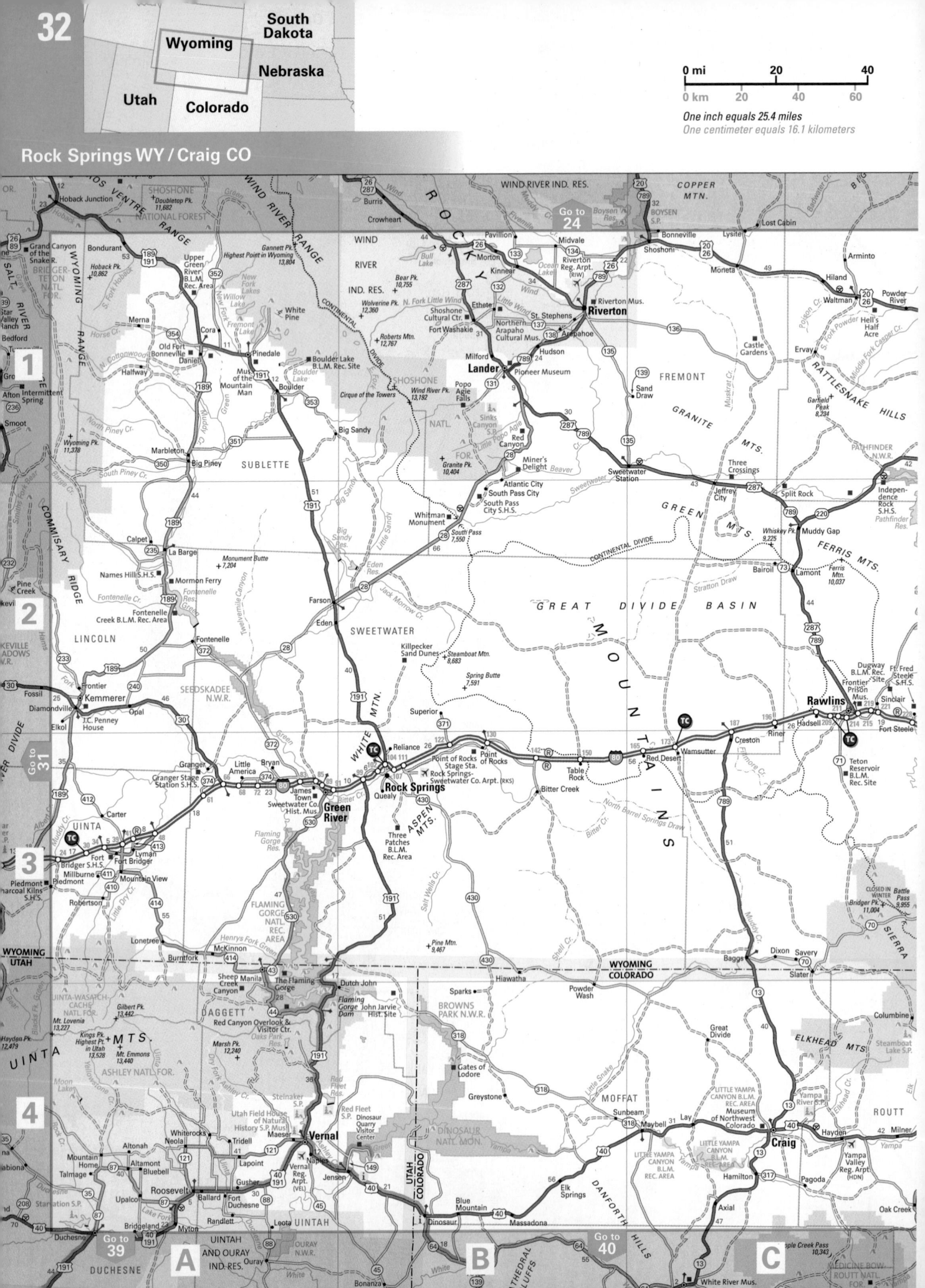

South Dakota
Wyoming
Nebraska
Utah   Colorado

South Dakota
Nebraska   Iowa
Colorado

North Platte NE / Chadron NE

0 mi   20   40
0 km   20   40   60
One inch equals 25.4 miles
One centimeter equals 16.1 kilometers

Go to 26
Go to 33
Go to 42

SOUTH DAKOTA
NEBRASKA

NEBRASKA
COLORADO

COLORADO
NEBRASKA

MOUNTAIN TIME ZONE
CENTRAL TIME ZONE

SAND HILLS
SURVEY VALLEY
PINE RIDGE
BOX BUTTE
MORRILL
GARDEN
ARTHUR
GRANT
HOOKER
THOMAS
BLAINE
MCPHERSON
LOGAN
CUSTER
KEITH
LINCOLN
PERKINS
CHASE
HAYES
FRONTIER
GOSPER
HITCHCOCK
RED WILLOW
FURNAS
DUNDY
CHEYENNE
DEUEL
SEDGWICK
PHILLIPS
YUMA
WASHINGTON
LOGAN
PEETZ TABLE
DAWES
SHERIDAN
CHERRY
BROWN
BENNETT
TODD
TRIPP
SHANNON
FALL RIVER
ROSEBUD IND. RES.
PINE RIDGE IND. RES.
BUFFALO GAP NATL. GRASSLAND
OGLALA NATL. GRASSLAND

Chadron
Alliance
Scottsbluff
Sidney
Sterling
Ogallala
North Platte
McCook
Lexington
Valentine
Winner
Cozad
Gothenburg

Museum of the Fur Trade
Museum of High Plains Heritage
Knight Mus. of High Plains Heritage
Carhenge
Fort Sidney Mus. and Post Commander's Home
Lake McConaughy St. Rec. Area
Ash Hollow St. Hist. Park
Kingsley Dam
Lake Ogallala S.R.A.
Bailey R.R. Yard & Golden Spike Tower
North Platte Reg. Arpt. (LBF)
Buffalo Bill Ranch S.R.A. & S.H.P.
Mari Sandoz St. Hist. Marker
Crescent Lake N.W.R.
Valentine N.W.R.
Samuel R. McKelvie Natl. For.
Nebraska Natl. For.
Merritt Res. St. Rec. Area
Medicine Creek S.R.A.
Museum of the High Plains
Pony Express Sta.

DRIVING DISTANCES IN MILES

	CHADRON, NE	GRAND ISLAND, NE	LINCOLN, NE	McCOOK, NE	NORFOLK, NE	NORTH PLATTE, NE	OGALLALA, NE	OMAHA, NE	SCOTTSBLUFF, NE	SIOUX CITY, IA	STERLING, CO	YANKTON, SD
GRAND ISLAND, NE	373		95	147	105	143	196	150	318	180	281	167
LINCOLN, NE	453	95		226	119	223	275	58	397	153	361	218
NORTH PLATTE, NE	230	143	223		67	248		53	278	175	373	138	310
OMAHA, NE	508	150	58	281	115	278	330		452	99	416	163

SEE ALSO DISTANCE AND DRIVING TIME MAP ON PAGES 286–287

California   Nevada

0 mi   20   40
0 km   20   40   60

One inch equals 25.4 miles
One centimeter equals 16.1 kilometers

San Francisco CA / Sacramento CA

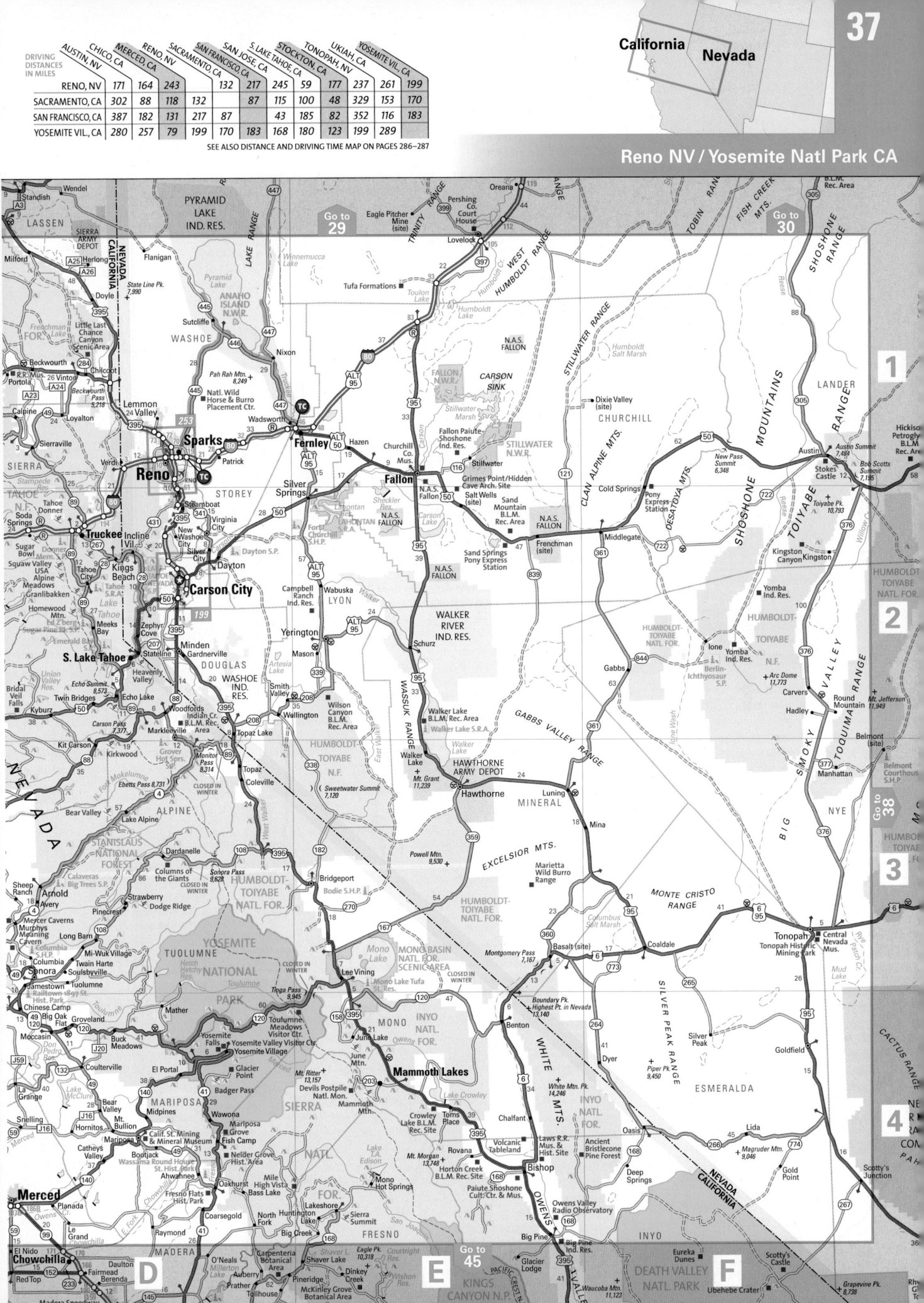

California Nevada

DRIVING DISTANCES IN MILES	AUSTIN, NV	CHICO, CA	MERCED, CA	RENO, NV	SACRAMENTO, CA	SAN FRANCISCO, CA	SAN JOSE, CA	S. LAKE TAHOE, CA	STOCKTON, CA	TONOPAH, NV	UKIAH, CA	YOSEMITE VIL., CA
RENO, NV	171	164	243		132	217	245	59	177	237	261	199
SACRAMENTO, CA	302	88	118	132		87	115	100	48	329	153	170
SAN FRANCISCO, CA	387	182	131	217	87		43	185	82	352	116	183
YOSEMITE VIL., CA	280	257	79	199	170	183	168	180	123	199	289	

SEE ALSO DISTANCE AND DRIVING TIME MAP ON PAGES 286–287

Nevada

Utah

0 mi 20 40
0 km 20 40 60
One inch equals 25.4 miles
One centimeter equals 16.1 kilometers

A **B** **C**

1 **2** **3** **4**

Go to 30
Go to 37
Go to 45
Go to 46

SHOSHONE RANGE
CORTEZ MTS.
PINE CR.
B.L.M. Rec. Area
305
278
LANDER
EUREKA
RUBY VALLEY
HUMBOLDT-TOIYABE NATL. FOR.
RUBY LAKE N.W.R.
Ruby Lake
Shantytown
ELKO
White Horse Pass 6,031
Dutch Mtn. 7,794
Gold Hill Ghost Town
93
ALT 93
Currie
50
59
Ibapah
Callao
Lages
Goshute Canyon and Cave
Cherry Creek
GOSHUTE IND. RES.
Goshute
Ibapah Pk. 12,087
Trout Creek
Blue Mass Scenic Area
Tonkin Spring B.L.M. Rec. Area
SULPHUR SPRING RANGE
Henderson Cr.
Collis Cr.
Newark Lake
DIAMOND MTS.
BUTTE MOUNTAINS
WHITE PINE
CHERRY CREEK RANGE
Duck Cr.
STEPTOE
SCHELL CR. RANGE
Spring Valley Cr.
Salt Marsh Lake
Gandy
HUMBOLDT-TOIYABE NATL. FOR.
DEEP CREEK RANGE
NEVADA UTAH
Austin
Austin Summit 7,484
Hickison Petroglyph B.L.M. Rec. Area
Bob Scotts Summit 7,195
Stokes Castle
58
50
Eureka
Eureka Sentinel Mus.
Eureka Opera House
Diamond Pk. 10,614
892
Little Antelope Summit 7,438
Robinson Summit 7,539
Steptoe (site)
McGill
Ely Arpt. (ELY)
Nev. Northern Railway Mus.
North Schell Pk. 11,883
Sacramento Pass 7,136
Mt. Moriah 12,050
Eskdale
50
305
376
FISH CREEK RANGE
Antelope Wash
Fish Cr.
Summit Mtn. 10,461
Toiyabe Pk. 10,793
Mt. Hamilton 10,745
Illipah Res. B.L.M. Rec. Area
Ward Mtn. B.L.M. Rec. Area
Garnet Hill
Ruth
Ely
E. Ely
Lane
EGAN RANGE
Cleve Creek B.L.M. Rec. Site
Cave Lake S.R.A.
Connors Pass 7,733
Majors Place
Wheeler Pk. 13,063
Lehman Caves
GREAT BASIN NATL. PARK
Baker
Garrison
Pruess Lake
DESERT RANGE EXPERIMENTAL STATION
488
487
159
CONFUSION RANGE
HUMBOLDT-TOIYABE NATL. FOR.
77
23
26
6 50
30
5
7
21
TOIYABE RANGE
TOQUIMA RANGE
SMOKY VALLEY
MONITOR RANGE
Potts (site)
Duckwater
Duckwater Ind. Res.
Currant Mtn. 11,513
Currant Summit 6,999
Preston
Lund
Currant
Shoshone
Minerva (site)
HUMBOLDT-TOIYABE NATL. FOR.
Mt. Jefferson 11,949
Round Mountain
Carvers
Belmont (site)
Belmont Courthouse S.H.P.
Manhattan
377
376
HOT CREEK RANGE
PANCAKE RANGE
RAILROAD VALLEY
White
GRANT RANGE
White
Ward Charcoal Ovens S.H.P.
894
6
50
318
379
93
6
318
SNAKE RANGE
LAKE VALLEY
WILSON CREEK RANGE
Mt. Wilson 9,296
Spring Valley S.P.
Meadow Valley B.L.M. Rec. Site
Hamlin Valley
INDIAN PEAK RANGE
Meadow Valley Wash
81
Warm Springs Summit 6,293
Warm Springs (site)
Lunar Crater Volcanic Field Natl. Natural Landmark
Nyala (site)
Troy Pk. 11,298
Adams-McGill Res.
Sunnyside
Central Nev. Mus.
Tonopah Hist. Mining Park
NYE
KAWICH RANGE
REVEILLE RANGE
EXTRATERRESTRIAL HIGHWAY
375
6
44
111
Pioche
Caselton
Ursine
Cathedral Gorge S.P.
Echo Canyon S.P.
Modena
Zane
Beryl
320
322
11
Queen City Summit 5,935
98
Tempiute (site)
Rachel
SEAMAN RANGE
GROOM RANGE
HUMBOLDT-TOIYABE NATL. FOR.
LINCOLN
Caliente
Caliente Railroad Depot
Kershaw-Ryan S.P.
Rainbow Canyon
Panaca
Uvada
Newcastle
Enterprise
14
20
19
25
56
18
319
TONOPAH TEST RANGE
CACTUS RANGE
BELTED RANGE
Mud Lake
Goldfield
Scotty's Junction
PAHUTE MESA
NELLIS AIR FORCE RANGE COMPLEX
Groom Lake
PAHRANAGAT RANGE
Hiko
Ash Springs
Ash Springs B.L.M. Rec. Site
Alamo
PAHRANAGAT N.W.R.
DELAMAR MTS.
Delamar Lake
Elgin
CLOVER MTS.
Beaver Dam S.P.
Lost Pk. 7,514
DIXIE NATL. FOR.
Mountain Meadows Monument
Central Baker Dam B.L.M. Rec. Site
Pinto
WASHINGTON
Gunlock S.P.
Snow Canyon S.P.
Veyo
Pine Valley
Dixie State Univ.
42
317
15
18
Grapevine Pk. 8,738
Beatty
NEVADA NATIONAL SECURITY SITE
DESERT NATL. WILDLIFE RANGE
Carp
MORMON MTS.
PAIUTE IND. RES. Shivwits
Ivins
Santa Clara
Jacob Hamblin Home
St. George
Joshua Tree Natural Area
NEVADA UTAH
PACIFIC TIME ZONE
MOUNTAIN TIME ZONE
95
93
62
36
16

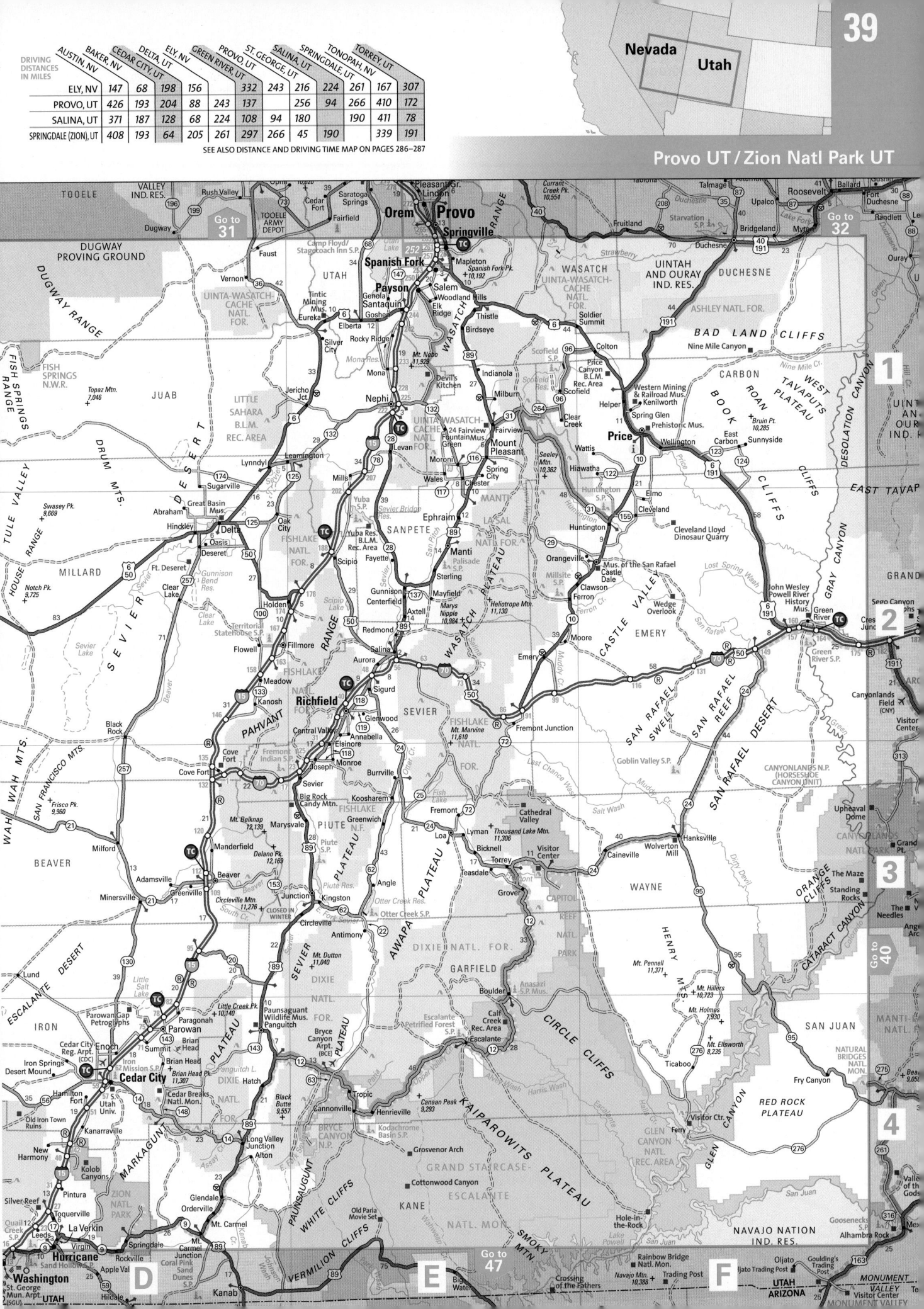

DRIVING DISTANCES IN MILES

	AUSTIN, NV	BAKER, NV	CEDAR CITY, UT	DELTA, UT	ELY, NV	GREEN RIVER, UT	PROVO, UT	ST. GEORGE, UT	SALINA, UT	SPRINGDALE, UT	TONOPAH, NV	TORREY, UT
ELY, NV	147	68	198	156		332	243	216	224	261	167	307
PROVO, UT	426	193	204	88	243	137		256	94	266	410	172
SALINA, UT	371	187	128	68	224	108	94	180		190	411	78
SPRINGDALE (ZION), UT	408	193	64	205	261	297	266	45	190		339	191

SEE ALSO DISTANCE AND DRIVING TIME MAP ON PAGES 286–287

0 mi 20 40
0 km 20 40 60
One inch equals 25.4 miles
One centimeter equals 16.1 kilometers

Go to 32

Go to 39

Go to 48

UINTAH AND OURAY INDIAN RESERVATION

EAST TAVAPUTS PLATEAU

ROAN CLIFFS

BOOK CLIFFS

ROAN PLATEAU

RIO BLANCO

GARFIELD

THE FLAT TOPS

WHITE RIVER NATL. FOR.

ROUTT

EAGLE

SAWATCH

Grand Junction
Fruita
Rifle
Glenwood Springs
Carbondale
Aspen
Delta
Montrose
Gunnison
Moab
Cortez
Durango

ARCHES NATL. PARK

CANYONLANDS NATL. PARK

MANTI-LA SAL NATL. FOR.

UNCOMPAHGRE PLATEAU

UNCOMPAHGRE NATL. FOR.

GRAND MESA

GRAND MESA NATL. FOR.

WEST ELK MTS.

GUNNISON NATL. FOR.

SAN JUAN MOUNTAINS

SAN JUAN NATL. FOR.

MESA VERDE

DOLORES

SAN MIGUEL

MONTROSE

OURAY

HINSDALE

MINERAL

RIO GRANDE NATL. FOR.

LA GARITA

COCHETOPA

SAN JUAN

NAVAJO NATION IND. RES.

UTE MOUNTAIN IND. RES.

SOUTHERN UTE IND. RES.

ARCHULETA

MONUMENT VALLEY

GLEN CANYON NATL. REC. AREA

UTAH ARIZONA

COLORADO NEW MEXICO

MONTEZUMA

A   B   C

Utah   Colorado

DRIVING DISTANCES IN MILES	ASPEN, CO / ALAMOSA, CO	CORTEZ, CO / COLORADO SPRS., CO	DENVER, CO	DURANGO, CO / GRAND JUNCTION, CO	GREEN RIVER, UT / MOAB, UT	MONTROSE, CO	PUEBLO, CO / TRINIDAD, CO
COLORADO SPRS., CO	162	157	359	70	314	318	418	404	236	43	127
DENVER, CO	230	164	70	452		337	250	350	337	277	111	196
DURANGO, CO	152	244	314	45	337		169	214	160	107	271	260
GRAND JUNCTION, CO	261	135	318	203	250	169		102	88	62	360	444

SEE ALSO DISTANCE AND DRIVING TIME MAP ON PAGES 286–287

Nebraska

Colorado   Kansas

One inch equals 25.4 miles
One centimeter equals 16.1 kilometers

SEE ALSO DISTANCE AND DRIVING TIME MAP ON PAGES 286–287

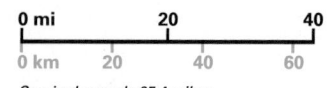

Nevada

California

0 mi   20   40
0 km   20   40   60
One inch equals 25.4 miles
One centimeter equals 16.1 kilometers

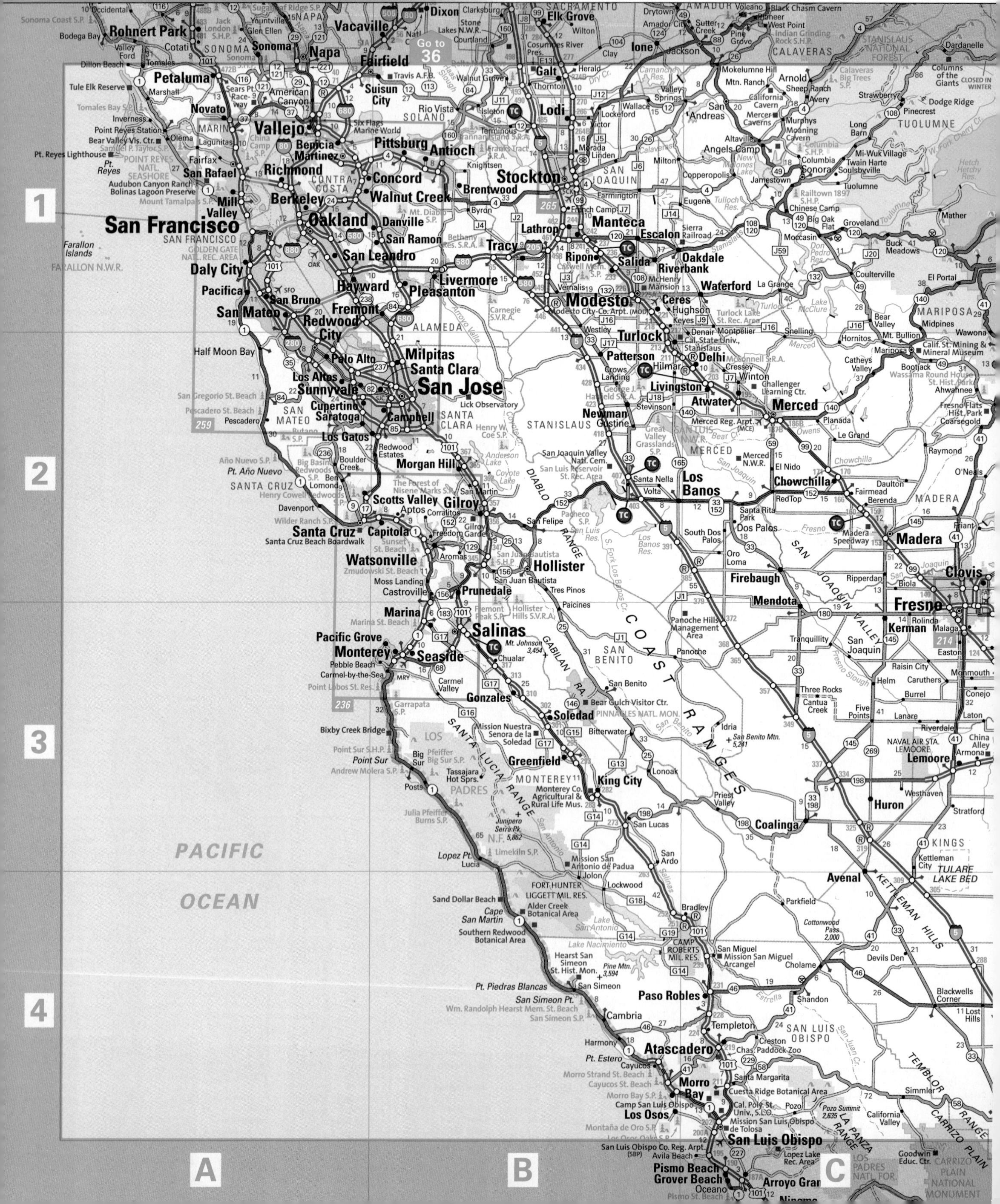

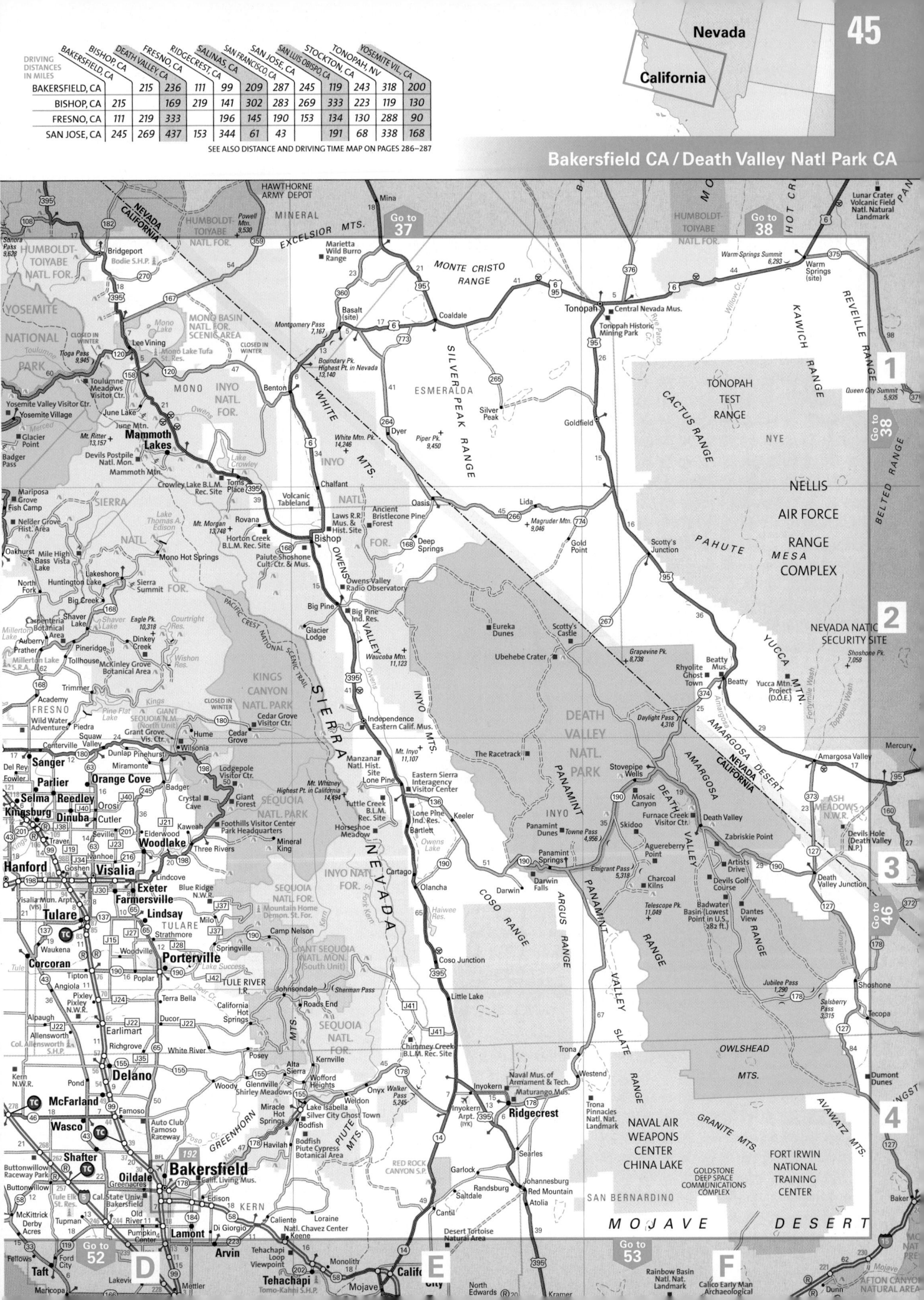

NEVADA · Utah · California · Arizona

0 mi — 20 — 40
0 km — 20 — 40 — 60
One inch equals 25.4 miles
One centimeter equals 16.1 kilometers

Go to 38

Go to 45

Go to 53

Go to 54

A **B** **C**

1 **2** **3** **4**

MESA
NYE
NELLIS AIR FORCE RANGE COMPLEX
NEVADA NATIONAL SECURITY SITE
Yucca Lake
Shoshone Pk. 7,058
Frenchman Lake
DESERT RANGE
Groom Lake
Dog Bone Lake
Desert Lake
Lake
PAHRANAGAT N.W.R.
LINCOLN
DELAMAR MTS.
MEADOW VALLEY MTS.
Carp
Kane Springs Wash
MORMON MTS.
Toquop Wash
WASHINGTON
ZION NATL. PARK
Gunlock
Veyo
Silver Reef
Toquerville
La Verkin
Virgin
Rockville
Springdale
13
Snow Canyon S.P.
Dixie State Univ.
Shivwits
Santa Clara
Jacob Hamblin Home
Ivins
St. George
Washington
St. George Mun. Arpt. (SGU)
Hurricane
Apple Valley
Leeds
Quail Lake
Sand Hollow S.P.
PAIUTE IND. RES.
Joshua Tree Natural Area
UTAH
ARIZONA
Colorado City
Cane Beds
Hildale
389
Beaver Dam
Littlefield
Mt. Bangs 8,012
Virgin River Canyon B.L.M. Rec. Area
HURRICANE CLIFFS
UINKARET PLATEAU
Mesquite
Bunkerville
VIRGIN MTS.
Virgin River Rec. Area
SHIVWITS PLATEAU
GRAND WASH CLIFFS
Mormon Pk. 7,411
Glendale
Moapa
Logandale
Overton
Lost City Mus.
VALLEY OF FIRE S.P.
MOAPA RIVER IND. RES.
Moapa Valley N.W.R.
PACIFIC TIME ZONE / MOUNTAIN TIME ZONE
Grand Wash
Parashant Wash
GRAND CANYON-PARASHANT NATL. MONUMENT
Poverty Mtn. 6,791
Mt. Trumbull
Mt. Trumbull 8,028
Ranger Station
Toroweap Overlook
Amargosa Valley
Mercury
Indian Springs
Creech A.F.B.
Hayford Pk. 9,912
SHEEP RANGE
NATL. WILDLIFE RANGE
CLARK
ASH MEADOWS N.W.R.
Devils Hole (Death Valley N.P.)
SPRING MOUNTAINS N.R.A.
Las Vegas Ski and Snowboard
Charleston Pk. 11,918
Death Valley Junction
Pahrump
Las Vegas
RED ROCK CANYON N.C.A.
North Las Vegas
NELLIS AIR FORCE RANGE COMPLEX
MUDDY MTS.
LAKE MEAD NATL. REC. AREA
Temple Bar
Meadview
Grand Canyon West & Skywalk
Grand Canyon West Arpt. (GCW)
GRAND CANYON NATL. PARK
Natural Bridge
LAKE MEAD N.R.A.
Shoshone
Tecopa
INYO
Floyd Lamb S.P.
Spring Mtn. Ranch S.P.
Blue Diamond
Henderson
Boulder City
Hoover Dam
Fortification Hill 3,718
Sloan
SLOAN CANYON N.C.A.
Willow Beach
WHITE HILLS
Joshua Tree Forest
Garnet Mtn. 8,440
Red Lake
GRAND WASH CLIFFS
HUALAPAI IND. RES.
Goodsprings
Sandy Valley
Jean
Nelson
ELDORADO MTS.
ARIZONA / NEVADA
BLACK MTS.
Dolan Springs
Mt. Tipton 7,148
MOHAVE
AUBREY CLIFFS
KINGSTON RANGE
Mesquite Lake
Roach Lake
Primm
Buffalo Bill's
Desert
Clark Mtn. 7,929
Mountain Pass
Nipton
Searchlight
Mt. Perkins 5,456
Cottonwood Cove
Lake Mohave
Windy Point B.L.M. Rec. Site
Chloride
Mt. Tipton 7,148
CERBAT MTS.
Peach Springs
Nelson
Yampai
Truxton
Grand Canyon Caverns
DUMONT DUNES
Halloran Springs
Silver Lake
Baker
Cima Dome
Cinder Cones
Cima
MOJAVE NATIONAL PRESERVE
NEW YORK MTS.
LANFAIR VALLEY
Ivanpah
Cal-Nev-Ari
Davis Dam
Colorado River Museum
ROAD CLOSED INDEFINITELY
Kingman
Kingman Arpt. (IGM)
HUALAPAI VALLEY
Hackberry
Valentine
Truxton Wash
SELIGMAN
Seligman
AFTON CANYON NATURAL AREA
CADY MTS.
DESERT
DEVILS PLAYGROUND
Kelso
Kelso Dunes
Providence Mountains St. Rec. Area
Mitchell Caverns
SAN BERNARDINO
Goffs
Fenner
Big Bend of the Colorado S.R.A.
Laughlin
Laughlin/Bullhead Intl. Arpt. (IFP)
McConnico
Bullhead City
Oatman
SACRAMENTO MTS.
Mohave Mus. of History & Arts and Historic Rt. 66 Mus.
Hualapai Mtn. Park
Hualapai Pk. 8,417
Wild Cow Springs B.L.M. Rec. Site
Yucca
Snow Mtn. 5,879
Cross Mtn. 6,463
AQUARIUS MOUNTAINS
JUNIPER MTS.
PRESCOTT NATL. FOR.
Mohon Pk. 7,499
Mt. Hope 7,263
Hyde Creek Mtn. 7,272
BRISTOL MTS.
Ludlow
Bagdad
Essex
Danby
South Pass 2,750
Needles
Golden Shores
HAVASU N.W.R.
Mohave Valley
FORT MOHAVE IND. RES.
BLACK MESA
HUALAPAI MTS.
DUTCH FLAT
Granite Pk. 7,069
Wikieup
MC CRACKEN MTS.
Aubrey Pk. 5,078
Burro Creek B.L.M. Rec. Site
Burro Creek
Bagdad
POACHIE RANGE
JOSHUA FOREST PARKWAY
Cypress Mtn. 6,251
MOJAVE
Amboy Crater Natl. Nat. Landmark
Amboy
Cadiz
Bristol Lake
OLD NATIONAL TRAIL HWY
Danby
OLD WOMAN MTS.
CHEMEHUEVI VALLEY
Topock
Moabi Reg. Park
MOHAVE MTS.
Lake Havasu City Arpt. (HII)
Lake Havasu City
Lake Havasu
Lake Havasu S.P.
CHEMEHUEVI IND. RES.
Hillside
Date
WEAVER MTS.
MARINE CORPS AIR GROUND COMBAT CENTER TWENTYNINE PALMS
Cadiz Lake
PIUTE MTS.
TURTLE MTS.
Danby Lake
London Bridge
WHIPPLE MTS.
Cattail Cove S.P.
Parker Dam
Bill Williams River N.W.R.
Alamo Lake
Tres Alamos 4,293
Alamo Dam
Congress
Joshua Tree
Twentynine Palms
Oasis Visitor Ctr.
Twentynine Palms Ind. Res.
JOSHUA TREE NATL. PARK
SHEEP HOLE MTS.
COXCOMB MTS.
Vidal Jct.
Parker Strip B.L.M. Rec. Area
BUCKSKIN MTS.
Buckskin Mountain S.P.
Swansea Ghost Town
Santa Maria River
Hot Sprs.
Lost Horse Mine
Cholla Cactus Garden
PINTO MTS.
RIVERSIDE
Vidal
Big River
Earp
Parker
Colorado River Indian Tribes Mus.
Poston
CACTUS PLAIN
LA PAZ
Robson's Mining World
Forepaugh
Aquila
Quail Mtn. 5,814
Keys View
Hidden Valley
Black Canyon Rd
Bouse Wash
Bouse

Nevada · Utah · California · Arizona

DRIVING DISTANCES IN MILES

	CHINLE, AZ	FLAGSTAFF, AZ	GRAND CANYON, AZ	HOLBROOK, AZ	KAYENTA, AZ	KINGMAN, AZ	LAKE HAVASU CITY, AZ	LAS VEGAS, NV	LAUGHLIN, NV	PAGE, AZ	PRESCOTT, AZ	ST. GEORGE, UT
FLAGSTAFF, AZ	216		89	93	152	148	209	249	182	135	89	271
GRAND CANYON, AZ	232	89		182	153	175	236	276	209	136	131	272
LAS VEGAS, NV	465	249	276	341	374	103	154		94	277	251	118
ST. GEORGE, UT	358	271	272	353	255	221	272	118	212	159	369	

SEE ALSO DISTANCE AND DRIVING TIME MAP ON PAGES 286–287

0 mi | 20 | 40
0 km | 20 | 40 | 60

One inch equals 25.4 miles
One centimeter equals 16.1 kilometers

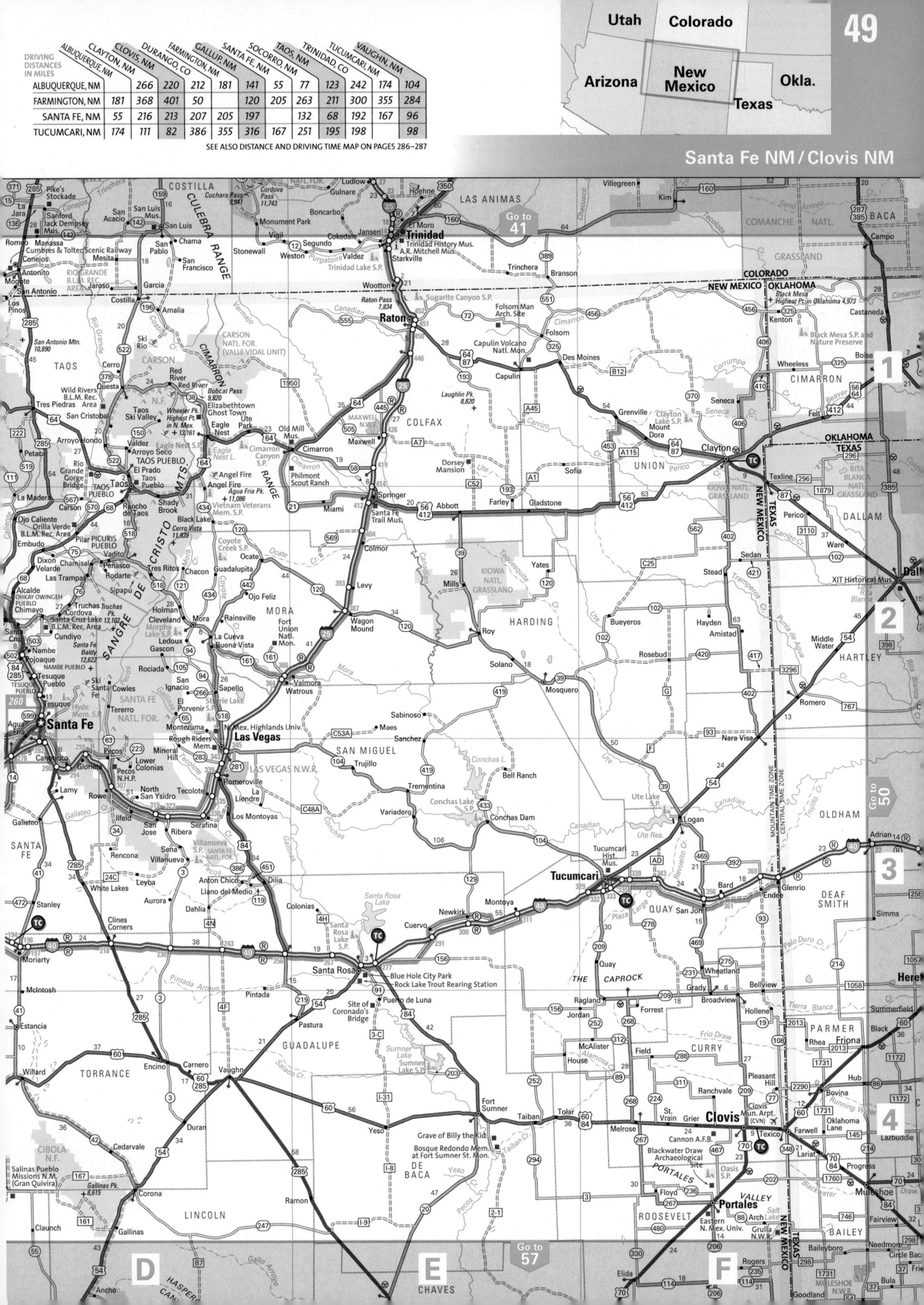

DRIVING DISTANCES IN MILES	ALBUQUERQUE, NM	CLAYTON, NM	CLOVIS, NM	DURANGO, CO	FARMINGTON, NM	GALLUP, NM	SANTA FE, NM	SOCORRO, NM	TAOS, NM	TRINIDAD, CO	TUCUMCARI, NM	VAUGHN, NM
ALBUQUERQUE, NM		266	220	212	181	141	55	77	123	242	174	104
FARMINGTON, NM	181	368	401	50		120	205	263	211	300	355	284
SANTA FE, NM	55	216	213	207	205	197		132	68	192	167	96
TUCUMCARI, NM	174	111	82	386	355	316	167	251	195	198		98

SEE ALSO DISTANCE AND DRIVING TIME MAP ON PAGES 286–287

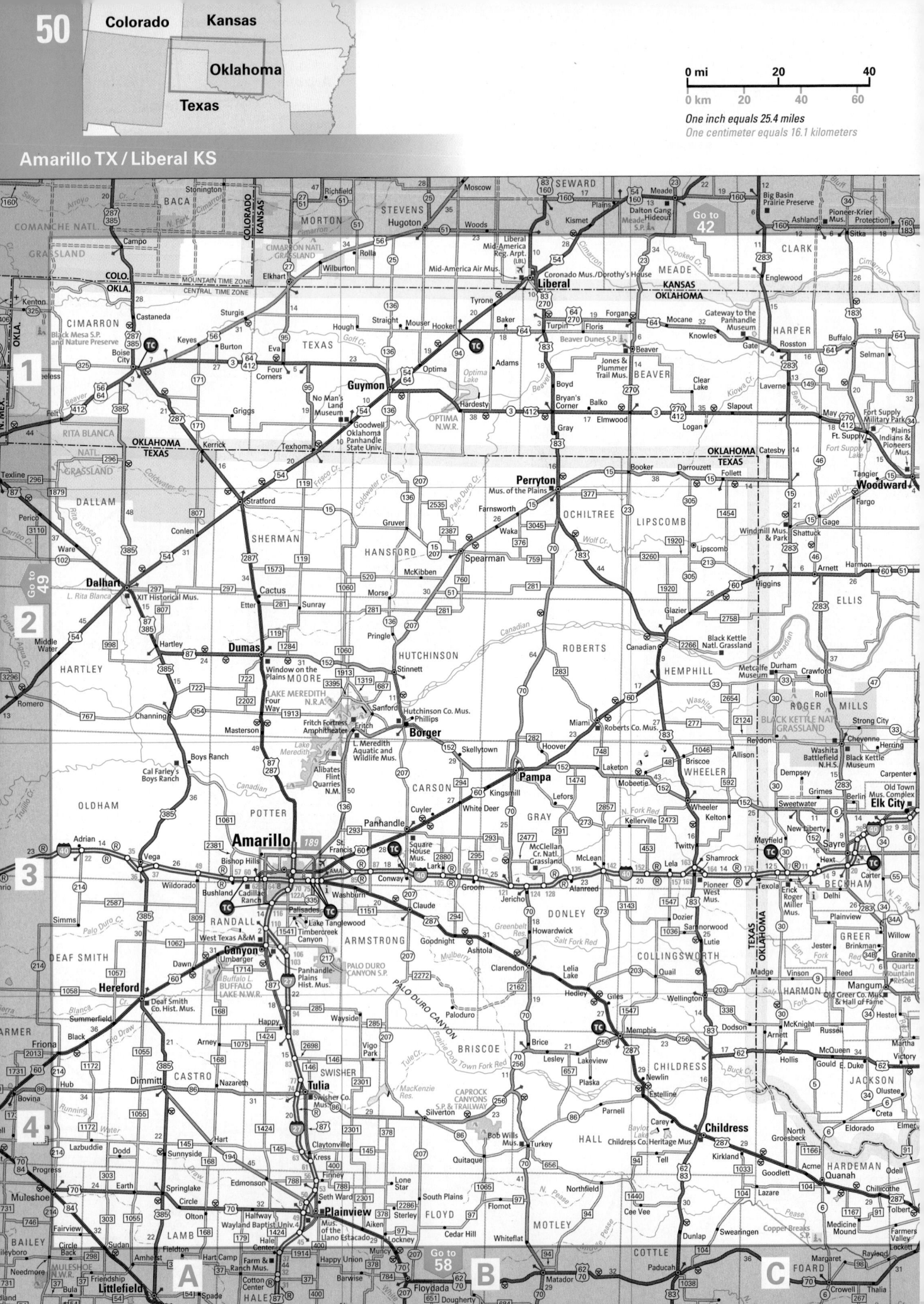

DRIVING DISTANCES IN MILES

	AMARILLO, TX	ARDMORE, OK	BARTLESVILLE, OK	CHILDRESS, TX	CLINTON, OK	ENID, OK	LAWTON, OK	LIBERAL, KS	OKLAHOMA CITY, OK	STILLWATER, OK	TULSA, OK	WOODWARD, OK
AMARILLO, TX		361	419	118	177	298	240	165	262	329	371	177
LAWTON, OK	240	103	243	124	98	142		287	85	152	194	175
OKLAHOMA CITY, OK	262	99	157	225	85	84	85	259		67	109	143
TULSA, OK	371	206	48	334	194	117	194	321	109	71		205

SEE ALSO DISTANCE AND DRIVING TIME MAP ON PAGES 286–287

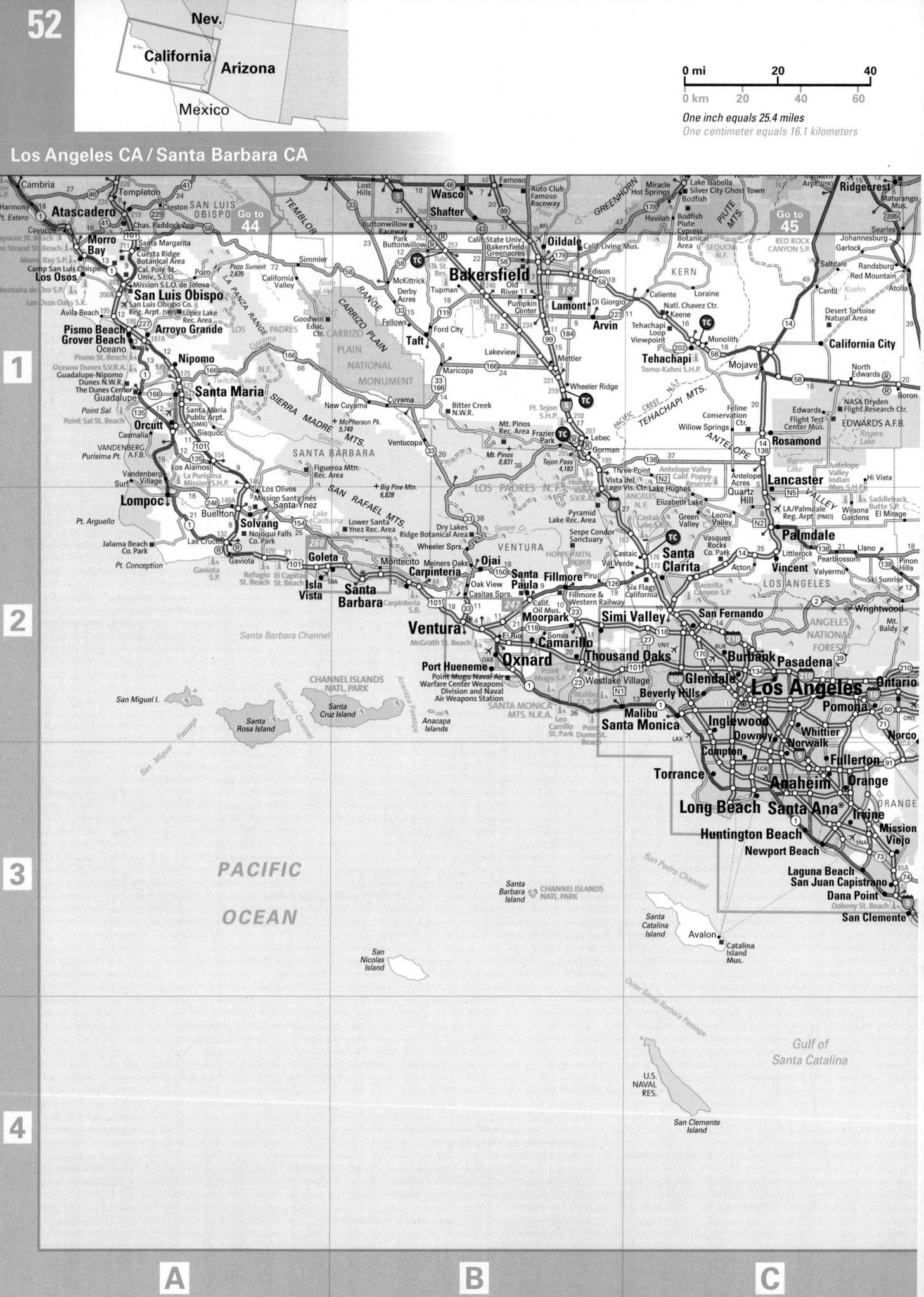

One inch equals 25.4 miles
One centimeter equals 16.1 kilometers

PACIFIC

OCEAN

San Diego CA / Palm Springs CA

53

California Arizona New Mexico

Mexico

0 mi   20   40
0 km   20   40   60
One inch equals 25.4 miles
One centimeter equals 16.1 kilometers

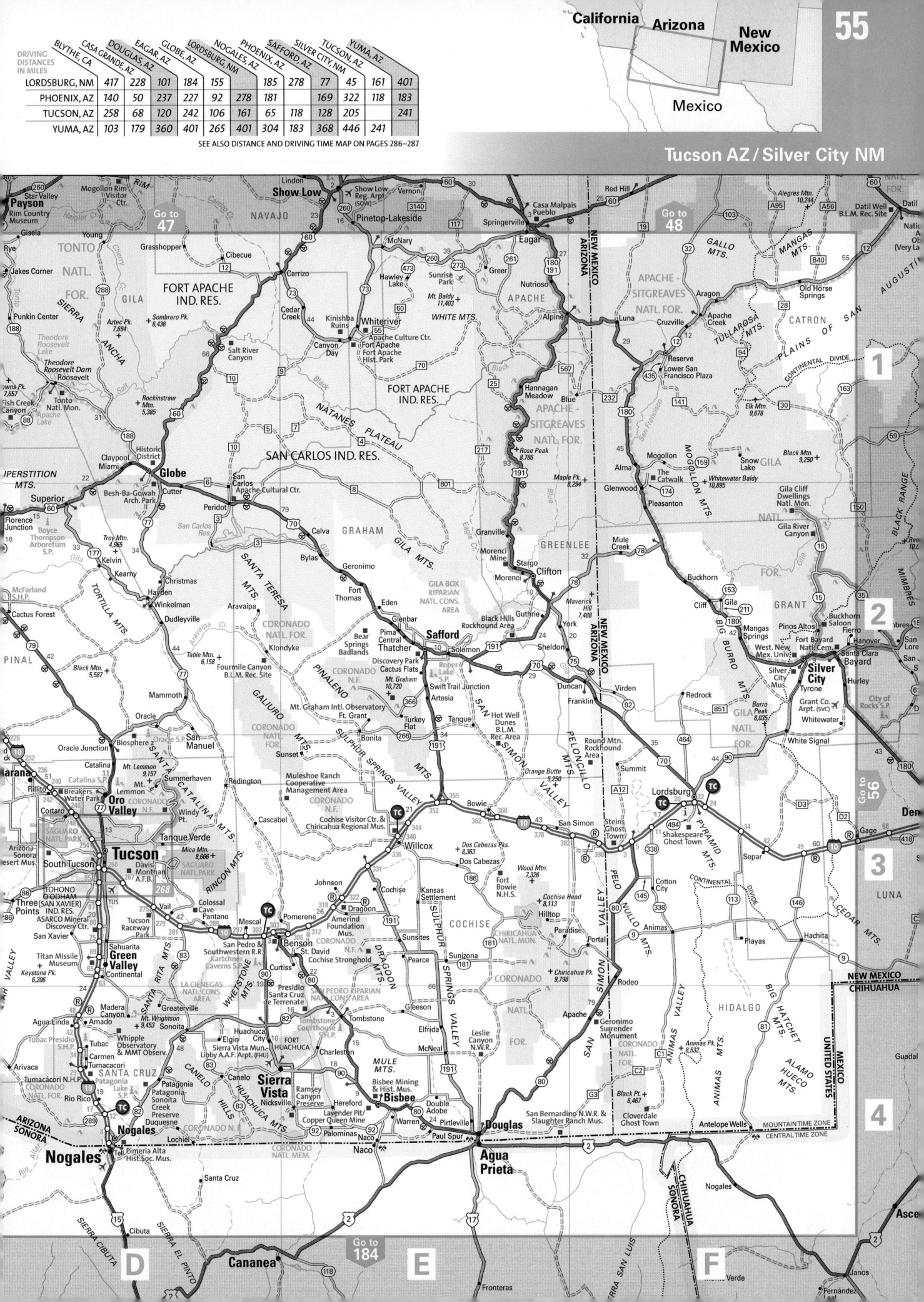

California Arizona New Mexico
Mexico

Go to 47

Go to 48

Go to 56

Go to 184

DRIVING DISTANCES IN MILES	BLYTHE, CA	CASA GRANDE, AZ	DOUGLAS, AZ	EAGAR, AZ	GLOBE, AZ	LORDSBURG, NM	NOGALES, AZ	PHOENIX, AZ	SAFFORD, AZ	SILVER CITY, NM	TUCSON, AZ	YUMA, AZ
LORDSBURG, NM	417	228	101	184	155		185	278	77	45	161	401
PHOENIX, AZ	140	50	237	227	92	278	181		169	322	118	183
TUCSON, AZ	258	68	120	242	106	161	65	118	128	205		241
YUMA, AZ	103	179	360	401	265	401	304	183	368	446	241	

SEE ALSO DISTANCE AND DRIVING TIME MAP ON PAGES 286–287

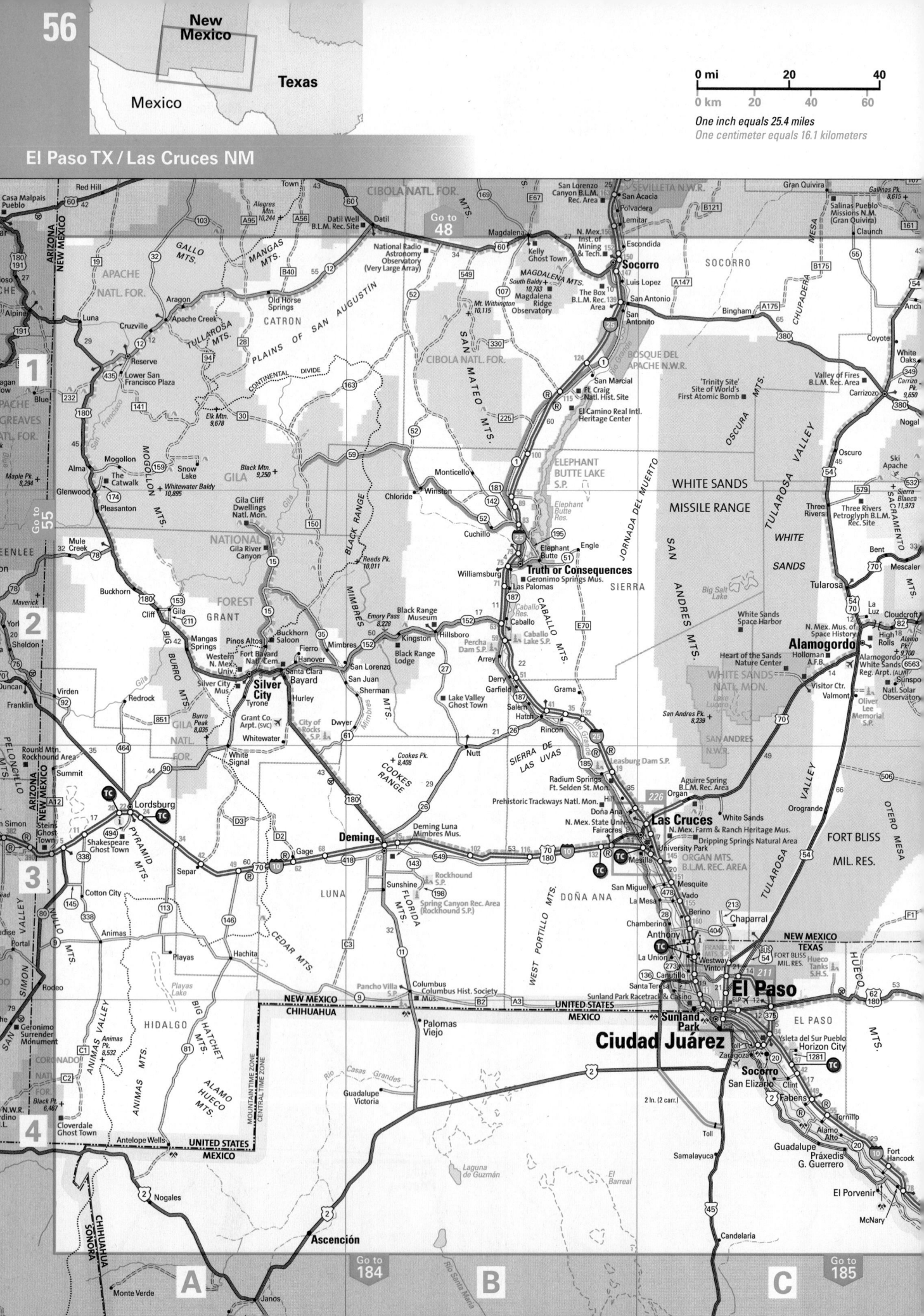

DRIVING DISTANCES IN MILES

SEE ALSO DISTANCE AND DRIVING TIME MAP ON PAGES 286–287

	ALAMOGORDO, NM	CARLSBAD, NM	EL PASO, TX	HOBBS, NM	LAS CRUCES, NM	LORDSBURG, NM	ODESSA, TX	PECOS, TX	PORTALES, NM	ROSWELL, NM	SILVER CITY, NM	SOCORRO, NM
CARLSBAD, NM	144		162	70	203	321	137	87	168	76	311	241
EL PASO, TX	86	162		232	42	160	285	209	295	203	150	190
LAS CRUCES, NM	65	203	42	250		122	325	250	274	182	111	146
ROSWELL, NM	117	76	203	117	182	304	201	163	92		293	164

Oklahoma

Texas

0 mi　　20　　40

0 km　20　40　60

One inch equals 25.4 miles
One centimeter equals 16.1 kilometers

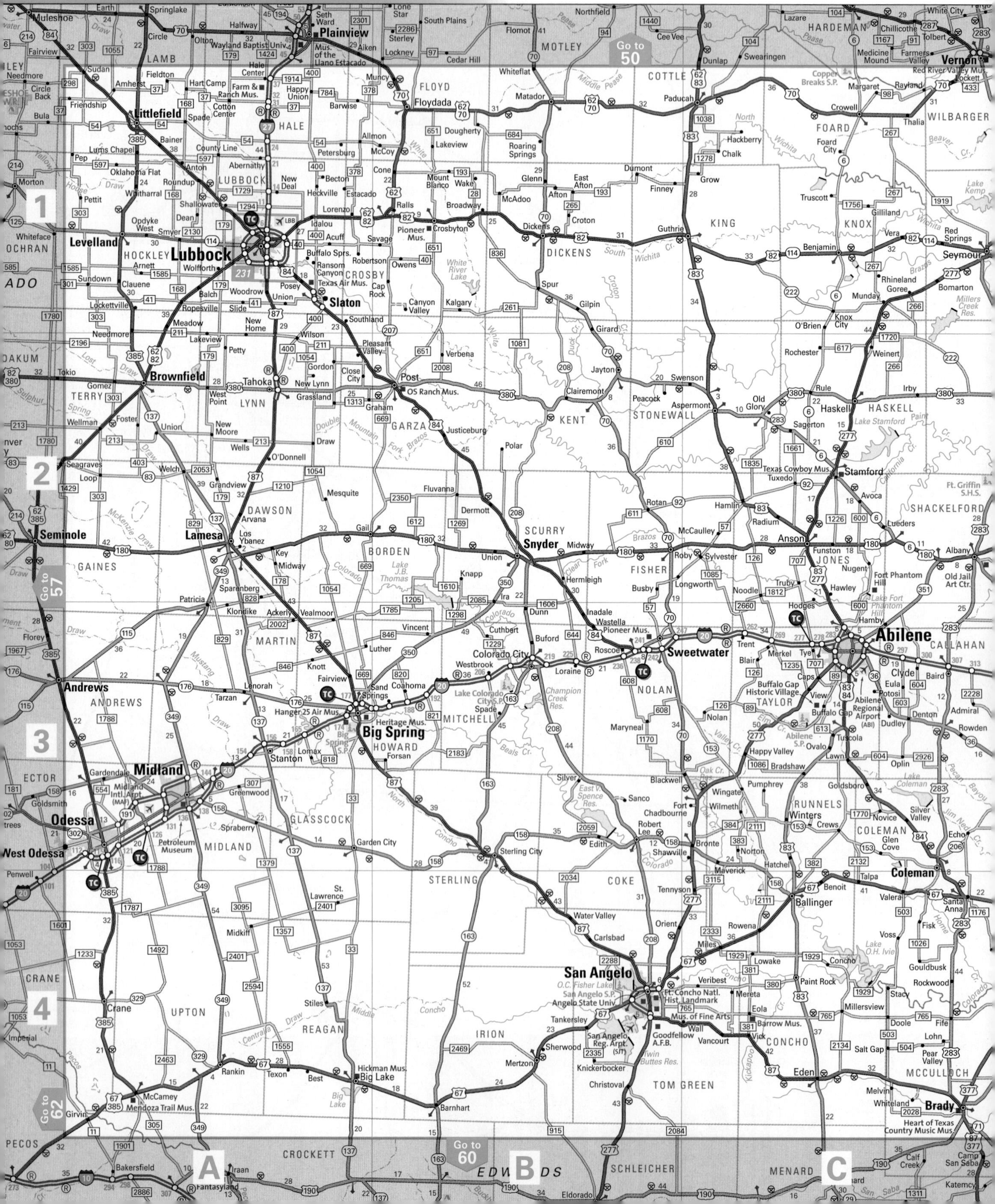

DRIVING DISTANCES IN MILES	ABILENE, TX	BIG SPRING, TX	BROWNWOOD, TX	DALLAS, TX	FORT WORTH, TX	LUBBOCK, TX	ODESSA, TX	SAN ANGELO, TX	SHERMAN, TX	TEMPLE, TX	WACO, TX	WICHITA FALLS, TX
ABILENE, TX		110	78	191	153	166	176	91	249	194	235	144
DALLAS, TX	191	298	190		32	354	364	265	64	130	94	141
LUBBOCK, TX	166	106	247	354	317		142	185	322	358	399	207
WACO, TX	235	343	124	94	87	399	409	219	159	40		201

SEE ALSO DISTANCE AND DRIVING TIME MAP ON PAGES 286-287

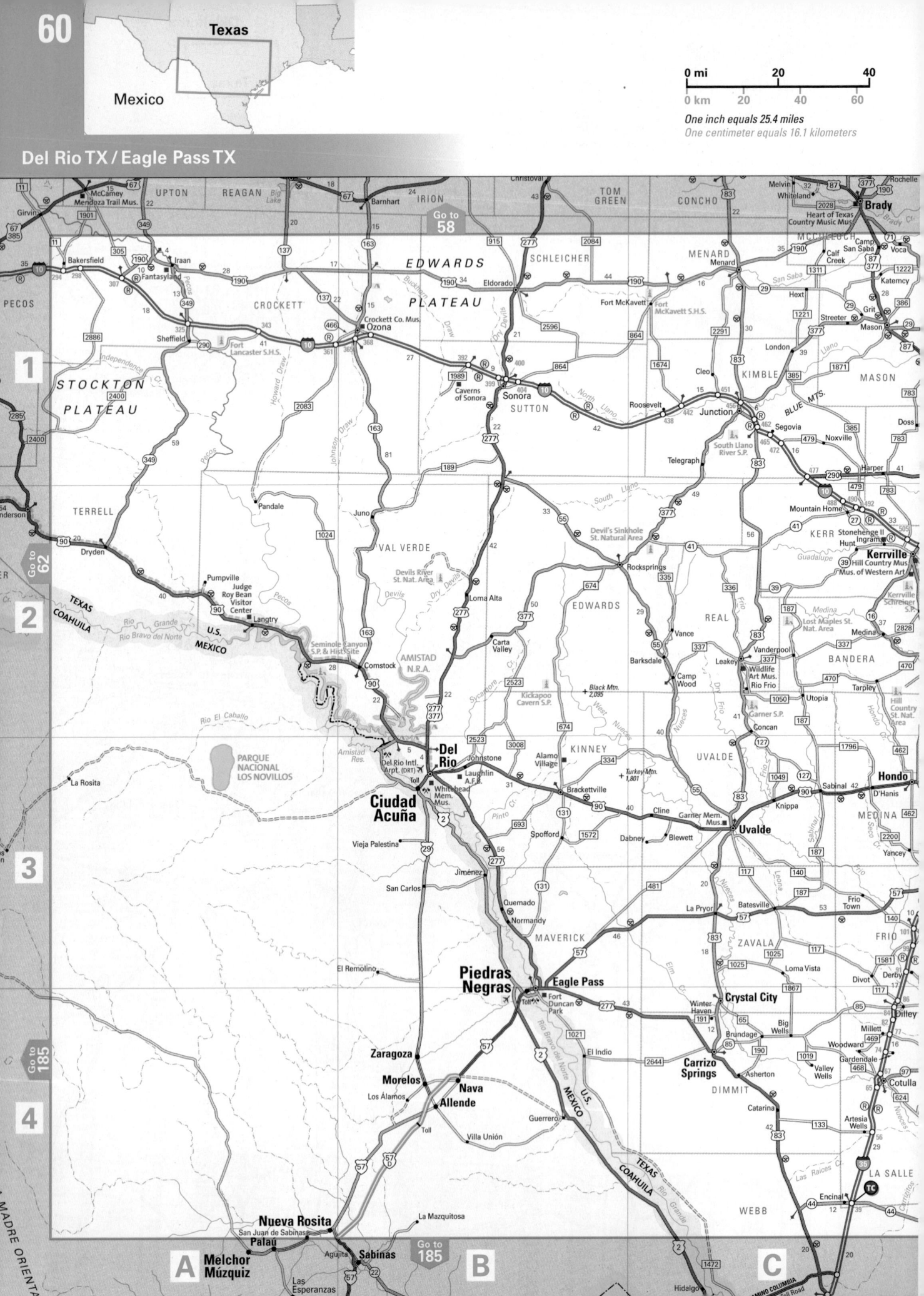

Texas

Mexico

0 mi 20 40
0 km 20 40 60
One inch equals 25.4 miles
One centimeter equals 16.1 kilometers

UPTON REAGAN Big Lake IRION Christoval TOM GREEN CONCHO Melvin Whiteland Brady

Go to 58

McCamey Mendoza Trail Mus. Barnhart Heart of Texas Country Music Mus.

Girvin EDWARDS PLATEAU Eldorado SCHLEICHER MENARD Menard San Saba Calf Creek San Saba Voca Camp Katemcy

Bakersfield Iraan Fantasyland Fort McKavett Fort McKavett S.H.S. London KIMBLE Mason Grit

PECOS CROCKETT Crockett Co. Mus. Ozona Sheffield Fort Lancaster S.H.S. Cleo Streeter

STOCKTON PLATEAU Caverns of Sonora Sonora SUTTON Roosevelt Junction Segovia Noxville Doss

Pandale South Llano River S.P. Telegraph BLUE MTS. Harper

Juno North Llano Mountain Home Hunt Stonehenge II Ingram KERR Kerrville Hill Country Mus. Mus. of Western Art

anderson Dryden Devil's Sinkhole St. Natural Area Guadalupe Kerrville Schreiner S.P.

Go to 62 TERRELL VAL VERDE Rocksprings EDWARDS REAL Lost Maples St. Nat. Area Medina

Pumpville Judge Roy Bean Visitor Center Devils River St. Nat. Area Vance BANDERA

TEXAS COAHUILA Langtry Loma Alta Barksdale Leakey Vanderpool Wildlife Art Mus. Rio Frio Tarpley Hill Country St. Nat. Area

Rio Grande U.S. MEXICO Seminole Canyon S.P. & Hist Site Carta Valley Camp Wood Utopia

Rio Bravo del Norte Comstock AMISTAD N.R.A. Black Mtn. 2,095 Garner S.P. Concan

La Rosita Kickapoo Cavern S.P. KINNEY UVALDE

PARQUE NACIONAL LOS NOVILLOS Amistad Res. Del Rio Johnstone Alamo Village Turkey Mtn. 1,801 Hondo D'Hanis

Del Rio Intl. Arpt. (DRT) Toll Laughlin A.F.B. Brackettville Cline Garner Mem. Mus. Knippa MEDINA

Ciudad Acuña Whitehead Mem. Mus. Spofford Dabney Blewett Uvalde Yancey

Vieja Palestina Jiménez Spofford FRIO

San Carlos Quemado La Pryor Batesville Frio Town

Normandy MAVERICK ZAVALA Loma Vista Dilley

El Remolino Piedras Negras Eagle Pass Crystal City Millett

Go to 185 Zaragoza Fort Duncan Park Winter Haven Brundage Woodward Gardendale Cotulla

Morelos Nava El Indio Carrizo Springs Asherton Valley Wells

Los Álamos Allende DIMMIT Catarina Artesia Wells

Guerrero Villa Unión LA SALLE

Nueva Rosita San Juan de Sabinas Palaú La Mazquitosa WEBB Encinal

MADRE ORIENTAL Melchor Múzquiz Aguijita Sabinas Go to 185 Hidalgo

Las Esperanzas

DRIVING DISTANCES IN MILES	AUSTIN, TX	BEEVILLE, TX	COLLEGE STATION TX	COLUMBUS, TX	DEL RIO, TX	EAGLE PASS, TX	FREDERICKSBURG, TX	SAN ANTONIO TX	SONORA, TX	TEMPLE, TX	UVALDE, TX	VICTORIA, TX
AUSTIN, TX		136	108	92	229	226	78	78	244	67	159	123
DEL RIO, TX	229	235	322	277		55	178	152	89	295	70	268
SAN ANTONIO, TX	78	110	171	128	152	145	67		172	144	82	118
VICTORIA, TX	123	56	160	87	268	254	186	118	292	187	198	

SEE ALSO DISTANCE AND DRIVING TIME MAP ON PAGES 286–287

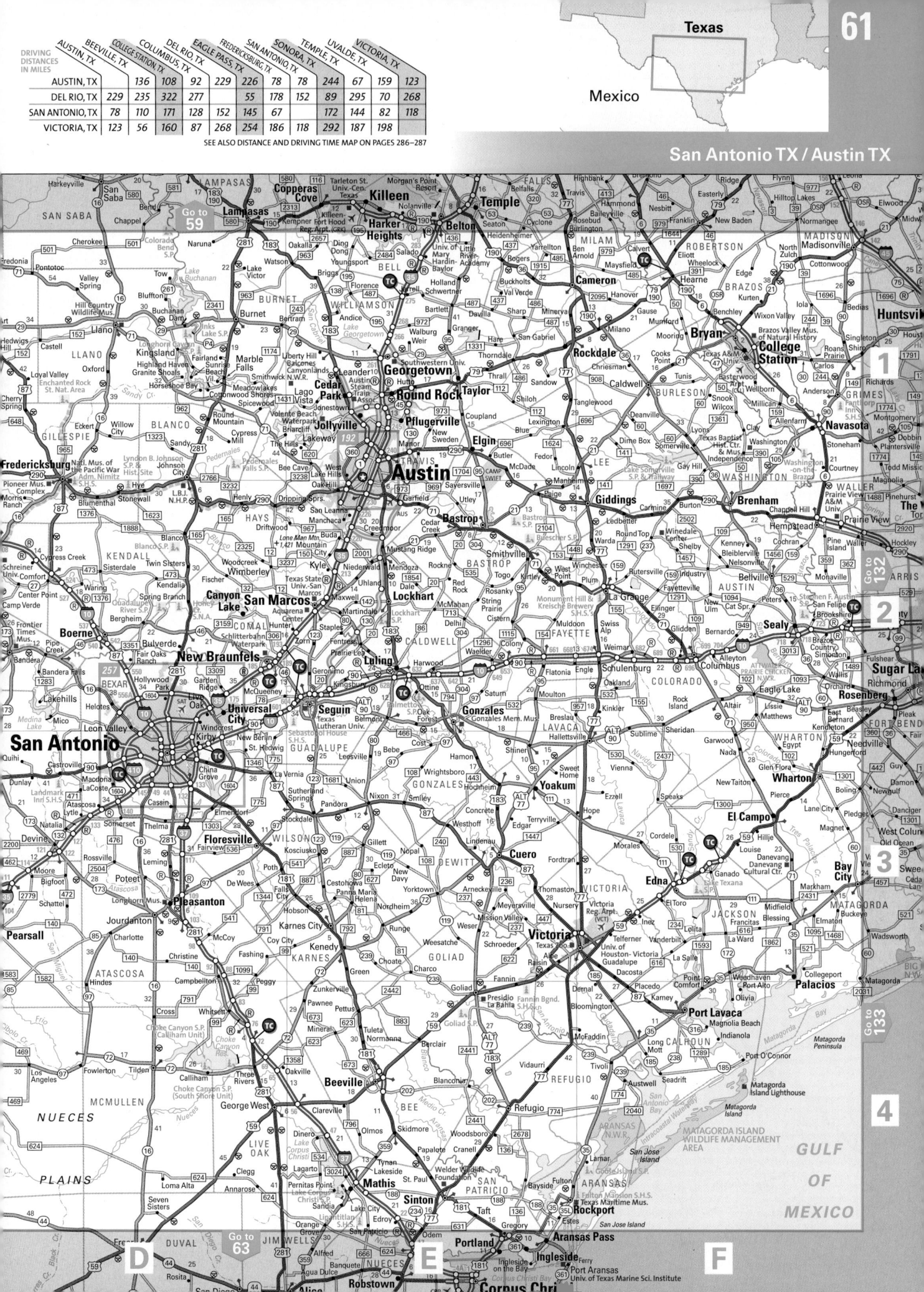

DRIVING DISTANCES IN MILES	ALPINE, TX	BIG BEND NP, TX	FORT STOCKTON, TX	ODESSA, TX	PECOS, TX	VAN HORN, TX
ALPINE, TX			97	65	151	96	110
FORT STOCKTON, TX	65	123		86	58	119
ODESSA, TX	151	209	86		76	163
VAN HORN, TX	110	207	119	163	87	

SEE ALSO DISTANCE AND DRIVING TIME MAP ON PAGES 286–287

One inch equals 25.4 miles
One centimeter equals 16.1 kilometers

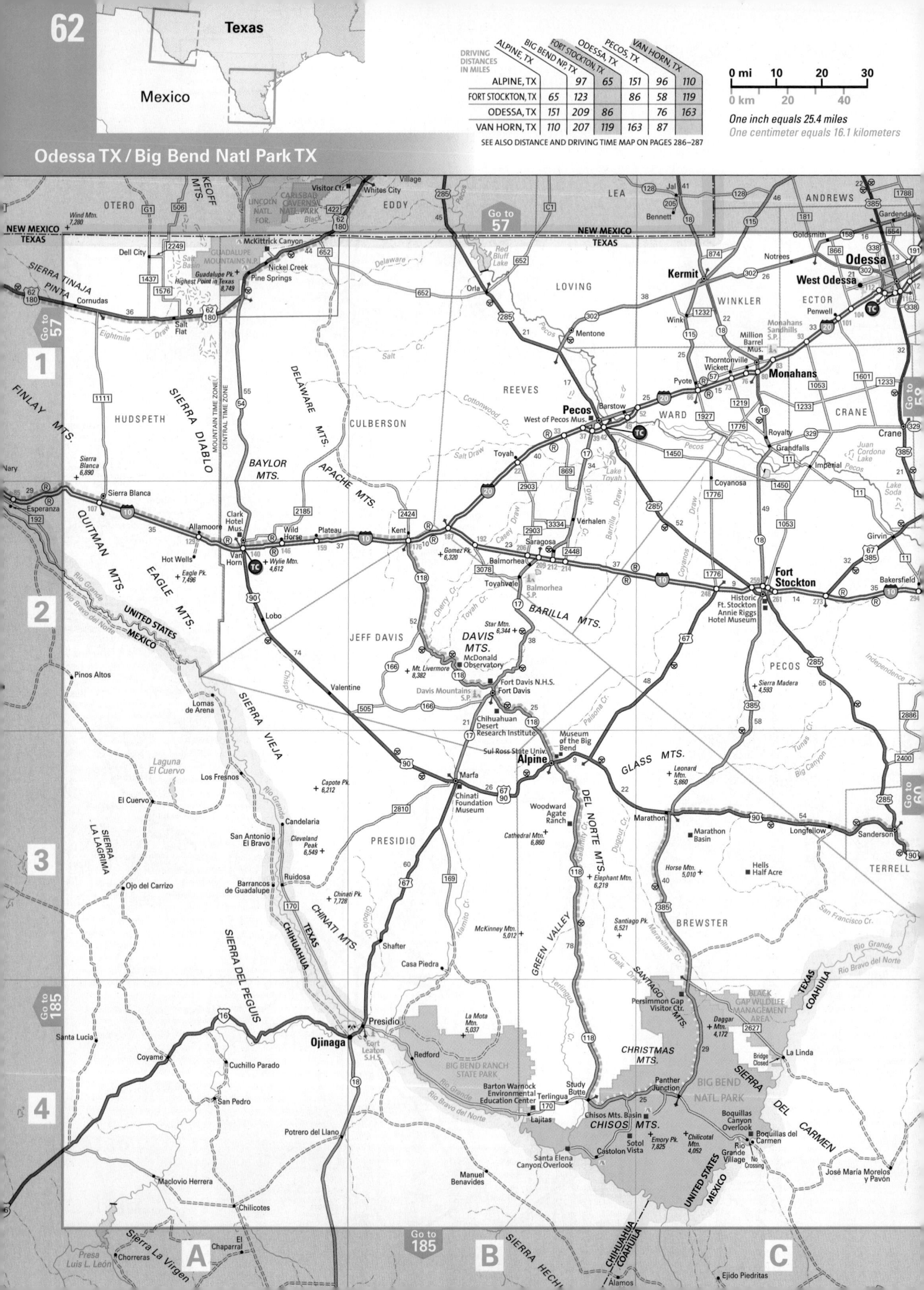

Manitoba   Ontario

Minnesota

Michigan

Wisconsin

0 mi   20   40
0 km   20   40   60
One inch equals 25.4 miles
One centimeter equals 16.1 kilometers

Duluth MN / International Falls MN

DRIVING DISTANCES IN MILES

	ASHLAND, WI	BEMIDJI, MN	BRAINERD, MN	DETROIT LAKES, MN	DULUTH, MN	GRAND PORTAGE, MN	HOUGHTON, MI	INTERNAT'L FALLS, MN	IRONWOOD, MI	ISHPEMING, MI	THUNDER BAY, ON	VIRGINIA, MN
BEMIDJI, MN	239		96	91	153	295	362	109	254	384	314	124
DULUTH, MN	92	153	116	202		143	215	157	107	238	183	61
HOUGHTON, MI	132	362	325	412	215	358		370	108	87	654	274
INTERNAT'L FALLS, MN	247	109	190	200	157	245	370		262	393	205	97

SEE ALSO DISTANCE AND DRIVING TIME MAP ON PAGES 286–287

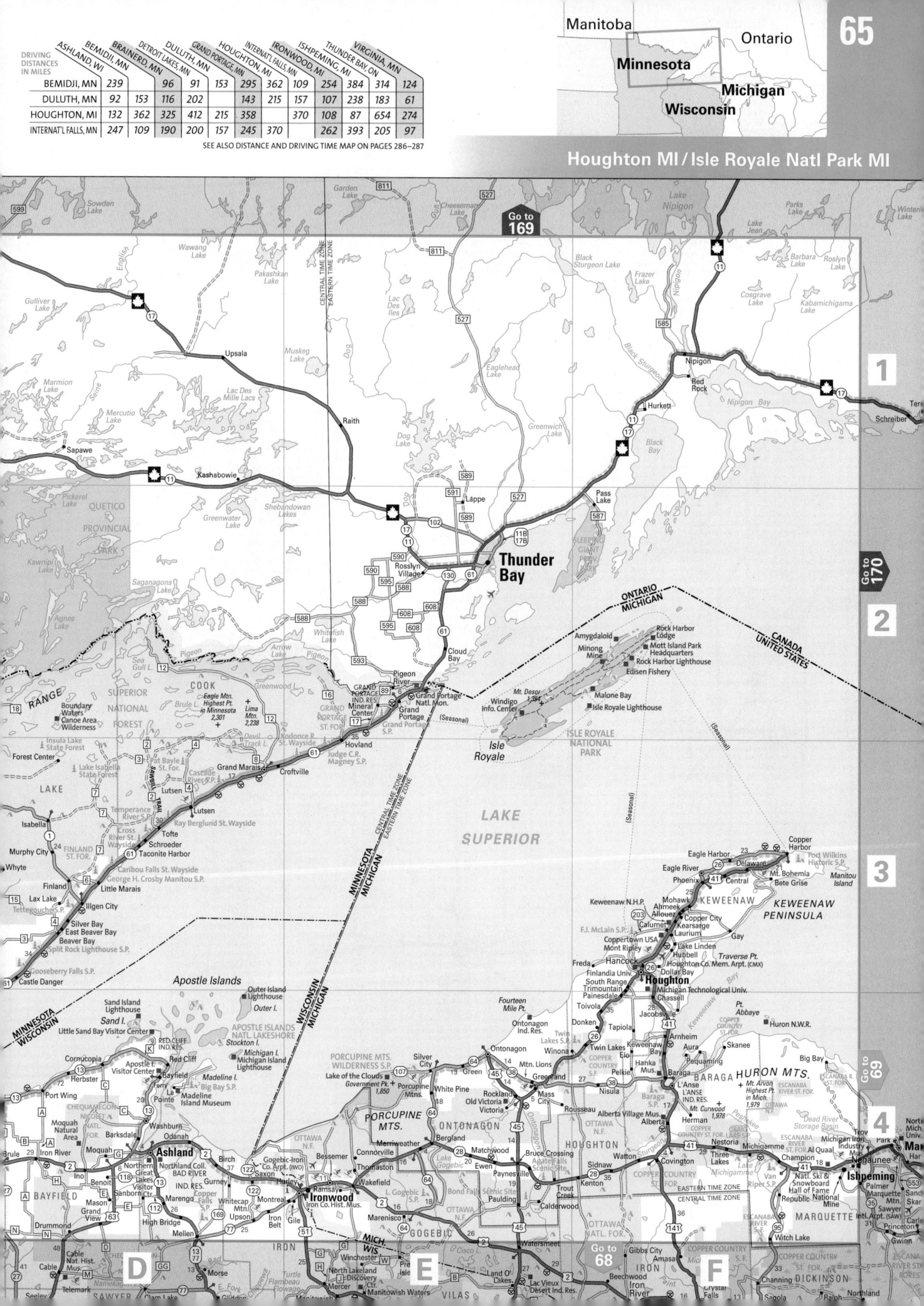

0 mi 10 20 30 40
0 km 10 20 30 40 50 60

One inch equals 18.4 miles
One centimeter equals 11.7 kilometers

Green Bay WI / Wausau WI

A B C
1 2 3 4

DRIVING DISTANCES IN MILES

	ESCANABA, MI	GREEN BAY, WI	IRON MOUNTAIN, MI	IRONWOOD, MI	L'ANSE, MI	MANISTIQUE, MI	MARINETTE, WI	MARQUETTE, MI	RHINELANDER, WI	STEVENS POINT, WI	TRAVERSE CITY, MI	WAUSAU, WI
ESCANABA, MI		111	52	178	134	54	57	65	132	185	252	171
GREEN BAY, WI	111		96	202	178	165	54	175	124	87	363	93
MARQUETTE, MI	65	175	79	145	70	86	122		147	238	269	204
WAUSAU, WI	171	93	133	121	176	225	112	204	58	35	423	

SEE ALSO DISTANCE AND DRIVING TIME MAP ON PAGES 286–287

Ontario

Michigan

0 mi 10 20 30 40
0 km 10 20 30 40 50 60
One inch equals 18.4 miles
One centimeter equals 11.7 kilometers

LAKE SUPERIOR

Go to 170

CANADA / U.S.
ONTARIO / MICHIGAN

Searchmont
Heyden
Goulais
Gros Cap
Sault Ste. Marie (Ontario)
Echo Lake
Echo Bay
Desbarats

Sault Ste. Marie
Soo Locks
Valley Camp
Lake Superior State Univ.
Brimley
Bay Mills Ind. Res.
Sugar I.
Rosedale
Bay Mills Ind. Res.
Richards Landing
Hilton Beach
Kentvale

Au Sable Pt.
Grand Marais
Deer Park
Muskallonge Lake S.P.
Great Lakes Shipwreck Museum
Whitefish Point
Whitefish Pt. N.W.R. & Bird Observatory
Paradise
Lower Falls
Point Iroquois Light

PICTURED ROCKS NATIONAL LAKESHORE
Grand Sable Dunes
Beaver Basin Overlook
Chapel Basin
Grand Island
GRAND ISLAND NATL. REC. AREA
Miners Castle
Melstrand
Munising Falls
Christmas
Au Train
Munising
Chatham

LUCE
TAHQUAMENON FALLS S.P.
Upper Falls
Natl. Fish Hatchery
Eckerman
Strongs
Raco
Brimley
Dafter
Kinross
Rudyard
Pickford
Stalwart
Goetzville
Cedarville
Hessel
Les Cheneaux Islands

CHIPPEWA
HIAWATHA NATIONAL FOREST

Wetmore
Shingleton
Seney
McMillan
Newberry
Dollarville
Soo Junction
Hulbert
McLeods Corner
Helmer
Germfask
Curtis
Gilchrist
Garnet
Rexton
Ozark
Trout Lake
Fibre

SENEY N.W.R.
SCHOOLCRAFT
Manistique Lake
Blaney Park
Engadine
Naubinway
Gould City
Epoufette
Brevort
Moran
Allenville
Sand Dunes

ALGER
Steuben
Big Spring
Palms Book S.P.
Indian Lake S.P.
Gulliver
Manistique
Thompson
Cooks
Isabella
Garden Corners
Nahma
Garden

DELTA
HIAWATHA NATIONAL FOREST
Fayette Historic S.P.
Fairport
Pt. Detour

Go to 69

LAKE SUPERIOR STATE FOREST

Father Marquette Natl. Mem.
Gros Cap
St. Ignace
Fort Mackinac
Mackinac Island S.P.
Mackinac Island
Straits of Mackinac
Colonial Michilimackinac
Mackinaw City
Historic Mill Creek
Pointe Aux Pins
Bois Blanc I.
MACKINAC ST. FOR.

LAKE HURON

St. Martin I.
Poverty I.
Summer I.
Little Summer I.

Garden I.
Hog I.
High I.
Gull I.
St. James
Welke Arpt. (6Y8)
Michigan Islands N.W.R.
Beaver Island Marine Museum
Beaver Island
MACKINAC ST. FOR.

Sturgeon Bay
WILDERNESS ST. PK.
Bliss
Cross Village
Levering
Carp Lake
Mackinaw St. For.
Cheboygan
Cheboygan S.P.
Mullett Lake
Alverno
Grace
Hammond Bay
Huron Beach

LAKE MICHIGAN

North Fox I.
South Fox I.
North Manitou I.
South Manitou I.

MICHIGAN / WISCONSIN
CENTRAL TIME ZONE / EASTERN TIME ZONE

Good Hart
Pellston Reg. Arpt. (PLN)
Pellston
Brutus
Alanson
EMMET
MACKINAW ST. FOR.
Pleasant View
Nub's Nob
Boyne Highlands
Harbor Springs
Wequetonsing
Conway
Oden
Indian River
Burt Lake
Topinabee
Aloha
Onaway S.P.
Ocqueoc
Ocqueoc Falls
Millersburg

Mt. McSauba
Petoskey
Petoskey S.P.
Bay View
Epsilon
CHEBOYGAN
Afton
Tower
Onaway
PRESQUE ISLE
MACKINAW STATE FOREST

Fisherman's Island S.P.
Charlevoix Mun. Arpt. (CVX)
Charlevoix
Little Traverse Bay
Bay Shore
Horton Bay
Walloon Lake
Clarion
Wolverine
Hillman

Norwood
Ironton
Boyne City
East Jordan
Boyne Mtn.
Boyne Falls
CHARLEVOIX
Vanderbilt
OTSEGO
Otsego Club
Treetops Resort
Clear Lake S.P.

Grand Traverse Lighthouse
Leelanau S.P.
Cathead Pt.
Northport
Omena
Ellsworth
Atwood
Eastport
Torch Lake
Central Lake
ANTRIM
MACKINAW ST. FOR.
Elmira
Johannesburg
Vienna
Atlanta
MONTMORENCY
Lewiston

North Manitou I.
Grand Traverse I.R.
Leland
Peshawbestown
Suttons Bay
Old Mission Point Lighthouse
Old Mission
Bellaire
Shanty Creek
Alba
Oak Grove
Otsego Lake S.P.
Otsego Lake
Waters
Gaylord
Arbutus Beach
Comins
Fairview
McKinley

SLEEPING BEAR DUNES NATL. LAKESHORE
Visitor Center
The Homestead
Glen Haven
Pierce Stocking Scenic Drive
Glen Arbor
Maple City
Cedar
LEELANAU
L. Leelanau
Greilickville
Lake Leelanau
Hickory Hills
Acme
Kewadin
Spirit of the Woods
Alden
Rapid City
Mancelona
CAMP GRAYLING ARMY & AIR NATL. GUARD TRAINING CTR.
Lovells
Frederic
Hartwick Pines Logging Mus.
HARTWICK PINES S.P.
Red Oak
Luzerne
OSCODA
Kirtlands Warbler Wildlife Management Area
Mio

Sleeping Bear Dune Natl. Lakeshore Visitors Center
Empire
BENZIE
Dennos Mus. Ctr.
Traverse City
Cherry Capital Arpt. (TVC)
Bates
Williamsburg
Mt. Holiday
Music House Mus.
Darragh
Kalkaska
KALKASKA
CRAWFORD
Grayling
Hanson Hills
Hartwick Pines S.P.

Pt. Betsie
Crystal L.
Frankfort
Elberta
Honor
Beulah
Benzie Area Hist. Mus.
Bendon
Center for the Arts
PERE MARQUETTE S.F.
Interlochen
Lake Ann
Interlochen S.P.
Grawn
Karlin
Kingsley
Fife Lake
South Boardman
Spencer
Skyline
CAMP GRAYLING MIL. RES.
Higgins Lake
North Higgins Lake S.P.
Roscommon
HURON NATL. FOR.

Arcadia
Crystal Mtn.
Thompsonville
Mayfield
GRAND TRAVERSE
Buckley
Copemish
Manton
MANISTEE
WEXFORD
Sherman
MISSAUKEE
Moorestown
Civilian Conservation Corps Museum
Higgins Lake
St. Helen
Rose City
Rifle River Rec. Area
OGEMAW

Go to 75
Go to 76

Ontario

Michigan

DRIVING DISTANCES IN MILES	ALPENA, MI	CHEBOYGAN, MI	GAYLORD, MI	GRAYLING, MI	MACKINAW CITY, MI	MANISTIQUE, MI	MUNISING, MI	PETOSKEY, MI	ROGERS CITY, MI	SAULT STE. MARIE, MI	SUDBURY, ON	TRAVERSE CITY, MI
ALPENA, MI		78	76	95	94	187	215	101	38	148	334	141
MACKINAW CITY, MI	94	16	60	87		95	123	38	58	57	242	106
SAULT STE. MARIE, MI	148	71	114	142	57	120	120	93	112		186	160
TRAVERSE CITY, MI	141	115	65	52	106	198	226	67	135	160	346	

SEE ALSO DISTANCE AND DRIVING TIME MAP ON PAGES 286–287

Minn. Wisconsin

Iowa Illinois

0 mi 10 20 30 40
0 km 10 20 30 40 50 60
One inch equals 18.4 miles
One centimeter equals 11.7 kilometers

Mankato MN / Fort Dodge IA

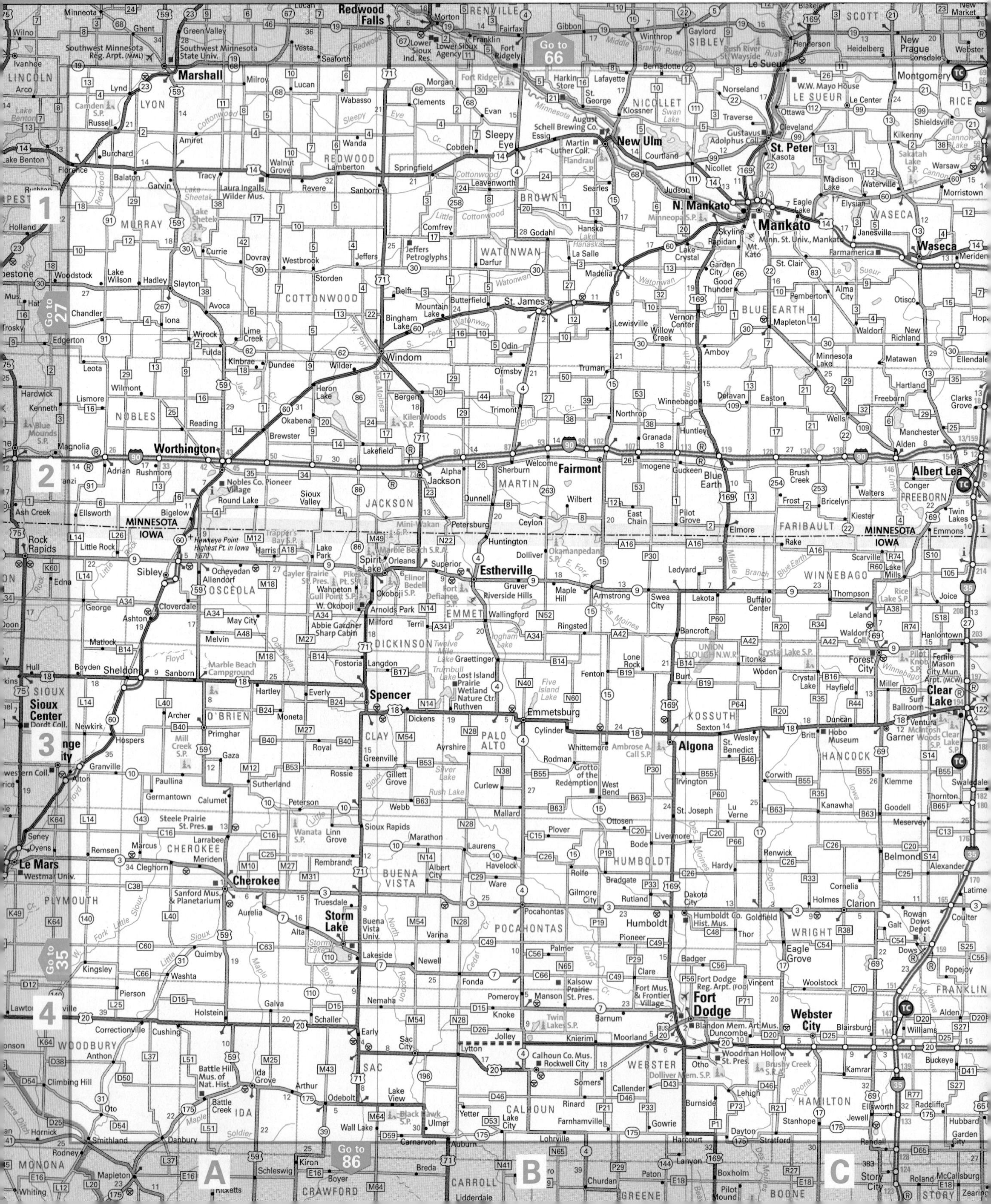

SEE ALSO DISTANCE AND DRIVING TIME MAP ON PAGES 286-287

DRIVING DISTANCES IN MILES	ALBERT LEA, MN	DECORAH, IA	DUBUQUE, IA	FORT DODGE, IA	LA CROSSE, WI	MANKATO, MN	MASON CITY, IA	ROCHESTER, MN	SPENCER, IA	WATERLOO, IA	WINONA, MN	WORTHINGTON, MN
FORT DODGE, IA	124	186	200		245	138	97	183	95	108	225	148
MANKATO, MN	56	151	253	138	149		100	80	123	186	128	108
ROCHESTER, MN	62	68	170	183	71	80	103		189	116	51	174
WATERLOO, IA	130	79	93	108	138	186	79	116	189		144	244

0 mi 10 20 30 40
0 km 10 20 30 40 50 60
One inch equals 18.4 miles
One centimeter equals 11.7 kilometers

DRIVING DISTANCES IN MILES

	CADILLAC, MI	DUBUQUE, IA	GRAND RAPIDS, MI	GREEN BAY, WI	KALAMAZOO, MI	MADISON, WI	MILWAUKEE, WI	MUSKEGON, MI	OSHKOSH, WI	ROCKFORD, IL	SHEBOYGAN, WI	TOMAH, WI
GRAND RAPIDS, MI	99	364		393	53	335	277	40	363	271	332	424
GREEN BAY, WI	492	229	393		362	135	115	400	50	211	61	162
MADISON, WI	434	93	335	135	304		78	341	86	78	132	98
MILWAUKEE, WI	377	167	277	115	247	78		285	87	95	54	168

SEE ALSO DISTANCE AND DRIVING TIME MAP ON PAGES 286–287

Ontario

Michigan

Detroit MI / Lansing MI

| 0 mi | 10 | 20 | 30 | 40 |

| 0 km | 10 | 20 | 30 | 40 | 50 | 60 |

One inch equals 18.4 miles
One centimeter equals 11.7 kilometers

DRIVING DISTANCES IN MILES

	ANN ARBOR, MI	BAD AXE, MI	BATTLE CREEK, MI	CADILLAC, MI	DETROIT, MI	FLINT, MI	HAMILTON, ON	LANSING, MI	LONDON, ON	MT. PLEASANT, MI	PORT HURON, MI	SAGINAW, MI
DETROIT, MI	42	107	116	209		62	203	86	128	149	58	97
LANSING, MI	63	140	56	131	86	53	270		191	67	117	86
PORT HURON, MI	101	81	175	211	58	64	154	117		75	155		100
SAGINAW, MI	87	64	142	116	97	36	253	86	174	60	100	

SEE ALSO DISTANCE AND DRIVING TIME MAP ON PAGES 286–287

One inch equals 18.4 miles
One centimeter equals 11.7 kilometers

Ontario

New York

DRIVING DISTANCES IN MILES

	BATH, NY	BUFFALO, NY	ITHACA, NY	NIAGARA FALLS, NY	ONEONTA, NY	OSWEGO, NY	ROCHESTER, NY	SYRACUSE, NY	TORONTO, ON	TUPPER LAKE, NY	UTICA, NY	WATERTOWN, NY
BUFFALO, NY	113		153	20	263	158	74	152	106	321	199	210
ROCHESTER, NY	78	74		89	88	200	73		88	181	257	135	146
SYRACUSE, NY	105	152	59	166	118	38	88			260	176	53	65
UTICA, NY	152	199	108	213	65	81	135	53	307	131		86

SEE ALSO DISTANCE AND DRIVING TIME MAP ON PAGES 286–287

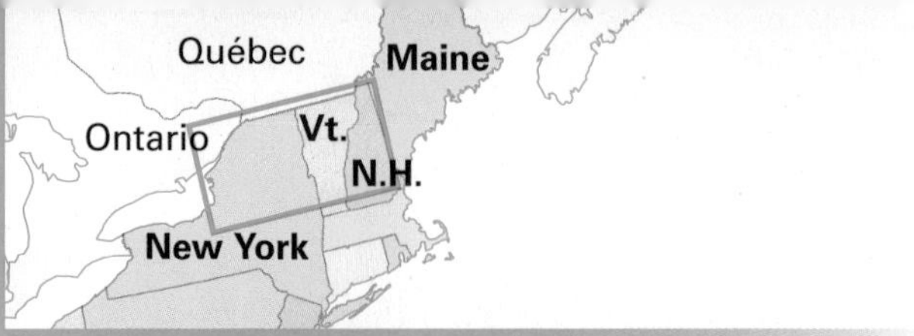

Québec Maine
Ontario Vt. N.H.
New York

0 mi   10   20   30   40
0 km 10 20 30 40 50 60
One inch equals 18.4 miles
One centimeter equals 11.7 kilometers

Go to 174

Carleton Place
Perth
Smiths Falls
Brockville
Ogdensburg
Prescott
Gananoque
Kingston
Massena
Cornwall
Salaberry-de-Valleyfield
Beauharnois
Huntingdon
Malone
QUÉBEC
NEW YORK
CANADA
U.S.
Potsdam
Canton
ST. LAWRENCE
Gouverneur
FRANKLIN
Saranac Lake
Lake Placid
Tupper Lake
Mount Van Hoevenberg Olympic Sports Complex
Mt. Marcy Highest Pt. in New York 5,344 ft
ESSEX
ADIRONDACK
PARK
MOUNTAINS
Watertown
FORT DRUM MIL. RES.
Carthage
Lowville
LEWIS
JEFFERSON
LAKE ONTARIO
Go to 79
Long Lake
Blue Mountain Lake
Raquette Lake
Old Forge
HAMILTON
HERKIMER
WARREN
Oswego
Fulton
Baldwinsville
Syracuse
ONONDAGA
OSWEGO
ONEIDA
Rome
Utica
Oneida
Herkimer Little Falls
Ilion
Gloversville
Johnstown
Saratoga Springs
Amsterdam
FULTON
SARATOGA
MONTGOMERY
Go to 79

DRIVING
DISTANCES
IN MILES

	BURLINGTON, VT	CONCORD, NH	LAKE PLACID, NY	OGDENSBURG, NY	PLATTSBURGH, NY	RUTLAND, VT	ST. JOHNSBURY, VT	SARATOGA SPRS., NY	SYRACUSE, NY	UTICA, NY	WATERTOWN, NY	WHITE RIVER JCT., VT
BURLINGTON, VT		150	68	208	51	69	76	115	230	183	195	91
CONCORD, NH	150		215	357	198	104	104	173	280	228	312	59
LAKE PLACID, NY	68	215		96	49	133	141	106	192	148	126	156
WATERTOWN, NY	195	312	126	68	167	244	319	179	65	86		289

SEE ALSO DISTANCE AND DRIVING TIME MAP ON PAGES 286–287

Québec   Maine
Ontario   Vt.
    N.H.
New York

Québec
Maine
N.B.
Nova Scotia
Vt.
N.H.

0 mi   10   20   30   40
0 km 10 20 30 40 50 60
One inch equals 18.4 miles
One centimeter equals 11.7 kilometers

Gulf of Maine

Go to 84
Go to 81
Go to 95

DRIVING DISTANCES IN MILES	AUGUSTA, ME	BANGOR, ME	BAR HARBOR, ME	BERLIN, NH	CALAIS, ME	CONCORD, NH	CONWAY, NH	LEWISTON, ME	MACHIAS, ME	PORTLAND, ME	PORTSMOUTH, NH	WATERVILLE, ME
AUGUSTA, ME		77	120	110	173	141	97	35	158	58	110	20
BANGOR, ME	77		45	160	97	214	170	108	83	131	184	56
BAR HARBOR, ME	120	45		204	112	257	214	151	71	175	227	100
PORTLAND, ME	58	131	175	93	228	83	62	36	213		53	84

SEE ALSO DISTANCE AND DRIVING TIME MAP ON PAGES 286–287

Québec
N.B.
Maine
N.H.

0 mi 10 20 30 40
0 km 10 20 30 40 50 60
One inch equals 18.4 miles
One centimeter equals 11.7 kilometers

Go to 176
Go to 175
Go to 82

LAURENTIAN MOUNTAINS
NOTRE DAME MTS.
APPALACHIAN MOUNTAINS
RÉS. FAUNIQUE DES LAURENTIDES
PARC DE LA JACQUES-CARTIER
ZEC BATISCAN-NEILSON
ZEC CHAPAIS
ALLAGASH WILDERNESS WATERWAY
CHAMBERLAIN LAKE PUBLIC RESERVED LAND
BAXTER STATE PARK
ROUND POND PUBLIC RESERVED LAND
PARC RÉGIONAL DU MASSIF DU SUD
PARC DE FRONTENAC
PARC DU MONT-MÉGANTIC
PISCATAQUIS
SOMERSET
OXFORD
COOS
QUÉBEC / MAINE
CANADA / UNITED STATES
QUE. / N.H.
MAINE / NEW HAMPSHIRE
St. Lawrence

Québec
Ste-Foy
Charlesbourg
Loretteville
Charny
Montmagny
Donnacona
Pont-Rouge
St-Raymond
Shannon
Château-Richer
L'Ange-Gardien
Beaupré
Ste-Anne-de-Beaupré
St-Féréol-les-Neiges
Ste-Famille
St-Jean
Île d'Orléans
St-Michel-de-Bellechasse
St-Charles-de-Bellechasse
St-Raphaël
Ste-Euphémie
Notre-Dame-du-Rosaire
St-Paul-de-Montminy
Ste-Apolline
Ste-Lucie-de-Beauregard
Lac-Frontière
St-Adalbert
St-Pamphile
St-Marcel
Daaquam
St-Just-de-Bretenières
St-Camille-de-Lellis
Ste-Sabine
Ste-Sabine-Station
St-Cyprien
Ste-Justine
Ste-Germaine-Station
Ste-Rose-de-Watford
St-Benjamin
St-Louis-de-Gonzague
St-Prosper
Beauceville
Notre-Dame-des-Pins
St-Georges
Jersey Mills
St-Côme–Linière
St-Benoît-Labre
St-René
St-Théophile
Armstrong
St-Martin
St-Honoré
La Guadeloupe
Adstock
Black Lake
Thetford Mines
Robertsonville
St-Jean-de-Brébeuf
St-Adrien-d'Irlande
Bernierville
Vianney
Kinnear's Mills
East Broughton
Broughton Station
Ste-Clotilde-de-Beauce
St-Victor
St-Frédéric
St-Joseph-de-Beauce
Tring-Jonction
St-Éphrem-de-Tring
St-Pierre-de-Broughton
St-Jacques-de-Leeds
St-Séverin
Vallée-Jonction
Ste-Marie
St-Elzéar
Ste-Agathe
St-Sylvestre
St-Odilon
Sts-Anges
Ste-Hénédine
St-Isidore
St-Anselme
St-Henri
St-Gervais
Armagh
St-Nérée
St-Damien-de-Buckland
Buckland
St-Nazaire-de-Buckland
St-Léon-de-Standon
St-Luc
Lac-Etchemin
St-Malachie
St-Édouard-de-Frampton
Honfleur
St-Apollinaire
St-Agapit
St-Flavien
Laurier-Station
St-Gilles
Dosquet
Joly
Val-Alain
Lyster
Laurierville
Inverness
Plessisville
Princeville
Norbertville
Victoriaville
Warwick
Chesterville
St-Fortunat
St-Daniel
St-Jacques-le-Majeur-de-Wolfestown
Disraëli
Ste-Praxède
St-Joseph-de-Coleraine
Vimy-Ridge
Ham-Nord
St-Rémi-de-Tingwick
St-Christophe-d'Arthabaska
Princeville
Plessisville
Asbestos
Wottonville
Ham-Sud
St-Gérard
St-Adrien
St-Aymer
Beaulac
Stratford
St-Romain
St-Sébastien
Courcelles
St-Hilaire-de-Dorset
St-Gédéon
Lambton
Sts-Martyrs-Canadiens
Stornoway
Fontainebleau
Weedon Centre
St-Samuel-Station
St-Ludger
Lac-Drolet
St-Robert-Bellarmin
Audet
Ste-Cécile-de-Whitton
Nantes
Lac-Mégantic
Frontenac
Marsboro
Piopolis
Val-Racine
Milan
Gould
Marbleton
Scotstown
Nantes
Woburn
Notre-Dame-des-Bois
La Patrie
Island Brook
Cookshire-Eaton
West Ditton
Bury
Dudswell (Bishopton)
East Angus
Ascot Corner
Sherbrooke
Lennoxville
Eaton
Sawyerville
Randboro
St-Isidore-d'Auckland
Chartierville
Martinville
Ste-Catherine-de-Hatley
Coaticook
Ste-Herménégilde
St-Malo
Barnston
East Hereford
Dixville
Hatley
Waterville

St-Urbain
Baie-St-Paul
St-Joseph-de-la-Rive
St-Placide-de-Charlevoix
Les Éboulements
St-Bernard-sur-Mer
La Baleine
Île aux Coudres
Cap-à-l'Aigle
Petite-Rivière-St-François
St-Cassien-des-Caps
St-Tite-des-Caps
La Miche
Grosse Île Natl. Hist. Site
Cap-Tourmente
St-François
St-Jean-Port-Joli
L'Islet-sur-Mer
L'Islet
L'Isle-aux-Grues
Île aux Oies
St-Aubert
St-Eugène
St-Cyrille-de-l'Islet
Tourville
Ste-Perpétue
St-Omer
Ste-Félicité
Lac Trois Saumons
Ste-Louise
La Pocatière
St-Roch-des-Aulnaies
Village-des-Aulnaies
St-Damase-des-Aulnaies
Mont-Carmel
St-Pacôme
Ste-Anne-de-Beaupré
St-Philippe-de-Néri
St-Denis
St-Pascal
St-Bruno-de-Kamouraska
Pohénégamook
St-Éleuthère
Pied-du-Lac
Kamouraska
Glazier Lake
Allagash Hist. Soc.
Dickey
Gate Allagash
Kelly Brook Mtn. 1,483
Clayton Lake
Long Lake
First Musquacook Lake
Fourth Musquacook L.
Priestly Mtn. 1,900
Priestly Lake
Harrow Lake
Hudson Mtn. 1,935
Clear Lake
Pleasant Lake
Spider Lake
Munsungan Lake
Crescent Pond
Churchill Lake
Allagash L.
Haymock Lake
Telos PUBLIC RESERVED LAND
GERO ISLAND PUBLIC RESERVED LAND
Chesuncook Village
Chesuncook Lake
Strickland Mtn. 2,390
Center Mtn. 2,902
North Brother 4,143
Doubletop Mtn. 3,488
Hardwood Mtn. 1,518
Poland Mtn. 2,390
Caucomgomoc Lake
Chamberlain Lake
Telos Mtn. 1,329
Loon Lake
Seboomook Mtn. 2,390
Green Mtn. 2,395
Seboomook Lake
Little Russell Mtn. 2,376
Penobscot Lake
Pittston Farm
Seboomook
Lobster Lake
Ripogenus Dam
Canada Falls Lake
Moosehead Lake
Big Spencer Mtn. 3,230
Ragged Lake
NAHMAKANTA PUBLIC RESERVED LAND
MOOSEHEAD LAKE PUBLIC RESERVED LAND
Rockwood
Kokadjo
Wadleigh Mtn. 1,863
Mt. Kineo 1,789
Brassua Lake
Lily Bay
Lily Bay S.P.
Baker Mtn. 3,520
Jo-Mary Mtn. 2,904
Upper Jo-Mary Lake
White Cap Mtn. 3,644
Jackman
Jackman Station
Attean Pond
Attean Mtn. 2,442
Big Moose Mtn. 3,196
Big Squaw
Greenville
Greenville Junction
Moosehead Marine Mus.
Gulf Hagas Br.
Saddleback Mtn. 2,998
Barren Mtn. 2,660
Katahdin Iron Works S.H.S.
Long Pond
Parlin Pond
Dennistown
Moose River
Sandy Stream Mtn. 2,869
Sandy Bay Mtn. 3,117
Tumbledown Mtn. 3,542
Three Slide Mtn. 3,112
Kibby Mtn. 3,638
Coburn Mtn. 3,718
Gerard
Spencer Lake
Hurricane Mtn. 2,142
Snow Mtn. 3,948
Lake Parlin
West Forks
The Forks
Lake Moxie
Moxie Pond
Moxie Mtn. 2,925
Indian Pond
LITTLE MOOSE PUBLIC RESERVED LAND
Shirley Mills
Little Wilson Falls
Bodfish
Onawa
Willimantic
Monson
North Guilford
Blanchard
Abbot Village
Guilford
Greeley Landing
Dover-Foxcroft
Sebec Lake
Sebec
Bowerbank
Brownville
Brownville Junction
Milo
Atkinson Corners
Blacksmith Shop Mus.
Sangerville
Mayfield Corner
Kingsbury
Pleasant Pond
Russell Mtn. 2,187
Caratunk
Carrabassett
Eustis
Flagstaff L.
Grand Falls
Dead River
Stratton
West Peak 4,150
Stewart Mtn. 2,671
Wyman L.
Bigelow
E. Kennebago Mtn. 3,825
W. Kennebago Mtn. 3,705
Parmachenee L.
Aziscohos L.
Rump Mtn. 3,647
White Cap Mtn. 3,815
Snow Mtn. 3,755
Boil Mtn. 3,601
Deer Mtn. 3,005
Salmon Mtn. 3,864
Second Conn. Lakes St. Forest
COBURN GORE
CHAIN OF PONDS PUBLIC RESERVED LAND
ZEC LOUISE-GOSFORD (SECTEUR GOSFORD)
ZEC LOUISE-GOSFORD (SECTEUR LOUISE)
ZEC JARO
BIGELOW PRESERVE
DEAD RIVER PUBLIC RESERVED LAND
ATTEAN PUBLIC RESERVED LAND
HOLEB PUBLIC RESERVED LAND
NORTH EAST CARRY
Boundary Bald Mtn. 3,640
Dole Pond
Depot Lake
Baker Lake
Southwest Br.
Big Black R.
St. Johns R.
Penobscot R.
W. Branch Penobscot
S. Branch Penobscot
Riviere Chaudière
Magalloway R.
Connecticut R.
Rivière Bécancour
Rivière St-François
Lac Saint-Joseph
Lac William
Lac Aylmer
Lac Drolet
Lac Mégantic
Lac aux Araignées
Lac Louise
Lac Elgin
Lac Moffat
Lac McGill
Lac Saint-François
Lac-Drolet
RESTRICTED ROADS
RESTRICTED ROAD
APPALACHIAN N.S.T.
Knight Landing
Sebec Lake

85

SEE ALSO DISTANCE AND DRIVING TIME MAP ON PAGES 286–287

DRIVING DISTANCES IN MILES

	BANGOR, ME	CALAIS, ME	CARIBOU, ME	FREDERICTON, NB	GREENVILLE, ME	HOULTON, ME	JACKMAN, ME	LINCOLN, ME	MADAWASKA, ME	MILLINOCKET, ME	PRESQUE ISLE, ME	QUEBEC, QC
HOULTON, ME	122	91	55	73	155		204	83	102	73	42	286
LINCOLN, ME	51	77	135	114	83	83	132		174	35	122	231
MADAWASKA, ME	214	207	50	167	212	102	269	174		164	62	182
PRESQUE ISLE, ME	162	133	13	113	166	42	215	122	62	113		246

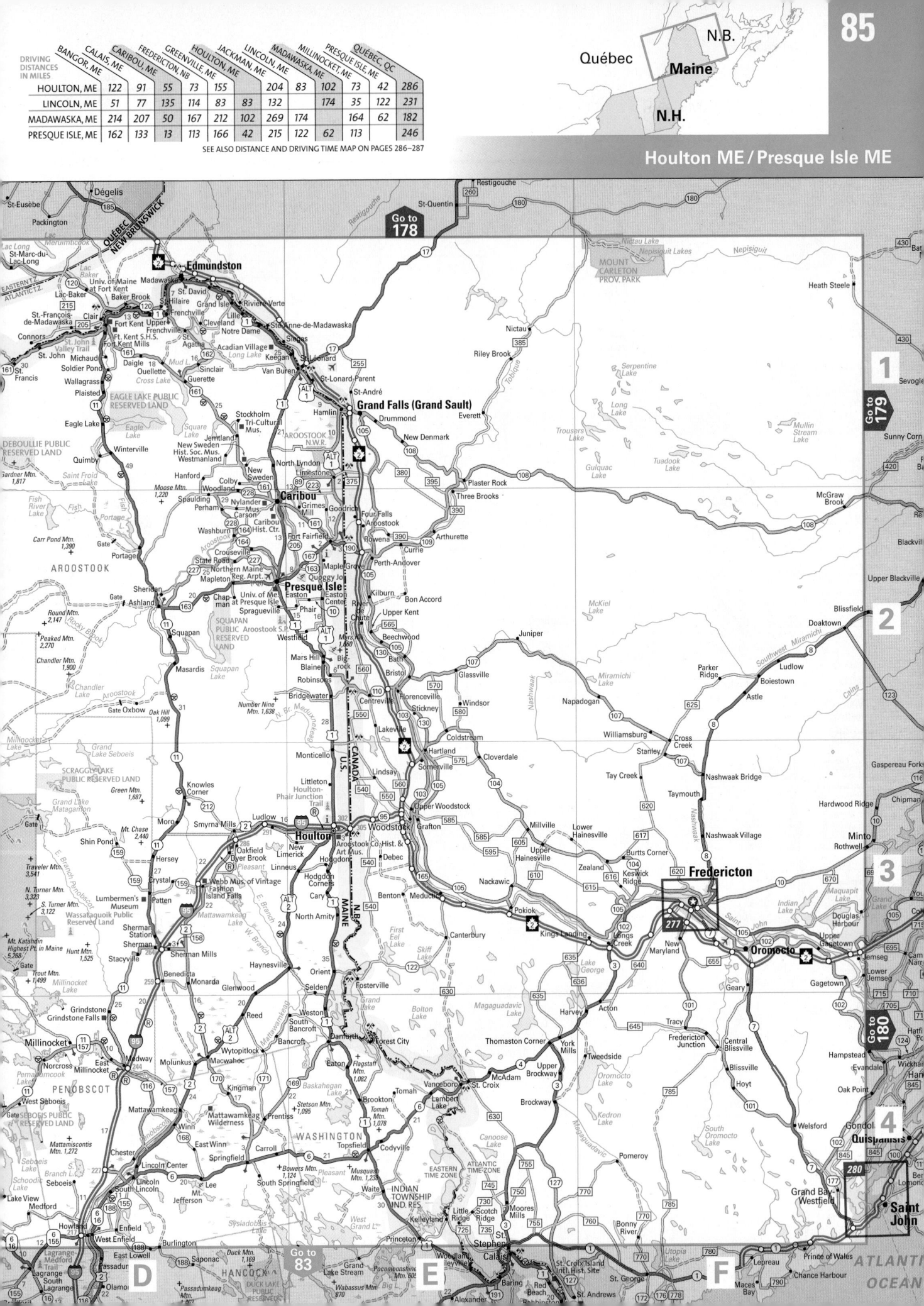

0 mi   10   20   30   40
0 km 10   20   30   40   50   60
One inch equals 18.4 miles
One centimeter equals 11.7 kilometers

Nebraska   Iowa

Illinois

Missouri

DRIVING DISTANCES IN MILES	AMES, IA	BURLINGTON, IA	CARROLL, IA	CEDAR RAPIDS, IA	CRESTON, IA	DAVENPORT, IA	DES MOINES, IA	IOWA CITY, IA	KIRKSVILLE, MO	MARYVILLE, MO	OMAHA, NE	OTTUMWA, IA
CEDAR RAPIDS, IA	108	106	173		211	87	129	28	170	276	266	111
DES MOINES, IA	34	157	90	129	81	171		113	145	146	136	86
IOWA CITY, IA	136	82	195	28	195	59	113		143	260	250	83
OMAHA, NE	171	328	97	266	98	308	136	250	275	112		221

SEE ALSO DISTANCE AND DRIVING TIME MAP ON PAGES 286–287

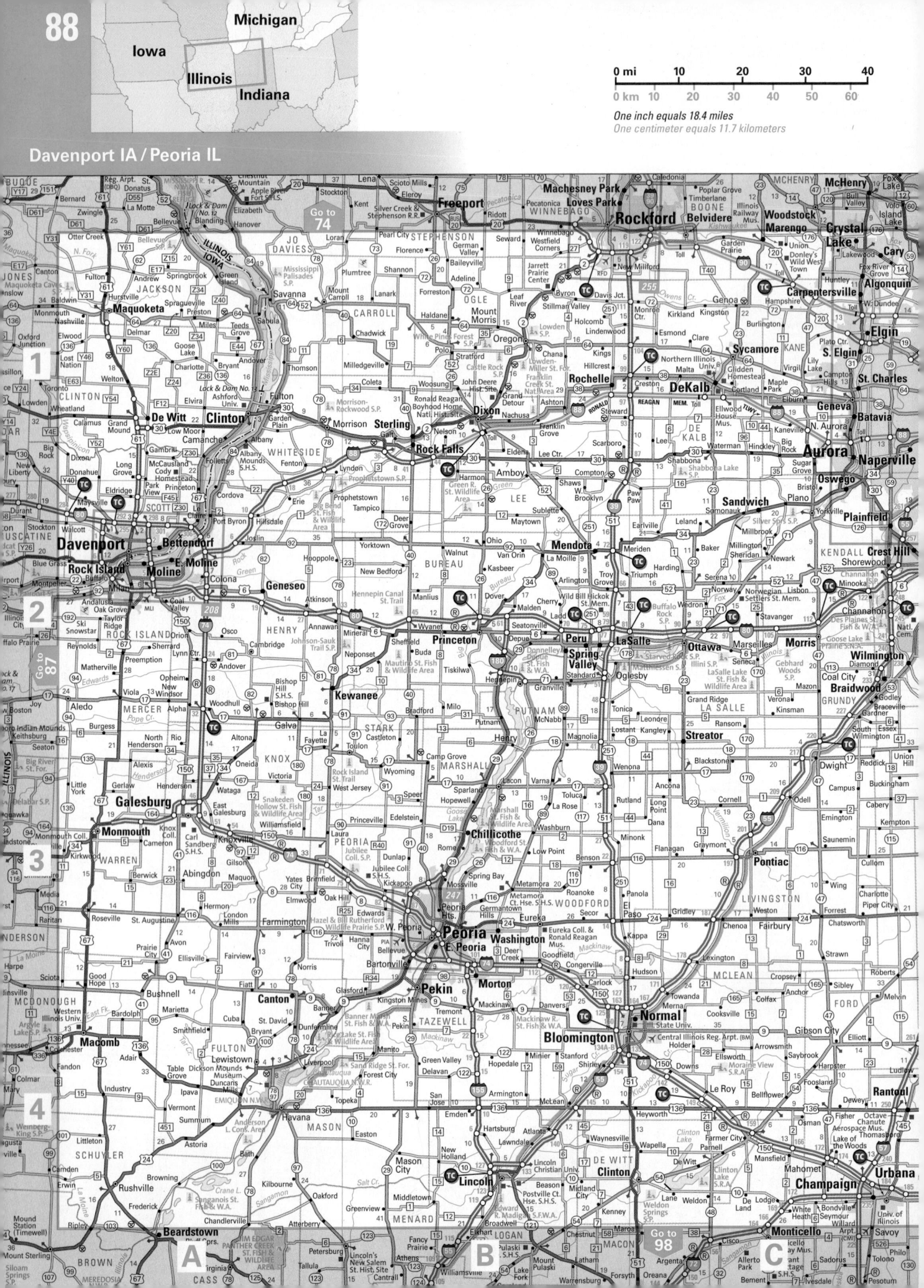

Michigan
Iowa
Illinois
Indiana

0 mi   10   20   30   40
0 km 10 20 30 40 50 60
One inch equals 18.4 miles
One centimeter equals 11.7 kilometers

Michigan   Ont.
Pennsylvania
Ohio
Indiana   W.Va.

0 mi   10   20   30   40
0 km   10   20   30   40   50   60
One inch equals 18.4 miles
One centimeter equals 11.7 kilometers

Michigan Ont.

Pennsylvania

Ohio

Indiana W.Va.

DRIVING DISTANCES IN MILES	ALLENTOWN, PA	ALTOONA, PA	BINGHAMTON, NY	ELMIRA, NY	ERIE, PA	HARRISBURG, PA	JOHNSTOWN, PA	PITTSBURGH, PA	READING, PA	SCRANTON, PA	STATE COLLEGE, PA	WILLIAMSPORT, PA
ALLENTOWN, PA		218	132	188	361	82	217	284	37	76	165	116
HARRISBURG, PA	82	140	181	157	298		138	205	65	119	88	83
PITTSBURGH, PA	284	99	363	284	126	205	73		262	301	139	215
SCRANTON, PA	76	185	61	117	317	119	233	301	103		149	83

SEE ALSO DISTANCE AND DRIVING TIME MAP ON PAGES 286–287

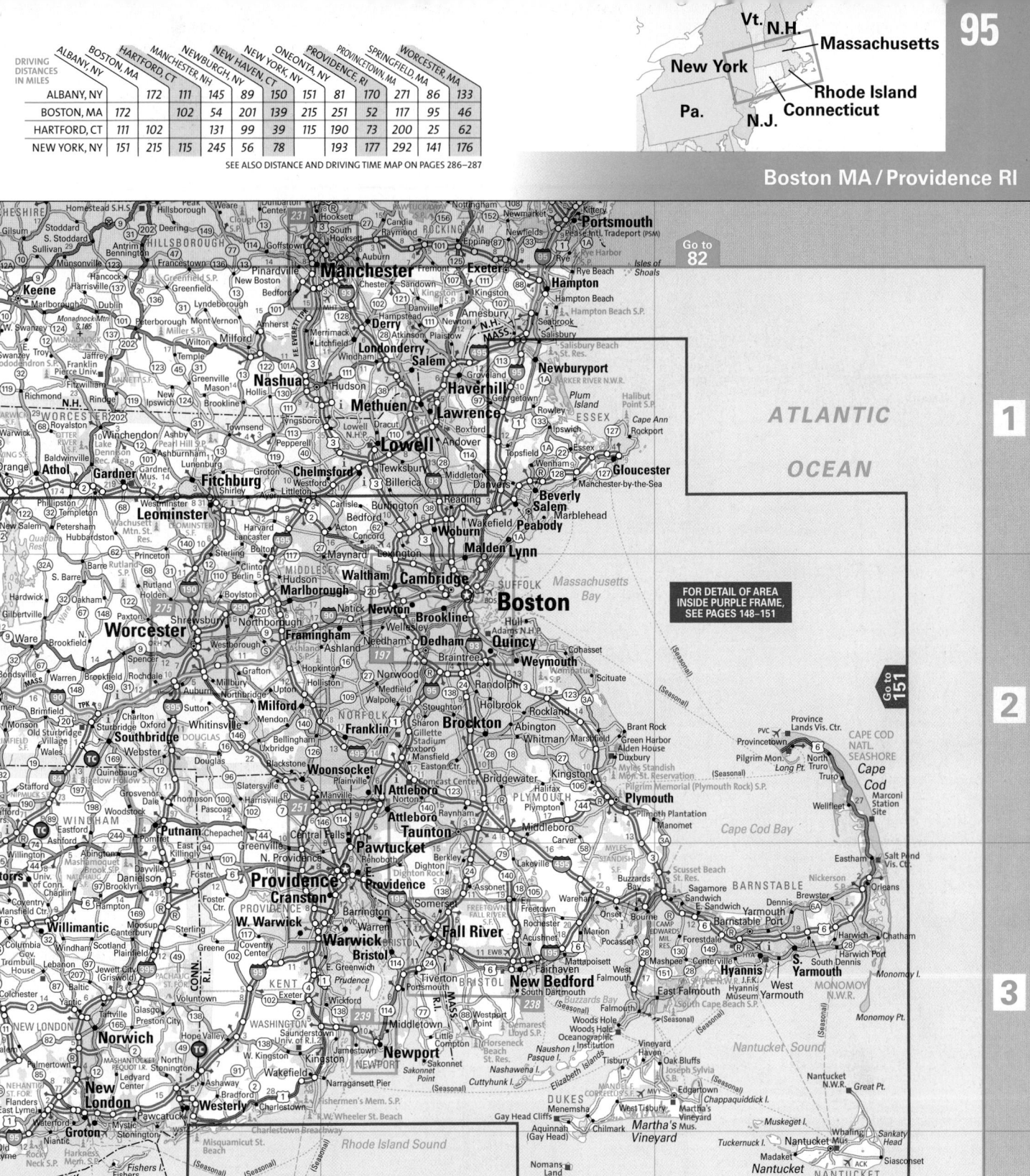

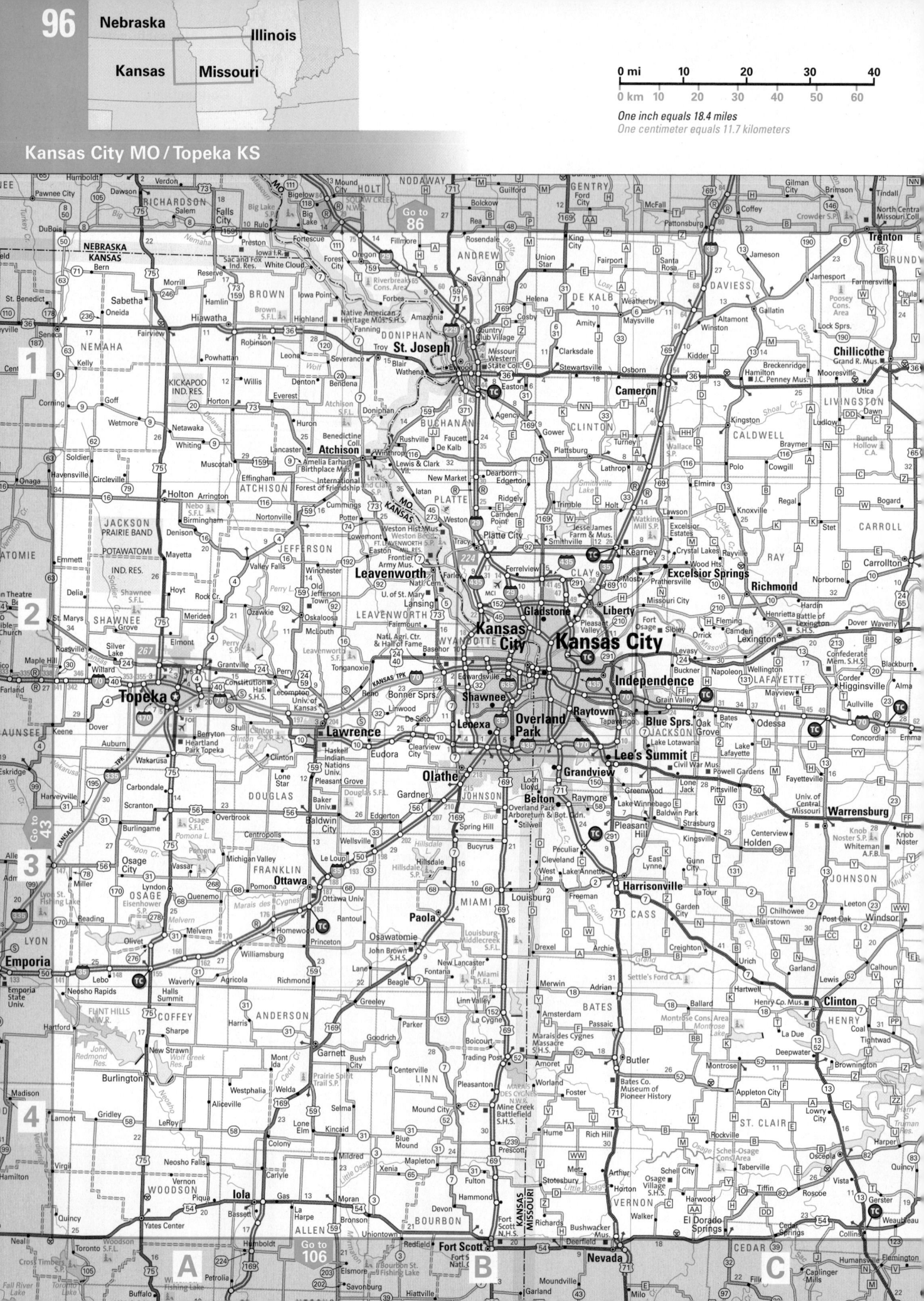

0 mi   10   20   30   40
0 km   10   20   30   40   50   60
One inch equals 18.4 miles
One centimeter equals 11.7 kilometers

DRIVING DISTANCES IN MILES	IOLA, KS COLUMBIA, MO	JEFFERSON CITY, MO	KANSAS CITY, MO	LAWRENCE, KS	MACON, MO	OSAGE BEACH, MO	QUINCY, IL	ROLLA, MO	ST. JOSEPH, MO	SEDALIA, MO	TOPEKA, KS
JEFFERSON CITY, MO	32	263		161	198	88	44	131	65	217	64	225
KANSAS CITY, MO	129	106	161		37	148	173	251	226	56	97	63
ST. JOSEPH, MO	185	154	217	56	76	131	229	210	282		153	71
TOPEKA, KS	193	100	225	63	26	209	236	314	289	71	161	

SEE ALSO DISTANCE AND DRIVING TIME MAP ON PAGES 286–287

Illinois
Indiana
Missouri
Kentucky

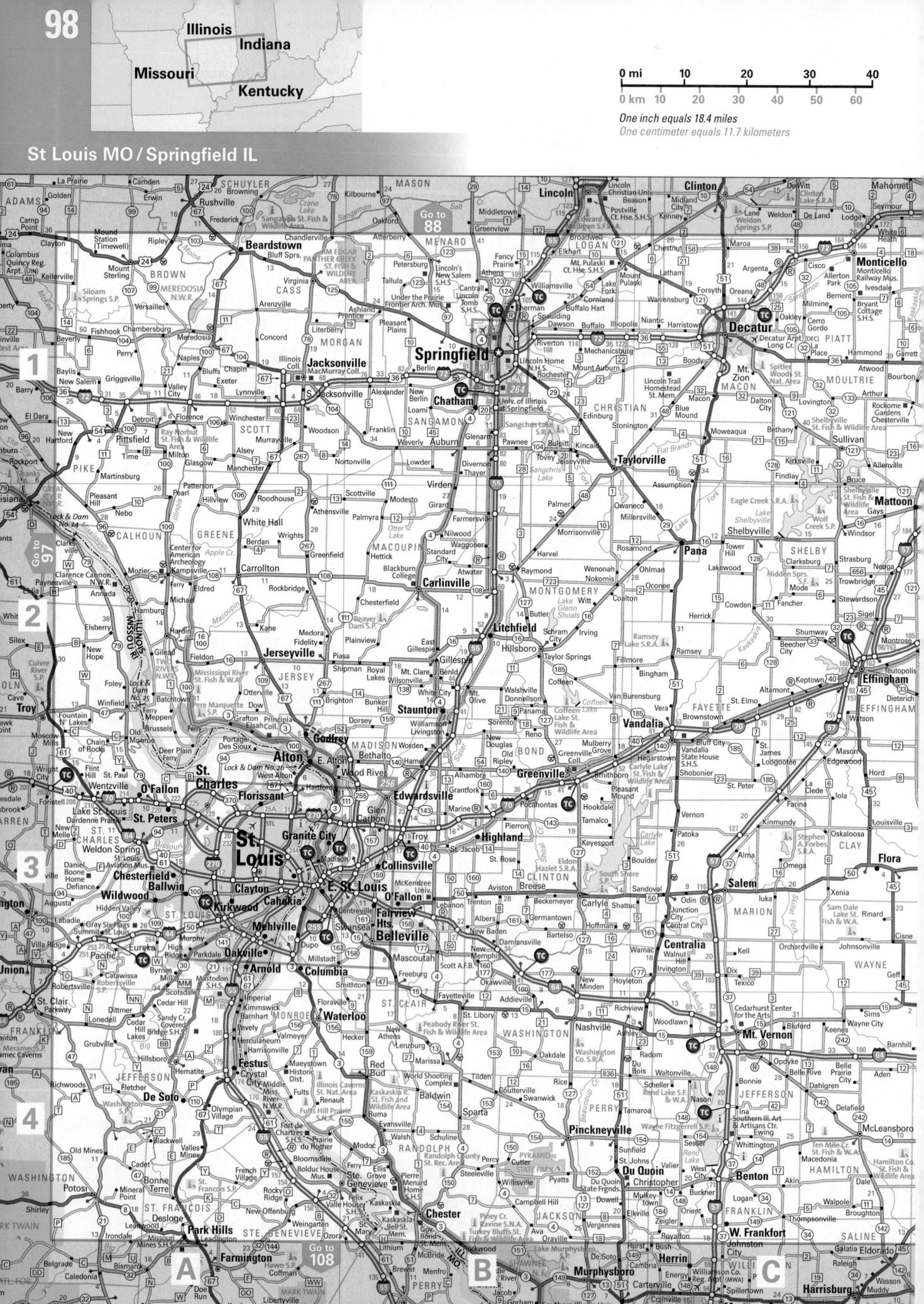

One inch equals 18.4 miles
One centimeter equals 11.7 kilometers

Ohio

Indiana W. Va.

Kentucky

0 mi 10 20 30 40
0 km 10 20 30 40 50 60
One inch equals 18.4 miles
One centimeter equals 11.7 kilometers

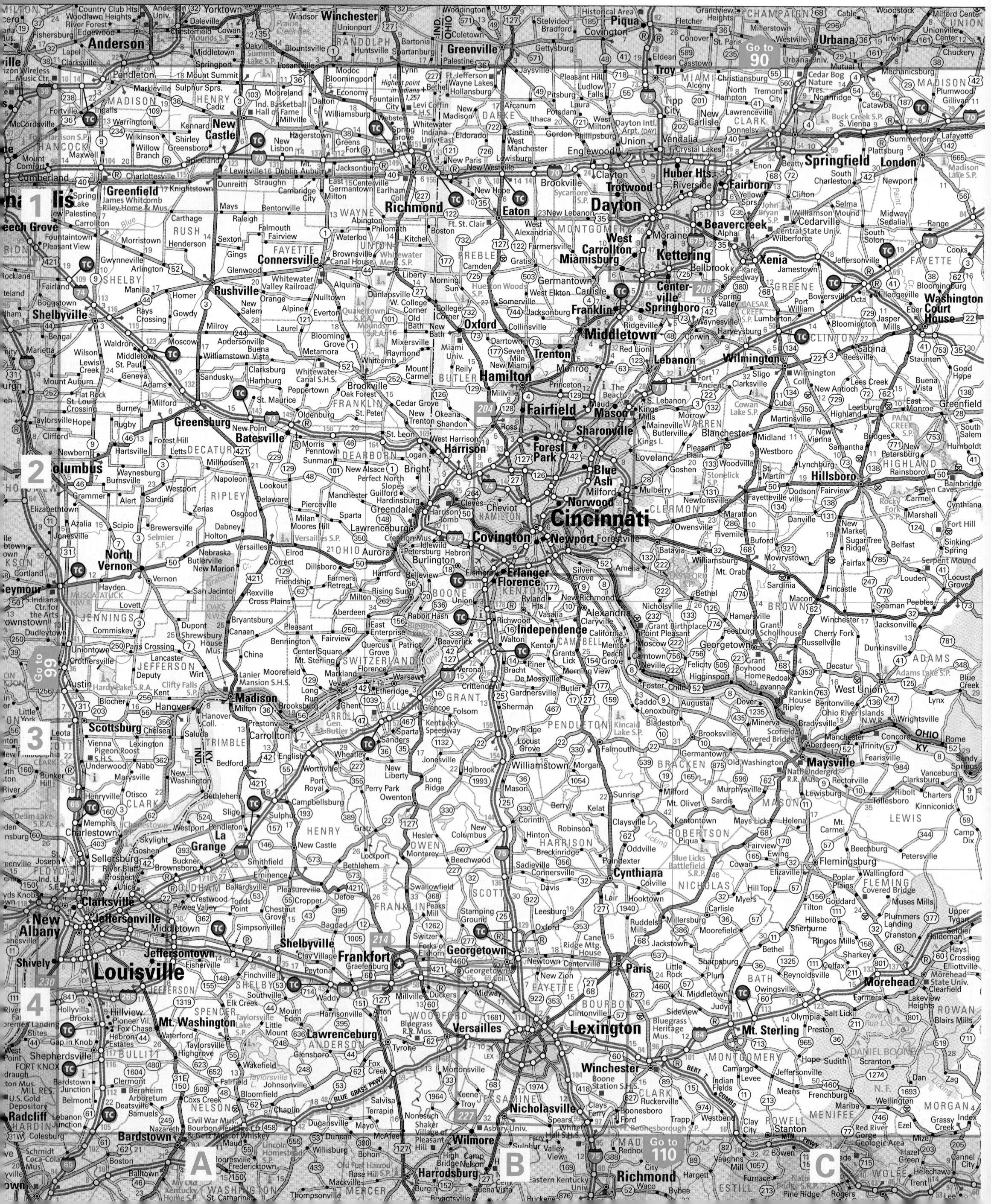

Ohio · Indiana · W.Va. · Kentucky

DRIVING DISTANCES IN MILES

	CHARLESTON, WV	CHILLICOTHE, OH	CINCINNATI, OH	COLUMBUS, OH	DAYTON, OH	HUNTINGTON, OH	LEXINGTON, KY	LOUISVILLE, KY	MAYSVILLE, KY	PARKERSBURG, WV	WHEELING, WV	ZANESVILLE, OH
CHARLESTON, WV		121	202	168	198	52	176	251	155	73	176	155
CINCINNATI, OH	202	108		109	52	150	85	100	63	191	235	164
COLUMBUS, OH	168	47	109		70	135	193	207	114	108	130	58
LEXINGTON, KY	176	191	85	193		135	126	80	67	249	319	247

SEE ALSO DISTANCE AND DRIVING TIME MAP ON PAGES 286–287

102

Pennsylvania
Ohio
Md. — Delaware
W.Va.
Virginia

Charlottesville VA / Morgantown WV

0 mi   10   20   30   40
0 km   10   20   30   40   50   60

One inch equals 18.4 miles
One centimeter equals 11.7 kilometers

Wheeling
Morgantown
Fairmont
Clarksburg
Bridgeport
Buckhannon
Elkins
Cumberland
Frostburg
Keyser
Uniontown
Connellsville
Somerset
Bedford
Harrisonburg
Staunton
Waynesboro
Charlottesville
Front Royal
Woodstock
Strasburg
Bridgewater
Stuarts Draft
Covington
Lexington
Summersville
Moundsville
New Martinsville
Martins Ferry
Monessen
Washington

Go to 92
Go to 101
Go to 112
Go to 201

DRIVING DISTANCES IN MILES

	Baltimore, MD	Charlottesville, VA	Cumberland, MD	Elkins, WV	Fredericksburg, VA	Front Royal, VA	Gettysburg, PA	Hagerstown, MD	Morgantown, WV	Salisbury, MD	Washington, DC	Wheeling, WV
BALTIMORE, MD		161	140	229	98	110	62	76	211	106	38	290
CHARLOTTESVILLE, VA	161		163	142	70	74	190	141	204	235	118	279
MORGANTOWN, WV	211	204	71	62	252	161	181	138		317	205	76
WASHINGTON, DC	38	118	134	192	54	73	80	70	205	115		284

SEE ALSO DISTANCE AND DRIVING TIME MAP ON PAGES 286–287

N.Y.
Pennsylvania
New Jersey
Md. Delaware
Virginia

Sept 7-16, 2012 York Fair, York PA

0 mi   10   20   30   40
0 km 10 20 30 40 50 60

One inch equals 18.4 miles
One centimeter equals 11.7 kilometers

Philadelphia PA / Harrisburg PA

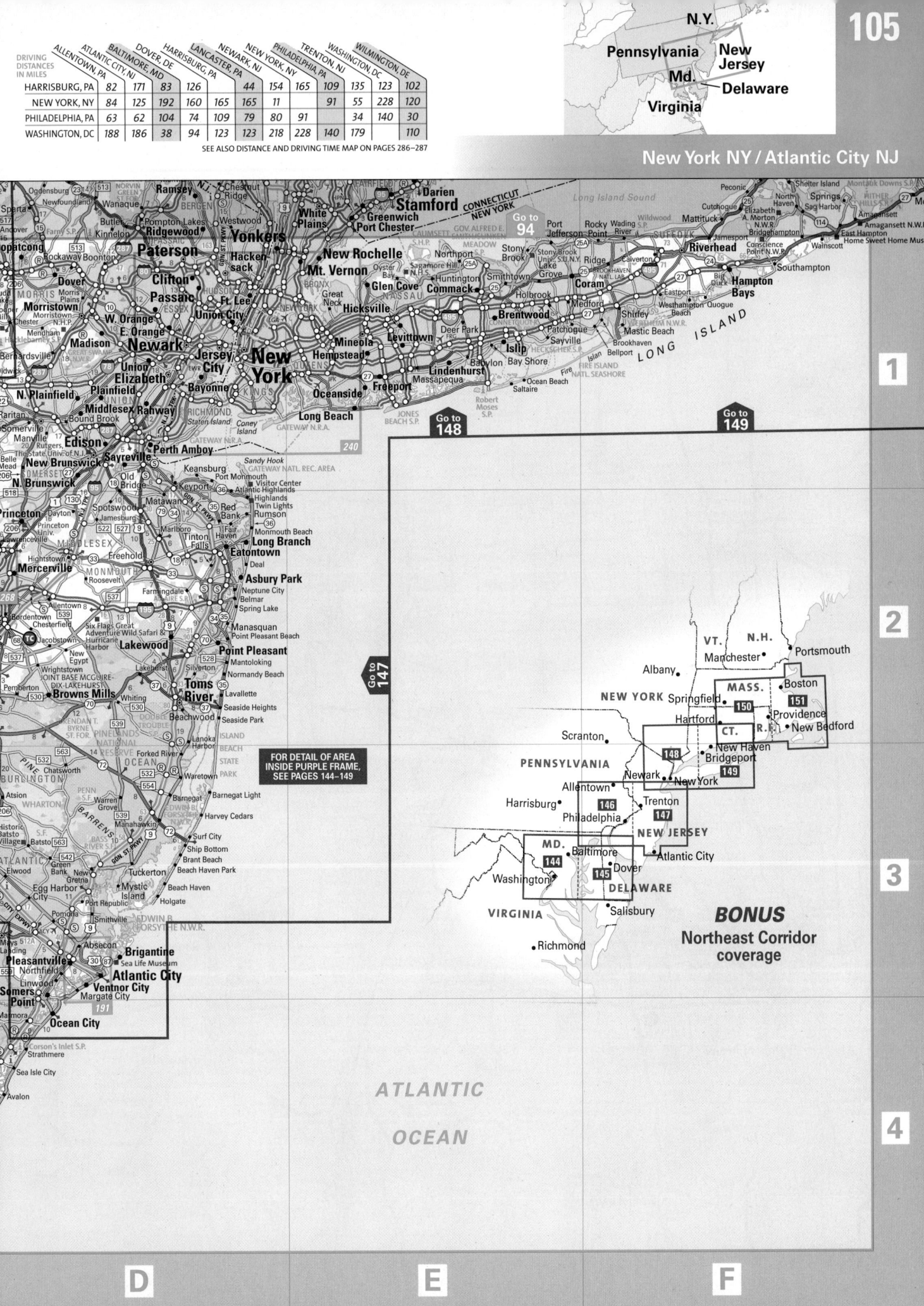

One inch equals 18.4 miles
One centimeter equals 11.7 kilometers

Kansas Missouri

Oklahoma Arkansas

DRIVING DISTANCES IN MILES	BARTLESVILLE, OK	BRANSON, MO	FAYETTEVILLE, AR	INDEPENDENCE, KS	JOPLIN, MO	MOUNTAIN HOME, AR	MUSKOGEE, OK	NEWPORT, AR	ROLLA, MO	SPRINGFIELD, MO	TULSA, OK	WEST PLAINS, MO
BRANSON, MO	213		95	188	111	84	181	178	147	41	225	109
FAYETTEVILLE, AR	154	95		165	88	127	86	241	227	121	113	182
SPRINGFIELD, MO	177	41	121	153	70	112	193	219	110		189	109
TULSA, OK	48	225	113	86	116	237	52	344	295	189		293

SEE ALSO DISTANCE AND DRIVING TIME MAP ON PAGES 286–287

108

Illinois Ind.
Missouri
Kentucky
Tennessee
Arkansas

Jonesboro AR / Cape Girardeau MO

One inch equals 18.4 miles
One centimeter equals 11.7 kilometers

Go to 98

Go to 107

Go to 118

DRIVING DISTANCES IN MILES	BOWLING GREEN, KY	CAPE GIRARDEAU, MO	CARBONDALE, IL	CLARKSVILLE, TN	DYERSBURG, TN	HOPKINSVILLE, KY	JACKSON, TN	JONESBORO, AR	NASHVILLE, TN	OWENSBORO, KY	PADUCAH, KY	POPLAR BLUFF, MO
BOWLING GREEN, KY		199	206	63	217	63	196	349	68	76	135	239
CAPE GIRARDEAU, MO	199		46	155	112	136	161	155	197	168	67	75
JONESBORO, AR	349	155	199	268	101	249	160		285	304	178	81
NASHVILLE, TN	68	197	204	46	178	68	132	285		141	133	237

SEE ALSO DISTANCE AND DRIVING TIME MAP ON PAGES 286-287

W. Va.
Virginia
Kentucky
North Carolina
Tennessee

0 mi 10 20 30 40
0 km 10 20 30 40 50 60
One inch equals 18.4 miles
One centimeter equals 11.7 kilometers

Knoxville TN / Richmond KY

W.Va. Virginia
Kentucky
North Carolina
Tennessee

Go to 101
Go to 112
Go to 121

DRIVING DISTANCES IN MILES	ASHEVILLE, NC	BECKLEY, WV	BRISTOL, TN/VA	COOKEVILLE, TN	GATLINBURG, TN	HICKORY, NC	JOHNSON CITY, TN	KNOXVILLE, TN	LONDON, KY	MAMMOTH CAVE NP, KY	PIKEVILLE, KY	RICHMOND, KY
Bristol, TN/VA	83	140		224	118	98	24	117	213	348	116	265
Hickory, NC	78	196	98	291	147		98	185	280	415	214	332
Knoxville, TN	109	256	117	107	40	185	107		100	234	202	151
London, KY	205	287	213	129	136	280	203	100		136	121	53

SEE ALSO DISTANCE AND DRIVING TIME MAP ON PAGES 286-287

112

W.Va.
Virginia
North
Carolina

Greensboro NC / Roanoke VA

0 mi   10   20   30   40
0 km   10   20   30   40   50   60
One inch equals 18.4 miles
One centimeter equals 11.7 kilometers

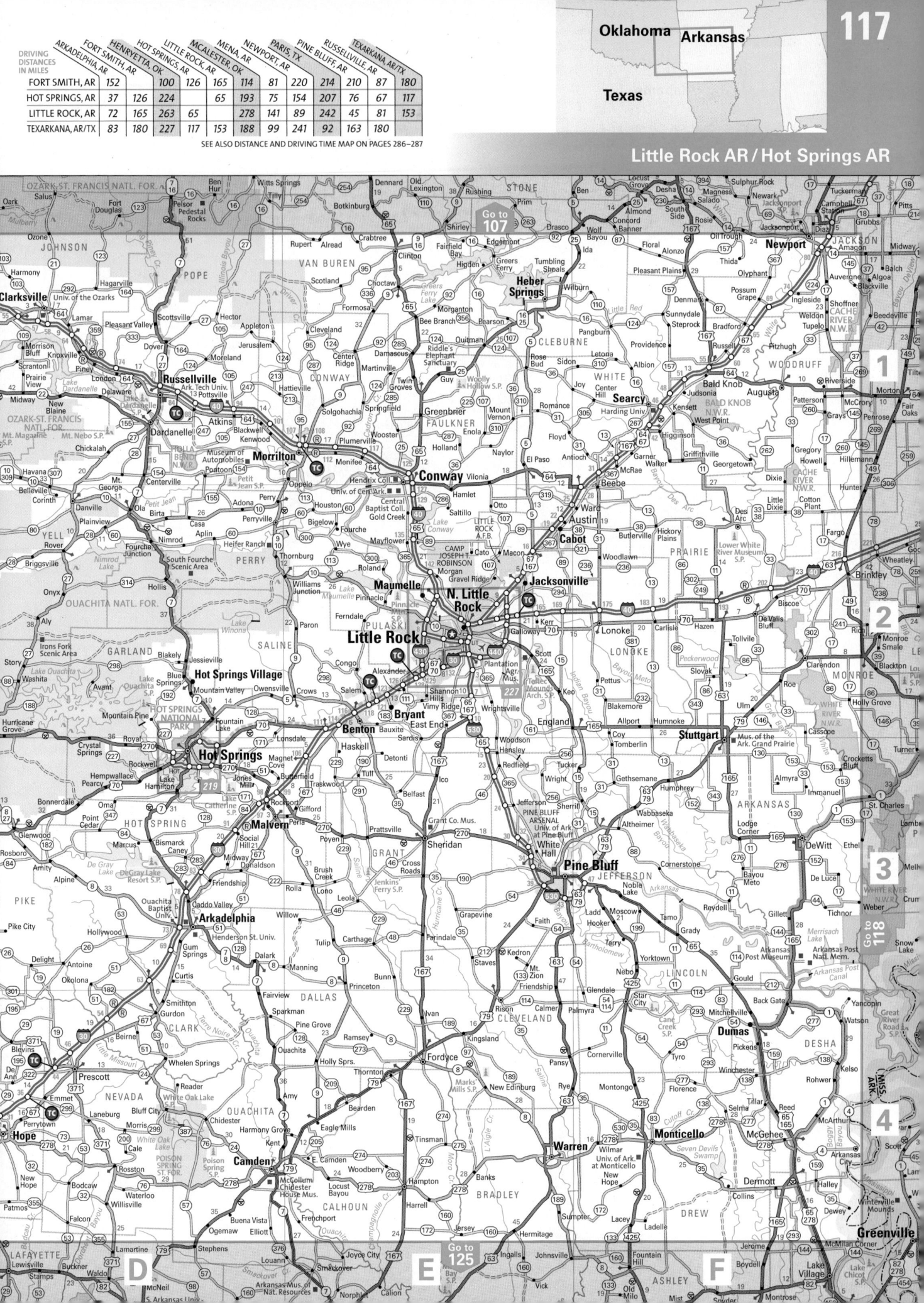

DRIVING DISTANCES IN MILES

	ARKADELPHIA, AR	FORT SMITH, AR	HENRYETTA, OK	HOT SPRINGS, AR	LITTLE ROCK, AR	MCALESTER, OK	MENA, AR	NEWPORT, AR	PARIS, TX	PINE BLUFF, AR	RUSSELLVILLE, AR	TEXARKANA, AR/TX
FORT SMITH, AR	152		100	126	165	114	81	220	214	210	87	180
HOT SPRINGS, AR	37	126	224		65	193	75	154	207	76	67	117
LITTLE ROCK, AR	72	165	263	65		278	141	89	242	45	81	153
TEXARKANA, AR/TX	83	180	227	117	153	188	99	241	92	163	180	

SEE ALSO DISTANCE AND DRIVING TIME MAP ON PAGES 286–287

Tennessee
Arkansas
Miss. Alabama

0 mi 10 20 30 40
0 km 10 20 30 40 50 60
One inch equals 18.4 miles
One centimeter equals 11.7 kilometers

Memphis

Germantown

Go to 109

Go to 120

Go to 127

SEE ALSO DISTANCE AND DRIVING TIME MAP ON PAGES 286–287

DRIVING DISTANCES IN MILES	BIRMINGHAM, AL	CLARKSDALE, MS	COLUMBIA, TN	COLUMBUS, MS	DECATUR, AL	FLORENCE, AL	GREENVILLE, MS	HUNTSVILLE, AL	JACKSON, TN	MEMPHIS, TN	OXFORD, MS	TUPELO, MS
BIRMINGHAM, AL		248	161	122	83	121	286	101	223	241	185	136
HUNTSVILLE, AL	101	260	79	163	25	65	318		205	216	196	148
MEMPHIS, TN	241	76	210	175	191	156	148	216	91		85	109
TUPELO, MS	136	113	159	66	123	92	172	148	107	109	50	

Arkansas Tennessee

Miss. Alabama

0 mi   10   20   30   40
0 km   10   20   30   40   50   60

One inch equals 18.4 miles
One centimeter equals 11.7 kilometers

Tennessee
North Carolina
South Carolina
Alabama Georgia

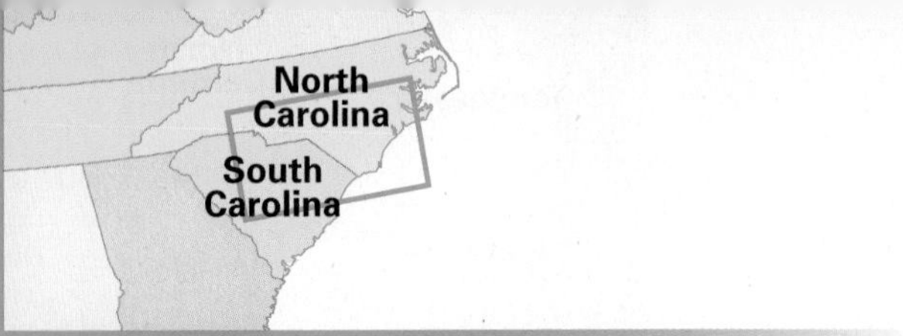

North Carolina
South Carolina

0 mi 10 20 30 40
0 km 10 20 30 40 50 60
One inch equals 18.4 miles
One centimeter equals 11.7 kilometers

Go to 111
Go to 112
Go to 121
Go to 130
Go to 131

Hickory
Conover
Newton
Salisbury
Asheboro
Siler City
Mooresville
Davidson
Kannapolis
Concord
Huntersville
Cornelius
Albemarle
Lincolnton
Shelby
Gastonia
Charlotte
Mint Hill
Matthews
Pinehurst
Southern Pines
Gaffney
York
Indian Trail
Monroe
Rock Hill
Wadesboro
Rockingham
Hamlet
Laurinburg
Chester
Lancaster
Cheraw
Bennettsville
Union
Dillon
Newberry
Camden
Hartsville
Darlington
Florence
Marion
Mullins
Irmo
Dentsville
Columbia
Cayce
Sumter
Lake City
Lexington
Manning
Kingstree
Batesburg-Leesville
Aiken
Orangeburg
Georgetown

U.S. DEPT.
OF ENERGY
SAVANNAH

A   B   C

DRIVING DISTANCES IN MILES	CHARLOTTE, NC	COLUMBIA, SC	FAYETTEVILLE, SC	FLORENCE, SC	GOLDSBORO, NC	HICKORY, NC	LUMBERTON, NC	MOREHEAD CITY, NC	MYRTLE BEACH, SC	ROCK HILL, SC	SUMTER, SC	WILMINGTON, NC
CHARLOTTE, NC		91	139	107	208	47	128	298	173	26	115	205
COLUMBIA, SC	91		170	80	240	139	139	289	146	70	45	199
MYRTLE BEACH, SC	173	146	116	66	170	220	83	165		181	93	71
WILMINGTON, NC	205	199	92	120	100	292	77	95	71	220	158	

SEE ALSO DISTANCE AND DRIVING TIME MAP ON PAGES 286–287

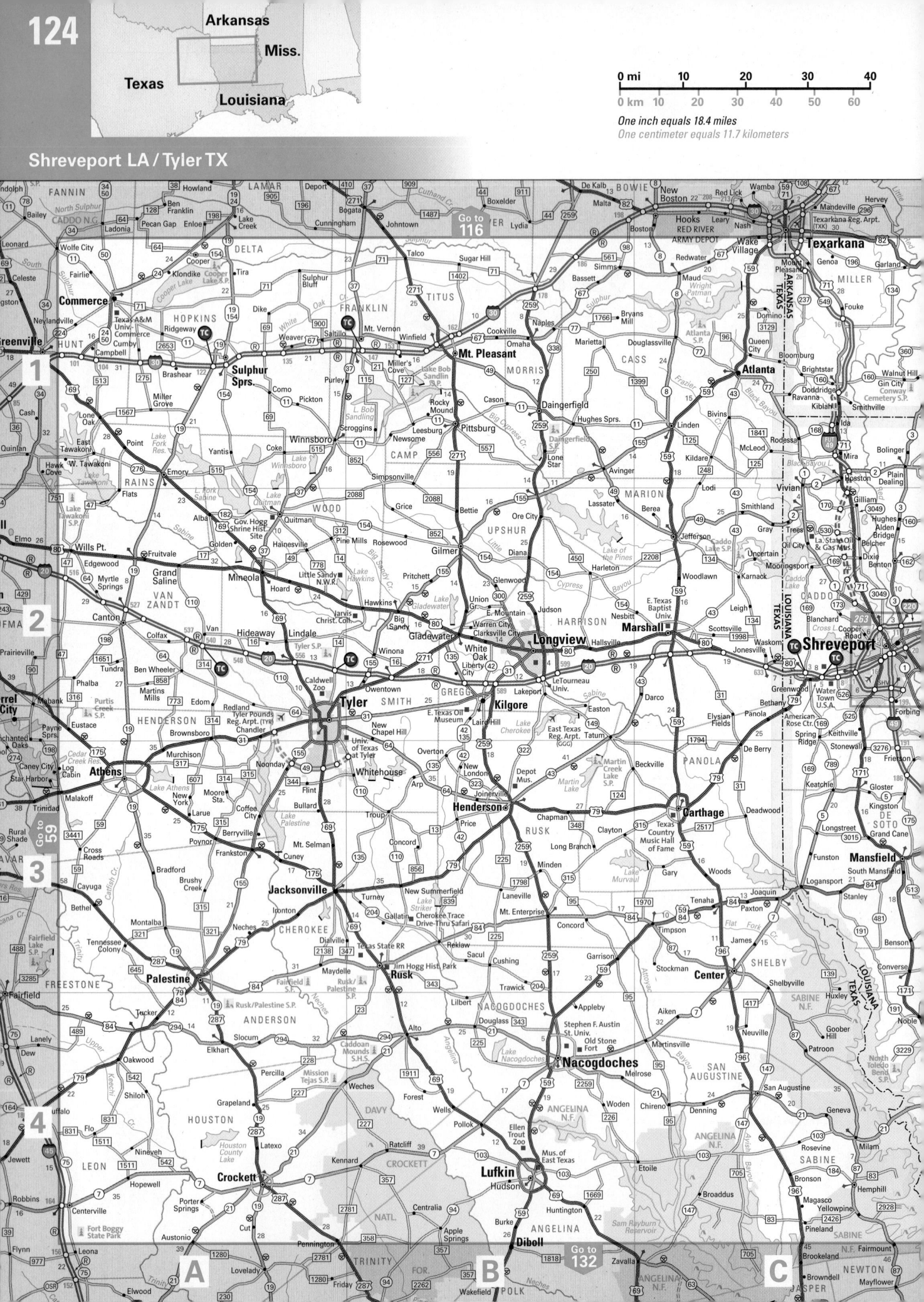

Arkansas

Miss.

Texas

Louisiana

0 mi   10   20   30   40

0 km   10   20   30   40   50   60

One inch equals 18.4 miles
One centimeter equals 11.7 kilometers

SEE ALSO DISTANCE AND DRIVING TIME MAP ON PAGES 286–287

DRIVING DISTANCES IN MILES	ALEXANDRIA, LA	EL DORADO, AR	GREENVILLE, TX	LONGVIEW, TX	LUFKIN, TX	MONROE, LA	NACOGDOCHES, TX	NATCHEZ, MS	NATCHITOCHES, LA	SHREVEPORT, LA	TEXARKANA, AR/TX	TYLER, TX
ALEXANDRIA, LA		147	276	179	160	96	167	76	55	121	190	213
MONROE, LA	96	86	267	170	223		203	95	100	103	172	204
SHREVEPORT, LA	121	96	165	68	121	103	101	198	73		69	102
TYLER, TX	213	196	77	42	82	204	76	288	164	102	118	

Arkansas

Miss. Alabama

Louisiana

0 mi 10 20 30 40
0 km 10 20 30 40 50 60
One inch equals 18.4 miles
One centimeter equals 11.7 kilometers

DRIVING DISTANCES IN MILES	BIRMINGHAM, AL	EVERGREEN, AL	GREENVILLE, AL	HATTIESBURG, MS	JACKSON, MS	MCCOMB, MS	MERIDIAN, MS	NATCHEZ, MS	SELMA, AL	TUSCALOOSA, AL	VICKSBURG, MS	WINONA, MS
HATTIESBURG, MS	239	184	215		90	75	89	142	193	183	132	180
JACKSON, MS	241	243	125	90		76	91	102	195	185	42	94
MERIDIAN, MS	149	152	216	89	91	167		194	104	94	133	113
TUSCALOOSA, AL	61	211	225	183	185	261	94	287	82		227	144

SEE ALSO DISTANCE AND DRIVING TIME MAP ON PAGES 286–287

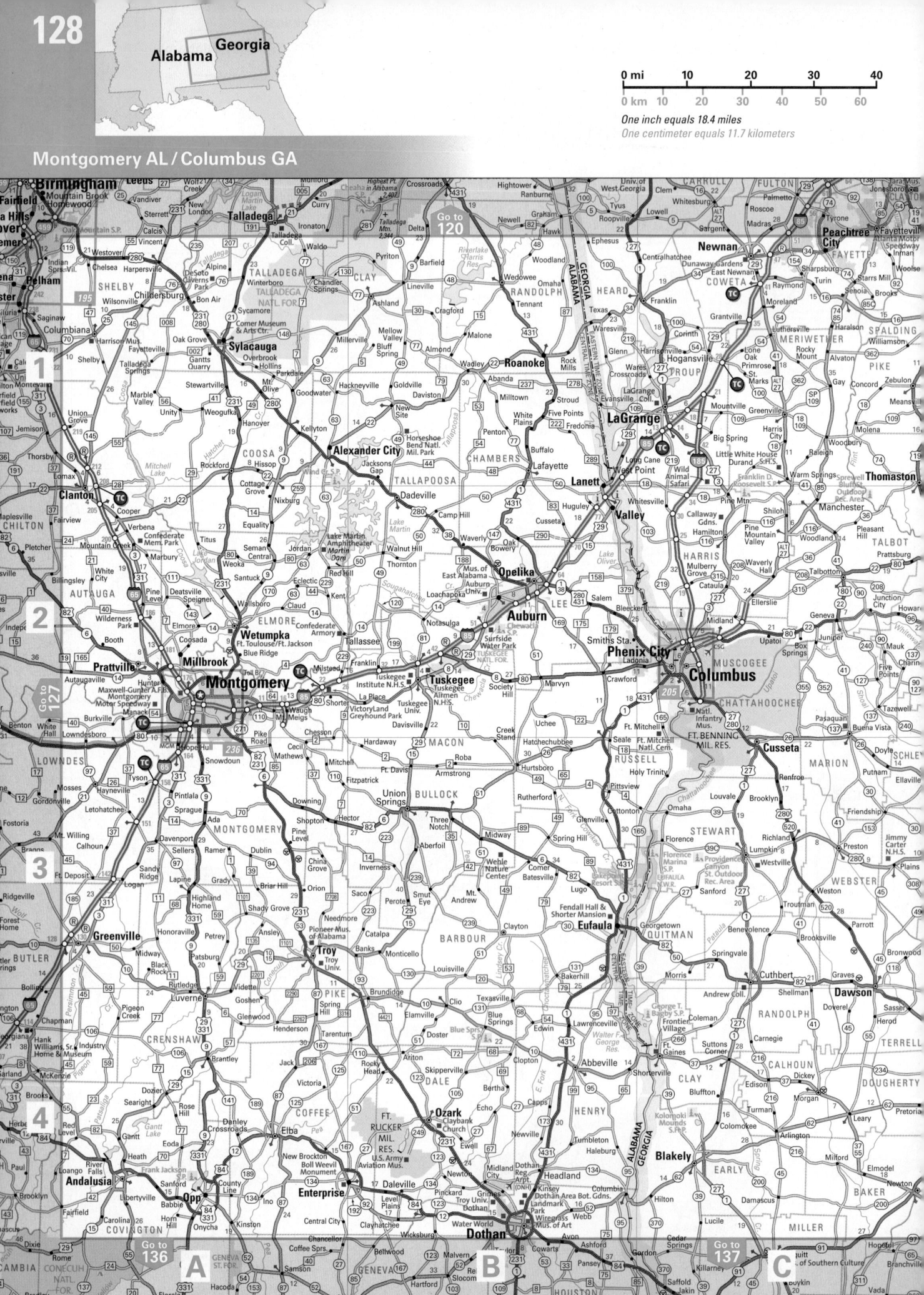

Alabama   Georgia

One inch equals 18.4 miles
One centimeter equals 11.7 kilometers

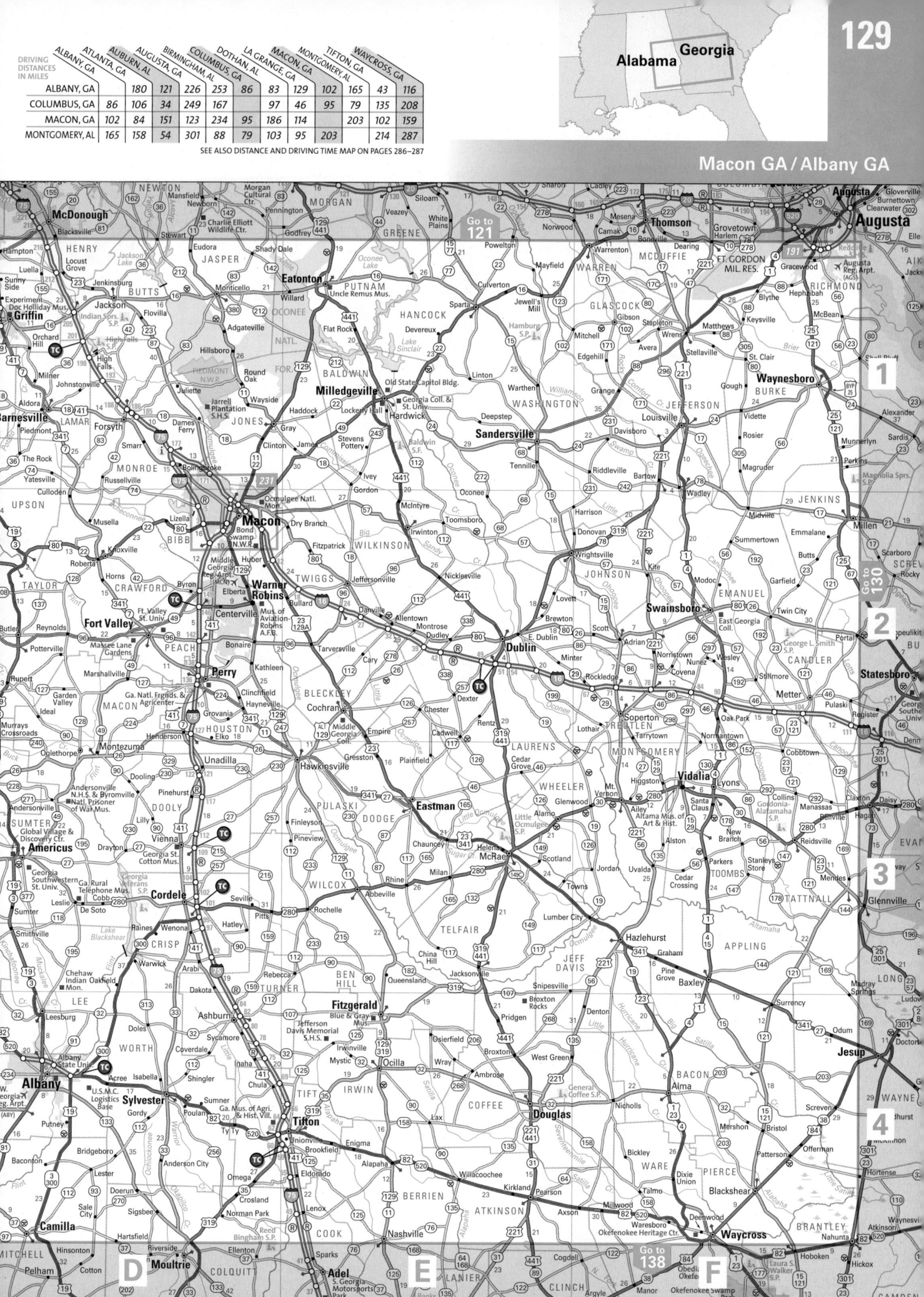

Georgia
Alabama

DRIVING DISTANCES IN MILES

	ALBANY, GA	ATLANTA, GA	AUBURN, AL	AUGUSTA, GA	BIRMINGHAM, AL	COLUMBUS, GA	DOTHAN, AL	LA GRANGE, GA	MACON, GA	MONTGOMERY, AL	TIFTON, GA	WAYCROSS, GA
ALBANY, GA		180	121	226	253	86	83	129	102	165	43	116
COLUMBUS, GA	86	106	34	249	167		97	46	95	79	135	208
MACON, GA	102	84	151	123	234	95	186	114		203	102	159
MONTGOMERY, AL	165	158	54	301	88	79	103	95	203		214	287

SEE ALSO DISTANCE AND DRIVING TIME MAP ON PAGES 286–287

0 mi 10 20 30 40

0 km 10 20 30 40 50 60

One inch equals 18.4 miles
One centimeter equals 11.7 kilometers

Savannah GA / Hilton Head Island SC

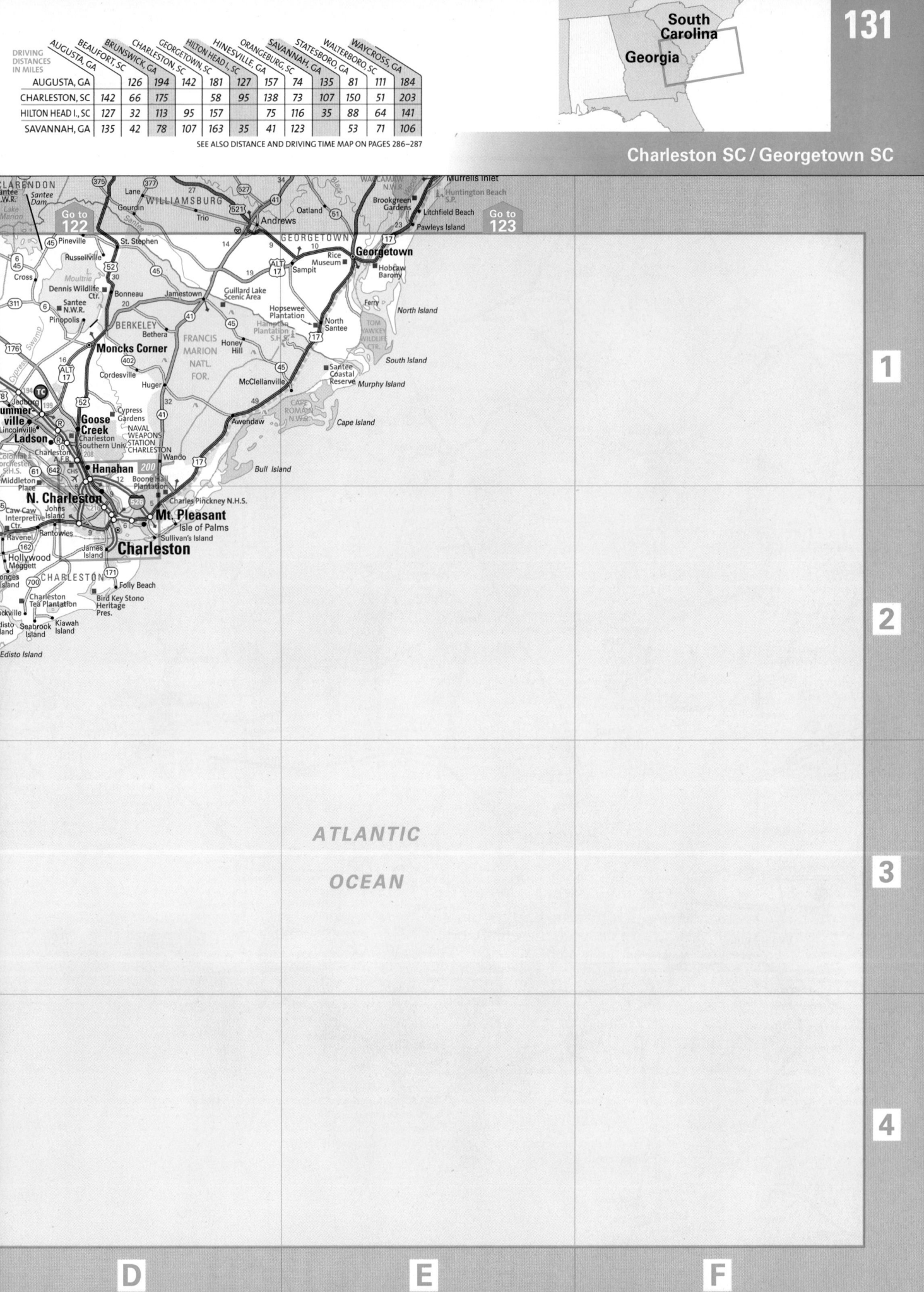

DRIVING DISTANCES IN MILES	AUGUSTA, GA	BEAUFORT, SC	BRUNSWICK, GA	CHARLESTON, SC	GEORGETOWN, SC	HILTON HEAD I, SC	HINESVILLE, GA	ORANGEBURG, SC	SAVANNAH, GA	STATESBORO, GA	WALTERBORO, SC	WAYCROSS, GA
AUGUSTA, GA		126	194	142	181	127	157	74	135	81	111	184
CHARLESTON, SC	142	66	175		58	95	138	73	107	150	51	203
HILTON HEAD I., SC	127	32	113	95	157		75	116	35	88	64	141
SAVANNAH, GA	135	42	78	107	163	35	41	123		53	71	106

SEE ALSO DISTANCE AND DRIVING TIME MAP ON PAGES 286–287

Miss.

Texas

Louisiana

0 mi · 10 · 20 · 30 · 40
0 km · 10 · 20 · 30 · 40 · 50 · 60
One inch equals 18.4 miles
One centimeter equals 11.7 kilometers

Houston TX / Beaumont TX

GULF OF MEXICO

Go to 124
Go to 61

FOR CONTINUATION
SEE INSET AT RIGHT

A · B · C

DRIVING DISTANCES IN MILES

	ALEXANDRIA, LA	BEAUMONT, TX	DE RIDDER, LA	FREEPORT, TX	GALVESTON, TX	HOUSTON, TX	HUNTSVILLE, TX	LAFAYETTE, LA	LAKE CHARLES, LA	LUFKIN, TX	OPELOUSAS, LA	PORT ARTHUR, TX
BEAUMONT, TX	157		82	143	75	84	157	133	57	112	144	18
HOUSTON, TX	241	84	166	61	53		75	217	141	121	228	93
LAFAYETTE, LA	87	133	119	276	208	217	290		76	216	27	130
LAKE CHARLES, LA	100	57	49	200	132	141	214	76		140	87	54

SEE ALSO DISTANCE AND DRIVING TIME MAP ON PAGES 286–287

DRIVING DISTANCES IN MILES

	BATON ROUGE, LA	BILOXI, MS	GULFPORT, MS	GULF SHORES, AL	HAMMOND, LA	HATTIESBURG, MS	HOUMA, LA	McCOMB, MS	MOBILE, AL	NEW ORLEANS, LA	PASCAGOULA, MS	PENSACOLA, FL
BATON ROUGE, LA		151	140	254	51	174	101	102	205	91	170	264
BILOXI, MS	151		12	110	106	82	148	161	61	93	20	120
MOBILE, AL	205	61	75	48	159	97	201	215		146	41	58
NEW ORLEANS, LA	91	93	81	195	57	115	57	111	146		112	205

SEE ALSO DISTANCE AND DRIVING TIME MAP ON PAGES 286–287

Alabama Georgia

Florida

0 mi   10   20   30   40
0 km 10   20   30   40   50   60
One inch equals 18.4 miles
One centimeter equals 11.7 kilometers

Pensacola FL / Panama City FL

GULF OF MEXICO

DRIVING DISTANCES IN MILES

	BREWTON, AL	DE FUNIAK SPRS, FL	DOTHAN, AL	FT. WALTON BEACH, FL	MARIANNA, FL	MOBILE, AL	PANAMA CITY, FL	PENSACOLA, FL	PERRY, FL	TALLAHASSEE, FL	THOMASVILLE, GA	VALDOSTA, GA
PANAMA CITY, FL	143	65	82	64	61	160		102	160	104	134	186
PENSACOLA, FL	57	82	152	39	138	58	102		256	200	230	282
TALLAHASSEE, FL	201	123	110	166	68	247	104	200	52		35	85
VALDOSTA, GA	283	204	133	247	149	329	186	282	66	85	42	

SEE ALSO DISTANCE AND DRIVING TIME MAP ON PAGES 286–287

Georgia

Florida

0 mi 10 20 30 40
0 km 10 20 30 40 50 60
One inch equals 18.4 miles
One centimeter equals 11.7 kilometers

Gainesville FL / Ocala FL

GULF OF MEXICO

Tallahassee

Valdosta

Live Oak

Lake City

Gainesville

Ocala

Perry

Moultrie

Adel

Thomasville

Camilla

Cairo

Waycross

OKEFENOKEE

GEORGIA
FLORIDA

Go to 129

Go to 137

Go to 140

A B C

1 2 3 4

DRIVING DISTANCES IN MILES	BRUNSWICK, GA	DAYTONA BEACH, FL	GAINESVILLE, FL	JACKSONVILLE, FL	LAKE CITY, FL	OCALA, FL	PERRY, FL	ST. AUGUSTINE, FL	STARKE, FL	TALLAHASSEE, FL	VALDOSTA, GA	WAYCROSS, GA
DAYTONA BEACH, FL	160		99	91	154	77	225	53	92	258	209	173
JACKSONVILLE, FL	69	91	70		62	101	133	41	45	166	117	78
OCALA, FL	171	77	40	101	80		120	81	57	186	137	170
TALLAHASSEE, FL	235	258	152	166	109	186	52	207	145		85	146

SEE ALSO DISTANCE AND DRIVING TIME MAP ON PAGES 286–287

Tampa FL / Sarasota FL

0 mi 10 20 30 40
0 km 10 20 30 40 50 60
One inch equals 18.4 miles
One centimeter equals 11.7 kilometers

1 **2** **3** **4**

A **B** **C**

GULF

OF

MEXICO

Go to 138

Go to 142

Yankeetown Inglis 19 98 336 41 Springs S.P. Marion Oaks R Belleview Candler FOREST
Crystal Sprs. 488 484 Dunnellon 484 Florida Horse Park 25 Ocklawaha MARION
Citrus Sprs. 41 200 Ross Prairie State Forest 27 Summerfield Eastlake Weir
Crystal River Pres. S.P. & Archaeological S.P. 475 Beverly Hills Holder 341 Pedro Dallas 31 Weirsdale 42
Crystal River N.W.R. Hernando 1066 Oxford The Villages 450
Crystal River 44 Inverness 44 470 19 TC Lady Lake Fruitland Pk. Lake Griffin S.P. 19
14 Lecanto 490 Homosassa Sprs. Fort Cooper S.P. 470 309 328 304 Wildwood Leesburg 44 441 14 Tavares 448
Homosassa Springs Wildlife S.P. 491 Panasoffkee Coleman 301 27 Yalaha 48
Homosassa Floral City Sumterville FLORIDA'S TPK. Howey-in-the-Hills 289 Astatula
Yulee Sugar Mill Ruins Historic S.P. 581 Lake 321 27 Mascotte 455
Homosassa Bay Chassahowitzka CITRUS 491 Pineola 48 Fla. Natl. Cem. Bushnell 48 Center Hill Montverde
CHASSAHOWITZKA 98 McKethan Lake Rec. Area Istachatta 314 476 469 33 Clermont 561 27
N.W.R. Toll Nobleton 478 Webster 21 Groveland 50 Citrus Tower
HERNANDO 19 Dade Battlefield Historic S.P. ST. FOR. Minneola Lake Louisa S.P.

Bayport 50 Brooksville R St. Catherine 301 Bay Lake 561 16
Weeki Wachee Gardens 50 98 WITHLACOOCHEE 565
Weeki Wachee Springs and Buccaneer Bay Weeki Wachee 574 Spring Lake 301 Ridge Manor 575 ST. FOR.
Hernando Beach Spring Hill 19 Trilby 41 575 Lacoochee 471
Aripeka 578 Masaryktown 15 Blanton Pioneer Florida Museum 474
Hudson 41 PASCO 233 578 10 33 Berry Eva
Bayonet Point 52 Gower's Corner San Antonio 285 St. Leo Colt Creek S.P. 33
Port Richey 12 11 Pasco 12 St. Leo Univ. 54 Zephyrhills Polk City Fantasy of Flight
Jasmine Estates 10 583 TC Wesley Chapel 279 Crystal Sprs. 35A 4
New Port Richey Trinity Coll. of Florida Toll Land O' Lakes Betmar Acres 54 Providence 570 559 17
Anclote Key Preserve S.P. ALT 19 Elfers 54 Odessa Denham R 579 Lumberton Kathleen 22 582 Auburndale Lake 92 557
Tarpon Sprs. Holiday 587 Lutz 275 301 39 Alfred 92
Palm Harbor 19 584 597 Temple Terrace 92 Thonotosassa Lakeland Winter Haven 542
Honeymoon Island S.P. 16 Oldsmar 580 589 10 21 570 Eagle Lake Legoland Florida
Caladesi Island S.P. 15 580 TPA Tampa Dover 574 Plant City Medulla Highland City Inwood
Dunedin 60 Safety Harbor Brandon Toll 10 98 17
Clearwater PINELLAS 18 275 618 13 256 Riverview Nichols 37 Bartow 98
Belleair Belleair Beach PIE 24 Gibsonton 254 Mulberry 640 Alturas
Largo 688 Seminole 693 92 41 Boyette Pinecrest 39 Bradley Jct. Homeland Ft. Meade
Indian Rocks Beach 699 31B Sun City Center Alafia River S.P. Picnic Brewster 630 Pembroke 98 15
Pinellas Park 92 HILLSBOROUGH Balm 672 POLK 17
Redington Beach 19 Tampa Bay Ruskin Little Manatee River St. Rec. Area 674 Baird Bowling Green 19
Madeira Beach St. Petersburg Wimauma 240 37 Paynes Creek Historic S.P.
Treasure Island South Pasadena 33 Sun City Ft. Green 664 62
Gulfport 679 275 41 Parrish 228 62 Quette Ft. Green Wauchula 636
St. Pete Beach 15 301 MANATEE HARDEE 64A
Fort De Soto Memphis 675 Lake Manatee S.P. Ona 64 Griffins Corner
Egmont Key S.P. Palmetto 224 TC Zolfo Sprs. 634
Anna Maria Bradenton 220 64 661 663 19
Holmes Beach Cortez 684 Oneco 217 70 Verna Solomon's Castle Limestone Gardner 665
Bradenton Beach Whitfield 41 213 Myakka City 46 661 17
Longboat Key 789 SRQ 780 210 Old Myakka 780 Pine Level Brownsville
Sarasota 780 MYAKKA Sandy 17
Ringling Mus. of Art Bee Ridge 207 72 RIVER S.P. Arcadia 70
Siesta Key 205 Vamo 115 SARASOTA 761 Nocatee DE SOTO
Coral Cove Osprey 200 72 Hull 26
Vamo Oscar Scherer S.P. Laurel Nokomis 30 183 Ft. Ogden
Laurel 75 191 769 31
Venice 266 Venice Gardens 182 170 Harbour Heights
South Venice 41 25 167 Cleveland
North Port Myakka S.F. 776 777 Port Charlotte 74 Babcock
Englewood Murdock Charlotte Harbor 161 TC CHARLOTTE
Englewood Beach Grove City 776 771 Punta Gorda 158 Babcock Wilderness Adventures
Rotonda R 23 31
Don Pedro Island S.P. 775 Charlotte Harbor Pres. S.P. Island Bay N.W.R. Pirate Harbor 214
Placida 78
Gasparilla Island Boca Grande Charlotte Harbor
Gasparilla Island S.P. Old Port Boca Grande Lighthouse Bokeelia 765 Pinelake 80 Ft. Myers Shores
Cayo Costa S.P. Pine Island N.W.R. Matlacha 41 Ft. Myers Tice
Ft. Myers LEE 75
Fort Myers

DRIVING DISTANCES IN MILES

	FORT MYERS, FL	FORT PIERCE, FL	LAKELAND, FL	MELBOURNE, FL	OKEECHOBEE, FL	ORLANDO, FL	PUNTA GORDA, FL	ST. PETERSBURG, FL	SARASOTA, FL	TAMPA, FL	TITUSVILLE, FL	W. PALM BEACH, FL
FORT PIERCE, FL	126		122	57	36	120	127	197	150	172	95	57
ORLANDO, FL	155	120	56	72	108		131	107	130	82	40	169
SARASOTA, FL	74	150	85	190	114	130	50	35		60	170	184
TAMPA, FL	123	172	37	142	162	82	99	25	60		121	223

SEE ALSO DISTANCE AND DRIVING TIME MAP ON PAGES 286–287

Florida

Fort Myers FL / Key West FL

0 mi   10   20   30   40
0 km 10 20 30 40 50 60

One inch equals 18.4 miles
One centimeter equals 11.7 kilometers

GULF

OF

MEXICO

Don Pedro Island S.P.
Charlotte Harbor Pres. S.P.
Babcock Wilderness Adventures
Placida
Island Bay N.W.R.
Pirate Harbor
Gasparilla Island
Boca Grande
Old Port Boca Grande Lighthouse
Gasparilla Island S.P.
Charlotte Harbor

Go to 140

Cayo Costa S.P.
Pine Island N.W.R.
Bokeelia
Pineland
Matlacha
N. Ft. Myers
Ft. Myers Shore
Fort Myers
Cape Coral
Ft. Myers Villa
Captiva I.
Captiva
St. James City
Punta Rassa
Iona
San Carlos Park
Sanibel
Estero
Sanibel I.
Ft. Myers Beach
Everglade Wonder Gardens
Lovers Key S.P.
Bonita Springs
214
LEE
RSW

Delnor-Wiggins Pass S.P.
Naples Park
Golden Gate
North Naples
Philharmonic Ctr. for the Arts
Naples Zoo at Caribbean Gardens
Naples Municipal Arpt. (APF)
Naples
Naples Botanical Garden
E. Naples
Naples Manor

Marco Island
Marco Island
Marco I. Trolley Tours
Cape Romano

DRY TORTUGAS NATL. PARK
Fort Jefferson

KEY WEST N.W.R.
224
Marquesas Keys
Stock Island
Key West
EYW

1

2

3

4

A   **B**   **C**

DRIVING DISTANCES IN MILES	ANNAPOLIS, MD	BALTIMORE, MD	CAMBRIDGE, MD	DOVER, DE	ELKTON, MD	FREDERICK, MD	HAGERSTOWN, MD	LEESBURG, VA	MANASSAS, VA	REHOBOTH BEACH, DE	VINELAND, NJ	WASHINGTON, DC
BALTIMORE, MD	25		78	98	58	51	76	71	67	111	109	38
DOVER, DE	62	98	64		40	135	160	135	131	43	77	94
FREDERICK, MD	73	51	128	135	106		28	25	61	161	158	44
WASHINGTON, DC	31	38	87	94	94	44	70	38	31	120	145	

SEE ALSO DISTANCE AND DRIVING TIME MAP ON PAGES 286–287

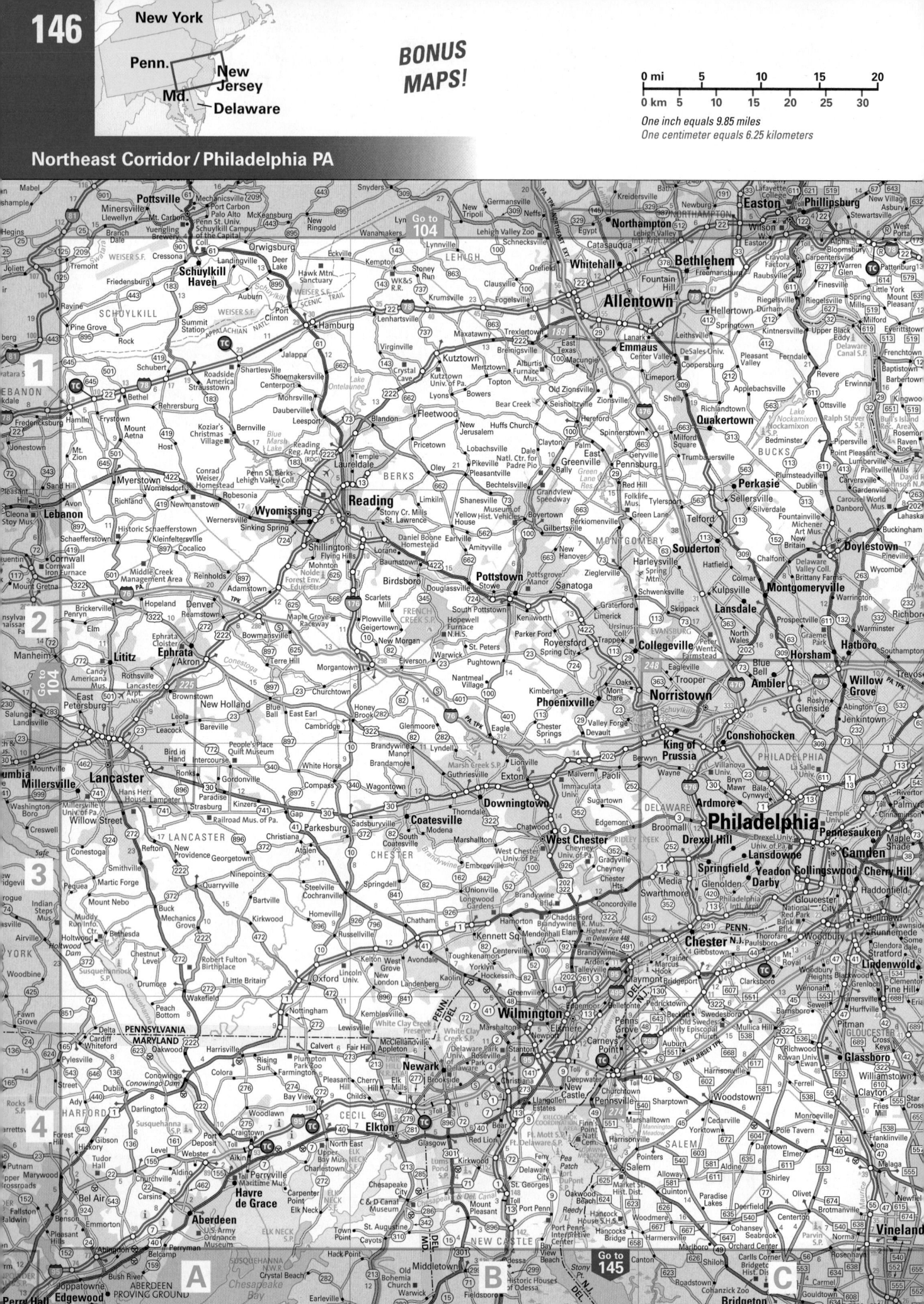

BONUS MAPS!

One inch equals 9.85 miles
One centimeter equals 6.25 kilometers

BONUS MAPS!

DRIVING DISTANCES IN MILES	ALLENTOWN, PA	ATLANTIC CITY, NJ	ELKTON, MD	LANCASTER, PA	LONG BRANCH, NJ	NEW BRUNSWICK, NJ	NEW YORK, NY	PHILADELPHIA, PA	READING, PA	TOMS RIVER, NJ	TRENTON, NJ	WILMINGTON, DE
NEW YORK, NY	84	125	137	165	55	34		91	118	75	55	120
PHILADELPHIA, PA	63	62	50	79	77	55	91		63	58	34	30
TRENTON, NJ	66	77	88	105	53	22	55	34		89	48	68
WILMINGTON, DE	77	86	20	53	106	90	120	30	56	85	68	

SEE ALSO DISTANCE AND DRIVING TIME MAP ON PAGES 286–287

New York
Penn.
New Jersey
Md.
Delaware

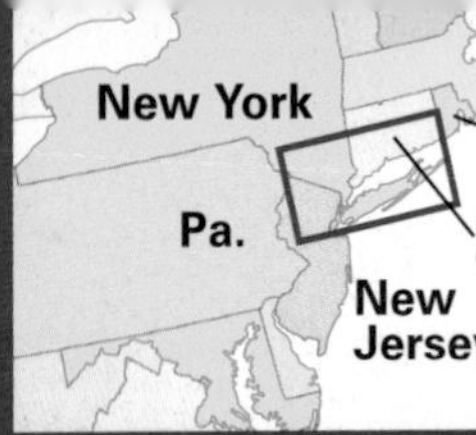

New York

Pa.

Rhode Island

Conn.

New Jersey

0 mi 5 10 15 20
0 km 5 10 15 20 25 30
One inch equals 9.85 miles
One centimeter equals 6.25 kilometers

Go to 94

Go to 147

BONUS MAPS!

New York
Pa.
Rhode Island
Conn.
New Jersey

DRIVING DISTANCES IN MILES

	Bridgeport, CT	Danbury, CT	Hartford, CT	Newark, NJ	Newburgh, NY	New Haven, CT	New London, CT	New York, NY	Paterson, NJ	Riverhead, NY	Stamford, CT	Waterbury, CT
BRIDGEPORT, CT		31	56	69	73	19	64	60	71	115	21	33
NEWARK, NJ	69	79	125		66	88	134	11	18	88	48	108
NEW HAVEN, CT	19	35	39	88	78		46	78	89	133	40	30
NEW YORK, NY	60	69	115	11	56	78	124		16	78	38	99

SEE ALSO DISTANCE AND DRIVING TIME MAP ON PAGES 286–287

Massachusetts
Rhode Island
Connecticut

BONUS MAPS!

0 mi   5   10   15   20
0 km 5 10 15 20 25 30
One inch equals 9.85 miles
One centimeter equals 6.25 kilometers

Northeast Corridor / Hartford CT

DRIVING DISTANCES IN MILES	GLOUCESTER, MA	HARTFORD, CT	HYANNIS, MA	NEW BEDFORD, MA	NEW LONDON, CT	NEWPORT, RI	PLYMOUTH, MA	PROVIDENCE, RI	PROVINCETOWN, MA	SPRINGFIELD, MA	WORCESTER, MA
BOSTON, MA	35	102	72	60	109	73	41	52	117	95	46
HARTFORD, CT	102	136	155	104	46	85	127	73	200	25	62
PROVIDENCE, RI	52	92	73	71	33	58	33	41	117	75	43
SPRINGFIELD, MA	95	129	25	148	127	71	111	120	75	193	55

SEE ALSO DISTANCE AND DRIVING TIME MAP ON PAGES 286–287

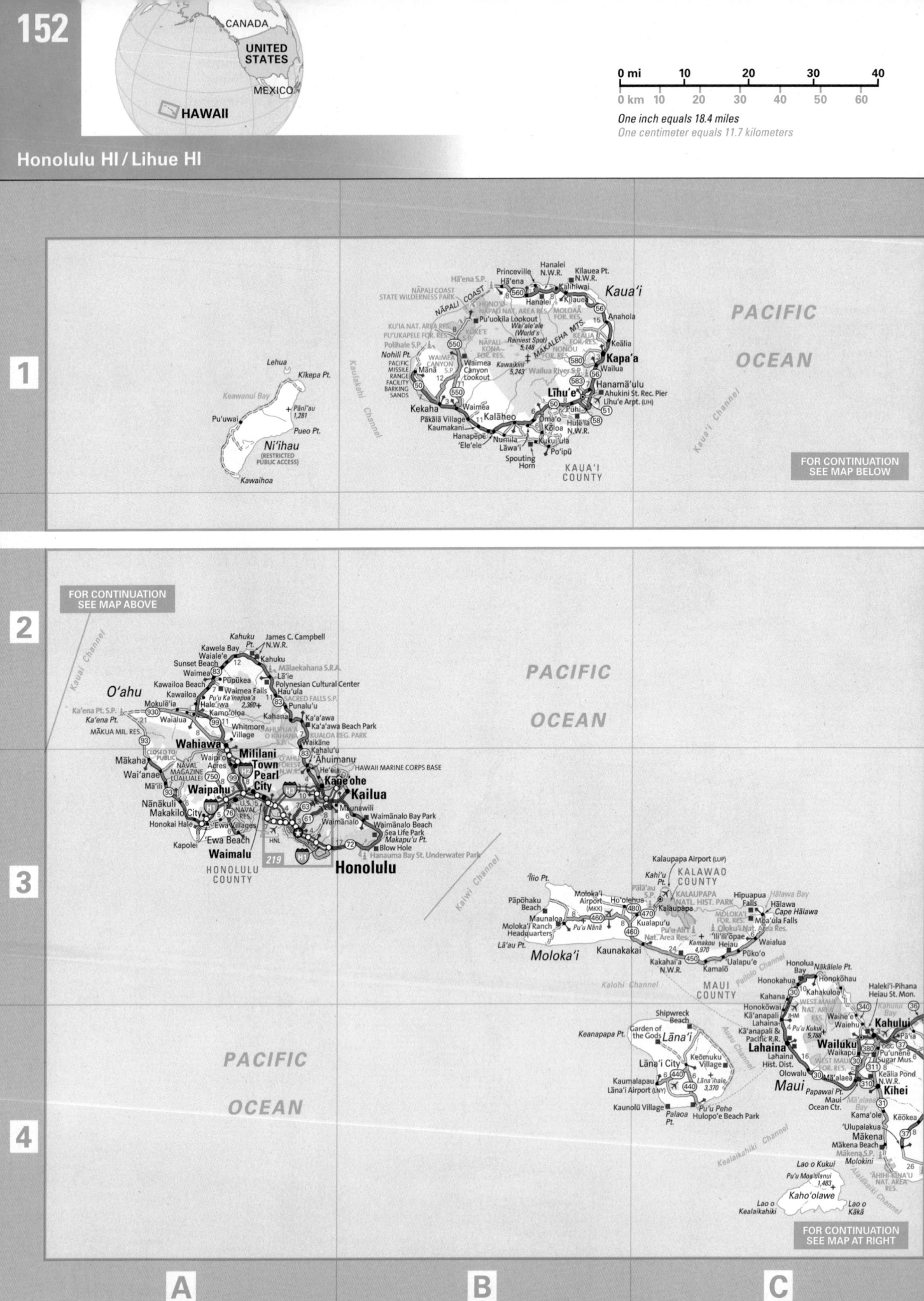

0 mi 10 20 30 40
0 km 10 20 30 40 50 60
One inch equals 18.4 miles
One centimeter equals 11.7 kilometers

1

Lehua
Kīkepa Pt.
Keawanui Bay
Puʻuwai
Pāniʻau 1,281
Pueo Pt.
Niʻihau
(RESTRICTED PUBLIC ACCESS)
Kawaihoa

Kauaʻi
Princeville
Hanalei N.W.R.
Hanalei
Hāʻena S.P.
Hāʻena
Kilauea Pt. N.W.R.
Kalihiwai
Kīlauea
NĀPALI COAST STATE WILDERNESS PARK
Anahola
KU'IA NAT. AREA RES.
PUʻUKAPELE FOR. RES.
Polihale S.P.
Nohili Pt.
PACIFIC MISSILE RANGE FACILITY BARKING SANDS
Manā
WAIMEA CANYON
Waimea Canyon Lookout
Waiʻaleʻale (World's Rainiest Spot) 5,148
MAKALEHA MTS.
KEĀLIA FOR. RES.
Keālia
Kapaʻa
Wailua
Kawaikini 5,243
Wailua River S.P.
Hanamāʻulu
Kekaha
Pākālā Village
Kaumakani
Waimea
Kalāheo
Hanapēpē
ʻEleʻele
Numila
Lāwaʻi
Kōloa
Ōmaʻo
Huleʻia N.W.R.
Kukuiʻula
Poʻipū
Spouting Horn
Puhi
Līhuʻe
Ahukini St. Rec. Pier
Lihuʻe Arpt. (LIH)
Kauaʻi County

Kaulakahi Channel
Kauaʻi Channel

PACIFIC OCEAN

FOR CONTINUATION SEE MAP BELOW

2

FOR CONTINUATION SEE MAP ABOVE

Oʻahu
Kauai Channel
Kaʻena Pt. S.P.
Kaʻena Pt.
MĀKUA MIL. RES.
Mokulēʻia
Waialua
Kawailoa Beach
Kawailoa
Haleʻiwa
Kamoʻoloa
Puʻu Kaʻinapuaʻa 2,360
Waimea Falls
Pūpūkea
Kahuku Pt.
Kahuku
James C. Campbell N.W.R.
Kawela Bay
Waialeʻe
Sunset Beach
Waimea
Mālaekahana S.R.A.
Lāʻie
Polynesian Cultural Center
Hauʻula
SACRED FALLS S.P.
Punaluʻu
Kahana
KAHANA
KUALOA REG. PARK
Kaʻaʻawa
Kaʻaʻawa Beach Park
Kaʻōhana
Waikāne
Whitmore Village
Mililani
Waipiʻo
Acres
Wahiawā
NAVAL MAGAZINE LUALUALEI
Mākaha
Waiʻanae
Māʻili
Nānākuli
Makakilo City
Honokai Hale
Kapolei
Ewa Villages
Ewa Beach
Waimalu
Waipahu
Pearl City
Mililani Town
Ahuimanu
Heʻeia
Kāneʻohe
HAWAII MARINE CORPS BASE
Kailua
Maunawili
Waimānalo
Waimānalo Bay Park
Waimānalo Beach
Sea Life Park
Makapuʻu Pt.
Blow Hole
Hanauma Bay St. Underwater Park
Honolulu
HNL
HONOLULU COUNTY
OʻAHU FOREST N.W.R.
U.S. NAVAL RES.

PACIFIC OCEAN

3

Kaiwi Channel

Kalaupapa Airport (LUP)
KALAWAO COUNTY
KALAUPAPA NATL. HIST. PARK
Kalaupapa
MOLOKAʻI FOR. RES.
Hipuapua Falls
Moaʻula Falls
Hālawa
Cape Hālawa
Hālawa Bay
MOʻahu
Īlio Pt.
Kahiʻu Pt.
Palaʻau
Pāpōhaku Beach
Molokaʻi Airport (MKK)
Hoʻolehua
Maunaloa
Molokaʻi Ranch Headquarters
Lāʻau Pt.
Kualapuʻu
ʻIliʻiliʻōpae Heiau
Kamakou 4,970
Waialua
Pukoʻo
Honouli
Ualapuʻe
Kamalō
Honouliwai
Kaunakakai
Kakahaiʻa N.W.R.
Moloka'i
OLOKUʻI NAT. AREA RES.
Puʻu Aliʻi

Kalohi Channel
Pailolo Channel

MAUI COUNTY

Nākālele Pt.
Honokōhau
Honolua Bay
Honokahua
Kahakuloa
HALEKIʻI-PIHANA HEIAU ST. MON.
WEST MAUI NAT. AREA RES.
WEST MAUI FOR. RES.
Kahana
Honokōwai
Kāʻanapali
Lahaina
Kāʻanapali & Pacific R.R.
Puʻu Kukui 5,788
Lahaina Hist. Dist.
Olowalu
Māʻalaea
Waiheʻe
Waiehu
Wailuku
Waikapū
Kahului
OGG
Pāʻia
Puʻu nēnē
Sugar Mus.
Waiheʻe
Kihei
Māʻalaea Bay
Maui Ocean Ctr.
Papawai Pt.
Keālia Pond N.W.R.
Maui
Kamaʻole
Kēōkea
ʻUlupalakua
Mākena
Mākena Beach
Mākena S.P.
Molokini
ʻĀHIHI-KĪNAʻU NAT. AREA RES.

Shipwreck Beach
Keanapapa Pt.
Garden of the Gods
Lānaʻi
Kānepuʻu
Keōmuku Village
Lānaʻi City
Kaumalapau
Lānaʻi Airport (LNY)
Lānaʻ ihale 3,370
Kaunolū Village
Palaoa Pt.
Hulopoʻe Beach Park
Puʻu Pehe
Lao o Kukui
Puʻu Moaʻilanui 1,483
Kahoʻolawe
Lao o Kealaikahiki
Lao o Kākā
KanapouBay
Au'au Channel
Kealaikahiki Channel
Alalākeiki Channel
Kahoʻolawe

PACIFIC OCEAN

4

FOR CONTINUATION SEE MAP AT RIGHT

A   **B**   **C**

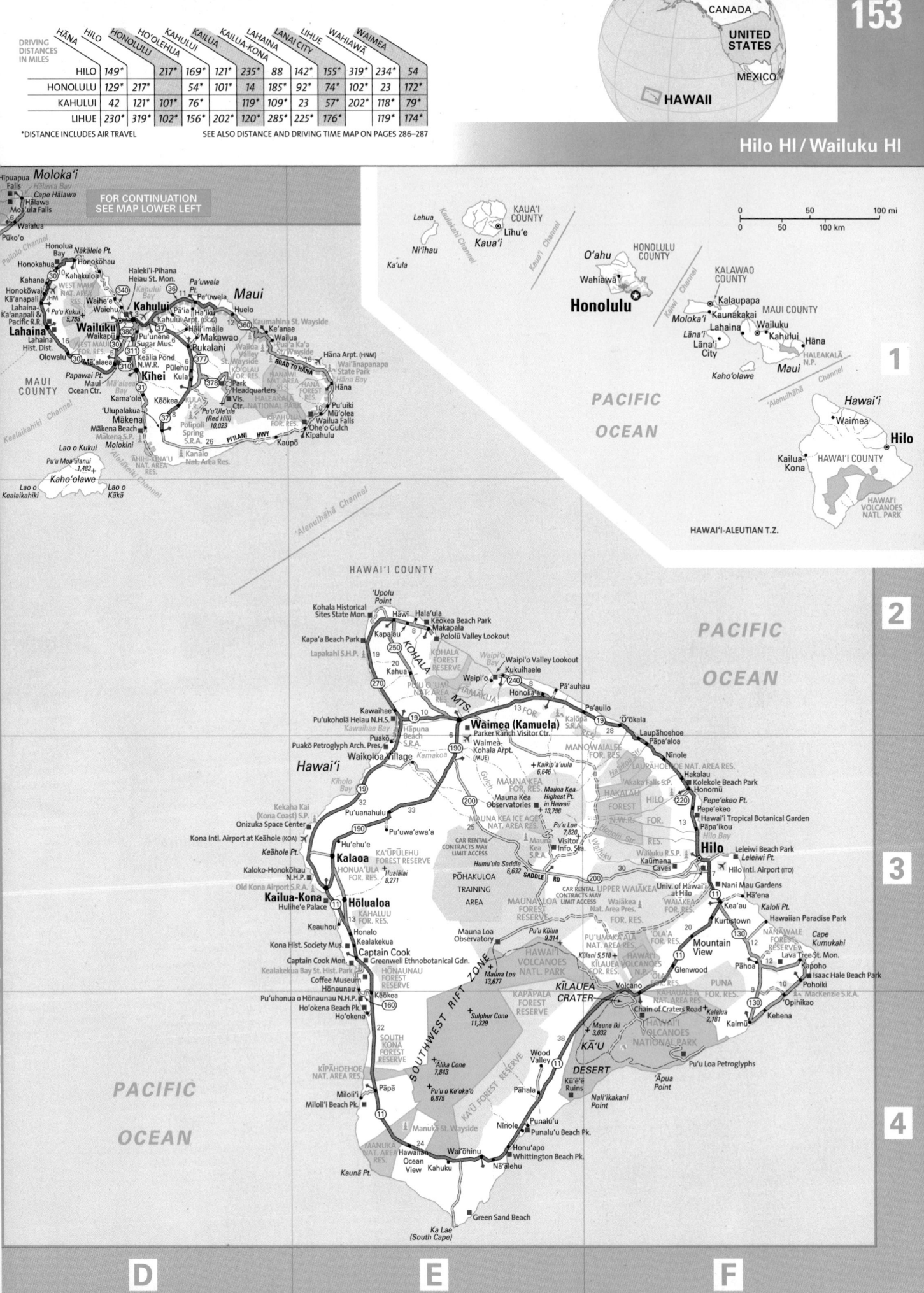

DRIVING DISTANCES IN MILES	HĀNA	HILO	HONOLULU	HO'OLEHUA	KAHULUI	KAILUA	KAILUA-KONA	LAHAINA	LANAI CITY	LIHUE	WAHIAWĀ	WAIMEA
HILO	149*		217*	169*	121*	235*	88	142*	155*	319*	234*	54
HONOLULU	129*	217*		54*	101*	14	185*	92*	74*	102*	23	172*
KAHULUI	42	121*	101*	76*		119*	109*	23	57*	202*	118*	79*
LIHUE	230*	319*	102*	156*	202*	120*	285*	225*	176*		119*	174*

*DISTANCE INCLUDES AIR TRAVEL   SEE ALSO DISTANCE AND DRIVING TIME MAP ON PAGES 286–287

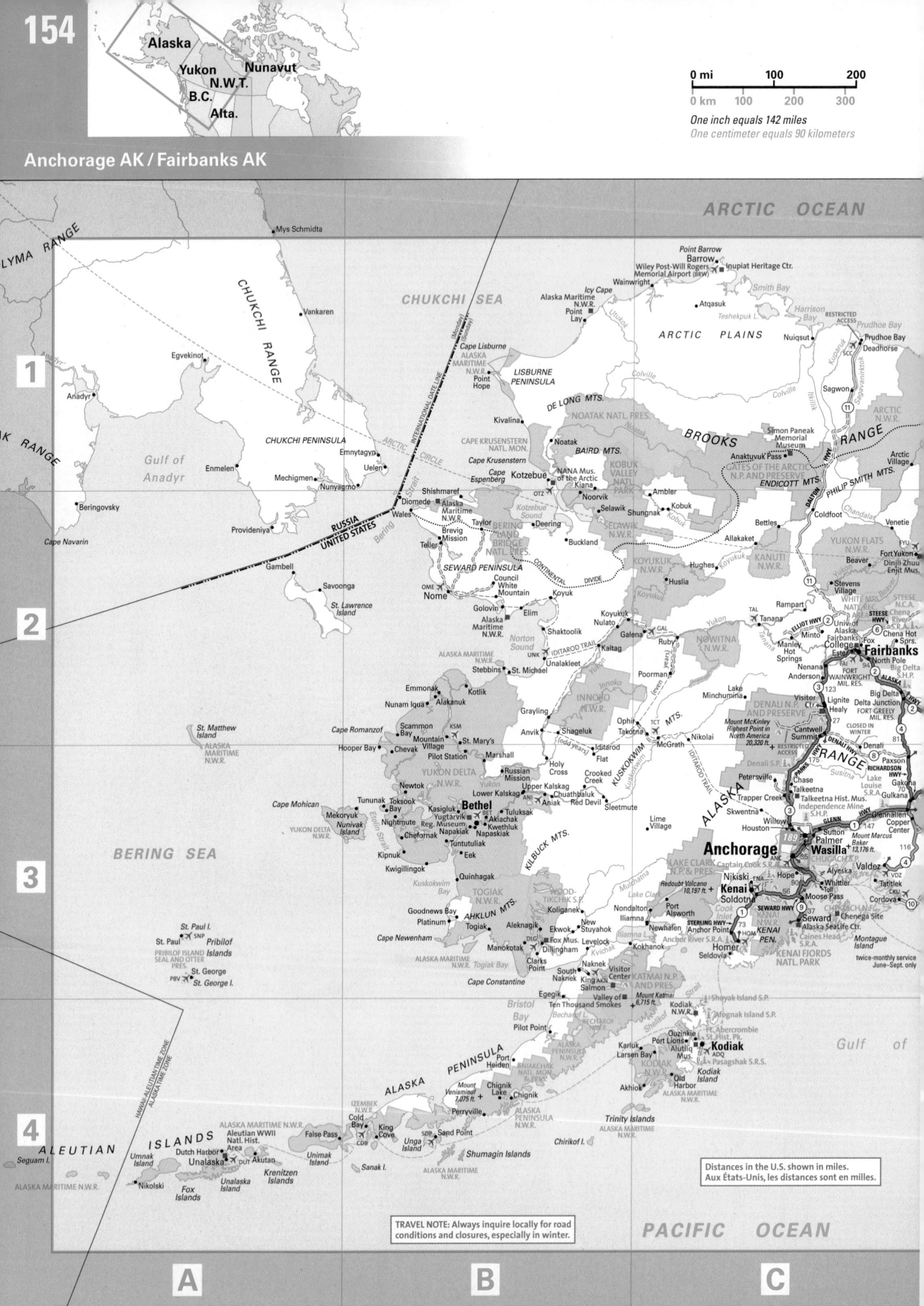

Alaska
Yukon Nunavut
N.W.T.
B.C.
Alta.

0 mi   100   200
0 km   100   200 300
One inch equals 142 miles
One centimeter equals 90 kilometers

ARCTIC OCEAN

Point Barrow
Barrow
Wiley Post-Will Rogers
Memorial Airport (BRW)   Inupiat Heritage Ctr.
Wainwright
Icy Cape   Smith Bay   Harrison RESTRICTED
Alaska Maritime   Atqasuk   Teshekpuk L.   Bay   ACCESS Prudhoe Bay
N.W.R.   Prudhoe Bay
Point   ARCTIC   PLAINS   Nuiqsut   Deadhorse
Lay
CHUKCHI SEA   Sagwon   ARCTIC
Cape Lisburne   N.W.R.
ALASKA   Colville
MARITIME   Simon Paneak
Point   N.W.R.   NOATAK NATL. PRES.   Memorial Museum
LISBURNE   Hope   BROOKS   RANGE
PENINSULA   Noatak   BAIRD MTS.   Anaktuvuk Pass   Arctic
DE LONG MTS.   KOBUK   GATES OF THE ARCTIC   Village
Kivalina   CAPE KRUSENSTERN   VALLEY   N.P. AND PRESERVE
NATL. MON.   NANA Mus.   NATL   ENDICOTT MTS.   PHILIP SMITH MTS.
Cape Krusenstern   of the Arctic   PARK   Ambler   Venetie
CHUKCHI PENINSULA   Cape   Kiana   Bettles   Fort Yukon
Espenberg   Kotzebue   Kobuk   Coldfoot   YUKON FLATS   Dinjii Zhuu
Shishmaref   OTZ   Noorvik   Shungnak   N.W.R.   Beaver Enjit Mus.
BERING   Selawik   KANUTI
Diomede   Taylor   LAND   SELAWIK   Hughes   KOYUKUK   N.W.R.   Stevens
Wales   BRIDGE   Deering   N.W.R.   Allakaket   N.W.R.   Village
Brevig   NATL. PRES.   Buckland   Huslia   WHITE MTS.   STEESE
Mission   CONTINENTAL   N.C.A. N.C.A.
SEWARD PENINSULA   DIVIDE   Koyuk   Minto Fox Chena Hot
Teller   Council   Koyukuk   NOWITNA   TAL Rampart   ELLIOT HWY   Sprs.
White   Golovin   Nulato   N.W.R.   Tanana   Univ. of
OME Mountain   Elim   Galena   GAL   Alaska-
Nome   Shaktoolik   Ruby   Manley   Fairbanks Fairbanks
Alaska   Koyukuk   Hot   FAI College
Maritime   Norton   UNK   Kaltag   Poorman   Springs Nenana   North Pole
N.W.R.   Sound   IDITAROD TRAIL   Anderson   Big Delta
Stebbins   Unalakleet   FORT   S.H.P.
St. Michael   Iditarod   WAINWRIGHT   123   Big Delta
Emmonak   Kotlik   Grayling   INNOKO   McGrath   MIL. RES.   Healy   Delta Junction
Nunam Iqua   Alakanuk   N.W.R.   Ophir   TCT MTS.   DENALI N.P.   FORT GREELY
Scammon   KSM   Anvik   Takotna   Nikolai   AND PRESERVE   MIL. RES.
St. Matthew   Bay   Mountain   St. Mary's   Flat   Mount McKinley   Lignite
Island   Hooper Bay   Chevak   Holy   Crooked   IDITAROD TRAIL   Highest Point in   Cantwell
Pilot Station   Cross   Creek   North America   Summit Denali
ALASKA   Marshall   Sleetmute   20,320 ft.   Paxson
MARITIME   YUKON DELTA   Russian   Upper Kalskag   Lime   Petersville RICHARDSON
N.W.R.   N.W.R.   Mission   Lower Kalskag   Chuathbaluk   Village   RANGE   Chase   HWY.
Newtok   Aniak   Red Devil   Talkeetna   Lake
Cape Mohican   Tununak   Toksook   Kasigluk   Tuluksak   Skwentna   Talkeetna Hist. Mus.   Louise Gakona
Mekoryuk   Bay   BET   Akiachak   Independence Mine   S.R.A. 70 Gulkana
YUKON DELTA   Nunivak   Nightmute   Yugtarvik   Kwethluk   Willow   S.H.P.
N.W.R.   Island   Reg. Museum   Napaskiak   Houston   1   Glennallen
Chefornak   Napakiak   Mount Marcus   Copper
Kipnuk   Tuntutuliak   KILBUCK MTS.   Baker 13,176 ft.   Palmer   Center
Eek   Anchorage   Wasilla   Sutton   116
BERING SEA   Kwigillingok   Quinhagak   Captain Cook S.R.A.   Glenn 147 Valdez
Kuskokwim   WOOD-   Hope   Nikiski   CHUGACH N.F.   VDZ
Bay   TIKCHIK S.P.   Kenai   90   Whittier   4
Goodnews Bay   Koliganek   New   Redoubt Volcano   Soldotna   Moose Pass   10
Platinum   Togiak   AHKLUN MTS.   Aleknagik   Stuyahok   10,197 ft.   KENAI   Seward   Tatitlek
St. Paul I.   Fox Mus.   Ekwok   Port   N.W.R.   Cordova
St. Paul   SNP   Pribilof   Manokotak   DLG   Alsworth   Nondalton   Anchor Point   Seward   Chenega Site
Pribilof Island   Dillingham   Levelock   Iliamna   Newhalen   STERLING HWY   HOM   Alaska Sealife Ctr.
SEAL AND OTTER   Clarks   73   Homer   KENAI   Caines Head
PRES.   St. George   Point   South   Kokhanok   Anchor River   PEN.   S.R.A.
PBV   St. George I.   Naknek   Naknek   S.R.A.   Seldovia   KENAI FJORDS   Montague
King   Visitor   NATL. PARK   Island
Egegik   Center   twice-monthly service
Ten Thousand   Mount Katmai   Shuyak Island S.P.   June–Sept. only
Bristol   Smokes   6,715 ft.   Kodiak
Bay   Pilot Point   KATMAI N.P.   N.W.R.   Afognak Island S.P.   Gulf   of
BECHAROF   AND PRES.   Ft. Abercrombie
Port   N.W.R.   Ouzinkie   Hist. Pk.
ALASKA   Heiden   ALASKA   Port Lions   Kodiak
ANIAKCHAK   Karluk   Alutiiq   Kodiak   ADQ   Pasagshak S.R.S.
NATL. MON.   KODIAK   Mus.   Island
Chignik   Larsen Bay   N.W.R.   Old
Mount   Chignik   Akhiok   Harbor
Veniaminof   Lake   Chignik
ALASKA   PENINSULA   7,075 ft.   ALASKA   Trinity Islands
IZEMBEK   Perryville   PENINSULA
N.W.R.   Cold   King   Sand Point   Chirikof I.   N.W.R.
Bay   Cove   Unga   ALASKA MARITIME
False Pass   CDB   Island   N.W.R.   PACIFIC   OCEAN
ALASKA MARITIME N.W.R.   King Cove   Shumagin Islands
Aleutian WWII   Unimak   Sanak I.
ALEUTIAN   ISLANDS   Natl. Hist.   Island
Seguam I.   Area   Krenitzin
Dutch Harbor   DUT Akutan   Islands
Unalaska   Fox   Unalaska
Nikolski   Islands   Island
Umnak Island
ALASKA MARITIME N.W.R.

Distances in the U.S. shown in miles.
Aux États-Unis, les distances sont en milles.

TRAVEL NOTE: Always inquire locally for road
conditions and closures, especially in winter.

COLYMA RANGE
CHUKCHI RANGE
Mys Schmidta
Vankaren
Egvekinot
Anadyr
Beringovsky
Cape Navarin
Provideniya
Gambell
Savoonga
St. Lawrence
Island
Gulf of
Anadyr
Enmelen
Mechigmen
Nunyagmo
Emnytagyn
Uelen
ARCTIC CIRCLE
RUSSIA
UNITED STATES
Bering Strait
INTERNATIONAL DATE LINE

A   B   C
1   2   3   4

DRIVING DISTANCES IN MILES	ANCHORAGE, AK	DAWSON CREEK, BC	DENALI NP, AK	FAIRBANKS, AK	HOMER, AK	JUNEAU, AK	PRINCE GEORGE, BC	PRINCE RUPERT, BC	SKAGWAY, AK	TOK, AK	WHITEHORSE, YT	YELLOWKNIFE, NT
ANCHORAGE, AK		1516	275	378	225	841*	1679	1514	807	323	697	1844
DAWSON CREEK, BC	1516		1503	1400	1740	963*	224	625	862	1193	819	741
FAIRBANKS, AK	378	1400	103		603	726*	1564	1398	691	207	581	1729
WHITEHORSE, YT	697	819	684	581	921	211*	982	817	110	374		1147

*DISTANCE INCLUDES FERRY TRAVEL   SEE ALSO DISTANCE AND DRIVING TIME MAP ON PAGES 286–287

Distances in Canada shown in kilometers.
Au Canada, les distances sont en kilomètres.

The Alaska Marine Highway—with ferry service to 30 communities in Alaska, plus Bellingham WA and Prince Rupert BC—is an All-American Road

Go to 158

Go to 164

Go to 156

Go to 157

0 mi 20 40 60
0 km 20 40 60 80
One inch equals 40.3 miles/Un pouce équivaut à 40.3 milles
One centimeter equals 25.4 km/Un cm équivaut à 25.4 km

Go to 155
Go to 155

Coffman Cove
Heceta I.
Meyers Chuck
To Juneau
TONGASS
Cleveland Peninsula
Thorne Bay
Noyes I.
AKW
Klawock
Craig
Hollis
Kasaan
Revillagigedo Island
Baker I.
Waterfall
Suemez I.
Hydaburg
Prince of Wales
NATIONAL
Ketchikan
Saxman
KTN
Gravina Island
MISTY
FIORDS
NATIONAL
MONUMENT

1

Sukkwan I.
Island
FOREST
ANNETTE ISLAND IND. RES.
Dall I.
Metlakatla

Go to 155

Forrester I.
ALASKA MARITIME N.W.R.
Long I.
Cordova Bay
Clarence Strait
Duke I.

ALASKA
B.C.

Mt. Pattullo 2,729 m
Meziadin Lake
37
37A
65
Stewart
Hyder
Meziadin Junction
Meziadin Lake Provincial Park
80
Motase Pk. 2,411 m
Bear Lake
SUSTUT PROVINCIAL PARK
CONTINENTAL DIVIDE

SWAN LAKE-KISPIOX RIVER PROVINCIAL PARK
Shelagyote Pk. 2,466 m
Kisgegas Pk. 2,347 m
Kinskuch Lake
Cranberry Junction
Cutoff Mtn. 1,649 m
BABINE RIVER CORRIDOR PROVINCIAL PARK
Centre Pk. 1,990 m

Alice Arm
Lavender Pk. 2,323 m
Swan L.
37
73
Mt. Thomlinson 2,591 m
Mt. Lovell 1,995 m

New Aiyansh
Nass Camp
Mt. Weber 2,007 m
Kispiox
Hazelton
'Ksan Hist. Village & Mus.
New Hazelton
Ross Lake Prov. Park
Fort Babine
Gitwinksihlkw
NISGA'A MEMORIAL LAVA BED PROVINCIAL PARK
Kitwancool Lake
Gitanyow Totem Poles
Seeley Lake Prov. Pk.
South Hazelton
Blunt Mtn. 2,286 m
Babine Lake Smithers Landing Marine Prov. Park
Nilkitkwa L.

1

Laxgalts'ap
Alder Pk. 2,220 m
Kitwanga Fort N.H.S.
Kitwanga
Cedarvale
Moricetown
Smithers Landing

Gingolx
Oscar Pk. 2,304 m
Lava Lake
37
SEVEN SISTERS PROV. PARK
Kitseguecla
Granisle
Red Bluff Prov. Pk.

Nass Bay
Nasoga Gulf
Kitsumkalum Lake
Rosswood
Smithers Arpt. (YYD)
BABINE MOUNTAINS PROV. PARK
Fulton L.

KHUTZEYMATEEN GRIZZLY BEAR SANCTUARY
Mt. Kenney 2,073 m
Heritage Park Mus.
91
Smithers
Telkwa
Tyhee Lake Provincial Park
118

U.S. CANADA
Chatham Sound
Lax Kw'alaams
Usk
Kleanza Creek Prov. Park
Ski Smithers
257
Eagle Pk. 2,093 m

ALASKA TIME ZONE
PACIFIC TIME ZONE
Dundas I.
Dixon Entrance
Shames Mountain
Terrace
Houston
16

2

Masset Arpt. (ZMT)
Masset
Mus. of Northern B.C.
Prodhomme Lake Prov. Park
Prince Rupert
Prince Rupert Arpt. (YPR)
Exchamsiks River Prov. Pk.
Terrace Arpt. (YXT)
Lakelse Lake Prov. Park
Lakelse Lake
58
37
McBride
Noralee

North Pacific Hist. Fishing Village
Stephens I.
Port Edward
147
Skeena
GITNADOIKS RIVER PROVINCIAL PARK
Khtada Lake
Morice Lake
Kidprice Lake
Tagetochlain

Graham Island
NAIKOON PROV. PARK
Diana Lake Prov. Park
Porcher Island
Port Essington
Kitimat
Kitamaat Village
Nadina Lake
Wistaria Prov. Park
Little Andrews Bay Marine Prov. Park
Ootsa Lake

Ian Lake
Oona River
2

Port Clements
16
Juskatla
Tlell
101
Kitkatla
McCauley I.
Pitt Island
Klewnuggit Inlet Marine Prov. Park
Nanika Lake
Tahtsa L.
Powell Pk. 2,012 m
Tweedsmuir Prov. Park 2,182 m
Glathell Lake
Michel Pk. 2,252 m

Yakoun L.
Banks Island
Cowe Inlet Marine Prov. Park
Hawkesbury Island
Kemano
Troitsa L.
Whtesail Lake
Fenton L.

Queen
Qay'llnagaay Heritage Center
Skidegate
Sandspit Arpt. (YZP)
Union Passage Marine Prov. Park
Hartley Bay
Gribbell Island
COAST
TWEEDSMUIR NORTH PROVINCIAL PARK
Eutsuk Lake
Oppy L.

Charlotte
Queen Charlotte
Sandspit
Alliford Bay
Gil I.
Anchor Lake
Surel L.
Pondosy L.
Tesla L.

Moresby Camp
Islands
Campania I.
HUCHSDUWACHSDU NUYEM JEES/ KITLOPE HERITAGE CONSERVANCY
Kynoch Inlet
Sigutlat L.

3

Sewell Inlet
Aristazabal Island
Princess Royal Island
Green Inlet Marine Prov. Park
Mussel Inlet
FIORDLAND CONSERVANCY
Kimsquit
Kalone Pk. 2,557 m

GWAII HAANAS NATIONAL PARK RESERVE & HAIDA HERITAGE SITE
Laredo Inlet
Pooley I.
Roderick I.
Jackson Narrows Marine Prov. Park
Thunder Mtn. 2,681 m

Moresby Island
Price I.
Klemtu
Swindle I.
QBC
Firvale
Bella
Hagensborg
20
Bella Coola

Oliver Cove Marine Prov. Pk.
St. Alexander Mackenzie Prov. Park
Ocean Falls
Link Lake
Cascade Inlet
MOUNTAINS
Mt. Saugstad 2,972 m

King I.
ZEL
Bella Bella
Shearwater
Codville Lagoon Marine Prov. Park

Goose I.
Hunter I.
Burke Channel

Namu
Oweikeno Lake

HAKAI LUXVBALIS CONSERVANCY
Mt. Buxton 1,045 m
Calvert I.
Dawsons Landing
Rivers Inlet

4

PACIFIC

OCEAN

Distances in Canada shown in kilometers.
Au Canada, les distances sont en kilomètres.

Good Hope
Draney Inlet
Penrose Island Marine Prov. Park

Smith Sound
Long I.
Belize Inlet

Go to 162

LANZ & COX ISLANDS PROV. PARK
CAPE SCOTT PROV. PARK
Lanz I.
Cox I.
Hope I.
Nigei I.
To Port Hardy
God's Pocket Marine Prov. Park
Sullivan Bay

A **B** **C**

DRIVING DISTANCES IN KM / DISTANCES ROUTIÈRES EN KM

	GRANDE PRAIRIE, AB	KAMLOOPS, BC	KITIMAT, BC	100 MILE HOUSE, BC	PRINCE GEORGE, BC	PRINCE RUPERT, BC	SMITHERS, BC	STEWART, BC	TERRACE, BC	VALEMOUNT, BC	WILLIAMS LAKE, BC
DAWSON CREEK, BC	124	931	1041	734	406	1130	777	1109	983	642	644
PRINCE GEORGE, BC	406	530	525	635	328		724	371	703	577	295	238
PRINCE RUPERT, BC	1130	1254	1249	205	1052	724		353	463	147	1019	962
WILLIAMS LAKE, BC	644	768	287	873	90	238	962	609	941	815	332

SEE ALSO DISTANCE AND DRIVING TIME MAP ON PAGES 286–287 / VOIR AUSSI CARTE DES DISTANCES ET DES TEMPS DE PARCOURS PAGES 286–287

Go to 158
Go to 158
Go to 164
Go to 163

British Columbia | Alberta | Sask.

0 mi 20 40 60
0 km 20 40 60 80
One inch equals 40.3 miles/Un pouce équivaut à 40.3 milles
One centimeter equals 25.4 km/Un cm équivaut à 25.4 km

Go to 155
Go to 157
Go to 164

Grid labels: 1, 2, 3, 4 (rows); A, B, C (columns)

Place names and features:

Buckinghorse River Wayside Prov. Park, Sikanni Chief, Pink Mountain, Beatton River, Milligan Hills Provincial Park, Etthithun Lake, Paddle Prairie, Chinchaga, Buffalo Head Prairie, Carcajou, Keg River, Prespatou, Altona, Wonowon, Buick, Doig, Chinchaga Wildland Prov. Park, Hotchkiss, Notikewin Prov. Park, Bison Lake, Russell Lake, Sawn Lake, Gods Lake, Peerless Lake

Charlie Lake Prov. Park, Montney, North Pine, Rose Prairie, Worsley, Eureka River, Hines Creek, Notikewin, Manning, North Star, Deadwood, Dixonville, Haig Lake, Otter Lakes, Red Earth Creek, Trout Lake, Graham Lake, Muskwa Lake, Peerless Lake

Fort St. John, Fort St. John Arpt. (YXJ), Baldonnel, Taylor, Taylor Landing Provincial Park, Cherry Point, Bear Canyon, Cleardale, Grimshaw, Queen Elizabeth Prov. Park, Brownvale, Whitelaw, Berwyn, Marie-Reine, Peace River, St. Isidore, Greene Valley Prov. Park, Cadotte Lake, Little Buffalo, Lubicon Lake, Cranberry Lake, Bat Lake

Hudson's Hope, W.A.C. Bennett Dam, Moberly Lake, Moberly Lake Prov. Park, Groundbirch, Chetwynd, East Pine Prov. Pk., Dawson Creek, Pouce Coupe, Farmington, Rolla, Bay Tree, Gordondale, Fairview, Historic Dunvegan, Dunvegan West Wildland Prov. Park, Blueberry Mountain, Rycroft, Dunvegan, Wanham, Eaglesham, Tangent, Girouxville, Falher, Donnelly, McLennan, Kathleen, Guy, Grouard Mission, Grouard, Winagami Wildland Prov. Park, Lesser Slave Lake, Marten Beach, Utikuma Lake, Nipisi Lake, Mistehae Lake, Randall Lake, Brintnell Lake

Lone Prairie, Gwillim Lake Prov. Park, Sukunka Falls Provincial Park, Tumbler Ridge, Swan Lake Prov. Park, Tomslake, Tupper, Demmitt, Valhalla Centre, Hythe, Buffalo Lake, La Glace, Sexsmith, Clairmont, Teepee Creek, Bezanson, DeBolt, Puskwaskau Lake, New Fish Creek, Young's Point Prov. Park, High Prairie, Enilda, Joussard, Driftpile, Kinuso, Faust, Canyon Creek, Widewater, Slave Lake

Goodfare, Beaverlodge, Elmworth, Huallen, Wembley, Grande Prairie, Grande Prairie Mus., O'Brien Prov. Park, Nitehawk, Crooked Creek, Sturgeon Heights, Williamson Prov. Park, Valleyview, Sunset House, Wallace Mtn. 1,259 m, Deer Mtn. 1,189 m, Grizzly Ridge Wildland Prov. Park, Hubert Lake Wildland Prov. Park, Ft. Assiniboine Sandhills Wildland Prov. Park

Bearhole Lake Provincial Park, Monkman Prov. Park, Quintette Mtn. 1,842 m, Wapiti Lake Prov. Park, Little Smoky, Fox Creek, Carson-Pegasus Prov. Park, Ft. Assiniboine, Fort Assiniboine, Vega, Neerlandia, Barrhead, Barrhead Centennial Mus., Birch Cove

Arctic Pacific Lakes Prov. Park, Ice Mtn. 2,286 m, Kakwa Prov. Park, Kakwa Prov. Park & Protected Area, Mt. Sir Alexander 3,274 m, Mt. May 2,450 m, Whitecourt, Forest Interpretive Center, Blue Ridge, Thunder Lake Prov. Park, Green Court, Lone Tiger Lily, Mayerthorpe, Sangudo, Cherhill, Ross Haven, West Cove, Gunn

Sinclair Mills, Longworth, Dome Creek, Intersection Mtn. 2,461 m, Grande Cache, Mt. De Veber 2,577 m, Willmore Wilderness Park, Silver Summit, Peers, Carrot Creek, MacKay, Evansburg, Gainford, Alberta Beach, Wabamun, Seba Beach, Wabamun Lake Prov. Pk.

Purden Lake, Purden Ski Village, Sugarbowl Prov. Park, Penny, Crescent Spur, Loos, Mt. Pauline 2,653 m, Mt. Chown 3,098 m, Resthaven Mtn. 3,098 m, William A. Switzer Prov. Park, Hook Lake Solomon Creek Wildland, Marlboro, Edson, Niton Junction, Nojack, Entwistle, Rocky Rapids, Lindale, Tomahawk

Wells, Barkerville, Barkerville Prov. Park, Barkerville Hist. Town, Bowron Lake Prov. Park, McBride, The Ranee 2,939 m, Jasper National Park, Brûlé, Pocahontas, Roche Miette 2,316 m, Luscar Mtn. 2,601 m, Robb, Cadomin, Obed Lake Prov. Park, Jasper Forestry Mus., Hinton, Cynthia, Drayton Valley, Lodgepole, Buck Creek, Brazeau Dam, Warburg, Breton, Buck Lake, Winfield, Alder Flats, Em-Te Town

Dunster, Mt. Robson 3,954 m, Resplendent Mtn. 3,426 m, Rearguard Falls Prov. Park, Tête Jaune Cache, Mt. Sir Wilfrid Laurier 3,505 m, Mt. Watt 2,519 m, Mount Robson Prov. Park, Jackman Flats Prov. Park, Valemount, Yellowhead Pass 1,131 m, Jasper, Jasper Tramway, Marmot Basin, Simon Peak 3,322 m, Mt. Edith Cavell 3,363 m, Athabasca Falls, Mt. Brazeau 3,470 m, Mt. Dalhousie 2,947 m

Likely, Horsefly Lake Prov. Park, Horsefly, Cariboo Mtn. 1,933 m, Wells Gray Prov. Park, Canoe, Mount Robson Prov. Park, Heritage Centre, Pas-Ka-Poo Park

ROCKY MOUNTAINS

Highways: 97, 29, 2, 49, 43, 40, 35, 88, 16, 101, 33, 22, 18, 47, 39, 20

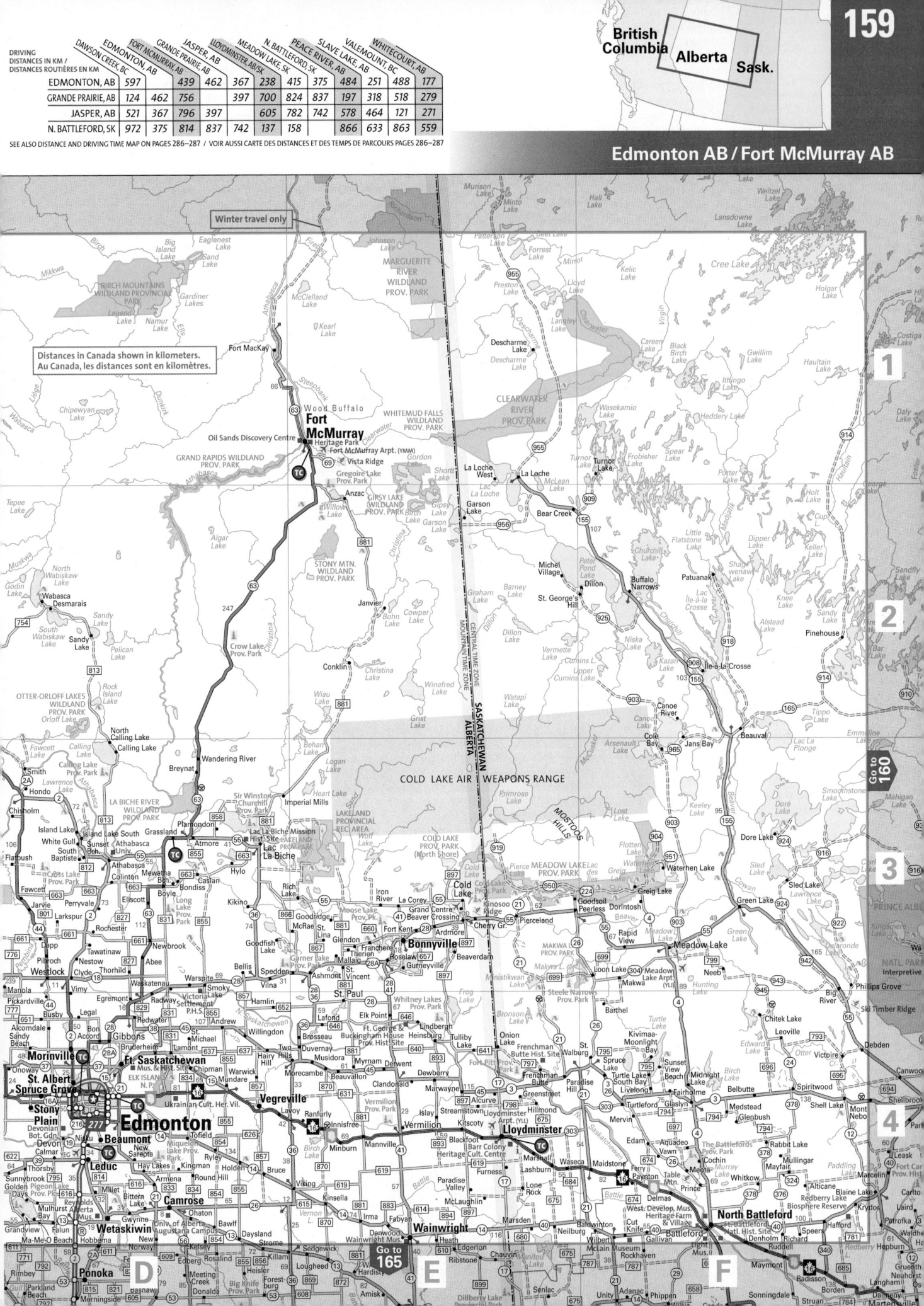

British
Columbia · Alberta · Sask.

SEE ALSO DISTANCE AND DRIVING TIME MAP ON PAGES 286–287 / VOIR AUSSI CARTE DES DISTANCES ET DES TEMPS DE PARCOURS PAGES 286–287

Distances in Canada shown in kilometers.
Au Canada, les distances sont en kilomètres.

Winter travel only

Alberta | Sask. | Manitoba
Ontario

Go to 159
Go to 165
Go to 166

One inch equals 40.3 miles/Un pouce équivaut à 40.3 milles
One centimeter equals 25.4 km/Un cm équivaut à 25.4 km

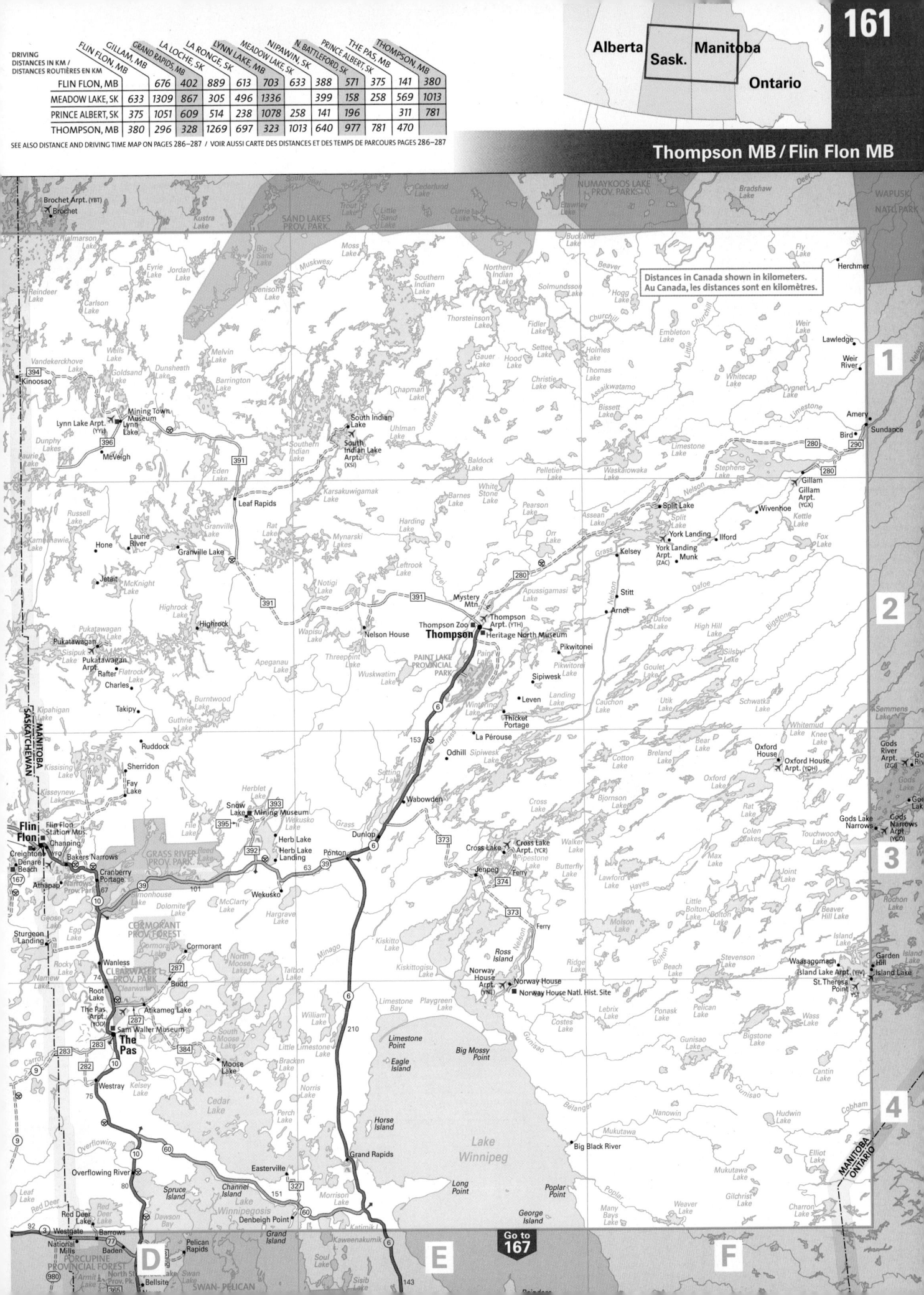

DRIVING DISTANCES IN KM / DISTANCES ROUTIÈRES EN KM	FLIN FLON, MB	GILLAM, MB	GRAND RAPIDS, MB	LA LOCHE, SK	LA RONGE, SK	LYNN LAKE, MB	MEADOW LAKE, SK	NIPAWIN, SK	N. BATTLEFORD, SK	PRINCE ALBERT, SK	THE PAS, MB	THOMPSON, MB
FLIN FLON, MB		676	402	889	613	703	633	388	571	375	141	380
MEADOW LAKE, SK	633	1309	867	305	496	1336		399	158	258	569	1013
PRINCE ALBERT, SK	375	1051	609	514	238	1078	258	141	196		311	781
THOMPSON, MB	380	296	328	1269	697	323	1013	640	977	781	470	

SEE ALSO DISTANCE AND DRIVING TIME MAP ON PAGES 286–287 / VOIR AUSSI CARTE DES DISTANCES ET DES TEMPS DE PARCOURS PAGES 286–287

Distances in Canada shown in kilometers.
Au Canada, les distances sont en kilomètres.

Go to 167

British Columbia

Washington

0 mi   20   40
0 km   20   40   60
One inch equals 25.4 miles/Un pouce équivaut à 25.4 milles
One cm equals 16.1 km/Un cm équivaut à 16.1 km

Go to 156

Go to 12

PACIFIC OCEAN

COAST MOUNTAINS

STRATHCONA PROV. PARK

Vancouver Island

Strait of Juan de Fuca

Strait of Georgia

Queen Charlotte Strait

Knight Inlet

Desolation Sound Marine Prov. Park

Distances in Canada shown in kilometers.
Au Canada, les distances sont en kilomètres.

B.C.
WASH.

Cities and towns:
Port Hardy, Holberg, Port Hardy Arpt. (YZT), Bear Cove, Coal Harbour, Quatsino, Winter Harbour, Sointula, Malcolm I., Port McNeill, Alert Bay, Telegraph Cove, Beaver Cove, U'Mista Cult. Ctr., Kokish, Port Alice, Woss, Mt. Cain, Zeballos, Tahsis, Yuquot, Gold River, Sayward, Rock Bay, Campbell River, Campbell River Arpt. (YBL), Quathiaski Cove, Kwagiulth Mus., Quadra I., Saratoga Beach, Black Creek, Miracle Beach, Powell River, Powell River Arpt. (YPW), Westview, Saltery Bay, Earls Cove, Merville, Little River, Comox, Comox Valley Arpt. (YQQ), Courtenay, Royston, Cumberland, Union Bay, Buckley Bay, Fanny Bay, Bowser, Qualicum Beach, Coombs, Errington, French Creek, Parksville, Nanoose Bay, Lantzville, Port Alberni, Tofino, Tofino Arpt. (YCD), Ucluelet, Bamfield, Clo-oose, Nanaimo, Nanaimo Arpt. (YCD), Cassidy, Ladysmith, Chemainus, Youbou, N. Cowichan, Duncan, Lake Cowichan, Honeymoon Bay, Mesachie L., Sooke, Port Renfrew, River Jordan, Milnes Landing, Sechelt, Madeira Park, Kleindale, Halfmoon Bay, Gabriola Island

Washington:
Neah Bay, MAKAH IND. RES., Clallam Bay, Sappho, Forks, La Push, OLYMPIC NATL. PARK, OLYMPIC NATL. FOR.

Parks:
CAPE SCOTT PROV. PARK, Quatsino Prov. Park, Marble River Prov. Pk., Lawn Point Prov. Pk., MUQUIN-BROOKS PENINSULA PROV. PARK, Nimpkish Lake Prov. Park, Woss Lake Prov. Park, Schoen Lake Prov. Park, Rugged Point Marine Prov. Park, Catala Island Marine Prov. Pk., Nuchatlitz Prov. Park, Bligh Island Marine Prov. Pk., HESQUIAT PEN. PROV. PARK, Hesquiat Lake Prov. Park, Maquinna Marine Prov. Pk., Flores Island Prov. Park, Gibson Marine Prov. Pk., Vargas Island Prov. Park, PACIFIC RIM NATIONAL PARK RESERVE (Long Beach Unit), PACIFIC RIM NATIONAL PARK RESERVE (Broken Group Islands Unit), PACIFIC RIM NATIONAL PARK RESERVE (West Coast Trail Unit), CARMANAH WALBRAN PROV. PARK, TS'IL-OS PROV. PARK, BISHOP RIVER PROV. PARK, UPPER LILLOOET PROV. PARK, CLENDINNING PROV. PK., Princess Louisa Marine Prov. Pk., Walsh Cove Prov. Park, Harmony Islands Marine Prov. Pk., Jedediah Island Marine Prov. Pk., Sandy I. Marine Prov. Pk., Fillongley Prov. Park, Horne Lake Caves Prov. Park, Stamp River Prov. Park, Taylor Arm Prov. Park, MacMillan Prov. Park, Little Qualicum Falls Prov. Park, Englishman River Falls Prov. Park, Rathtrevor Beach Prov. Park

Mountains and peaks:
Mt. Tatlow 3,066 m, Mt. Queen Bess 3,298 m, Good Hope Mtn. 3,240 m, Monmouth Mtn. 3,194 m, Mt. Grenville 3,109 m, Mt. Raleigh 3,078 m, Superb Mtn. 2,469 m, Mt. Gilbert 3,109 m, Toba Pk. 2,896 m, Mt. Everard 2,182 m, Costello Peak 1,713 m, Mt. Rodell 2,187 m, Mt. Cridge 1,795 m, Mt. Kennedy 2,028 m, Mt. Smith 2,299 m, Granite Pk. 2,048 m, Victoria Pk. 2,163 m, Mt. Washington

Highways: 19, 19A, 1, 30, 28, 36, 62, 64, 68, 89, 4, 34, 101, 14, 18, 92, 35, 46, 47, 72, 31, 81, 102, 110, 112, 113

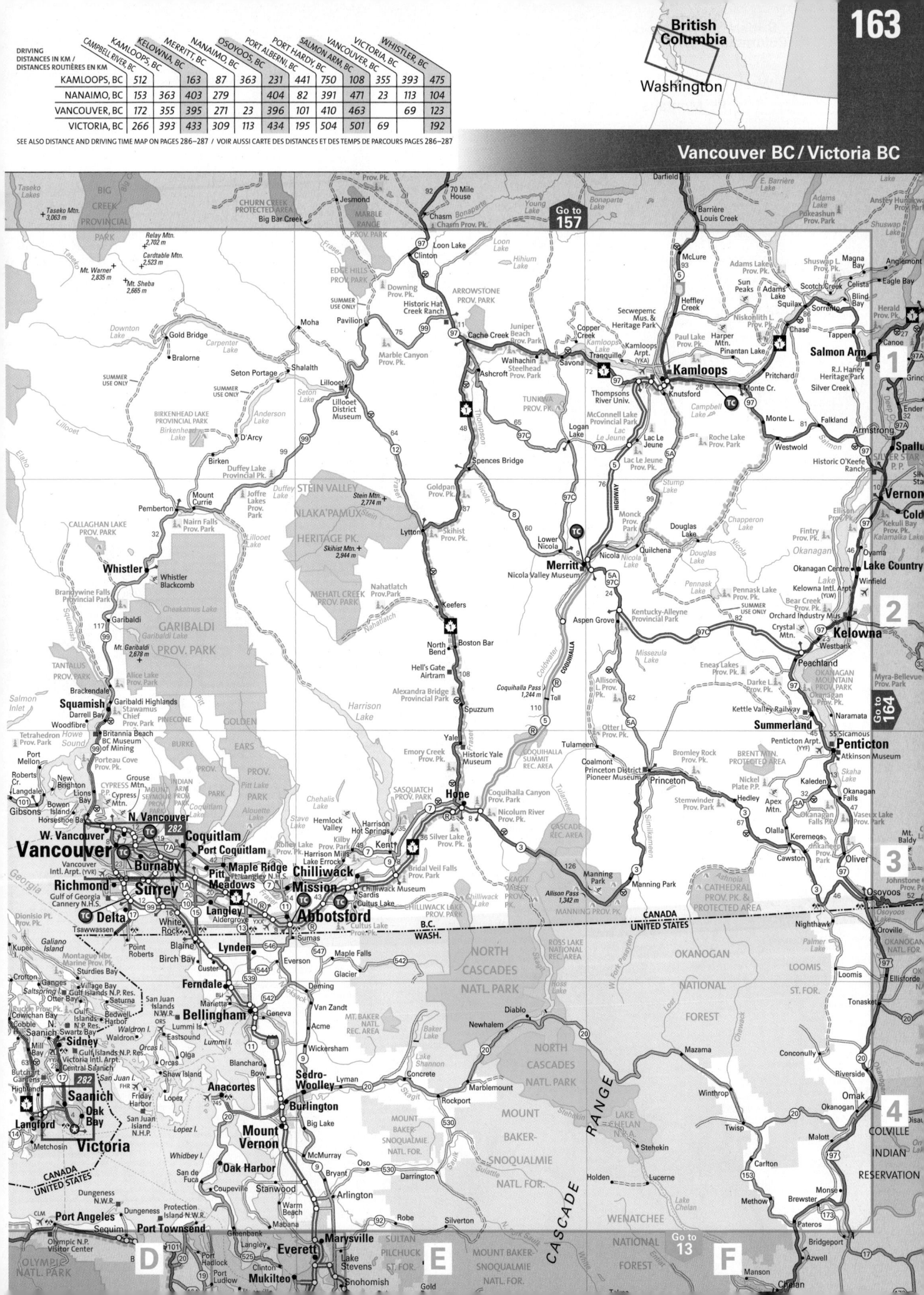

0 mi 20 40 60
0 km 20 40 60 80

One inch equals 40.3 miles/Un pouce équivaut à 40.3 milles
One centimeter equals 25.4 km/Un cm équivaut à 25.4 km

Go to 158
Go to 157
Go to 163

ROCKY MOUNTAINS

JASPER NATIONAL PARK

BANFF NATIONAL PARK

YOHO NATL. PARK

MOUNT REVELSTOKE N.P.

GLACIER NATL. PARK

Edmonton

Calgary

Banff

Canmore

Cochrane

Airdrie

Okotoks

Red Deer

Lacombe

Ponoka

Wetaskiwin

Leduc

Beaumont

Spruce Grove

Stony Plain

Ft. Saskatchewan

Morinville

Drayton Valley

Rocky Mountain House

Nordegg

Innisfail

Olds

Didsbury

Three Hills

Strathmore

High River

Claresholm

Jasper

Hinton

Edson

Tête Jaune Cache

Valemount

Blue River

Clearwater

Revelstoke

Golden

Field

Lake Louise

Kelowna

Penticton

Vernon

Salmon Arm

Spallumcheen

Coldstream

Nelson

Castlegar

Trail

Rossland

Creston

Cranbrook

Kimberley

Invermere

Windermere

Radium Hot Springs

Fairmont Hot Springs

Golden

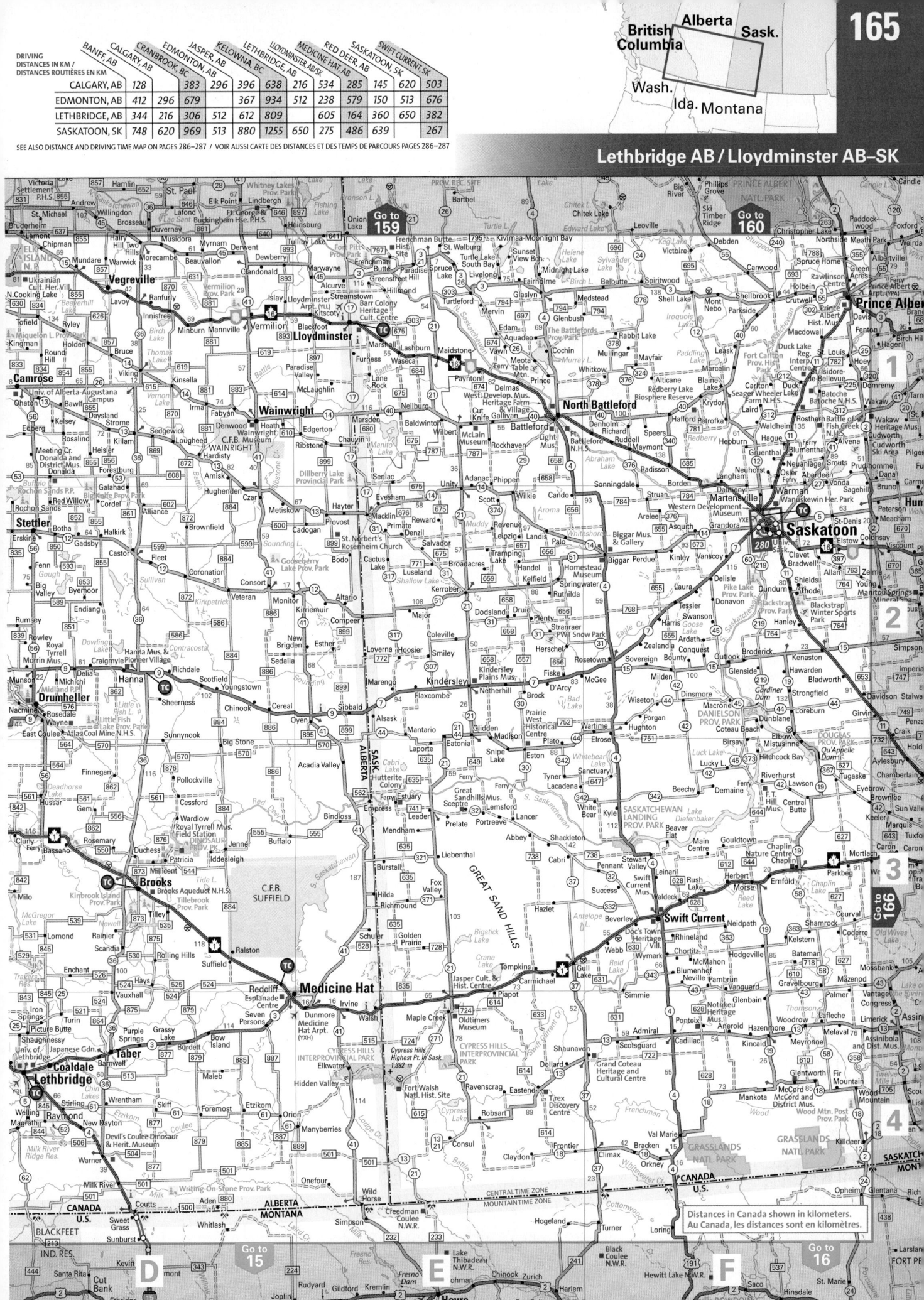

DRIVING DISTANCES IN KM / DISTANCES ROUTIÈRES EN KM	BANFF, AB	CALGARY, AB	CRANBROOK, BC	EDMONTON, AB	JASPER, AB	KELOWNA, BC	LETHBRIDGE, AB	LLOYDMINSTER AB/SK	MEDICINE HAT, AB	RED DEER, AB	SASKATOON, SK	SWIFT CURRENT, SK
CALGARY, AB	128		383	296	396	638	216	534	285	145	620	503
EDMONTON, AB	412	296	679		367	934	512	238	579	150	513	676
LETHBRIDGE, AB	344	216	306	512	612	809		605	164	360	650	382
SASKATOON, SK	748	620	969	513	880	1255	650	275	486	639		267

SEE ALSO DISTANCE AND DRIVING TIME MAP ON PAGES 286–287 · VOIR AUSSI CARTE DES DISTANCES ET DES TEMPS DE PARCOURS PAGES 286–287

Distances in Canada shown in kilometres.
Au Canada, les distances sont en kilomètres.

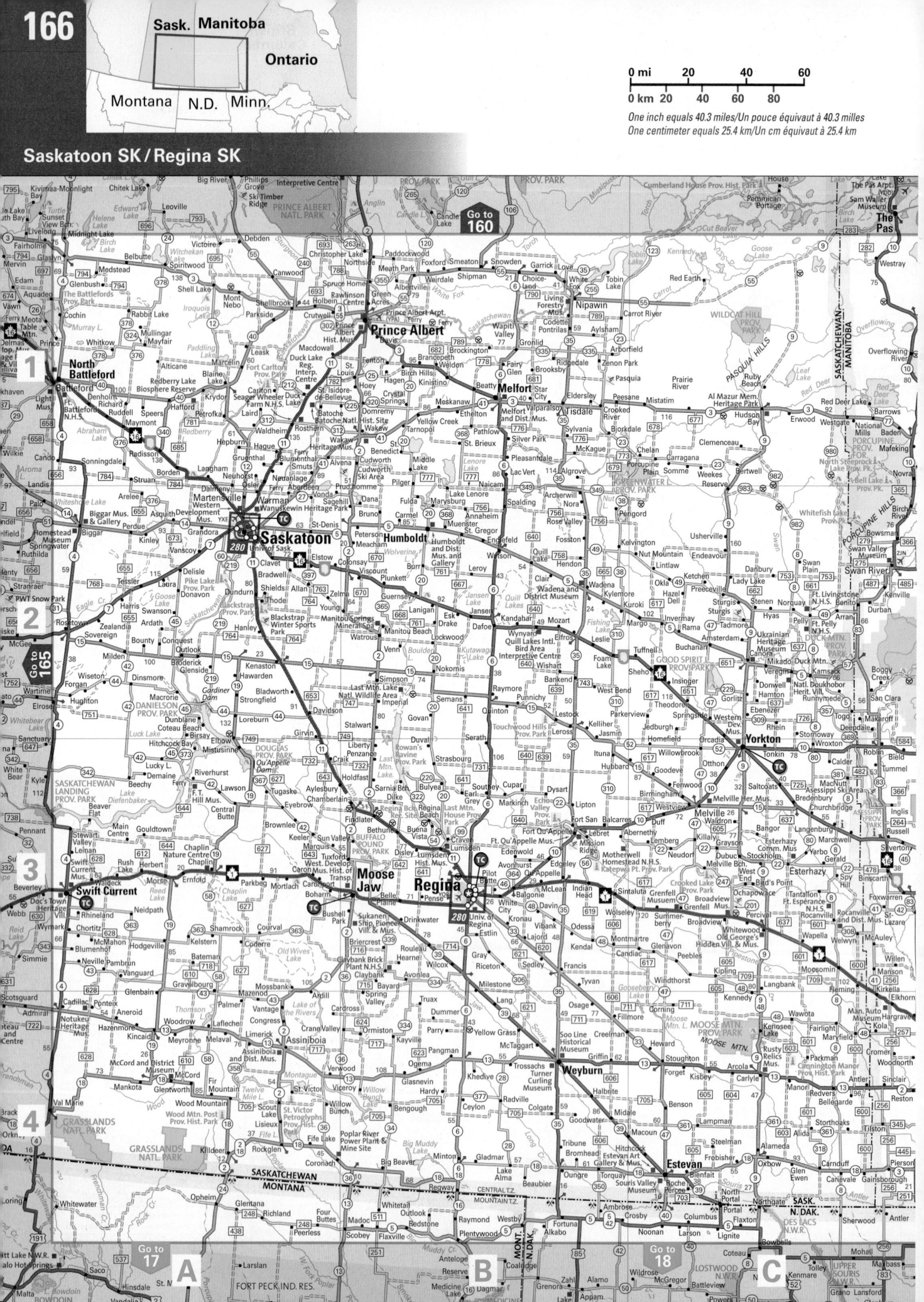

DRIVING DISTANCES IN KM /
DISTANCES ROUTIÈRES EN KM

	BRANDON, MB	DAUPHIN, MB	GRAND RAPIDS, MB	MOOSE JAW, SK	PORTAGE LA PRAIRIE, MB	PRINCE ALBERT, SK	REGINA, SK	SASKATOON, SK	SWIFT CURRENT, SK	THE PAS, MB	WINNIPEG, MB	YORKTON, SK
BRANDON, MB		166	525	448	134	745	377	639	618	570	216	270
REGINA, SK	377	366	787	68	511	368		261	241	557	593	195
SASKATOON, SK	639	502	689	224	691	141	261		267	578	773	331
WINNIPEG, MB	216	322	430	664	82	819	593	773	834	611		442

SEE ALSO DISTANCE AND DRIVING TIME MAP ON PAGES 286–287 · VOIR AUSSI CARTE DES DISTANCES ET DES TEMPS DE PARCOURS PAGES 286–287

Distances in Canada shown in kilometers.
Au Canada, les distances sont en kilomètres.

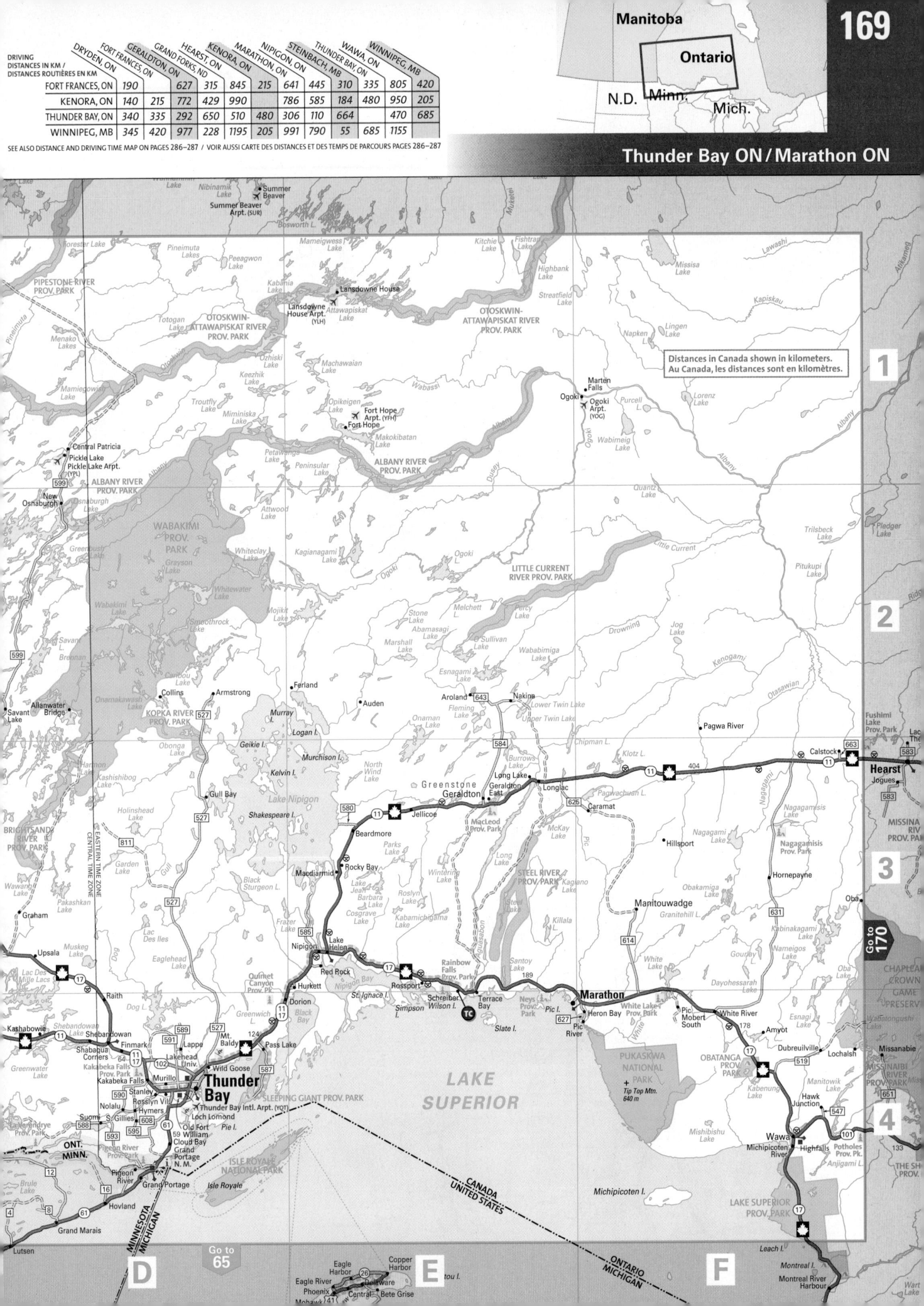

DRIVING DISTANCES IN KM /
DISTANCES ROUTIÈRES EN KM

	DRYDEN, ON	FORT FRANCES, ON	GERALDTON, ON	GRAND FORKS, ND	HEARST, ON	KENORA, ON	MARATHON, ON	NIPIGON, ON	STEINBACH, MB	THUNDER BAY, ON	WAWA, ON	WINNIPEG, MB
FORT FRANCES, ON	190		627	315	845	215	641	445	310	335	805	420
KENORA, ON	140	215	772	429	990		786	585	184	480	950	205
THUNDER BAY, ON	340	335	292	650	510	480	306	110	664		470	685
WINNIPEG, MB	345	420	977	228	1195	205	991	790	55	685	1155	

SEE ALSO DISTANCE AND DRIVING TIME MAP ON PAGES 286–287 / VOIR AUSSI CARTE DES DISTANCES ET DES TEMPS DE PARCOURS PAGES 286–287

Distances in Canada shown in kilometers.
Au Canada, les distances sont en kilomètres.

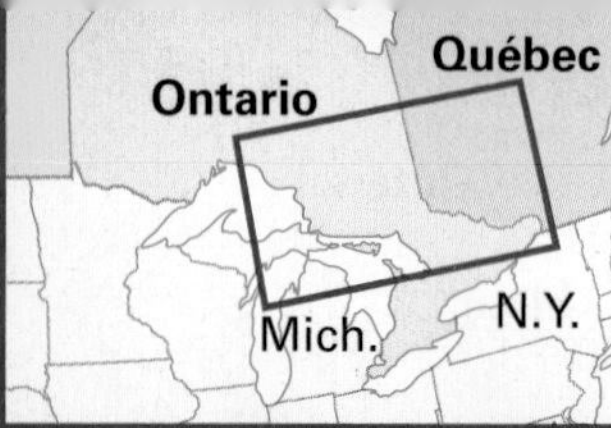

Ontario Québec
Mich. N.Y.

0 mi 20 40 60
0 km 20 40 60 80

One inch equals 40.3 miles/Un pouce équivaut à 40.3 milles
One centimeter equals 25.4 km/Un cm équivaut à 25.4 km

Distances in Canada shown in kilometers.
Au Canada, les distances sont en kilomètres.

LAKE SUPERIOR

LAKE MICHIGAN

LAKE HURON

Georgian Bay

ONTARIO / MICHIGAN

CANADA / UNITED STATES

Go to 169

Go to 65

Go to 69

Go to 70

Go to 172

Hearst Kapuskasing Cochrane Iroquois Falls Timmins Sudbury

Marathon Wawa Chapleau Sault Ste. Marie Elliot Lake Blind River Espanola

Schreiber Terrace Bay Manitouwadge White River

Munising Newberry Manistique Escanaba Gladstone

Petoskey Boyne City Gaylord Cheboygan Alpena Traverse City

Bruce Peninsula Natl. Park Tobermory Manitoulin Island Killarney

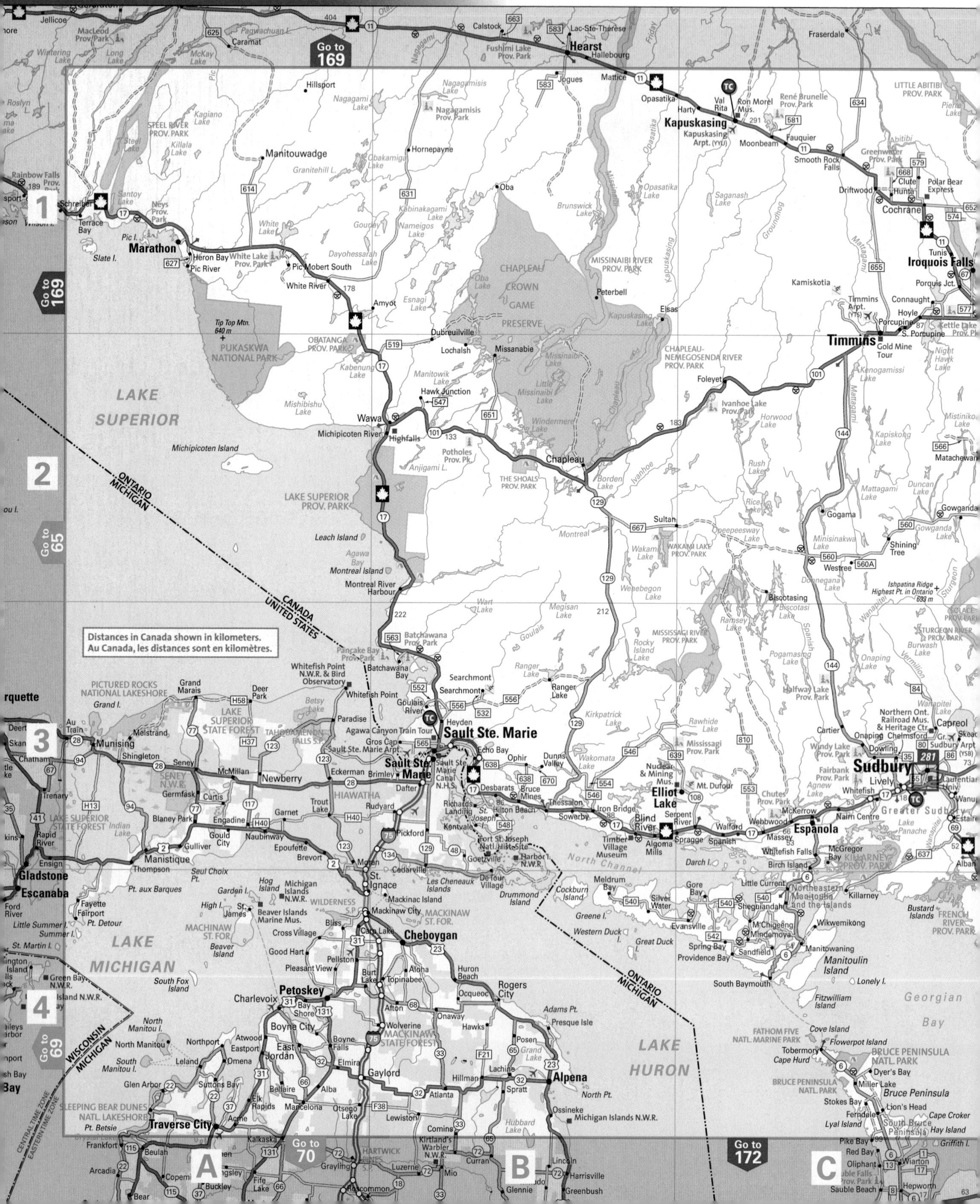

DRIVING DISTANCES IN KM / DISTANCES ROUTIÈRES EN KM

	HEARST, ON	HUNTSVILLE, ON	KIRKLAND LAKE, ON	MONT-LAURIER, QC	NORTH BAY, ON	ORILLIA, ON	OTTAWA, ON	ROUYN-NORANDA, QC	SAULT STE. MARIE, ON	SUDBURY, ON	TIMMINS, ON	WAWA, ON
KIRKLAND LAKE, ON	370	370		505	250	578	610	154	580	315	140	475
OTTAWA, ON	955	350	610	209	364	415		456	787	488	730	1015
SAULT STE. MARIE, ON	545	560	580	1004	430	562	787	734		305	440	225
SUDBURY, ON	550	250	315	699	124	263	488	469	305		290	530

SEE ALSO DISTANCE AND DRIVING TIME MAP ON PAGES 286–287 / VOIR AUSSI CARTE DES DISTANCES ET DES TEMPS DE PARCOURS PAGES 286–287

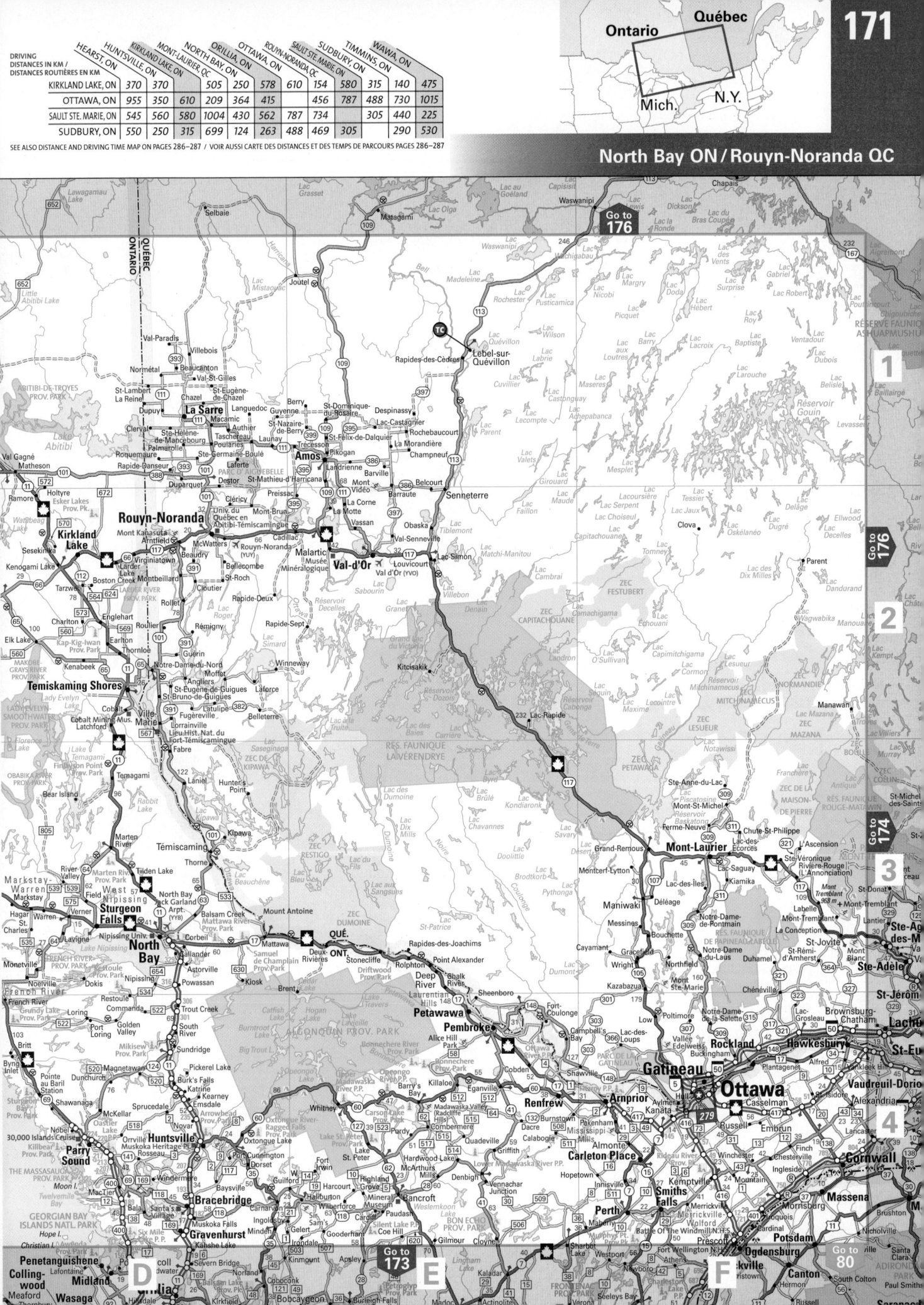

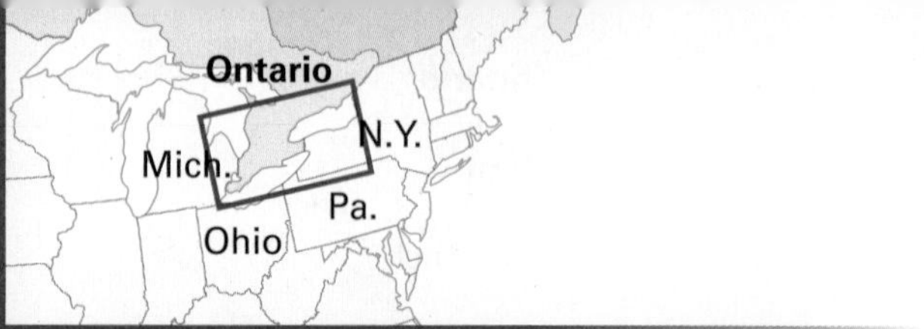

Ontario
Mich.
N.Y.
Pa.
Ohio

London ON / Windsor ON

0 mi — 20 — 40
0 km — 20 — 40 — 60

One inch equals 25.4 miles/Un pouce équivaut à 25.4 milles
One cm equals 16.1 km/Un cm équivaut à 16.1 km

Go to 170

Distances in Canada shown in kilometers.
Au Canada, les distances sont en kilomètres.

Go to 76

Go to 90

Go to 91

A   B   C

1   2   3   4

DRIVING DISTANCES IN KM / DISTANCES ROUTIÈRES EN KM

	BARRIE, ON	HAMILTON, ON	KINGSTON, ON	KITCHENER, ON	LONDON, ON	NIAGARA FALLS, ON	ORILLIA, ON	OWEN SOUND, ON	PETERBOROUGH, ON	SARNIA, ON	TORONTO, ON	WINDSOR, ON
KINGSTON, ON	350	330		430	430	390	317	430	180	530	260	620
NIAGARA FALLS, ON	200	68	390	130	190		237	260	260	290	130	380
TORONTO, ON	90	70	260	105	185	130	127	190	135	280		370
WINDSOR, ON	430	310	620	285	190	380	467	390	490	160	370	

SEE ALSO DISTANCE AND DRIVING TIME MAP ON PAGES 286–287 / VOIR AUSSI CARTE DES DISTANCES ET DES TEMPS DE PARCOURS PAGES 286–287

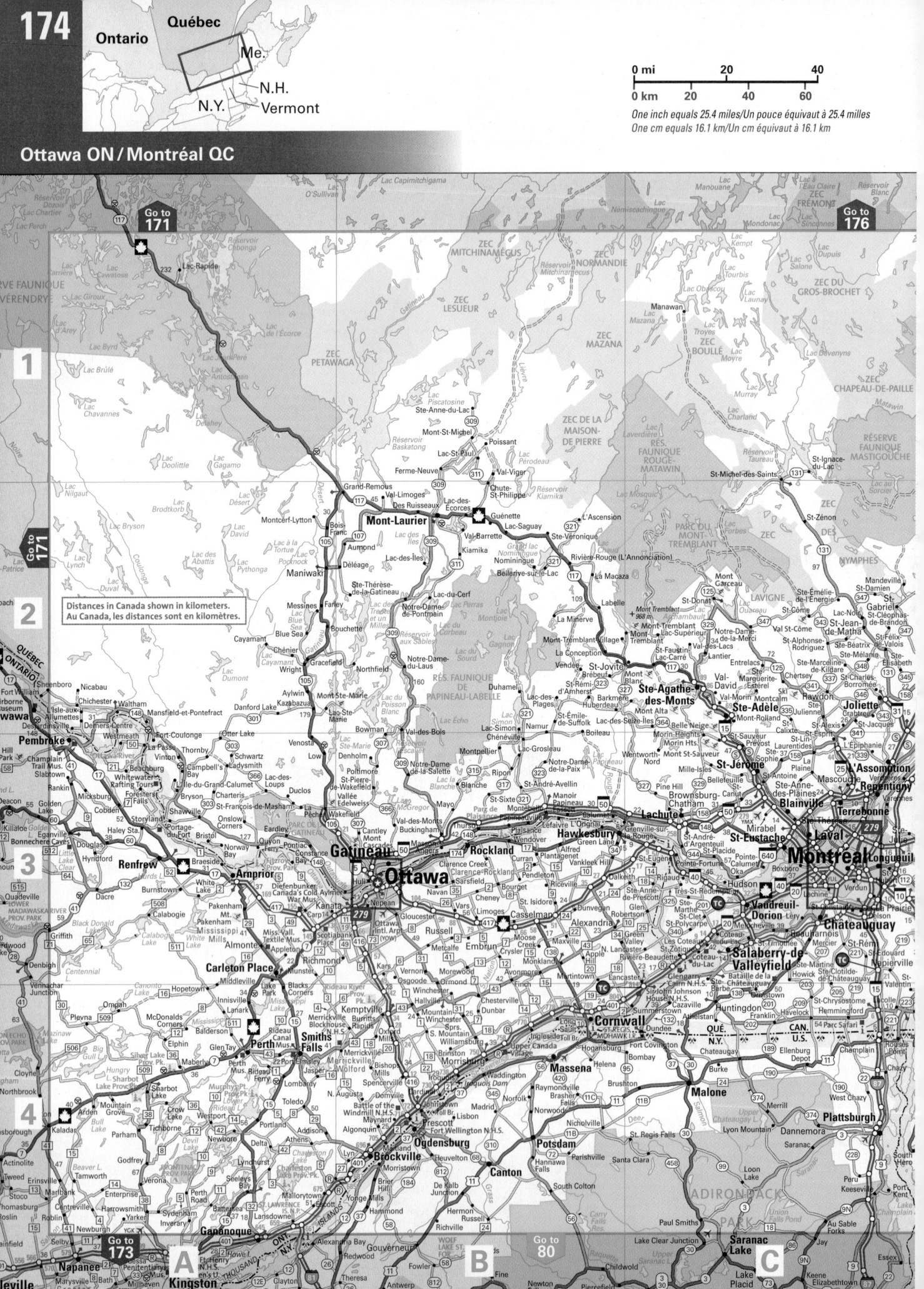

Ottawa ON / Montréal QC

Ontario / Québec / Me. / N.H. / Vermont / N.Y.

DRIVING DISTANCES IN KM / DISTANCES ROUTIÈRES EN KM

	BURLINGTON, VT	CORNWALL, ON	DRUMMONDVILLE, QC	KINGSTON, ON	MONT-LAURIER, QC	MONTRÉAL, QC	MONT-TREMBLANT, QC	OTTAWA, ON	QUÉBEC, QC	ST-GEORGES, QC	SHERBROOKE, QC	TROIS-RIVIÈRES, QC
MONTRÉAL, QC	153	103	116	283	230		126	194	250	325	143	146
OTTAWA, ON	360	97	310	175	209	194	208		444	485	337	340
QUÉBEC, QC	394	353	151	533	445	250	298	444		102	233	135
SHERBROOKE, QC	174	246	82	426	402	143	269	337	233	148		158

SEE ALSO DISTANCE AND DRIVING TIME MAP ON PAGES 286–287 / VOIR AUSSI CARTE DES DISTANCES ET DES TEMPS DE PARCOURS PAGES 286–287

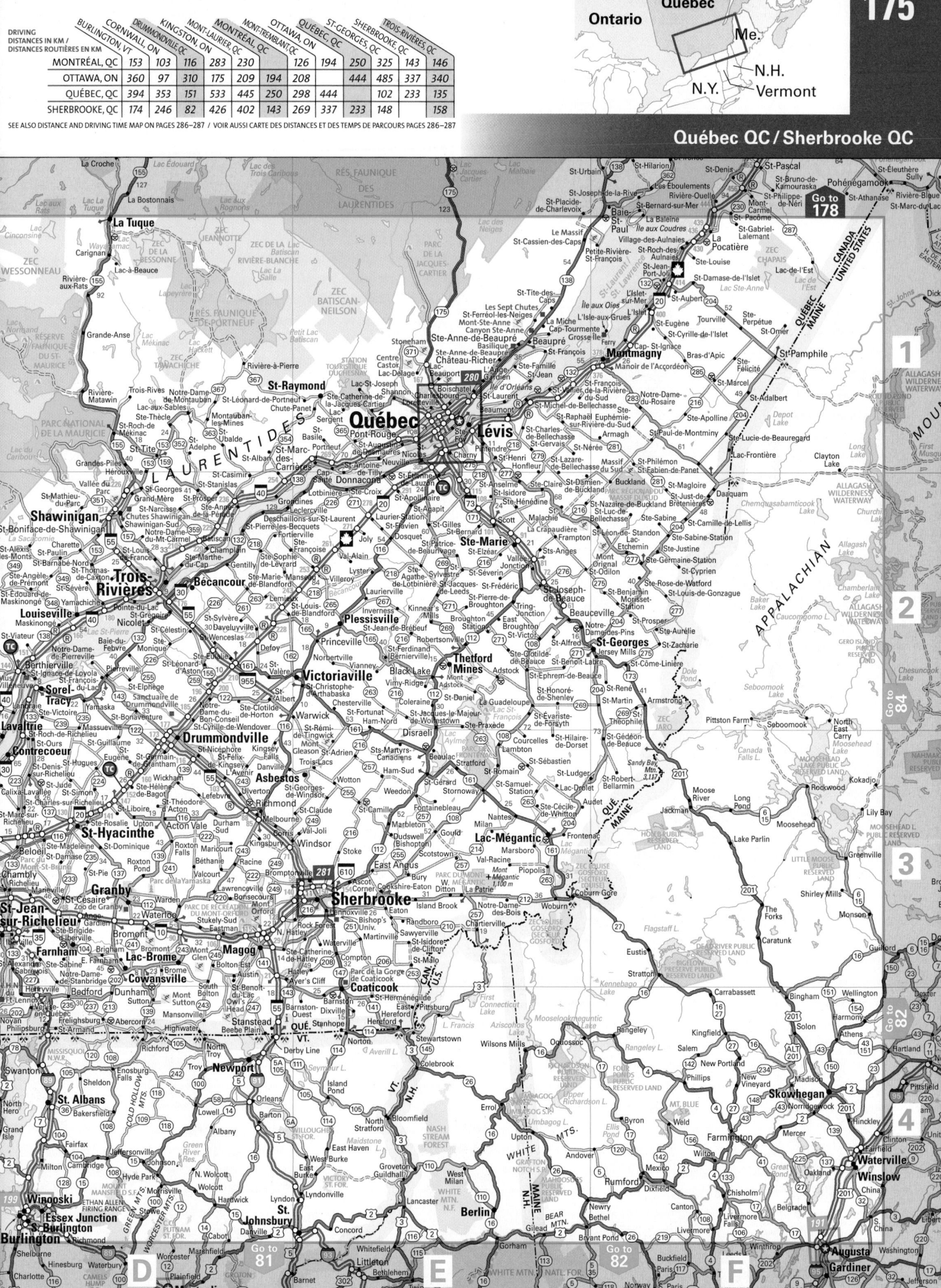

176

Québec
P.E.I.
N.B.
Maine

Chicoutimi QC / Chibougamau QC

0 mi 20 40 60
0 km 20 40 60 80
One inch equals 40.3 miles/Un pouce équivaut à 40.3 milles
One centimeter equals 25.4 km/Un cm équivaut à 25.4 km

Distances in Canada shown in kilometers.
Au Canada, les distances sont en kilomètres.

Go to 171

Go to 174

Go to 174

A B C

1 2 3 4

DRIVING DISTANCES IN KM / DISTANCES ROUTIÈRES EN KM

	BAIE-COMEAU, QC	CAMPBELLTON, NB	CHIBOUGAMAU, QC	CHICOUTIMI, QC	EDMUNDSTON, NB	GASPÉ, QC	HAVRE-ST-PIERRE, QC	MATANE, QC	MIRAMICHI, NB	QUÉBEC, QC	RIMOUSKI, QC	SEPT-ÎLES, QC
CHICOUTIMI, QC	435	444	359		269	771	884	348	622	211	253	667
EDMUNDSTON, NB	368	188	628	269		534	817	249	268	317	180	600
GASPÉ, QC	287	340	1130	771	534		743	294	518	706	389	526
QUÉBEC, QC	408	508	570	211	317	706	857	412	582		507	640

SEE ALSO DISTANCE AND DRIVING TIME MAP ON PAGES 286–287 / VOIR AUSSI CARTE DES DISTANCES ET DES TEMPS DE PARCOURS PAGES 286–287

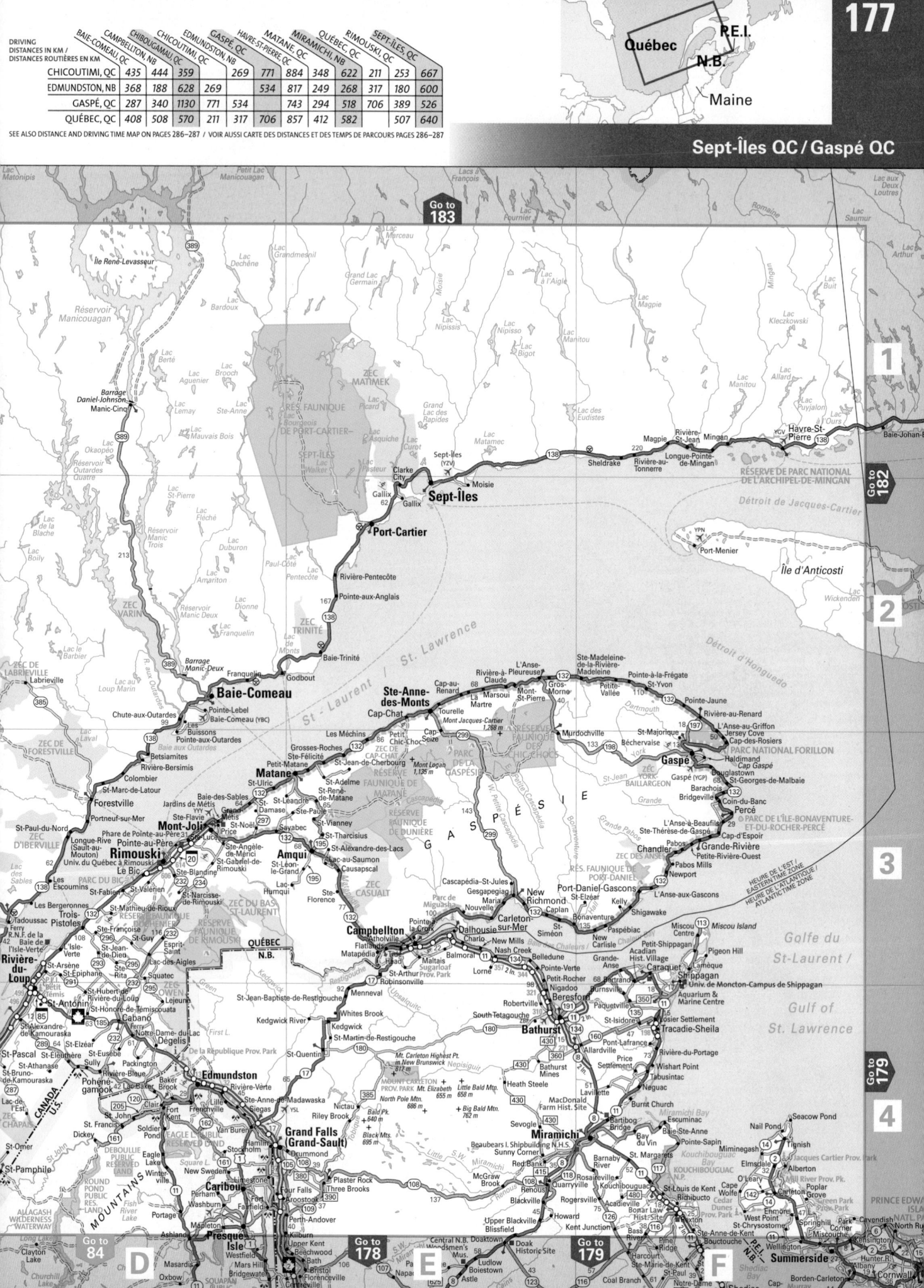

Québec
P.E.I.
N.B.
Maine

0 mi 20 40
0 km 20 40 60
One inch equals 25.4 miles/Un pouce équivaut à 25.4 milles
One cm equals 16.1 km/Un cm équivaut à 16.1 km

Go to 177

Go to 176

Go to 175

Go to 84

Go to 85

Go to 180

Baie-Comeau
Pointe-Lebel
Chute-aux-Outardes
Baie-Comeau (YBC)
Les Buissons
Pointe-aux-Outardes
Rivière-à-Claude
La Martre
Tourelle
Cap-au-Renard
Marsoui
Mont-St-Pierre
Ste-Anne-des-Monts
Cap-Chat
Cap-Seize
Mont Jacques-Cartier 1,268 m
Betsiamites
Rivière-Bersimis
Colombier
St-Marc-de-Latour
Forestville
Les Méchins
Grosses-Roches
Mont Logan 1,135 m
Portneuf-sur-Mer
Longue-Rive (Sault-au-Mouton)
St-Paul-du-Nord
Pointe-à-Boisvert
Baie-des-Bacon
Matane
St-Ulric
St-Adelme
St-Luc-de-Matane
St-Félicité
St-Jean-de-Cherbourg
GASPÉSIE
Baie-des-Sables
Métis-sur-Mer
Grand-Métis
St-Léandre
Mont-Castor
St-Damase
St-René-de-Matane
RÉSERVE FAUNIQUE DE MATANE
RÉSERVE FAUNIQUE DE DUNIÈRE
Ste-Flavie
Jardins Boules de Métis
Price
St-Noël
Padoue
Sayabec
St-Vianney
Mont-Joli
St-Luce
Ste-Angèle-de-Mérici
Val-Brillant
St-Tharcisius
St-Donat
Pointe-au-Père
Rimouski-Est
St-Gabriel-de-Rimouski
La Rédemption
St-Léon-le-Grand
Amqui
St-Alexandre-des-Lacs
Univ. du Québec à Rimouski
Mont-Comi
Rimouski
Ste-Blandine
Les Hauteurs
Lac-au-Saumon
Causapscal
Le Bic
St-Valérien
St-Narcisse-de-Rimouski
Mont-Lebel
St-Charles-Garnier
Lac-Humqui
Albertville
Ste-Marguerite
PARC DU BIC
St-Fabien
St-Eugène-de-Ladrière
Ste-Florence
Cascapédia-St-Jules
St-Mathieu-de-Rioux
ZEC DU BAS-ST-LAURENT
Gesgapegiag
Maria
St-Simon
Lac Inférieur
CASUALT
Nouvelle
Trois-Pistoles
St-François
St-André-de-Restigouche
New Richmond
Carleton-sur-Mer
St-Éloi
St-Médard
St-Guy
Esprit-Saint
Pointe-à-la-Croix
Point La Nim
Escuminac
St-Mathieu
St-Paul-de-la-Croix
Ste-Rita
RÉSERVE FAUNIQUE DE RIMOUSKI
Campbellton
Atholville
Dalhousie
Eel River Crossing
Charlo
L'Isle-Verte
St-Jean-de-Dieu
Biencourt
St-François-d'Assise
Matapédia
Tide Head
Dundee
New Mills
Black Point
Nash Creek
R.N.F. de la Baie de l'Isle-Verte
St-Cyprien
Squatec
QUÉBEC NEW BRUNSWICK
L'Ascension-de-Patapédia
Mann Rd
Glencoe
Balmoral
Belledune
Rivière-du-Loup
St-Georges-de-Cacouna
St-François-Xavier-de-Viger
Lejeune
Dawsonville
Sugarloaf Prov. Park
Maltais
Lorne
Pointe-Verte
Notre-Dame-des-Sept-Douleurs
L'Anse-au-Persil
St-Hubert-de-Rivière-du-Loup
St-Pierre-de-Lamy
Robinsonville
St-Arthur
Nicholas Denys
Robertville
St-Antonin
Chemin-du-Lac
St-Honoré-de-Témiscouata
Fort Ingall
Cabano
Menneval
St-Jean-Baptiste-de-Restigouche
North Tetagouche
South Tetagouche
St-André-de-Kamouraska
St-Joseph-de-Kamouraska
St-Elzéar
St-Juste-du-Lac
Notre-Dame-du-Lac
Whites Brook
Kedgwick River
Kedgwick
St-Martin-de-Restigouche
St-Pascal
St-Hélène
Dégelis
Cabano
St-Bruno-de-Kamouraska
Pohénégamook
St-Éleuthère
St-Jean-de-la-Lande
De la République Prov. Park
St-Quentin
MOUNT CARLETON PROV. PARK
Bathurst Mines
La Pocatière
Lac-à-l'Est
Packington
Pied-du-Lac
Univ de Moncton-Campus d'Edmundston
Mt. Carleton Highest Pt. in New Brunswick 817 m
Mt. Elizabeth 655 m
Little Bald Mtn. 658 m
Heath Steele
St-Pacôme
St-Gabriel-Lalemant
Rivière-Bleue
St-Marc-du-Lac-Long
Lac Baker
Madawaska
Edmundston
Rivière-Verte
Nictau
St-François-de-Madawaska
Baker Brook
St-Hilaire
Grand Isle
Lille
St-Anne-de-Madawaska
North Pole Mtn. 686 m
Big Bald Mtn. 762 m
Clair
Frenchville
Siegas
St-Léonard (St-Léonard)
Bald Pk. 640 m
Black Mts. 695 m
Fort Kent
Connors
St. John
Van Buren
Riley Brook
Dickey
St. Francis
Soldier Pond
Sinclair
Léonard-Parent
St-André
Grand Falls Gorge
Grand Falls (Grand-Sault)
Sunny Corner
Eagle Lake
Winterville
Stockholm
Hamlin
Drummond
New Denmark
McGraw Brook
Renous
Quarryville
Red Bank
Clayton Lake
New Sweden
Limestone
Caribou
Plaster Rock
Three Brooks
Blackville
Ashland
Perham
Washburn
Fort Fairfield
Aroostook
Arthurette
Portage
Mapleton
Bon Accord
Perth-Andover
Upper Blackville
Presque Isle
Currie
Kilburn
River de Chute
Upper Kent
Beechwood
Juniper
Blissfield
Doaktown
Doak Historic Site
Masardis
Westfield
Mars Hill
Bath
Glassville
Parker Ridge
Napadogan
Central N.B. Woodsmen's Mus.
Ludlow
Boiestown
Oxbow
Bridgewater
Centreville
Florenceville
Stickney
Windsor
Hartland Covered Bridge (World's Longest)
Astle
Williamsburg
Cross Creek
Gaspereau Forks
Monticello
Lakeville
Coldstream
Hartland
Somerville
Cloverdale
Stanley
Nashwaak Bridge
Tay Creek
Hardwood Ridge
Chipman
Littleton
Lindsay
Upper Woodstock
Taymouth
Minto
Houlton
Smyrna Mills
Grafton
Millville
Crabbe Mtn.
Lower Hainesville
Nashwaak Village
Rothwell
Coles Island
Woodstock
Upper Hainesville
Zealand
Keswick Ridge
Burtts Corner
Linneus
Debec
Benton
Meductic
Nackawic
Fredericton
Island Falls
Patten
Canterbury
Pokiok
Fredericton Jct.

ST. LAWRENCE / St-Laurent
APPALACHIAN MOUNTAINS
ALLAGASH WILDERNESS WATERWAY
MAINE
CANADA / UNITED STATES
QUÉBEC / MAINE
ZEC DE FORESTVILLE
ZEC D'IBERVILLE
ZEC NORDIQUE
ZEC HAUVIN
ZEC CHAPAIS
ZEC DE CAP-CHAT
PARC DE LA GASPÉSIE

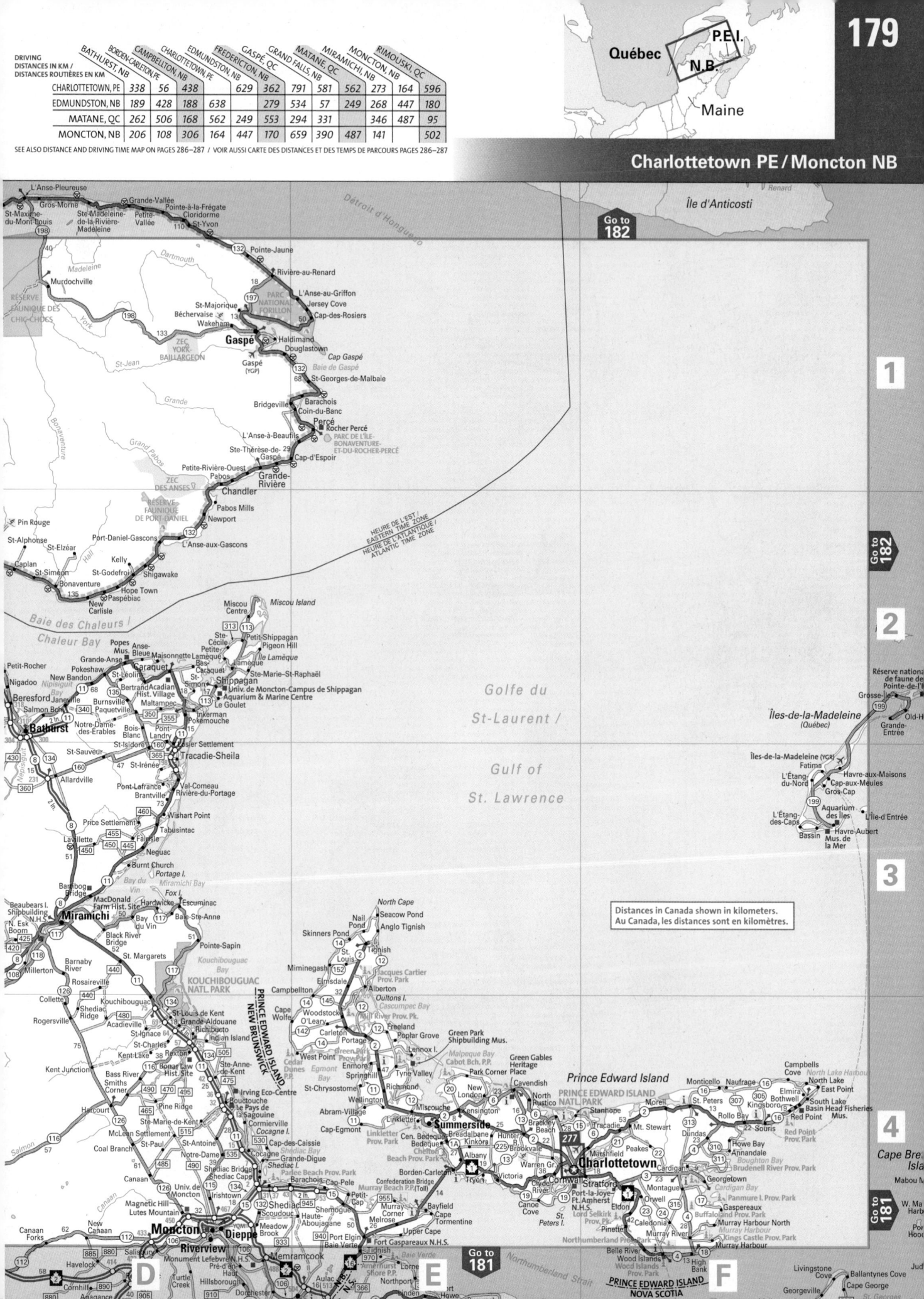

DRIVING DISTANCES IN KM / DISTANCES ROUTIÈRES EN KM

	BATHURST, NB	BORDEN-CARLETON, NB	CAMPBELLTON, NB	CHARLOTTETOWN, PE	EDMUNDSTON, NB	FREDERICTON, NB	GASPÉ, QC	GRAND FALLS, NB	MATANE, QC	MIRAMICHI, NB	MONCTON, NB	RIMOUSKI, QC
CHARLOTTETOWN, PE	338	56	438		629	362	791	581	562	273	164	596
EDMUNDSTON, NB	189	428	188	638		279	534	57	249	268	447	180
MATANE, QC	262	506	168	562	249	553	294	331		346	487	95
MONCTON, NB	206	108	306	164	447	170	659	390	487	141		502

SEE ALSO DISTANCE AND DRIVING TIME MAP ON PAGES 286–287 / VOIR AUSSI CARTE DES DISTANCES ET DES TEMPS DE PARCOURS PAGES 286–287

Distances in Canada shown in kilometers.
Au Canada, les distances sont en kilomètres.

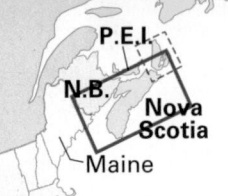

P.E.I.

N.B.

Nova
Scotia

Maine

Saint John NB / Yarmouth NS

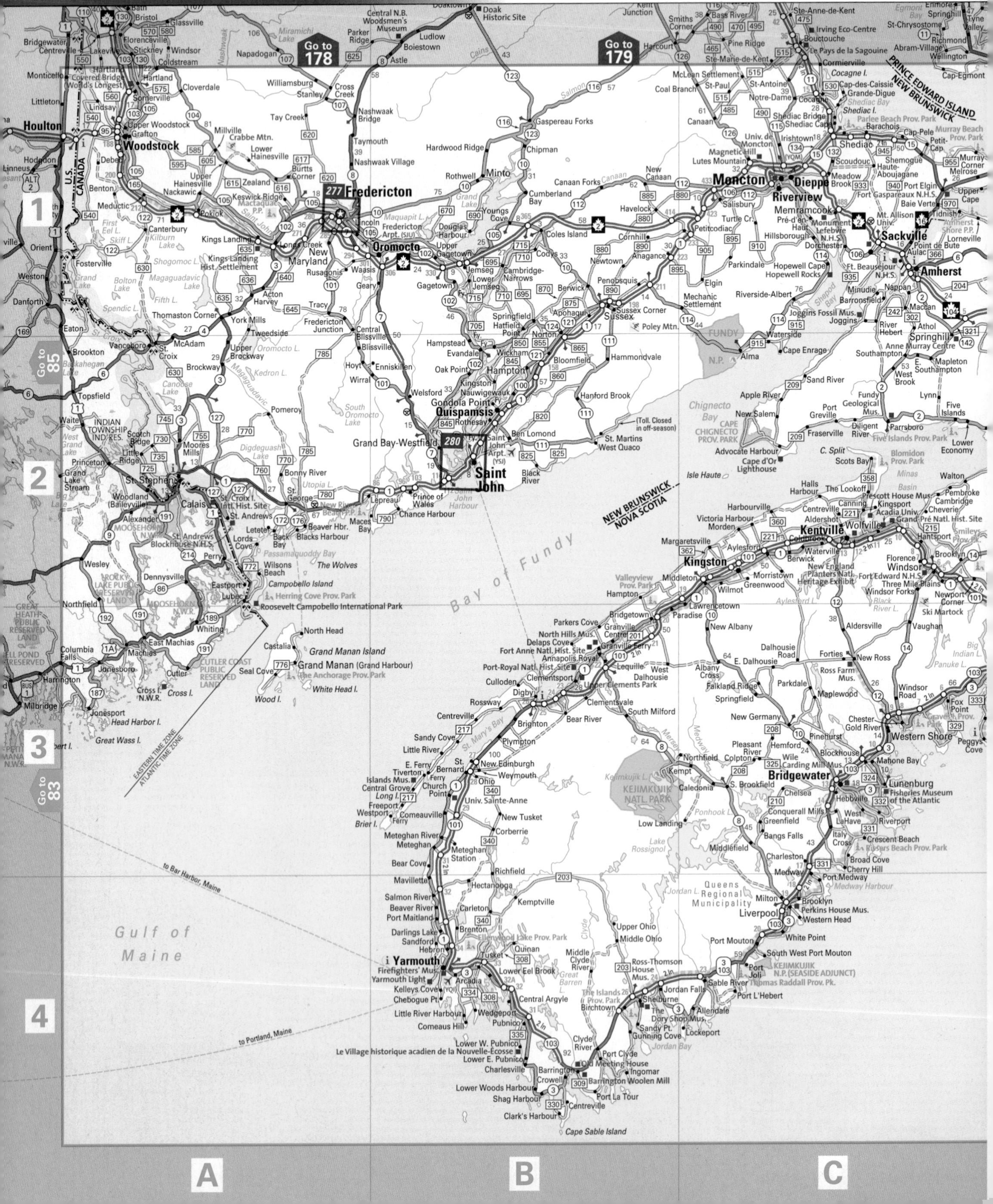

0 mi ——— 20 ——— 40
0 km ——— 20 ——— 40 ——— 60
One inch equals 25.4 miles/Un pouce équivaut à 25.4 milles
One cm equals 16.1 km/Un cm équivaut à 16.1 km

Go to **178**

Go to **179**

Houlton

Woodstock

277 Fredericton

Oromocto

Saint John

Moncton Dieppe

Riverview

Memramcook

Sackville

Amherst

Springhill

Go to **85**

St. Stephens

Calais

Go to **83**

Grand Manan Island

Grand Manan (Grand Harbour)

Bay of Fundy

NEW BRUNSWICK
NOVA SCOTIA

Digby

Kentville Wolfville

Kingston

Windsor

Bridgewater

Lunenburg

Liverpool

*Gulf of
Maine*

to Bar Harbor, Maine

to Portland, Maine

Yarmouth

A   B   C

DRIVING DISTANCES IN KM /
DISTANCES ROUTIÈRES EN KM

	CHARLOTTETOWN, PE	CHETICAMP, NS	DIGBY, NS	FREDERICTON, NB	HALIFAX, NS	MONCTON, NB	PORT HAWKESBURY, NS	SAINT JOHN, NB	ST. STEPHEN, NB	SYDNEY, NS	TRURO, NS	YARMOUTH, NS
HALIFAX, NS	322	425	235	462		260	265	410	515	415	89	339
MONCTON, NB	164	481	231	170	260		374	150	278	497	182	599
SAINT JOHN, NB	350	640	72	114	410	150	497		119	647	321	176
SYDNEY, NS	374	173	623	689	415	497	123	647	766		326	727

SEE ALSO DISTANCE AND DRIVING TIME MAP ON PAGES 286–287 / VOIR AUSSI CARTE DES DISTANCES ET DES TEMPS DE PARCOURS PAGES 286–287

P.E.I.
N.B.
Nova Scotia
Maine

Distances in Canada shown in kilometers.
Au Canada, les distances sont en kilomètres.

Go to 182

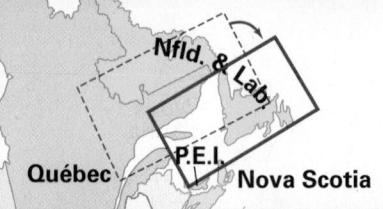

Nfld. & Lab.
Québec
P.E.I.
Nova Scotia

0 mi 20 40 60
0 km 20 40 60 80
One inch equals 40.3 miles/Un pouce équivaut à 40.3 milles
One centimeter equals 25.4 km/Un cm équivaut à 25.4 km

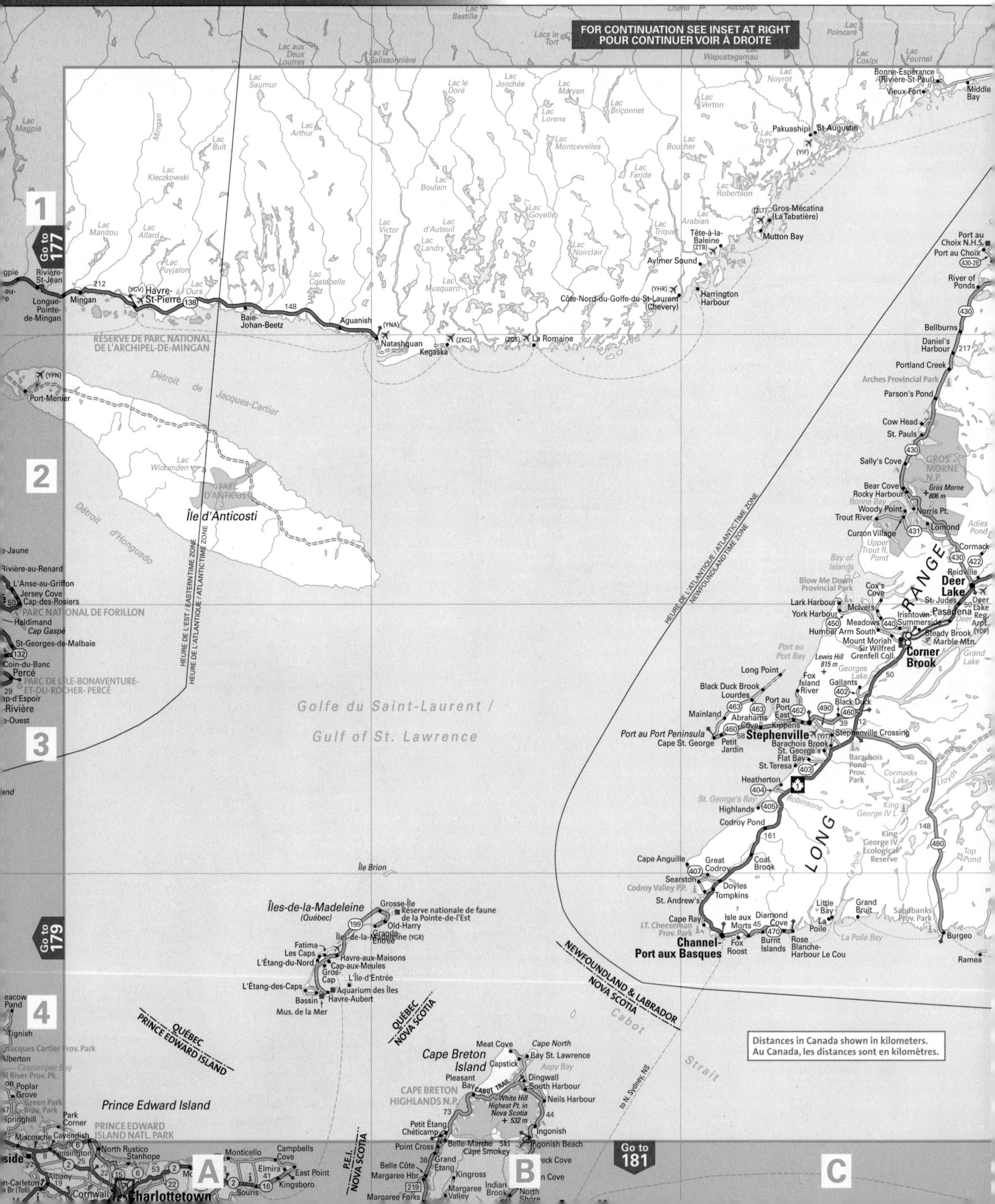

FOR CONTINUATION SEE INSET AT RIGHT
POUR CONTINUER VOIR À DROITE

1
2
3
4

Go to 177
Go to 179
Go to 181

Distances in Canada shown in kilometers.
Au Canada, les distances sont en kilomètres.

Golfe du Saint-Laurent /
Gulf of St. Lawrence

Île d'Anticosti

Détroit de Jacques-Cartier
Détroit d'Honguedo

PARC D'ANTICOSTI

RÉSERVE DE PARC NATIONAL
DE L'ARCHIPEL-DE-MINGAN

Île Brion
Îles-de-la-Madeleine
(Québec)

Prince Edward Island

Cape Breton
Island
CAPE BRETON
HIGHLANDS N.P.

NEWFOUNDLAND & LABRADOR
NOVA SCOTIA

Cabot Strait

GROS MORNE N.P.

Deer Lake
Corner Brook
Stephenville
Channel-
Port aux Basques

LONG RANGE

DRIVING
DISTANCES IN KM /
DISTANCES ROUTIÈRES EN KM

	ARGENTIA, NL	BISHOP'S FALLS, NL	BONAVISTA, NL	CHAN.-PT. AUX BASQUES, NL	CORNER BROOK, NL	DEER LAKE, NL	GANDER, NL	GRAND FALLS-WINDSOR, NL	MARYSTOWN, NL	ST. ANTHONY, NL	ST. JOHN'S, NL	STEPHENVILLE, NL
BISHOP'S FALLS, NL	363		307	482	280	225	72	18	384	628	393	339
CHAN.-PT. AUX BASQUES, NL	845	482	789		202	257	554	464	866	660	875	151
CORNER BROOK, NL	643	280	587	202		55	352	262	664	458	673	59
ST. JOHN'S, NL	134	393	296	875	673	618	321	411	293	1021		732

SEE ALSO DISTANCE AND DRIVING TIME MAP ON PAGES 286–287 / Voir aussi carte des distances et des temps de parcours pages 286–287

Ariz. N.M.
Texas
MEXICO

0 mi   50   100   150
0 km   50   100   150   200
One inch equals 83.75 miles/Una pulgada igual a 83.75 millas
One centimeter equals 53 km/Un centímetro igual a 53 km

CALIFORNIA
San Diego
Tijuana
Phoenix
El Centro
Go to 53
Go to 55
Casa Grande
Rosarito
El Descanso
La Rumorosa Par. Nac. Constitución de 1857
Tecate
Calexico
Mexicali
San Luis Río Colorado
ARIZONA
Safford
Francisco Zarco
Ojos Negros
El Faro
Guadalupe Victoria
Yuma
Lordsburg
El Sauzal
Ensenada
Maneadero
196
148
209
Riito
Tucson
Deming
Isla de Todos Santos
La Bufadora
Puerto Santo Tomás
Santo Tomás
Golfo de Santa Clara
SAGUARO N.P.
SAGUARO NATL. PARK
Palomas Viejo
San Vicente
Isla Montague
RESERVA DE LA BIÓSFERA ALTO GOLFO DE CALIFORNIA Y DELTA DEL RÍO COLORADO
RESERVA DE LA BIÓSFERA EL PINACATE Y GRAN DESIERTO DE ALTAR
Sonoyta
UNITED STATES
MÉXICO
Nogales
Douglas
Guadalupe Victoria
222
Villa Hidalgo
Pico del Diablo 3,100 m
San Felipe
Punta Estrella
Puerto Peñasco
División del Norte
El Sásabe
Nogales
NOG
Cibuta
Naco
Agua Prieta
Ascensión
Janos
Fernández Leal
Nogales
162
Colonet
Vicente Guerrero
254
Parque Nacional Sierra de San Pedro Mártir
Puertecitos
El Arenoso
Sáric
64
Imuris
40
Cananea
Fronteras
Esqueda
SIERRA
Casas Grandes
Bavispe
Bacerac
Casas Grandes Paquime (ruinas)
Galeana
Ricardo Flores Magón
2 ln.
Lázaro Cárdenas
Isla San Martín
San Quintín
El Desemboque
La Tubutama
Atil
Caborca
Magdalena de Kino
Bacoachi
La Angostura
Villa Hidalgo
Huásabas
Buenaventura
Ignacio Zaragoza
10
El Rosario
Punta Baja
Cabo Tepoca
Pitiquito
Altar
Santa Ana
Nacozari de García
Arizpe
17
Cumpas
Nacori Chico
28
Las Varas
Gómez Farías
Namiquipa
28
Lázaro Cárdenas
Cataviña
288
Punta Final
Cabo Lobos
Puerto Libertad
260
El Claro
Cucurpe
Querobabi
Banamichi
118
Moctezuma
Baviácora
Tepachi
Madera
Nicolás Bravo
Punta San Carlos
Punta Canoas
Chapala
BAJA CALIFORNIA
Isla Ángel de la Guarda
Cabo Tepopa
176
ÁREA DE PROTECCIÓN ISLAS DEL GOLFO DE CALIFORNIA
Opodepe
Aconchi
Rayón
Carbó
Divisaderos
Mazocahui
14
San Pedro de la Cueva
Ures
Tamósachi
Matachi
Bachiniva
Álvaro Obregón
Punta María
Punta Prieta
Santa Rosalita
Bahía de los Ángeles
Isla Tiburón
Punta de las Animas
3
Kino Nuevo
Bahía Kino
ÁREA DE PROTECCIÓN ISLAS DEL GOLFO DE CALIFORNIA
HMO
Hermosillo
Miguel Alemán
100
20
Mazatán
Pueblo de Álamo
Presa P.E. Calles
Bacanora
Sahuaripa
Rebeico
Madera
16
Cd. Guerrero
Adolfo López Madero
Islas San Benito
Isla Cedros
La Gringa
Santa Rosalía
Bahía Sebastián Vizcaíno
Misión Santa Gertrudis
Puerto San Francisquito
Santa Eduwiges
Santa Misa
La Colorada
Pinturas Rupestres
San Javier
Soyopa
Tonichi
Yepachi
418
Basaseachi
16
174
Cuauhtémoc
Cusihuiriachi
Isla Natividad
Punta Eugenia
Bahía de Tortugas
GUB
Guerrero Negro
Complejo Lagunar Ojo de Liebre
El Arco
304
Punta San Carlos
15
Ortiz
134
Mazatán
16
Tecoripa
Suaqui Grande
Onavas
Movas
Nuri
Par. Nac. Cascada de Basaseachi
Maguarichi
San Juanito
Bocoyna
Creel
Barranca del Cobre (Copper Canyon)
Samachique
Morro Hermoso
Punta San Pablo
Bahía Asunción
RESERVA DE LA BIÓSFERA EL VIZCAÍNO
Volcán las Vírgenes 1,920 m
Santa Rosalía
GYM
Guaymas
San Carlos
Empalme
Cabo Haro
Presa Álvaro Obregón
138
Vicam
Potam
12
Rosario
Yécora
San Rafael
Urique
La Bufa
Batopilas
Uruachi
Carichi
Laguna San Ignacio
Punta Abreojos
San Ignacio
BAJA CALIFORNIA SUR
SIERRA DE LA
Mulegé
Punta Concepción
El Rosarito
Punta Púlpito
204
Isla Lobos
Ciudad Obregón
CEN
Fundición
Chinipas
Guazapares
Témoris
Guachochi
Morelos
Las Táscates
Baborigame
Punta San Juanico
La Purísima
Misión San Javier
Comondú
53
Loreto
LTO
Isla Carmen
Puerto Escondido
Isla Danzante
Isla Santa Catalina
Bácum
Pueblo Yaqui
Villa Juárez
Bacobampo
Etchojoa
Navojoa
San Bernardo
Álamos
SINALOA
23
OCCIDENTAL
Santo Domingo
149
Puerto Agua Verde
Punta San Marcial
Gustavo Díaz Ordaz
San Miguel Zapotitlán
15
Huatabampo
Punta Rosa
Yávaros
228
Las Bocas
El Fuerte
San Blas
San José de Gracia
Guadalupe y Calvo
Puerto Adolfo López Mateos
Ciudad Insurgentes
Isla Magdalena
22
Ciudad Constitución
Isla San José
Isla Espíritu Santo
ÁREA DE PROTECCIÓN ISLAS DEL GOLFO DE CALIFORNIA
Bahía DE CALIFORNIA
La Paz
Higuera de Zaragoza
Charay
Ahome
Los Mochis
LMM
Topolobampo
Gral. Juan J. Ríos
Guasave
Naranjo
Leyva Solano
Guamúchil
Sinaloa de Leyva
Tameapa
Santiago de los Caballeros
Badiraguato
GIGANTA
Cabo San Lázaro
San Carlos
Puerto Cancún
Santa Rita
Puerto Cortés
Isla Santa Margarita
218
Pichilingue
Isla Cerralvo
24
Las Glorias
Angostura
La Reforma
Pericos
Presa A. López Mateos
Navolato
Altata
Villa Juárez
Costa Rica
15
Culiacán
CUL
OCÉANO PACÍFICO / PACIFIC OCEAN
La Paz
LAP
San Pedro
Punta Arena
Los Planes
San Antonio
San Bartolo
19
El Triunfo
Buenavista
1
Península de Lucenilla
El Dorado
Quila
216
Península de Quevedo
La Cruz
Todos Santos
Santiago
Cabo Pulmo
Parque Nacional Cabo Pulmo
El Pescadero
163
211
Miraflores
Dimas
223
RESERVA DE LA BIÓSFERA SIERRA LA LAGUNA
2 ln.
SID
Santa Rosa
San José del Cabo
Cabo Falso
Cabo San Lucas

Distances in Mexico shown in kilometers.
Distancias en México constan en kilómetros.

SONORA
SIERRA MADRE OCCIDENTAL
Salton Sea
Golfo de California
Bahía de los Ángeles

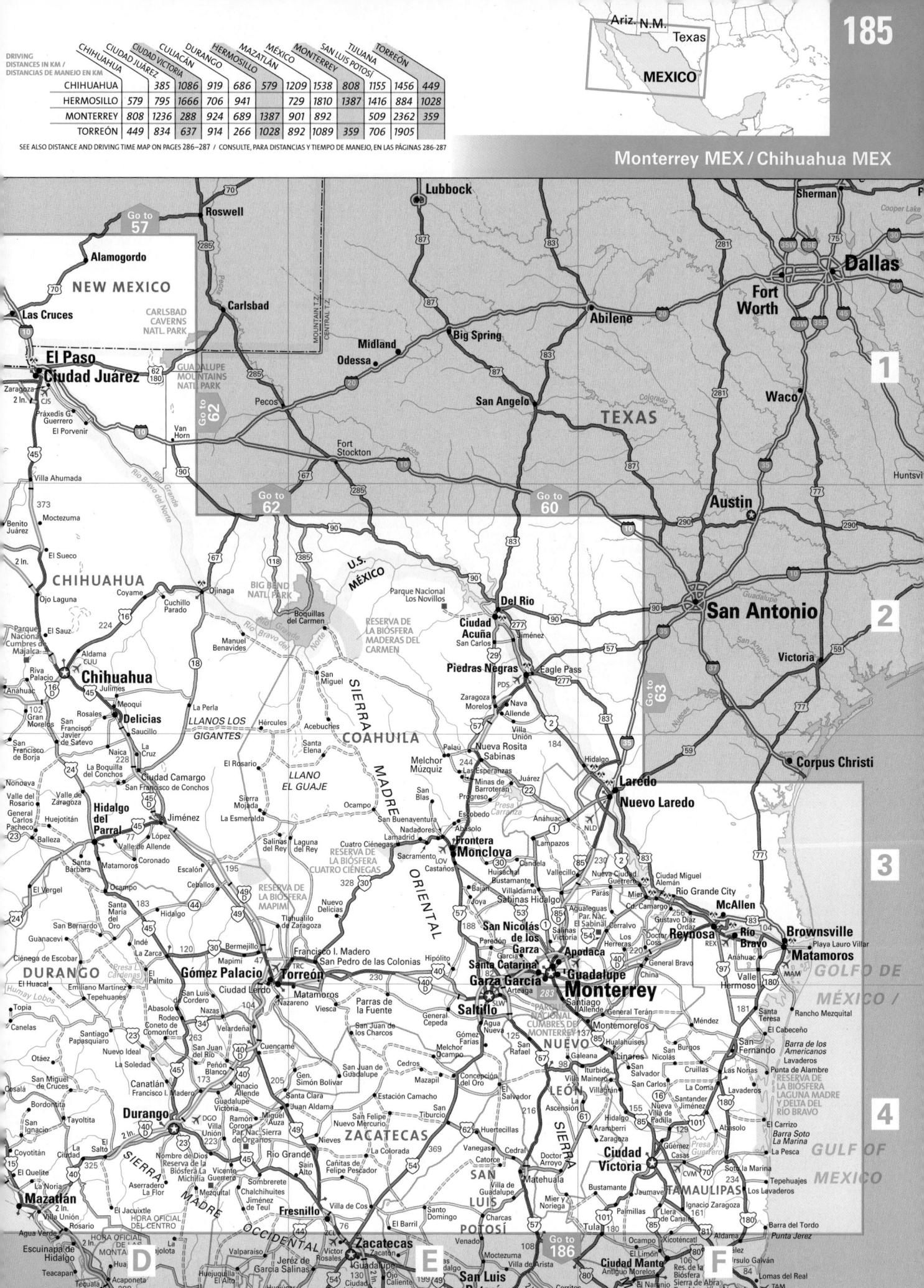

DRIVING DISTANCES IN KM / DISTANCIAS DE MANEJO EN KM

	CHIHUAHUA	CIUDAD JUÁREZ	CIUDAD VICTORIA	CULIACÁN	DURANGO	HERMOSILLO	MAZATLÁN	MÉXICO	MONTERREY	SAN LUIS POTOSÍ	TIJUANA	TORREÓN
CHIHUAHUA		385	1086	919	686	579	1209	1538	808	1155	1456	449
HERMOSILLO	579	795	1666	706	941		729	1810	1387	1416	884	1028
MONTERREY	808	1236	288	924	689	1387	901	892		509	2362	359
TORREÓN	449	834	637	914	266	1028	892	1089	359	706	1905	

SEE ALSO DISTANCE AND DRIVING TIME MAP ON PAGES 286–287 / Consulte, para distancias y tiempo de manejo, en las páginas 286–287

MEXICO

MEXICO

Puerto Rico

0 mi 50 100 150
0 km 50 100 150 200

One inch equals 83.75 miles/Una pulgada igual a 83.75 millas
One centimeter equals 53 km/Un centímetro igual a 53 km

Distances in Mexico shown in kilometers.
Distancias en México constan en kilómetros.

OCÉANO PACÍFICO /

PACIFIC OCEAN

DURANGO · Gómez Palacio · Torreón · Garza García · Guadalupe · Monterrey · Saltillo · NUEVO LEÓN · Montemorelos · Linares · TAMAULIPAS · Ciudad Victoria · Ciudad Mante · Tampico · Ciudad Madero

Mazatlán · Durango · SIERRA MADRE OCCIDENTAL · ZACATECAS · Fresnillo · Zacatecas · SAN LUIS POTOSÍ · San Luis Potosí · Soledad de Graciano Sánchez · Matehuala

NAYARIT · Tepic · Aguascalientes · Lagos de Moreno · León · GUANAJUATO · Guanajuato · San Miguel de Allende · QUERÉTARO · HIDALGO · Pachuca

Puerto Vallarta · JALISCO · Zapopan · Guadalajara · Tonalá · Ocotlán · La Piedad de Cabadas · Irapuato · Celaya · Salamanca · Querétaro · San Juan del Río · Tulancingo · Poza Rica · Tuxpam

Manzanillo · Colima · COLIMA · Ciudad Guzmán · Uruapan · Morelia · Zitácuaro · Toluca · México · Netzahualcóyotl · Tlaxcala · PUEBLA · Puebla · Cholula · Córdoba · Orizaba · Xalapa

MICHOACÁN · Lázaro Cárdenas · Zihuatanejo · GUERRERO · Chilpancingo · Cuernavaca · Cuautla · Iguala · MORELOS · Tehuacán · Oaxaca · PUEBLA

Acapulco · SIERRA MADRE DEL SUR · Puerto Escondido

A B C

1 2 3 4

MEXICO — Puerto Rico

DRIVING DISTANCES IN KM / DISTANCIAS DE MANEJO EN KM

	ACAPULCO	CANCÚN	CIUDAD VICTORIA	DURANGO	GUADALAJARA	MAZATLÁN	MÉRIDA	MÉXICO	PUEBLA	SAN LUIS POTOSÍ	TUXTLA GUTIÉRREZ	VERACRUZ
GUADALAJARA	897	2275	774	599		523	1904	578	691	336	1510	943
MÉRIDA	1777	321	1725	2182	1904	2408		1326	1282	1707	786	995
MÉXICO	422	1736	682	856	578	1081	1326		133	381	932	365
SAN LUIS POTOSÍ	834	2161	438	475	336	687	1707	381	496		1313	747

SEE ALSO DISTANCE AND DRIVING TIME MAP ON PAGES 286–287 / CONSULTE, PARA DISTANCIAS Y TIEMPO DE MANEJO, EN LAS PÁGINAS 286–287

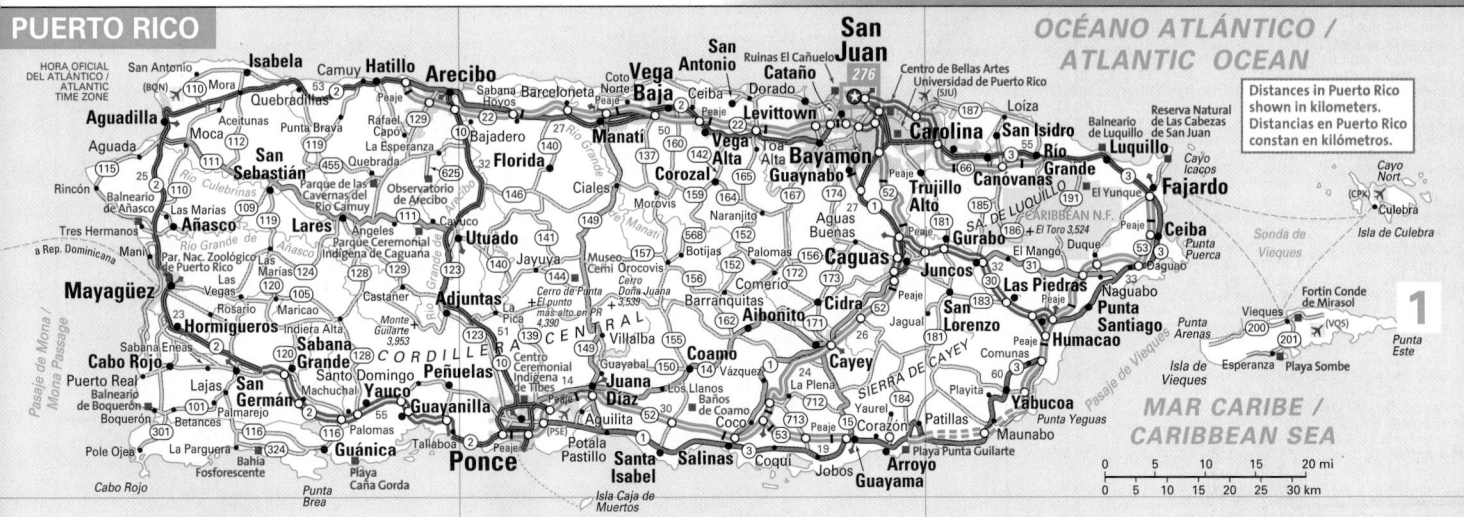

188
Abbeville – Allerton

Figures after entries indicate population, page number, and grid reference.

UNITED STATES

A

Abbeville AL, *2688* 128 B4
Abbeville GA, *2908* 129 E3
Abbeville LA, *12257* 133 F3
Abbeville MS, *419* 118 C3
Abbeville SC, *5237* 121 E3
Abbeville Co. SC, *25417* 121 E3
Abbotsford WI, *2310* 68 A4
Abbottstown PA, *1011* 103 E1
Abercrombie ND, *263* 19 F4
Aberdeen ID, *1994* 31 E1
Aberdeen MD, *14959* 145 D1
Aberdeen MS, *5612* 119 D4
Aberdeen NC, *6350* 122 C1
Aberdeen OH, *1638* 100 C3
Aberdeen SD, *26091* 27 E2
Aberdeen WA, *16896* 12 B4
Abernathy TX, *2805* 58 A1
Abilene KS, *6844* 43 E2
Abilene TX, *117063* 58 C3
Abingdon IL, *3319* 88 A3
Abingdon MD, *950* 145 D1
Abingdon VA, *8191* 111 E3
Abington MA, *15985* 151 D2
Abita Sprs. LA, *2365* 134 B2
Absarokee MT, *1150* 24 B2
Absecon NJ, *8411* 147 F4
Acadia Par. LA, *61773* 133 E2
Accokeek MD, *10573* 144 B4
Accokeek Acres MD, *1500* 144 B4
Accomac VA, *519* 114 C3
Accomack Co. VA, *33164* 114 C3
Accord MA, *2300* 151 D2
Accord NY, *562* 94 A3
Achille OK, *492* 59 F1
Achilles VA, *650* 113 F2
Ackerman MS, *1510* 126 C1
Ackley IA, *1589* 73 D4
Acme MI, *650* 69 F4
Acomita Lake NM, *416* 48 B3
Acton CA, *7596* 52 C2
Acton MA, *21924* 150 C1
Acushnet MA, *3073* 151 D3
Acworth GA, *20425* 120 C3
Ada MN, *1707* 19 F3
Ada OH, *5952* 90 B3
Ada OK, *16810* 51 F4
Ada Co. ID, *392365* 22 B4
Adair IA, *781* 86 B2
Adair OK, *790* 106 A3
Adair Co. IA, *7682* 86 B2
Adair Co. KY, *18656* 110 B2
Adair Co. MO, *25607* 87 D4
Adair Co. OK, *22683* 106 B4
Adairsville GA, *4648* 120 B3
Adair Vil. OR, *840* 20 B3
Adairville KY, *852* 109 F3
Adams MA, *5515* 94 C1
Adams MN, *787* 73 D2
Adams NE, *573* 35 F4
Adams NY, *1775* 79 E2
Adams OR, *350* 21 F1
Adams TN, *633* 109 E3
Adams WI, *1967* 74 A1
Adams Ctr. NY, *1568* 79 E2
Adams Co. CO, *441603* 41 F1
Adams Co. ID, *3976* 22 B2
Adams Co. IL, *67103* 87 F4
Adams Co. IN, *34387* 90 A3
Adams Co. IA, *4029* 86 B3
Adams Co. MS, *32297* 126 A4
Adams Co. NE, *31364* 35 D4
Adams Co. ND, *2343* 26 A1
Adams Co. OH, *28550* 100 C3
Adams Co. PA, *101407* 103 E1
Adams Co. WA, *18728* 13 F4
Adams Co. WI, *20875* 74 A2
Adamston NJ, *4900* 147 E3
Adamstown MD, *2372* 144 A2
Adamstown PA, *1789* 146 A2
Adamsville AL, *4522* 119 F4
Adamsville RI, *550* 151 D4
Adamsville TN, *2207* 119 D1
Addis LA, *3593* 134 A2
Addison AL, *758* 119 E3
Addison IL, *36942* 203 C4
Addison ME, *300* 83 E2
Addison MI, *605* 90 B1
Addison NY, *1763* 93 D1
Addison TX, *13056* 207 D1
Addison Co. VT, *36821* 81 D3
Adel GA, *5334* 137 F1
Adel IA, *3682* 86 C2
Adelanto CA, *31765* 53 D2
Adelphi MD, *15086* 270 E1
Adelphia NJ, *700* 147 E2
Adena OH, *759* 91 F4
Adrian GA, *664* 129 F2
Adrian MI, *21133* 90 B1
Adrian MN, *1209* 72 A2
Adrian MO, *1677* 96 B4
Advance IN, *477* 99 E1
Advance MO, *1347* 108 B2
Adwolf VA, *1530* 111 F2
Affton MO, *20307* 256 B3
Afton IA, *845* 86 C3
Afton NY, *822* 93 F1
Afton OK, *1049* 106 B3
Afton WY, *1911* 31 F1
Agawam MA, *28438* 150 A2
Agency IA, *638* 87 E3
Agency MO, *684* 96 B1
Agoura Hills CA, *20330* 228 A2
Agua Dulce TX, *3014* 63 E2
Agua Fria NM, *2800* 49 D2
Aguilar CO, *538* 41 E4
Ahoskie NC, *5039* 113 F3
Ahsahka ID, *600* 14 B4
Ahuimanu HI, *8810* 152 A3
Aiken SC, *29524* 121 F4
Aiken Co. SC, *160099* 122 A4
Ainsworth IA, *567* 87 F2
Ainsworth NE, *1728* 34 C1
Airmont NY, *8628* 148 B3
Airport Drive MO, *698* 106 B2
Airway Hts. WA, *6114* 13 F3
Aitkin MN, *2165* 64 B4
Aitkin Co. MN, *16202* 64 B4
Ajo AZ, *3304* 54 B3
Ak-Chin Vil. AZ, *862* 54 C2
Akiachak AK, *627* 154 B3
Akins OK, *493* 116 B1
Akron AL, *356* 127 E1
Akron CO, *1702* 41 F1
Akron IN, *1167* 89 F3
Akron IA, *1486* 35 F1
Akron MI, *402* 76 B2
Akron NY, *2868* 78 B3

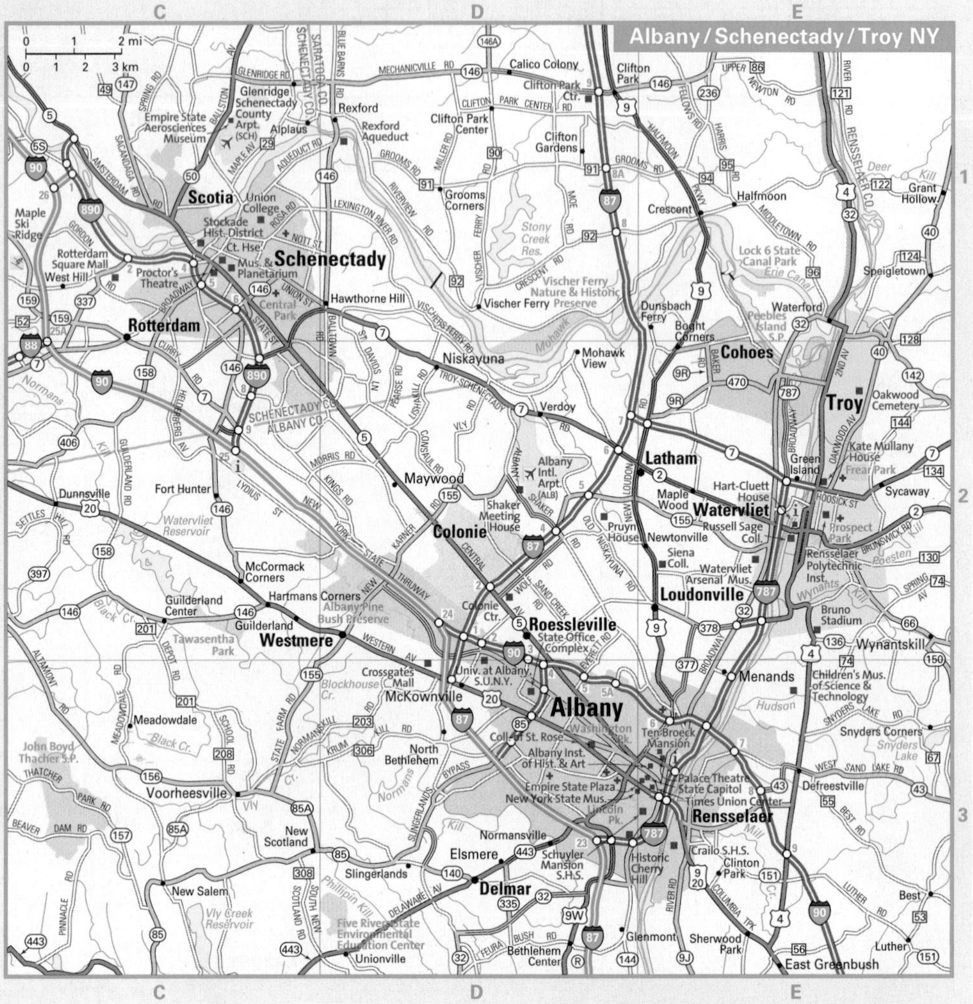
Albany / Schenectady / Troy NY
C
D
E
0 1 2 mi
0 1 2 3 km
1
2
3
Scotia
Schenectady
Rotterdam
Niskayuna
Colonie
Latham
Cohoes
Troy
Watervliet
Loudonville
Roessleville
Westmere
Albany
Rensselaer
Delmar
Voorheesville
Guilderland
Rexford
Waterford
Menands
Elsmere
Slingerlands
East Greenbush

Albany D3
Alplaus C1
Best E3
Bethlehem Ctr. D3
Boght Corners E1
Calico Colony D1
Clifton Gardens D1
Clifton Park D1
Clifton Park Ctr. D1
Clinton Park E3
Cohoes E2
Colonie D2
Crescent E1
Defreestville E3
Delmar D3
Dunnsville C2
Dunsbach Ferry E1
E. Greenbush E3
Elsmere D3
Ft. Hunter C2
Glenmont D3
Glenridge C1
Grant Hollow E1
Green Island E2
Grooms Corners D1
Guilderland C2
Guilderland Ctr. C2
Halfmoon E1
Hartmans Corners C2
Hawthorne Hill D1
Latham E2
Loudonville E2
Luther E3
Maple Wood E2
Maywood D2
McCormack Corners C2
McKownville D3
Meadowdale C3
Menands E3
Mohawk View D2
New Salem C3
New Scotland C3
Newtonville E2
Niskayuna D2
Normanville D3
N. Bethlehem D3
Rensselaer E3
Rexford D1
Roessleville D2
Rotterdam C1
Schenectady C1
Scotia C1
Sherwood Park E3
Slingerlands D3
Snyders Corners E3
Speigletown E1
Sycaway E2
Troy E2
Unionville D3
Verdoy D2
Vischer Ferry D1
Voorheesville C3
Waterford E1
Watervliet E2
W. Hill C1
Westmere D2
Wynantskill E2

Akron OH, *199110* 91 E3
Akron PA, *3876* 146 A2
Akutan AK, *1027* 154 A4
Alabaster AL, *30352* 127 F1
Alachua FL, *9059* 138 C3
Alachua Co. FL, *247336* 138 C3
Alakanuk AK, *677* 154 B2
Alamance Co. NC, *151131* 112 C4
Alameda CA, *73812* 259 C3
Alameda NM, *4200* 48 C3
Alameda Co. CA, *1510271* 36 B4
Alamo CA, *14570* 259 D2
Alamo GA, *2797* 129 E3
Alamo NM, *1085* 48 B4
Alamo TN, *2461* 108 C4
Alamo TX, *18353* 63 E4
Alamogordo NM, *30403* 56 C2
Alamo Hts. TX, *7031* 257 E2
Alamosa CO, *8780* 41 D4
Alamosa Co. CO, *15445* 41 D4
Alanson MI, *738* 70 C3
Alapaha GA, *668* 129 E4
Alba MO, *555* 106 B2
Albany CA, *18539* 259 C2
Albany GA, *77434* 129 D4
Albany IL, *891* 88 A1
Albany IN, *2165* 90 A4
Albany KY, *2033* 110 B3
Albany LA, *1088* 134 B2
Albany MN, *2561* 66 B2
Albany MO, *1730* 86 B4
Albany NY, *97856* 94 B1
Albany OH, *828* 101 E2
Albany OR, *50158* 20 B3
Albany TX, *2034* 58 C2
Albany WI, *1018* 74 B4
Albany Co. NY, *304204* 94 B1
Albany Co. WY, *36299* 33 E2
Albemarle NC, *15903* 122 B1
Albemarle Co. VA, *98970* 102 C4
Albers IL, *1190* 98 B3
Albert City IA, *699* 72 B4
Albert Lea MN, *18016* 72 C2
Alberton MT, *420* 15 D4
Albertville AL, *21160* 120 A3
Albertville MN, *7044* 66 C3
Albia IA, *3766* 87 D3
Albin VA, *700* 102 C2
Albion ID, *267* 31 D2
Albion IL, *1988* 99 D4
Albion IN, *2349* 90 A2
Albion IA, *505* 87 D1
Albion MI, *8616* 76 A4

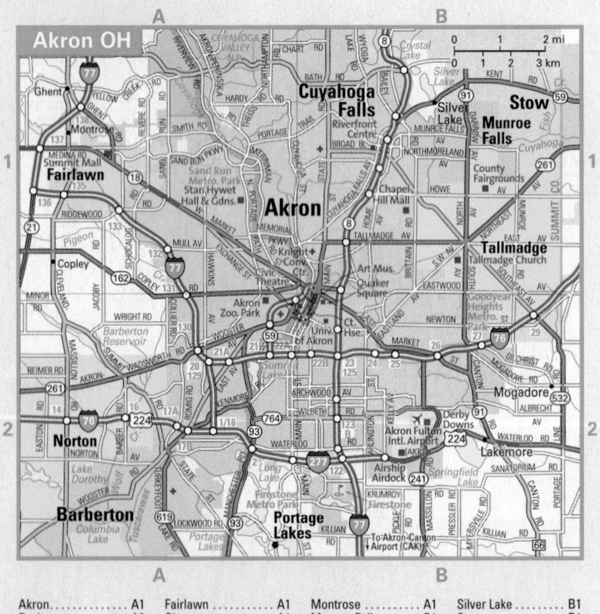
Akron OH
A
B
0 1 2 mi
0 1 2 3 km
1
2
Cuyahoga Falls
Stow
Munroe Falls
Fairlawn
Akron
Tallmadge
Norton
Mogadore
Barberton
Portage Lakes
Lakemore

Akron A1
Barberton A2
Copley A1
Cuyahoga Falls B1
Fairlawn A1
Ghent A1
Lakemore B2
Mogadore B2
Montrose A1
Munroe Falls B1
Norton A2
Portage Lakes A2
Silver Lake B1
Stow B1
Tallmadge B1

Albion NE, *1650* 35 E3
Albion NY, *6056* 78 B3
Albion PA, *1516* 91 F1
Albion WA, *579* 14 A4
Albuquerque NM, *545852* 48 C3
Alburg VT, *497* 81 D1
Alburnett IA, *673* 87 E1
Alburtis PA, *2361* 146 B1
Alcalde NM, *285* 49 D2
Alcester SD, *807* 35 F1
Alcoa TN, *8449* 110 C4
Alcona Co. MI, *10942* 71 D4
Alcorn MS, *1017* 126 A3
Alcorn Co. MS, *37057* 119 D2
Alda NE, *642* 35 D4
Aldan PA, *4152* 248 B4
Alden IA, *787* 72 C4
Alden MN, *661* 72 C2
Alden NY, *2605* 78 B3
Alderson WV, *1184* 112 A1
Alderwood Manor WA, *8442* 262 B2
Aldine TX, *15869* 220 C1
Aledo IL, *3640* 87 F2
Aledo TX, *2716* 59 E2
Alex OK, *550* 51 E3
Alexander AR, *2901* 117 E2
Alexander ND, *223* 17 F2
Alexander City AL, *14875* 128 A1
Alexander Co. IL, *8238* 108 C2
Alexander Co. NC, *37198* 112 A4
Alexandria AL, *3917* 120 A4
Alexandria IN, *5145* 89 F4
Alexandria KY, *8477* 100 B3
Alexandria LA, *47723* 125 E4
Alexandria MN, *11070* 66 B2
Alexandria SD, *615* 27 E4
Alexandria TN, *966* 110 A4
Alexandria VA, *139966* 144 B3
Alexandria Bay NY, *1078* 79 E1
Alexis IL, *831* 88 A3
Alfalfa Co. OK, *5642* 51 D1
Alford FL, *489* 136 C1
Alfred ME, *2497* 82 B4
Alfred NY, *4174* 92 C1
Alger OH, *860* 90 B3
Alger Co. MI, *9601* 69 E1
Algoa TX, *900* 132 B4
Algodones NM, *814* 48 C3
Algoma MS, *590* 118 C3
Algoma WI, *3167* 69 D4
Algona IA, *5560* 72 B3
Algona WA, *3014* 262 B5
Algonac MI, *4110* 76 C4
Algonquin IL, *30046* 88 C1
Algood TN, *3495* 110 A3
Alhambra CA, *83089* 228 D2
Alhambra IL, *681* 98 B3
Alice TX, *19104* 63 E2
Aliceville AL, *2486* 127 E1
Ali Chuk AZ, *161* 54 B3
Aliquippa PA, *9438* 91 F3
Aliso Viejo CA, *47823* 229 G6
Allamakee Co. IA, *14330* 73 F3
Allamuchy NJ, *78* 94 A4
Allardt TN, *634* 110 B3
Allegan MI, *4998* 75 F4
Allegan Co. MI, *111408* 75 F4
Allegany NY, *1816* 92 C1
Allegany Co. MD, *75087* 102 C1
Allegany Co. NY, *48946* 78 C4
Alleghany Co. NC, *11155* 111 F3
Alleghany Co. VA, *16250* 102 A4
Allegheny Co. PA, *1223348* 92 A4
Allen NE, *377* 35 F2
Allen OK, *932* 51 F3
Allen SD, *420* 26 B4
Allen TX, *84246* 59 F2
Allen Co. IN, *355329* 90 A3
Allen Co. KS, *13371* 96 A4
Allen Co. KY, *19956* 109 F2
Allen Co. OH, *106331* 90 B3
Allendale MI, *17579* 75 F3
Allendale NJ, *6505* 148 B3
Allendale SC, *3482* 130 B1
Allendale Co. SC, *10419* 130 B1
Allenhurst GA, *695* 130 B3
Allenhurst NJ, *496* 147 F2
Allen Par. LA, *25764* 133 E1
Allen Park MI, *28210* 210 B4
Allenspark CO, *528* 41 D1
Allenton RI, *1400* 150 C4
Allenton WI, *823* 74 C2
Allentown NJ, *1828* 147 D2
Allentown PA, *118032* 146 B1
Allenwood NJ, *925* 147 E2
Allerton IA, *501* 87 D3

Entries in **bold black** indicate counties or parishes.
Entries in **bold color** indicate cities with detailed inset maps.

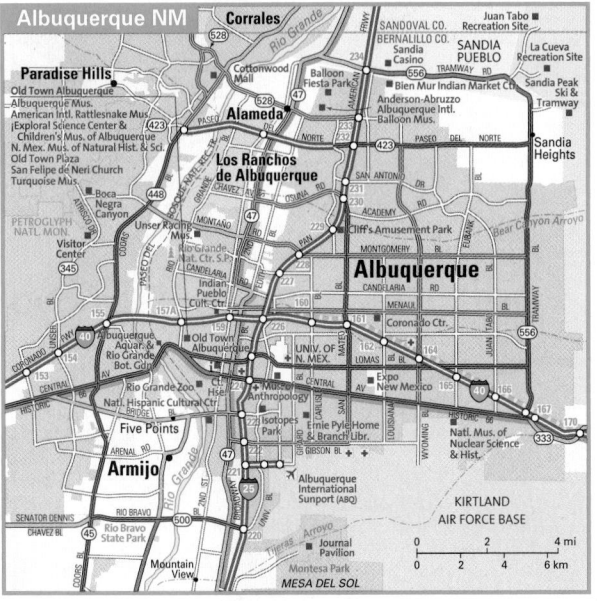

Albuquerque NM

Amarillo TX

Anchorage AK

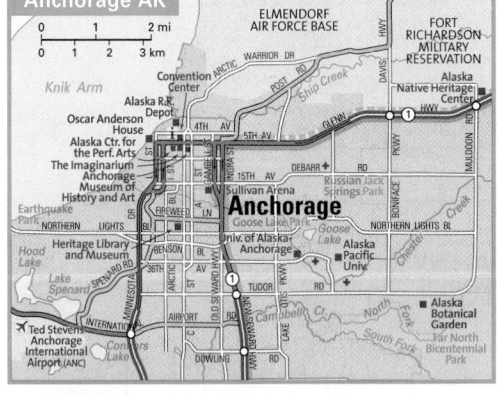

Allentown / Bethlehem PA

Annapolis MD

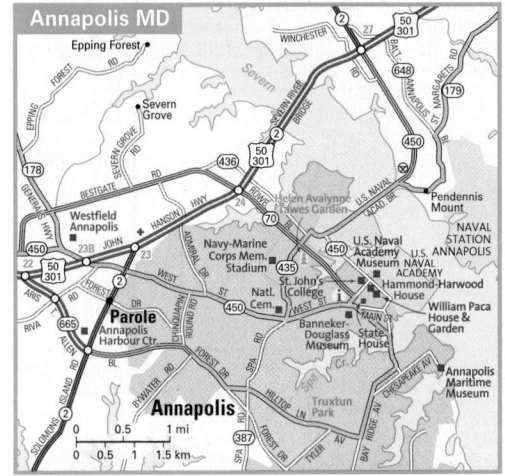

190

Anoka County–Arcade

Figures after entries indicate population, page number, and grid reference.

Ann Arbor MI

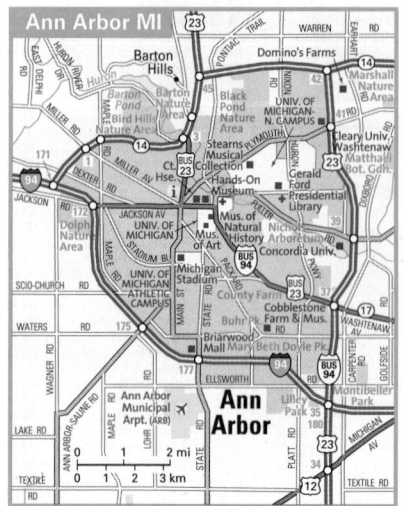

Asheville NC

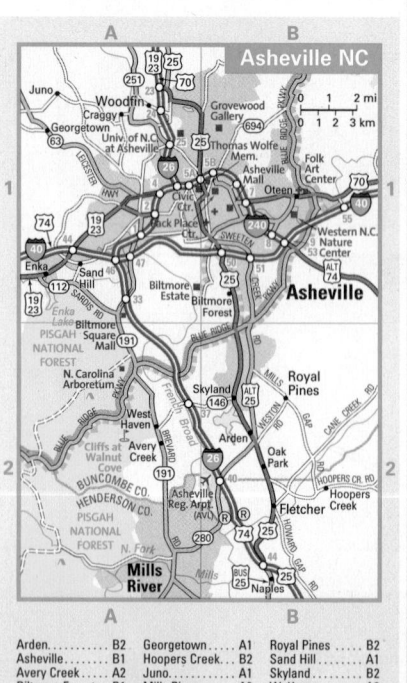

Atlanta GA

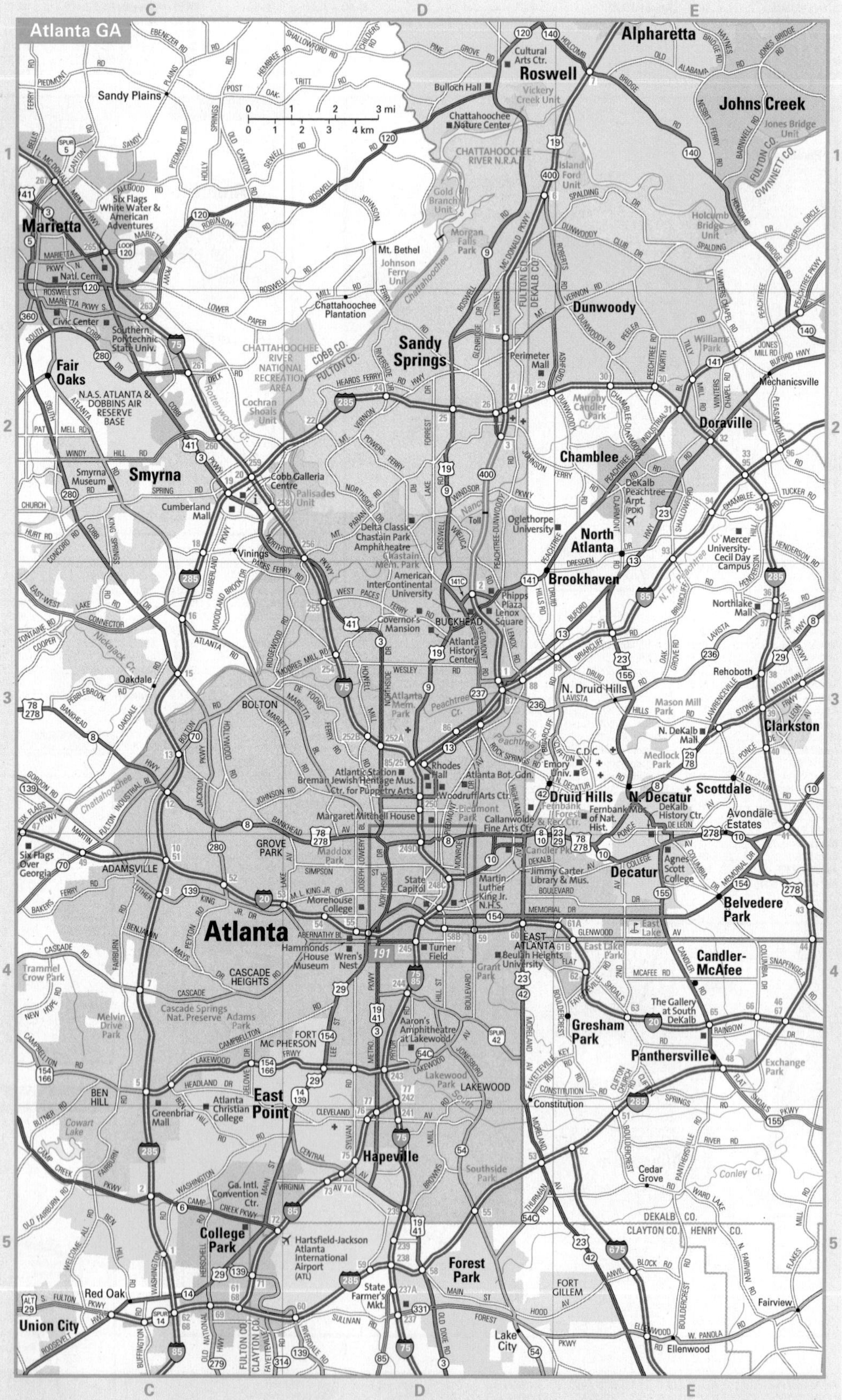

(second column of Atlanta index)

Entries in **bold black** indicate counties or parishes.
Entries in **bold color** indicate cities with detailed inset maps.

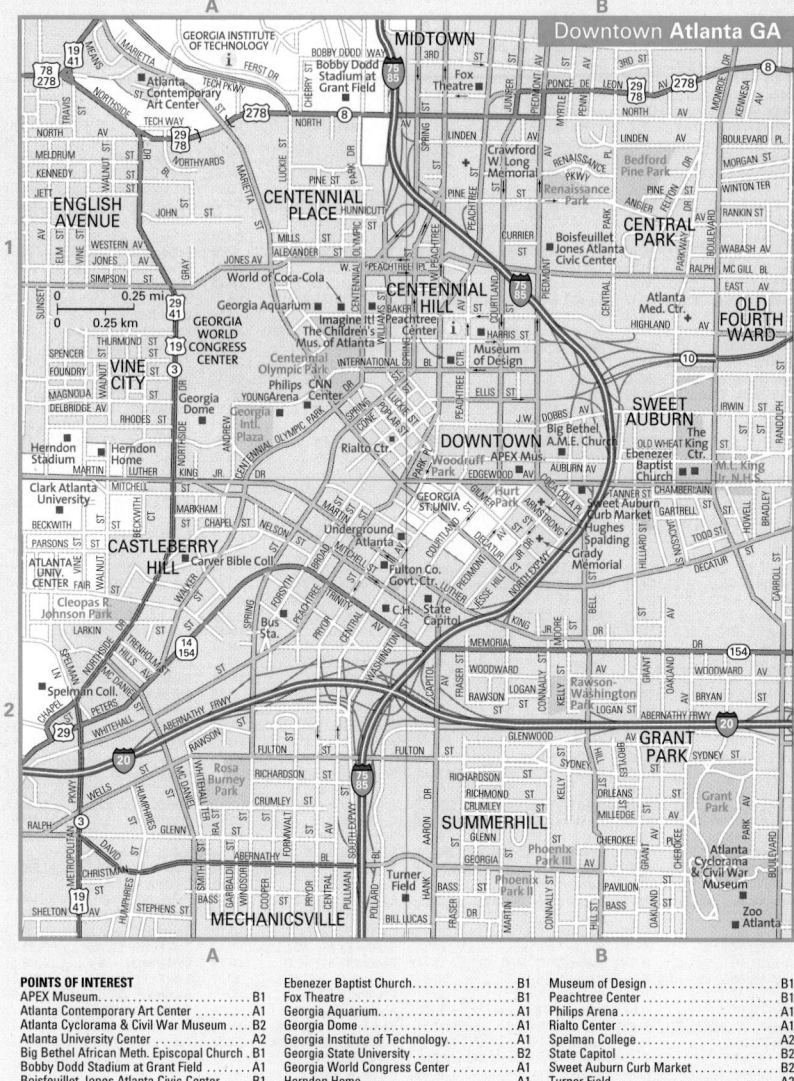

Downtown Atlanta GA

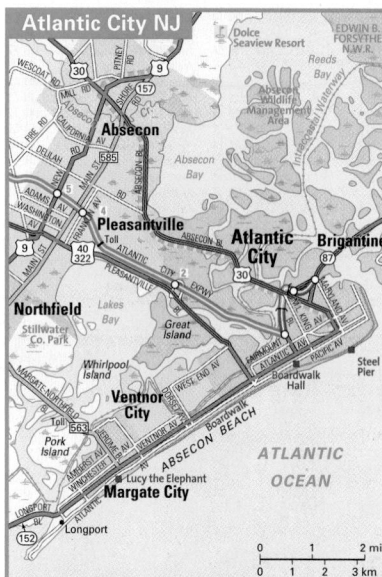

Atlantic City NJ

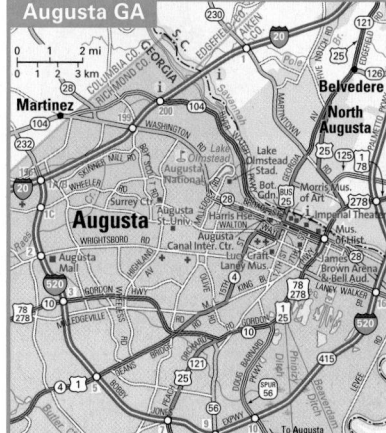

Augusta GA

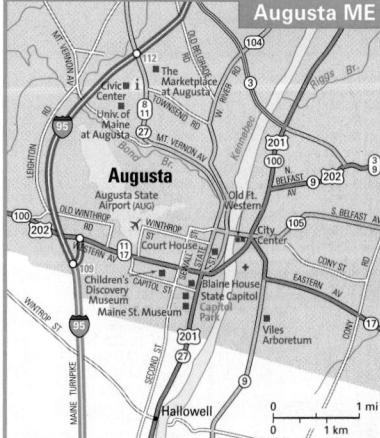

Augusta ME

POINTS OF INTEREST

APEX Museum	B1
Atlanta Contemporary Art Center	A1
Atlanta Cyclorama & Civil War Museum	B2
Atlanta University Center	A2
Big Bethel African Meth. Episcopal Church	B1
Bobby Dodd Stadium at Grant Field	A1
Boisfeuillet Jones Atlanta Civic Center	B1
Carver Bible College	A2
City Hall	B2
Clark Atlanta University	A2
CNN Center	A1
Ebenezer Baptist Church	B1
Fox Theatre	B1
Georgia Aquarium	A1
Georgia Dome	A1
Georgia Institute of Technology	A1
Georgia State University	B2
Georgia World Congress Center	A1
Herndon Home	A1
Herndon Stadium	A1
Imagine It! The Children's Mus. of Atlanta	A1
The King Center	B2
Martin Luther King, Jr. Natl. Hist. Site	B1
Museum of Design	B1
Peachtree Center	B1
Philips Arena	A1
Rialto Center	A1
Spelman College	A2
State Capitol	B2
Sweet Auburn Curb Market	B2
Turner Field	B2
Underground Atlanta	A2
World of Coca-Cola	A1
Zoo Atlanta	B2

192
Aulander – Belmont

Figures after entries indicate population, page number, and grid reference.

Aulander NC, 895 113 E3
Ault CO, 1519 33 E4
Aumsville OR, 3584 20 B2
Aurelia IA, 1036 72 A4
Aurora CO, 325078 41 E1
Aurora IL, 197899 88 C1
Aurora IN, 3750 100 B2
Aurora MN, 1682 64 C3
Aurora MO, 7508 106 C2
Aurora NE, 4479 35 E4
Aurora NY, 724 79 D4
Aurora NC, 520 115 D3
Aurora OH, 15548 91 E2
Aurora OR, 918 20 C2
Aurora SD, 532 27 F3
Aurora TX, 1220 59 E2
Aurora UT, 1016 39 E2
Aurora Co. SD, 2710 27 D4
Au Sable MI, 1404 76 C1
Autaugaville AL, 870 127 F2
Auxvasse MO, 983 97 E2
Ava IL, 654 98 B4
Ava MO, 2993 107 E2
Avalon CA, 3728 52 C3
Avalon NJ, 1334 105 D4
Avalon PA, 4705 250 A1
Avawam KY, 450 111 D2
Avella PA, 804 91 F4
Avenal CA, 15505 44 C3
Avenel NJ, 17011 147 E1
Aventura FL, 35762 143 F2
Averill Park NY, 1693 94 B1
Avery CA, 646 37 D3
Avery Co. NC, 17797 111 F4
Avery Creek NC, 1950 121 E1
Avilla IN, 2401 90 A2
Avis PA, 1484 93 D2
Aviston IL, 1945 98 B3
Avon MN, 1396 66 C2
Avon NY, 3394 78 C3
Avon NC, 776 115 F3
Avon OH, 21193 91 D2
Avon PA, 1667 146 A2
Avon SD, 590 35 E1
Avon-by-the-Sea NJ, 1901 147 F2
Avondale AZ, 76238 54 C1
Avondale CO, 674 41 E3
Avondale LA, 4954 134 B3
Avondale MO, 440 224 C2
Avondale PA, 1265 146 B3
Avondale RI, 425 149 F2
Avondale Estates GA, 2960 190 E3
Avonia PA, 1205 91 F1
Avon Lake OH, 22581 91 D2
Avonmore PA, 1011 92 A4
Avon Park FL, 8836 141 D3
Avoyelles Par. LA, 42073 125 F4

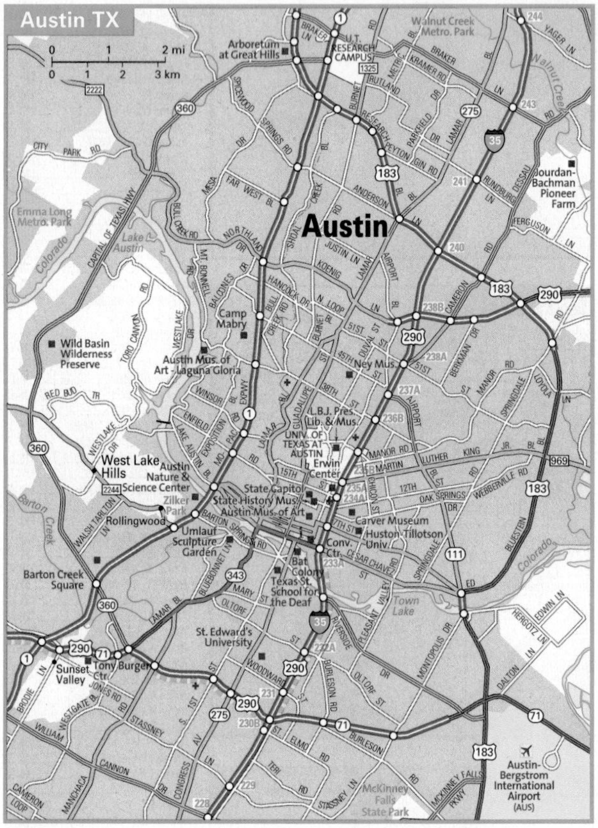
Austin TX
Austin
Arboretum at Great Hills
Wild Basin Wilderness Preserve
Camp Mabry
Austin Mus. of Art - Laguna Gloria
West Lake Hills
Austin Nature & Science Center
Zilker Park
State Capitol
Rollingwood
Umlauf Sculpture Garden
Barton Creek Square
Sunset Valley
St. Edward's University
Carver Museum
Huston-Tillotson Univ.
Texas Sch. School for the Deaf
UNIV. OF TEXAS AT AUSTIN
Austin-Bergstrom International Airport
McKinney Falls State Park
Bourdan-Bachman Pioneer Farm
Walnut Creek Metro. Park
Emma Long Metro. Park

Au Sable Forks NY, 559 81 D2
Austin AR, 2038 117 E2
Austin IN, 4295 99 F3
Austin MN, 24718 73 D2
Austin NV, 192 37 F1
Austin PA, 562 92 C2
Austin TX, 790390 61 E1
Austin Co. TX, 28417 61 F2
Austintown OH, 29677 91 F3
Autauga Co. AL, 54571 127 F2
Avoca AR, 488 106 C3
Avoca IA, 1506 86 A2
Avoca NY, 946 78 C4
Avoca PA, 2661 261 C2
Avoca WI, 637 74 A3
Avon AL, 543 137 D1
Avon CO, 6447 40 C1
Avon CT, 18098 94 C3
Avon IL, 799 88 A3
Avon IN, 12446 99 F1
Awendaw SC, 1294 131 D1
Axtell KS, 406 43 F1
Axtell NE, 726 35 D4
Ayden NC, 4932 115 D3
Ayer MA, 2868 95 D1
Aynor SC, 560 122 C3
Azalea Park FL, 12556 246 D2
Azle TX, 10947 59 E2
Aztec NM, 6763 48 B1
Azusa CA, 46361 228 E2

B

Babbie AL, 603 128 A4
Babbitt MN, 1475 64 C3
Babson Park FL, 1356 141 D3
Babylon NY, 12166 148 C4
Baca Co. CO, 3788 42 A4
Bacon Co. GA, 11096 129 F4
Baconton GA, 915 129 D4
Bad Axe MI, 3129 76 C2
Baden PA, 4135 92 A3
Badger IA, 561 72 C4
Badin NC, 1974 122 B1
Bagdad AZ, 1876 46 C4
Bagdad FL, 3761 135 F2
Baggs WY, 440 32 C3
Bagley MN, 1392 64 A3
Bahama NC, 550 112 C4
Bailey NC, 569 113 D4
Bailey Co. TX, 7165 49 F4
Bailey Island ME, 400 82 B3
Bailey's Crossroads VA, 23643 270 B4
Bailey's Prairie TX, 727 132 A4
Baileyton AL, 610 119 F3
Baileyton TN, 431 111 D3
Bainbridge GA, 12697 137 D1
Bainbridge IN, 746 99 E1
Bainbridge NY, 1355 79 E4
Bainbridge OH, 3267 101 D2

Bakersfield CA
Bakersfield
Oildale
Meadows Field (BFL)
Standard Park
Panorama Park
Sam Lynn Ballpark
College Park
Sierron Park
Kern Co. Mus.
Beach Park
Buena Vista Mus. of Nat. Hist.
Rabobank Arena Theater & Conv. Ctr.
Kern County Fairgrounds
Valley Plaza
Casa Loma Park
Planz Park

Bainbridge Island WA, 23025 12 C3
Baird TX, 1496 58 C3
Baiting Hollow NY, 1642 149 E3
Baker LA, 13895 134 A2
Baker MT, 1741 17 F4
Baker City OR, 9828 21 F2
Baker Co. FL, 27115 138 C2
Baker Co. GA, 3451 128 C4
Baker Co. OR, 16134 21 F3
Bakersfield CA, 347483 45 D4
Bakersville NC, 464 111 E4
Bala-Cynwyd PA, 10300 146 C3
Balaton MN, 643 72 A1
Balch Sprs. TX, 23728 207 E3
Balcones Hts. TX, 2941 257 E2
Bald Knob AR, 2897 117 F1
Baldwin FL, 1425 139 D2
Baldwin GA, 3279 121 D3
Baldwin IL, 373 98 B4
Baldwin LA, 2436 133 F3
Baldwin MD, 850 144 C1
Baldwin MI, 1208 75 F2
Baldwin PA, 19767 250 C3
Baldwin WI, 3957 67 E4
Baldwin City KS, 4515 96 A3
Baldwin Co. AL, 182265 135 E1
Baldwin Co. GA, 45720 129 E1
Baldwin Harbor NY, 8102 147 F1
Baldwin Park CA, 75390 228 E2
Baldwinsville NY, 7378 79 D3
Baldwinville MA, 2028 95 D1
Baldwyn MS, 3297 119 D3
Balfour NC, 1187 121 E1
Bal Harbour FL, 2513 233 B3
Ball LA, 4000 125 E4
Ballantine MT, 320 24 C1
Ballard UT, 801 32 A4
Ballard Co. KY, 8249 108 C2
Ballentine SC, 850 122 A3
Ball Ground GA, 1433 120 C3
Ballinger TX, 3767 58 C4
Ballouville CT, 950 150 B3
Ballston Spa NY, 5409 80 C4
Ballville OH, 2976 90 C2
Ballwin MO, 30404 98 A3
Bally PA, 1090 146 B1
Balmorhea TX, 479 62 B2
Balmville NY, 3178 148 B1
Balsam Lake WI, 1009 67 E3
Baltic CT, 1250 149 F1
Baltic OH, 795 91 E4
Baltic SD, 1089 27 F4
Baltimore MD, 620961 144 C2
Baltimore OH, 2966 101 D1
Baltimore Co. MD, 805029 144 C1
Baltimore Highlands MD, 7019 193 C4
Bamberg SC, 3607 130 C1
Bamberg Co. SC, 15987 130 B1
Bancroft ID, 377 31 E1
Bancroft IA, 732 72 B3
Bancroft KY, 494 230 F1
Bancroft MI, 545 76 B3
Bancroft NE, 495 35 F2
Bancroft WV, 587 101 E3
Bandera TX, 857 61 D2
Bandera Co. TX, 20485 60 C2
Bandon OR, 3066 28 A1
Bangor ME, 33039 83 D1
Bangor MI, 1885 75 E4
Bangor PA, 5273 93 F3
Bangor WI, 1459 73 F2
Bangs TX, 1603 59 D4
Banks OR, 1777 20 B1
Banks Co. GA, 18395 121 D3
Banner Co. NE, 690 33 F3
Banner Elk NC, 1028 111 F4
Banner Hill TN, 1497 111 E4
Bannertown NC, 950 112 A3
Banning CA, 29603 53 D2
Bannockburn IL, 1583 203 C2
Bannock Co. ID, 82839 31 E1
Banquete TX, 726 63 F2
Bantam CT, 759 94 C3
Baraboo WI, 12048 74 A2
Baraga MI, 2053 65 F4
Baraga Co. MI, 8860 65 F4
Barataria LA, 1109 134 B3
Barber Co. KS, 4861 43 D4
Barberton OH, 26550 91 E3
Barbour Co. AL, 27457 128 B3
Barbour Co. WV, 16589 102 A2
Barbourmeade KY, 1218 230 F1
Barboursville WV, 3964 101 E4
Barbourville KY, 3165 110 C2
Bardstown KY, 11700 110 A1
Bardwell KY, 723 108 C2
Bardwell TX, 649 59 F3
Bareville PA, 6625 146 A2
Bargersville IN, 4013 99 F1
Bar Harbor ME, 2552 83 D2
Barker NY, 533 78 B3
Barling AR, 4649 116 C1
Barlow KY, 675 108 C2
Bar Mills ME, 800 82 B3
Barnegat NJ, 2817 147 E4
Barnegat Light NJ, 574 147 E4
Barnegat Pines NJ, 1300 147 E3
Barnes Co. ND, 11066 19 D4
Barnesville GA, 6755 129 D1
Barnesville MN, 2563 19 F4
Barnesville OH, 4193 101 F1
Barneveld WI, 1231 74 A3
Barnhart MO, 5682 98 A4
Barnsboro NJ, 2500 146 C4
Barnsdall OK, 1243 51 F1
Barnstable MA, 45193 151 F3
Barnstable Co. MA, 215888 151 E4
Barnum MN, 613 64 C4
Bar Nunn WY, 2213 33 D1
Barnwell SC, 4750 130 B1
Barnwell Co. SC, 22621 130 B1
Baroda MI, 873 89 E1
Barrackville WV, 1302 102 A1
Barre MA, 1009 150 B1
Barre VT, 9052 81 E2
Barren Co. KY, 42173 110 A2
Barre Plains MA, 1200 150 B1
Barrett TX, 3199 132 B3
Barrington IL, 10327 203 B2
Barrington NH, 8576 81 F4
Barrington NJ, 6983 248 D4
Barrington RI, 16310 151 D3
Barrington Hills IL, 4209 203 A2
Barron WI, 3423 67 E3
Barron Co. WI, 45870 67 E3
Barrow AK, 4212 154 C1
Barrow Co. GA, 69367 121 D3
Barry IL, 1318 97 F1
Barry Co. MI, 59173 75 F4
Barry Co. MO, 35597 106 C2
Barstow CA, 22639 53 D1
Barstow MD, 750 144 C4
Bartelso IL, 595 98 B3
Bartholomew Co. IN, 76794 99 F2
Bartlesville OK, 35750 51 F1
Bartlett IL, 41208 203 A3
Bartlett NE, 117 35 D2
Bartlett NH, 373 81 F2
Bartlett TN, 54613 118 B1
Bartlett TX, 1623 61 E1
Barton MD, 457 102 C1
Barton VT, 737 81 E1
Barton Co. KS, 27674 43 D3
Barton Co. MO, 12402 106 B1
Bartonsville MD, 1451 144 A1
Bartonville IL, 6471 88 B3
Bartow FL, 17298 140 C2
Bartow Co. GA, 100157 120 B3
Barview OR, 1844 20 A4
Basalt CO, 3857 40 C2
Basalt ID, 394 23 E4
Basehor KS, 4613 96 B2
Basile LA, 1821 133 E2
Basin MT, 212 15 E4
Basin WY, 1285 24 C3
Basin City WA, 1092 13 E4
Baskett KY, 550 99 E4
Basking Ridge NJ, 3600 148 A4
Bassett NE, 619 35 D1
Bassett VA, 1100 112 B2
Bass Harbor ME, 600 83 D2
Bass Lake IN, 1195 89 E2
Bastrop LA, 11365 125 F2
Bastrop TX, 7218 61 E2
Bastrop Co. TX, 74171 61 E2
Basye VA, 1253 102 C3
Batavia IL, 26045 88 C1
Batavia IA, 499 87 E3
Batavia NY, 15465 78 B3
Batavia OH, 1509 100 B2
Batesburg-Leesville SC, 5362 122 A4
Bates Co. MO, 17049 96 B4
Batesville AR, 10248 107 F4
Batesville IN, 6520 100 A2
Batesville MS, 7463 118 B3
Batesville TX, 1068 60 C3
Bath ME, 8514 82 C3
Bath MI, 2083 76 A3
Bath NY, 5786 78 C4
Bath PA, 2693 93 F3
Bath Co. KY, 11591 100 C4
Bath Co. VA, 4731 102 B4
Baton Rouge LA, 229493 134 A2
Battle Creek IA, 713 72 A4
Battle Creek MI, 52347 75 F4
Battle Creek NE, 1207 35 E2
Battlefield MO, 5590 107 D2
Battle Ground IN, 1334 89 E4
Battle Ground WA, 17571 20 C1
Battle Lake MN, 875 19 F4
Battlement Mesa CO, 4471 40 B2
Battle Mtn. NV, 3635 30 A4
Baudette MN, 1106 64 A1
Baumstown PA, 422 146 B2
Bauxite AR, 487 117 E2
Bawcomville LA, 3588 125 E2
Baxley GA, 4400 129 F3
Baxter IA, 1101 87 D1
Baxter MN, 7610 64 A4
Baxter TN, 1365 110 A4
Baxter Co. AR, 41513 107 E4
Baxter Estates NY, 999 241 G2
Baxter Sprs. KS, 4238 106 B2
Bay AR, 1801 108 A4
Bayard IA, 471 86 B1
Bayard NE, 1209 33 F2
Bayard NM, 2328 55 F3
Bayboro NC, 1263 115 D3
Bay City MI, 34932 76 B2
Bay City OR, 1286 20 B2
Bay City TX, 17614 61 F3
Bay Co. FL, 168852 136 C2
Bay Co. MI, 107771 76 B2
Bayfield CO, 2333 40 C4
Bayfield WI, 487 65 D4
Bayfield Co. WI, 15014 65 D4
Bay Harbor Islands FL, 5628 233 C4
Bay Head NJ, 968 147 E3
Bay Hill FL, 4884 246 B3
Baylor Co. TX, 3726 59 D1
Bay Minette AL, 8044 135 E1
Bayonet Pt. FL, 23467 140 B2
Bayonne NJ, 63024 148 B4
Bayou Cane LA, 19355 134 A3
Bayou George FL, 800 136 C2
Bayou Goula LA, 612 134 A2
Bayou La Batre AL, 2558 135 E2
Bayou Vista LA, 4652 134 A3
Bayou Vista TX, 1537 132 B4
Bay Park NY, 2212 241 G5
Bay Pines FL, 2931 266 A3
Bay Pt. CA, 21349 259 D1
Bayport MN, 3471 67 D4
Bayport NY, 8896 149 D4
Bay Ridge MD, 2300 144 C3
Bay St. Louis MS, 9260 134 C2
Bay Shore NY, 26337 149 D4
Bayshore Gardens FL, 16323 266 B5
Bay Side NJ, 1800 147 E4
Bayside WI, 4389 234 D1
Bay Sprs. MS, 1786 126 C3
Baytown TX, 71802 132 B3
Bay View OH, 632 91 D2
Bay Vil. OH, 15651 204 D2
Bayville NJ, 4700 147 E3
Bayville NY, 6669 148 C3
Beach ND, 1019 17 F4
Beach City OH, 1033 91 E3
Beach City TX, 2198 132 B3
Beach Haven NJ, 1170 147 E4
Beach Haven Gardens
NJ, 1200 147 E4
Beach Haven Terrace NJ, 1100 147 E4
Beachwood NJ, 11045 147 E3
Beachwood OH, 11953 204 G2
Beacon IA, 494 87 D2
Beacon NY, 15541 148 B1
Beacon Falls CT, 5596 149 D1
Beadle Co. SD, 17398 27 D3
Bealeton VA, 4435 103 D3
Beals ME, 618 83 E2
Bean Sta. TN, 2826 111 D3
Bear DE, 19371 145 E1
Bear Creek AL, 1070 119 E3
Bearden AR, 966 117 E4
Beardstown IL, 6123 98 A1
Bear Lake Co. ID, 5986 31 F2
Bear River City UT, 853 31 E3
Beasley TX, 641 132 A4
Beatrice AL, 301 127 F4
Beatrice NE, 12459 35 F4
Beatty NV, 1010 45 F2
Beattyville KY, 1307 110 C1
Beatyestown NJ, 3223 94 A4
Beaufort NC, 4039 115 E4
Beaufort SC, 12361 130 C2
Beaufort Co. NC, 47759 113 F4
Beaufort Co. SC, 162233 130 C3
Beaumont CA, 36877 53 D2
Beaumont MS, 951 135 D1
Beaumont TX, 118296 132 C3
Beaumont Place TX, 4500 220 D2
Beauregard Par. LA, 35654 133 D2
Beaver OK, 1515 50 C1
Beaver PA, 4531 91 F3
Beaver UT, 3112 39 D3
Beaver WV, 1308 111 F1
Beaver City NE, 609 42 C1
Beaver Co. OK, 5636 50 C1
Beaver Co. PA, 170539 91 F3
Beaver Co. UT, 6629 39 D3
Beavercreek OH, 45193 100 C1
Beaver Crossing NE, 403 35 E4
Beaverdale PA, 1035 92 B4
Beaver Dam KY, 3409 109 E1
Beaver Dam WI, 16214 74 B2
Beaver Falls PA, 8987 91 F3
Beaverhead Co. MT, 9246 23 D2
Beaver Meadows PA, 869 93 E3
Beaver Sprs. PA, 674 93 D3
Beaverton MI, 1071 76 A2
Beaverton OR, 89803 20 C2
Beavertown PA, 965 93 D3
Bechtelsville PA, 942 146 B1
Beckemeyer IL, 1040 98 B3
Becker MN, 4538 66 C3
Becker Co. MN, 32504 19 F3
Beckett NJ, 4847 146 C4
Beckham Co. OK, 22119 50 C3
Beckley WV, 17614 111 F1
Beckville TX, 847 124 C3
Bedford IN, 13413 99 F3
Bedford IA, 1440 86 B3
Bedford KY, 599 100 A3
Bedford MA, 13320 151 D1
Bedford NH, 21203 95 D1
Bedford NY, 1834 148 C2
Bedford OH, 13074 204 G3
Bedford PA, 2841 102 C1
Bedford TX, 46979 207 B2
Bedford VA, 6222 112 B1
Bedford Co. PA, 49762 92 C4
Bedford Co. TN, 45058 120 A1
Bedford Co. VA, 68676 112 B1
Bedford Hts. OH, 10751 204 G3
Bedford Hills NY, 3001 148 C2
Bedford Park IL, 580 203 D5
Beebe AR, 7315 117 F2
Bee Cave TX, 3925 61 E1
Beech Bottom WV, 523 91 F4
Beech Creek PA, 701 93 D3
Beecher IL, 4359 89 D2
Beech Grove IN, 14192 99 F1
Beechwood Vil. KY, 1324 230 E1
Bee Co. TX, 31861 61 E4
Beemer NE, 678 35 F2
Bee Ridge FL, 9598 140 B4
Beersheba Sprs. TN, 477 120 A1
Beesleys Pt. NJ, 1400 147 F4
Beeville TX, 12863 61 E4
Beggs OK, 1321 51 F2
Bel Air MD, 10120 145 D1
Belcamp MD, 1900 145 D1
Belchertown MA, 2899 150 A1
Belcourt ND, 2078 18 C1
Belding MI, 5757 75 F3
Belen NM, 7269 48 C4
Belfair WA, 3931 12 C3
Belfast ME, 6668 82 C2
Belfast NY, 837 78 B4
Belfast PA, 1257 93 F3
Belfield ND, 800 18 A4
Belford NJ, 1768 147 E1
Belfry MT, 218 24 B2
Belgium WI, 2245 75 D2
Belgrade MN, 740 66 B3
Belgrade MT, 7389 23 F1
Belgrade Lakes ME, 350 82 B2
Belhaven NC, 1688 115 E3
Belinda City TN, 2100 109 F4
Belington WV, 1921 102 A2
Belknap Co. NH, 60088 81 F4
Bell CA, 35477 228 D3
Bellair FL, 16539 222 C4
Bellaire MI, 1086 69 F4
Bellaire OH, 4278 101 F1
Bellaire TX, 16855 132 A3
Bellamy AL, 543 127 E2
Bella Villa MO, 729 256 B3
Bella Vista AR, 26461 106 C3
Bella Vista CA, 2781 28 C4
Bellbrook OH, 6943 100 C1
Bell Buckle TN, 500 119 F1
Bell Co. KY, 28691 110 C3
Bell Co. TX, 310235 61 E1
Belle MO, 1545 97 F4
Belle WV, 1260 101 F4
Belleair FL, 3869 140 B2
Belleair Beach FL, 1560 140 B2
Belleair Bluffs FL, 2031 266 A2
Belle Ctr. OH, 813 90 C4
Belle Chasse LA, 12679 134 B3
Bellefontaine OH, 13370 90 B4
Bellefontaine Neighbors
MO, 10860 256 C1
Bellefonte AR, 454 107 D3
Bellefonte DE, 1193 146 B4
Bellefonte KY, 888 101 D3
Bellefonte PA, 6187 92 C3
Belle Fourche SD, 5594 25 F3
Belle Glade FL, 17467 143 E1
Belle Haven VA, 532 114 B3
Belle Isle FL, 5988 141 D1
Bellemeade KY, 865 230 F2
Belle Plaine IA, 2534 87 E1
Belle Plaine KS, 1681 43 E4
Belle Plaine MN, 6661 66 C4
Belle Rose LA, 1902 134 A3
Bellerose NY, 1193 241 G3
Bellerose Terrace NY, 2198 241 G3
Belle Terre NY, 792 149 D3
Belle Vernon PA, 1093 92 A4
Belleview FL, 4492 139 D4
Belleville IL, 44478 98 B3
Belleville KS, 1991 43 E1
Belleville MI, 3991 90 C1
Belleville NJ, 35926 148 B4
Belleville PA, 1827 92 C4
Belleville WI, 2385 74 B3
Bellevue ID, 2287 22 C4
Bellevue IL, 1978 88 B3
Bellevue IA, 2191 74 A4
Bellevue KY, 5955 204 B3
Bellevue MI, 1282 76 A4
Bellevue NE, 50137 86 A2
Bellevue OH, 8202 204 B3
Bellevue PA, 8370 92 A4
Bellevue WA, 122363 12 C3
Bellevue WI, 14570 74 C1
Bellflower CA, 76616 228 D3
Bell Gardens CA, 42072 228 D3
Bellingham MA, 4854 150 C2
Bellingham WA, 80885 12 C1
Bellmawr NJ, 11583 146 C3
Bellmead TX, 9901 59 E4
Bellows Falls VT, 3148 81 E4
Bellport NY, 2084 149 D4
Bells TN, 2437 108 C4
Bells TX, 1392 59 F1
Bellview FL, 23355 247 A1
Bellville OH, 1918 91 D3
Bellville TX, 4097 61 F2
Bellwood IL, 19071 203 C4
Bellwood NE, 435 35 E3
Bellwood PA, 1828 92 C4
Bellwood VA, 6352 254 B3
Belmar NJ, 5794 147 F2
Belmond IA, 2376 72 C3
Belmont CA, 25835 259 B5
Belmont MA, 24729 151 D1
Belmont MS, 2021 119 D3
Belmont NH, 1301 81 F4

Entries in **bold black** indicate counties or parishes.
Entries in **bold color** indicate cities with detailed inset maps.

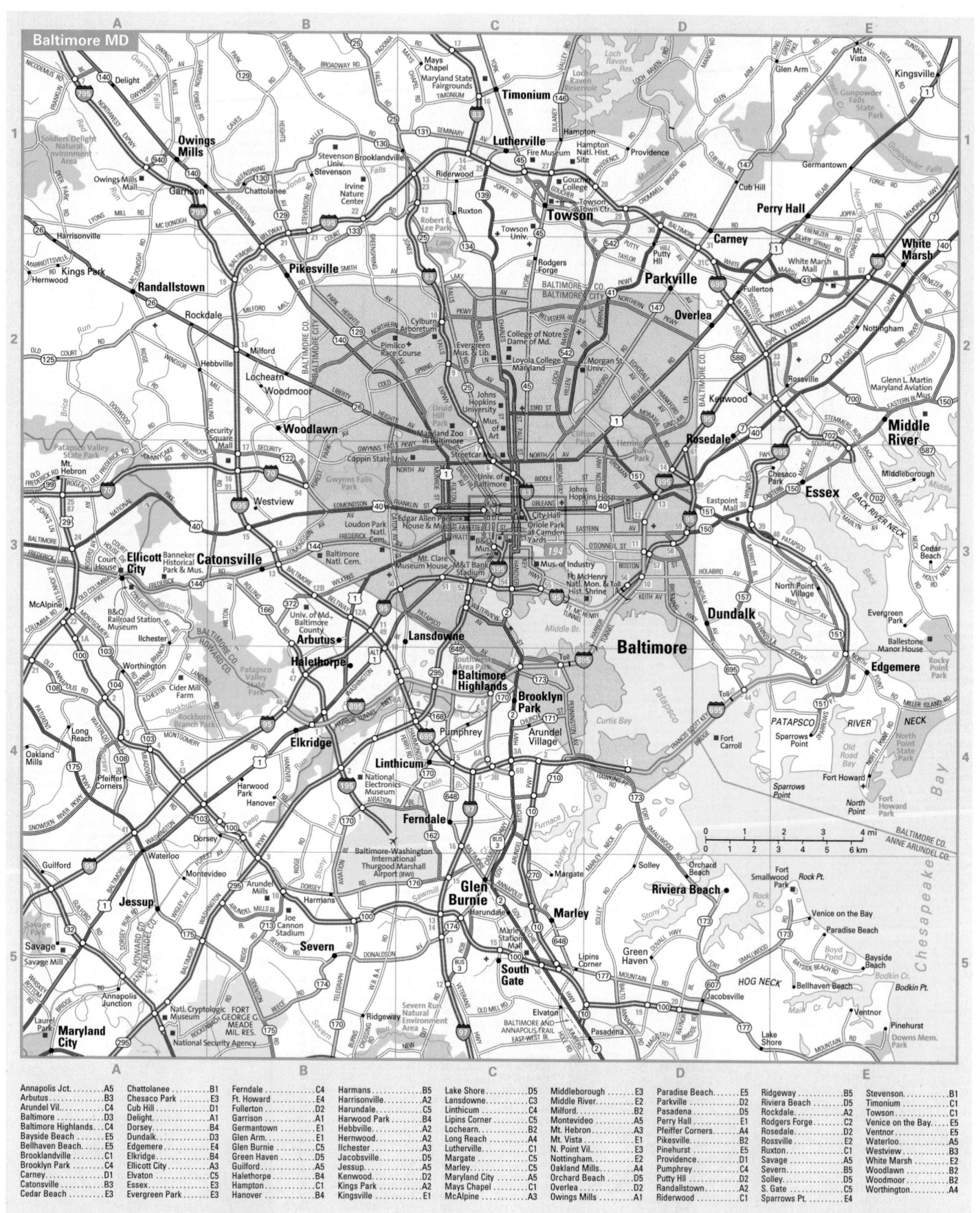

Baltimore MD

194
Belmont–Blairstown

Figures after entries indicate population, page number, and grid reference.

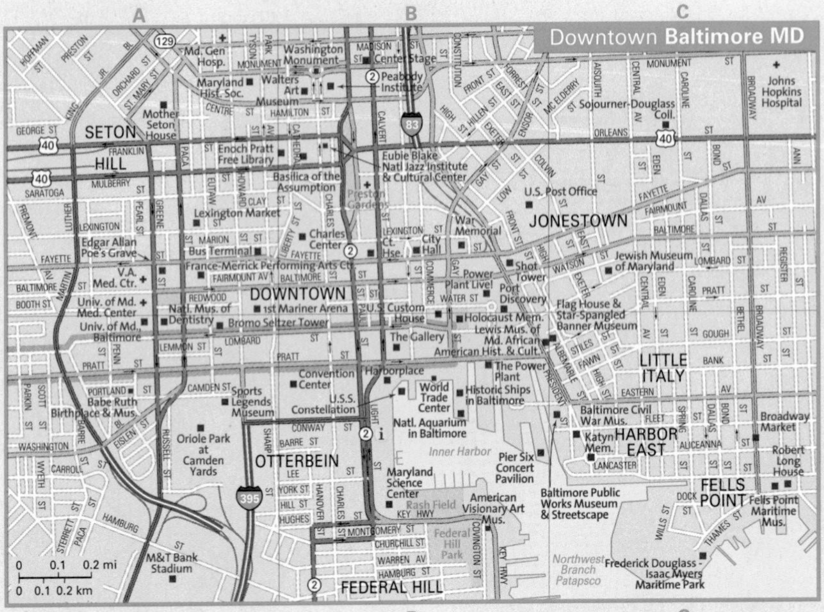
Downtown Baltimore MD
A
B
C
1
2
SETON HILL
DOWNTOWN
JONESTOWN
LITTLE ITALY
HARBOR EAST
FELLS POINT
OTTERBEIN
FEDERAL HILL
Inner Harbor
Johns Hopkins Hospital
Oriole Park at Camden Yards
M&T Bank Stadium
Washington Monument
Lexington Market
Northwest Branch Patapsco
0 0.1 0.2 mi
0 0.1 0.2 km

POINTS OF INTEREST

1st Mariner Arena ... A1
American Visionary Art Museum ... B2
Babe Ruth Birthplace & Museum ... A2
Baltimore Civil War Museum ... C2
Baltimore Maritime Museum ... B2
Baltimore Public Works Mus. & Streetscape .. C2
Basilica of the Assumption ... B1
Broadway Market ... C2
Bromo Seltzer Tower ... A2
Bus Terminal ... A1
Charles Center ... B1
Convention Center ... B2
Edgar Allan Poe's Grave ... A1
Enoch Pratt Free Library ... A1
Eubie Blake Natl. Jazz Institute & Cult. Ctr. ... B1
Fells Point Maritime Museum ... C2
Flag House & Star-Spangled Banner Mus. ... C2
France-Merrick Performing Arts Center ... A1
The Gallery ... B2
Harborplace ... B2
Jewish Mus. of Maryland ... C1
Lewis Mus. of MD. African-American History & Culture ... B2
Lexington Market ... A1
M&T Bank Stadium ... A2
Maryland Historical Society ... A1
Maryland Science Center ... B2
Mother Seton House ... A1
Natl. Aquarium in Baltimore ... B2
Oriole Park at Camden Yards ... A2
Peabody Institute ... B1
Pier Six Concert Pavilion ... B2
Port Discovery ... B1
Power Plant Live ... B1
Robert Long House ... C2
Shot Tower ... B1
Sports Legends Museum ... A2
U.S. Custom House ... B2
Univ. of Maryland, Baltimore ... A2
U.S.S. Constellation ... B2
Walters Art Museum ... B1
War Memorial ... B1
Washington Monument ... B1
World Trade Center ... B2

Belmont NY, 969 ... 92 C1
Belmont NC, 10076 ... 122 A1
Belmont WV, 903 ... 101 F2
Belmont WI, 986 ... 74 A4
Belmont Corner ME, 375 ... 82 C2
Belmont Co. OH, 70400 ... 101 F1
Bel-Nor MO, 1499 ... 256 B2
Beloit KS, 3835 ... 43 E1
Beloit OH, 978 ... 91 F3
Beloit WI, 36966 ... 74 B4
Belpre OH, 6441 ... 101 E2
Bel-Ridge MO, 2737 ... 256 B2
Belt MT, 597 ... 15 F3
Belton KY, 500 ... 109 E2
Belton MO, 23116 ... 96 B3
Belton SC, 4134 ... 121 E3
Belton TX, 18216 ... 59 E4
Beltrami Co. MN, 44442 ... 64 A2
Beltsville MD, 16772 ... 144 B3
Belvedere CA, 2068 ... 259 B2
Belvedere SC, 5792 ... 121 F4
Belvedere Park GA, 15152 ... 190 E4
Belvidere IL, 25585 ... 74 B4
Belvidere NJ, 2681 ... 93 F3
Belwood NC, 950 ... 121 F1
Belzoni MS, 2235 ... 126 B1
Bement IL, 1730 ... 98 C1
Bemidji MN, 13431 ... 64 A3
Bemiss GA, 1500 ... 137 F1
Benavides TX, 1362 ... 63 E2
Ben Avon PA, 1781 ... 250 A1
Benbrook TX, 21234 ... 207 A3
Bend OR, 76639 ... 21 D3
Bendersville PA, 641 ... 103 E1
Benewah Co. ID, 9285 ... 14 B3
Benham KY, 500 ... 111 D2
Ben Hill Co. GA, 17634 ... 129 E3
Benicia CA, 26997 ... 36 B3
Benjamin TX, 258 ... 58 C1
Benkelman NE, 953 ... 42 B1
Benld IL, 1556 ... 98 B2
Ben Lomond CA, 6234 ... 44 A2
Bennet NE, 719 ... 35 F4
Bennett CO, 2308 ... 41 E1
Bennett Co. SD, 3431 ... 26 B4
Bennettsville SC, 9069 ... 122 C2
Bennington KS, 672 ... 43 E2
Bennington NE, 1458 ... 35 F3
Bennington NH, 381 ... 81 E4
Bennington VT, 9074 ... 94 C1
Bennington Co. VT, 37125 ... 81 D4
Benoit MS, 477 ... 118 A4
Bensenville IL, 18352 ... 203 C4
Bensley VA, 5819 ... 113 E1
Benson AZ, 5105 ... 55 D3
Benson MD, 950 ... 144 C1
Benson MN, 3240 ... 66 A3
Benson NC, 3311 ... 123 D1
Benson Co. ND, 6660 ... 19 D2
Bent Co. CO, 6499 ... 41 F3
Bent Creek NC, 1287 ... 121 E1
Bentleyville OH, 864 ... 204 G3
Bentleyville PA, 2581 ... 92 A4
Benton AR, 30681 ... 117 E2
Benton IL, 7087 ... 98 C4
Benton KS, 880 ... 43 F4
Benton KY, 4349 ... 109 D2
Benton LA, 1948 ... 124 C2
Benton ME, 2557 ... 82 C2
Benton MO, 863 ... 108 B2
Benton PA, 824 ... 93 E2
Benton TN, 1385 ... 120 C1
Benton WI, 973 ... 74 A4
Benton City WA, 3038 ... 21 E1
Benton Co. AR, 221339 ... 106 B3
Benton Co. IN, 8854 ... 89 D3
Benton Co. IA, 26076 ... 87 E1
Benton Co. MN, 38451 ... 66 C2
Benton Co. MS, 8729 ... 118 C2
Benton Co. MO, 19056 ... 97 D4
Benton Co. OR, 85579 ... 20 B3
Benton Co. TN, 16489 ... 109 D4
Benton Co. WA, 175177 ... 21 E1
Benton Harbor MI, 10038 ... 89 E1
Bentonia MS, 440 ... 126 B2
Bentonville AR, 35301 ... 106 C3
Benzie Co. MI, 17525 ... 69 F4
Benzonia MI, 497 ... 69 E4
Berea KY, 13561 ... 110 C1
Berea OH, 19093 ... 91 E2
Berea SC, 14295 ... 217 A2
Beresford SD, 2005 ... 35 F1
Bergen NY, 1176 ... 78 B3
Bergen Co. NJ, 905116 ... 148 B3
Bergenfield NJ, 26764 ... 148 B3
Bergholz OH, 664 ... 91 F4
Bergman AR, 439 ... 107 D3
Berino NM, 1441 ... 56 C3
Berkeley CA, 112580 ... 36 B4
Berkeley IL, 5209 ... 203 C4
Berkeley MO, 8978 ... 256 B1
Berkeley RI, 2800 ... 150 C3
Berkeley Co. SC, 177843 ... 131 D1
Berkeley Co. WV, 104169 ... 103 D2
Berkeley Hts. NJ, 13183 ... 148 A4
Berkeley Sprs. WV, 624 ... 102 C1
Berkley MA, 5749 ... 151 D3
Berkley MI, 14970 ... 210 B2
Berks Co. PA, 411442 ... 146 B1
Berkshire CT, 950 ... 149 D2
Berkshire Co. MA, 131219 ... 94 C2
Berlin CT, 19590 ... 149 E1
Berlin GA, 551 ... 137 F1
Berlin MD, 4485 ... 114 C2
Berlin MA, 2866 ... 150 C1
Berlin NH, 10051 ... 81 F2
Berlin NJ, 7588 ... 147 D3
Berlin OH, 898 ... 91 E4
Berlin PA, 2104 ... 102 C1
Berlin WI, 5524 ... 74 B1
Berlin Hts. OH, 714 ... 91 D2
Bermuda Run NC, 1725 ... 112 A4
Bernalillo NM, 8320 ... 48 C3
Bernalillo Co. NM, 662564 ... 48 C3
Bernardston MA, 2155 ... 94 C1
Bernardsville NJ, 7707 ... 148 A4
Berne IN, 3999 ... 90 A3
Bernice LA, 1689 ... 125 E1
Bernice OK, 562 ... 106 B3
Bernie MO, 1958 ... 108 B3
Bernstadt KY, 475 ... 110 C2
Bernville PA, 955 ... 146 A1
Berrien Co. GA, 19286 ... 129 E4
Berrien Co. MI, 156813 ... 89 E1
Berrien Sprs. MI, 1800 ... 89 E1
Berry AL, 1148 ... 119 E4
Berryville AR, 5356 ... 106 C3
Berryville TX, 975 ... 124 A3
Berryville VA, 4185 ... 103 D2
Berthold ND, 454 ... 18 B2
Berthoud CO, 5105 ... 33 E4
Bertie Co. NC, 21282 ... 113 F4
Bertram IA, 294 ... 87 F1
Bertram TX, 1353 ... 61 D1
Bertrand MI, 1700 ... 89 F1
Bertrand MO, 821 ... 108 B2
Bertrand NE, 750 ... 35 D4
Berwick LA, 4946 ... 134 A3
Berwick ME, 2187 ... 82 A4
Berwick PA, 10477 ... 93 E3
Berwyn IL, 56657 ... 89 D1
Berwyn PA, 3631 ... 146 B3
Berwyn Hts. MD, 3123 ... 270 E2
Bessemer AL, 27456 ... 127 F1
Bessemer MI, 1905 ... 65 E4
Bessemer PA, 1111 ... 91 F3
Bessemer City NC, 5340 ... 122 A1
Bethalto IL, 9521 ... 98 B3
Bethany CT, 5473 ... 149 D1
Bethany IL, 1352 ... 98 C1
Bethany MO, 3292 ... 86 C4
Bethany OK, 19051 ... 51 E3
Bethany WV, 1036 ... 91 F4
Bethany Beach DE, 1060 ... 145 F4
Bethel AK, 6080 ... 154 B3
Bethel CT, 9549 ... 148 C2
Bethel DE, 171 ... 145 E4
Bethel ME, 2411 ... 82 B2
Bethel NC, 1577 ... 113 E4
Bethel OH, 2711 ... 100 C2
Bethel VT, 569 ... 81 E3
Bethel VA, 500 ... 103 D3
Bethel Acres OK, 2895 ... 51 F3
Bethel Hts. AR, 2372 ... 106 C3
Bethel Park PA, 32313 ... 92 A4
Bethel Sprs. TN, 718 ... 119 D1
Bethesda MD, 60858 ... 144 B3
Bethesda OH, 1256 ... 101 F1
Bethlehem CT, 3596 ... 149 D1
Bethlehem GA, 601 ... 121 D4
Bethlehem MD, 600 ... 145 D4
Bethlehem NH, 972 ... 81 F2
Bethlehem NC, 4214 ... 111 F4
Bethlehem PA, 74982 ... 146 C1
Bethlehem Ctr. NY, 2500 ... 188 D3
Bethpage NY, 16429 ... 148 C4
Betmar Acres FL, 4000 ... 140 C2
Bettendorf IA, 33217 ... 88 A2
Bettsville OH, 661 ... 90 C2
Beulah CO, 1164 ... 41 E3
Beulah MI, 342 ... 69 E4
Beulah MS, 348 ... 118 A4
Beulah ND, 3121 ... 18 B3
Beulaville NC, 1296 ... 123 E2
Beverly MA, 39502 ... 151 F1
Beverly NJ, 2577 ... 147 D3
Beverly OH, 1313 ... 101 E1
Beverly WV, 702 ... 102 B3
Beverly Beach FL, 338 ... 139 E4
Beverly Beach MD, 1600 ... 144 C3
Beverly Hills CA, 34109 ... 52 C2
Beverly Hills FL, 8445 ... 140 B1
Beverly Hills MI, 10267 ... 210 B2
Beverly Hills MO, 574 ... 256 B2
Beverly Shores IN, 613 ... 89 E2
Bevier MO, 718 ... 97 E1
Bevil Oaks TX, 1274 ... 132 C2
Bevis OH, 5700 ... 204 A1
Bexar Co. TX, 1714773 ... 61 D2
Bexley OH, 13057 ... 206 C2
Bibb Co. AL, 22915 ... 127 F1
Bibb Co. GA, 155547 ... 129 D2
Bicknell IN, 2915 ... 99 E3
Bicknell UT, 327 ... 39 E3
Biddeford ME, 21277 ... 82 B4
Bienville Par. LA, 14353 ... 125 D2
Big Bear City CA, 12304 ... 53 D2
Big Bear Lake CA, 5019 ... 53 D2
Big Beaver PA, 1970 ... 91 F3
Big Bend WI, 1290 ... 74 C3
Big Chimney WV, 627 ... 101 F3
Big Coppitt Key FL, 2458 ... 143 D4
Big Delta AK, 591 ... 154 C2
Big Flats NY, 5277 ... 93 D1
Bigfork MT, 4270 ... 15 D2
Biggs CA, 1707 ... 36 B2
Big Horn Co. MT, 12865 ... 24 C2
Big Horn Co. WY, 11668 ... 24 C3
Big Lake MN, 443 ... 66 C3
Big Lake TX, 2936 ... 58 A4
Big Lake WA, 1835 ... 12 C2
Biglerville PA, 1200 ... 103 E1
Big Oak Flat CA, 3388 ... 37 D4
Big Pine CA, 1756 ... 37 E4
Big Pine Key FL, 4252 ... 143 D4
Big Piney WY, 552 ... 32 A1
Big Rapids MI, 10601 ... 75 F2
Big River CA, 1327 ... 46 B4
Big Run PA, 624 ... 92 B3
Big Sandy MT, 598 ... 16 B2
Big Sandy TN, 557 ... 109 D3
Big Sandy TX, 1343 ... 124 B2
Big Sky MT, 2308 ... 23 F2
Big Spr. TX, 27282 ... 58 A3
Big Sprs. NE, 400 ... 34 B3
Big Stone City SD, 467 ... 27 F2
Big Stone Co. MN, 5269 ... 27 F2
Big Stone Gap VA, 5614 ... 111 E2
Big Timber MT, 1641 ... 24 A1
Big Water UT, 475 ... 47 D1
Big Wells TX, 697 ... 60 C4
Billerica MA, 40243 ... 95 E1
Billings MO, 1035 ... 106 C2
Billings MT, 104170 ... 24 C1
Billings NY, 800 ... 148 B1
Billings OK, 509 ... 51 E1
Billings Co. ND, 783 ... 18 A3
Billington Hts. NY, 1685 ... 78 B4
Biloxi MS, 44054 ... 135 D2
Biltmore Forest NC, 1343 ... 121 E1
Bingen PA, 1300 ... 189 B2
Binger OK, 672 ... 51 D3
Bingham ME, 758 ... 82 B1
Bingham Co. ID, 45607 ... 23 E4
Bingham Farms MI, 1111 ... 210 B2
Binghamton NY, 47376 ... 93 E1
Biola CA, 1623 ... 44 C2
Birch Bay WA, 8413 ... 12 C1
Birch Run MI, 1555 ... 76 B3
Birch Tree MO, 679 ... 107 F2
Birchwood Vil. MN, 870 ... 235 E1
Bird City KS, 447 ... 42 B1
Bird Island MN, 1042 ... 66 B4
Birdsboro PA, 5163 ... 146 B2
Birmingham AL, 212237 ... 119 F4
Birmingham MI, 20103 ... 76 C4
Birnamwood WI, 818 ... 68 B4
Biron WI, 839 ... 74 A1
Bisbee AZ, 5575 ... 55 E4
Biscayne Park FL, 3055 ... 233 B4
Biscoe AR, 476 ... 117 F2
Biscoe NC, 1700 ... 122 C1
Bishop CA, 3879 ... 37 E4
Bishop TX, 3134 ... 63 F2
Bishopville SC, 3471 ... 122 B3
Bismarck MO, 1546 ... 108 A1
Bismarck ND, 61272 ... 18 C4
Bison SD, 333 ... 26 A2
Bithlo FL, 8268 ... 141 D1
Bitter Sprs. AZ, 452 ... 47 D1
Biwabik MN, 969 ... 64 C3
Bixby OK, 20884 ... 106 A4
Blackbird DE, 700 ... 145 E1
Black Canyon City AZ, 2837 ... 47 D4
Black Creek NC, 769 ... 123 E1
Black Creek WI, 1316 ... 68 C4
Black Diamond WA, 4151 ... 12 C3
Blackduck MN, 785 ... 64 A3
Black Eagle MT, 904 ... 15 F3
Black Earth WI, 1338 ... 74 A3
Blackfoot ID, 11899 ... 31 E1
Blackford Co. IN, 12766 ... 90 A4
Black Forest CO, 13116 ... 41 E2
Blackhawk SD, 2892 ... 26 A3
Black Hawk Co. IA, 131090 ... 73 E4
Black Jack MO, 6929 ... 256 B1
Black Lick PA, 1462 ... 92 B4
Blacklick Estates OH, 8682 ... 206 C3
Black Mtn. NC, 7848 ... 121 E1
Black River NY, 1348 ... 79 E1
Black River Falls WI, 3622 ... 73 F1
Black Rock AR, 662 ... 107 F4
Black Rock NM, 1323 ... 48 A3
Blacksburg SC, 1848 ... 122 A1
Blacksburg VA, 42620 ... 112 A2
Blackshear GA, 3445 ... 129 F4
Blackstone MA, 9026 ... 150 C2
Blackstone VA, 3621 ... 113 D2
Blackville SC, 2406 ... 130 B1
Blackwell OK, 7092 ... 51 E1
Blackwells GA, 2200 ... 120 C3
Blackwood NJ, 4545 ... 146 C3
Bladenboro NC, 1750 ... 123 D3
Bladen Co. NC, 35190 ... 123 D2
Bladensburg MD, 9148 ... 270 E3
Blades DE, 1241 ... 145 E4
Blaine ME, 301 ... 85 E2
Blaine MN, 57186 ... 67 D3
Blaine TN, 1856 ... 110 C4
Blaine WA, 4684 ... 12 C1
Blaine Co. ID, 21376 ... 23 D4
Blaine Co. MT, 6491 ... 16 B2
Blaine Co. NE, 478 ... 34 C2
Blaine Co. OK, 11943 ... 51 D2
Blair NE, 7990 ... 35 F3
Blair OK, 818 ... 51 D4
Blair WI, 1366 ... 73 F1
Blair Co. PA, 127089 ... 92 C4
Blairs VA, 916 ... 112 C3
Blairstown IA, 692 ... 87 E1

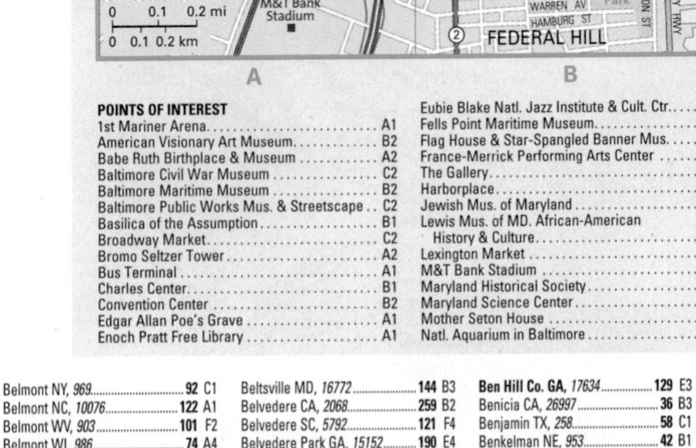
Baton Rouge LA
Baton Rouge Metropolitan Airport (BTR)
Southern University & A&M College
Central
Merrydale
Baton Rouge
Port Allen
Westminster
Inniswold
Mall of Louisiana
Independence Park
City Park
University Lake
Tiger Stadium
Louisiana State University & A&M Coll.
Magnolia Mound Plantation
Belle of Baton Rouge Casino
0 1 2 mi
0 1 2 3 km

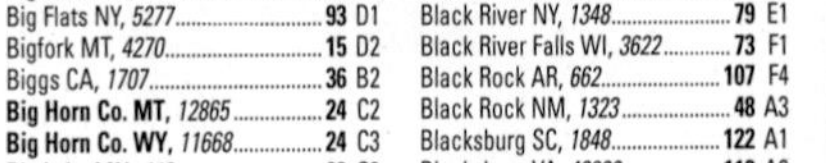
Billings MT
Billings
Billings Logan International Airport (BIL)
Yellowstone Co. Museum
Rocky Mountain College
Alberta Bair Theater
Moss Mansion
Yellowstone Art Mus.
Western Heritage Ctr.
Pioneer Park
Central Park
Amend Park
0 0.5 1 mi
0 0.5 1 1.5 km

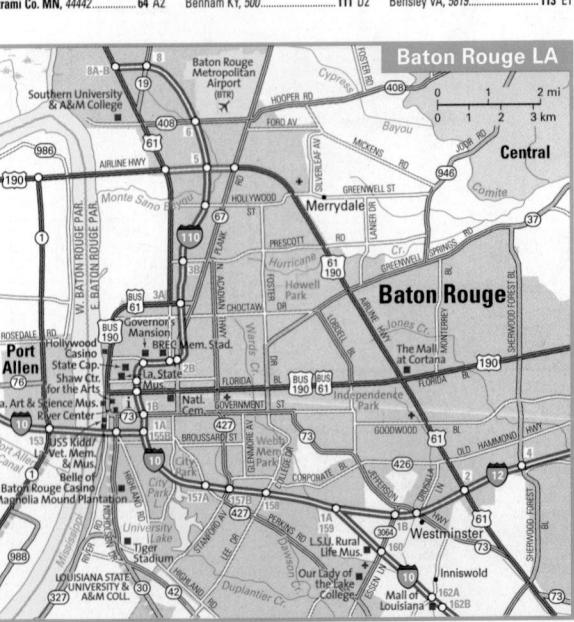

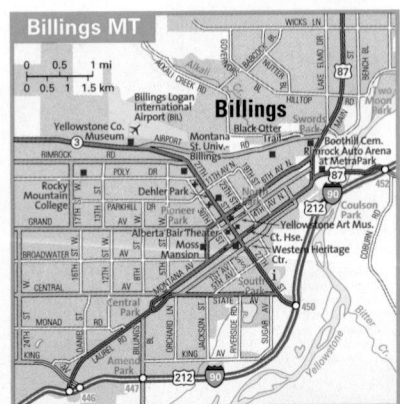

Entries in **bold black** indicate counties or parishes.
Entries in **bold color** indicate cities with detailed inset maps.

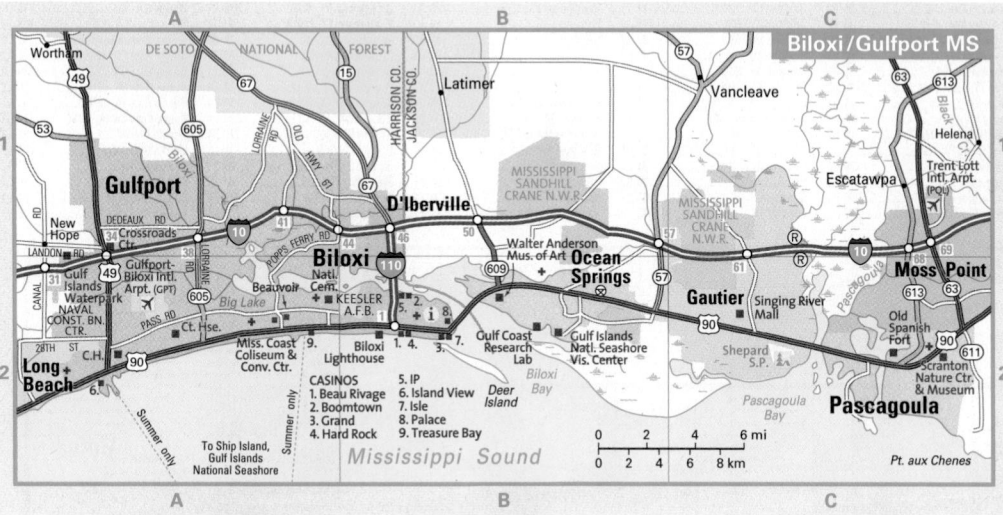

Birmingham AL

196
Bowers – Burgettstown

Figures after entries indicate population, page number, and grid reference.

Bowers DE, 335 145 F3
Bowie AZ, 449 55 E3
Bowie MD, 54727 144 C3
Bowie TX, 5218 59 E1
Bowie Co. TX, 92565 116 B4
Bowleys Quarters MD, 6755 144 C2
Bowling Green FL, 2930 140 C3
Bowling Green KY, 58067 109 F2
Bowling Green MO, 5334 97 F2
Bowling Green OH, 30028 90 C2
Bowling Green VA, 1111 103 D4
Bowman GA, 862 121 E3
Bowman ND, 1650 25 F1
Bowman SC, 968 130 C1
Bowman Co. ND, 3151 25 F1
Bow Mar CO, 866 209 B4
Boxborough MA, 4996 150 C1
Box Butte Co. NE, 11308 34 A2
Box Elder MT, 87 16 B2
Box Elder SD, 7800 26 A3
Box Elder Co. UT, 49975 31 D3
Boxford MA, 2339 151 F1
Boyce LA, 1004 125 E4
Boyce VA, 589 103 D2
Boyceville WI, 1086 67 E3
Boyd TX, 1207 59 E2
Boyd WI, 552 67 F4
Boyd Co. KY, 49542 101 D4
Boyd Co. NE, 2099 35 D1
Boyden IA, 707 35 F1
Boydton VA, 431 113 D3
Boyertown PA, 4055 146 B2
Boyette FL, 5895 140 C3
Boykins VA, 564 113 E3
Boyle MS, 650 118 A4
Boyle Co. KY, 28432 110 B1
Boyne City MI, 3735 70 B3
Boynton Beach FL, 68217 143 F1
Boys Town NE, 745 245 A2
Bozeman MT, 37280 23 F1
Braceville IL, 793 88 C2
Bracken Co. KY, 8488 100 C3
Brackettville TX, 1688 60 B3
Bradbury CA, 1048 228 E2
Braddock PA, 2159 250 C2
Braddock Hts. MD, 2608 144 A1
Braddock Hills PA, 1880 250 C2
Bradenton FL, 49546 140 B3
Bradenton Beach FL, 1171 140 B3
Bradford AR, 759 117 F1
Bradford IL, 768 88 B2
Bradford NH, 356 81 E4
Bradford OH, 1842 90 B4
Bradford PA, 8770 92 B1
Bradford RI, 1406 150 C4
Bradford TN, 1048 108 C4
Bradford VT, 788 81 E3
Bradford Co. FL, 28520 138 C3
Bradford Co. PA, 62622 93 E2
Bradfordville FL, 1100 137 E2
Bradford Woods PA, 1171 92 A3
Bradley AR, 628 125 D1
Bradley IL, 15895 89 D3
Bradley ME, 1242 83 D1
Bradley WV, 2040 101 F4
Bradley Beach NJ, 4298 147 F2
Bradley Co. AR, 11508 117 E4
Bradley Co. TN, 98963 120 C1
Bradley Jct. FL, 686 140 C3
Bradner OH, 985 90 C2
Brady TX, 5528 58 C4
Braham MN, 1793 67 D2
Braidwood IL, 6191 88 C2
Brainerd MN, 13590 64 B4
Braintree MA, 35744 151 D2
Bramwell WV, 364 111 F1
Branch Co. MI, 45248 90 A1
Branchville AL, 825 119 F4
Branchville NJ, 841 94 A4
Branchville SC, 1024 130 C1
Brandenburg KY, 2643 99 F4
Brandon FL, 103483 140 C2
Brandon MS, 21705 126 B3
Brandon SD, 8785 27 F4
Brandon VT, 1648 81 D3
Brandon WI, 879 74 C2
Brandywine MD, 6719 144 B4
Brandywine Manor PA, 1200 146 B3
Branford CT, 29089 149 D2
Branford FL, 712 138 B3
Branson MO, 10520 107 D3
Brant Beach NJ, 800 147 E4
Brantley AL, 809 128 A4
Brantley Co. GA, 18411 129 F4
Brant Rock MA, 5100 151 E2
Braselton GA, 7511 121 D3
Brasher Falls NY, 669 80 B1
Bratenahl OH, 1197 204 F1
Brattleboro VT, 7414 94 C1
Brawley CA, 24953 53 E4
Braxton Co. WV, 14523 101 F3
Bray OK, 1209 51 E4
Braymer MO, 878 96 C1
Brazil IN, 7912 99 E1
Brazoria TX, 3019 132 A4
Brazoria Co. TX, 313166 132 A4
Brazos Co. TX, 194851 61 F1
Brea CA, 39282 229 F3
Breathitt Co. KY, 13878 111 D1
Breaux Bridge LA, 8139 133 F2
Breckenridge CO, 4540 41 D1
Breckenridge MI, 1328 76 A2
Breckenridge MN, 3386 27 F1
Breckenridge TX, 5780 59 D2
Breckenridge Hills MO, 4746 256 B2
Breckinridge Co. KY, 20059 99 F4
Brecksville OH, 13656 204 F3
Breese IL, 4442 98 B3
Breezy Pt. MD, 800 144 C4
Breezy Pt. MN, 2346 64 B4
Breinigsville PA, 4138 146 B1
Bremen GA, 6227 120 B4
Bremen IN, 4588 89 F2
Bremen KY, 197 109 E1
Bremen OH, 1425 101 D1
Bremer Co. IA, 24276 73 E3
Bremerton WA, 37729 12 C3
Bremond TX, 929 59 F4
Brenham TX, 15716 61 F2
Brent AL, 4947 127 F1
Brent FL, 21804 135 F2
Brentsville VA, 650 144 A4
Brentwood CA, 51481 36 B3
Brentwood MD, 3046 270 E2
Brentwood MO, 8055 256 B2
Brentwood NY, 60664 149 D4
Brentwood PA, 9643 250 B3
Brentwood TN, 37060 109 F4
Bressler PA, 1437 218 C2
Brevard NC, 7609 121 E1
Brevard Co. FL, 543376 141 E2
Brewer ME, 9482 83 D1
Brewerton NY, 4029 79 D3
Brewster MA, 2000 151 F3
Brewster MN, 473 72 A2
Brewster NE, 17 34 C2
Brewster NY, 2390 148 C2
Brewster OH, 2112 91 E3
Brewster WA, 2370 13 E2
Brewster Co. TX, 9232 62 C3
Brewster Hill NY, 2089 148 C1
Brewton AL, 5408 135 F1
Briar TX, 5665 59 E2
Briarcliff TX, 1438 61 D1
Briarcliffe Acres SC, 457 123 D4
Briarcliff Manor NY, 7867 148 B2
Briar Creek PA, 660 93 E3
Briarwood KY, 435 230 F1
Briceville TN, 650 110 C4
Brickerville PA, 1309 146 A2
Bridge City LA, 7706 239 B2
Bridge City TX, 7840 132 C3
Bridgehampton NY, 1756 149 F3
Bridgeport AL, 2418 120 A2
Bridgeport CA, 575 37 E3
Bridgeport CT, 144229 149 D2
Bridgeport IL, 1886 99 D3
Bridgeport MD, 2700 144 A1
Bridgeport MI, 6950 76 B3
Bridgeport NE, 1545 34 A3
Bridgeport NY, 1490 79 E3
Bridgeport PA, 4554 248 A1
Bridgeport TX, 5976 59 E2
Bridgeport WA, 2409 13 E2
Bridgeport WV, 8149 102 A2
Bridger MT, 708 24 B2
Bridgeton MO, 11550 256 B1
Bridgeton NJ, 25349 145 F1
Bridgetown OH, 14407 204 A2
Bridgeview IL, 16446 203 D5
Bridgeville DE, 2048 145 E4
Bridgeville PA, 5148 250 A3
Bridgewater MA, 7841 151 D2
Bridgewater NJ, 44464 147 D1
Bridgewater NY, 470 79 E3
Bridgewater SD, 492 27 E4
Bridgewater VA, 5644 102 C4
Bridgman MI, 2291 89 E1
Bridgton ME, 2071 82 B3
Brielle NJ, 4774 147 E2
Brier WA, 6087 262 B2
Brigantine NJ, 9450 147 F4
Brigham City UT, 17899 31 E3
Bright IN, 5693 100 B2
Brighton AL, 2945 195 D2
Brighton CO, 33352 41 E1
Brighton IL, 2254 98 A2
Brighton IA, 652 87 E2
Brighton MI, 7444 76 B4
Brighton NY, 36609 78 C3
Brighton TN, 2735 118 B1
Brightwaters NY, 3103 149 D4
Brightwood VA, 1001 102 C3
Brilliant AL, 900 119 E3
Brilliant OH, 1482 91 F4
Brillion WI, 3148 74 C1
Brimfield IL, 868 88 B3
Brinckerhoff NY, 2900 148 B1
Brinkley AR, 3188 117 F2
Brinnon WA, 797 12 C3
Brisbane CA, 4282 259 B3
Briscoe Co. TX, 1637 50 B4
Bristol CT, 60477 149 D1
Bristol FL, 996 137 D2
Bristol IN, 1602 89 F1
Bristol NH, 1688 81 F3
Bristol PA, 9726 147 D2
Bristol RI, 22954 151 D3
Bristol SD, 341 27 E2
Bristol TN, 26702 111 E3
Bristol VT, 2030 81 D2
Bristol VA, 17835 111 E3
Bristol WI, 2584 74 C4
Bristol Co. MA, 548285 151 D2
Bristol Co. RI, 49875 151 D3
Bristow OK, 4222 51 F2
Britt IA, 2069 72 C3
Brittany Farms PA, 3695 146 C2
Britton MI, 586 90 B1
Britton SD, 1241 27 E1
Broadalbin NY, 1327 80 C4
Broad Brook CT, 4069 150 A3
Broadmoor CA, 4176 259 B3
Broadus MT, 468 25 E2
Broadview IL, 7932 203 C4
Broadview Hts. OH, 19400 204 F3
Broadwater Co. MT, 5612 15 F4
Broadway NC, 1229 123 D1
Broadway VA, 3691 102 C3
Brock Hall MD, 9552 144 C3
Brockport NY, 8366 78 C3
Brockton MA, 93810 151 D2
Brockton MT, 255 17 E2
Brockway PA, 2072 92 B2
Brocton NY, 1486 78 A4
Brodhead KY, 1211 110 C1
Brodhead WI, 3293 74 B4
Brodheadsville PA, 1800 93 F3
Brogden NC, 2633 123 E1
Broken Arrow OK, 98850 106 A4
Broken Bow NE, 3559 35 D3
Broken Bow OK, 4120 116 B3
Bromley KY, 763 204 A3
Bronson FL, 1113 138 C4
Bronson MI, 2349 90 A1
Bronte TX, 999 58 C3
Bronwood GA, 225 128 C3
Bronx Co. NY, 1385108 148 B4
Brook IN, 997 89 D3
Brookdale SC, 4873 122 A4
Brooke VA, 650 103 D4
Brooke Co. WV, 24069 91 F4
Brookfield CT, 16354 148 C1
Brookfield IL, 18978 203 C5
Brookfield MA, 833 150 B2
Brookfield MO, 4542 97 D1
Brookfield OH, 1288 276 C1
Brookfield WI, 37920 234 B2
Brookfield Ctr. CT, 1800 148 C1
Brookhaven MS, 12513 126 B4
Brookhaven NY, 3451 149 D4
Brookhaven PA, 8006 248 A4
Brookings OR, 6336 28 A2
Brookings SD, 22056 27 F3
Brookings Co. SD, 31965 27 F3
Brookland AR, 1642 108 A4
Brooklandville MD, 2200 193 C1
Brooklawn NJ, 1955 248 C4
Brooklet GA, 1395 130 B2
Brookline MA, 58732 151 D1
Brookline NH, 4991 95 D1
Brooklyn CT, 981 150 B3
Brooklyn IL, 749 256 C2
Brooklyn IN, 1598 99 F1
Brooklyn IA, 1468 87 E1
Brooklyn MI, 1206 90 B1
Brooklyn OH, 11169 204 E2
Brooklyn WI, 1401 74 B3
Brooklyn Ctr. MN, 30104 235 B1
Brooklyn Hts. OH, 1543 204 F2
Brooklyn Park MD, 14373 193 C4
Brooklyn Park MN, 75781 235 B1
Brookneal VA, 1112 112 C2
Brook Park OH, 19212 204 E3
Brookport IL, 984 108 C2
Brooks GA, 524 128 D1
Brooks KY, 2401 100 A4
Brooks ME, 1022 82 C2
Brooks Co. GA, 16243 137 F1
Brooks Co. TX, 7223 63 E3
Brookshire TX, 4702 61 F2
Brookside AL, 1363 195 D1
Brookside DE, 14353 146 B4
Brookside OH, 632 91 F4
Brookside Vil. TX, 1523 220 C4
Brookston IN, 1554 89 E3
Brooksville FL, 7719 140 C1
Brooksville KY, 642 100 C3
Brooksville MS, 1223 127 D1
Brookville IN, 2596 100 A2
Brookville NY, 3465 148 C4
Brookville OH, 5884 100 B1
Brookville PA, 3924 92 B2
Brookwood AL, 1828 127 F1
Broomall PA, 10789 146 C3
Broome Co. NY, 200600 93 F1
Broomfield CO, 55889 41 E1
Broomfield Co. CO, 55889 41 E1
Brooten MN, 743 66 B3
Broussard LA, 8197 133 F2
Broward Co. FL, 1748066 143 E1
Browerville MN, 790 66 B2
Brown City MI, 1325 76 C3
Brown Co. IL, 6937 87 F4
Brown Co. IN, 15242 99 F2
Brown Co. KS, 9984 96 A1
Brown Co. MN, 25893 72 B1
Brown Co. NE, 3145 34 C1
Brown Co. OH, 44846 100 C3
Brown Co. SD, 36531 27 E1
Brown Co. TX, 38106 59 D3
Brown Co. WI, 248007 74 C1
Brown Deer WI, 11999 234 C1
Brownfield TX, 9657 58 A2
Browning MT, 1016 15 E2
Brownsboro TX, 1039 124 A3
Brownsburg IN, 21285 99 F1
Brownsdale MN, 676 73 D2
Browns Mills NJ, 11223 147 D3
Brownstown IL, 759 98 C2
Brownstown IN, 2947 99 F3
Browns Valley MN, 589 27 F1
Brownsville CA, 1069 36 C1
Brownsville KY, 836 109 F2
Brownsville MN, 466 73 F2
Brownsville OR, 1668 20 B3
Brownsville PA, 2331 102 B1
Brownsville TN, 10292 118 C1
Brownsville TX, 175023 63 F4
Brownsville WI, 581 74 C2
Brownton MN, 762 66 C4
Brownville NY, 1119 79 E1
Brownville Jct. ME, 750 84 C4
Brownwood TX, 19288 59 D4
Broxton GA, 1189 129 E4
Broyhill Park VA, 17000 270 B4
Bruce MS, 1939 118 C3
Bruce SD, 204 27 F3
Bruce WI, 779 67 F3
Bruceton TN, 1478 109 D4
Bruceville-Eddy TX, 1475 59 E4
Brule Co. SD, 5255 27 D4
Brundidge AL, 2076 128 B4
Brunson SC, 554 130 B1
Brunswick GA, 15383 139 D1
Brunswick ME, 15175 82 B3
Brunswick MD, 5870 144 A2
Brunswick MO, 858 97 D2
Brunswick OH, 34255 91 E2
Brunswick Co. NC, 107431 123 E3
Brunswick Co. VA, 17434 113 D3
Brush CO, 5463 33 F4
Brush Prairie WA, 2652 20 C1
Brushy OK, 900 116 B1
Brusly LA, 2589 134 A2
Bryan OH, 8545 90 B2
Bryan TX, 76201 61 F1
Bryan Co. GA, 30233 130 B3
Bryan Co. OK, 42416 59 F1
Bryans Road MD, 7244 144 B4
Bryant AR, 16688 117 E2
Bryant SD, 456 27 E3
Bryantville MA, 2600 151 E2
Bryn Athyn PA, 1375 248 D1
Bryn Mawr PA, 3779 146 C3
Bryson TX, 539 59 D2
Bryson City NC, 1424 121 D1
Buchanan GA, 1104 120 B4
Buchanan MI, 4456 89 E1
Buchanan NY, 2230 148 B2
Buchanan VA, 1178 112 B1
Buchanan Co. IA, 20958 73 E4
Buchanan Co. MO, 89201 96 B1
Buchanan Co. VA, 24098 111 F2
Buchanan Dam TX, 1519 61 D1
Buchtel OH, 558 101 E2
Buckeye AZ, 50876 54 B1
Buckeye Lake OH, 2746 101 D1
Buckfield ME, 1723 82 B2
Buckhannon WV, 5639 102 A2
Buckhead Ridge FL, 1450 141 E4
Buckingham PA, 1400 146 C2
Buckingham VA, 133 113 D1
Buckingham Co. VA, 17146 113 D1
Buckland AK, 416 154 B2
Buckley IL, 600 89 D4
Buckley MI, 697 69 F4
Buckley WA, 4354 12 C3
Bucklin KS, 794 42 C4
Bucklin MO, 467 97 D1
Buckner KY, 5837 100 A4
Buckner MO, 3076 96 C2
Bucks Co. PA, 625249 146 C1
Bucksport ME, 2885 83 D2
Bucksport SC, 876 123 D4
Bucoda WA, 562 12 C4
Bucyrus OH, 12362 90 C3
Buda IL, 538 88 B2
Buda TX, 7295 61 E2
Budd Lake NJ, 8968 94 A4
Bude MS, 1063 126 A4
Buellton CA, 4828 52 A2
Buena NJ, 4603 147 D4
Buena WA, 990 13 D4
Buena Park CA, 80530 228 E3
Buena Ventura Lakes FL, 26079 246 C5
Buena Vista CO, 2617 41 D2
Buena Vista GA, 2173 128 C2
Buena Vista MI, 6816 76 B2
Buena Vista VA, 6650 112 C1
Buena Vista Co. IA, 20260 72 B4
Buffalo IN, 692 89 E3
Buffalo IA, 1270 87 F2
Buffalo KY, 498 110 A1
Buffalo MN, 15453 66 C3
Buffalo MO, 3084 107 D1
Buffalo NY, 261310 78 B3
Buffalo ND, 188 19 E4
Buffalo OK, 1299 50 C1
Buffalo SC, 1266 121 F2
Buffalo SD, 330 25 F1
Buffalo TX, 1856 59 F4
Buffalo WV, 1236 101 E3
Buffalo WY, 4585 25 D3
Buffalo Ctr. IA, 905 72 C2
Buffalo City WI, 1023 73 E1
Buffalo Co. NE, 46102 35 D4
Buffalo Co. SD, 1912 27 D3
Buffalo Co. WI, 13587 67 E4
Buffalo Grove IL, 41496 203 C2
Buffalo Lake MN, 733 66 B4
Buford GA, 12225 120 C3
Buhl ID, 4122 30 C1
Buhl MN, 1000 64 C3
Buhler KS, 1327 43 E3
Buies Creek NC, 2942 123 D1
Bullard TX, 2463 124 A3
Bullhead SD, 348 26 C1
Bullhead City AZ, 39540 46 B3
Bullitt Co. KY, 74319 99 F4
Bulloch Co. GA, 70217 130 B2
Bullock Co. AL, 10914 128 B3
Bulls Gap TN, 738 111 D3
Bull Shoals AR, 1950 107 E3
Bull Valley IL, 1077 74 C4
Bulverde TX, 4630 61 D2
Buna TX, 2142 132 C2
Buncombe Co. NC, 238318 111 E4
Bunker Hill IL, 1774 98 B2
Bunker Hill IN, 888 89 F3
Bunker Hill OR, 1444 20 A4
Bunker Hill WV, 700 103 D2
Bunker Hill Vil. TX, 3633 220 B2
Bunkerville NV, 1303 46 B1
Bunkie LA, 4171 133 E1
Bunnell FL, 2676 139 E4
Buras LA, 945 134 C4
Burbank CA, 103340 52 C2
Burbank IL, 28925 203 D5
Burbank WA, 3291 21 E1
Burden KS, 535 43 F4
Bureau Co. IL, 34978 88 B2
Burgaw NC, 3872 123 E2
Burgettstown PA, 1388 91 F4

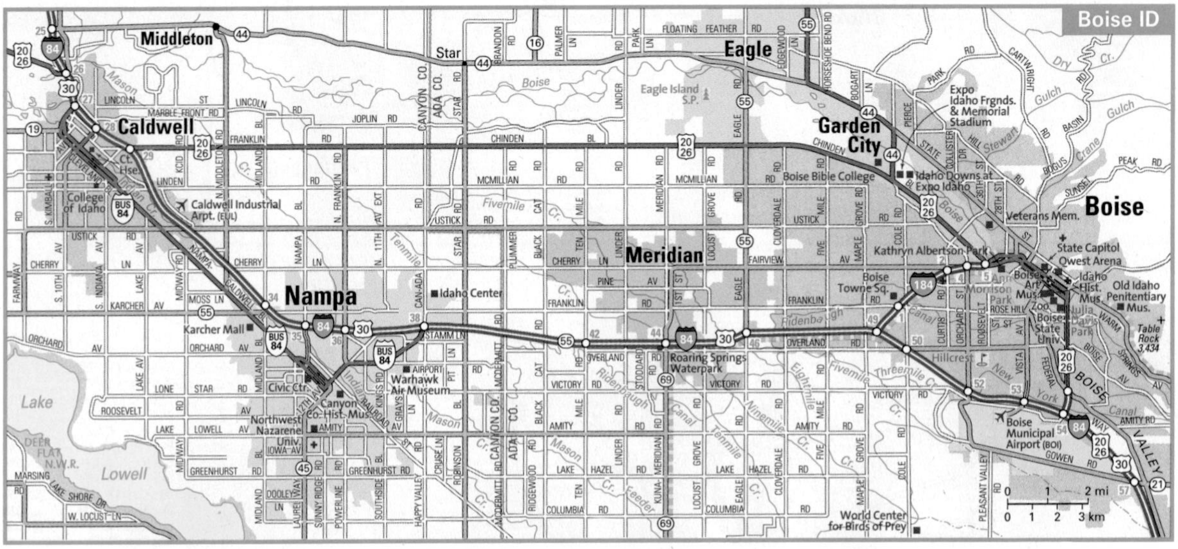
Boise ID
Middleton
Star
Eagle
Caldwell
Garden City
Boise
Meridian
Nampa
College of Idaho
Caldwell Industrial Arpt. (EUL)
Idaho Center
Karcher Mall
Warhawk Air Museum
Canyon Co. Hist. Mus.
Northwest Nazarene Univ.
Eagle Island S.P.
Expo Idaho Frgnds. & Memorial Stadium
Boise Bible College
Idaho Downs at Expo Idaho
Veterans Mem.
State Capitol
Qwest Arena
Kathryn Albertson Park
Boise Towne Sq.
Roaring Springs Waterpark
Boise State Univ.
Boise Municipal Airport (BOI)
Old Idaho Penitentiary
World Center for Birds of Prey
Deer Flat N.W.R.
Lake Lowell
Table Rock 3,434
0 1 2 mi
0 1 2 3 km

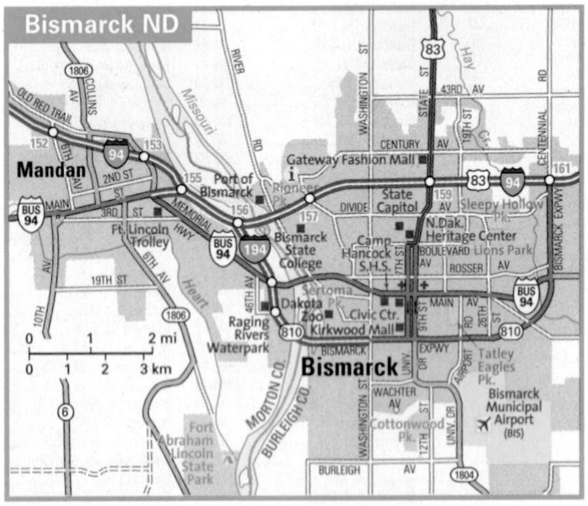
Bismarck ND
Mandan
Bismarck
Gateway Fashion Mall
Port of Bismarck
State Capitol
Sleepy Hollow Pk.
N. Dak. Heritage Center
Camp Hancock S.H.S.
Bismarck State College
Ft. Lincoln Trolley
Dakota Zoo
Civic Ctr.
Kirkwood Mall
Raging Rivers Waterpark
Tatley Eagles Pk.
Cottonwood Pk.
Bismarck Municipal Airport (BIS)
Fort Abraham Lincoln State Park
Missouri
0 1 2 mi
0 1 2 3 km

Entries in **bold black** indicate counties or parishes.
Entries in **bold color** indicate cities with detailed inset maps.

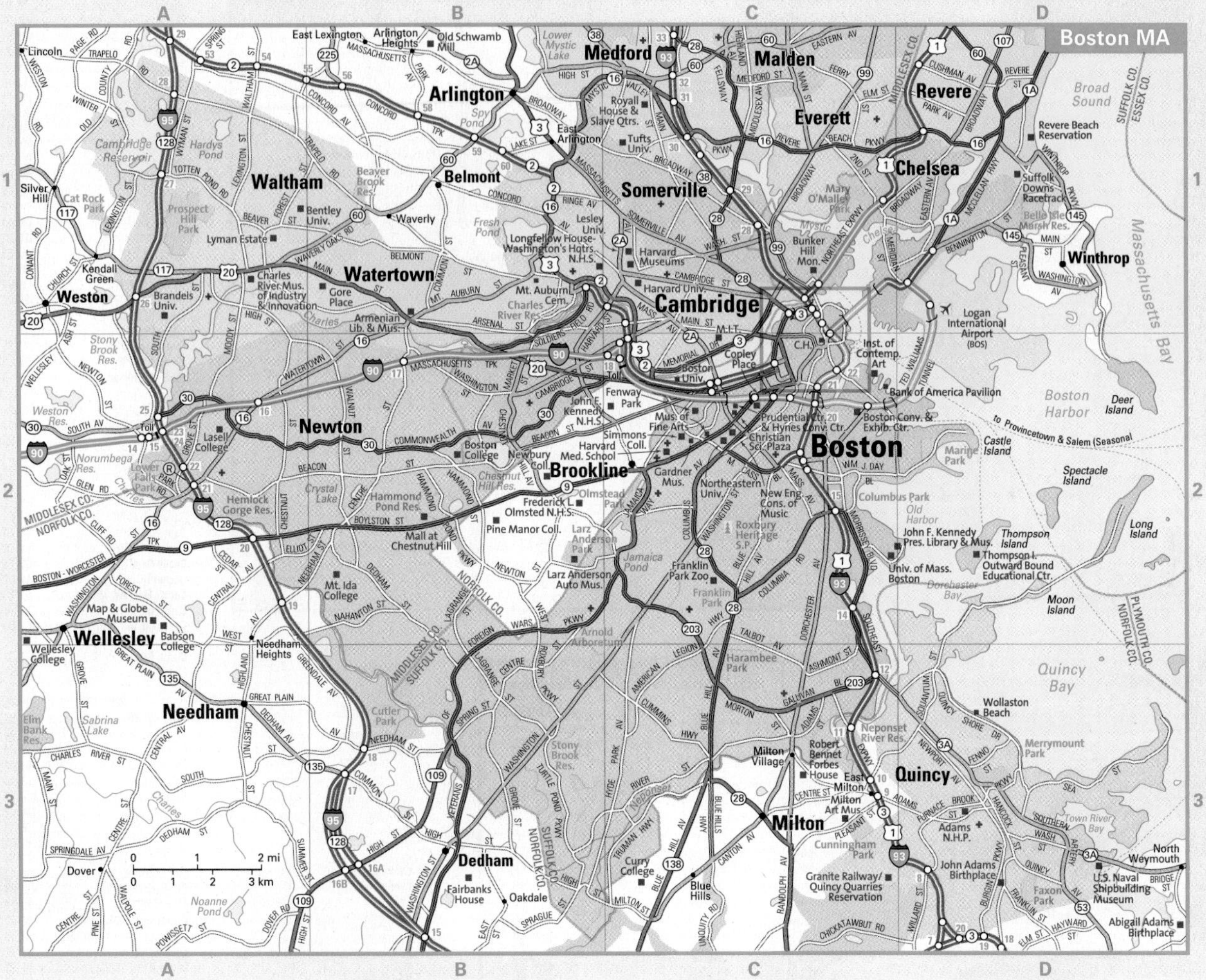

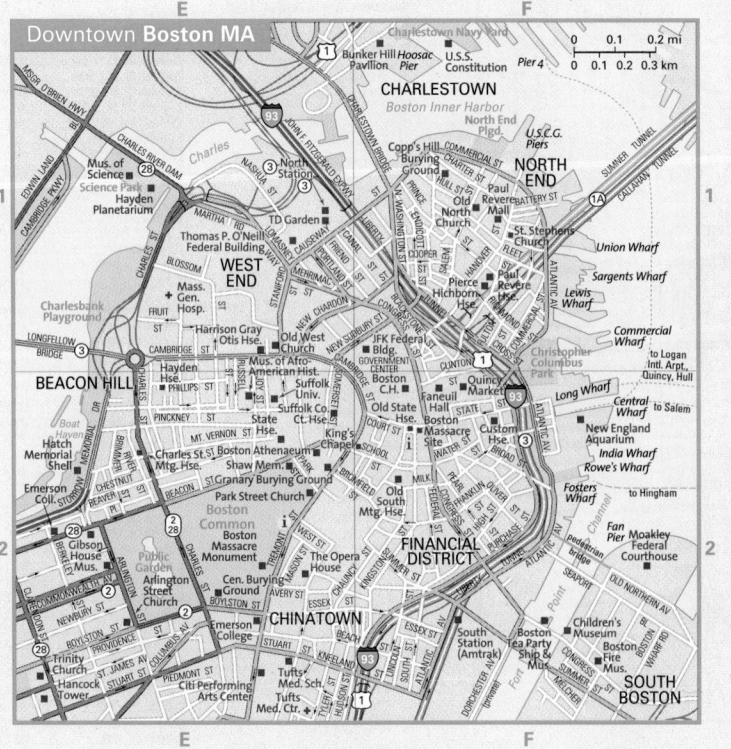

Boston MA

Downtown Boston MA

POINTS OF INTEREST

Arlington Street Church.................... E2
Boston Athenaeum........................ E2
Boston City Hall.......................... F2
Boston Fire Museum....................... F2
Boston Massacre Monument................. F2
Boston Massacre Site...................... F2
Boston Tea Party Ship & Museum........... F2
Bunker Hill Pavilion....................... F1
Central Burying Ground.................... E2
Charles Street Meeting House............... E2
Children's Museum........................ F2
Citi Performing Arts Center................. E2
Copp's Hill Burying Ground................. F1
Custom House............................ F2
Emerson College.......................... E2
Faneuil Hall.............................. F2
Gibson House Museum..................... E2
Granary Burying Ground................... E2
Hancock Tower........................... E2
Harrison Gray Otis House................... E1
Hatch Memorial Shell...................... E2
Hayden House............................ E2
Hayden Planetarium....................... E1
JFK Federal Building...................... F1
King's Chapel............................ F2
Moakley Federal Courthouse............... F2
Museum of Afro-American Hist............. E1
Museum of Science....................... E1
New England Aquarium.................... F2
North Station............................ E1
Old North Church......................... F1
Old South Meeting House.................. F2
Old State House.......................... F2
Old West Church......................... E1
The Opera House......................... E2
Park Street Church........................ E2
Paul Revere House........................ F1
Paul Revere Mall......................... F1
Pierce Hichborn House.................... F1
Quincy Market........................... F2
St. Stephens Church....................... F1
Shaw Memorial........................... E2
South Station (Amtrak).................... F2
State House.............................. E2
Suffolk County Court House................ E1
Suffolk University........................ E1
TD Garden.............................. E1
Thomas P. O'Neill Federal Building.......... E1
Trinity Church........................... E2
U.S.S. Constitution....................... F1

198

Butterfield–Callahan

Figures after entries indicate population, page number, and grid reference.

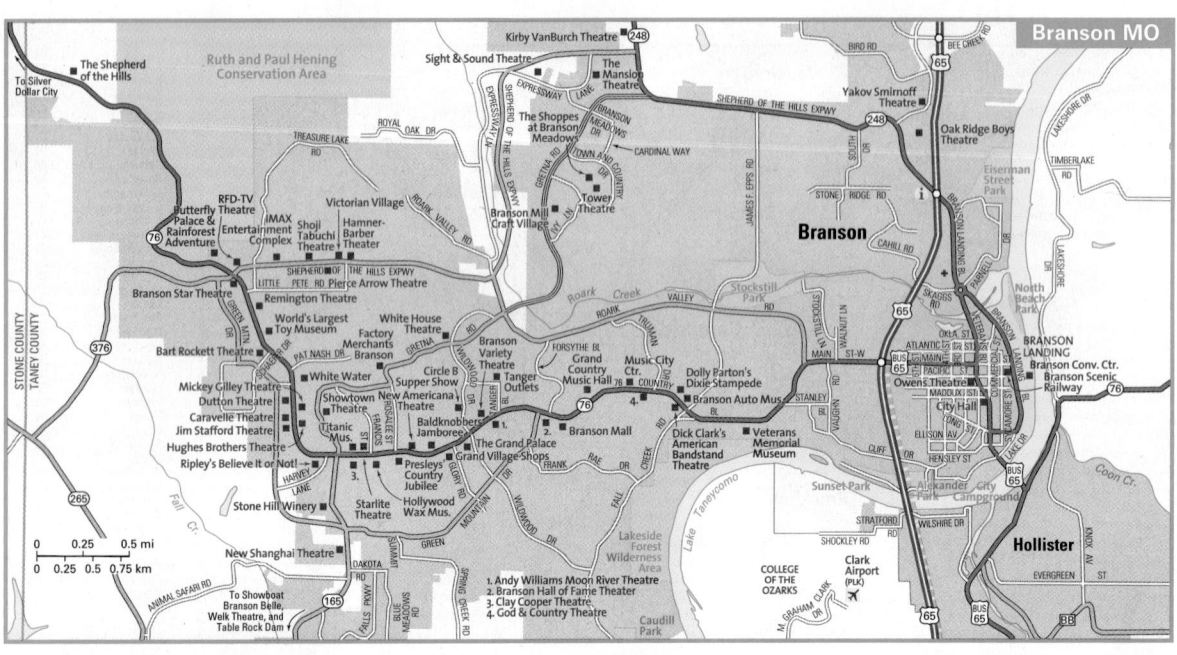

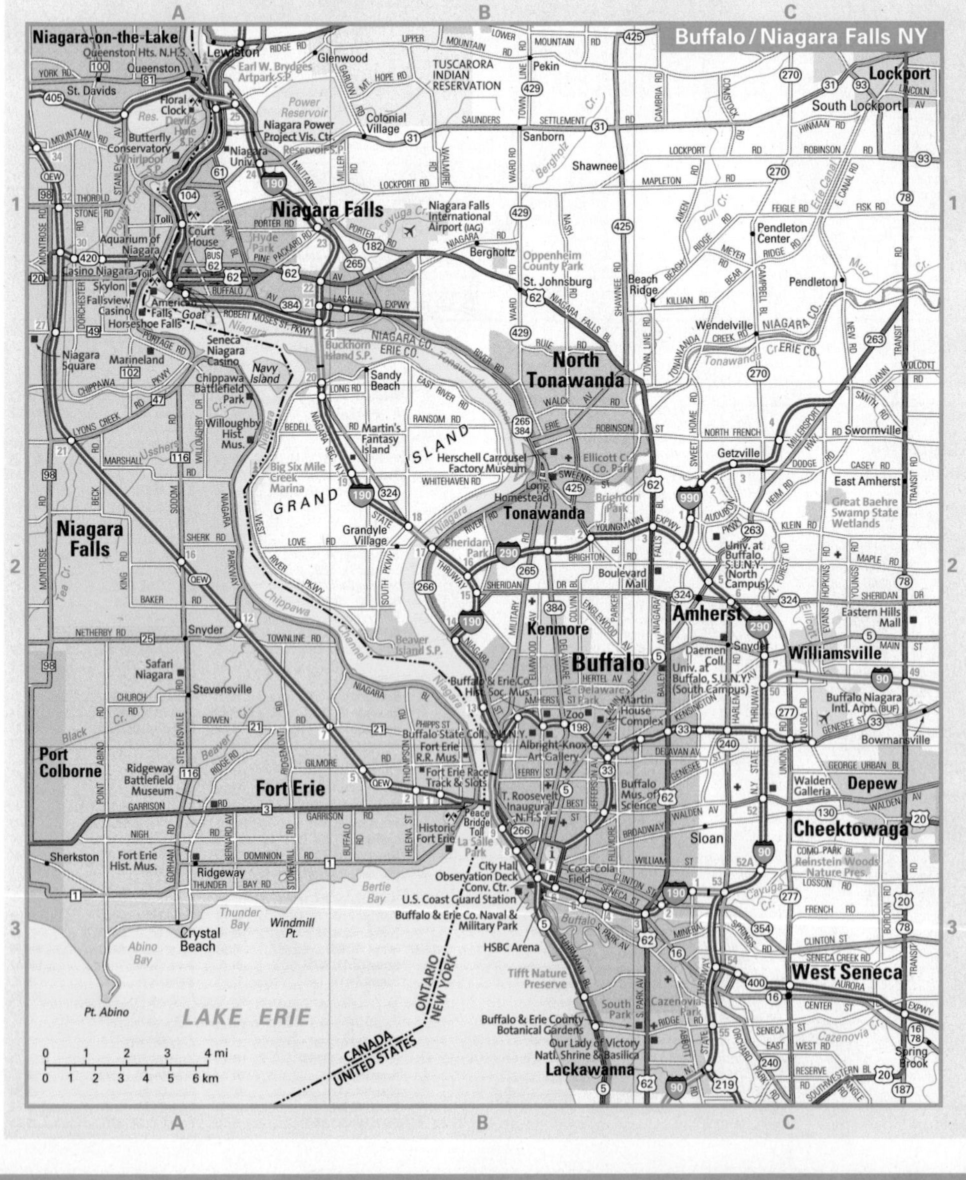

Branson MO

Buffalo / Niagara Falls NY

Entries in **bold black** indicate counties or parishes.
Entries in **bold color** indicate cities with detailed inset maps.

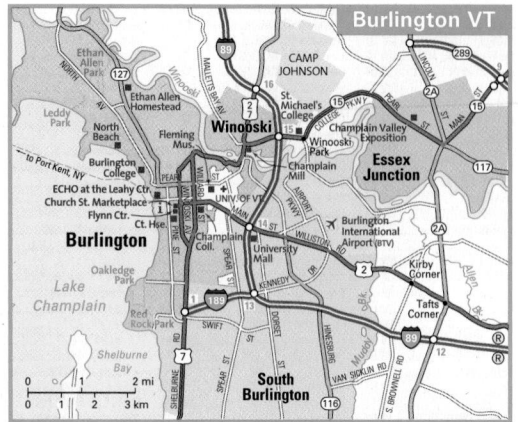

Burlington VT

Canton OH

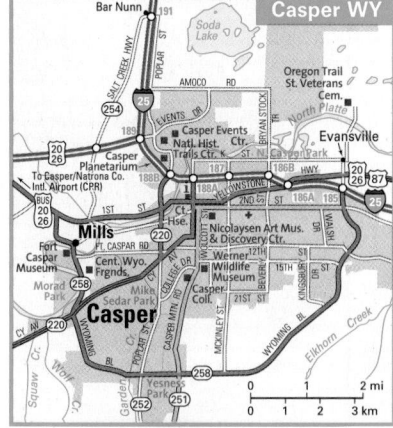

Carson City NV

Casper WY

200
Cave City–Chisago County

Figures after entries indicate population, page number, and grid reference.

Cave City AR, 1904 107 F4
Cave City KY, 2240 110 A2
Cave Creek AZ, 5015 54 C1
Cave Jct. OR, 1883 28 B2
Cave Spr. GA, 1200 120 B3
Cave Spr. VA, 24922 112 B2
Cave Sprs. AR, 1729 106 C3
Cavetown MD, 1473 144 A1
Cawker City KS, 469 43 D1
Cawood KY, 731 111 D2
Cayce SC, 12528 122 A3
Cayucos CA, 2592 44 B4
Cayuga IN, 1162 99 E1
Cayuga NY, 549 79 D3
Cayuga Co. NY, 80026 79 D4
Cayuga Hts. NY, 3729 79 D4
Cazenovia NY, 2835 79 E3
Cecil PA, 2476 92 A4
Cecil Co. MD, 101108 145 E1
Cecilia KY, 572 110 A1
Cecilia LA, 1980 133 F2
Cecilton MD, 663 145 E1
Cedar Bluff AL, 1820 120 A3
Cedar Bluff VA, 1137 111 F2
Cedar Bluffs NE, 610 35 F3
Cedar Brook NJ, 1100 147 D4
Cedarburg WI, 11412 74 C3
Cedar City UT, 28857 39 D4
Cedar Co. IA, 18499 87 F1
Cedar Co. MO, 13982 106 C1
Cedar Co. NE, 8852 35 E1
Cedar Creek NE, 390 35 F3
Cedar Crest NM, 958 48 C3
Cedaredge CO, 2253 40 B2
Cedar Falls IA, 39260 73 D4
Cedar Fort UT, 368 31 E4
Cedar Grove FL, 3397 136 C2
Cedar Grove MD, 950 144 B2
Cedar Grove NJ, 12411 148 A3
Cedar Grove NM, 747 48 C3
Cedar Grove WV, 997 101 F4
Cedar Grove WI, 2113 75 D2
Cedar Hill MO, 1721 98 A4
Cedar Hill TX, 45028 207 C3
Cedar Hills OR, 8300 251 C2
Cedarhurst NY, 6592 241 G5
Cedar Key FL, 702 138 B4
Cedar Lake IN, 11560 89 D2
Cedar Park TX, 48937 61 E1
Cedar Pt. NC, 1279 115 D4
Cedar Rapids IA, 126326 87 E1
Cedar Rapids NE, 382 35 E3
Cedar Sprs. MI, 3509 75 F3
Cedartown GA, 9750 120 B3
Cedar Vale KS, 579 51 F1
Cedarville AR, 1394 116 C1
Cedarville IL, 741 74 B4
Cedarville NJ, 776 145 F2
Cedarville OH, 4019 100 C1
Celebration FL, 7427 141 D1
Celeste TX, 814 59 F2
Celina OH, 10400 90 B4
Celina TN, 1495 110 A3
Celina TX, 6028 59 F2
Celoron NY, 1112 92 B1
Cement OK, 501 51 E3
Cement City MI, 438 90 B1
Centennial CO, 100377 209 C4
Center CO, 2230 41 D4
Center MO, 508 97 F1
Center NE, 94 35 E1
Center ND, 571 18 B3
Center TX, 5193 124 C3
Center Barnstead NH, 500 81 F4
Centerbrook CT, 950 149 E2
Center Brunswick NY, 900 94 B1
Centerburg OH, 1773 91 D4
Center City MN, 628 67 D3
Centereach NY, 31578 149 D3
Centerfield UT, 1367 39 E2
Center Harbor NH, 1096 81 F3
Center Hill FL, 988 140 C1
Center Line MI, 8257 210 C2
Center Moriches NY, 7580 149 D4
Center Ossipee NH, 561 81 F3
Center Pt. AL, 16921 119 F4
Center Pt. IA, 2421 87 E1
Center Pt. TX, 750 61 D2
Centerport NY, 5508 148 C3
Centerton AR, 9515 106 C3
Centerton NJ, 2000 147 D3
Centertown KY, 423 109 E1
Center Valley PA, 1600 146 C1
Centerville GA, 7148 129 D2
Centerville IN, 2552 100 B1
Centerville IA, 5528 87 D3
Centerville LA, 800 133 F3
Centerville MA, 9200 151 F3
Centerville MO, 191 108 A1
Centerville OH, 103 100 B1
Centerville PA, 3263 92 A4
Centerville SC, 6586 121 E3
Centerville SD, 882 35 F1
Centerville TN, 3644 109 E4
Centerville TX, 892 124 A4
Centerville UT, 15335 31 E4
Central AZ, 645 55 E2
Central SC, 5159 121 E2
Central TN, 2279 111 E3
Central Bridge NY, 593 79 F4
Central City AR, 502 116 C1
Central City CO, 663 41 D1
Central City IL, 1172 98 C3
Central City IA, 1257 87 F1
Central City KY, 5978 109 E1
Central City NE, 2934 35 E3
Central City PA, 1124 92 B4
Central Falls RI, 19376 150 C3
Central High OK, 1199 51 E4
Centralia IL, 13032 98 C3
Centralia KS, 512 43 F1
Centralia MO, 4027 97 E2
Centralia WA, 16336 12 B4
Central Islip NY, 34450 149 D4
Central Lake MI, 952 69 F3
Central Park WA, 2685 12 B4
Central Pt. OR, 17169 28 B2
Central Square NY, 1848 79 D3
Central Valley (Woodbury) NY, 1857 148 B2
Central Vil. CT, 1400 150 B3
Central Vil. MA, 600 151 D4
Centre AL, 3489 120 A3
Centre Co. PA, 153990 92 C3
Centre Hall PA, 1265 92 C3
Centreville AL, 2778 127 F1
Centreville IL, 5309 98 A3
Centreville MD, 4285 145 D3
Centreville MI, 1425 89 F1
Centreville MS, 1684 134 A1
Centreville VA, 71135 144 A3
Centuria WI, 948 67 E3
Century FL, 1698 135 F1
Ceres CA, 45417 36 C4
Ceresco NE, 889 35 F3
Cerritos CA, 49041 228 E4
Cerro Gordo IL, 1403 98 C1
Cerro Gordo Co. IA, 44151 73 D3
Chackbay LA, 5177 134 A3
Chadbourn NC, 1856 123 D3
Chadron NE, 5851 34 A1
Chaffee MO, 2955 108 B2
Chaffee Co. CO, 17809 41 D2
Chaffinville MA, 3100 150 B1
Chagrin Falls OH, 4113 91 E2
Chalco NE, 10994 35 F3
Chalfant PA, 800 250 D2
Chalfont PA, 4009 146 C2
Chalkville AL, 3829 195 F1
Challenge CA, 1069 36 C1
Challis ID, 1081 23 D3
Chalmers IN, 508 89 E3
Chalmette LA, 16751 134 B3
Chama NM, 1022 48 C1
Chamberino NM, 919 56 C3
Chamberlain SD, 2387 27 D4
Chamberlayne Farms VA, 5456 254 B1
Chambersburg PA, 20268 103 D1
Chambers Co. AL, 34215 128 B1
Chambers Co. TX, 35096 132 B3
Chamblee GA, 9892 120 C4
Chamisal NM, 310 49 D2
Champaign IL, 81055 88 C4
Champaign Co. IL, 201081 89 D4
Champaign Co. OH, 40097 90 C4
Champion Hts. OH, 6498 91 F2
Champlain NY, 1101 81 D1
Chancellor SD, 264 27 F4
Chandler AZ, 236123 54 C2
Chandler IN, 2887 99 E4
Chandler OK, 3100 51 F2
Chandler TX, 2734 124 A2
Chandler Hts. AZ, 950 54 C2
Chandlerville IL, 553 88 A4
Chanhassen MN, 22952 66 C4
Channahon IL, 12560 88 C2
Channel Lake IL, 1664 74 C4
Channelview TX, 38289 132 B3
Channing TX, 363 50 A2
Chantilly VA, 23039 144 A3
Chanute KS, 9119 106 A1
Chaparral NM, 14631 56 C3
Chapel Hill NC, 57233 112 C4
Chapel Hill TN, 1445 119 F1
Chapin IL, 512 98 A1
Chapin SC, 1445 122 A3
Chaplin KY, 418 100 A4
Chapman KS, 1393 43 F2
Chapmanville WV, 1256 101 E4
Chappaqua NY, 1436 148 B2
Chappell NE, 929 34 A3
Chardon OH, 5148 91 E2
Charenton LA, 1903 133 F3
Chariton IA, 4321 87 D3
Chariton Co. MO, 7831 97 D1
Charlack MO, 1363 256 B2
Charleroi PA, 4120 92 A4
Charles City IA, 7652 73 D3
Charles City VA, 133 113 E1
Charles City Co. VA, 7256 113 E1
Charles Co. MD, 146551 144 B4
Charles Mix Co. SD, 9129 27 D4
Charleston AR, 2494 116 C1
Charleston IL, 21838 99 D2
Charleston ME, 300 82 C1
Charleston MS, 2193 118 B3
Charleston MO, 5947 108 C2
Charleston SC, 120083 131 D2
Charleston TN, 651 120 C1
Charleston UT, 415 31 F4
Charleston WV, 51400 101 E4
Charleston Co. SC, 350209 131 D2
Charlestown IN, 7585 100 A3
Charlestown MD, 1183 145 D1
Charlestown NH, 1152 81 E4
Charlestown RI, 7827 150 C4
Charles Town WV, 5259 103 D2
Charlevoix MI, 2513 69 F3
Charlevoix Co. MI, 25949 70 B3
Charlo MT, 379 15 D3
Charlotte MI, 9074 76 A4
Charlotte NC, 731424 122 A1
Charlotte TN, 1235 109 E4
Charlotte TX, 1715 61 D3
Charlotte Co. FL, 159978 140 C4
Charlotte Co. VA, 12586 113 D2
Charlotte C.H. VA, 543 113 D2
Charlotte Hall MD, 1420 144 C4
Charlotte Harbor FL, 3714 140 C4
Charlottesville VA, 43475 102 C4
Charlton MA, 12981 150 B2
Charlton NY, 3954 94 B1
Charlton City MA, 1400 150 B2
Charlton Co. GA, 12171 138 C1
Charlton Depot MA, 1200 150 B2
Charter Oak CA, 9310 229 F2
Charter Oak IA, 502 86 A1
Chartley MA, 1600 151 D2
Chase KS, 477 43 D3
Chase City VA, 2351 113 D2
Chase Co. KS, 2790 43 F3
Chase Co. NE, 3966 34 B4
Chaska MN, 23770 66 C4
Chassahowitzka FL, 700 140 B1
Chassell MI, 800 65 F4
Chateaugay NY, 833 80 C1
Chatfield MN, 2779 73 E2
Chatham IL, 11500 98 B1
Chatham LA, 557 125 E2
Chatham MA, 1421 151 F3
Chatham NJ, 8962 148 A4
Chatham NY, 1770 94 B2
Chatham VA, 1269 112 C2
Chatham Co. GA, 265128 130 B3
Chatham Co. NC, 63505 112 C4
Chatom AL, 1288 127 D4
Chatsworth GA, 4299 120 C2
Chatsworth IL, 1205 88 C3
Chattahoochee FL, 3652 137 D1
Chattahoochee Co. GA, 11267 128 C2
Chattanooga OK, 461 51 D4
Chattanooga TN, 167674 120 B2
Chattaroy WV, 756 111 E1
Chattooga Co. GA, 26015 120 B3
Chatwood PA, 3600 146 B3
Chaumont NY, 624 79 D1
Chauncey OH, 1049 101 E2
Chautauqua Co. KS, 3669 43 F4
Chautauqua Co. NY, 134905 78 A4
Chauvin LA, 2912 134 B4
Chaves Co. NM, 65645 57 E2
Chazy NY, 565 81 D1
Cheatham Co. TN, 39105 109 E3
Cheat Lake WV, 7988 102 B1
Chebanse IL, 1062 89 D3
Cheboygan MI, 4867 70 C2
Cheboygan Co. MI, 26152 70 C3
Checotah OK, 3335 116 A1
Cheektowaga NY, 75178 78 B3
Chefornak AK, 418 154 B3
Chehalis WA, 7259 12 B4
Chelan WA, 3890 13 E3
Chelan Co. WA, 72453 13 D2
Chelmsford MA, 33802 95 E1
Chelsea AL, 10183 127 F1
Chelsea MA, 35177 151 D1
Chelsea MI, 4944 76 B4
Chelsea NY, 2300 148 B1
Chelsea OK, 1964 106 A3
Chelsea VT, 1250 81 E3
Cheltenham MD, 650 144 C4
Cheltenham PA, 5500 248 C2
Chelyan WV, 776 101 F4
Chemung Co. NY, 88830 93 E1
Chenango Bridge NY, 2883 93 E1
Chenango Co. NY, 50477 79 E4
Chenequa WI, 590 74 C3
Cheney KS, 2094 43 E4
Cheney WA, 10590 13 F3
Cheneyville LA, 625 133 E1
Chenoa IL, 1785 88 C3
Chenoweth OR, 1855 21 D1
Chepachet RI, 1675 150 C3
Cheraw SC, 5851 122 C2
Cheriton VA, 487 114 B3
Cherokee AL, 1048 119 D2
Cherokee IA, 5253 72 A4
Cherokee KS, 714 106 B1
Cherokee OK, 1498 51 D1
Cherokee Co. AL, 25989 120 A3
Cherokee Co. GA, 214346 120 C3
Cherokee Co. IA, 12072 72 A3
Cherokee Co. KS, 21603 106 B2
Cherokee Co. NC, 27444 121 D1
Cherokee Co. OK, 46987 106 B4
Cherokee Co. SC, 55342 121 F2
Cherokee Co. TX, 50845 124 A3
Cherokee Forest SC, 8000 217 A1
Cherokee Vil. AR, 4671 107 F3
Cherry Co. NE, 5713 34 B1
Cherry Creek NY, 461 78 A4
Cherryfield ME, 1157 83 E2
Cherry Grove OH, 4378 204 C3
Cherry Hill NJ, 71045 146 C3
Cherry Hills Vil. CO, 5987 209 C4
Cherryvale KS, 2367 106 A2
Cherryvale SC, 2496 122 B4
Cherry Valley AR, 651 118 A1
Cherry Valley NY, 520 79 F4
Cherryville NC, 5760 122 A1
Chesaning MI, 2394 76 B3
Chesapeake OH, 745 101 D3
Chesapeake VA, 222209 113 F3
Chesapeake WV, 1554 101 F4
Chesapeake Beach MD, 5753 144 C4
Chesapeake City MD, 673 145 E1
Chesapeake Ranch Estates MD, 10519 103 F4
Cheshire CT, 29097 149 D1
Cheshire MA, 514 94 C1
Cheshire Co. NH, 77117 81 E4
Chesilhurst NJ, 1634 147 D4
Chesnee SC, 868 121 F1
Chester CA, 2144 29 D4
Chester CT, 3832 149 E2
Chester IL, 8586 98 B4
Chester MD, 4167 145 D3
Chester MA, 627 94 C2
Chester MT, 847 15 F2
Chester NH, 4768 81 F4
Chester NJ, 1649 94 A4
Chester NY, 3969 148 A2
Chester PA, 33972 146 C3
Chester SC, 5607 122 A2
Chester VT, 1005 81 E4
Chester VA, 20987 113 E1
Chester WV, 2585 91 F3
Chester Co. PA, 498886 146 B3
Chester Co. SC, 33140 122 A2
Chester Co. TN, 17131 119 D1
Chester Depot VT, 850 81 E4
Chesterfield IN, 2547 89 F4
Chesterfield MO, 47484 98 A3
Chesterfield SC, 1472 122 B2
Chesterfield VA, 3558 113 E1
Chesterfield Co. SC, 46734 122 B2
Chesterfield Co. VA, 316236 113 E1
Chester Hts. PA, 2531 146 B3
Chester Hill PA, 883 92 C3
Chesterland OH, 2521 91 E2
Chesterton IN, 13068 89 E2
Chestertown MD, 5252 145 D2
Chestnut Mtn. GA, 650 121 D3
Chestnut Ridge NY, 7916 148 B3
Cheswick PA, 1746 250 D1
Cheswold DE, 1380 145 E2
Chetek WI, 2221 67 E3
Chetopa KS, 1125 106 B2
Chevak AK, 938 154 B3
Cheverly MD, 6173 144 B3
Cheviot OH, 8375 100 B2
Chevy Chase MD, 1953 270 C2
Chevy Chase View MD, 920 270 C1
Chewelah WA, 2607 13 F2
Cheyenne OK, 801 50 C3
Cheyenne WY, 59466 33 E3
Cheyenne Co. CO, 1836 42 A2
Cheyenne Co. KS, 2726 42 B1
Cheyenne Co. NE, 9998 34 A3
Cheyenne Wells CO, 846 42 A2
Cheyney PA, 1600 146 B3
Chicago IL, 2695598 89 D1
Chicago Hts. IL, 30276 89 D2
Chicago Ridge IL, 14305 203 D5
Chichester NH, 2523 81 F4
Chickamauga GA, 3101 120 B2
Chickasaw AL, 6106 135 E1
Chickasaw Co. IA, 12439 73 E3
Chickasaw Co. MS, 17392 118 C4
Chickasha OK, 16036 51 E3
Chico CA, 86187 36 B1
Chico TX, 1002 59 E2
Chicopee MA, 55298 150 A2
Chicora PA, 1043 92 A3
Chicot Co. AR, 11800 125 F1
Chiefland FL, 2245 138 B4
Chilchinbito AZ, 506 47 F1
Chilcoot CA, 387 37 D1
Childersburg AL, 5175 128 A1
Childress TX, 6105 50 C4
Childress Co. TX, 7041 50 C4
Chilhowie VA, 1781 111 F2
Chillicothe IL, 6097 88 B3
Chillicothe MO, 9515 96 C1
Chillicothe OH, 21901 101 D2
Chillicothe TX, 707 50 C4
Chillum MD, 33513 270 D2
Chiloquin OR, 734 28 C1
Chilton WI, 3933 74 C1
Chilton Co. AL, 43643 127 F2
Chimayo NM, 3177 49 D2
China TX, 1160 132 C3
China Grove NC, 3563 122 B1
China Grove TX, 1179 61 D3
Chinchilla PA, 2098 261 E1
Chincoteague VA, 2941 114 C2
Chinle AZ, 4518 47 F2
Chino CA, 77983 229 G3
Chino Hills CA, 74799 229 G3
Chinook MT, 1203 16 B2
Chinook WA, 466 20 B1
Chino Valley AZ, 10817 47 D4
Chipita Park CO, 1709 205 C1
Chipley FL, 3605 136 C1
Chippewa Co. MI, 38520 70 B1
Chippewa Co. MN, 12441 66 A3
Chippewa Co. WI, 62415 67 F3
Chippewa Falls WI, 13661 67 F4
Chippewa Lake OH, 711 91 E3
Chisago City MN, 4967 67 D3
Chisago Co. MN, 53887 67 D3

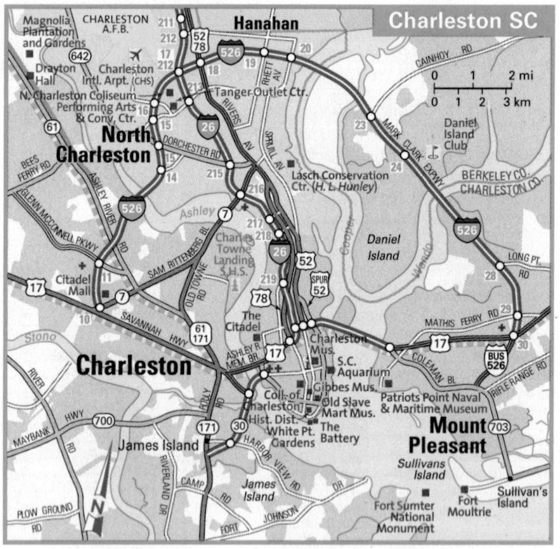
Charleston SC
Hanahan
North Charleston
Charleston
Mount Pleasant
James Island
Daniel Island
Sullivans Island
Magnolia Plantation and Gardens
Drayton Hall
Charleston Intl. Arpt. (CHS)
Tanger Outlet Ctr.
Citadel Mall
The Citadel
Charleston Mus.
S.C. Aquarium
Patriots Point Naval & Maritime Museum
Fort Sumter National Monument
Fort Moultrie

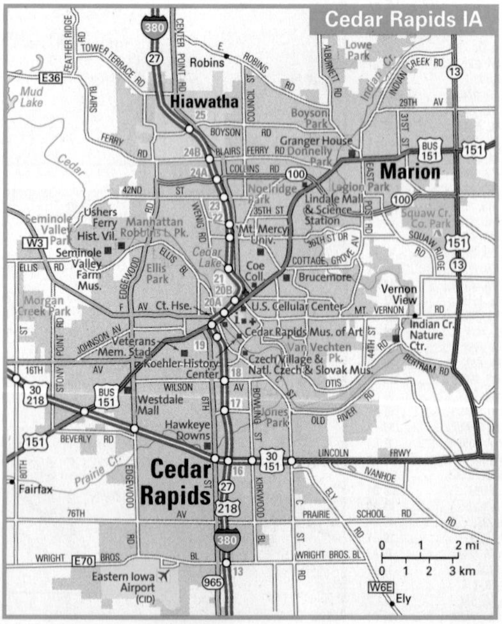
Cedar Rapids IA
Cedar Rapids
Hiawatha
Marion
Robins
Fairfax
Eastern Iowa Airport (CID)
Ely

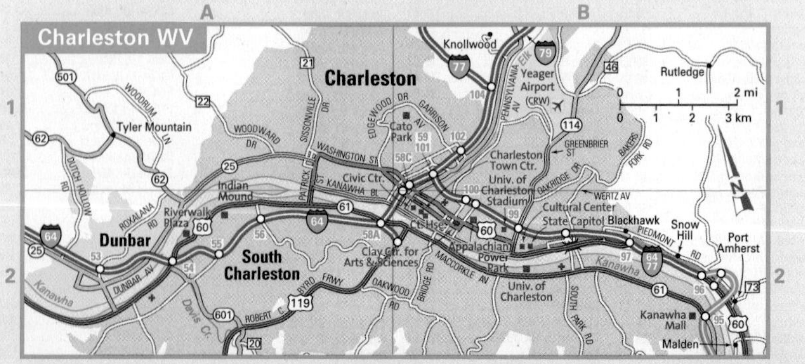
Charleston WV
Charleston
South Charleston
Dunbar
Tyler Mountain
Knollwood
Rutledge
Snow Hill
Port Amherst
Malden
Blackhawk
Yeager Airport (CRW)

Blackhawk B2
Charleston A1
Dunbar A2
Knollwood B1
Malden B2
Port Amherst B2
Rutledge B1
Snow Hill B2
S. Charleston A2
Tyler Mtn. A1

Entries in **bold black** indicate counties or parishes.
Entries in **bold color** indicate cities with detailed inset maps.

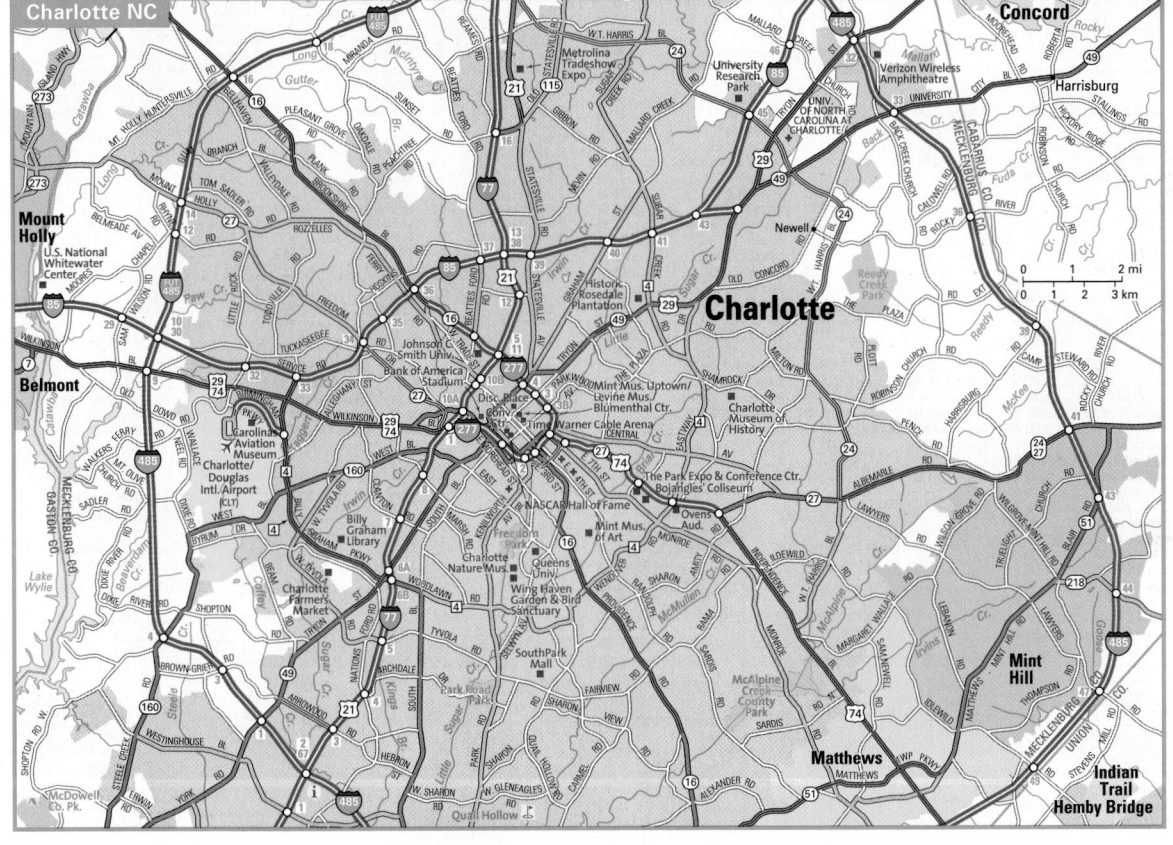

Charlotte NC

Mount Holly — Belmont — Concord — Harrisburg — Newell — Charlotte — Mint Hill — Matthews — Indian Trail — Hemby Bridge

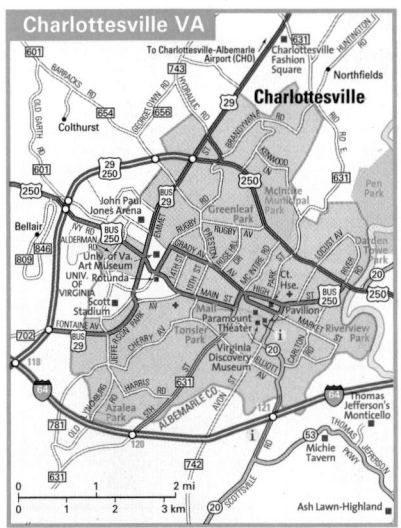

Charlottesville VA

Charlottesville — Northfields — Colthurst — Bellair

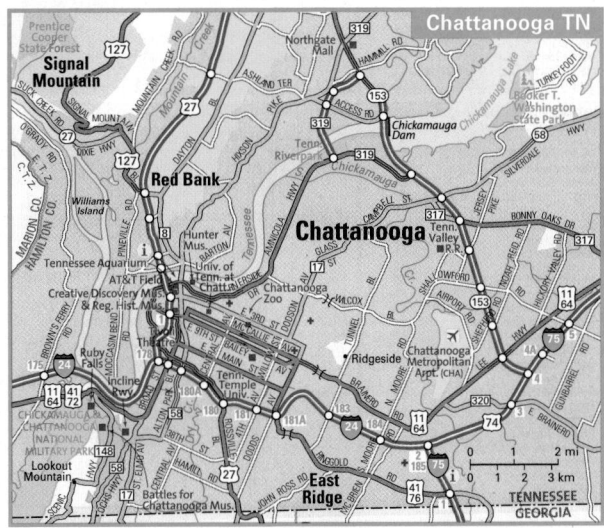

Chattanooga TN

Signal Mountain — Red Bank — Chattanooga — East Ridge — Lookout Mountain

Figures after entries indicate population, page number, and grid reference.

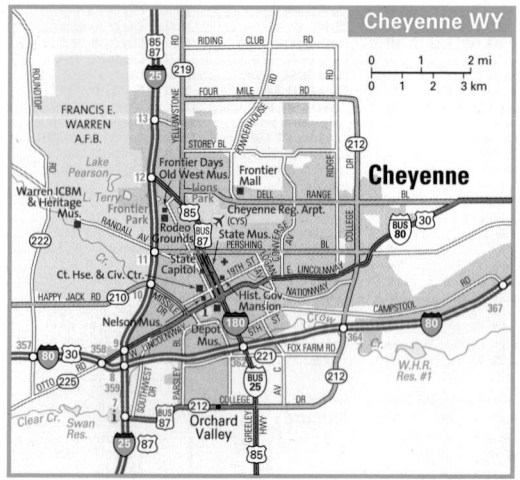

Cheyenne WY

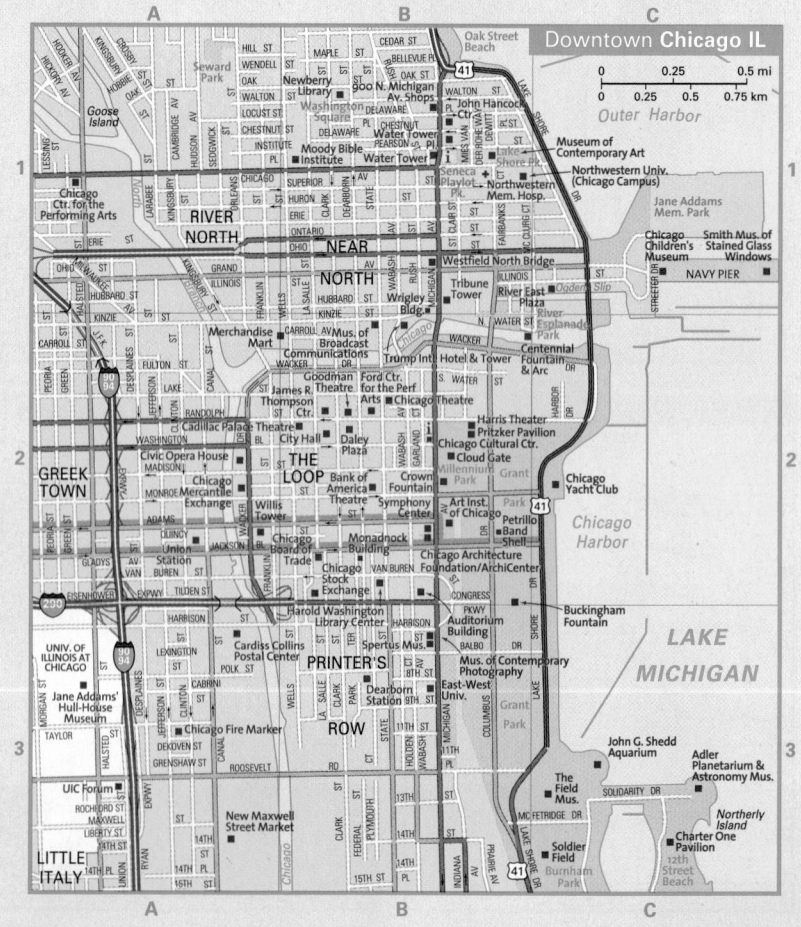

Downtown **Chicago IL**

POINTS OF INTEREST

Entries in **bold black** indicate counties or parishes.
Entries in **bold color** indicate cities with detailed inset maps.

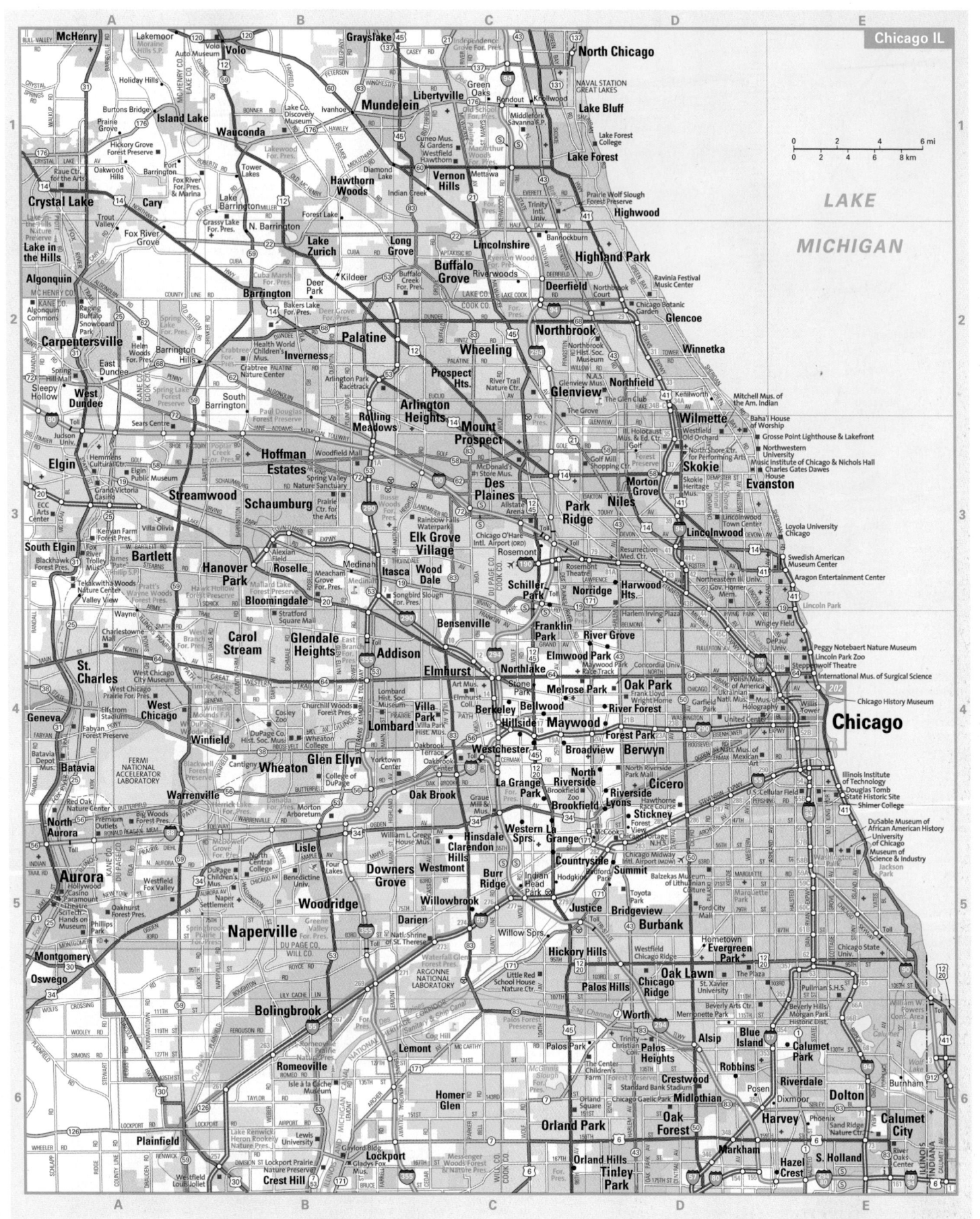

Chicago IL

LAKE MICHIGAN

204

Columbus–Concord

Figures after entries indicate population, page number, and grid reference.

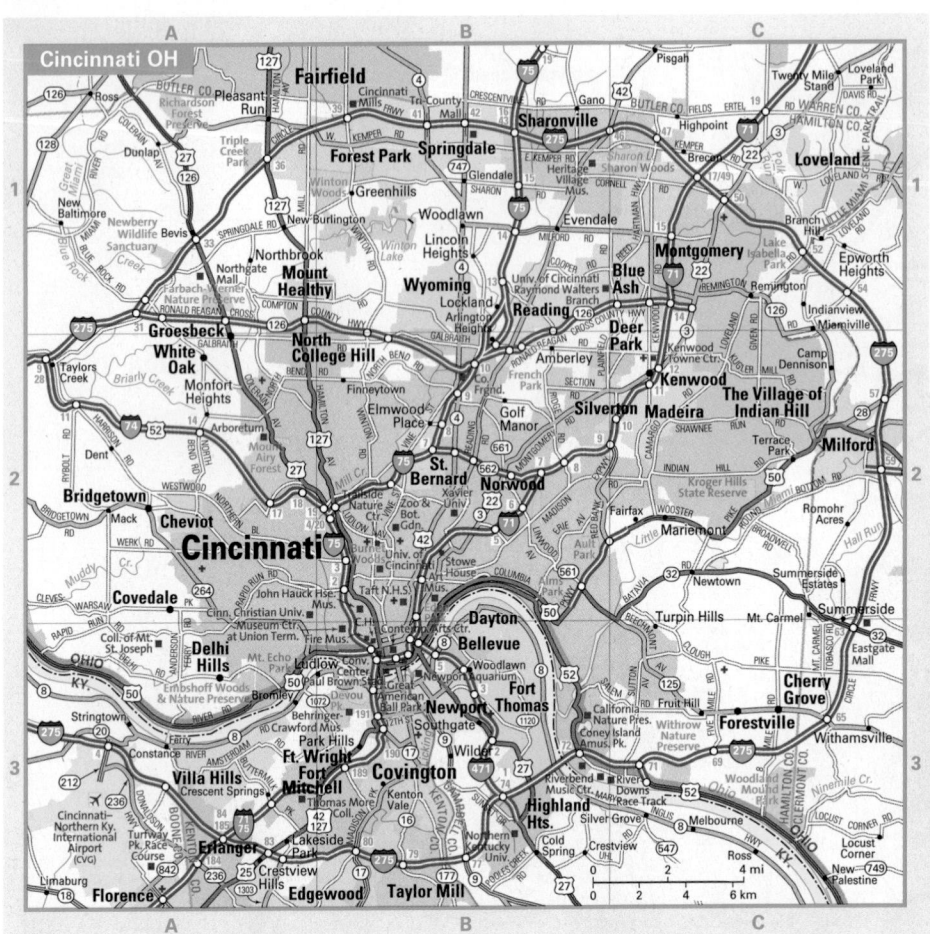

Cincinnati OH

Cleveland OH

Cincinnati index

Amberley	B2	Ft. Mitchell	A3
Arlington Hts.	B2	Ft. Thomas	B3
Bellevue	B3	Ft. Wright	B3
Bevis	A1	Fruit Hill	C2
Blue Ash	C1	Gano	B1
Branch Hill	C1	Glendale	B1
Brecon	C1	Golf Manor	B2
Bridgetown	A2	Greenhills	A2
Bromley	A3	Groesbeck	A2
Camp Dennison	C1	Highland Hts.	B3
Cherry Grove	C2	Highpoint	C1
Cheviot	A2	Indianview	C2
Cincinnati	A2	Kenton Vale	B3
Cold Spr.	B3	Kenwood	C2
Constance	A2	Lakeside Park	A3
Covedale	A2	Limaburg	A3
Covington	A3	Lincoln Hts.	B1
Crescent Sprs.	A3	Lockland	B1
Crestview	A3	Locust Corner	C3
Crestview Hills	A3	Loveland	C1
Dayton	B2	Loveland Park	C1
Deer Park	C2	Ludlow	A3
Delhi Hills	A2	Mack	A2
Dent	A2	Madeira	C2
Dunlap	A1	Mariemont	C2
Edgewood	B3	Melbourne	C3
Elmwood Place	B2	Miamiville	C1
Epworth Hts.	C1	Milford	C2
Erlanger	B3	Monfort Hts.	A2
Evendale	B1	Montgomery	C1
Fairfax	B2	Mt. Carmel	C2
Fairfield	B1	Mt. Healthy	A1
Finneytown	A2	New Baltimore	A1
Florence	A3	New Burlington	A1
Forest Park	B1	New Palestine	C3
Forestville	C3	Newport	B3

Newtown	C2
Northbrook	A1
N. College Hill	A2
Norwood	B2
Park Hills	B3
Pisgah	C1
Pleasant Run	A1
Reading	B1
Remington	C1
Romohr Acres	C2
Ross, KY	C3
Ross, OH	A1
St. Bernard	B2
Sharonville	B1
Silver Grove	C3
Silverton	B2
Southgate	B3
Springdale	B1
Stringtown	A3
Summerside	C2
Summerside Estates	C2
Taylor Mill	B3
Taylors Creek	A2
Terrace Park	C2
The Vil. of Indian Hill	C2
Turpin Hills	C3
Twenty Mile Stand	C1
Villa Hills	A3
White Oak	A2
Wilder	B3
Withamsville	C3
Woodlawn, KY	B3
Woodlawn, OH	B1
Wyoming	B1

Cleveland index

Cleveland	E1
Cleveland Hts.	F2
Cuyahoga Hts.	F2
E. Cleveland	F1
Euclid	G1
Fairview Park	D2
Garfield Hts.	F3
Gates Mills	G1
Glenwillow	G3
Highland Hts.	G1
Highland Hills	G2
Hunting Valley	G2
Independence	F3
Lakewood	E2
Linndale	E2
Lyndhurst	G2
Macedonia	G3
Maple Hts.	F3
Mayfield	G1
Mayfield Hts.	G1
Middleburg Hts.	E3
Moreland Hills	G2
Newburgh Hts.	F2
Northfield	G3
N. Olmsted	D2
N. Randall	G2
N. Ridgeville	D3
N. Royalton	E3
Oakwood	G3
Olmsted Falls	D3
Orange	G2
Parma	E3
Parma Hts.	E3
Pepper Pike	G2
Richmond Hts.	G1
Rocky River	E2
Sagamore Hills	F3
Seven Hills	F3
Shaker Hts.	G2
Solon	G3
S. Euclid	G1
Strongsville	E3
Twinsburg	G3
University Hts.	G2
Valley View	F3
Walton Hills	G3
Warrensville Hts.	G2
Westlake	D2
Wickliffe	G1
Willoughby Hills	G1
Woodmere	G2

Avon	D2	Bedford	G3	Bratenahl	F1	Broadview Hts.	F3	Brooklyn Hts.	F2
Avon Lake	D2	Bedford Hts.	G3	Brecksville	F3	Brooklyn	E2	Brook Park	E3
Bay Vil.	D2	Bentleyville	G3					Woodmere	G2
Beachwood	G2	Berea	D3						

LAKE ERIE

Entries in **bold black** indicate counties or parishes.
Entries in **bold color** indicate cities with detailed inset maps.

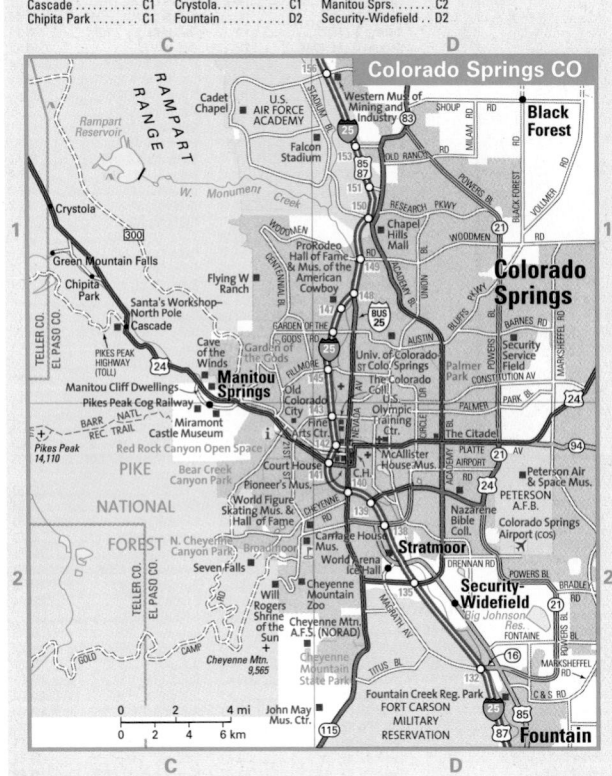

Colorado Springs CO

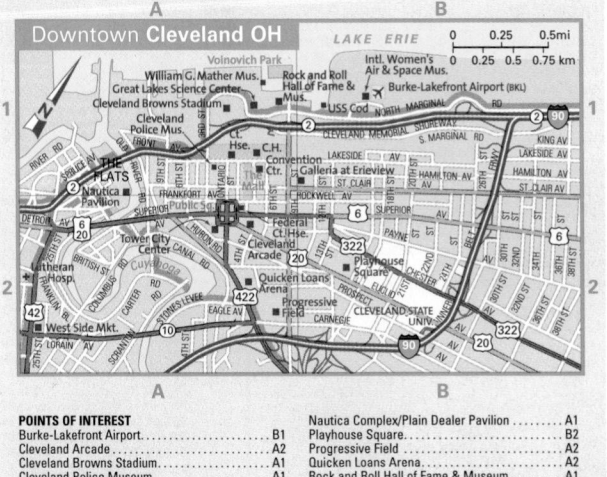

Downtown **Cleveland OH**

POINTS OF INTEREST
Burke-Lakefront Airport B1
Cleveland Arcade A2
Cleveland Browns Stadium A1
Cleveland Police Museum A2
Cleveland State University B2
Convention Center B1
Galleria at Erieview B1
Great Lakes Science Center A1
International Women's Air & Space Museum ... B1
Nautica Complex/Plain Dealer Pavilion ... A1
Playhouse Square B2
Progressive Field A2
Quicken Loans Arena A2
Rock and Roll Hall of Fame & Museum ... A1
Terminal Tower/Tower City A2
U.S.S. Cod A1
West Side Market A2
William G. Mather Museum B1

Columbia SC

Columbus GA

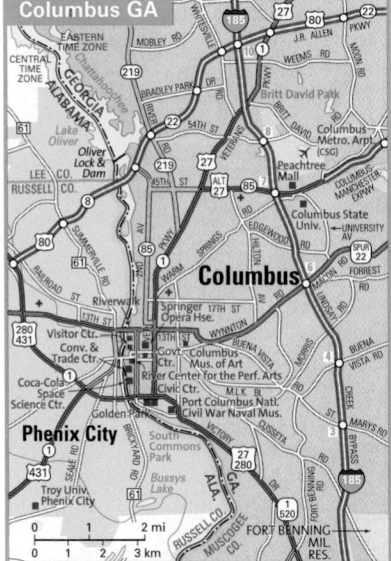

206
Crescent City – Decatur

Figures after entries indicate population, page number, and grid reference.

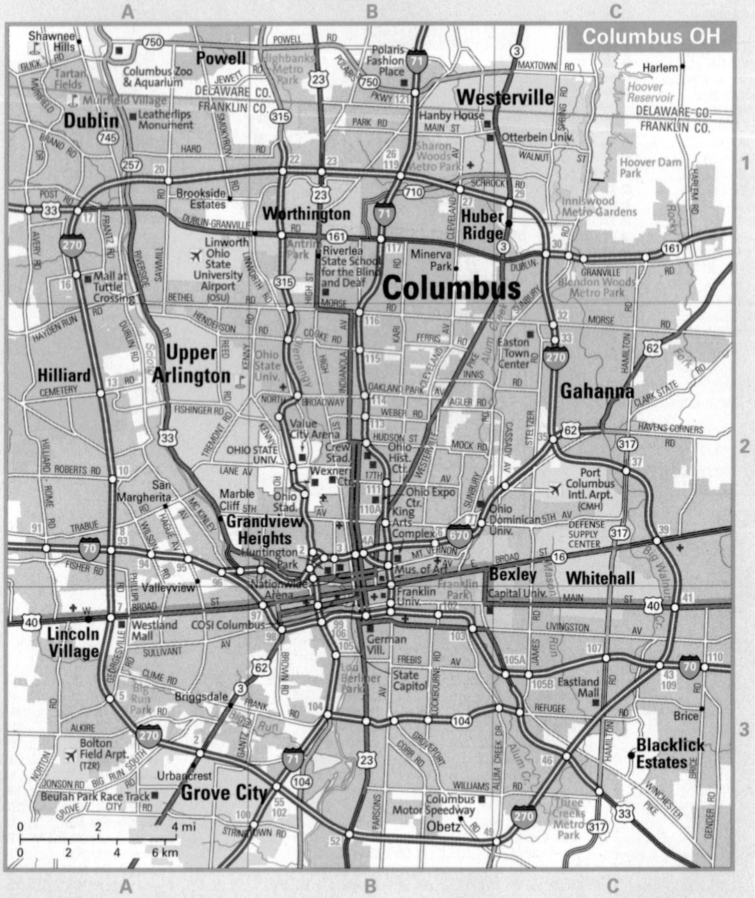
Columbus OH
Powell
Westerville
Dublin
Worthington
Huber Ridge
Columbus
Upper Arlington
Hilliard
Gahanna
Grandview Heights
Bexley
Whitehall
Lincoln Village
Blacklick Estates
Grove City
Obetz
Brice
Urbancrest
Valleyview
Briggsdale
San Margherita
Marble Cliff
Minerva Park
Linworth
Riverlea
Harlem
0 2 4 mi
0 2 4 6 km
A
B
C
1
2
3

Bexley C2
Blacklick Estates C3
Brice C3
Briggsdale A3
Brookside Estates A1
Columbus B1
Dublin A1
Gahanna C2
Grandview Hts. B2
Grove City A3
Harlem C1
Hilliard A2
Huber Ridge C1
Lincoln Vil. A3
Linworth B1
Marble Cliff A2
Minerva Park B1
New Rome A3
Obetz B3
Powell A1
Riverlea B1
San Margherita A2
Shawnee Hills A1
Upper Arlington A2
Urbancrest A3
Valleyview A2
Westerville C1
Whitehall C2
Worthington B1

Crescent City IL, 615 89 D3
Crescent Sprs. KY, 3801 204 A3
Cresco IA, 3868 73 E2
Cresson PA, 1711 92 B4
Cressona PA, 1651 146 A1
Crested Butte CO, 1487 40 C2
Crest Hill IL, 20837 89 D2
Crestline CA, 10770 53 D2
Crestline OH, 4630 91 D3
Creston IA, 7834 86 B3
Creston OH, 2171 91 E3
Crestview FL, 20978 136 B1
Crestview KY, 475 204 B3
Crestview Hills KY, 3148 204 A3
Crestwood IL, 10950 203 D6
Crestwood KY, 4531 100 A4
Crestwood MO, 11912 256 B3
Crestwood Vil. NJ, 7907 147 E3
Creswell OR, 5031 20 B4
Crete IL, 8259 89 D2
Crete NE, 6960 35 F4
Creve Coeur MO, 17833 256 A2
Crewe VA, 2326 113 D2
Cricket NC, 1855 111 F4
Cridersville OH, 1852 90 B3
Crimora VA, 2209 102 C4
Cripple Creek CO, 1189 41 E2
Crisfield MD, 2726 103 F4
Crisp Co. GA, 23439 129 D3
Crittenden KY, 3815 100 B3
Crittenden Co. AR, 50902 118 B1
Crittenden Co. KY, 9315 109 D2
Crivitz WI, 984 68 C3
Crocker MO, 1110 97 E4
Crockett CA, 3094 259 C1
Crockett TX, 6950 124 A4
Crockett Co. TN, 14586 108 C4
Crockett Co. TX, 3719 60 A1
Crofton KY, 749 109 E2
Crofton MD, 27348 144 C3
Crofton NE, 726 35 E1
Croghan NY, 618 79 E2
Crompond NY, 2292 148 B2
Cromwell CT, 13594 149 E1
Crook Co. OR, 20978 21 D3
Crook Co. WY, 7083 25 F3
Crooked Lake Park FL, 1722 141 D3
Crooks SD, 1269 27 F4
Crookston MN, 7891 19 F3
Crooksville OH, 2534 101 E1
Crosby MN, 2386 64 B4
Crosby ND, 1070 18 A1
Crosby TX, 2299 132 B3
Crosby Co. TX, 6059 58 A1
Crosbyton TX, 1741 58 B1
Cross City FL, 1728 137 F3
Cross Co. AR, 17870 118 A1
Crossett AR, 5507 125 F1
Cross Hill SC, 507 121 F3
Cross Keys NJ, 3600 146 C4
Crosslake MN, 2141 64 B4
Cross Plains TN, 1714 109 F3
Cross Plains TX, 982 59 D3
Cross Plains WI, 3538 74 B3
Cross Roads TX, 1563 59 F2
Crossville AL, 1862 120 A3
Crossville IL, 745 99 D4
Crossville TN, 10795 110 B4
Crosswicks NJ, 900 147 D2
Croswell MI, 2447 76 C3
Crothersville IN, 1591 99 F3
Croton Falls NY, 1200 148 C2
Croton-on-Hudson NY, 8070 148 B2
Crow Agency MT, 1616 24 C1
Crowder MS, 712 118 B3
Crowder OK, 430 116 A1
Crowell TX, 948 58 C1
Crowley LA, 13265 133 E2
Crowley TX, 12838 59 E2
Crowley Co. CO, 5823 41 F3
Crown Hts. NY, 2840 148 B1
Crown Pt. IN, 27317 89 D2
Crown Pt. LA, 650 134 B3
Crownpoint NM, 2278 48 B2
Crown Pt. NY, 2119 81 D3
Crownsville MD, 1757 144 C3
Crow Wing Co. MN, 62500 66 C1
Croydon PA, 9950 248 E2
Crozet VA, 5565 102 C4
Cruger MS, 386 126 B1
Crump TN, 1428 119 D1
Crystal MN, 22151 235 B2
Crystal NM, 311 48 A2
Crystal Beach FL, 4000 266 A1
Crystal City MO, 4855 98 A4
Crystal City TX, 7138 60 C4
Crystal Falls MI, 1469 68 C2
Crystal Lake CT, 1945 150 A3
Crystal Lake IL, 40743 88 C1
Crystal Lakes OH, 1483 100 C1
Crystal River FL, 3108 140 B1
Crystal Sprs. FL, 1327 140 C2
Crystal Sprs. MS, 5044 126 B3
Cuba IL, 1294 88 A4
Cuba MO, 3356 97 F4
Cuba NM, 731 48 C2
Cuba NY, 1575 92 C1
Cuba City WI, 2086 74 A4
Cudahy CA, 23805 228 D3
Cudahy WI, 18267 75 D3
Cuddebackville NY, 750 148 A1
Cudjoe Key FL, 1763 143 D4
Cuero TX, 6841 61 E3
Culberson Co. TX, 2398 57 E4
Culbertson MT, 714 17 F2
Culbertson NE, 595 34 C4
Culdesac ID, 380 14 B4
Cullen LA, 1163 125 D1
Cullman AL, 14775 119 F3
Cullman Co. AL, 80406 119 F3
Culloden WV, 3061 101 E3
Cullowhee NC, 6228 121 D1
Culpeper VA, 16379 103 D3
Culpeper Co. VA, 46689 103 D3
Culver IN, 1353 89 E2
Culver OR, 1357 21 D3
Culver City CA, 38883 228 C3
Cumberland IN, 5169 99 F1
Cumberland KY, 2237 111 D2
Cumberland MD, 20859 102 C1
Cumberland NC, 4400 123 D2
Cumberland VA, 393 113 D1
Cumberland WI, 2170 67 E3
Cumberland Ctr. ME, 2499 82 B3
Cumberland Co. IL, 11048 99 D2
Cumberland Co. KY, 6856 110 A2
Cumberland Co. ME, 281674 82 B3
Cumberland Co. NJ, 156898 145 F2
Cumberland Co. NC, 319431 123 D2
Cumberland Co. PA, 235406 103 D1
Cumberland Co. TN, 56053 110 B4
Cumberland Co. VA, 10052 113 D1
Cumberland Foreside ME, 500 82 B3
Cumberland Hill RI, 7934 150 C2
Cumby TX, 777 124 A1
Cuming Co. NE, 9139 35 F2
Cumming GA, 5430 120 C3
Cunningham KS, 454 43 D4
Cupertino CA, 58302 36 B4
Curlew FL, 5900 266 A1
Currituck NC, 125 115 E1
Currituck Co. NC, 23547 115 E1
Curry Co. NM, 48376 49 F4
Curry Co. OR, 22364 28 A2
Curtis NE, 939 34 C4
Curwensville PA, 2542 92 B3
Cushing OK, 7826 51 F2
Cushing TX, 612 124 B3
Cushman AR, 452 107 F4
Cusseta GA, 11267 128 C3
Custer SD, 2067 25 F4
Custer Co. CO, 4255 41 E3
Custer Co. ID, 4368 23 D3
Custer Co. MT, 11699 25 E1
Custer Co. NE, 10939 34 C3
Custer Co. OK, 27469 51 D2
Custer Co. SD, 8216 25 F4
Cut and Shoot TX, 1070 132 A2
Cut Bank MT, 2869 15 E1
Cutchogue NY, 3349 149 E3
Cuthbert GA, 3873 128 C3
Cutler CA, 5000 45 D3
Cutler Ridge FL, 24781 143 E3
Cutlerville MI, 14370 75 F3
Cut Off LA, 5976 134 B3
Cutten CA, 3108 28 A4
Cuyahoga Co. OH, 1280122 91 E2
Cuyahoga Falls OH, 49652 91 E3
Cuyahoga Hts. OH, 638 204 F2
Cygnet OH, 597 90 C2
Cynthiana IN, 545 99 D4
Cynthiana KY, 6402 100 B4
Cypress CA, 47802 228 E4
Cypress Quarters FL, 1215 141 E4
Cyril OK, 1059 51 E3

D

Dacono CO, 4152 41 E1
Dacula GA, 4442 121 D3
Dade City FL, 6437 140 C2
Dade Co. GA, 16633 120 B2
Dade Co. MO, 7883 106 C1
Dadeville AL, 3230 128 B2
Daggett CA, 600 53 D1
Daggett Co. UT, 1059 32 A4
Dagsboro DE, 805 145 F4
Dahlgren VA, 2653 103 E4
Dahlonega GA, 5242 120 C3
Daingerfield TX, 2560 124 B1
Daisetta TX, 966 132 B2
Dakota City IA, 843 72 C4
Dakota City NE, 1919 35 F2
Dakota Co. MN, 398552 67 D4
Dakota Co. NE, 21006 35 F2
Dale IN, 1593 99 E4
Dale City VA, 65969 144 A4
Dale Co. AL, 50251 128 B4
Daleville AL, 5295 128 B4
Daleville IN, 1647 89 F4
Daleville VA, 2557 112 B1
Dalhart TX, 7930 50 A2
Dallam Co. TX, 6703 50 A2
Dallas GA, 11544 120 B4
Dallas NC, 4488 122 A1
Dallas OR, 14583 20 B2
Dallas PA, 2804 93 E2
Dallas TX, 1197816 59 F2
Dallas Ctr. IA, 1623 86 C2
Dallas City IL, 945 87 F3
Dallas Co. AL, 43820 127 F3
Dallas Co. AR, 8116 117 E4
Dallas Co. IA, 66135 86 C2
Dallas Co. MO, 16777 107 D1
Dallas Co. TX, 2368139 59 F2
Dallastown PA, 4049 103 E1
Dalton GA, 33128 120 B2
Dalton MA, 6892 94 C1
Dalton OH, 1830 91 E3
Dalton PA, 1234 93 F2
Dalton City IL, 544 98 C1
Dalton Gardens ID, 2335 14 B3
Dalworthington Gardens TX, 2259 207 B3
Daly City CA, 101123 36 B4
Dalzell SC, 3059 122 B3
Damariscotta ME, 1142 82 C3
Damascus MD, 15257 144 B2
Damascus OR, 10539 20 C2
Damascus VA, 814 111 F3
Damon TX, 552 132 A4
Dana IN, 608 99 E1
Dana Pt. CA, 33351 52 C3
Danboro PA, 1500 146 C2
Danbury CT, 80893 148 C2
Danbury NC, 189 112 B3
Danbury TX, 1715 132 A4
Dandridge TN, 2812 111 D4
Dane WI, 995 74 B3
Dane Co. WI, 488073 74 B3
Danforth IL, 604 89 D3
Dania Beach FL, 29639 143 F2
Daniel MD, 650 144 B1
Daniels Co. MT, 1751 17 E1
Danielson CT, 4051 150 B3
Danielsville GA, 560 121 D3
Dannemora NY, 3936 80 C1
Dansville NY, 4719 78 C4
Dante VA, 649 111 E2
Danube MN, 505 66 B4
Danvers IL, 1154 88 B4
Danvers MA, 26493 151 F1
Danville AR, 2409 117 D2
Danville CA, 42039 36 B4
Danville IL, 33027 89 D4
Danville IN, 9001 99 F1
Danville IA, 934 87 F3
Danville KY, 16218 110 B1
Danville NH, 4387 95 E1
Danville OH, 1044 91 D4
Danville PA, 4699 93 E3
Danville VT, 383 81 E2
Danville VA, 43055 112 C3
Danville WV, 691 101 E4
Daphne AL, 21570 135 E2
Darby MT, 720 23 D1
Darby PA, 10687 146 C3
Dardanelle AR, 4745 117 D1
Dardenne Prairie MO, 11494 98 A3
Dare Co. NC, 33920 115 F2
Dares Beach MD, 1400 144 C4
Darien CT, 20732 148 C3
Darien GA, 1975 130 B4
Darien IL, 22086 203 C5
Darien WI, 1580 74 C4
Darke Co. OH, 52959 100 B1
Darlington IN, 843 89 E4
Darlington SC, 6289 122 C3
Darlington WI, 2451 74 A4
Darlington Co. SC, 68681 122 B3
Darmstadt IN, 1407 99 D4
Darnestown MD, 6802 144 B2
Darrington WA, 1347 12 C2
Dasher GA, 912 137 F1
Dassel MN, 1469 66 C3
Dauphin PA, 791 93 D4
Dauphin Co. PA, 268100 93 D4
Dauphin Island AL, 1238 135 E2
Davenport FL, 2888 141 D2
Davenport IA, 99685 88 A2
Davenport ND, 252 19 E4
Davenport OK, 814 51 F2
Davenport WA, 1734 13 F3
David City NE, 2906 35 F3
Davidson NC, 10944 122 A1
Davidson Co. NC, 162878 112 B4
Davidson Co. TN, 626681 109 F4
Davidsville PA, 1130 92 B4
Davie FL, 91992 143 E2
Davie Co. NC, 41240 112 A4
Daviess Co. IN, 31648 99 E3
Daviess Co. KY, 96656 109 E1
Daviess Co. MO, 8433 96 C1
Davis CA, 65622 36 B3
Davis IL, 677 74 B4
Davis OK, 2683 51 F4
Davis WV, 660 102 B2
Davisboro GA, 2010 129 F1
Davis Co. IA, 8753 87 E3
Davis Co. UT, 306479 31 E3
Davison MI, 5173 76 B3
Davison Co. SD, 19504 27 E4
Davy WV, 420 111 F1
Dawes Co. NE, 9182 34 A1
Dawson GA, 4540 128 C3
Dawson MN, 1540 27 F2
Dawson TX, 807 59 F3
Dawson Co. GA, 22330 120 C3
Dawson Co. MT, 8966 17 F3
Dawson Co. NE, 24326 35 D4
Dawson Co. TX, 13833 58 A2
Dawson Sprs. KY, 2764 109 E2
Dawsonville GA, 2536 120 C3
Day Co. SD, 5710 27 E2
Dayton ID, 463 31 E2
Dayton IN, 1420 89 E4
Dayton IA, 837 72 C4
Dayton KY, 5338 204 B2
Dayton MN, 4671 66 C3
Dayton NV, 8964 37 D2
Dayton NJ, 7063 147 D1
Dayton OH, 141527 100 B1
Dayton OR, 2534 20 B2
Dayton TN, 7191 120 B1
Dayton TX, 7242 132 B3
Dayton VA, 1530 102 C3
Dayton WA, 2526 13 F4
Dayton WY, 757 24 C2
Daytona Beach FL, 61005 139 E4
Daytona Beach Shores FL, 4247 139 E4
Dayville CT, 1600 150 B3
Deadwood SD, 1270 25 F3
Deaf Smith Co. TX, 19372 49 F3
Deal NJ, 750 147 F2
Deale MD, 4945 144 C3
Deal Island MD, 471 103 F4
Dearborn MI, 98153 76 C4
Dearborn MO, 496 96 B1
Dearborn Co. IN, 50047 100 B2
Dearborn Hts. MI, 57774 210 B3
Dearing KS, 431 106 A2
DeArmanville AL, 700 120 A4
Deary ID, 506 14 B4
Deaver WY, 178 24 B2
De Baca Co. NM, 2022 49 E4
DeBary FL, 19320 141 D1
De Beque CO, 504 40 B2
Decatur AL, 55683 119 F2
Decatur AR, 1699 106 B3
Decatur GA, 19335 120 C4
Decatur IL, 76122 98 C1
Decatur IN, 9405 90 A3
Decatur MI, 1819 89 F1

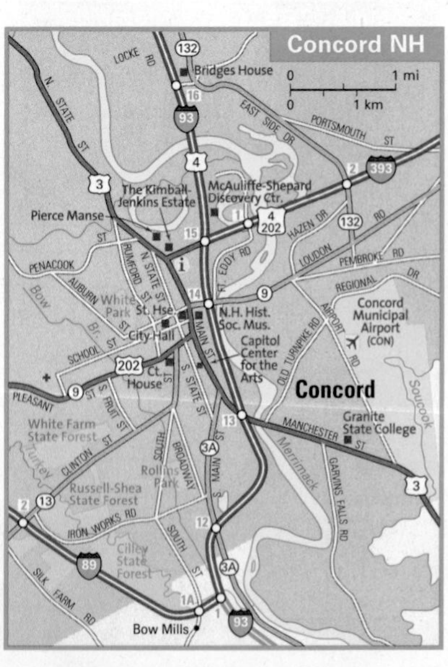
Concord NH
0 1 mi
0 1 km
Bridges House
The Kimball-Jenkins Estate
McAuliffe-Shepard Discovery Ctr.
Pierce Manse
St. Hse.
City Hall
N.H. Hist. Soc. Mus.
Capitol Center for the Arts
Concord Municipal Airport (CON)
Concord
Granite State College
White Farm State Forest
Russell-Shea State Forest
Cilley State Forest
Bow Mills

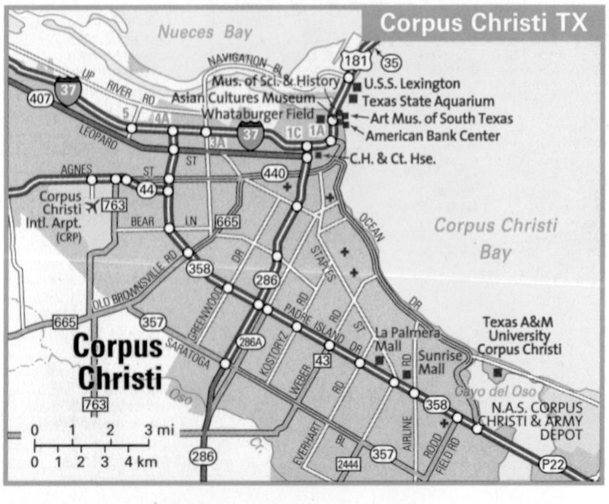
Corpus Christi TX
Nueces Bay
Mus. of Sci. & History
Asian Cultures Museum
Whataburger Field
U.S.S. Lexington
Texas State Aquarium
Art Mus. of South Texas
American Bank Center
C.H. & Ct. Hse.
Corpus Christi Intl. Arpt. (CRP)
Corpus Christi Bay
Corpus Christi
La Palmera Mall
Sunrise Mall
Texas A&M University Corpus Christi
N.A.S. CORPUS CHRISTI & ARMY DEPOT
0 1 2 3 mi
0 1 2 3 4 km

Entries in **bold black** indicate counties or parishes.
Entries in **bold color** indicate cities with detailed inset maps.

Dallas / Fort Worth TX

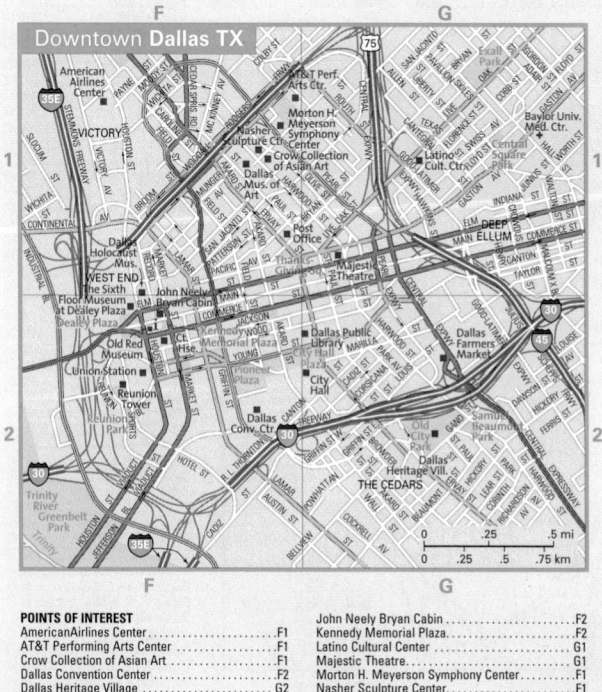

Downtown Dallas TX

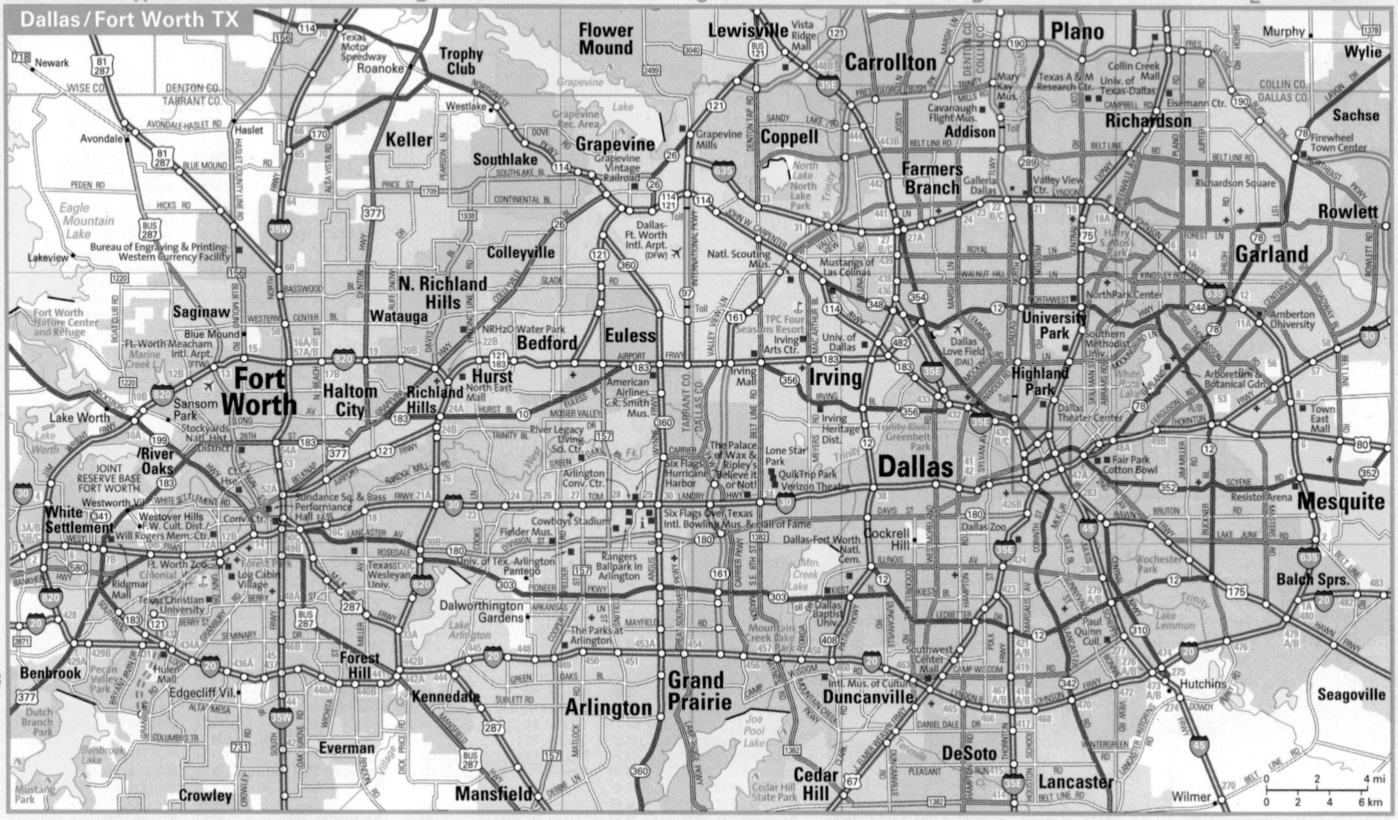

POINTS OF INTEREST

AmericanAirlines Center F1	John Neely Bryan Cabin F2	
AT&T Performing Arts Center F1	Kennedy Memorial Plaza F2	
Crow Collection of Asian Art F1	Latino Cultural Center G1	
Dallas Convention Center F2	Majestic Theatre F2	
Dallas Heritage Village G2	Morton H. Meyerson Symphony Center F1	
Dallas Holocaust Museum F1	Nasher Sculpture Center F1	
Dallas Museum of Art F1	Old Red Museum F2	
Dallas Public Library G2	Reunion Arena F2	
Farmers Market G2	Reunion Tower F2	
	The Sixth Floor Museum at Dealey Plaza F2	

208

Detroit–Dudley

Figures after entries indicate population, page number, and grid reference.

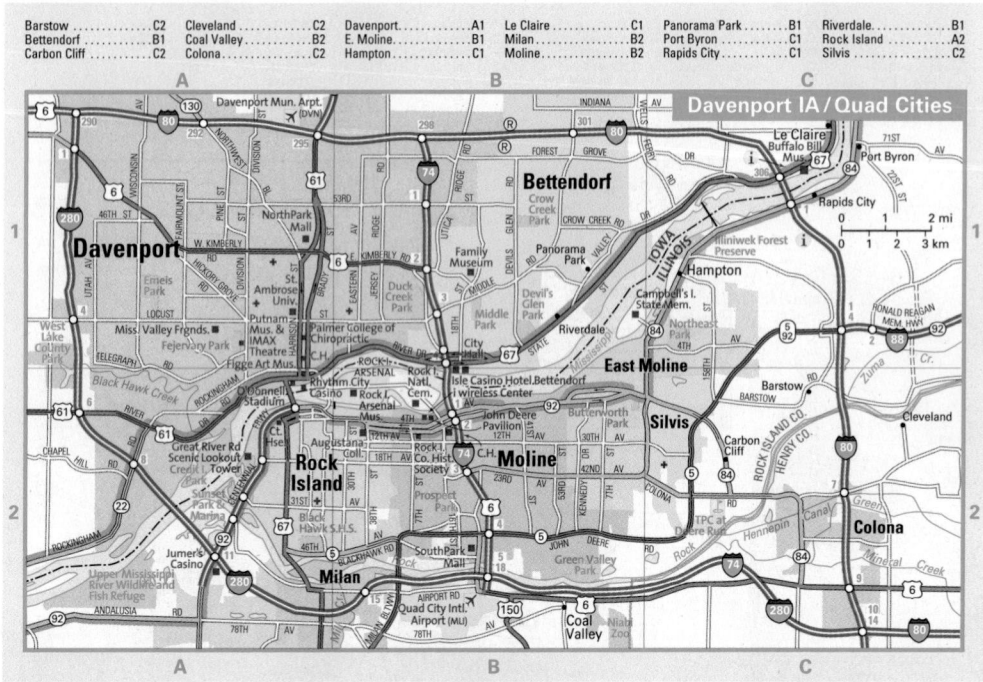

Davenport IA / Quad Cities

Barstow	C2	Cleveland	C2	Davenport	A1	Le Claire	C1	Panorama Park	B1	Riverdale	B1
Bettendorf	B1	Coal Valley	B2	E. Moline	B1	Milan	B2	Port Byron	C1	Rock Island	A2
Carbon Cliff	C2	Colona	C2	Hampton	C1	Moline	B2	Rapids City	C1	Silvis	C2

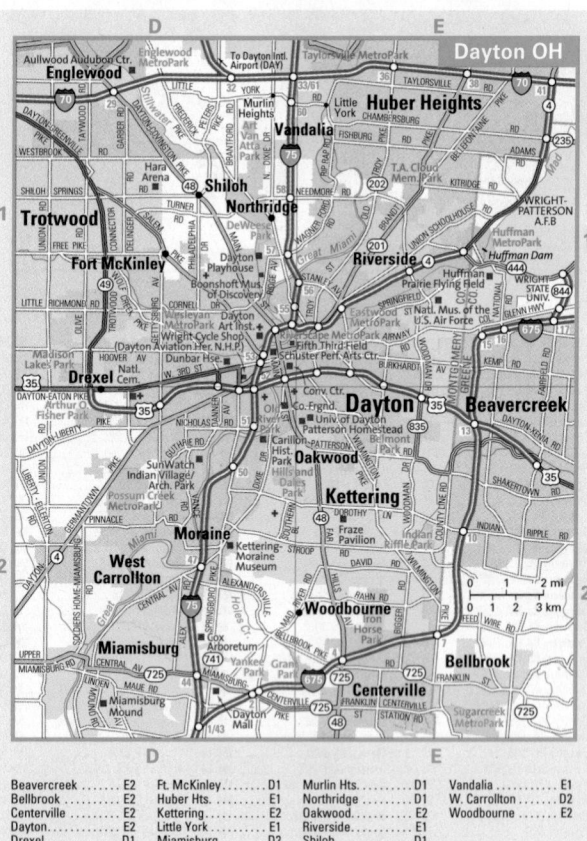

Dayton OH

Beavercreek	E2	Ft. McKinley	D1	Murlin Hts.	D1	Vandalia	E1
Bellbrook	E2	Huber Hts.	E1	Northridge	D1	W. Carrollton	D2
Centerville	E2	Kettering	E2	Oakwood	E2	Woodbourne	E2
Dayton	E2	Little York	E1	Riverside	E1		
Drexel	D1	Miamisburg	D2	Shiloh	D1		
Englewood	D1	Moraine	D2	Trotwood	D1		

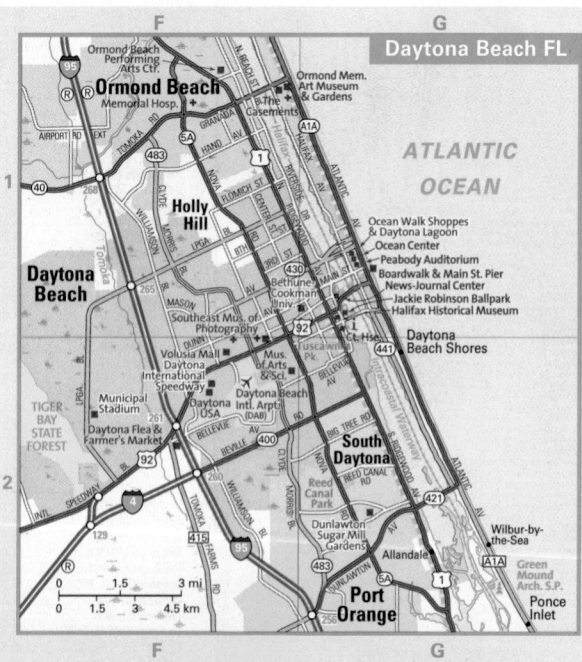

Daytona Beach FL

Allandale	G2	Holly Hill	F1	Port Orange	G2
Daytona Beach	F1	Ormond Beach	F1	S. Daytona	G2
Daytona Beach Shores	F1	Ponce Inlet	G2	Wilbur-by-the-Sea	G2

Detroit MI, 713777 .... 76 C4
Detroit TX, 732 .... 116 A4
Detroit Beach MI, 2087 .... 90 C1
Detroit Lakes MN, 8569 .... 19 F4
Deuel Co. NE, 1941 .... 34 A3
Deuel Co. SD, 4364 .... 27 F2
De Valls Bluff AR, 619 .... 117 F2
Deville LA, 1764 .... 125 E4
Devils Lake ND, 7141 .... 19 D2
Devine TX, 4350 .... 61 D3
Devola OH, 2652 .... 101 F2
Devon PA, 1515 .... 248 A2
Dewar OK, 888 .... 116 A1

Dewey OK, 3432 .... 51 F1
Dewey Beach DE, 341 .... 145 F4
Dewey Co. OK, 4810 .... 51 D2
Dewey Co. SD, 5301 .... 26 C2
Dewey-Humboldt AZ, 3894 .... 47 D4
Deweyville TX, 1023 .... 132 C2
Deweyville UT, 332 .... 31 E3
DeWitt AR, 3292 .... 117 F3
De Witt IA, 5322 .... 88 A1
DeWitt MI, 4507 .... 76 A3
De Witt NE, 513 .... 35 F4
De Witt NY, 24071 .... 79 E3
De Witt Co. IL, 16561 .... 88 B4

DeWitt Co. TX, 20097 .... 61 E3
Dexter GA, 575 .... 129 E2
Dexter IA, 611 .... 86 C2
Dexter ME, 2158 .... 82 C1
Dexter MI, 4067 .... 76 B4
Dexter MO, 7864 .... 108 B3
Dexter NM, 1266 .... 57 E2
Dexter NY, 1052 .... 79 E2
Dexter OR, 750 .... 20 C4
Diablo CA, 1158 .... 259 D2
Diamond IL, 2527 .... 88 C2
Diamond MO, 902 .... 106 C2
Diamond Bar CA, 55544 .... 229 D4

Diamond City AR, 782 .... 107 D3
Diamondhead MS, 8425 .... 134 C2
Diamond Hill RI, 1100 .... 150 C2
Diamond Sprs. CA, 11037 .... 36 C2
Diamondville WY, 737 .... 31 E3
Diaz AR, 1318 .... 107 F4
D'Iberville MS, 9486 .... 135 D2
Diboll TX, 4776 .... 132 B1
Dickens TX, 286 .... 58 B1
Dickens Co. TX, 2444 .... 58 B1
Dickenson Co. VA, 15903 .... 111 E2
Dickey Co. ND, 5289 .... 27 D1
Dickeyville WI, 1061 .... 73 F4
Dickinson ND, 17787 .... 18 A4
Dickinson TX, 18680 .... 132 B4
Dickinson Co. IA, 16667 .... 72 B3
Dickinson Co. KS, 19754 .... 43 E2
Dickinson Co. MI, 26168 .... 69 D2
Dickson OK, 1207 .... 51 F4
Dickson TN, 14538 .... 109 E4
Dickson City PA, 6070 .... 93 F2

Dickson Co. TN, 49666 .... 109 E4
Dierks AR, 1133 .... 116 C3
Dieterich IL, 617 .... 98 C2
Dighton KS, 1038 .... 42 C3
Dighton MA, 6175 .... 151 D3
Dike IA, 1209 .... 73 D4
Dilkon AZ, 1184 .... 47 F3
Dill City OK, 562 .... 51 D3
Dilley TX, 3894 .... 60 C4
Dillingham AK, 2329 .... 154 B3
Dillon CO, 904 .... 41 D1
Dillon MT, 4134 .... 23 E2
Dillon SC, 6788 .... 122 C3
Dillon Co. SC, 32062 .... 122 C3
Dillonvale OH, 3474 .... 91 F4
Dillsboro IN, 1327 .... 100 A2
Dillsburg PA, 2563 .... 93 D4
Dillwyn VA, 447 .... 113 D1
Dilworth MN, 4024 .... 19 F4
Dimmit Co. TX, 9996 .... 60 C4
Dimmitt TX, 4393 .... 50 A4

Dimondale MI, 1234 .... 76 A4
Dinosaur CO, 339 .... 32 B4
Dinuba CA, 21453 .... 45 D3
Dinwiddie VA, 350 .... 113 E2
Dinwiddie Co. VA, 28001 .... 113 E2
District Hts. MD, 5837 .... 271 F4
Divernon IL, 1172 .... 98 B1
Dixfield ME, 1076 .... 82 B2
Dixie Co. FL, 16422 .... 137 F3
Dixmoor IL, 3644 .... 203 E6
Dixon CA, 18351 .... 36 B3
Dixon IL, 15733 .... 88 B2
Dixon KY, 786 .... 109 E1
Dixon NM, 1549 .... 97 E4
Dixon MT, 203 .... 15 D3
Dixon Co. NE, 6000 .... 35 F3
D'Lo MS, 394 .... 126 B3
Dobbins Hts. NC, 866 .... 122 C2
Dobbs Ferry NY, 10875 .... 148 B3
Dobson NC, 1586 .... 112 A3
Dock Jct. GA, 7721 .... 139 D1
Doctor Phillips FL, 10981 .... 246 B3
Doctors Inlet FL, 1400 .... 139 D2
Doddridge Co. WV, 8202 .... 102 A2
Dodge NE, 612 .... 35 F2
Dodge Ctr. MN, 2670 .... 73 D1
Dodge City AL, 593 .... 119 F3
Dodge City KS, 27340 .... 42 C4
Dodge Co. GA, 21796 .... 129 E3
Dodge Co. MN, 20087 .... 73 D1
Dodge Co. NE, 36691 .... 35 F3
Dodge Co. WI, 88759 .... 74 C2
Dodgeville WI, 4693 .... 74 A3
Doerun GA, 774 .... 129 D4
Doland SD, 180 .... 27 E2
Dolan Sprs. AZ, 2033 .... 46 B3
Dolgeville NY, 2206 .... 79 F3
Dollar Bay MI, 1082 .... 65 F3
Dolores CO, 936 .... 40 B4
Dolores Co. CO, 2064 .... 40 B4
Dolton IL, 23153 .... 203 E6
Doña Ana NM, 1211 .... 56 B3
Dona Ana Co. NM, 209233 .... 56 B3
Donald OR, 979 .... 20 B2
Donaldsonville LA, 7436 .... 134 A2
Donalsonville GA, 2650 .... 137 D1
Dongola IL, 726 .... 108 C1
Doniphan MO, 1997 .... 108 A3
Doniphan NE, 829 .... 35 D4
Doniphan Co. KS, 7945 .... 96 B1
Donley Co. TX, 3677 .... 50 B3
Donna TX, 15798 .... 63 E4
Donnellson IA, 912 .... 87 F3
Donora PA, 4781 .... 92 A4
Doolittle MO, 630 .... 97 E3
Dooly Co. GA, 14918 .... 129 D3
Doon IA, 577 .... 27 F4
Dora AL, 2025 .... 119 F4
Doral FL, 45704 .... —
Doraville GA, 8330 .... 120 C4
Dorchester NE, 586 .... 35 F4
Dorchester WI, 876 .... 68 A4
Dorchester Co. MD, 32618 .... 103 F4
Dorchester Co. SC, 136555 .... 130 C1
Dormont PA, 8593 .... 250 B3

Dorr MI, 2800 .... 75 F4
Dorris CA, 939 .... 28 C2
Dorset VT, 249 .... 81 D4
Dorsey MD, 1000 .... 193 B4
Dortches NC, 835 .... 113 D4
Dos Palos CA, 4950 .... 44 C2
Dothan AL, 65496 .... 128 B4
Double Sprs. AL, 1083 .... 119 E3
Dougherty Co. GA, 94565 .... 128 C4
Douglas AL, 744 .... 120 A3
Douglas AZ, 17378 .... 55 F4
Douglas GA, 11589 .... 129 E4
Douglas MA, 8471 .... 150 C1
Douglas MI, 1232 .... 75 E4
Douglas WY, 6120 .... 33 E1
Douglas Co. CO, 285465 .... 41 E2
Douglas Co. GA, 132403 .... 120 C4
Douglas Co. IL, 19980 .... 99 D1
Douglas Co. KS, 110826 .... 96 A3
Douglas Co. MN, 36009 .... 66 B2
Douglas Co. MO, 13684 .... 107 E2
Douglas Co. NE, 517110 .... 35 F3
Douglas Co. NV, 46997 .... 37 D2
Douglas Co. OR, 107667 .... 20 B4
Douglas Co. SD, 3002 .... 27 E4
Douglas Co. WA, 38431 .... 13 E3
Douglas Co. WI, 44159 .... 64 C4
Douglass KS, 1700 .... 43 F4
Douglass Hills KY, 5484 .... 230 E2
Douglassville PA, 448 .... 146 B2
Douglasville GA, 30961 .... 120 C4
Dousman WI, 2302 .... 74 C3
Dove Creek CO, 735 .... 40 A4
Dover AR, 1378 .... 117 D1
Dover DE, 36047 .... 145 E2
Dover FL, 3702 .... 140 C2
Dover ID, 556 .... 14 B2
Dover MA, 2265 .... 151 D1
Dover NH, 29987 .... 82 A4
Dover NJ, 18157 .... 148 A3
Dover OH, 12826 .... 91 E4
Dover PA, 2007 .... 103 E1
Dover TN, 1417 .... 109 D3
Dover-Foxcroft ME, 2528 .... 82 C1
Dover Plains NY, 1323 .... 94 B3
Dowagiac MI, 5879 .... 89 F1
Dowling Park FL, 650 .... 137 F2
Downers Grove IL, 47833 .... 89 D1
Downey CA, 111772 .... 52 C2
Downey ID, 625 .... 31 E2
Downieville CA, 282 .... 36 C1
Downingtown PA, 7891 .... 146 B3
Downs IL, 1005 .... 88 C4
Downs KS, 900 .... 43 D1
Downs IA, 538 .... 72 C4
Doyle CA, 539 .... 37 D4
Doyle TN, 537 .... 110 A4
Doylestown OH, 3051 .... 91 E3
Doylestown PA, 8380 .... 146 C2
Doyline LA, 818 .... 125 D2
Drain OR, 1151 .... 20 B4
Drake ND, 275 .... 18 C2
Drakesboro KY, 515 .... 109 E2
Drakes Branch VA, 530 .... 113 D2
Draper UT, 42274 .... 31 E4
Dravosburg PA, 1792 .... 250 C3
Drayton ND, 824 .... 19 E2
Dresden OH, 1529 .... 91 E4
Dresden TN, 3005 .... 108 C3
Dresser WI, 895 .... 67 D3
Drew MS, 1927 .... 118 A4
Drew Co. AR, 18509 .... 117 F4
Drexel MO, 965 .... 96 B3
Drexel NC, 1858 .... 111 F4
Drexel OH, 2076 .... 208 D1
Drexel Hill PA, 28043 .... 146 C3
Driggs ID, 1660 .... 23 F4
Dripping Sprs. TX, 1788 .... 61 D2
Driscoll TX, 739 .... 63 F2
Druid Hills GA, 14568 .... 190 D3
Drummond MT, 309 .... 15 E4
Drumright OK, 2907 .... 51 F2
Dryden ME, 1100 .... 82 B2
Dryden MI, 951 .... 76 C3
Dryden NY, 1890 .... 79 D4
Dryden VA, 1200 .... 111 D2
Dry Mills ME, 700 .... 82 B3
Dry Prong LA, 436 .... 125 E4
Dry Ridge KY, 2191 .... 100 B3
Duarte CA, 21321 .... 228 E2
Dubach LA, 961 .... 125 E2
Dublin CA, 46036 .... 259 E3
Dublin GA, 16201 .... 129 E2
Dublin IN, 790 .... 100 A1
Dublin NH, 650 .... 145 D1
Dublin OH, 41751 .... 90 C4
Dublin PA, 2158 .... 146 C2
Dublin TX, 3654 .... 59 D3
Dublin VA, 2534 .... 112 A2
Dubois ID, 677 .... 23 E3
DuBois PA, 7794 .... 92 B3
Dubois WY, 971 .... 24 B4
Dubois Co. IN, 41889 .... 99 E3
Duboistown PA, 1205 .... 93 D2
Dubuque IA, 57637 .... 73 F4
Dubuque Co. IA, 93653 .... 73 F4
Duchesne UT, 1690 .... 32 A4
Duchesne Co. UT, 18607 .... 39 F1
Duck Hill MS, 732 .... 118 B4
Ducktown TN, 475 .... 120 C2
Ducor CA, 612 .... 45 D4
Dudley MA, 11390 .... 150 B2

Entries in **bold black** indicate counties or parishes.
Entries in **bold color** indicate cities with detailed inset maps.

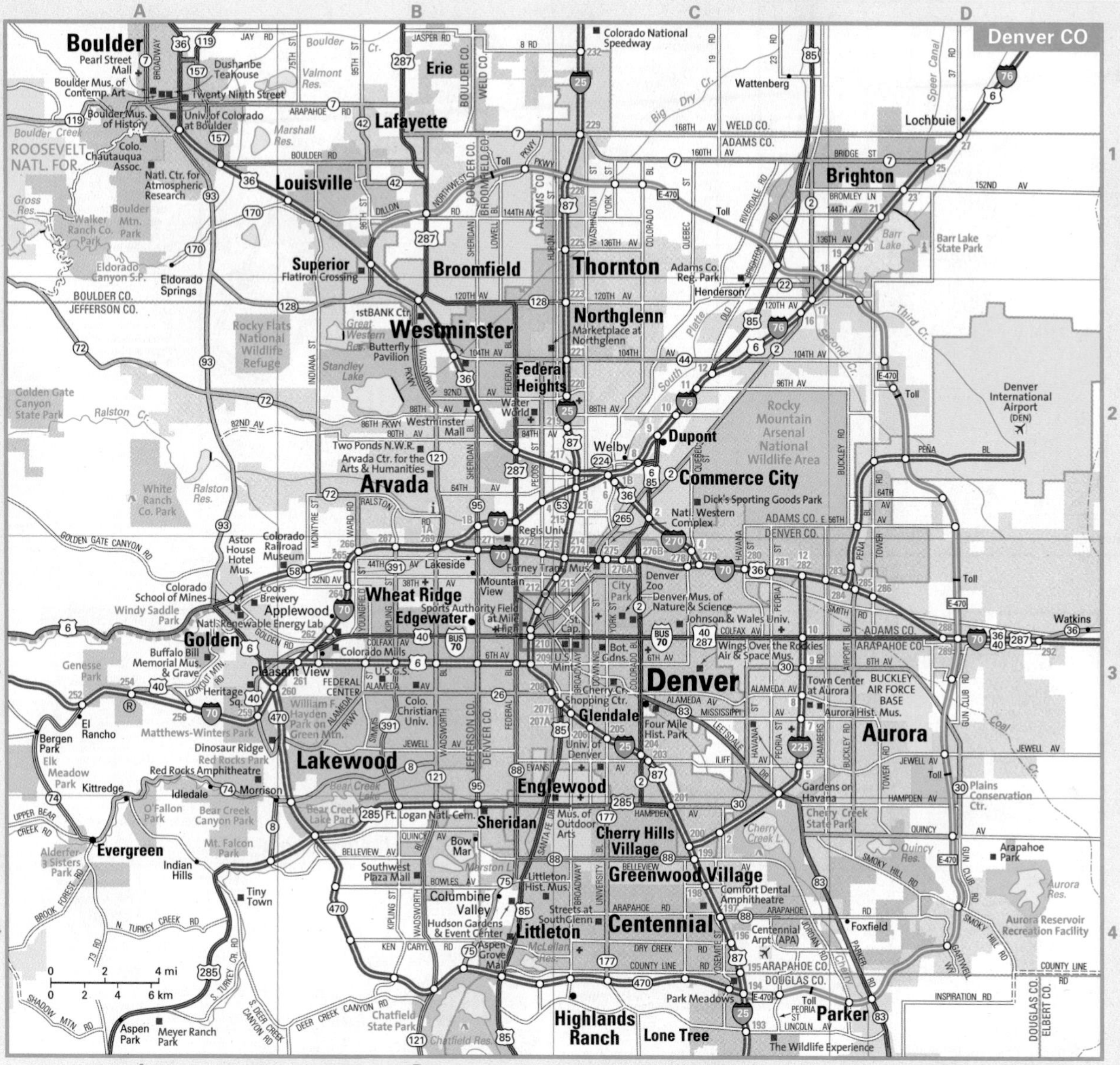

Denver CO

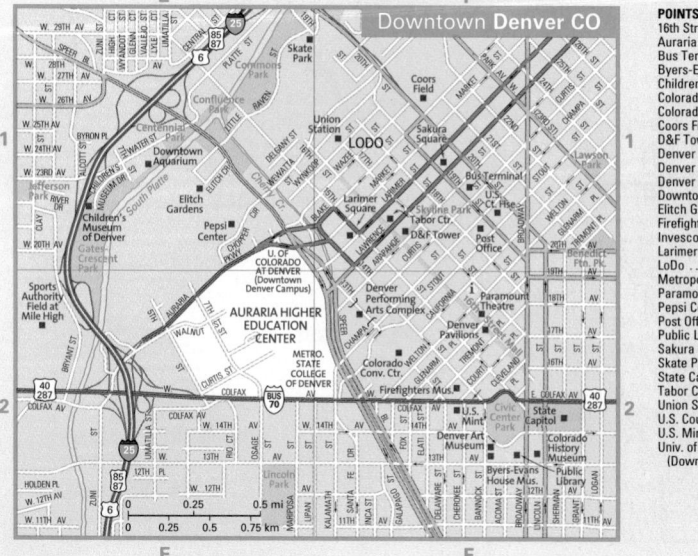

Downtown Denver CO

POINTS OF INTEREST

Figures after entries indicate population, page number, and grid reference.

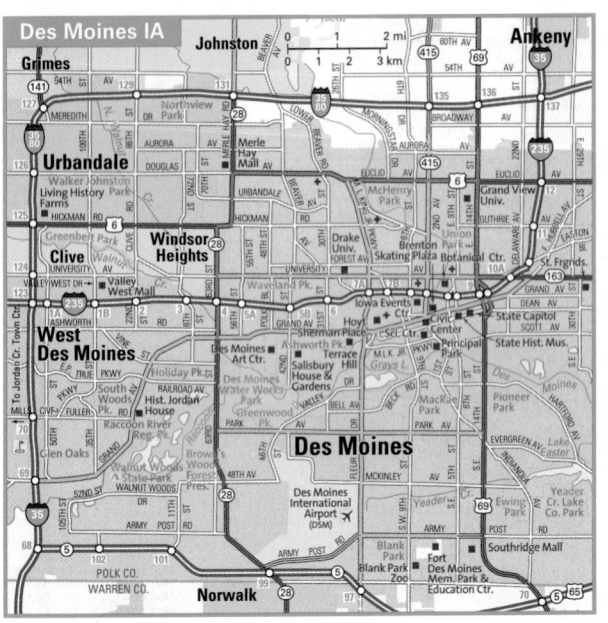

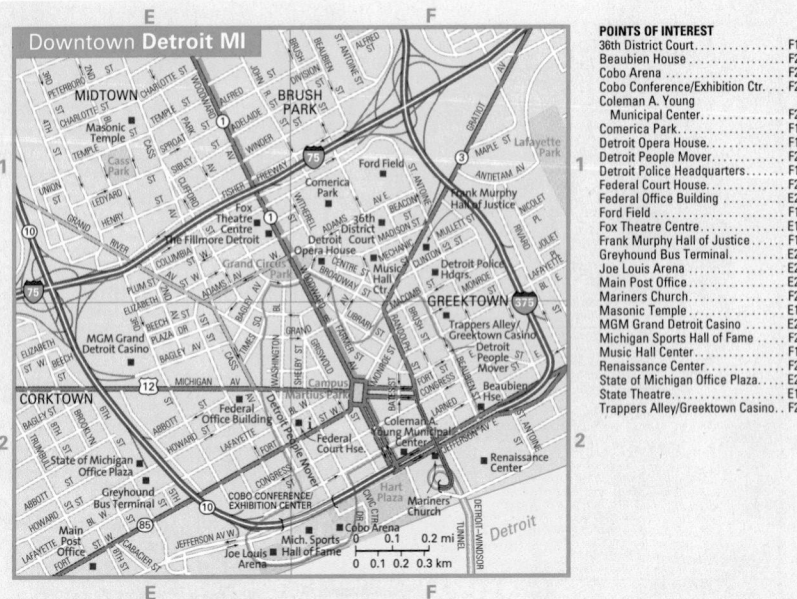

Downtown Detroit MI

Detroit MI

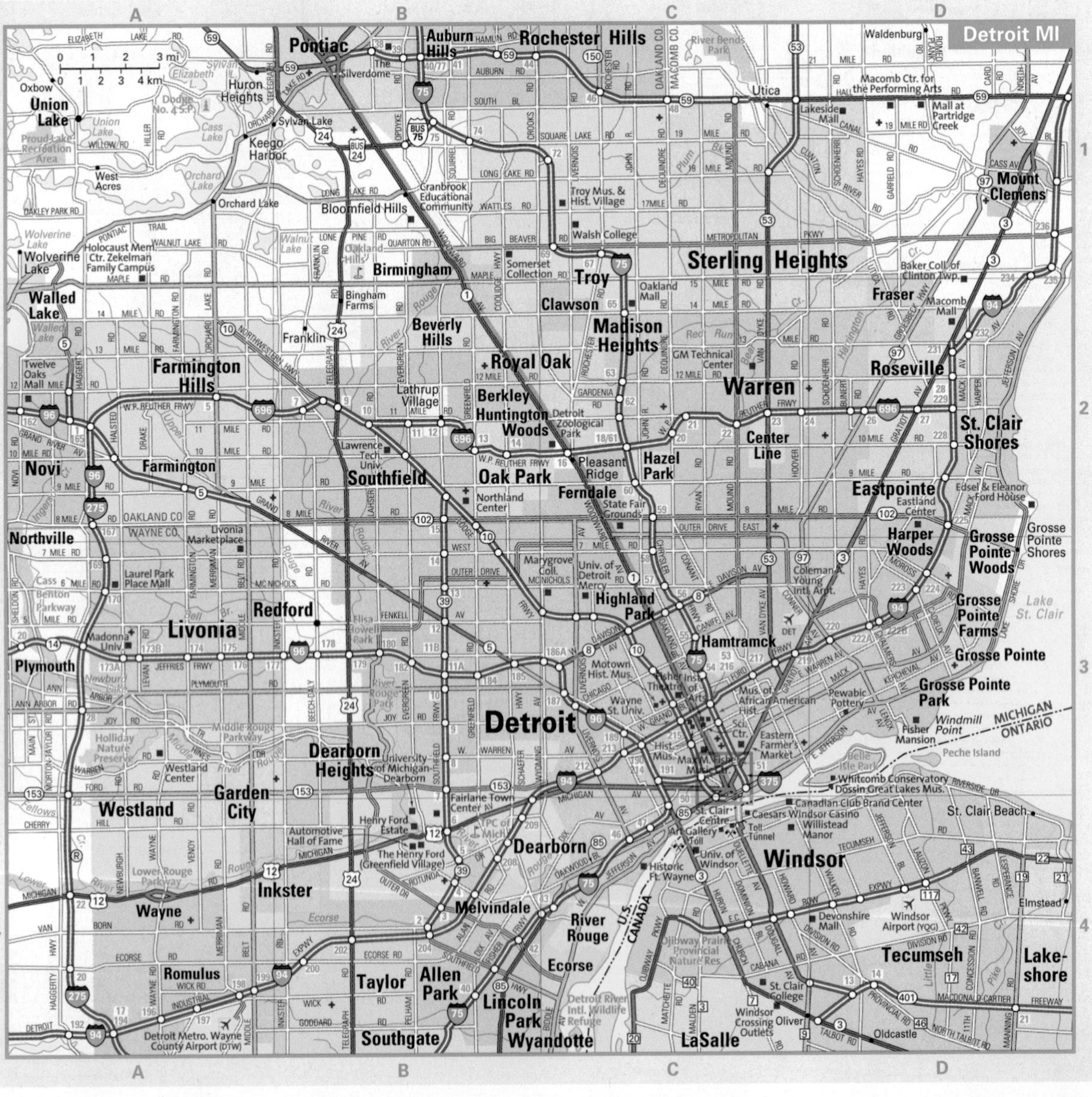

Entries in **bold black** indicate counties or parishes.
Entries in **bold color** indicate cities with detailed inset maps.

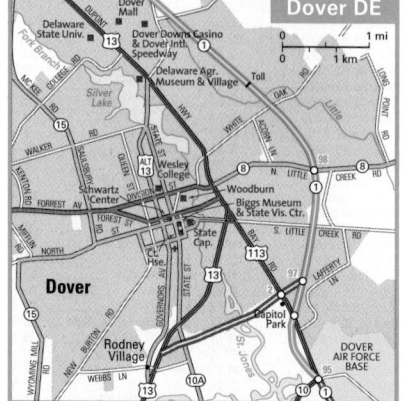

Dover DE

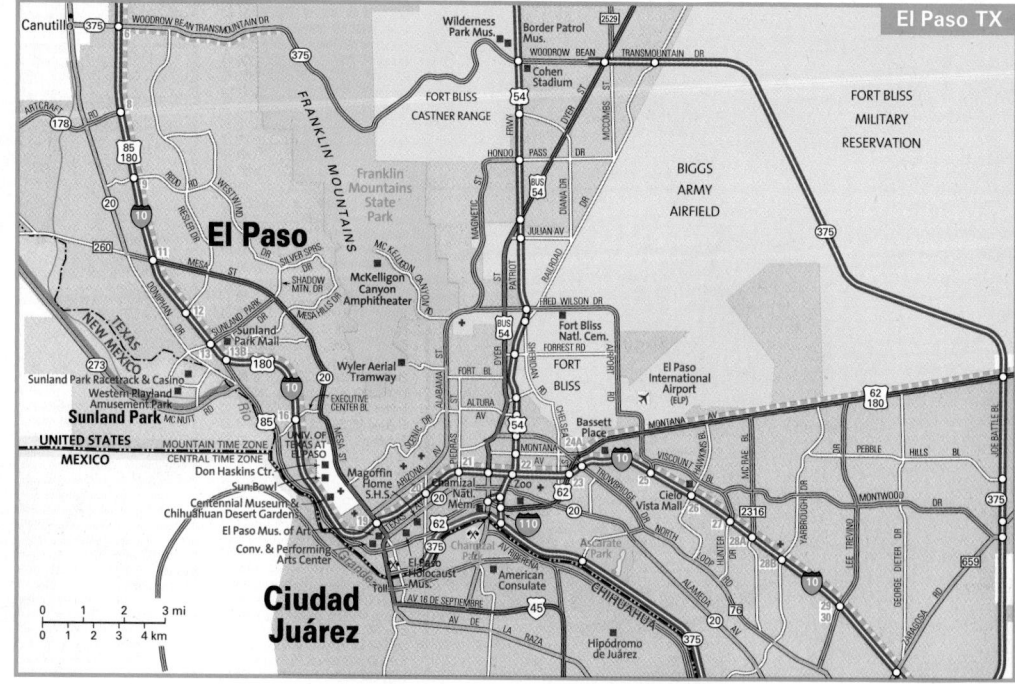

El Paso TX

Figures after entries indicate population, page number, and grid reference.

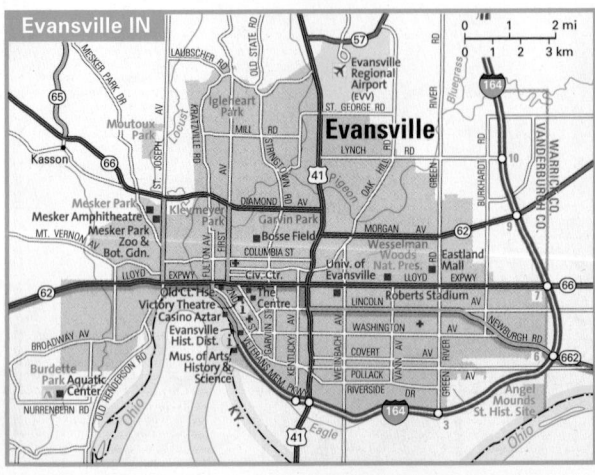

Erie PA

Eugene OR

Evansville IN

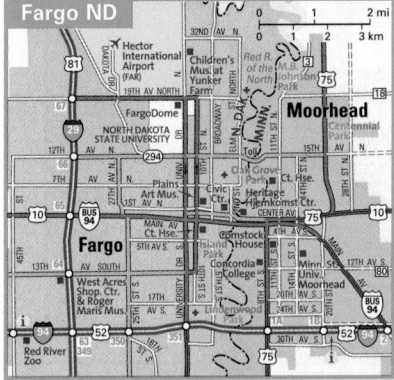

Fargo ND

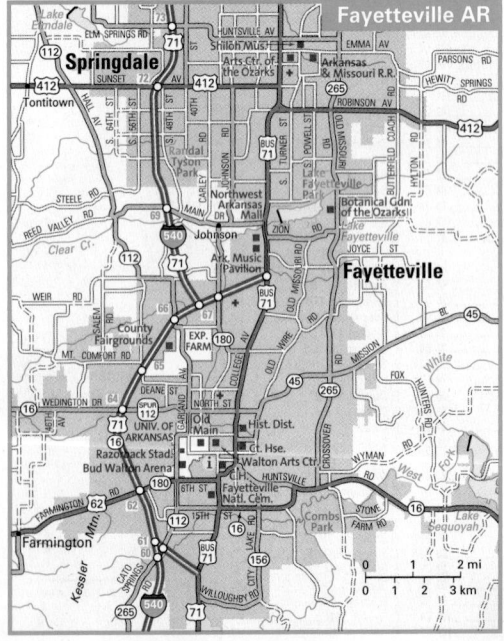

Fayetteville AR

Entries in **bold black** indicate counties or parishes.
Entries in **bold color** indicate cities with detailed inset maps.

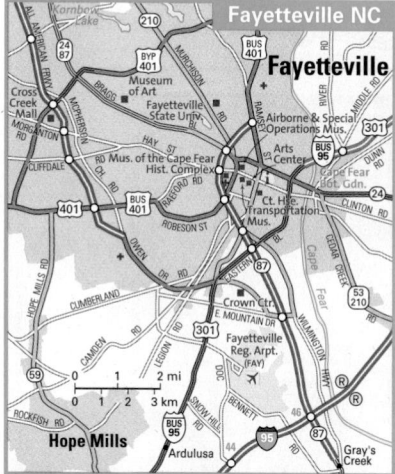

Fayetteville NC

Fayetteville

Hope Mills

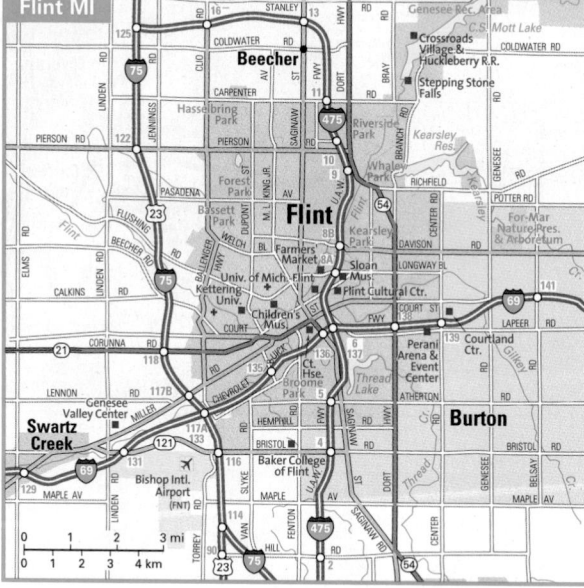

Flint MI

Beecher

Flint

Burton

Swartz Creek

Flagstaff AZ

Flagstaff

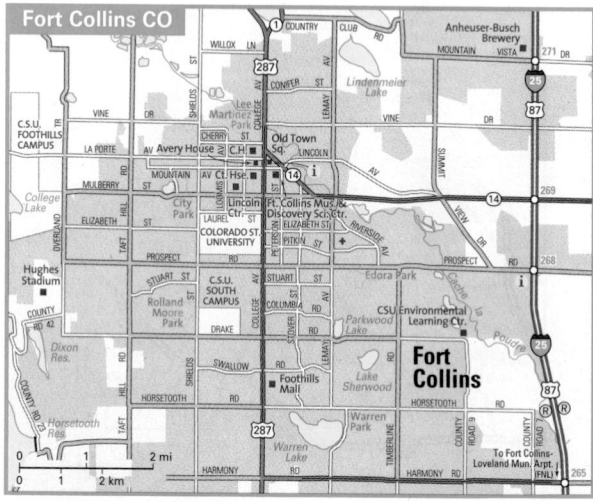

Fort Collins CO

Fort Collins

Figures after entries indicate population, page number, and grid reference.

Fort Myers FL

Frankfort KY

Fresno CA

Fort Wayne IN

Entries in **bold black** indicate counties or parishes.
Entries in **bold color** indicate cities with detailed inset maps.

Franklin Co. ME, *30768* 82 B1
Franklin Co. MA, *71372* 150 A1
Franklin Co. MS, *8118* 126 A4
Franklin Co. MO, *101492* 97 F3
Franklin Co. NE, *3225* 43 D1
Franklin Co. NY, *51599* 80 C2
Franklin Co. NC, *60619* 113 D4
Franklin Co. OH, *1163414* 101 D1
Franklin Co. PA, *149618* 103 D1
Franklin Co. TN, *41052* 120 A1
Franklin Co. TX, *10605* 124 B1
Franklin Co. VT, *47746* 81 D1
Franklin Co. VA, *56159* 112 B2
Franklin Co. WA, *78163* 13 F4
Franklin Furnace OH, *1660* 101 D3
Franklin Grove IL, *1021* 88 B1
Franklin Par. LA, *20767* 125 F2
Franklin Park IL, *18333* 203 C4
Franklin Park PA, *13470* 92 A3
Franklin Sprs. GA, *952* 121 E3
Franklin Square NY, *29320* 241 G4
Franklinton LA, *3857* 134 B1
Franklinton NC, *2023* 113 D4
Franklinville NJ, *1500* 145 F1
Franklinville NY, *1740* 78 B4
Franklinville NC, *1164* 112 B4
Frankston TX, *1229* 124 A3
Frankton IN, *1862* 89 F4
Frannie WY, *157* 24 B2
Fraser CO, *1224* 41 D1
Fraser MI, *14480* 210 D2
Frazee MN, *1350* 19 F4
Frazer MT, *362* 17 E2
Frazeysburg OH, *1326* 91 D4
Frazier Park CA, *2691* 52 B1
Frederic WI, *1137* 67 E2
Frederica DE, *774* 145 E3
Frederick CO, *8679* 41 E1
Frederick MD, *65239* 144 A1
Frederick OK, *3940* 51 D4
Frederick SD, *199* 27 D1
Frederick Co. MD, *233385* 144 A1
Frederick Co. VA, *102* 102 C2
Fredericksburg IA, *931* 73 E3
Fredericksburg PA, *1357* 92 A2
Fredericksburg TX, *10530* 61 D2
Fredericksburg VA, *24286* 103 D4
Fredericktown MO, *3985* 108 A1
Fredericktown OH, *2493* 91 D4
Fredonia AZ, *1314* 47 D1
Fredonia KS, *2482* 106 A1
Fredonia NY, *11230* 78 A4
Fredonia PA, *502* 91 F2
Fredonia WI, *2160* 74 C2
Freeborn Co. MN, *31255* 72 C2
Freeburg IL, *4354* 98 B3
Freeburg PA, *575* 93 D3
Freedom CA, *3070* 44 B2
Freedom WI, *1500* 74 C1
Freehold NJ, *12052* 147 E2
Freeland MI, *6969* 76 B2
Freeland PA, *3531* 93 E3
Freeland WA, *2045* 262 A1
Freeman MO, *482* 96 B3
Freeman SD, *1306* 27 E4
Freemansburg PA, *2636* 146 C1
Freeport FL, *1787* 136 B2
Freeport IL, *25638* 74 B4
Freeport ME, *1485* 82 B3
Freeport NY, *42860* 147 F1
Freeport PA, *1813* 92 A3
Freeport TX, *12049* 133 E4
Freer TX, *2818* 63 E2
Freestone Co. TX, *19816* 59 F4
Freetown IN, *385* 99 F2
Freetown NY, *2400* 149 F3
Freeville NY, *520* 79 D4
Freewood Acres NJ, *3100* 147 E2
Fremont CA, *214089* 36 B4
Fremont IN, *2138* 90 A1
Fremont IA, *743* 87 E2
Fremont MI, *4081* 75 F2
Fremont NE, *26397* 35 F3
Fremont NH, *4283* 81 F4
Fremont NC, *1255* 123 E1
Fremont OH, *16734* 90 C2
Fremont WI, *679* 74 C1
Fremont Co. CO, *46824* 41 D3
Fremont Co. ID, *13242* 23 F3
Fremont Co. IA, *7441* 86 A3
Fremont Co. WY, *40123* 32 C1
Fremont Hills MO, *826* 107 D2
Frenchburg KY, *486* 100 C4
French Camp CA, *3376* 36 C4
French Lick IN, *1807* 99 F3
French Settlement LA, *1116* 134 A2
Frenchtown MT, *1825* 15 D4
Frenchtown NJ, *1373* 146 C1
Frenchville ME, *1225* 85 D1
Fresno CA, *494665* 44 C3
Fresno TX, *19069* 220 B4
Fresno Co. CA, *930450* 37 E4
Frewsburg NY, *1906* 92 B1
Friant CA, *509* 44 C2
Friars Pt. MS, *1200* 118 A3
Friday Harbor WA, *2162* 12 B2
Fridley MN, *27208* 67 D3
Friedens PA, *1523* 92 B4
Friedensburg PA, *858* 146 A1
Friend NE, *1027* 35 E4
Friendly MD, *9250* 144 B4

G

Gabbs NV, *269* 37 F2
Gackle ND, *310* 19 D4
Gadsden AL, *36856* 120 A3
Gadsden AZ, *678* 53 F4
Gadsden TN, *470* 108 C4
Gadsden Co. FL, *46389* 137 D2
Gaffney SC, *12414* 121 F2
Gage Co. NE, *22311* 35 F4
Gahanna OH, *33248* 101 D1
Gail TX, *231* 58 B2
Gainesboro TN, *962* 110 A3
Gaines Co. TX, *17526* 57 F2
Gainesville FL, *124354* 138 C3
Gainesville GA, *33804* 121 D3
Gainesville MO, *773* 107 E3
Gainesville TX, *16002* 59 E1
Gainesville VA, *11481* 144 A3
Gaithersburg MD, *59933* 144 B2
Galatia IL, *933* 108 C1
Galax VA, *7042* 112 A3
Galena AK, *470* 154 C2
Galena IL, *3429* 74 A4
Galena IN, *1818* 99 F4
Galena KS, *3085* 106 B2
Galena MO, *440* 107 D2
Galena Park TX, *10887* 220 C3
Galesburg IL, *32195* 88 A3
Galesburg MI, *2009* 75 F4
Gales Ferry CT, *1162* 149 F1
Galesville WI, *1481* 73 F1
Galeton PA, *1149* 92 C1
Galeville NY, *4617* 265 A1
Galien MI, *549* 89 E1
Galilee RI, *700* 150 C4
Galion OH, *10512* 91 D3
Galisteo NM, *210* 49 D3
Gallatin MO, *1786* 96 C1
Gallatin TN, *30278* 109 F3
Gallatin Co. IL, *5589* 109 D1
Gallatin Co. KY, *8589* 100 B3
Gallatin Co. MT, *89513* 23 F2
Gallatin Gateway MT, *856* 23 F1
Gallia Co. OH, *30934* 101 E3
Galliano LA, *7676* 134 B4
Gallipolis OH, *3641* 101 E3
Gallitzin PA, *1668* 92 B4
Gallup NM, *21678* 48 A3

Galt CA, *23647* 36 C3
Gale Mill SC, *913* 122 A2
Galva IL, *2589* 88 A2
Galva KS, *870* 43 E3
Galveston IN, *1311* 89 F3
Galveston KY, *450* 111 E1
Galveston TX, *47743* 132 B4
Galveston Co. TX, *291309* 132 B4
Gamaliel KY, *376* 110 A3
Gambell AK, *491* 154 A2
Gamber MD, *1000* 144 B1
Gambier OH, *2391* 91 D4
Gamewell NC, *4051* 111 F4
Ganado AZ, *1210* 47 F2
Ganado TX, *2003* 61 F3
Gang Mills NY, *4185* 93 D1
Gann Valley SD, *14* 27 D2
Gansevoort NY, *800* 81 D4
Gantt SC, *14229* 121 F3
Gap PA, *1931* 146 A3
Garber OK, *822* 51 E1
Gardena CA, *58829* 228 C4
Garden City AL, *492* 119 F3
Garden City CO, *234* 33 E4
Garden City GA, *8778* 130 B3
Garden City ID, *10972* 22 B4
Garden City KS, *26658* 42 B3
Garden City MI, *27692* 210 A3
Garden City MO, *1642* 96 C3
Garden City NY, *22371* 241 G3
Garden City SC, *9209* 123 D4
Garden City TX, *334* 58 A3
Garden Co. NE, *2057* 34 A3
Gardendale AL, *13893* 119 F4
Gardendale MI, *800* 76 C3
Gardendale TX, *1574* 58 A3
Garden Grove CA, *170883* 228 E4
Garden Home OH, *6674* 251 C2
Garden Plain KS, *849* 43 E4
Garden Ridge TX, *3259* 61 E1
Garden View PA, *2503* 93 D2
Garfield Co. AR, *1000* 146 C1
Gardiner ME, *5800* 82 C3
Gardiner MT, *875* 23 F2
Gardiner NY, *950* 148 B1
Gardner IL, *1463* 88 C1
Gardner KS, *19123* 96 B3
Gardner MA, *20228* 95 D1
Gardnertown NY, *4395* 148 B1
Gardnerville NV, *5656* 37 D2
Garfield AR, *502* 106 C3
Garfield NJ, *30487* 148 B3
Garfield TX, *1698* 61 E2
Garfield WA, *597* 14 B4
Garfield Co. CO, *56389* 40 B1
Garfield Co. MT, *1206* 17 D2
Garfield Co. NE, *2049* 35 D2
Garfield Co. OK, *60580* 51 E1
Garfield Co. UT, *5172* 39 E1
Garfield Co. WA, *2266* 14 A4
Garfield Hts. OH, *28849* 91 E2
Garibaldi OR, *779* 20 B2
Garland NC, *625* 123 D2
Garland TX, *226876* 59 F2
Garland UT, *2400* 31 E2
Garland Co. AR, *96024* 117 D2
Garnavillo IA, *745* 73 F3
Garner IA, *3129* 72 C3
Garner KY, *600* 111 D1
Garner NC, *25745* 113 D4
Garnett KS, *3415* 96 A4
Garrard Co. KY, *16912* 110 A1
Garretson SD, *1166* 27 F4
Garrett IN, *6286* 90 A2
Garrett Co. MD, *30097* 102 B2
Garrett Park MD, *992* 270 C1
Garrettsville OH, *2325* 91 F2
Garrison KY, *866* 101 D3
Garrison ND, *8823* 193 A1
Garrison ND, *1453* 18 B3
Garrison TX, *895* 124 B3
Garrisonville VA, *2700* 144 A4
Garvin Co. OK, *27576* 51 E3
Garwin IA, *527* 87 D1
Gary IN, *80294* 89 D2
Gary SD, *227* 27 F2
Gary WV, *968* 111 F1
Garysburg NC, *1057* 113 E3
Garyville LA, *2811* 134 B3

Gautier MS, *18572* 135 D2
Gayle Mill SC, *913* 122 A2
Gaylesville AL, *141* 120 A2
Gaylord MI, *3645* 70 C3
Gaylord MN, *2305* 66 C4
Gaylordsville CT, *750* 148 C1
Gayville SD, *407* 35 E1
Gays Mills WI, *491* 73 F3
Gearhart OR, *1462* 20 B1
Geary OK, *1268* 51 D4
Geauga Co. OH, *93389* 91 E2
Geary Co. KS, *34362* 43 F2
Geddes SD, *208* 35 D1
Geistown PA, *2467* 92 B4
Gem Co. ID, *16719* 22 B3
Gem Co. ID, *16719* 22 B3
Geneseo IL, *6586* 88 A2
Geneseo NY, *8031* 78 C4
Geneva AL, *4452* 136 C1
Geneva FL, *2940* 141 D1
Geneva IL, *21495* 88 C1
Geneva IN, *1293* 90 A3
Geneva NE, *2217* 35 E4
Geneva NY, *13261* 79 D3
Geneva OH, *6215* 91 F1
Geneva WA, *2321* 12 C1
Geneva Co. AL, *26790* 136 C1
Geneva-on-the-Lake OH, *1288* 91 F1
Genoa IL, *5193* 88 C1
Genoa NE, *1003* 35 E3
Genoa OH, *2336* 90 C2
Genoa City WI, *3042* 74 C4
Genola UT, *1370* 39 E1
Gentry AR, *3158* 106 B3
Gentry Co. MO, *6738* 86 B4
George IA, *1080* 72 A2
George WA, *501* 13 E4
George Co. MS, *22578* 135 D1
Georgetown CO, *2367* 36 C2
Georgetown CO, *2367* 41 D1

Georgetown CT, *1805* 148 C2
Georgetown DE, *6422* 145 F4
Georgetown GA, *11823* 128 C3
Georgetown ID, *491* 31 F1
Georgetown IL, *1404* 99 D1
Georgetown IN, *2876* 99 F4
Georgetown KY, *29098* 100 B4
Georgetown MA, *8183* 151 F1
Georgetown OH, *4331* 100 C3
Georgetown PA, *174* 146 A3
Georgetown SC, *9163* 131 E1
Georgetown Co. SC, *60158* 122 C4
George West TX, *2445* 61 D4
George Vil. CT, *375* 81 D1
Georgiana AL, *1738* 127 F4
Gerald MO, *1345* 97 F3
Geraldine AL, *896* 120 A3
Geraldine MT, *261* 16 A3
Gerber CA, *1060* 36 B1
Gering NE, *8500* 33 F2
Gerlach NV, *206* 29 E4

Gila Co. AZ, *53597* 55 D1
Gilbert AZ, *208453* 54 C2
Gilbert IA, *1082* 86 C1
Gilbert LA, *521* 125 F3
Gilbert MN, *1799* 64 C3
Gilbert SC, *565* 122 A4
Gilbert WV, *450* 111 F1
Gilbert Co. KY, *14028* 110 A2
Gilbertsville PA, *4832* 146 B2
Gilbertville IA, *712* 73 E4
Gilbertville MA, *1000* 150 B1
Gilby ND, *237* 19 E2
Gilchrist Co. FL, *16939* 138 C3
Gilcrest CO, *1034* 33 E4
Giles Co. TN, *29485* 119 F1
Giles Co. VA, *17286* 112 A1
Gilford NH, *7126* 81 E3
Gilford Park NJ, *8700* 147 E3
Gillespie IL, *3319* 98 B2
Gillespie Co. TX, *24837* 61 D1
Gillett AR, *677* 117 F3
Gillett WI, *1386* 68 C4
Gillette WY, *29087* 25 E2

Gilman IL, *1814* 89 D3
Gilman IA, *509* 87 D1
Gilman VT, *375* 81 F2
Gilmer TX, *4905* 124 B2
Gilmer Co. GA, *28292* 120 C2
Gilmer Co. WV, *8693* 101 F2
Gilmore City IA, *504* 72 B4
Gilpin Co. CO, *5441* 41 D1
Gilroy CA, *48821* 44 B2
Gilt Edge TN, *477* 118 B3
Ginger Blue MO, *61* 106 B3
Girard IL, *2103* 98 B2
Girard KS, *2789* 106 B1
Girard OH, *9958* 91 F2
Girard PA, *3104* 91 F1
Girardville PA, *1519* 93 E3
Gisela AZ, *570* 47 E4
Glacier Co. MT, *13399* 15 E1
Gladbrook IA, *945* 87 D1
Gladden AZ, *400* 54 B1
Glades Co. FL, *12884* 141 D4
Glade Spr. VA, *1456* 111 F2
Gladewater TX, *6441* 124 B2
Gladstone MI, *4973* 69 D2
Gladstone MO, *25410* 96 B2
Gladstone ND, *284* 18 A4
Gladstone OR, *11497* 251 D3
Gladwin MI, *2933* 76 A1
Gladwin Co. MI, *25692* 76 A1
Glandorf OH, *1001* 90 B3
Glasco KS, *498* 43 E2
Glasco NY, *2099* 94 B3
Glasford IL, *1012* 88 B4
Glasgow DE, *14303* 145 E1
Glasgow KY, *14028* 110 A2
Glasgow MO, *1103* 97 D2
Glasgow MT, *3250* 17 D2
Glasgow VA, *1133* 112 B1
Glasgow WV, *905* 101 F4
Glasgow Vil. MO, *5429* 256 C2
Glascock Co. GA, *3082* 129 F1
Glascock Co. TX, *1226* 58 A3
Glassmanor MD, *17295* 270 D5
Glassport PA, *4483* 250 B3
Glastonbury CT, *33089* 150 A3
Gleason TN, *1445* 108 C3
Glenaire MO, *545* 224 C2
Glen Allen AL, *510* 119 E4
Glen Allen VA, *14774* 254 B1
Glen Alpine NC, *1517* 111 F4
Glenarden MD, *6000* 144 B3
Glenburn ND, *380* 18 B2
Glen Burnie MD, *67639* 144 C2
Glen Carbon IL, *12934* 98 B3
Glencoe AL, *5160* 120 A4
Glencoe IL, *8723* 89 D1
Glencoe KY, *601* 51 F2
Glen Cove ME, *375* 82 C2
Glen Cove NY, *26964* 148 C3
Glendale AZ, *226721* 54 C1
Glendale CA, *191719* 52 C2
Glendale CO, *4184* 209 C3
Glendale MO, *5925* 256 B2
Glendale OH, *2155* 204 B1
Glendale OR, *874* 28 B1
Glendale RI, *800* 150 C2
Glendale Vil. UT, *381* 39 D1
Glen Dale WV, *1526* 101 F1
Glendale IL, *12872* 234 C1
Glendale Hts. IL, *34208* 203 B4
Glendive MT, *4935* 17 F3
Glendo WY, *205* 33 E1
Glendora CA, *50073* 229 F2
Glendora NJ, *4750* 146 C3
Glenfield NY, *450* 79 F3
Glenn Co. CA, *28280* 36 B1
Glen Allen AL, *510* 119 E4
Glenham NY, *2570* 148 B1
Glen Ellen CA, *784* 36 B3
Glen Ellyn IL, *27450* 203 B4
Glen Gardner NJ, *1704* 104 C1
Glen Head NY, *4300* 148 B1
Glen Lyon PA, *1873* 93 E2
Glen Mills MA, *750* 151 F1

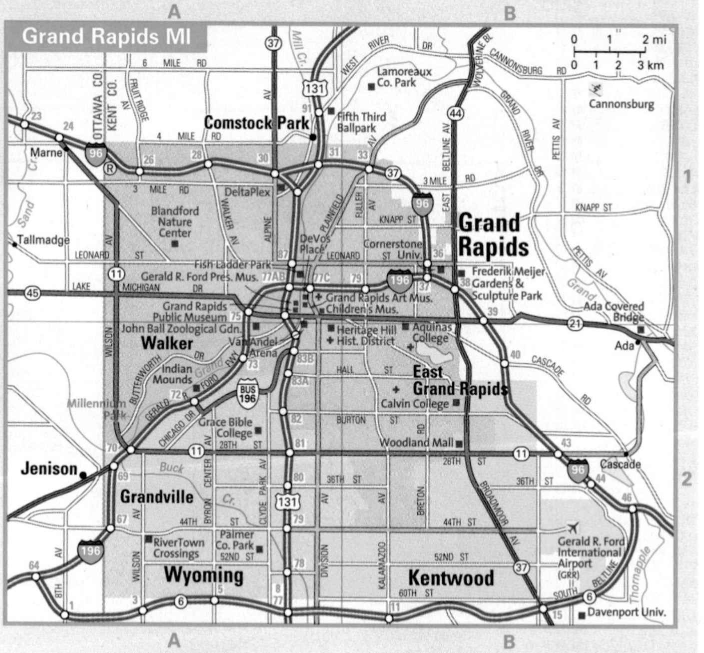

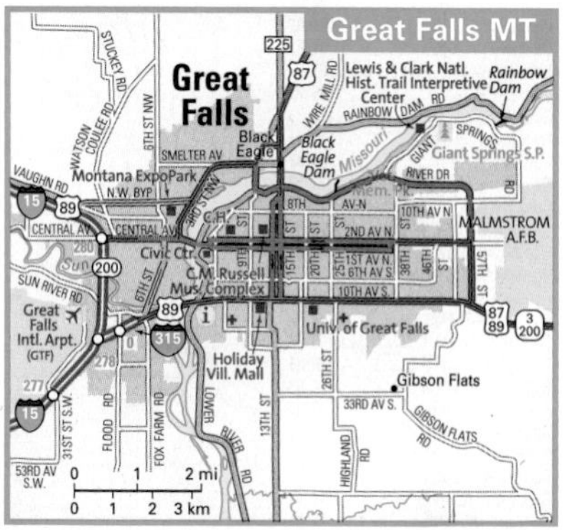

Figures after entries indicate population, page number, and grid reference.

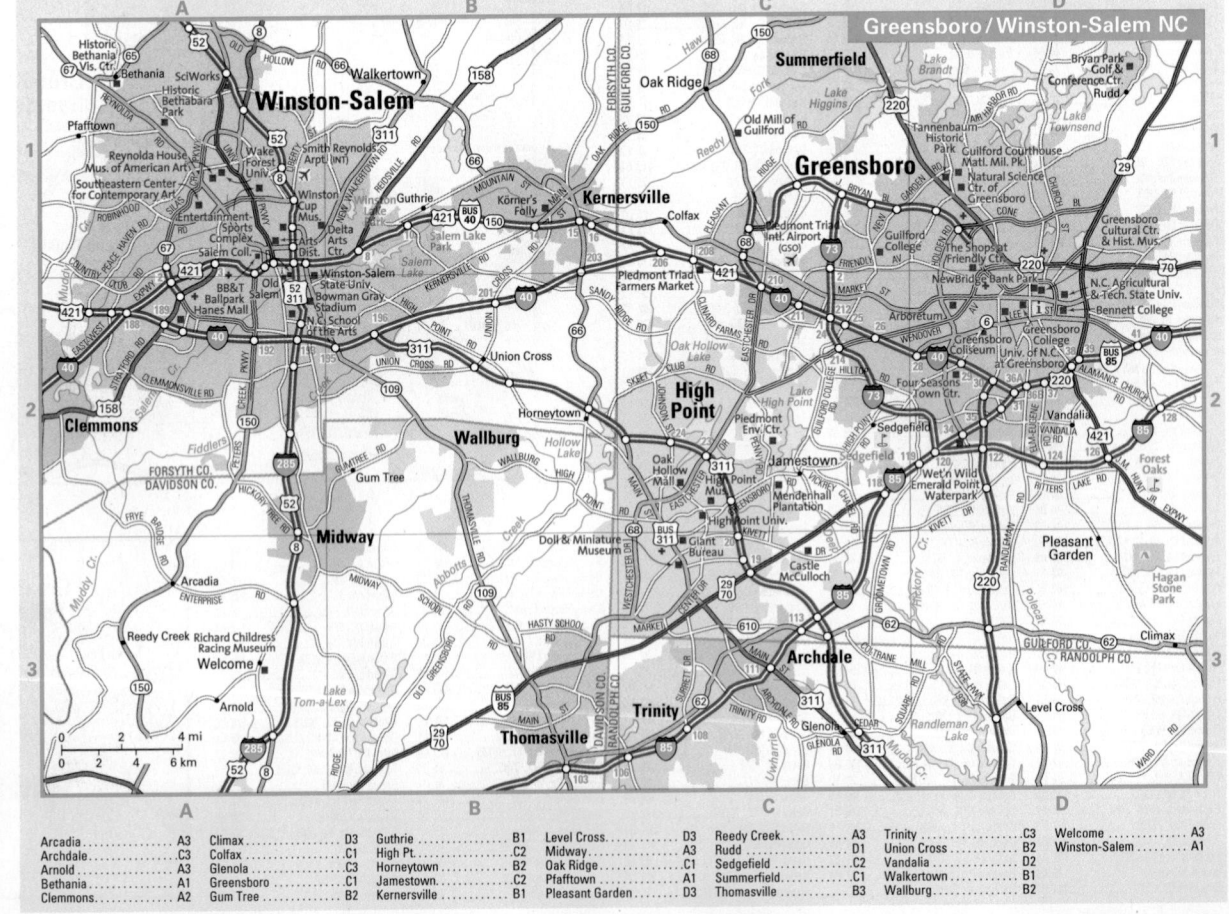

Green Bay WI

Howard · Hobart · Green Bay · Green Bay · Ashwaubenon · Bellevue · Allouez · De Pere

UNIV. OF WIS.–GREEN BAY

Greensboro / Winston-Salem NC

Winston-Salem · Summerfield · Oak Ridge · Walkertown · Greensboro · Kernersville · Colfax · Pfafftown · Clemmons · Wallburg · High Point · Jamestown · Midway · Horneytown · Pleasant Garden · Thomasville · Archdale · Trinity · Level Cross

217
Graysville–Harrisburg

Entries in **bold black** indicate counties or parishes.
Entries in **bold color** indicate cities with detailed inset maps.

Graysville AL, *2165* ... 119 F4
Graysville TN, *1502* ... 120 B1
Grayville IL, *1666* ... 99 D4
Greasewood AZ, *547* ... 47 F3
Great Barrington MA, *2231* ... 94 B2
Great Bend KS, *15995* ... 43 D3
Great Bend NY, *843* ... 79 E1
Great Bend PA, *734* ... 93 F1
Great Falls MT, *58505* ... 15 F3 (color)
Great Falls SC, *1979* ... 122 A2
Great Falls VA, *15427* ... 144 B3
Great Meadows NJ, *303* ... 94 A4
Great Mills MD, *2600* ... 103 E4
Great Neck NY, *9989* ... 148 B4
Great Neck Estates NY, *2761* ... 241 G3
Great Neck Gardens NY, *1186* ... 241 G2
Great Neck Plaza NY, *6707* ... 241 G2
Great River NY, *1489* ... 149 D4
Greece NY, *14519* ... 78 C3
Greeley CO, *92889* ... 33 E4
Greeley NE, *466* ... 35 D3
Greeley Co. KS, *1247* ... 42 B3
Greeley Co. NE, *2538* ... 35 D3
Greeleyville SC, *438* ... 122 B4
Green OH, *25699* ... 91 E3
Green OR, *7515* ... 28 B1
Greenacres CA, *5566* ... 45 D4
Greenacres FL, *37573* ... 143 F1
Greenback TN, *1064* ... 110 C4
Green Bay WI, *104057* ... 68 C4 (color)
Greenbelt MD, *23068* ... 144 B3
Greenbrier AR, *4706* ... 117 E1
Greenbrier TN, *6433* ... 109 F3
Greenbrier Co. WV, *35480* ... 102 A4
Greenbush MA, *550* ... 151 E2
Greenbush MN, *719* ... 19 F1
Greencastle IN, *10326* ... 99 E1
Greencastle PA, *3996* ... 103 D1
Green City MO, *657* ... 87 D4
Green Co. KY, *11258* ... 110 A1
Green Co. WI, *36842* ... 74 B4
Green Cove Sprs. FL, *6908* ... 139 D3
Green Creek NJ, *1300* ... 104 C4
Greendale IN, *4520* ... 100 B2
Greendale MO, *651* ... 256 B2
Greendale WI, *14046* ... 234 C3
Greene IA, *1130* ... 73 D3
Greene ME, *4076* ... 82 B2
Greene NY, *1580* ... 79 E4
Greene Co. AL, *9045* ... 127 E2
Greene Co. AR, *42090* ... 108 A3
Greene Co. GA, *15994* ... 121 E4
Greene Co. IL, *13886* ... 98 A2
Greene Co. IN, *33165* ... 99 E2
Greene Co. IA, *9336* ... 86 B1
Greene Co. MS, *14400* ... 127 D4
Greene Co. MO, *275174* ... 107 D1
Greene Co. NY, *49221* ... 94 A2
Greene Co. NC, *21362* ... 115 C3
Greene Co. OH, *161573* ... 100 C1
Greene Co. PA, *38686* ... 102 A1
Greene Co. TN, *68831* ... 111 D3
Greene Co. VA, *18403* ... 102 C4
Greenevers NC, *634* ... 123 E2
Greeneville TN, *15062* ... 111 D4
Greenfield CA, *3991* ... 44 B3
Greenfield IL, *1071* ... 98 A2
Greenfield IN, *20602* ... 99 F1
Greenfield IA, *1982* ... 86 B2
Greenfield MA, *17456* ... 94 C1
Greenfield MO, *1371* ... 106 C1
Greenfield NH, *375* ... 95 D1
Greenfield OH, *4639* ... 100 C2
Greenfield TN, *2182* ... 108 C4
Greenfield WI, *36720* ... 234 C3
Green Forest AR, *2761* ... 107 D3
Green Harbor MA, *2609* ... 151 E2
Green Haven MD, *24287* ... 144 C2
Green Haven NY, *3000* ... 148 C1
Green Hill TN, *6618* ... 109 F3
Greenhills OH, *3615* ... 204 B1
Green Island NY, *2620* ... 188 E2
Green Lake WI, *960* ... 74 B2
Green Lake Co. WI, *19051* ... 74 B2
Greenland AR, *1259* ... 106 C4
Greenland NH, *3549* ... 82 A4
Green Lane PA, *508* ... 146 B2
Greenleaf ID, *846* ... 22 A4
Greenlee Co. AZ, *8437* ... 55 E2
Greenmount MD, *600* ... 144 B1
Green Mtn. Falls CO, *640* ... 205 C1
Green Oaks IL, *3866* ... 203 C1
Green Park MO, *2622* ... 256 B3
Green Pond NJ, *1400* ... 148 A3
Greenport NY, *2197* ... 149 E3
Green River UT, *952* ... 39 F2
Green River WY, *12515* ... 32 A3
Greensboro AL, *2497* ... 127 E2
Greensboro FL, *602* ... 137 D2
Greensboro GA, *3359* ... 121 D4
Greensboro MD, *1931* ... 145 E3
Greensboro NC, *269666* ... 112 B4 (color)
Greensboro Bend VT, *232* ... 81 E2
Greensburg IN, *11492* ... 100 A2
Greensburg KS, *777* ... 43 D4
Greensburg KY, *2163* ... 110 A2
Greensburg LA, *718* ... 134 B1
Greensburg PA, *14892* ... 92 A4
Green Sprs. OH, *1368* ... 90 C2
Greensville Co. VA, *12243* ... 113 E2
Greentown IN, *2415* ... 89 F4
Greentown OH, *3804* ... 91 E3
Green Tree PA, *4432* ... 250 B2
Greenup IL, *1513* ... 99 D2
Greenup KY, *1188* ... 101 D3
Greenup Co. KY, *36910* ... 101 D3
Green Valley AZ, *21391* ... 55 D3
Green Valley CA, *600* ... 52 C2
Green Valley IL, *709* ... 88 B4
Green Valley MD, *12262* ... 144 B2
Greenview IL, *778* ... 88 B4
Green Vil. PA, *1100* ... 103 D1
Greenville AL, *8135* ... 128 A3
Greenville CA, *1129* ... 36 C4
Greenville DE, *2326* ... 146 B3
Greenville FL, *843* ... 137 F2
Greenville GA, *876* ... 128 C1
Greenville IL, *7000* ... 98 B3
Greenville IN, *595* ... 99 F4
Greenville KY, *4312* ... 109 E2
Greenville ME, *1257* ... 84 C4
Greenville MI, *8481* ... 75 F3
Greenville MS, *34400* ... 126 A1
Greenville MO, *511* ... 108 A2
Greenville NH, *1108* ... 95 D1
Greenville NY, *7116* ... 94 B2
Greenville NC, *84554* ... 115 D2
Greenville OH, *13227* ... 90 A4
Greenville PA, *5919* ... 91 F2
Greenville RI, *8658* ... 150 C3
Greenville SC, *58409* ... 121 E2 (color)
Greenville TX, *25557* ... 59 F2
Greenville VA, *832* ... 102 B4
Greenville WI, *950* ... 74 C1
Greenville Co. SC, *451225* ... 121 E2
Greenville Jct. ME, *850* ... 84 C4
Greenwich CT, *12942* ... 148 C3
Greenwich NY, *1777* ... 81 D4
Greenwich OH, *1476* ... 91 D3
Greenwood AR, *8952* ... 116 C1
Greenwood DE, *973* ... 145 E3
Greenwood FL, *686* ... 137 D1
Greenwood IN, *49791* ... 99 F1
Greenwood LA, *3219* ... 124 C2
Greenwood MS, *15205* ... 118 B4
Greenwood MO, *5221* ... 96 B3
Greenwood NE, *568* ... 35 F3
Greenwood SC, *23222* ... 121 F3
Greenwood WI, *1026* ... 68 A4
Greenwood Co. KS, *6689* ... 43 F3
Greenwood Co. SC, *69661* ... 121 F3
Greenwood Lake NY, *3154* ... 148 A2
Greenwood Vil. CO, *13925* ... 209 C4
Greer SC, *25515* ... 121 F2
Greer Co. OK, *6239* ... 50 C3
Greers Ferry AR, *891* ... 117 E1
Gregg Co. TX, *121730* ... 124 B2
Gregory SD, *1295* ... 35 D1
Gregory TX, *1907* ... 63 F2
Gregory Co. SD, *4271* ... 35 D1
Greilickville MI, *1530* ... 69 F4
Grenada MS, *13092* ... 118 B4
Grenada Co. MS, *21906* ... 118 B4
Gresham OR, *105594* ... 20 C2
Gresham WI, *586* ... 68 C4
Gresham Park GA, *7432* ... 190 E4
Gretna FL, *1460* ... 137 D2
Gretna LA, *17736* ... 134 B3
Gretna NE, *4441* ... 35 F3
Gretna VA, *1267* ... 112 C2
Greybull WY, *1847* ... 24 C3
Gridley CA, *6584* ... 36 B2
Gridley IL, *1432* ... 88 C3
Gridley KS, *341* ... 96 A4
Griffin GA, *23643* ... 129 D1
Griffith IN, *16893* ... 89 D2
Grifton NC, *2617* ... 115 D3
Griggs Co. ND, *2420* ... 19 D3
Griggsville IL, *1226* ... 98 A1
Grimes AL, *558* ... 128 B4
Grimes IA, *8246* ... 86 C2
Grimes Co. TX, *26604* ... 132 A2
Grinnell IA, *9218* ... 87 D1
Griswold IA, *1036* ... 86 B2
Groesbeck OH, *6788* ... 204 A2
Groesbeck TX, *4328* ... 59 F4
Groom TX, *574* ... 50 B3
Grosse Pointe MI, *5421* ... 210 D3
Grosse Pointe Farms MI, *9479* ... 210 D3
Grosse Pointe Park MI, *11555* ... 210 D3
Grosse Pointe Shores MI, *3008* ... 210 D3
Grosse Pointe Woods MI, *16135* ... 76 C4
Grosse Tete LA, *647* ... 133 F2
Grosvenor Dale CT, *700* ... 150 B2
Groton CT, *10389* ... 149 F2
Groton MA, *1124* ... 95 D1
Groton NY, *2363* ... 79 D4
Groton SD, *1458* ... 27 E2
Groton VT, *437* ... 81 E2
Groton Long Pt. CT, *518* ... 149 F2
Grottoes VA, *2668* ... 102 C4
Grove OK, *6623* ... 106 B3
Grove City FL, *1804* ... 140 C4
Grove City MN, *635* ... 66 B3
Grove City OH, *35575* ... 101 D1
Grove City PA, *8322* ... 92 A2
Grove Hill AL, *1570* ... 127 E4
Groveland CA, *601* ... 37 D4
Groveland FL, *8729* ... 140 C1
Groveland MA, *2800* ... 95 E1
Groveport OH, *5363* ... 101 D1
Grover NC, *708* ... 122 A1
Grover Beach CA, *13156* ... 52 A1
Groves TX, *16144* ... 132 C3
Groveton NH, *1118* ... 81 F2
Groveton TX, *1057* ... 132 B1
Groveton VA, *14598* ... 144 B4
Grovetown GA, *11216* ... 121 F4
Grubbs AR, *386* ... 107 F4
Gruetli-Laager TN, *1813* ... 120 A1
Grundy VA, *1021* ... 111 E2
Grundy Ctr. IA, *2706* ... 73 D4
Grundy Co. IL, *50063* ... 88 C2
Grundy Co. IA, *12453* ... 73 D4
Grundy Co. MO, *10261* ... 86 C4
Grundy Co. TN, *13703* ... 120 A1
Gruver TX, *1194* ... 50 B2
Guadalupe AZ, *5523* ... 249 C3
Guadalupe CA, *7080* ... 52 A1
Guadalupe Co. NM, *4687* ... 49 E4
Guadalupe Co. TX, *131533* ... 61 E3
Guerneville CA, *4534* ... 36 A3
Guernsey WY, *1147* ... 33 E2
Guernsey Co. OH, *40087* ... 91 E4
Gueydan LA, *1398* ... 133 E3
Guilderland NY, *35303* ... 188 C2
Guildhall VT, *268* ... 81 F2
Guilford CT, *22307* ... 149 E2
Guilford ME, *903* ... 82 C1
Guilford MD, *12918* ... 193 A5
Guilford Co. NC, *488406* ... 112 B4
Guin AL, *2376* ... 119 E4
Gulf Breeze FL, *5763* ... 135 F2
Gulf Co. FL, *15863* ... 137 D3
Gulfport FL, *12029* ... 140 B3
Gulfport MS, *67793* ... 135 D2
Gulf Shores AL, *9741* ... 135 E2
Gulf Stream FL, *786* ... 143 F1
Gun Barrel City TX, *5672* ... 59 F3
Gunnison CO, *5854* ... 40 C3
Gunnison MS, *452* ... 118 A4
Gunnison UT, *3285* ... 39 E2
Gunnison Co. CO, *15324* ... 40 C2
Gunter TX, *1498* ... 59 F1
Guntersville AL, *8197* ... 120 A3
Guntown MS, *2083* ... 119 D3
Gurdon AR, *2212* ... 117 D4
Gurley AL, *801* ... 119 F2
Gurn Spr. NY, *600* ... 80 C4
Gustavus AK, *442* ... 155 D4
Gustine CA, *5520* ... 36 C4
Guthrie KY, *1419* ... 109 E3
Guthrie OK, *10191* ... 51 E2
Guthrie TX, *160* ... 58 C1
Guthrie Ctr. IA, *1569* ... 86 B2
Guthrie Co. IA, *10954* ... 86 B2
Guthriesville PA, *1800* ... 146 B3
Guttenberg IA, *1919* ... 73 F4
Guttenberg NJ, *11176* ... 240 D2
Guymon OK, *11442* ... 50 B1
Guys TN, *466* ... 119 D2
Guyton GA, *1684* ... 130 B2
Gwinn MI, *1917* ... 69 D1
Gwinner ND, *753* ... 27 E1
Gwinnett Co. GA, *805321* ... 121 D4
Gwynn VA, *602* ... 113 F1
Gypsum CO, *6477* ... 40 C1
Gypsum KS, *405* ... 43 E2

H

Haakon Co. SD, *1937* ... 26 B3
Habersham Co. GA, *43041* ... 121 D2
Hacienda Hts. CA, *54038* ... 228 E3
Hackberry LA, *1261* ... 133 D3
Hackensack NJ, *43010* ... 148 B3
Hackett AR, *812* ... 116 C1
Hackettstown NJ, *9724* ... 94 A4
Hackleburg AL, *1516* ... 119 E3
Haddam CT, *7635* ... 149 E1
Haddonfield NJ, *11593* ... 146 C3
Haddon Hts. NJ, *7473* ... 248 D4
Hadley MA, *5093* ... 150 A1
Hadley NY, *1009* ... 80 C4
Hagaman NY, *1292* ... 80 C4
Hagan GA, *996* ... 129 F3
Hagerhill KY, *900* ... 111 D1
Hagerman ID, *872* ... 30 C1
Hagerman NM, *1257* ... 57 E2
Hagerstown IN, *1787* ... 100 A1
Hagerstown MD, *39662* ... 144 A1
Hahira GA, *2737* ... 137 F1
Hahnville LA, *3344* ... 134 B3
Haiku HI, *8118* ... 153 D1
Hailey ID, *7960* ... 22 C4
Haileyville OK, *813* ... 116 A2
Haines AK, *1713* ... 155 D3
Haines OR, *416* ... 21 F2
Haines City FL, *20535* ... 141 D2
Halaula HI, *469* ... 153 E2
Halawa HI, *14014* ... 152 C3
Hale Ctr. TX, *2252* ... 58 A1
Hale Co. AL, *15760* ... 127 E2
Hale Co. TX, *36273* ... 58 A1
Haledon NJ, *8318* ... 148 B3
Haleiwa HI, *3970* ... 152 A2
Hales Corners WI, *7692* ... 74 C3
Haleyville AL, *4173* ... 119 E3
Halfmoon NY, *18474* ... 188 E1
Half Moon NC, *8352* ... 115 D4
Half Moon Bay CA, *11324* ... 36 B4
Halfway MD, *10701* ... 144 A1
Halfway OR, *288* ... 22 A2
Halifax MA, *7500* ... 151 D2
Halifax NC, *234* ... 113 E3
Halifax PA, *841* ... 93 D4
Halifax VA, *1309* ... 112 C2
Halifax Co. NC, *54691* ... 113 E4
Halifax Co. VA, *36241* ... 112 C2
Haliimaile HI, *964* ... 153 D1
Hallam PA, *2673* ... 103 E1
Hallandale Beach FL, *37113* ... 143 F2
Hall Co. GA, *179684* ... 121 D3
Hall Co. NE, *58607* ... 35 D4
Hall Co. TX, *3353* ... 50 B4
Hallettsville TX, *2550* ... 61 F3
Halliday ND, *188* ... 18 A3
Hallock MN, *981* ... 19 E1
Hallowell ME, *2381* ... 82 C2
Halls TN, *2255* ... 108 C4
Hallsburg TX, *507* ... 59 F4
Halls Crossroads TN, *2100* ... 110 C4
Halls Gap KY, *450* ... 110 B1
Hallstead PA, *1303* ... 93 F1
Hallsville MO, *1491* ... 97 E2
Hallsville TX, *3577* ... 124 B2
Halsey OR, *904* ... 20 B3
Halstad MN, *597* ... 19 F3
Halstead KS, *2085* ... 43 E3
Haltom City TX, *42409* ... 207 B2
Hamblen Co. TN, *62544* ... 111 D3
Hamburg AR, *2857* ... 125 F1
Hamburg IA, *1187* ... 86 A3
Hamburg MN, *513* ... 66 C4
Hamburg NJ, *3277* ... 148 A2
Hamburg NY, *9409* ... 78 B4
Hamburg PA, *4289* ... 146 A1
Hamden CT, *58180* ... 149 D2
Hamden OH, *879* ... 101 D2
Hamel IL, *816* ... 98 B3
Hamilton AL, *6885* ... 119 D3
Hamilton GA, *1016* ... 128 C2
Hamilton IL, *2951* ... 87 F4
Hamilton IN, *1532* ... 90 A2
Hamilton MI, *1300* ... 75 F4
Hamilton MO, *1809* ... 96 C1
Hamilton MT, *4348* ... 23 D1
Hamilton NY, *4239* ... 79 E3
Hamilton NC, *408* ... 113 E4
Hamilton OH, *62477* ... 100 B2
Hamilton RI, *2500* ... 150 C4
Hamilton TX, *3095* ... 59 E4
Hamilton VA, *506* ... 144 A2
Hamilton City CA, *1759* ... 36 B1
Hamilton Co. FL, *14799* ... 138 C2
Hamilton Co. IL, *8457* ... 98 C4
Hamilton Co. IN, *274569* ... 99 F1
Hamilton Co. IA, *15673* ... 72 C4
Hamilton Co. KS, *2690* ... 42 A3
Hamilton Co. NE, *9124* ... 35 E4
Hamilton Co. NY, *4836* ... 79 F2
Hamilton Co. OH, *802374* ... 100 B2
Hamilton Co. TN, *336463* ... 120 B1
Hamilton Co. TX, *8517* ... 59 D4
Hamilton Square NJ, *12784* ... 147 D2
Ham Lake MN, *15296* ... 67 D3
Hamler OH, *576* ... 90 B2
Hamlet IN, *800* ... 89 E2
Hamlet NC, *6495* ... 122 C2
Hamlin TX, *2124* ... 58 C2
Hamlin WV, *1142* ... 101 E4
Hamlin Co. SD, *5903* ... 27 E3
Hammon OK, *568* ... 50 C3
Hammond IL, *509* ... 98 C1
Hammond IN, *80830* ... 89 D2
Hammond LA, *20019* ... 134 B2
Hammond WI, *1922* ... 67 E4
Hammondsport NY, *661* ... 78 C4
Hammondville AL, *488* ... 120 A2
Hammonton NJ, *14791* ... 147 D4
Hamorton PA, *1400* ... 146 B3
Hampden ME, *4343* ... 83 D1
Hampden Co. MA, *463490* ... 150 A2
Hampden Sydney VA, *1450* ... 113 D2
Hampshire IL, *5563* ... 88 C1
Hampshire Co. MA, *158080* ... 94 C2
Hampshire Co. WV, *23964* ... 102 C2
Hampstead MD, *6323* ... 144 B1
Hampstead NH, *8523* ... 95 E1
Hampton AR, *1324* ... 117 E4
Hampton FL, *500* ... 138 C3
Hampton GA, *6987* ... 129 D1
Hampton IL, *1863* ... 208 C1
Hampton IA, *4461* ... 73 D4
Hampton MD, *5052* ... 193 C1
Hampton NE, *423* ... 35 E4
Hampton NH, *9656* ... 95 E1
Hampton NJ, *1401* ... 104 C1
Hampton PA, *632* ... 103 D1
Hampton SC, *2808* ... 130 B2
Hampton TN, *1300* ... 111 E3
Hampton VA, *137436* ... 113 F2
Hampton Bays NY, *13603* ... 149 E3
Hampton Beach NH, *2275* ... 95 E1
Hampton Co. SC, *21090* ... 130 B2
Hampton Park NY, *950* ... 149 E3
Hamtramck MI, *22423* ... 210 C3
Hana HI, *1235* ... 153 E1
Hanahan SC, *17997* ... 131 D1
Hanamaulu HI, *3835* ... 152 B1
Hanapepe HI, *2638* ... 152 B1
Hanceville AL, *2982* ... 119 F3
Hancock MD, *1545* ... 102 C1
Hancock MI, *4634* ... 65 F3
Hancock MN, *765* ... 66 A3
Hancock NH, *204* ... 81 E4
Hancock NY, *1031* ... 93 F1
Hancock Co. GA, *9429* ... 129 E1
Hancock Co. IL, *19104* ... 87 F4
Hancock Co. IN, *70002* ... 100 A1
Hancock Co. IA, *11341* ... 72 C3
Hancock Co. KY, *8565* ... 109 F1
Hancock Co. ME, *54418* ... 83 D1
Hancock Co. MS, *43929* ... 134 C2
Hancock Co. OH, *74782* ... 90 B3
Hancock Co. TN, *6819* ... 111 D3
Hancock Co. WV, *30676* ... 91 F4
Hand Co. SD, *3431* ... 27 D3
Hanford CA, *53967* ... 45 D3
Hankinson ND, *919* ... 27 F1
Hanley Hills MO, *2101* ... 256 B2
Hanna WY, *841* ... 33 D2
Hanna City IL, *1225* ... 88 B3
Hannibal MO, *17916* ... 97 F1
Hannibal NY, *555* ... 79 D3
Hanover CT, *700* ... 149 F1
Hanover IL, *844* ... 74 A4
Hanover IN, *3546* ... 100 A3
Hanover KS, *682* ... 43 F1
Hanover MA, *13164* ... 151 E2
Hanover MN, *2938* ... 66 C3
Hanover NH, *8636* ... 81 E3
Hanover NJ, *13731* ... 148 A3
Hanover OH, *921* ... 91 D4
Hanover PA, *15289* ... 103 E1
Hanover VA, *252* ... 113 E1
Hanover Co. VA, *99863* ... 103 D4
Hanover Park IL, *37973* ... 203 B3
Hansen ID, *1144* ... 30 C1
Hansford Co. TX, *5613* ... 50 B2
Hanson KY, *742* ... 109 E1
Hanson MA, *2118* ... 151 D2
Hanson Co. SD, *3331* ... 27 E4
Hapeville GA, *6373* ... 190 D5
Happy TX, *678* ... 50 A4
Happy Camp CA, *1190* ... 28 B2
Happy Valley OR, *13903* ... 251 D2
Harahan LA, *9277* ... 239 B2
Haralson Co. GA, *28780* ... 120 B4
Harbert MI, *1619* ... 89 E1
Harbeson DE, *375* ... 145 F4
Harbor OR, *2391* ... 28 A2
Harbor Beach MI, *1703* ... 76 C2
Harbor Bluffs FL, *2860* ... 266 A2
Harbor Hills NY, *575* ... 241 G2
Harbor Hills OH, *1509* ... 101 D1
Harbor Sprs. MI, *1194* ... 70 B3
Harbour Hts. FL, *2987* ... 140 C4
Hardee Co. FL, *27731* ... 140 C3
Hardeeville SC, *2952* ... 130 B3
Hardeman Co. TN, *27253* ... 118 C1
Hardeman Co. TX, *4139* ... 50 C4
Hardin IL, *967* ... 98 A2
Hardin KY, *615* ... 109 D2
Hardin MO, *569* ... 96 C2
Hardin MT, *3505* ... 24 C1
Hardin TX, *819* ... 132 B2
Hardin Co. IL, *4320* ... 109 D1
Hardin Co. IA, *17534* ... 73 D4
Hardin Co. KY, *105543* ... 110 A1
Hardin Co. OH, *32058* ... 90 C3
Hardin Co. TN, *26026* ... 119 D1
Hardin Co. TX, *54635* ... 132 C2
Harding Co. NM, *695* ... 49 E2
Harding Co. SD, *1255* ... 25 F1
Hardinsburg KY, *2343* ... 109 F1
Hardwick GA, *3930* ... 129 E1
Hardwick VT, *1345* ... 81 E2
Hardy AR, *772* ... 107 F3
Hardy Co. WV, *14025* ... 102 C2
Harewood Park MD, *3400* ... 145 D1
Harford Co. MD, *244826* ... 144 C1
Hargill TX, *877* ... 63 E4
Harker Hts. TX, *26700* ... 59 E4
Harkers Island NC, *1207* ... 115 E4
Harlan IA, *5106* ... 86 A2
Harlan KY, *1745* ... 111 D2
Harlan Co. KY, *29278* ... 111 D2
Harlan Co. NE, *3423* ... 35 D4
Harlem FL, *2658* ... 141 D4
Harlem GA, *2666* ... 129 F1
Harlem MT, *808* ... 16 C2
Harleysville PA, *9286* ... 146 C2
Harleyville SC, *677* ... 130 C1
Harlingen TX, *64849* ... 63 F4
Harlowton MT, *997* ... 16 B4
Harmon Co. OK, *2922* ... 50 C4
Harmony IN, *656* ... 99 E1
Harmony MN, *1020* ... 73 E2
Harmony NC, *531* ... 112 A4
Harmony PA, *890* ... 92 A3
Harmony RI, *985* ... 150 C3
Harnett Co. NC, *114678* ... 123 D1
Harney Co. OR, *7422* ... 21 E4
Harold KY, *1400* ... 111 E1
Harper KS, *1473* ... 43 E4
Harper TX, *1192* ... 60 C1
Harper Co. KS, *6034* ... 43 E4
Harper Co. OK, *3685* ... 50 C1
Harpersville AL, *1637* ... 128 A1
Harper Woods MI, *14236* ... 210 D2
Harrah OK, *5095* ... 51 E3
Harrah WA, *625* ... 13 D4
Harriman NY, *2424* ... 148 B2
Harriman TN, *6350* ... 110 B4
Harrington DE, *3562* ... 145 E3
Harrington ME, *882* ... 83 E2
Harrington WA, *424* ... 13 F3
Harris MN, *1132* ... 67 D3
Harrisburg AR, *2288* ... 118 A1
Harrisburg IL, *9017* ... 109 D1
Harrisburg NE, *100* ... 33 F3

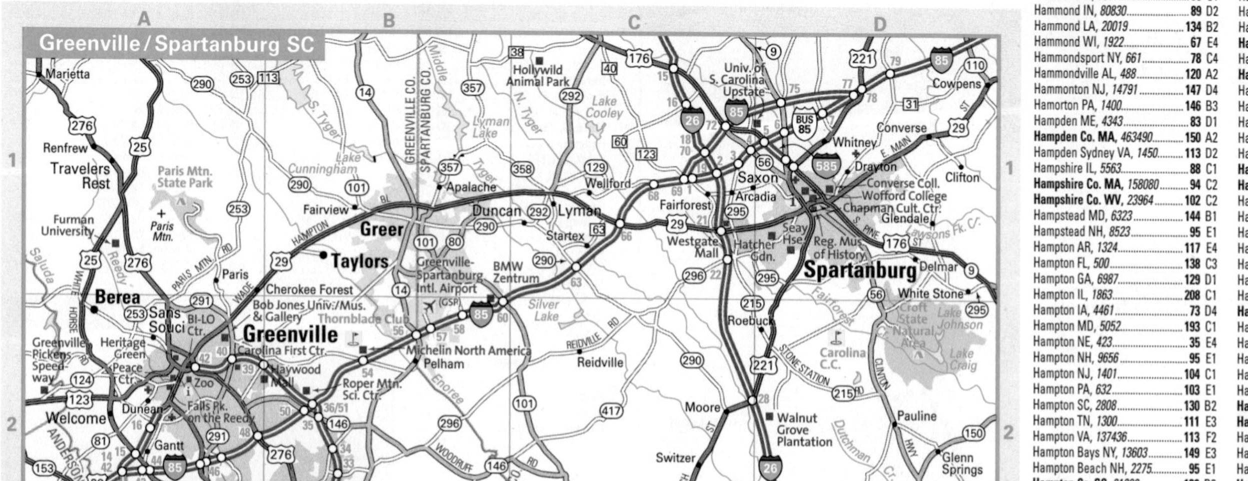

Apalache ... B1
Arcadia ... C1
Berea ... A2
Cherokee Forest ... A1
Clifton ... D1
Conestee ... A2
Converse ... D1
Cowpens ... D1
Crescent ... C2
Delmar ... D1
Drayton ... D1
Duncan ... C1
Dunean ... A2
E. Gantt ... A2
Fairforest ... C1
Fairview ... B1
Gantt ... A2
Glendale ... D1
Glenn Sprs. ... D2
Greenville ... A2
Greer ... B1
Lake Forest ... A2
Lyman ... C1
Marietta ... A1
Mauldin ... B2
Moore ... C2
Paris ... A1
Pauline ... D2
Pelham ... B2
Reidville ... C2
Renfrew ... A1
Roebuck ... D2
Sans Souci ... A2
Saxon ... C1
Simpsonville ... B2
Spartanburg ... D1
Startex ... C1
Switzer ... C2
Taylors ... B1
Travelers Rest ... A1
Welcome ... A2
Wellford ... C1
White Stone ... D1
Whitney ... D1

Figures after entries indicate population, page number, and grid reference.

Harrisburg NC, 11526	122 B1	Harris Co. TX, 4092459	132 A3	Harrison MI, 2114	76 A1	Harrison TN, 7769	120 B1
Harrisburg OR, 3567	20 B3	Harrison AR, 12943	107 D3	Harrison NE, 251	33 F1	Harrisonburg LA, 348	125 F3
Harrisburg PA, 49528	93 D4	Harrison GA, 489	129 F2	Harrison NJ, 13620	148 B4	Harrisonburg VA, 48914	102 C3
Harrisburg SD, 4089	27 F4	Harrison ID, 203	14 B3	Harrison NY, 27472	148 C3	Harrison Co. IN, 39364	99 F4
Harris Co. GA, 32024	128 C2	Harrison ME, 2315	82 B2	Harrison OH, 9897	100 B2	Harrison Co. IA, 14928	86 A1

Harrison Co. KY, 18846	100 B3	Hawaiian Paradise Park	
Harrison Co. MS, 187105	134 C2	HI, 11404	153 F3
Harrison Co. MO, 8957	86 C4	Hawaii Co. HI, 185079	153 E2
Harrison Co. OH, 15864	91 E4	Hawarden IA, 2546	35 F1
Harrison Co. TX, 65651	124 B2	Hawesville KY, 945	99 E4
Harrison Co. WV, 69099	102 A4	Hawi HI, 1081	153 E2
Harrisonville MO, 10019	96 B3	Hawkins TX, 1278	124 B2
Harristown IL, 1367	98 C1	Hawkins Co. TN, 56833	111 D3
Harrisville MD, 600	146 A4	Hawkinsville GA, 4589	129 E3
Harrisville MI, 493	71 D4	Hawley MN, 2067	19 F4
Harrisville NH, 961	95 D1	Hawley PA, 1211	93 F2
Harrisville NY, 628	79 E1	Hawley TX, 634	58 C2
Harrisville PA, 897	92 A3	Hawleyville CT, 800	148 C1
Harrisville RI, 1605	150 C2	Haw River NC, 2298	112 C4
Harrisville UT, 5567	31 E3	Hawthorn PA, 494	92 B3
Harrison IL, 101	99 F4	Hawthorne CA, 84293	228 C3
Harrodsburg KY, 8340	110 B1	Hawthorne FL, 1417	138 C3
Harrogate TN, 4389	110 C3	Hawthorne NV, 3269	37 E3
Harrold SD, 124	27 D3	Hawthorne NJ, 18791	148 B3
Hart MI, 2126	75 E2	Hawthorne NY, 4586	148 B3
Hart TX, 1114	50 A4	Hawthorn Woods IL, 7663	203 B1
Hart Co. GA, 25213	121 E3	Haxtun CO, 946	34 A4
Hart Co. KY, 18199	110 A2	Hayden AL, 914	119 F4
Hartford AL, 2624	136 C1	Hayden AZ, 662	55 D3
Hartford AR, 642	116 C2	Hayden CO, 1810	32 C4
Hartford CT, 124775	150 A3	Hayden ID, 13294	14 B3
Hartford IL, 1429	98 A3	Hayden Lake ID, 574	14 B3
Hartford IA, 771	86 C2	Haydenville MA, 700	150 A1
Hartford KS, 371	43 F3	Hayes LA, 780	133 E2
Hartford KY, 2672	109 E1	Hayes Ctr. NE, 214	34 B4
Hartford MI, 2688	89 F1	Hayes Co. NE, 967	34 B4
Hartford SD, 2534	27 F4	Hayesville NC, 311	121 D2
Hartford WV, 614	101 E2	Hayesville OR, 19936	20 B2
Hartford WI, 14223	74 C3	Hayfield MN, 1340	73 D2
Hartford City IN, 6220	90 A4	Hayfork CA, 2368	28 B4
Hartford Co. CT, 894014	150 A3	Haymarket VA, 1782	144 A3
Hartington NE, 1554	35 E1	Haynesville LA, 2327	125 D1
Hartland ME, 813	82 C1	Haynesville VA, 550	103 E4
Hartland VT, 380	81 E3	Hayneville AL, 932	128 A3
Hartland WI, 9110	74 C3	Hays KS, 20510	43 D2
Hartley IA, 1672	72 A3	Hays MT, 843	16 C2
Hartley Co. TX, 6062	50 A2	Hays Co. TX, 157107	61 D2
Hartman AR, 519	116 C1	Hartly DE, 74	145 E2
Harts WV, 656	101 E4	Hay Sprs. NE, 570	34 A1
Hartselle AL, 14255	119 F3	Haysville KS, 10826	43 E3
Hartshorne OK, 2125	116 A2	Hayti MO, 2939	108 B3
Hartsville SC, 7764	122 B3	Hayti SD, 381	27 F3
Hartsville TN, 7870	109 F3	Hayward CA, 144186	36 B4
Hartville MO, 613	107 E2	Hayward WI, 2318	67 F2
Hartville OH, 2944	91 E3	Haywood Co. NC, 59036	111 D4
Hartwell GA, 4469	121 E3	Haywood Co. TN, 18787	108 C4
Harvard MA, 6520	150 C1	Hazard KY, 4456	111 D2
Harvard NE, 1013	35 E4	Hazardville CT, 4599	150 A2
Harvest AL, 5281	119 F2	Hazel KY, 410	108 C2
Harvey IL, 25282	203 E6	Hazel Crest IL, 14100	203 E6
Harvey LA, 20348	239 C2	Hazel Green AL, 3630	119 F2
Harvey MI, 1393	69 D1	Hazel Green WI, 1256	74 A4
Harvey ND, 1783	18 C3	Hazel Park MI, 16422	210 C2
Harvey Co. KS, 34684	43 E3	Hazelton ID, 753	31 D1
Harveysburg OH, 546	100 C2	Hazelton ND, 235	18 C4
Harveys Lake PA, 2791	93 E2	Hazelwood MO, 25703	256 B1
Harwich MA, 1798	151 F3	Hazen AR, 1468	117 F2
Harwich Port MA, 1644	151 F3	Hazen ND, 2411	18 B3
Harwinton CT, 5571	94 C3	Hazlehurst GA, 4226	129 F3
Harwood ND, 19	19 F4	Hazlehurst MS, 4009	126 B3
Harwood Hts. IL, 8612	203 D3	Hazleton IA, 823	73 E4
Hasbrouck Hts. NJ, 11842	240 C1	Hazleton PA, 25340	93 E3
Haskell AR, 3990	117 E3	Hazlettville DE, 450	145 E2
Haskell OK, 2007	106 A4	Headland AL, 4510	128 B4
Haskell TX, 3322	58 C2	Head of the Harbor NY, 1472	149 D3
Haskell Co. KS, 4256	42 B4	Healdsburg CA, 11254	36 B3
Haskell Co. OK, 12769	116 B1	Healdton OK, 2788	51 E4
Haskell Co. TX, 5899	58 C2	Healy AK, 1021	154 C2
Haskins OH, 1186	90 C2	Heard Co. GA, 11834	128 B1
Haslet TX, 1517	207 E1	Hearne TX, 4459	61 F1
Haslett MI, 19220	76 A4	Heart Butte MT, 582	15 E2
Hastings FL, 580	139 D3	Heath OH, 10310	101 D1
Hastings MI, 7350	75 F4	Heathcote NJ, 5821	147 D1
Hastings MN, 22172	67 D4	Heath Sprs. SC, 790	122 B2
Hastings NE, 24907	35 E4	Heathsville VA, 142	103 E4
Hastings PA, 1278	92 B3	Heavener OK, 3414	116 B2
Hatboro PA, 7360	146 C2	Hebbronville TX, 4558	63 E2
Hatch NM, 1648	56 B2	Hebbville MD, 10900	193 A2
Hatfield AR, 413	116 C3	Heber AZ, 2722	47 E4
Hatfield IN, 813	99 E4	Heber CA, 4275	53 E4
Hatfield MA, 1318	150 A1		
Hatfield PA, 3290	146 C2		
Hatley MS, 482	119 D4		
Hatteras NC, 504	115 F3		
Hattiesburg MS, 45989	126 C4		
Hatton ND, 777	19 E3		
Haubstadt IN, 1577	99 D4		
Haughton LA, 3454	125 D2		
Hauppauge NY, 20882	149 D3		
Hauser ID, 678	14 B3		
Hauula HI, 4148	152 A2		
Havana FL, 1754	137 E2		
Havana IL, 3301	88 A4		
Havelock NC, 20735	115 D4		
Haven KS, 1237	43 E3		
Haverhill FL, 1873	143 F1		
Haverhill MA, 60879	95 E1		
Haverhill NH, 4697	81 E3		
Haverstraw NY, 11910	148 B2		
Havertown PA, 22300	248 A3		
Haviland KS, 701	43 D4		
Havre MT, 9310	16 B2		
Havre de Grace MD, 12952	145 D1		
Hawaiian Gardens CA, 14254	228 D4		
Hawaiian Ocean View HI, 4437	153 D4		

Heber City UT, 11362	31 E1		
Heber Sprs. AR, 7165	117 E1		
Hebron CT, 9198	149 E1		
Hebron IL, 1216	74 C4		
Hebron IN, 3724	89 E2		
Hebron KY, 5929	100 B2		
Hebron MD, 1084	103 F3		
Hebron NE, 1579	43 E1		
Hebron OH, 2336	101 D1		
Hebron Estates KY, 1087	100 A4		
Hecla SD, 227	27 E1		
Hector AR, 450	117 D1		
Hector MN, 1151	66 B4		
Hedrick IA, 764	87 E2		
Hedwig Vil. TX, 2557	220 B2		
Heeia HI, 4963	152 A3		
Heflin AL, 3480	120 A4		
Heidelberg MS, 718	127 D3		
Heidelberg PA, 1244	250 A3		
Heilwood PA, 711	92 B3		
Helena AL, 16793	127 F1		
Helena AR, 6323	118 A2		
Helena GA, 2883	129 E3		
Helena MS, 1184	195 C1		
Helena MT, 28190	15 E4		
Helena OK, 1403	51 D1		
Helendale CA, 5800	110 B3		
Hellertown PA, 5898	146 C1		
Helmetta NJ, 2178	147 E1		
Helotes TX, 7341	61 D2		
Helper UT, 2201	39 F1		
Hemet CA, 78657	53 D3		
Hemingford NE, 803	34 A2		
Hemingway SC, 459	122 C4		
Hemlock MI, 1466	76 B2		
Hemphill TX, 1198	124 C4		
Hemphill Co. TX, 3807	50 C2		
Hempstead NY, 53891	148 C4		
Hempstead TX, 5770	61 F2		
Hempstead Co. AR, 22609	116 C4		
Henagar AL, 2344	120 A2		
Henderson KY, 28757	109 E1		
Henderson LA, 1674	133 F2		
Henderson MN, 886	66 C4		
Henderson NE, 991	35 E4		
Henderson NV, 257729	46 B2		
Henderson NC, 15368	113 D3		
Henderson TN, 6309	119 D1		
Henderson TX, 13712	124 B3		
Henderson Co. IL, 7331	87 F3		
Henderson Co. KY, 46250	109 E1		
Henderson Co. NC, 106740	121 E1		
Henderson Co. TN, 27769	109 D4		
Henderson Co. TX, 78532	124 A2		
Hendersonville NC, 13137	121 E1		
Hendersonville TN, 51372	109 F3		
Hendricks MN, 713	27 F3		
Hendricks Co. IN, 145448	99 F1		
Hendron KY, 4687	108 C2		
Hendry Co. FL, 39140	143 D1		
Henlopen Acres DE, 122	145 F4		
Hennepin IL, 745	88 B2		
Hennepin Co. MN, 1152425	66 C4		
Hennessey OK, 2131	51 E2		
Henniker NH, 1747	81 F4		
Henning MN, 802	64 A4		
Henning TN, 945	108 B4		
Henrico Co. VA, 306935	113 E1		
Henrietta NY, 42581	78 C3		
Henrietta TX, 3141	59 D1		
Henry IL, 2464	88 B3		
Henry SD, 267	27 E2		
Henry TN, 464	109 D3		
Henry Co. AL, 17302	128 B4		
Henry Co. GA, 203922	129 D1		
Henry Co. IL, 50486	88 A2		
Henry Co. IN, 49462	100 A1		
Henry Co. IA, 20145	87 F3		
Henry Co. KY, 15416	100 A3		
Henry Co. MO, 22272	96 C4		
Henry Co. OH, 28215	90 B2		
Henry Co. TN, 32330	109 D3		
Henry Co. VA, 54151	112 B2		
Henryetta OK, 5927	51 F3		

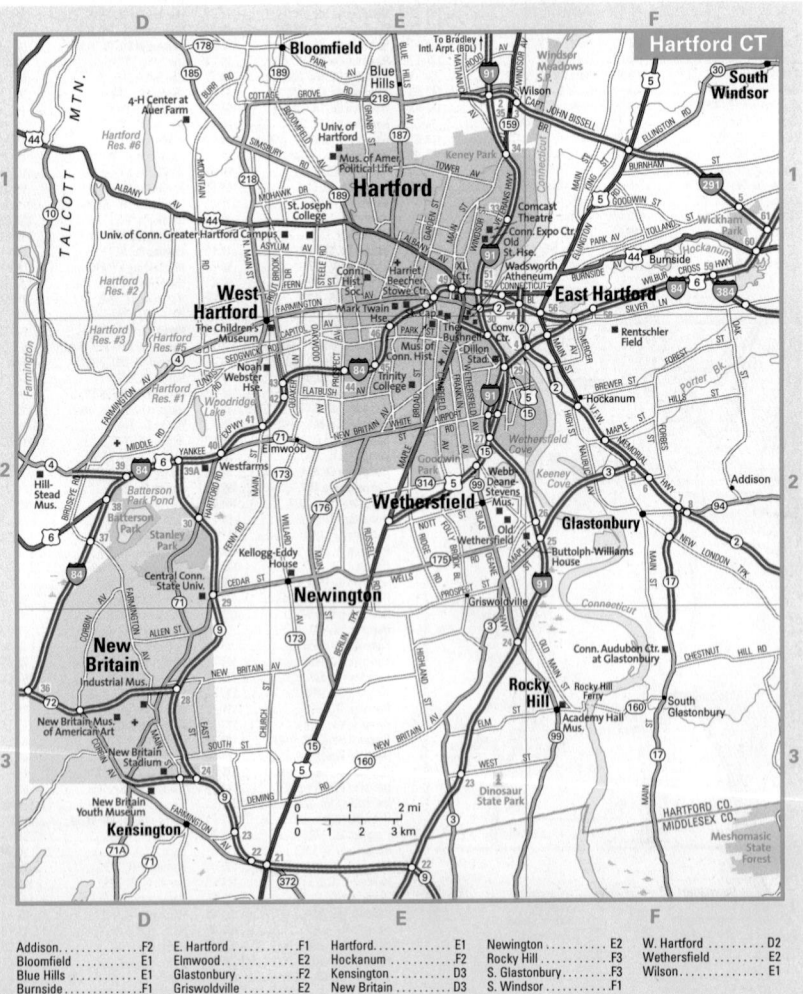

Harrisburg PA

Bressler	C2	Fair Acres	B2	Marsh Run	C2	Penbrook	B1	Summerdale	A1
Camp Hill	A2	Good Hope	B2	Mechanicsburg	A2	Progress	B1	W. Enola	A1
Colonial Park	C1	Green Lane Farms	B2	New Cumberland	B2	Reesers Summit	B2	W. Fairview	A1
Eberlys Mill	B2	Harrisburg	B1	Oakleigh	C2	Rossmoyne	A2	White Hill	A2
Edgemont	C1	Highland Park	B2	Oberlin	C2	Rossmoyne Manor	A2	Wormleysburg	B1
Enhaut	C2	Highspire	C2	Paxtang	B1	Rutherford Hts.	C1	
Enola	A1	Lawnton	C1	Paxtang Manor	C1	Shiremanstown	A2	
Estherton	B1	Lemoyne	B2	Paxtonia	C1	Steelton	B2	

Hartford CT

Addison	F2	E. Hartford	F1	Hartford	E1	Newington	E2	W. Hartford	D2
Bloomfield	E1	Elmwood	E2	Hockanum	F2	Rocky Hill	E2	Wethersfield	E2
Blue Hills	E1	Glastonbury	F2	Kensington	D3	S. Glastonbury	F3	Wilson	E1
Burnside	F1	Griswoldville	E2	New Britain	D3	S. Windsor	F1	

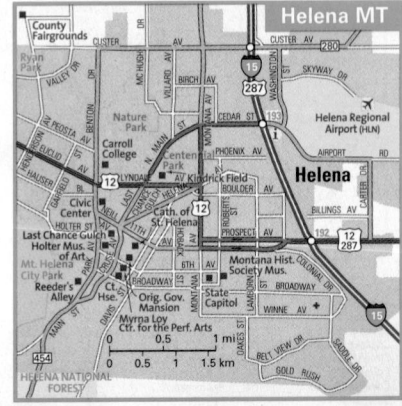

Helena MT

Entries in **bold black** indicate counties or parishes.
Entries in **bold color** indicate cities with detailed inset maps.

Henryville IN, 1905......100 A3
Hephzibah GA, 4011......129 F1
Heppner OR, 1291......21 E2
Herculaneum MO, 3468......98 A4
Hercules CA, 24060......259 C1
Hereford PA, 930......146 B1
Hereford TX, 15370......50 A4
Herington KS, 2526......43 E3
Herkimer NY, 7743......79 F3
Herkimer Co. NY, 64519......79 F2
Hermann MO, 2431......97 F3
Hermantown MN, 9414......64 C4
Hermiston OR, 16745......21 E1
Hermitage AR, 830......117 E4
Hermitage MO, 467......97 D4

Hiawassee GA, 880......121 D2
Hiawatha GA, 4011......129 F1
Hiawatha IA, 7024......87 E1
Hiawatha KS, 3172......96 A1
Hibbing MN, 16361......64 B3
Hickman KY, 2395......108 C3
Hickman NE, 1657......35 F4
Hickman Co. KY, 4902......108 C3
Hickman Co. TN, 24690......109 E4
Hickory MS, 530......126 C2
Hickory NC, 40010......111 F4
Hickory Co. MO, 9627......97 D4
Hickory Flat MS, 601......118 C2
Hickory Withe TN, 29354......118 C1
Hicksville NY, 41547......148 C4
Hicksville OH, 3581......90 A2

Highlands NJ, 5005......147 F1
Highlands NC, 924......121 D2
Highlands TX, 7522......132 B3
Highlands Co. FL, 98786......141 D4
Highland Spr. VA, 15711......254 C2
Highlands Ranch CO, 96713......209 C4
Highlandville MO, 911......107 D2
High Pt. FL, 3686......266 B2
High Pt. NC, 104371......112 B4
High Ridge MO, 4305......98 A3
High Rolls NM, 834......56 C2
High Shoals NC, 696......122 A1
Highspire PA, 2399......218 C2
High Spr. FL, 5350......138 C3
Hightstown NJ, 5494......147 D2

Hillsborough Co. FL, 1229226......140 C3
Hillsborough Co. NH, 400721......81 F4
Hillsdale IL, 523......88 A2
Hillsdale MI, 8305......90 B1
Hillsdale MO, 1478......256 B2
Hillsdale Co. MI, 46688......90 B1
Hillside IL, 8157......203 C4
Hillside NJ, 21404......148 A4
Hillside Lake NY, 1084......148 B1
Hillsville VA, 2681......112 A2
Hilltop NH, 744......235 C1
Hillview KY, 8172......100 A4
Hilmar CA, 4807......36 C4
Hilo HI, 43263......153 F3
Hilshire Vil. TX, 746......220 B2

Hodgkins IL, 1897......203 C5
Hoffman MN, 681......66 A2
Hoffman NC, 588......122 C2
Hoffman Estates IL, 51895......203 B3
Hogansville GA, 3060......128 C3
Hohenwald TN, 3757......119 E1
Hoisington KS, 2706......43 D3
Hokah MN, 580......73 F2
Hoke Co. NC, 46952......123 D2
Hokendauqua PA, 3378......189 A1
Hokes Bluff AL, 4286......120 A3
Holbrook AZ, 5053......47 F3
Holbrook MA, 10791......151 D2
Holcomb KS, 2094......42 B3
Holcomb MO, 635......108 A3

Holden MA, 17346......150 B1
Holden MO, 2252......96 C3
Holden UT, 378......39 E2
Holden WV, 876......111 E1
Holden Beach NC, 575......123 E4
Holdenville OK, 5771......51 F3
Holdingford MN, 708......66 B2
Holdrege NE, 5495......35 D4
Holgate OH, 1109......90 B2
Holiday FL, 22403......140 B2
Holiday Hills IL, 610......203 A1
Holiday Lakes TX, 1107......132 A4
Holladay UT, 26472......257 B2
Holland IN, 626......99 E4
Holland MA, 1464......150 B3
Holland MN, 213......72 A1
Holland NY, 1206......78 B4
Holland OH, 1764......90 C2
Holland TX, 1121......61 E1
Hollandale MS, 2702......126 A1
Holley FL, 1630......135 F2
Holley NY, 1811......78 B3
Holliday TX, 1758......59 D1
Hollidaysburg PA, 5791......92 C4
Hollins VA, 14673......112 B1
Hollis NH, 7684......95 D1
Hollis OK, 2060......50 C4
Hollis Ctr. ME, 450......82 B3
Hollister CA, 34928......44 B2
Hollister MO, 4426......107 D3
Hollister NC, 674......113 D3
Holliston MA, 13547......150 C2
Hollow Creek KY, 783......230 E3
Hollow Rock TN, 718......109 D4
Holly CO, 802......42 A3
Holly MI, 6086......76 B4
Holly Grove AR, 602......117 F2
Holly Hill FL, 11659......139 E4
Holly Hill SC, 1277......130 C1
Holly Park NJ, 2200......147 E3
Holly Pond AL, 798......119 F3
Holly Ridge NC, 1268......115 C4
Holly Spr. GA, 9189......120 C3
Holly Spr. MS, 7699......118 C2
Holly Spr. NC, 24661......112 C4
Hollyvilla KY, 537......100 A4
Hollywood AL, 1000......120 A2
Hollywood FL, 140768......143 F2
Hollywood MD, 650......103 E4
Hollywood SC, 4714......131 D2
Hollywood Park TX, 3062......61 D2
Holmdel NJ, 16773......147 E2
Holmen WI, 9005......73 F1
Holmes Beach FL, 3836......140 B3
Holmes Co. FL, 19927......136 C1
Holmes Co. MS, 19198......126 B1
Holmes Co. OH, 42366......91 D4
Holstein IA, 1396......72 A4
Holt AL, 3638......127 E1
Holt MI, 23973......76 A4
Holt Co. MO, 4912......86 A4
Holt Co. NE, 10435......35 D1
Holton KS, 3329......96 A2
Holts Summit MO, 3247......97 E3
Holtville CA, 5939......53 E4
Holualoa HI, 8538......153 E3
Holyoke CO, 2313......34 A4
Holyoke MA, 39880......150 A2
Holyrood KS, 447......43 D3
Homecroft IN, 722......99 F1
Homedale ID, 2633......22 C2
Home Gardens CA, 11570......229 H4
Homeland CA, 5969......229 K4
Homeland GA, 910......139 D1

Homeland Park SC, 6296......121 E3
Homer AK, 5003......154 C3
Homer GA, 1141......121 D3
Homer IL, 1193......99 E1
Homer LA, 3237......125 D2
Homer MI, 1668......90 A1
Homer NE, 549......35 F2
Homer NY, 3291......79 D4
Homer City PA, 1707......92 B4
Homer Glen IL, 14220......203 C6
Homerville GA, 2456......138 C1
Homestead FL, 60512......143 E3
Homestead PA, 3165......250 C2
Homestead Valley CA, 3032......259 A2
Hometown IL, 4349......203 D5
Hometown PA, 1349......93 E3
Hometown WV, 668......101 E3
Homewood AL, 25167......119 F4
Hominy OK, 3565......51 F1
Homosassa FL, 2578......140 B1
Homosassa Spr. FL, 13791......140 B1
Honaker VA, 1449......111 E2
Honalo HI, 2423......153 E3
Honaunau HI, 2567......153 E3
Hondo TX, 8803......60 C3
Honea Path SC, 3597......121 E3
Honeoye NY, 579......78 C4
Honeoye Falls NY, 2674......78 C3
Honesdale PA, 4480......93 F2
Honey Brook PA, 1713......146 B2
Honey Grove TX, 1668......59 F1
Honeyville UT, 1441......31 E3
Honoka'a HI, 2258......153 E2
Honokowai HI, 7261......153 D1
Hollow Rock TN, 718......109 D4
Honolulu HI, 337256......152 A3
Honolulu Co. HI, 953207......152 A3
Honomu HI, 509......153 F3
Hood Co. TX, 51182......59 E4
Hood River OR, 7167......21 E1
Hood River Co. OR, 22346......20 C2
Hooker OK, 1918......50 B1
Hooker Co. NE, 736......34 B2
Hooks TX, 2769......116 C4
Hooksett NH, 4147......81 F4
Hoonah AK, 760......155 D4
Hooper NE, 830......35 F3
Hooper UT, 7218......244 A2
Hooper Bay AK, 1093......154 B3
Hoopeston IL, 5351......89 D4
Hoople ND, 242......19 E2
Hoosick Falls NY, 3501......94 B1
Hoover AL, 81619......127 F1
Hooverson Hts. WV, 2590......91 F4
Hooversville PA, 645......92 B4
Hopatcong NJ, 15147......148 A3
Hope AR, 10095......117 D4
Hope IN, 2102......99 F2
Hope ND, 258......19 E3
Hope RI, 1900......150 C3
Hopedale IL, 865......88 B4
Hopedale MA, 3753......150 C2
Hopedale OH, 950......91 F4
Hope Mills NC, 15176......123 D2
Hope Valley RI, 1612......150 C4
Hopewell NJ, 1922......147 D1
Hopewell TN, 1874......120 B1
Hopewell VA, 22591......113 E1
Hopewell Jct. NY, 376......148 B1
Hopkins MI, 610......75 F4
Hopkins MN, 17591......235 A3
Hopkins MO, 532......86 B4
Hopkins Co. KY, 46920......109 E2
Hopkins Co. TX, 35161......124 A1
Hopkins Park IL, 603......89 D3
Hopkinsville KY, 31577......109 E2

Honolulu HI

Hermitage PA, 16220......91 F2
Hermon ME, 4437......83 D1
Hermosa CO, 700......40 B4
Hermosa SD, 398......26 A4
Hermosa Beach CA, 19506......228 C4
Hernandez NM, 946......48 C2
Hernando FL, 9054......140 C1
Hernando MS, 14090......118 B2
Hernando Beach FL, 2299......140 B1
Hernando Co. FL, 172778......140 B1
Herndon VA, 23292......144 A3
Heron Lake MN, 698......72 A2
Herreid SD, 438......26 C1
Herricks NY, 4295......241 G3
Herriman UT, 21785......31 E4
Herrin IL, 12501......108 C1
Herscher IL, 1591......89 D3
Hershey NE, 665......34 B3
Hershey PA, 14257......93 E4
Hertford NC, 2143......113 F3
Hertford Co. NC, 24669......113 F3
Hesperia CA, 90173......53 D2
Hesperia MI, 954......75 E2
Hessmer LA, 802......133 F1
Hesston KS, 3709......43 E3
Hettinger ND, 1226......26 A1
Hettinger Co. ND, 2477......18 A4
Heuvelton NY, 714......80 B2
Hewitt TX, 13549......59 E4
Hewitt WI, 828......68 A4
Hewlett NY, 6819......241 G4
Hewlett Harbor NY, 1263......241 G5
Hewlett Neck NY, 445......241 G5
Heyburn ID, 3089......31 D1
Heyworth IL, 2841......88 C4
Hialeah FL, 224669......143 E2
Hialeah Gardens FL, 21744......143 E2

Hico TX, 1379......59 E3
Hidalgo TX, 11198......63 E4
Hidalgo Co. NM, 4894......55 F3
Hidalgo Co. TX, 774769......63 E3
Hidden Hills CA, 1856......228 A3
Hiddenite NC, 536......112 A4
Hideaway TX, 3083......124 A2
Higbee MO, 568......97 E2
Higganum CT, 1698......149 E1
Higginsville MO, 4797......96 C2
High Bridge NJ, 3648......104 C1
Highgate Ctr. VT, 600......81 D1
Highgrove CA, 3988......229 J3
Highland AR, 1045......107 F3
Highland CA, 53104......229 K2
Highland IL, 9919......98 B3
Highland IN, 23777......89 D2
Highland KS, 1012......96 A1
Highland MD, 1034......144 B3
Highland NY, 5647......148 B1
Highland UT, 15523......31 F4
Highland WI, 842......74 A3
Highland City FL, 10834......140 C2
Highland Co. OH, 43589......100 C2
Highland Co. VA, 2321......102 B4
Highland Hts. KY, 6923......204 B3
Highland Hts. OH, 8345......204 G1
Highland Hills OH, 1130......204 G3
Highland Lakes NJ, 4933......148 A2
Highland Mills NY, 3468......148 B2
Highland Park IL, 29763......89 D1
Highland Park MI, 11776......210 C3
Highland Park NJ, 13982......147 E1
Highland Park PA, 1380......218 B2
Highland Park TX, 8564......207 D2

Hightsville NC, 739......275 A1
Highwood IL, 5405......203 D1
Hilbert WI, 1132......74 C1
Hilda SC, 447......130 B1
Hildale UT, 2726......46 C1
Hiles WI, 404......68 B2
Hillandale MD, 6043......270 E1
Hillburn NY, 951......148 B2
Hill City KS, 1474......42 C2
Hill City MN, 633......64 B4
Hill City SD, 948......25 F4
Hillcrest MO, 16096......142 B4
Hillcrest NY, 7558......148 B2
Hillcrest TX, 730......132 B4
Hillcrest Hts. MD, 16469......144 B3
Hilliard FL, 3086......139 D1
Hilliard OH, 28435......101 D1
Hillman MI, 701......70 C3
Hillman MN, 686......64 B4
Hills IA, 703......87 F2
Hills MN, 686......71 F2
Hillsboro AL, 552......119 E2
Hillsboro IL, 6207......98 B2
Hillsboro IN, 538......89 E4
Hillsboro KS, 2821......43 E3
Hillsboro MO, 2821......98 A4
Hillsboro ND, 1603......19 E3
Hillsboro OH, 6605......100 C2
Hillsboro OR, 91611......20 B1
Hillsboro TX, 8456......59 E4
Hillsboro WI, 1417......74 A2
Hillsboro Beach FL, 1875......143 F1
Hillsboro Pines FL, 10825......259 A4
Hillsboro Pk. NH, 1976......81 E4
Hillsboro NC, 6087......112 C4

Hilton NY, 5886......78 C3
Hilton Head Island SC, 37099......130 C3
Hinckley IL, 2070......88 C1
Hinckley MN, 1800......67 D2
Hinckley UT, 696......39 D2
Hindman KY, 777......111 D1
Hindsville AR, 928......35 F1
Hines OR, 1563......21 E4
Hinesburg VT, 658......81 D2
Hinesville GA, 33437......130 B3
Hingham MA, 5650......151 D1
Hinsdale IL, 16816......203 C5
Hinsdale MA, 1872......94 C1
Hinsdale NH, 1548......94 C1
Hinsdale Co. CO, 843......40 C4
Hinson FL, 750......137 E2
Hinton IA, 928......35 F1
Hinton OK, 3196......51 D3
Hinton WV, 2676......112 A1
Hiram GA, 3546......120 C4
Hiram OH, 1406......91 E2
Hobbs NM, 34122......57 F2
Hobe Sound FL, 11521......141 F4
Hoboken NJ, 50005......148 B4
Hobson MT, 215......16 B4
Hockessin DE, 13527......146 B3
Hocking Co. OH, 29380......101 D1
Hockley Co. TX, 22935......58 A3
Hodge LA, 470......125 E3
Hodgenville KY, 3206......110 A1
Hodgeman Co. KS, 1916......42 C3

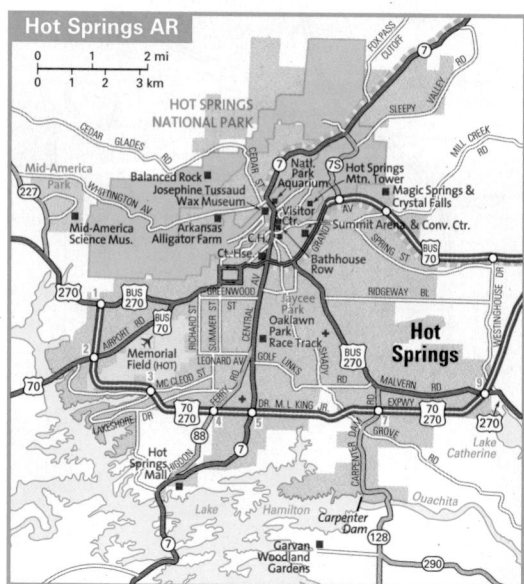

Hot Springs AR

Figures after entries indicate population, page number, and grid reference.

Houston TX

Downtown Houston TX

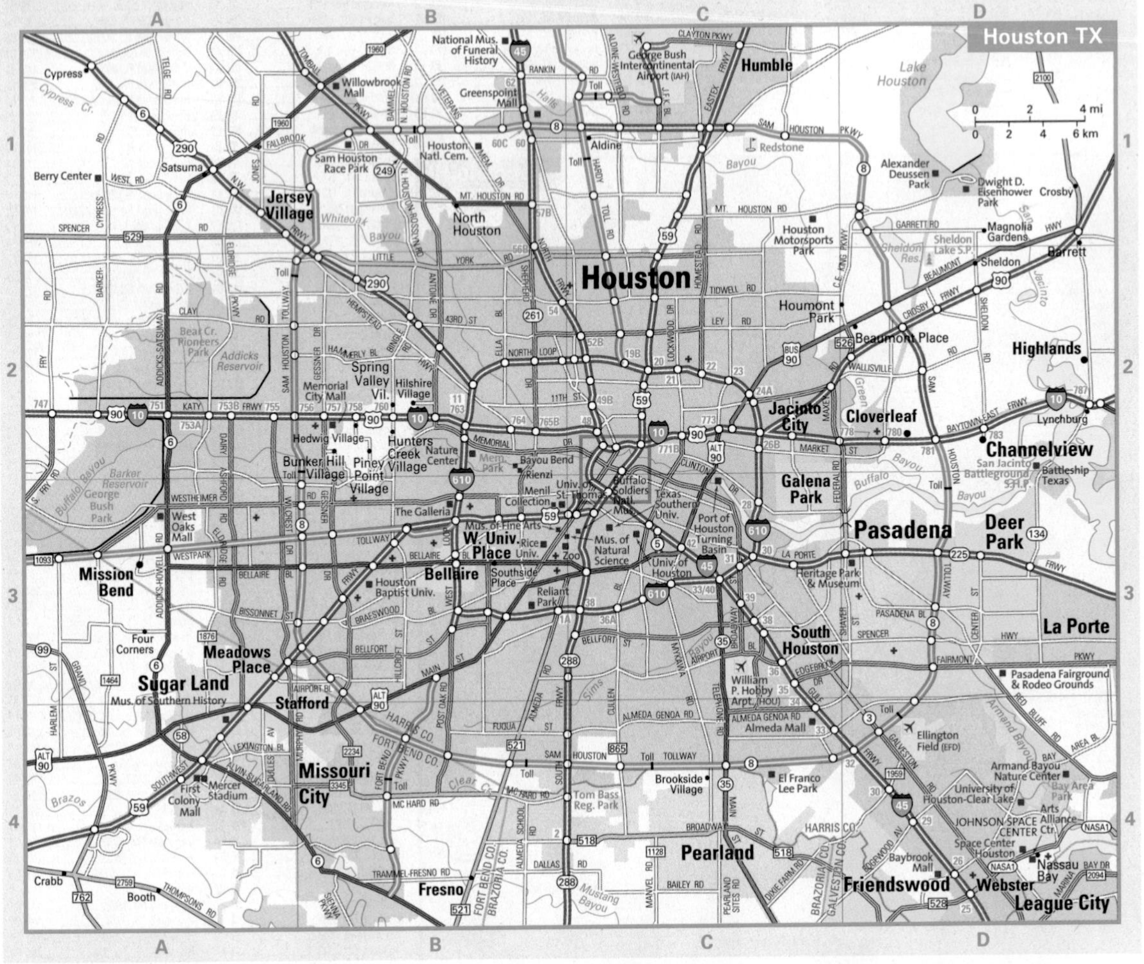

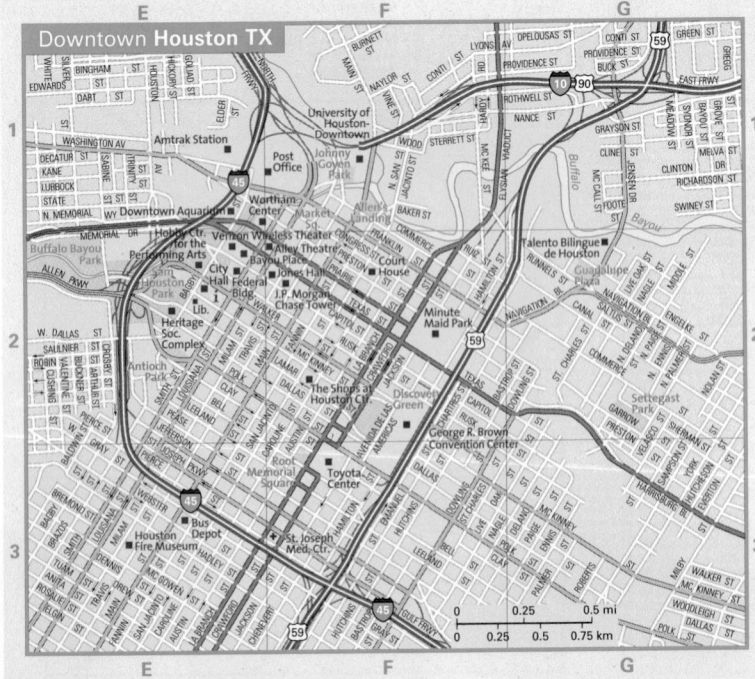

POINTS OF INTEREST

Allen's Landing F1	
Alley Theatre E1	
Amtrak Station E2	
Bayou Place F2	
Bus Depot E3	
City Hall E2	
Court House F2	
Downtown Aquarium E1	
Federal Building F2	
George R. Brown Convention Center F2	
Heritage Society Complex E2	
Hobby Center for the Performing Arts E2	
Houston Fire Museum E3	
Jones Hall F2	
J.P. Morgan Chase Tower F2	
Library F2	
Minute Maid Park G1	
Post Office F1	
The Shops at Houston Center G2	
Talento Bilingue de Houston G2	
Toyota Center F3	
Univ. of Houston-Downtown F1	
Verizon Wireless Theater E2	
Wortham Center E1	

Entries in **bold black** indicate counties or parishes.
Entries in *bold color* indicate cities with detailed inset maps.

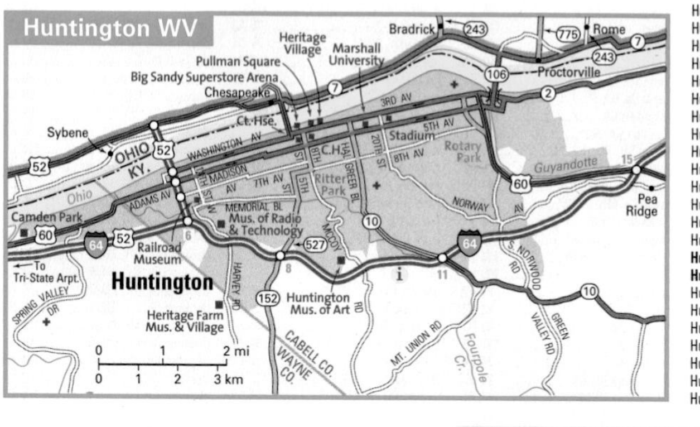

Huntington WV

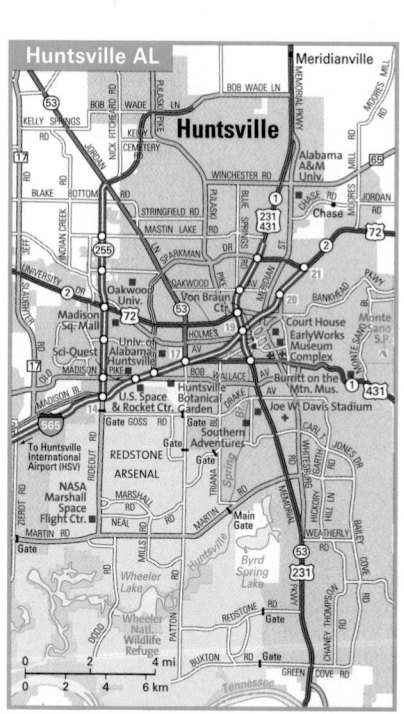

Huntsville AL

Idaho Falls ID

Indianapolis IN

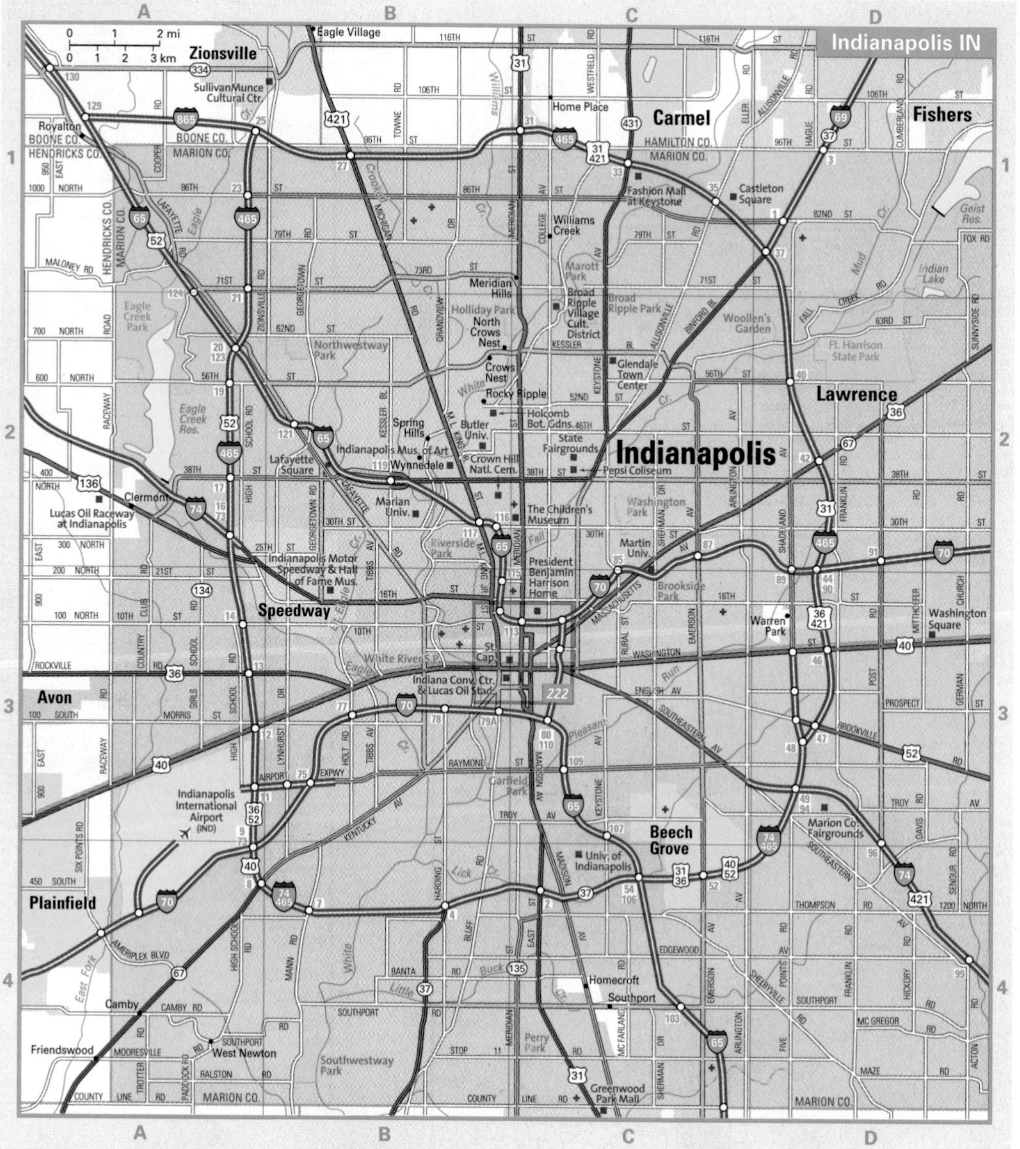

222

Indiantown–Jacksonville

Figures after entries indicate population, page number, and grid reference.

POINTS OF INTEREST

American Legion National Headquarters	A1
Artsgarden	A2
Canal & State Park Cultural District	A2
Circle Centre	A2
City Market	A2
Conseco Fieldhouse	B2
Eiteljorg Museum	A2
Herron School of Art	A1
Indiana Avenue Cultural District	A1
Indiana Convention Center	A2
Indiana State Museum	A2
Indiana Univ./Purdue Univ. Indianapolis	A1
Indiana War Memorial	A1
James Whitcomb Riley Home	B1
Lucas Oil Stadium	A2
Madame Walker Theatre Center	A1
Massachusetts Avenue Cultural District	B1
Morris-Butler House	B1
Murat Center	B1
NCAA Hall of Champions	A2
President Benjamin Harrison Home	B1
Scottish Rite Cathedral	A1
Soldiers & Sailors Monument	A2
State Capitol	A2
Victory Field	A2
White River State Park	A2
Zoo	A2

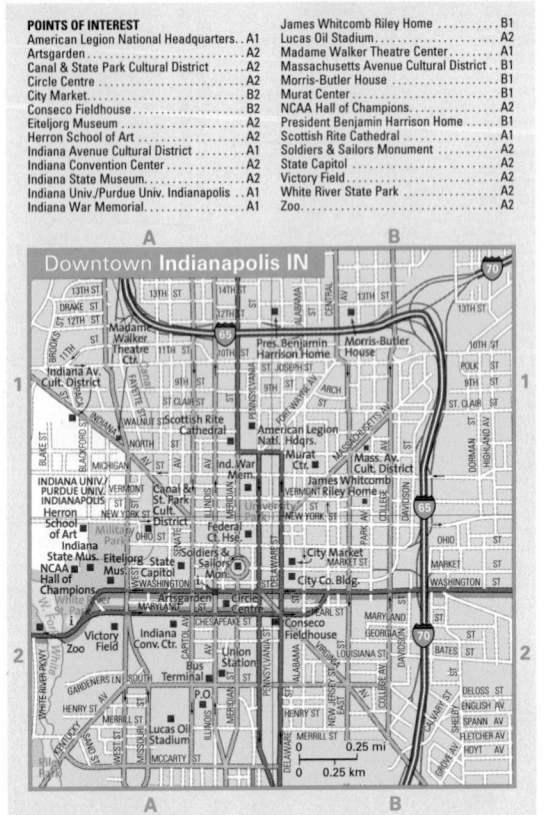

Downtown **Indianapolis IN**

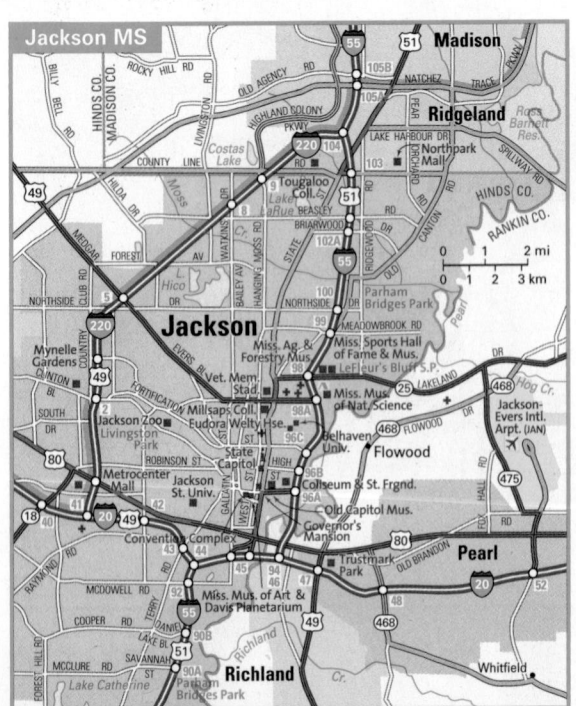

Jackson MS

Indiantown FL, 6083	141 E4	Inglis FL, 1325	138 C4
Indian Trail NC, 33518	122 B2	Ingold NC, 471	123 E2
Indian Wells CA, 4958	53 E3	Ingram PA, 3330	250 A2
Indio CA, 76036	53 E3	Ingram TX, 1804	60 C2
Indrio FL, 550	141 E3	Inkom ID, 854	31 E1
Industry CA, 219	228 E3	Inkster MI, 25369	210 B4
Industry PA, 1835	91 F3	Inman GA, 650	128 C1
Inez KY, 717	101 D4	Inman KS, 1377	43 E3
Inez TX, 2098	61 F3	Inman SC, 2321	121 F2
Ingalls IN, 2394	99 F1	Inola OK, 1788	106 A4
Ingham Co. MI, 280895	76 A4	Intercession City FL, 900	141 D2
Ingleside TX, 9387	63 F2	Interlachen FL, 1403	139 D3
Ingleside on the Bay TX, 615	63 F2	Interlaken NJ, 820	147 F2
Inglewood CA, 109673	52 C2	Interlaken NY, 602	79 D4

Iola WI, 1301	68 B4	Interlochen MI, 583	69 F4
Iona ID, 1803	23 E4	International Falls MN, 6424	64 B2
Ione CA, 7918	36 C3	Inver Grove Hts. MN, 33880	235 D4
Ione OR, 321	21 E2	Inverness CA, 1304	36 A3
Ione WA, 447	13 F1	Inverness FL, 7210	140 C1
Ionia MI, 11394	76 A3	Inverness IL, 7399	203 B2
Ionia Co. MI, 63905	75 F3	Inverness MS, 1019	126 B1
Iosco Co. MI, 25887	76 B1	Inwood FL, 6403	140 C2
Iota LA, 1500	133 E2	Inwood IA, 814	27 F4
Iowa LA, 2996	133 D2	Inwood NY, 9792	147 F1
Iowa City IA, 67862	87 F2	Inwood WV, 2954	103 D2
Iowa Colony TX, 1170	132 A4	Inyo Co. CA, 18546	37 F4
Iowa Co. IA, 16355	87 E2	Inyokern CA, 1099	45 E4
Iowa Co. WI, 23687	74 A3	Iola KS, 5704	96 A4
Iowa Falls IA, 5238	73 D4	
Iowa Park TX, 6355	59 D1	
Ipswich MA, 4222	151 F1	
Ipswich SD, 954	27 D2	
Iraan TX, 1229	60 A1	
Iredell Co. NC, 159437	112 A4	
Irene SD, 420	35 E1	
Ireton IA, 609	35 F1	
Irion Co. TX, 1599	58 B4	
Irmo SC, 11097	122 A3	
Iron City TN, 328	119 E2	
Iron Co. MI, 11817	68 C1	
Iron Co. MO, 10630	108 A1	
Iron Co. UT, 46163	39 D4	
Iron Co. WI, 5916	68 A1	
Irondale AL, 12349	119 F4	
Irondequoit NY, 51692	78 C3	
Iron Gate VA, 388	112 B1	
Iron Mtn. MI, 7624	68 C2	
Iron Mtn. Lake MO, 737	108 A1	
Iron Ridge WI, 929	74 C2	
Iron River MI, 3029	68 C2	
Ironton MN, 572	64 B4	
Ironton MO, 1460	108 A1	
Ironton OH, 11129	101 D3	
Ironwood MI, 5387	65 E4	

Iroquois SD, 266	27 E3	Isle of Wight Co. VA, 35270	113 F2
Iroquois Co. IL, 29718	89 D3	Isleta NM, 491	48 C3
Irrigon OR, 1826	21 E1	Isleton CA, 804	36 C3
Irvine CA, 212375	52 C3	Islip NY, 18689	149 A5
Irvine KY, 2715	110 C1	Isola MS, 713	126 B1
Irving IL, 495	98 B2	Issaquah WA, 30434	12 C3
Irving TX, 216290	59 F2	Issaquena Co. MS, 1406	126 A2
Irvington IL, 659	98 C3	Italy TX, 1863	59 F3
Irvington KY, 1181	99 F4	Itasca IL, 8649	203 B3
Irvington NE, 950	245 A1	Itasca TX, 1644	59 E3
Irvington NJ, 53926	148 A4	Itasca Co. MN, 45058	64 B3
Irvington NY, 6420	148 B3	Itawamba Co. MS, 23401	119 D3
Irvington VA, 432	113 F1	Ithaca MI, 3098	76 A3
Irwin PA, 3973	92 A4	Ithaca NY, 30014	79 D4
Irwin SC, 1405	122 B2	Itta Bena MS, 2049	118 B4
Irwin Co. GA, 9538	129 E4	Iuka IL, 489	98 C3
Irwindale CA, 1422	228 E2	Iuka MS, 3028	119 D2
Irwinton GA, 589	129 E2	Iva SC, 1218	121 E3
Isabel SD, 135	26 B2	Ivanhoe CA, 4495	45 D3
Isabella Co. MI, 70311	76 A2	Ivanhoe MN, 559	27 F2
Isanti MN, 5251	67 D3	Ivanhoe VA, 551	112 A2
Isanti Co. MN, 37816	67 D2	Ivey GA, 981	129 E1
Iselin NJ, 18895	147 E1	Ivins UT, 6753	38 C4
Ishpeming MI, 6470	65 F4	Ivins TX, 4511	59 D2
Islamorada FL, 6119	143 E4	Ixonia WI, 1624	74 C3
Island KY, 458	109 E1	Izard Co. AR, 13696	107 F4
Island City OR, 989	21 F2	
Island Co. WA, 78506	12 C2	**J**
Island Lake IL, 8080	74 C4	Jacinto City TX, 10553	220 C2
Island Hts. NJ, 1673	147 E3	Jack Co. TX, 9044	59 D2
Island Lake IL, 8080	74 C4	Jackman ME, 718	84 B4
Island Park ID, 286	23 F3	Jackman Sta. ME, 750	84 B4
Island Park NY, 4655	147 F1	Jackpot NV, 1195	30 C2
Island Pond VT, 821	81 E1	Jacksboro TN, 2020	110 C3
Isla Vista CA, 23096	52 A2	Jacksboro TX, 4511	59 D2
Isle MN, 751	67 D2	Jacksons Gap AL, 828	128 B3
Isle of Hope GA, 2402	130 C3	Jacksonville AL, 12548	120 A4
Isle of Palms SC, 4133	131 D2	Jacksonville AR, 28364	117 E2
Isle of Wight VA, 100	113 F2	Jacksonville FL, 821784	139 D3
		Jacksonville IL, 19446	98 A1

Jackson MN, 3299	72 B2
Jackson MS, 173514	126 B2
Jackson MO, 13758	108 B1
Jackson NC, 513	113 E3
Jackson OH, 6397	101 D2
Jackson SC, 1700	130 B1
Jackson TN, 65211	118 C1
Jackson WI, 6753	74 C3
Jackson WY, 9577	23 F4
Jackson Ctr. OH, 1462	90 B4
Jackson Co. AL, 53227	120 A2
Jackson Co. AR, 17997	118 A1
Jackson Co. CO, 1394	33 D4
Jackson Co. FL, 49746	137 D3
Jackson Co. GA, 60485	121 D3
Jackson Co. IL, 60218	98 B4
Jackson Co. IN, 42376	99 F3
Jackson Co. IA, 19848	87 F1
Jackson Co. KS, 13462	96 A2
Jackson Co. KY, 13494	110 C1
Jackson Co. MI, 160248	76 A4
Jackson Co. MN, 10266	72 B2
Jackson Co. MS, 139668	135 D2
Jackson Co. MO, 674158	96 C3
Jackson Co. NC, 40271	121 E1
Jackson Co. OH, 33225	101 D3
Jackson Co. OK, 26446	50 C4
Jackson Co. OR, 203206	28 B1
Jackson Co. SD, 3031	26 B4
Jackson Co. TN, 11638	110 A3
Jackson Co. TX, 14075	61 F3
Jackson Co. WV, 29211	101 E3
Jackson Co. WI, 20449	67 F4
Jackson Par. LA, 16274	125 E2
Jackson KY, 2231	111 D1
Jackson LA, 3842	134 A1
Jackson MI, 33534	76 A4

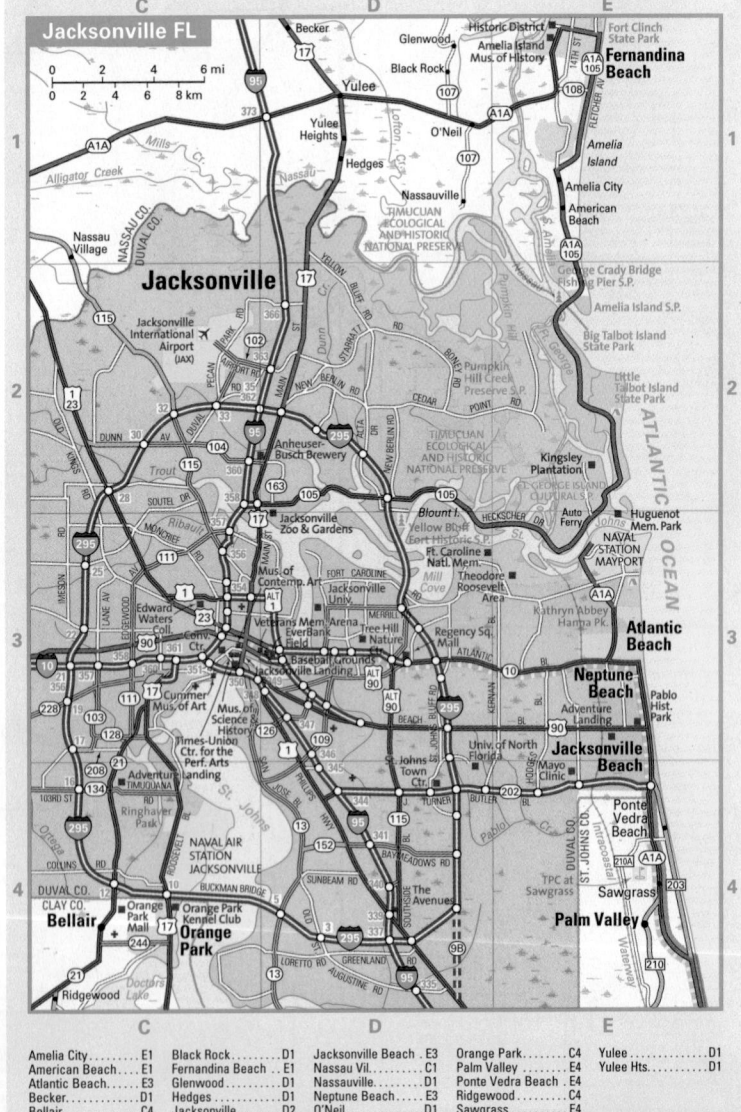

Jacksonville FL

Entries in **bold black** indicate counties or parishes.
Entries in **bold color** indicate cities with detailed inset maps.

Jacksonville NC, 70145 .... 115 D4
Jacksonville OR, 2785 .... 28 B2
Jacksonville PA, 637 .... 92 B4
Jacksonville TX, 14544 .... 124 A3
Jacksonville VT, 223 .... 94 C1
Jacksonville Beach FL, 21362 .. 139 D2
Jacobstown NJ, 950 .... 147 D2
Jacobus PA, 1841 .... 103 E1
Jaffrey NH, 2757 .... 95 D1
Jal NM, 2047 .... 57 F3
Jamaica Beach TX, 983 .... 132 B4
Jamesburg NJ, 5915 .... 147 E2
James City VA, 5899 .... 115 D3
James City Co. VA, 67009 .. 113 F1
Jamesport MO, 524 .... 96 C1
Jamesport NY, 1710 .... 149 E3
Jamestown CA, 3433 .... 37 D3
Jamestown IN, 958 .... 99 E1
Jamestown KS, 286 .... 43 E1
Jamestown KY, 1794 .... 110 B2
Jamestown MI, 31146 .... 75 F3
Jamestown NC, 3382 .... 112 B4
Jamestown ND, 15427 .... 19 D4
Jamestown OH, 1993 .... 100 C1
Jamestown PA, 617 .... 91 F2
Jamestown RI, 5405 .... 150 C4
Jamestown TN, 1959 .... 110 B3
James Town WY, 536 .... 32 A3
Jamesville NC, 491 .... 113 F4
Jamul CA, 6163 .... 53 D4
Jane Lew WV, 409 .... 102 A2
Janesville CA, 1408 .... 29 D4
Janesville IA, 930 .... 73 D4
Janesville MN, 2256 .... 72 C1
Janesville WI, 63575 .... 74 B4
Jarales NM, 2475 .... 48 C4
Jarratt VA, 638 .... 113 E2
Jarrell TX, 984 .... 61 E1
Jarrettsville MD, 2916 .... 144 C1
Jasmine Estates FL, 18989 .... 140 B2
Jasonville IN, 2222 .... 99 E2
Jasper AL, 14352 .... 119 E4
Jasper AR, 466 .... 107 D4
Jasper FL, 4546 .... 138 B2
Jasper GA, 3684 .... 120 C3
Jasper IN, 15038 .... 99 E4
Jasper MN, 633 .... 27 F4
Jasper MO, 931 .... 106 C1
Jasper OR, 700 .... 20 A4
Jasper TN, 3279 .... 120 A2
Jasper TX, 7590 .... 132 C1
Jasper Co. GA, 13900 .... 129 D1
Jasper Co. IL, 9698 .... 99 D2

Jasper Co. IN, 33478 .... 89 E3
Jasper Co. IA, 36842 .... 87 D2
Jasper Co. MS, 17062 .... 126 C3
Jasper Co. MO, 117404 ...... 106 C2
Jasper Co. SC, 24777 .... 130 C3
Jasper Co. TX, 35710 .... 132 C1
Jay OK, 2448 .... 106 B3
Jay, 533 .... 135 F1
Jay ME, 4985 .... 82 B2
Jay OK, 2448 .... 106 B3
Jay Co. IN, 21253 .... 90 A4
Jayton TX, 534 .... 58 B2
Jeanerette LA, 5530 .... 133 F3
Jean Lafitte LA, 1903 .... 134 B3
Jeannette PA, 9654 .... 92 A4
Jeddito AZ, 293 .... 47 F2
Jeff Davis Co. GA, 15068 ... 129 F3
Jeff Davis Co. TX, 2342 .... 62 B2
Jefferson GA, 9432 .... 121 D3
Jefferson IA, 4345 .... 86 B1
Jefferson LA, 11193 .... 239 B1
Jefferson MA, 1600 .... 150 B1
Jefferson NC, 1611 .... 111 F3
Jefferson OH, 3120 .... 91 F1
Jefferson OR, 3098 .... 20 B3
Jefferson PA, 631 .... 103 E1
Jefferson SC, 753 .... 122 B2
Jefferson SD, 547 .... 35 F1
Jefferson TX, 2106 .... 124 C2
Jefferson WI, 7973 .... 74 B3
Jefferson City MO, 43079 .... 97 E3
Jefferson City MT, 472 .... 15 E4
Jefferson City TN, 8047 .... 111 D4
Jefferson Co. AL, 658466 ... 119 F4
Jefferson Co. AR, 77435 .... 117 F3
Jefferson Co. CO, 534543 .... 41 E1
Jefferson Co. FL, 14761 .... 137 E2
Jefferson Co. GA, 16930 ... 129 F1
Jefferson Co. ID, 26140 ...... 23 E4
Jefferson Co. IL, 38827 .... 98 C4
Jefferson Co. IN, 32428 .... 100 A3
Jefferson Co. IA, 16843 ...... 87 E3
Jefferson Co. KS, 19126 ..... 96 A2
Jefferson Co. KY, 741096 .. 100 A4
Jefferson Co. MS, 7726 ..... 126 A3
Jefferson Co. MO, 218733 ... 98 A4
Jefferson Co. MT, 11406 ...... 23 E1
Jefferson Co. NE, 7547 .... 35 E4
Jefferson Co. NY, 111629 ... 79 E2
Jefferson Co. OH, 69709 .... 91 F4
Jefferson Co. OK, 6472 ...... 59 E1
Jefferson Co. OR, 21720 ..... 20 C3
Jefferson Co. PA, 45200 ...... 92 B2
Jefferson Co. TN, 51407 .... 111 D4
Jefferson Co. TX, 252273 ... 132 C3

Jefferson Co. WA, 29872 .... 12 B3
Jefferson Co. WV, 53498 .. 103 D2
Jefferson Co. WI, 83686 ...... 74 C3
Jefferson Davis Co. MS, 12487 .. 126 B4
Jefferson Davis Par. LA, 31594 .. 133 E2
Jefferson Hts. NY, 1094 .... 94 B2
Jefferson Davis Par. LA, 432552 .. 134 B3
Jeffersontown KY, 26595 ..... 100 A4
Jefferson Valley NY, 14142 .. 148 B2
Jeffersonville GA, 1035 .... 129 E2
Jeffersonville IN, 44953 ...... 100 A4
Jeffersonville KY, 1506 .... 100 C4
Jeffersonville OH, 1203 ...... 100 C1
Jeffersonville PA, 10200 ..... 248 A1
Jeffersonville VT, 729 .... 81 D1
Jellico TN, 2355 .... 110 C3
Jemez Pueblo NM, 1788 .... 48 C2
Jemez Sprs. NM, 250 .... 48 C2
Jemison AL, 2585 .... 125 E1
Jena LA, 3398 .... 125 E4
Jenkins KY, 2203 .... 111 E2
Jenkins Co. GA, 8340 .... 129 F2
Jenkintown PA, 4422 .... 146 C2
Jenks OK, 16924 .... 51 F2
Jennerstown PA, 695 .... 92 B4
Jennings FL, 878 .... 137 F2
Jennings LA, 10383 .... 133 E2
Jennings MO, 14712 .... 256 B1
Jennings Co. IN, 28525 ... 100 A3
Jenny Lind AR, 650 .... 116 C1
Jensen Beach FL, 11707 ..... 141 E4
Jerauld Co. SD, 2071 .... 27 D3
Jericho NY, 13567 .... 148 C3
Jericho VT, 1329 .... 81 D2
Jermyn PA, 2169 .... 93 F2
Jerome AZ, 444 .... 47 D4
Jerome ID, 10890 .... 30 C1
Jerome PA, 1017 .... 92 B4
Jerome Co. ID, 22374 .... 31 D1
Jersey City NJ, 247597 .... 148 B4
Jersey Co. IL, 22985 .... 98 A2
Jersey Shore PA, 4361 .... 93 D2
Jersey Vil. TX, 7620 .... 132 A3
Jerseyville IL, 8465 .... 98 A2
Jerseyville NJ, 1000 .... 147 E2
Jerusalem RI, 800 .... 150 C4
Jessamine Co. KY, 48586 .. 100 B4
Jessup MD, 7137 .... 144 C4
Jessup PA, 4676 .... 93 F2
Jessup IA, 10214 .... 130 A4
Jesup GA, 10214 .... 73 E4
Jetmore KS, 867 .... 42 C3

Johnson Co. GA, 9980 .... 129 F2
Johnson Co. IL, 12582 .... 108 C1
Johnson Co. IN, 139654 .... 99 F2
Johnson Co. IA, 130882 .... 87 F2
Johnson Co. KS, 544179 .... 96 B3
Johnson Co. KY, 23356 .... 111 D1
Johnson Co. MO, 52595 .... 96 C3
Johnson Co. NE, 5217 .... 35 F4
Johnson Co. TN, 18244 ...... 111 F3
Johnson Co. TX, 150934 .... 59 E3
Johnson Co. WY, 8569 .... 25 D4
Johnson Creek WI, 2738 .... 74 C3
Johnsonville SC, 1480 .... 122 C4
Johnston IA, 17278 .... 86 C2
Johnston SC, 2362 .... 121 F4
Johnston Co. NC, 168878 ... 113 D4
Johnston Co. OK, 10957 .... 51 F4
Johnstown CO, 9887 .... 33 E4
Johnstown NY, 4631 .... 79 F3
Johnstown OH, 4632 .... 91 D4
Johnstown PA, 20978 .... 92 B4
Joiner AR, 576 .... 118 B1
Joliet IL, 147433 .... 89 D2
Jollet MT, 595 .... 24 B2
Jollyville TX, 16151 .... 61 E1
Jones OK, 2692 .... 51 E3
Jonesboro AR, 67263 .... 108 A4
Jonesboro GA, 4724 .... 120 C4
Jonesboro IL, 1821 .... 108 C1
Jonesboro IN, 1756 .... 89 F4
Jonesboro LA, 4704 .... 125 E3
Jonesborough TN, 5051 ...... 111 E3
Jonesburg MO, 768 .... 97 F3
Jonesport ME, 1408 .... 83 E2
Jonestown MS, 1298 .... 118 A3
Jonestown PA, 64 .... 93 E4
Jonestown TX, 1834 .... 61 E1
Jonesville LA, 2265 .... 125 F4
Jonesville MI, 2258 .... 90 B1
Jonesville SC, 911 .... 121 F2
Jonesville VT, 375 .... 81 D2
Jonesville VA, 1034 .... 111 D3
Joplin MO, 50150 .... 106 B2
Joplin MT, 157 .... 15 F2
Joppatowne MD, 12616 .... 145 D1
Jordan MN, 5470 .... 66 C4
Jordan MT, 343 .... 17 D3
Jordan NY, 1368 .... 79 D3
Joseph OR, 1081 .... 22 A4
Joseph City AZ, 1386 .... 47 F3
Josephine TX, 812 .... 59 F2
Josephine Co. OR, 82713 ... 28 B2
Joshua TX, 5910 .... 59 E3
Joshua Tree CA, 7414 .... 53 E2
Jourdanton TX, 3871 .... 61 D3
Juab Co. UT, 10246 .... 39 D1
Judith Basin Co. MT, 2072 .. 16 A3
Judsonia AR, 2019 .... 117 F1
Julesburg CO, 1225 .... 34 A3
Julietta ID, 579 .... 14 B4
Julian CA, 1502 .... 53 D4
Julian NC, 600 .... 112 B4
Jumpertown MS, 480 .... 119 D2
Junction TX, 2574 .... 60 C1
Junction UT, 191 .... 39 E3
Junction City AR, 581 .... 125 E1
Junction City KS, 23353 .... 43 F2
Junction City KY, 2241 .... 110 B1
Junction City LA, 582 .... 125 E1
Junction City OH, 819 .... 101 E1
Junction City OR, 5392 .... 20 B3
Juneau AK, 31275 .... 155 E4
Juneau WI, 2814 .... 74 C2
Juneau Co. WI, 26664 .... 74 A1
Juniata NE, 755 .... 35 D4
Juniata Co. PA, 24636 .... 93 D3
Junior WV, 520 .... 102 A2
Juno Beach FL, 3176 .... 141 F4
Jupiter FL, 55156 .... 141 F4
Jupiter Island FL, 817 .... 141 F4
Jurupa Valley CA, 94235 .... 229 H3
Justice IL, 12926 .... 203 D5
Justin TX, 3246 .... 59 E2
Justus TX, 950 .... 261 E1

K

Kaaawa HI, 1379 .... 152 A2
Kaanapali HI, 1045 .... 153 D1
Kadoka SD, 654 .... 26 B4
Kahaluu HI, 4738 .... 152 A3
Kahoka MO, 2134 .... 87 E4
Kahuku HI, 2614 .... 152 A2
Kahului HI, 26337 .... 153 D1
Kaibab AZ, 124 .... 47 E1
Kaibito AZ, 1522 .... 47 F1
Kailua HI, 38635 .... 152 B3
Kailua-Kona HI, 11975 .... 153 F3
Kake AK, 557 .... 155 E4
Kaleheo HI, 4595 .... 152 B1
Kalama WA, 2344 .... 20 C1
Kalaoa HI, 9644 .... 153 E3
Kalaupapa HI, ... 152 C3

Kalawao Co. HI, 90 .... 152 C3
Kaleva HI, 470 .... 75 F1
Kalida OH, 1542 .... 90 B3
Kalihiwai HI, 428 .... 152 B1
Kalispell MT, 19927 .... 15 D2
Kalkaska MI, 2020 .... 69 F4
Kalkaska Co. MI, 17153 .... 70 B4
Kalona IA, 2363 .... 87 E2
Kamas UT, 1811 .... 31 F1
Kamiah ID, 1295 .... 22 B1
Kanab UT, 4312 .... 39 E4
Kanabec Co. MN, 16239 ...... 67 D2
Kanaranville UT, 355 .... 39 D4
Kanarraville UT, 652 .... 72 C3
Kanawha IA, 652 .... 72 C3
Kanawha Co. WV, 193063 ... 101 F2
Kandiyohi MN, 491 .... 66 B3
Kandiyohi Co. MN, 42239 ..... 66 B3
Kane PA, 3730 .... 92 B2
Kane Co. IL, 515269 .... 88 C1
Kane Co. UT, 7125 .... 39 E4
Kaneohe HI, 34597 .... 152 A3
Kankakee IL, 27537 .... 89 D3
Kankakee Co. IL, 113449 ...... 89 D2
Kannapolis NC, 42625 .... 122 B1
Kanopolis KS, 492 .... 43 E2
Kanosh UT, 474 .... 39 D2
Kansas IL, 787 .... 99 D1
Kansas OK, 802 .... 106 B3
Kansas City KS, 145786 .... 96 B2
Kansas City MO, 459787 .... 96 B2
Kapaa HI, 10699 .... 152 B1
Kapaau HI, 1734 .... 153 E2
Kapaa HI, 3730 .... 152 B1
Kaplan LA, 4600 .... 133 E3
Karlstad MN, 760 .... 19 F2
Karnak IL, 499 .... 108 C2
Karnes City TX, 3042 .... 61 E3
Karnes Co. TX, 14824 .... 61 E3
Karns TN, 3643 .... 110 C4
Kasigluk AK, 569 .... 154 B3
Kasota MN, 695 .... 72 C1
Kasson MN, 1500 .... 99 D4
Kasson MN, 5931 .... 73 D1
Kathleen FL, 6332 .... 140 C2
Kathleen GA, 650 .... 129 D2
Katonah NY, 1679 .... 148 C2
Katy TX, 14102 .... 132 A3

Kauai Co. HI, 67091 .... 152 B1
Kaufman TX, 6703 .... 59 F2
Kaufman Co. TX, 103350 .... 59 F3
Kaukauna WI, 15462 .... 74 C1
Kaumakani HI, 749 .... 152 B1
Kaunakakai HI, 3425 .... 152 C3
Kawkawlin MI, 1600 .... 76 B2
Kaycee WY, 263 .... 25 D4
Kayenta AZ, 5189 .... 47 F1
Kaysville UT, 27300 .... 31 E3
Keaau HI, 2253 .... 153 F3
Keachi LA, 369 .... 124 B2
Kealakekua HI, 2019 .... 153 E3
Keams Canyon AZ, 304 .... 47 F2
Keansburg NJ, 10105 .... 147 E1
Kearney MO, 8381 .... 96 B2
Kearney NE, 30787 .... 35 D4
Kearneysville WV, 650 .... 103 D2
Kearns UT, 35731 .... 257 A2
Kearny AZ, 1950 .... 55 D2
Kearny NJ, 40684 .... 148 B4
Kearny Co. KS, 3977 .... 42 B3

Kenly NC, 1339 .... 123 E1
Kechi KS, 1909 .... 43 E4
Kenmare ND, 1096 .... 18 B1
Kenmore NY, 15423 .... 78 A3
Kenmore WA, 20460 .... 262 B2
Kennebec Co. ME, 122151 .. 82 B2
Kennebunk ME, 5214 .... 82 B4
Kennebunkport ME, 1238 .... 82 B4
Kennedale TX, 6763 .... 207 B3
Kennedy AL, 447 .... 119 D4
Kenner LA, 66702 .... 134 B3
Kennesaw GA, 29783 .... 120 C3
Kenneth City FL, 4980 .... 266 A3
Kennett MO, 10932 .... 108 B3
Kennett Square PA, 6072 .. 146 B3
Kennewick WA, 73917 .... 21 E1
Keno OR, 850 .... 28 C2
Kenosha WI, 99218 .... 75 D4
Kenosha Co. WI, 166426 ..... 74 C4
Kenova WV, 3216 .... 101 D4
Kensett AR, 1648 .... 117 F1
Kensington CA, 5077 .... 259 C2
Kensington CT, 8459 .... 149 E1
Kensington KS, 473 .... 43 D1

Keavy KY, 450 .... 110 C2
Kechi KS, 1909 .... 43 E4
Keedysville MD, 1152 .... 144 A1
Keegan ME, 550 .... 85 E1
Keego Harbor MI, 2970 ...... 210 A1
Kent OH, 28904 .... 91 E3
Kent CT, 2962 .... 94 B3
Kent WA, 92411 .... 12 C3
Kent City MI, 1057 .... 75 F3
Kent Co. DE, 162310 .... 145 E3
Kent Co. MD, 20197 .... 145 D2
Kent Co. MI, 602622 .... 75 F3
Kent Co. RI, 166158 .... 150 C3
Kent City NY, 375 .... 100 B3
Kenton DE, 261 .... 145 E2
Kenton OH, 8262 .... 90 C3
Kenton TN, 1281 .... 108 C3
Kenton Co. KY, 159720 .... 100 B2
Kentfield CA, 6485 .... 259 A1
Kentland IN, 1748 .... 89 D3
Kentwood LA, 2198 .... 134 B1
Kentwood MI, 48707 .... 75 F3
Kenvil NJ, 3009 .... 148 A3
Kenwood MD, 9800 .... 193 D2
Kenwood OH, 6981 .... 204 C2
Kenwood Beach MD, 600 .. 144 C4
Kenyon MN, 1815 .... 73 D1
Keokuk IA, 10780 .... 87 F4
Keokuk Co. IA, 10511 .... 87 E2
Keosauqua IA, 1006 .... 87 E3
Keota IA, 1009 .... 87 E2
Keota OK, 564 .... 116 B1
Kerens TX, 1573 .... 59 F3
Kerhonkson NY, 1684 .... 94 A3
Kerkhoven MN, 759 .... 66 B3
Kerman CA, 13544 .... 44 C3
Kermit TX, 5708 .... 57 F3
Kern Co. CA, 839631 .... 45 D4
Kernersville NC, 23123 ...... 112 B4
Kernville CA, 1395 .... 45 E4
Kerr Co. TX, 49625 .... 60 C2
Kerrville TX, 22347 .... 60 C2
Kersey CO, 1454 .... 33 E4
Kershaw SC, 1803 .... 122 B2
Kershaw Co. SC, 61697 ... 122 B3
Keshena WI, 1262 .... 68 C4
Ketchikan AK, 8050 .... 155 E4
Ketchum ID, 2689 .... 22 C4

Kettering OH, 56163 .... 100 B1
Kettle Falls WA, 1595 .... 13 F1
Kettleman City CA, 1439 ...... 44 C4
Kevil KY, 376 .... 108 C2
Kewanee IL, 12916 .... 88 A2
Kewanna IN, 613 .... 89 E3
Kewaskum WI, 4004 .... 74 C2
Kewaunee WI, 20527 .... 75 D1
Kewaunee Co. WI, 20574 .... 69 D4
Keweenaw Co. MI, 2156 ...... 65 F3
Keya Paha Co. NE, 824 .... 35 D1
Key Biscayne FL, 12344 ..... 143 E3
Key Colony Beach FL, 797 .. 143 D4
Keyes CA, 5601 .... 36 C4
Key Largo FL, 10433 .... 143 E3
Keyport NJ, 7240 .... 147 E1
Keyser WV, 5439 .... 102 C2
Keystone CO, 1079 .... 41 D2
Keystone IA, 622 .... 87 E1
Keystone SD, 337 .... 25 F3
Keystone FL, 1111 .... 111 F1
Keystone Hts. FL, 1350 ...... 139 D3
Keysville VA, 832 .... 113 D2

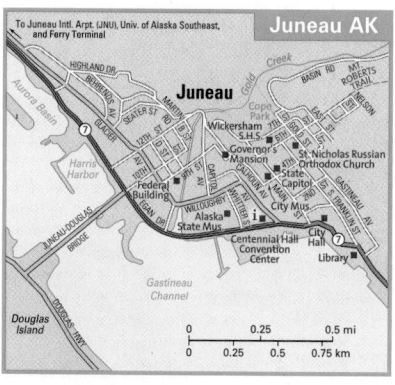

Jefferson City MO

Juneau AK

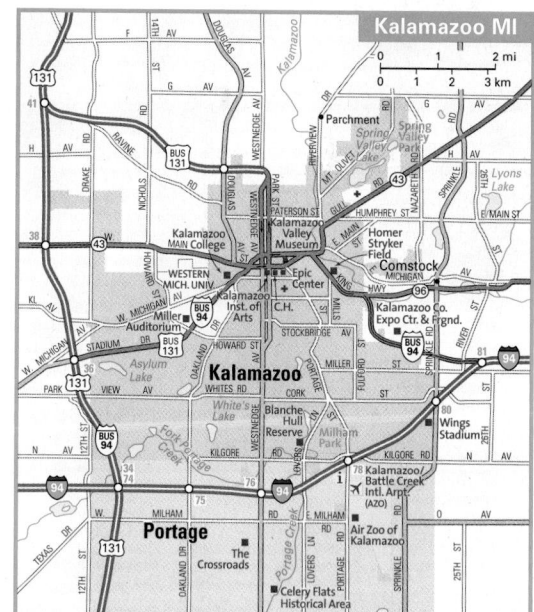

Kalamazoo MI

Portage

224

Keytesville–Kingston

Figures after entries indicate population, page number, and grid reference.

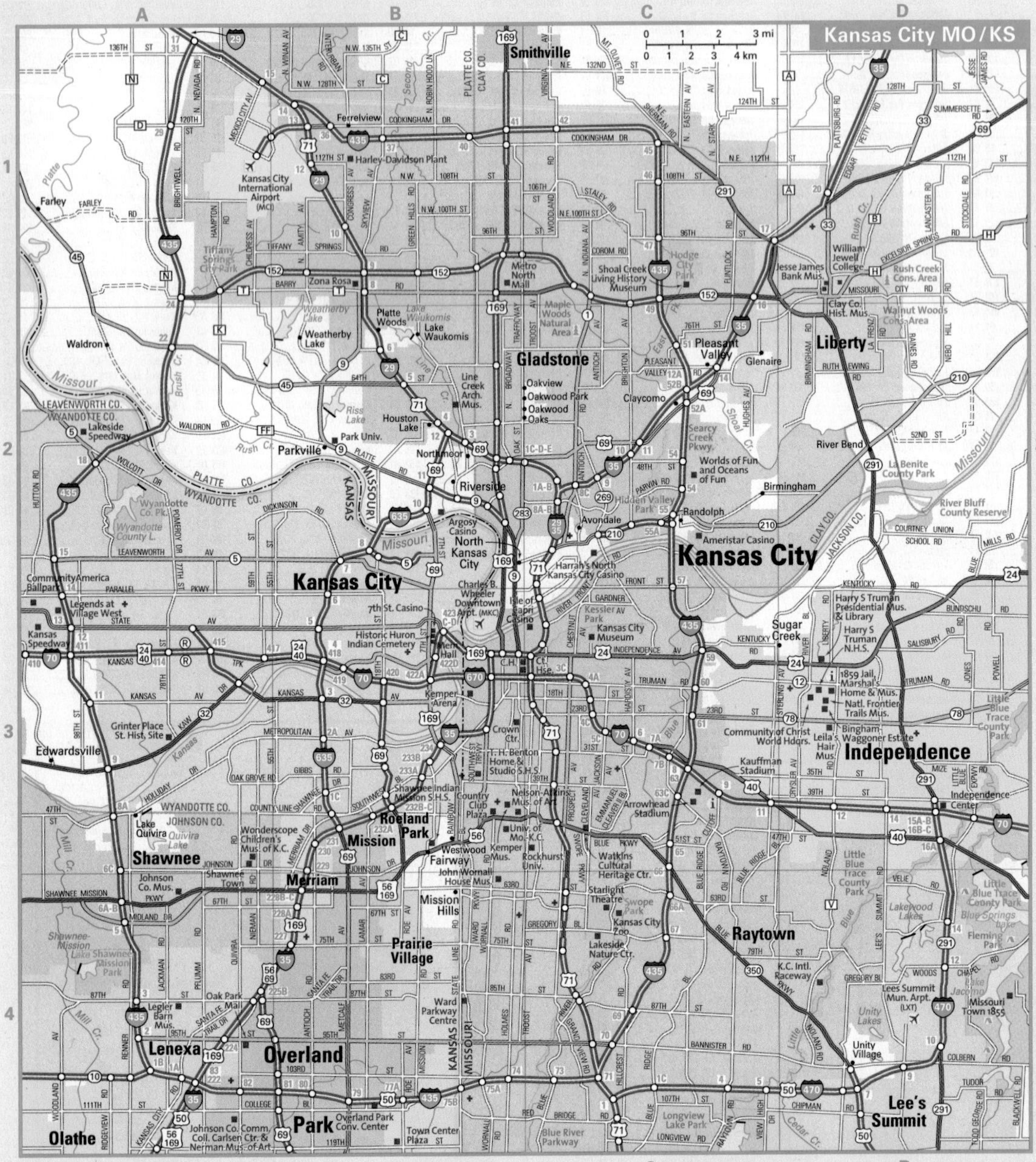

Kansas City MO/KS

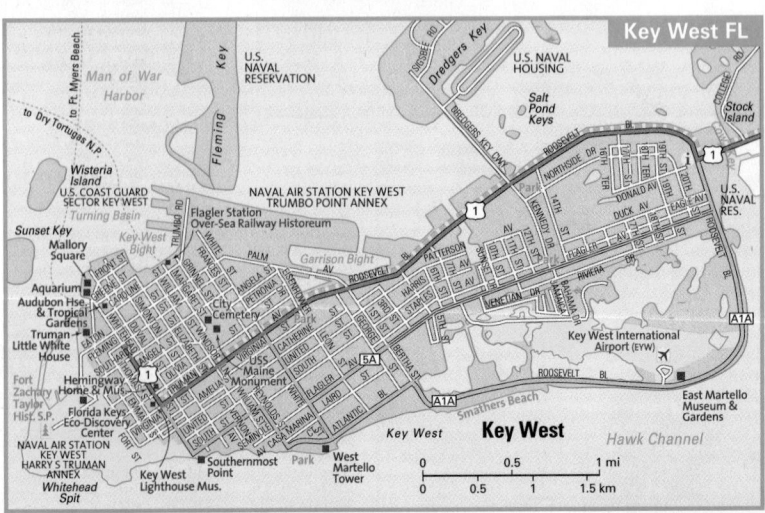

Key West FL

Entries in **bold black** indicate counties or parishes.
Entries in **bold color** indicate cities with detailed inset maps.

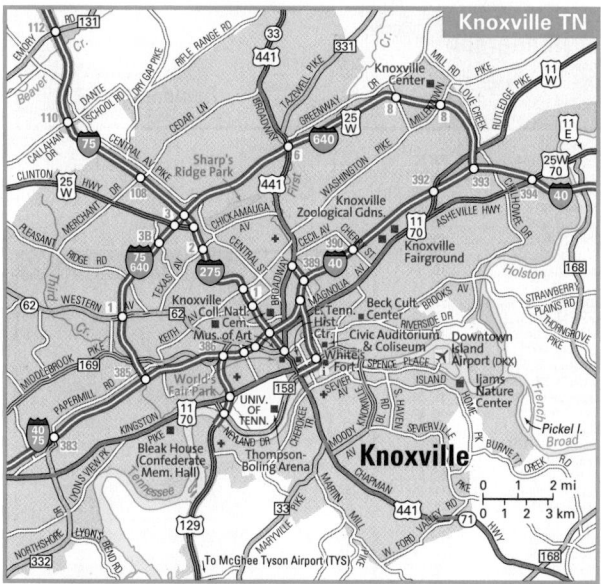

Knoxville TN

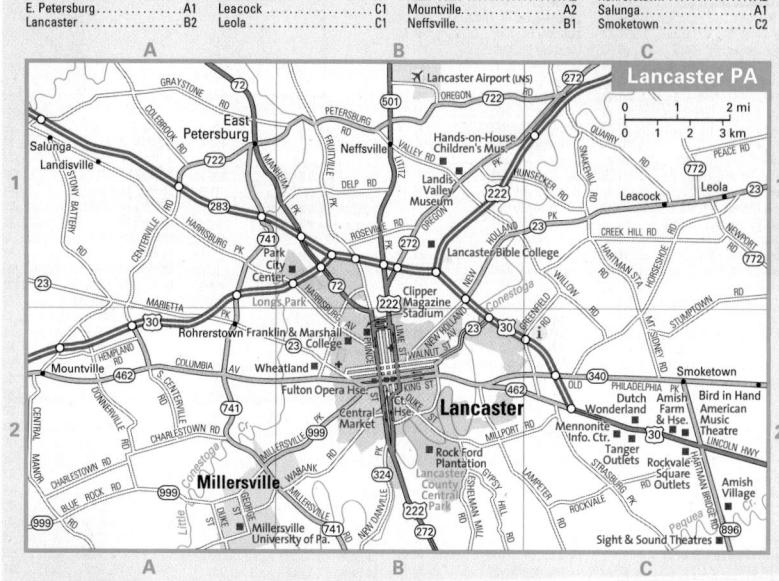

Bird in Hand C2	Landisville A1	Millersville A2	Rohrerstown A2
E. Petersburg A1	Leacock C1	Mountville A2	Salunga A1
Lancaster B2	Leola C1	Neffsville B1	Smoketown C2

Lancaster PA

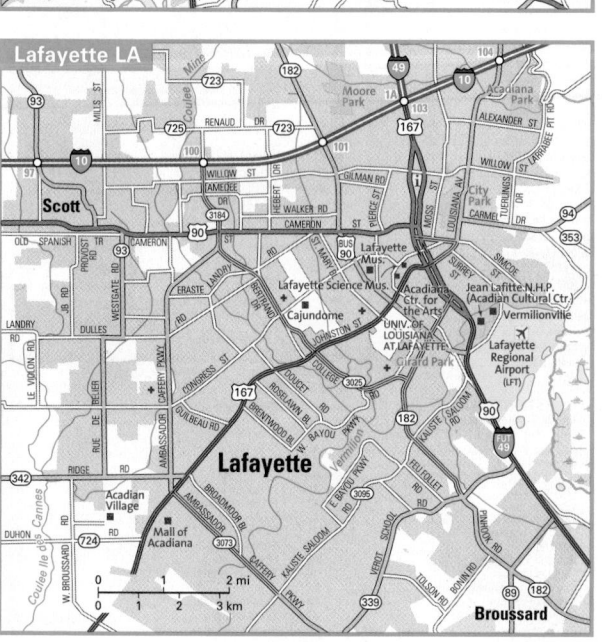

Lafayette LA

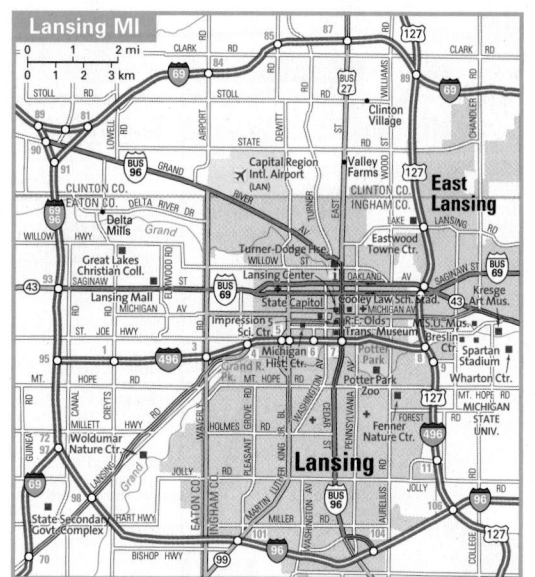

Lansing MI

Figures after entries indicate population, page number, and grid reference.

Las Vegas NV

North Las Vegas

NELLIS AIR FORCE BASE

Las Vegas–Dunes Recreation Lands

0 2 4 6 mi
0 2 4 6 8 km

Floyd Lamb Park at Tule Springs

Las Vegas

Nev. St. Mus. & Hist. Soc.

L.V. Natural Hist. Museum
Cashman Field
Old Las Vegas Mormon Fort S.H.P.

Las Vegas Motor Speedway
NELLIS AIR FORCE BASE

Sunrise Mtn.
+3,364

Sunrise Mtn. Natural Area

Meadows Mall

Sunrise Manor

Mob. Mus.

Callville Bay

Spring Valley

The Strip
U.N.L.V.

Blvd. Mall

Winchester

Lake Las Vegas Reflection Bay

SouthShore

Las Vegas Bay

PACIFIC TIME ZONE

MOUNTAIN TIME ZONE

Paradise
Whitney

Galleria at Sunset

Clark County Wetlands Park

Lake Mead

McCarran Intl. Airport (LAS)

Sam Boyd Stadium

LAKE MEAD NATIONAL RECREATION AREA

Boulder Beach

Enterprise

Clark County Museum

Alan Bible Visitor Center

Visitor Center

Hoover Dam

Henderson

Nevada State Coll.

Nev. St. Railroad Mus., Boulder City

Boulder City/ Hoover Dam Mus.

Henderson Executive Airport (HND)

SLOAN CANYON NATIONAL CONSERVATION AREA

Railroad Pass 2,367

Hist. Dist.

Boulder City

Boulder City Mun. Arpt. (61B)

Las Vegas Strip NV

Palace Station

Stratosphere

Circus Circus

Echelon Place
Riviera

Las Vegas Hilton
Las Vegas Conv. Center

Fashion Show Mall

Wynn Las Vegas

Treasure Island
The Palazzo

Monorail

The Mirage
The Venetian

Harrah's
Imperial Palace
Flamingo
Las Vegas

Caesars Palace

Bellagio

Bally's Las Vegas
Paris-Las Vegas

The Cosmopolitan
Planet Hollywood

Hard Rock

UNIV. OF NEVADA, LAS VEGAS

Atomic Testing Mus.

CityCenter

Monte Carlo

Showcase Mall

New York-New York

MGM Grand

Excalibur
Tropicana

McCarran Intl. Airport (LAS)

Luxor Las Vegas

Mandalay Bay

0 .25 .5 mi
0 .25 .5 .75 km

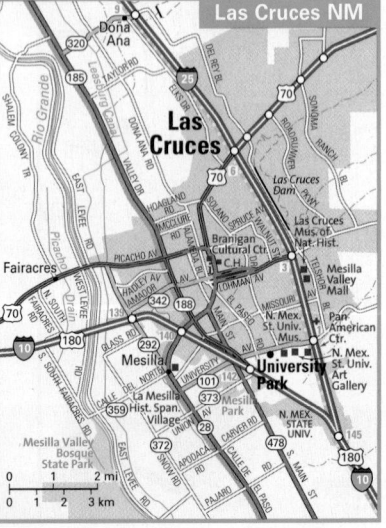

Las Cruces NM

Doña Ana

Las Cruces

Las Cruces Dam

Las Cruces Mus. of Nat. Hist.

La Mesilla Cultural Ctr.

Branigan Cultural Ctr.

Mesilla Valley Mall

Fairacres

N. Mex. St. Univ.

Pan American Ctr.

N. Mex. St. Univ. Art Gallery

Mesilla

University Park

La Mesilla Hist. Span. Village

N. MEX. STATE UNIV.

Mesilla Valley Bosque State Park

0 1 2 mi
0 1 2 3 km

Entries in **bold black** indicate counties or parishes.
Entries in **bold color** indicate cities with detailed inset maps.

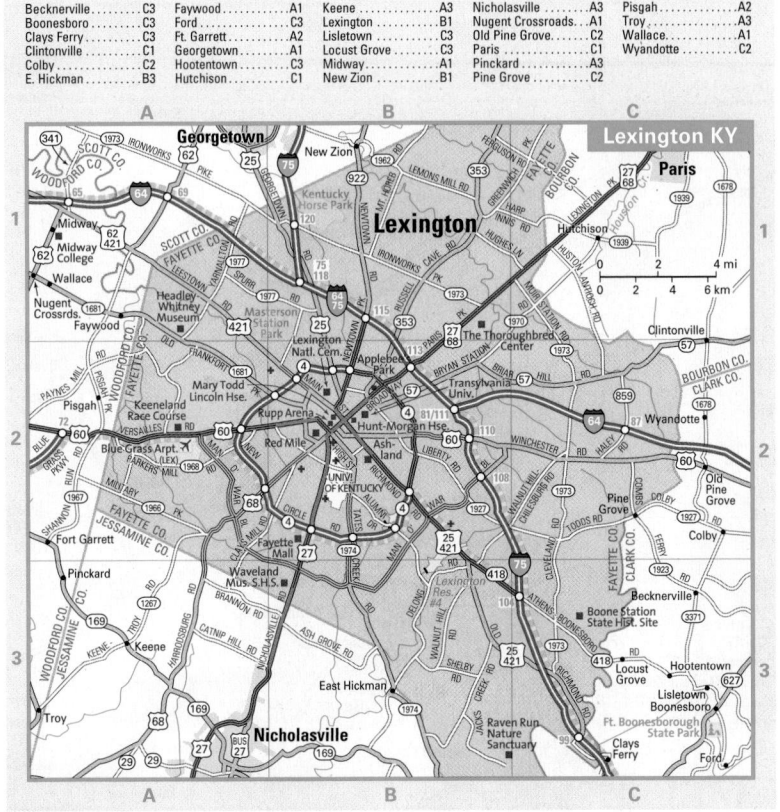

Lexington KY

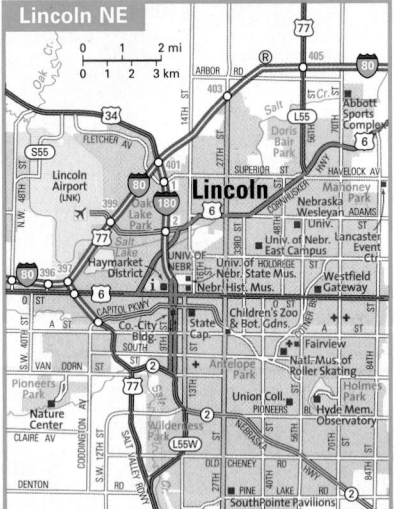

Lincoln NE

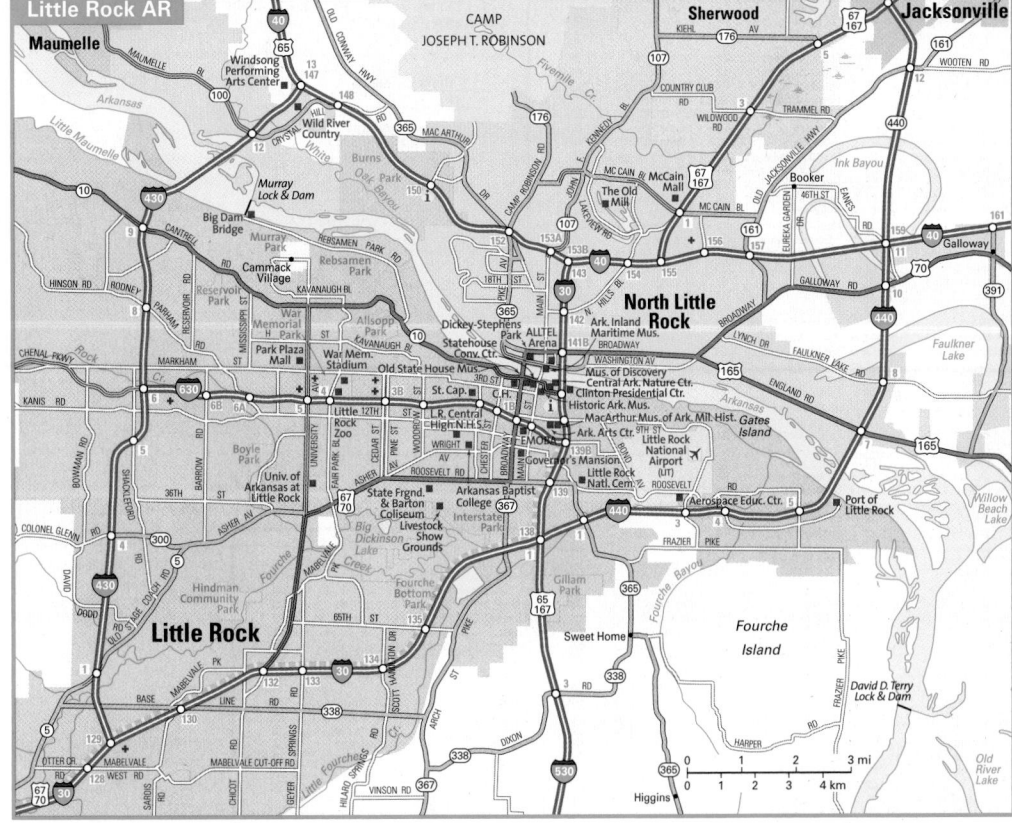

Little Rock AR

Figures after entries indicate population, page number, and grid reference.

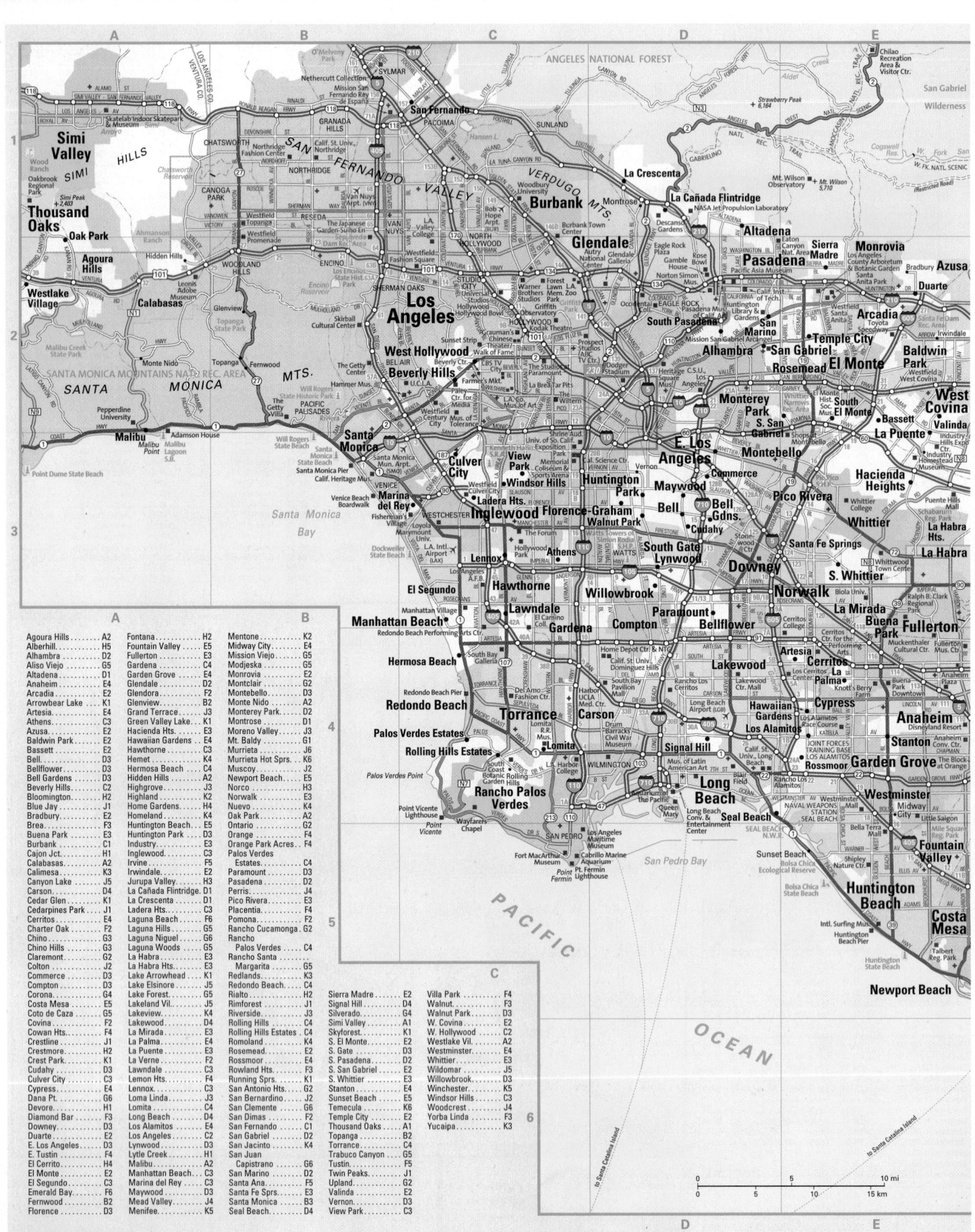

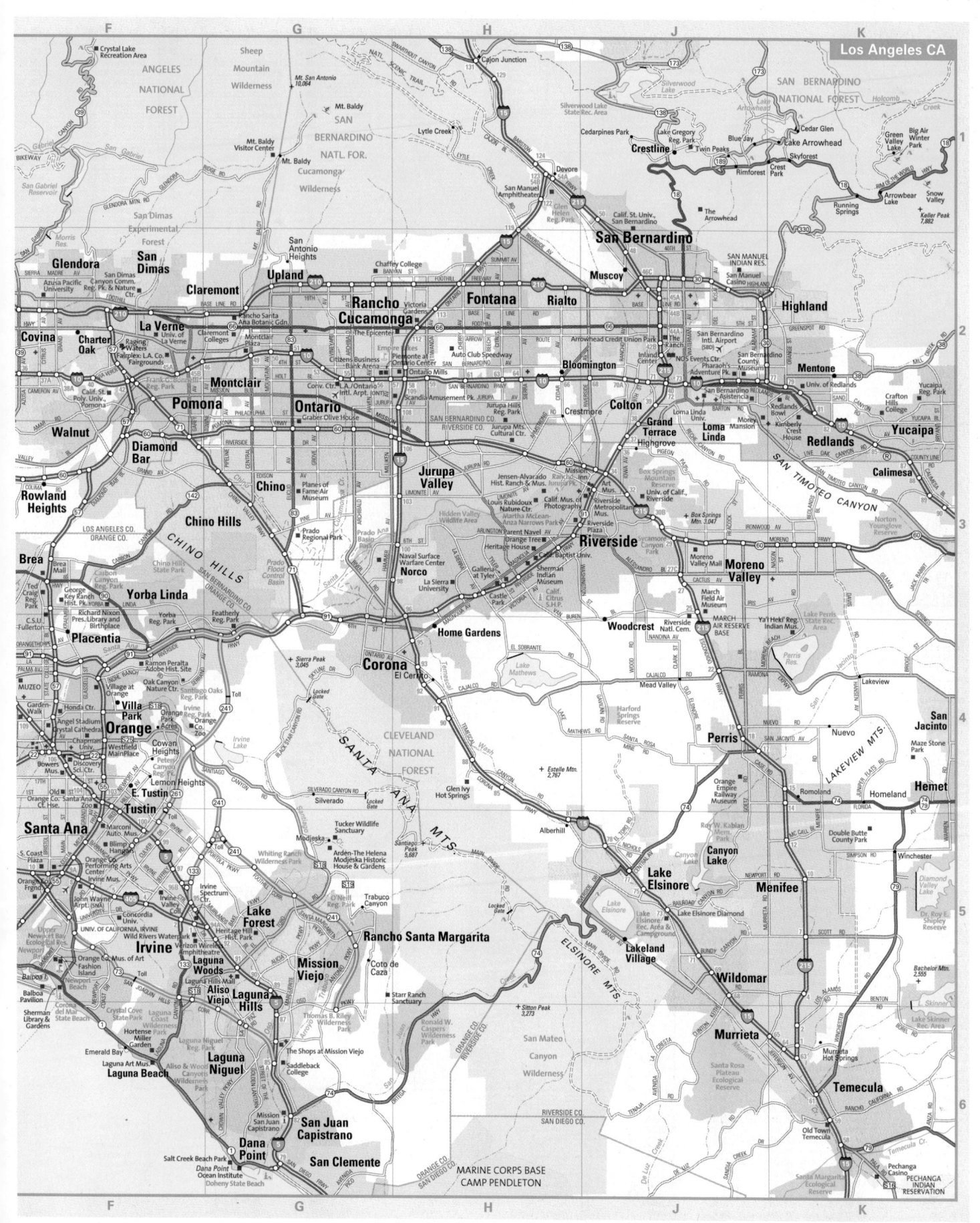

Los Angeles CA

230

Lexington–Lodi

Figures after entries indicate population, page number, and grid reference.

POINTS OF INTEREST

Angels Flight A1
Bradbury Building A1
California Plaza A1
Cathedral of Our Lady of the Angels .A1
Chinese American Museum B1
City Hall B1
Convention Center A2
Court House A1
Dodger Stadium B1

El Pueblo de Los Angeles Hist. Mon. .B1
Flower District A2
GRAMMY Museum A2
Japanese American Natl. Museum ..B1
Jewelry District A2
L.A. Center Studios A1
L.A. Live A2
Library A1
MOCA at the Geffen Contemporary ..B1
Mt. St. Mary's College A1

Museum of Contemporary Art
(MOCA) A1
Museum of Neon Art A2
Music Center A1
NOKIA Theatre A2
Olvera Street B1
Post Office B1
STAPLES Center A2
Union Station B1
Walt Disney Concert Hall A1

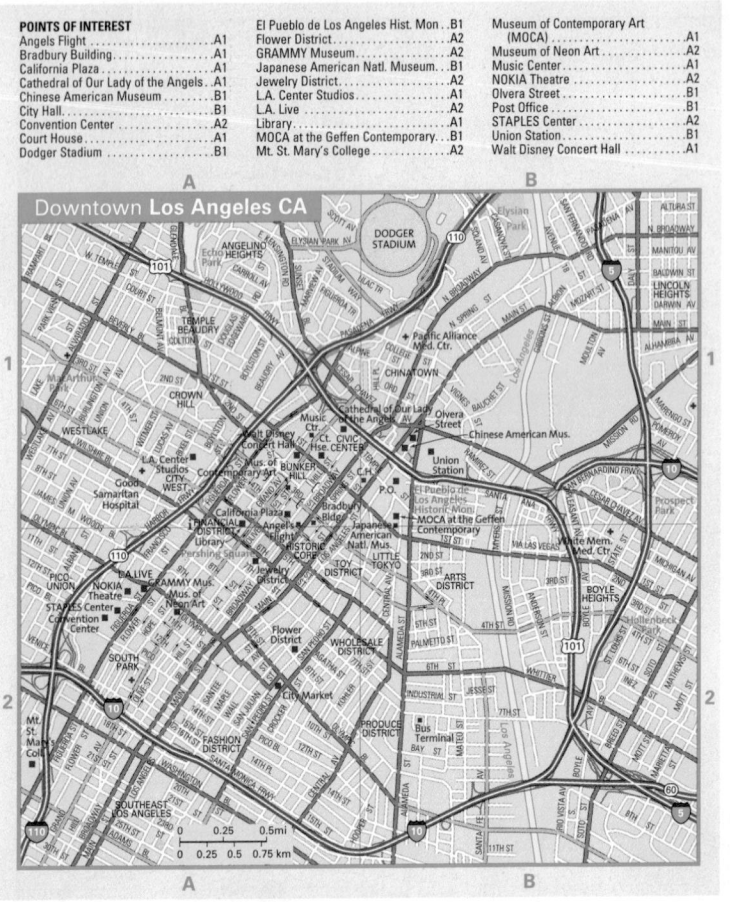

Downtown Los Angeles CA

Entry	Pop	Pg	Grid
Lincoln Hts. OH, 3286		204	B1
Lincolnia VA, 22855		270	B4
Lincoln Par. LA, 46735		125	E2
Lincoln Park CO, 3546		41	E3
Lincoln Park MI, 38144		90	C1
Lincoln Park NJ, 10521		148	A3
Lincolnshire IL, 7275		203	C2
Lincolnton GA, 1566		121	E4
Lincolnton NC, 10486		122	A1
Lincoln Vil. OH, 9032		206	A3
Lincolnville SC, 1139		131	D1
Lincolnville Ctr. ME, 325		82	C2
Lincolnwood IL, 12590		203	D3
Lincroft NJ, 6135		147	E2
Lind WA, 564		13	F4
Linda CA, 17773		36	C2
Lindale GA, 4191		120	B3
Lindale TX, 4818		124	A2
Lindcove CA, 406		45	D3
Linden CA, 1784		36	C3
Linden IN, 759		89	E4
Linden MI, 3991		76	B3
Linden NJ, 40499		147	E1
Linden TN, 908		119	E1
Linden TX, 1988		124	C1
Linden WI, 549		74	A1
Lindenhurst IL, 17462		74	C4
Lindenhurst NY, 27253		148	C4
Lindenwold NJ, 17613		146	C3
Lindon UT, 10070		31	D4
Lindsay CA, 11768		45	D3
Lindsay OK, 2840		51	E4
Lindsay TX, 1018		59	E1
Lindsborg KS, 3458		43	E3
Lindstrom MN, 4442		67	D3
Linesville PA, 1040		91	F2
Lineville AL, 2395		128	B1
Lingle WY, 468		33	F2
Linglestown PA, 6334		93	D4
Linn KS, 410		43	F1
Linn MO, 1459		97	D3
Linn TX, 801		63	E3
Linn Co. IA, 211226		87	E1
Linn Co. KS, 9656		96	B4
Linn Co. MO, 12761		97	D1
Linn Co. OR, 116672		20	C3
Linneus MO, 278		97	D1
Linn Valley KS, 804		96	B4
Lino Lakes MN, 20216		235	D7
Linthicum MD, 10324		193	C4
Linton IN, 5413		99	E2
Linton ND, 1097		26	C1
Linwood IN, 700		89	F4
Linwood KS, 375		96	B2
Linwood MI, 1200		76	B2
Linwood NJ, 7092		147	F4

Entry	Pop	Pg	Grid
Lionville PA, 6189		146	B3
Lipscomb AL, 2210		195	D2
Lipscomb TX, 37		50	C2
Lipscomb Co. TX, 3302		50	C2
Lisbon IA, 2152		87	F1
Lisbon ME, 9077		82	B3
Lisbon NH, 980		81	E2
Lisbon ND, 2154		19	E4
Lisbon OH, 2821		91	F3
Lisbon Falls ME, 4100		82	B3
Lisle IL, 22390		203	B5
Lisman AL, 539		127	D3
Litchfield CT, 1258		94	C3
Litchfield IL, 6939		98	B2
Litchfield ME, 3110		82	B2
Litchfield MN, 1369		90	A1
Litchfield MI, 6726		66	B3
Litchfield Co. CT, 189927		94	B3
Litchfield Park AZ, 5476		249	A2
Lithia Spgs. GA, 15491		120	C4
Lithonia GA, 1924		120	C4
Lithopolis OH, 1106		101	D1
Lititz PA, 9369		146	A2
Little Canada MN, 9773		235	D2
Little Chute WI, 10449		74	C1
Little Compton RI, 3492		151	D4
Little Creek DE, 224		145	E2
Little Cypress TX, 1800		132	C2
Little Eagle SD, 319		26	C1
Little Elm TX, 25898		59	F2
Little Falls MN, 8343		66	C2
Little Falls NJ, 11694		148	A3
Little Falls NY, 4946		79	F3
Little Ferry NJ, 10626		240	C2
Littlefield TX, 6372		58	A1
Little Flock AR, 2585		106	C2
Little Heaven DE, 1400		145	E3
Little River KS, 557		43	E3
Little River SC, 8960		123	D4
Little River-Academy TX, 1961		61	E1
Little River Co. AR, 13171		116	C4
Little Rock AR, 193524		117	D2
Littlerock CA, 1377		52	C2
Little Silver NJ, 5950		147	E2
Littlestown PA, 4434		103	E1
Littleton CO, 41737		41	E1
Littleton NH, 4412		81	F2
Littleton NC, 674		113	D3
Little Valley NY, 1143		92	B1
Littleville AL, 1011		119	E2
Live Oak CA, 17158		36	C2
Live Oak CA, 17158		236	D1
Live Oak FL, 6850		138	B2
Live Oak TX, 13131		61	D2
Live Oak Co. TX, 11531		61	D4
Livermore CA, 80968		36	B4

Entry	Pop	Pg	Grid
Livermore KY, 1365		109	E1
Livermore Falls ME, 1594		82	B2
Liverpool NY, 2347		265	A1
Liverpool PA, 955		93	D4
Livingston AL, 3485		127	D2
Livingston CA, 13058		36	C4
Livingston IL, 858		98	B2
Livingston LA, 1769		134	A2
Livingston MT, 7044		23	F1
Livingston NJ, 29366		148	A4
Livingston TN, 4058		110	A3
Livingston TX, 5335		132	B1
Livingston WI, 664		74	A3
Livingston Co. IL, 38950		88	C3
Livingston Co. KY, 9519		109	D2
Livingston Co. MI, 180967		76	B4
Livingston Co. MO, 15195		96	C1
Livingston Co. NY, 65383		78	C4
Livingston Par. LA, 128026		134	B2
Livonia LA, 1442		133	F2
Livonia MI, 96942		76	B4
Livonia NY, 1409		78	C3
Llangollen Estates DE, 5600		145	E1
Llano TX, 3232		61	D1
Llano Co. TX, 19301		61	D1
Lloyd Harbor NY, 3660		148	C3
Loa UT, 572		39	E3
Loami IL, 745		98	B1
Lobelville TN, 897		109	F4
Lochbuie CO, 4726		209	D1
Lochearn MD, 25333		144	C2
Loch Lynn Hts. MD, 552		102	F3
Loch Sheldrake NY, 800		94	A3
Lockeford CA, 3233		36	C3
Lockesburg AR, 739		116	C4
Lockhart AL, 516		136	B1
Lockhart FL, 13060		246	B1
Lockhart TX, 12698		61	E2
Lock Haven PA, 9772		93	D3
Lockland OH, 3449		204	B1
Lockney TX, 1842		50	B4
Lockport IL, 24839		89	D2
Lockport LA, 2578		134	B3
Lockport NY, 21165		78	B3
Lockwood MO, 936		106	C1
Locust NC, 2930		122	B4
Locust Fork AL, 1186		119	F4
Locust Grove GA, 5402		129	C5
Locust Grove OK, 1423		106	B3
Locust Valley NY, 3406		148	C3
Lodge Grass MT, 428		24	C2
Lodge Pole MT, 265		16	C2
Lodi CA, 62134		36	C3
Lodi NJ, 24136		240	C1
Lodi OH, 2746		91	D3
Lodi WI, 3050		74	B3

Entry	Pop	Pg	Grid
Lexington IL, 2060		88	C3
Lexington KY, 295803		100	B4
Lexington MA, 31394		151	D1
Lexington MI, 1178		76	C3
Lexington MN, 2049		235	C1
Lexington MS, 1731		126	B1
Lexington MO, 4726		96	C2
Lexington NE, 10230		34	C4
Lexington NC, 18931		112	B4
Lexington OH, 4822		91	D3
Lexington OK, 2152		51	E3
Lexington SC, 17870		122	A3
Lexington TN, 7652		109	D4
Lexington TX, 1177		61	E1
Lexington VA, 7042		112	C1
Lexington Co. SC, 262391		122	A4
Lexington Park MD, 11626		103	F4
Libby MT, 2628		14	C2
Liberal KS, 20525		50	B1
Liberal MO, 759		106	B1
Liberty IL, 516		97	F1
Liberty IN, 2133		100	B1
Liberty KY, 2168		110	B1
Liberty ME, 300		82	C2
Liberty MS, 658		134	A1
Liberty MO, 29149		96	B2
Liberty NY, 4392		94	A3
Liberty NC, 2656		112	B4
Liberty PA, 2551		250	C3
Liberty SC, 3269		121	E2
Liberty TN, 310		110	A4
Liberty TX, 8397		132	B3
Liberty Ctr. OH, 1180		90	B2
Liberty City TX, 2351		124	B2
Liberty Corner NJ, 1700		147	D1
Liberty Co. FL, 8365		137	D2
Liberty Co. GA, 63453		130	B3
Liberty Co. MT, 2339		15	F1
Liberty Co. TX, 75643		132	B2
Liberty Hill TX, 967		61	E1
Liberty Lake WA, 7591		14	B3
Libertyville IL, 20315		74	C4
Licking MO, 3124		107	E1
Licking Co. OH, 166492		91	D4
Lidgerwood ND, 652		27	E1
Lido Beach NY, 2897		147	E1
Lighthouse Pt. FL, 10344		143	F1
Ligonier IN, 4405		89	F2
Ligonier PA, 1573		92	B4
Lihue HI, 6455		152	B1
Lilburn GA, 11596		120	C4
Lillington NC, 3194		123	D1
Lilly PA, 968		92	B4
Lily KY, 1200		110	C2

Entry	Pop	Pg	Grid
Lilydale MN, 623		235	D3
Lily Lake IL, 993		88	C1
Lima MT, 221		23	E3
Lima NY, 2139		78	C3
Lima OH, 38771		90	B3
Lima PA, 2735		248	A4
Lime Lake NY, 867		78	B4
Limeport PA, 1100		146	C1
Limerick ME, 2240		82	A3
Limerick PA, 850		146	B2
Lime Spgs. IA, 496		73	E2
Limestone ME, 1075		85	E1
Limestone Co. AL, 82782		119	F2
Limestone Co. TX, 23384		59	F4
Limon CO, 1880		41	F2
Lincoln AR, 2249		106	C4
Lincoln CA, 42819		36	C2
Lincoln DE, 950		145	E3
Lincoln ID, 1087		23	F4
Lincoln IL, 14504		88	B4
Lincoln KS, 1253		43	E2
Lincoln ME, 2884		85	D4
Lincoln MA, 6362		197	A1
Lincoln MO, 1190		97	D4
Lincoln MT, 1013		15	E4
Lincoln NE, 258379		35	F4
Lincoln NH, 993		81	F2
Lincoln ND, 2406		18	C4
Lincoln RI, 5241		150	C4
Lincoln VT, 358		80	C3
Lincoln Beach OR, 2045		20	B2
Lincoln Co. AR, 14134		117	F3
Lincoln Co. CO, 5467		41	F2
Lincoln Co. GA, 7996		121	E4
Lincoln Co. ID, 5208		31	D1
Lincoln Co. KY, 24742		110	B1
Lincoln Co. ME, 34457		82	C3
Lincoln Co. MN, 5896		27	F3
Lincoln Co. MS, 34869		126	B4
Lincoln Co. MT, 19687		14	C2
Lincoln Co. NE, 36288		34	C3
Lincoln Co. NV, 5345		38	B4
Lincoln Co. NM, 20497		49	D4
Lincoln Co. NC, 78265		122	A1
Lincoln Co. OK, 34273		51	E2
Lincoln Co. OR, 46034		20	B2
Lincoln Co. SD, 44828		35	F3
Lincoln Co. TN, 33361		119	F1
Lincoln Co. WA, 10570		13	F3
Lincoln Co. WV, 21720		101	E4
Lincoln Co. WI, 28743		68	A3
Lincoln Co. WY, 18106		32	A2
Lincolndale NY, 1521		148	B4

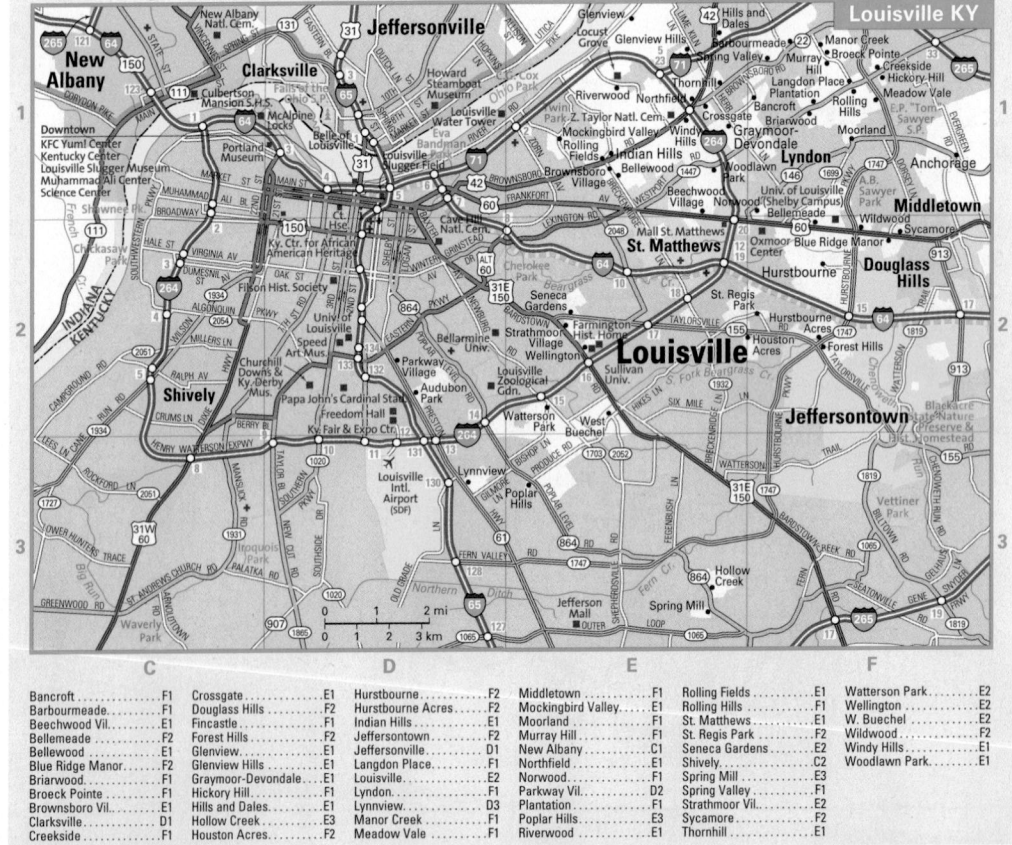

Louisville KY

Place	Grid
Bancroft	F1
Barbourmeade	F1
Beechwood Vil.	F2
Bellemeade	F2
Bellewood	F1
Blue Ridge Manor	F2
Briarwood	F1
Broeck Pointe	E1
Brownsboro Vil.	E1
Clarksville	D1
Creekside	F1
Crossgate	E1
Douglass Hills	F1
Fincastle	F1
Forest Hills	F2
Glenview	E1
Glenview Hills	E1
Graymoor-Devondale	E1
Hickory Hill	F1
Hills and Dales	E3
Hollow Creek	F2
Houston Acres	F2
Hurstbourne	F2
Hurstbourne Acres	F2
Indian Hills	E1
Jeffersontown	F2
Jeffersonville	D1
Langdon Place	E1
Louisville	E2
Lyndon	F1
Lynnview	D3
Manor Creek	F1
Meadow Vale	F1
Middletown	F1
Mockingbird Valley	E1
Moorland	E1
Murray Hill	E1
New Albany	C1
Northfield	E1
Norwood	D2
Parkway Vil.	E2
Plantation	E1
Poplar Hills	E2
Riverwood	E1
Rolling Fields	E1
Rolling Hills	F1
St. Matthews	E1
St. Regis Park	F2
Seneca Gardens	E2
Shively	C2
Spring Mill	E3
Spring Valley	E1
Strathmoor Vil.	E2
Sycamore	F1
Thornhill	F1
Watterson Park	E2
Wellington	E2
W. Buechel	E2
Wildwood	F1
Windy Hills	E1
Woodlawn Park	E1

Lubbock TX

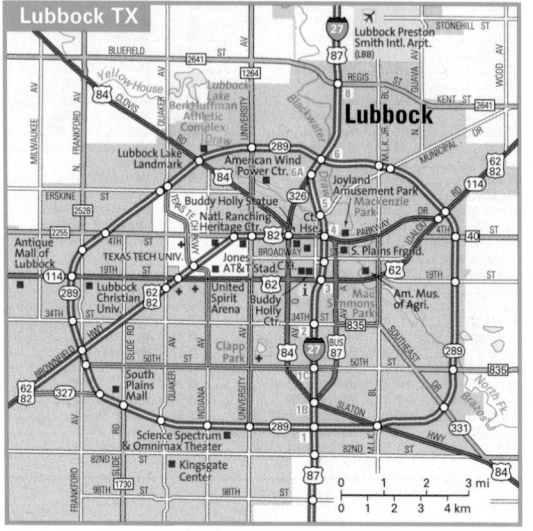

Macon GA

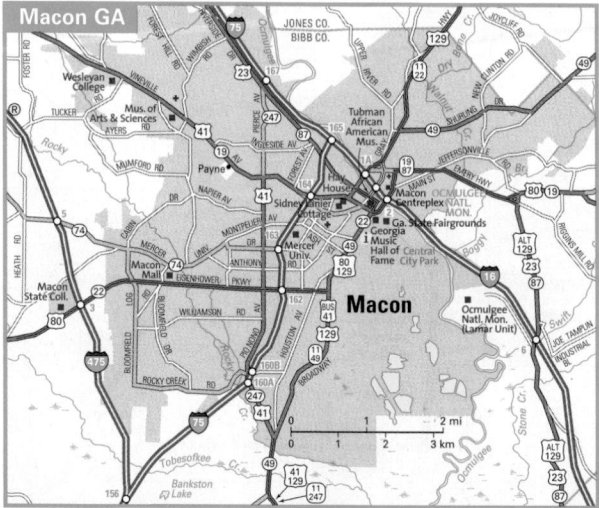

Madison WI

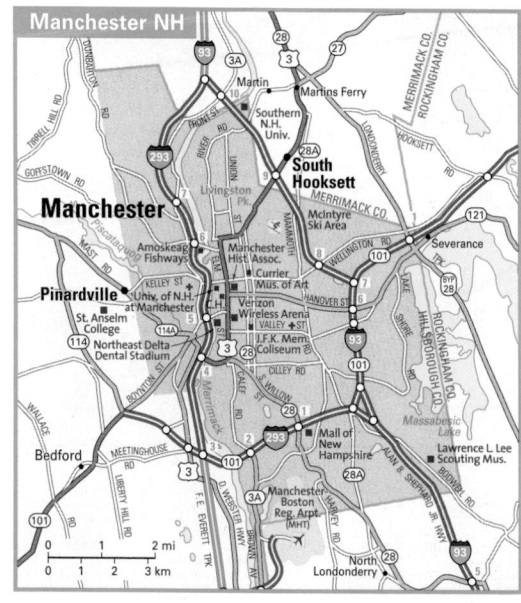

Manchester NH

232

Macon County–Many Farms

Figures after entries indicate population, page number, and grid reference.

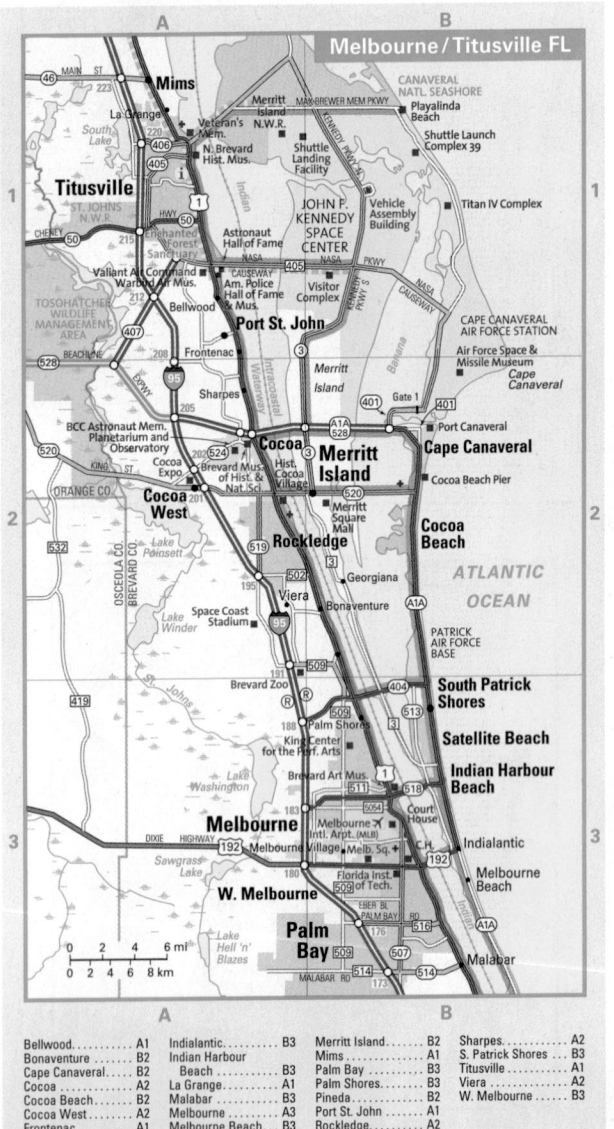

Melbourne / Titusville FL

Memphis TN

Entries in **bold black** indicate counties or parishes.
Entries in **bold color** indicate cities with detailed inset maps.

Miami / Fort Lauderdale FL

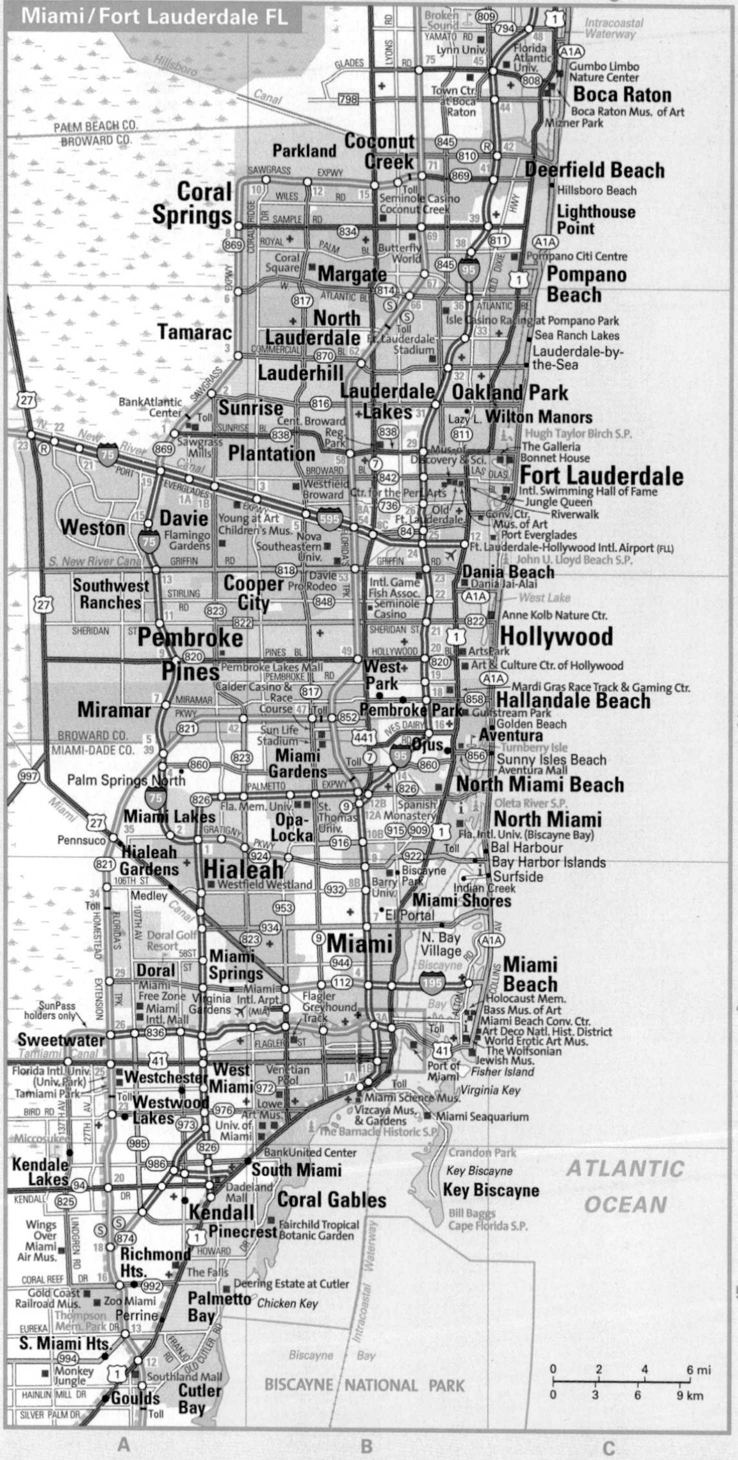

Aventura B3
Bal Harbour B3
Bay Harbor Islands C4
Biscayne Park B4
Boca Raton C1
Coconut Creek B1
Cooper City A3
Coral Gables B5
Coral Sprs. A1
Cutler Ridge A5
Dania Beach B3
Davie A2
Deerfield Beach C1
El Portal B4
Ft. Lauderdale C2
Golden Beach C3
Goulds A5
Hallandale Beach C3
Hialeah A4
Hialeah Gardens A4
Hillsboro Beach C1
Hollywood B3
Indian Creek B4
Kendale Lakes A5
Kendall A5
Key Biscayne B5
Lauderdale-by-the-Sea C2
Lauderdale Lakes B2
Lauderhill B2
Lazy Lake B2
Lighthouse Pt. C1
Margate B1
Medley A4
Miami B4
Miami Beach C4
Miami Gardens B3
Miami Lakes A3
Miami Shores B4
Miami Sprs. A4
Miramar A3
N. Bay Vil. B4
N. Lauderdale B2
N. Miami C3
N. Miami Beach B3
Oakland Park B2
Opa-Locka B3
Ojus B3
Palmetto Bay A5
Palm Springs North A3
Parkland B1
Pembroke Park B3
Pembroke Pines A3
Perrine A5
Pinecrest A5
Plantation B2
Pompano Beach C1
Richmond Hts. A5
Rockdale A5
S. Miami A5
S. Miami Hts. A5
Southwest Ranches A3
Sunny Isles Beach C3
Sunrise B2
Surfside C4
Sweetwater A4
Tamarac A2
Virginia Gardens A4
W. Miami A4
Westchester A4
Weston A2
West Park B3
Westwood Lakes A4
Wilton Manors C2

Downtown Miami FL

POINTS OF INTEREST

AmericanAirlines Arena E1
Amphitheatre E2
Bayside Marketplace E2
Flagler Palm Cottage D2
Freedom Tower D1
Gusman Center D2
James L. Knight Center D2
Knight Concert Hall E1
Miami Arena D1
Miami Children's Museum E1
Miami-Dade Cultural Center/Historical Museum of Southern Florida D2
Miami Herald Building E1
Miami Seaplane Base E1
Parrot Jungle Island E1
Port of Miami E2
Sanford & Dolores Ziff Ballet Opera House D1

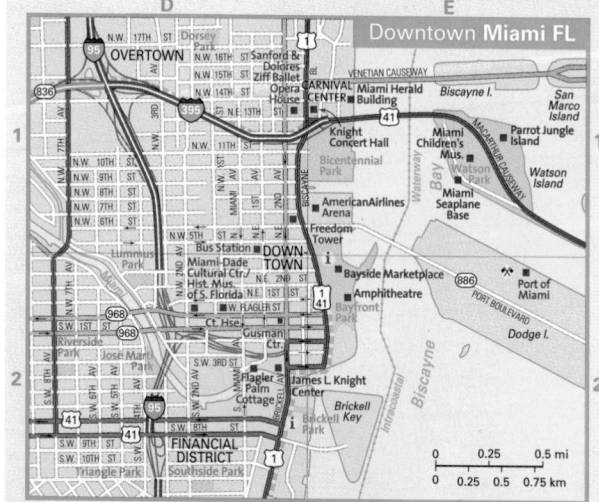

234

Marysvale–Medina County

Figures after entries indicate population, page number, and grid reference.

Marysvale UT, 408 .... 39 E3
Marysville CA, 12072 .... 36 C2
Marysville KS, 3294 .... 43 F1
Marysville MI, 9959 .... 76 C3
Marysville OH, 22094 .... 90 C4
Marysville PA, 2534 .... 93 D4
Marysville WA, 60020 .... 12 C2
Maryville IL, 7487 .... 256 D1
Maryville MO, 11972 .... 88 B4
Maryville TN, 27465 .... 110 C4
Marywood MD, 6000 .... 145 D1
Masaryktown FL, 1040 .... 140 B1
Mascot TN, 2411 .... 110 C4
Mascotte FL, 5101 .... 140 B1
Mascoutah IL, 7483 .... 98 B3
Mashpee MA, 1000 .... 151 E3

Mason MI, 8252 .... 76 A4
Mason NV, 500 .... 37 C2
Mason NH, 1382 .... 95 D1
Mason OH, 30712 .... 100 B2
Mason TN, 1609 .... 118 C1
Mason TX, 2114 .... 60 C1
Mason WV, 968 .... 101 E2
Masonboro NC, 11812 .... 123 E3
Mason City IL, 2343 .... 88 B4
Mason City IA, 28079 .... 73 D3
Mason Co. IL, 14666 .... 88 A4
Mason Co. KY, 17490 .... 100 C3
Mason Co. MI, 28705 .... 75 E1
Mason Co. TX, 4012 .... 60 C1
Mason Co. WA, 60699 .... 12 A3
Mason Co. WV, 27324 .... 101 E3

Masontown PA, 3450 .... 102 B1
Masontown WV, 546 .... 102 B1
Masonville KY, 1014 .... 109 E1
Masonville NJ, 7300 .... 147 D3
Mason Co. VA, 555 .... 113 F1
Massac Co. IL, 15429 .... 108 C2
Mathews Co. VA, 8978 .... 113 F1
Massapequa NY, 21685 .... 148 C4
Massapequa Park NY, 17008 .... 148 C4
Massena NY, 10936 .... 80 B1
Massillon OH, 32149 .... 91 E3
Massugansville MD, 3071 .... 103 D1
Mattapoisett MA, 2915 .... 151 E3
Mattawa WA, 4437 .... 13 E4
Mattawamkeag ME, 825 .... 85 D4
Mattawan MI, 1997 .... 89 F1

Matewan WV, 499 .... 111 E1
Matherville IL, 723 .... 88 A2
Mathews LA, 2209 .... 134 B3
Mathews VA, 555 .... 113 F1
Mathis TX, 4942 .... 61 E4
Mathiston MS, 698 .... 118 C4
Matlacha FL, 677 .... 142 C1
Mattoon IL, 18555 .... 98 C2
Mattydale NY, 6446 .... 79 D3
Matunuck RI, 750 .... 150 C4
Maud FL, 4800 .... 100 B2
Maud OK, 1048 .... 51 F3
Maud TX, 1056 .... 124 C1
Maui Co. HI, 154834 .... 153 D1
Mauldin SC, 22889 .... 121 F2
Maumee OH, 14286 .... 90 C2
Maumelle AR, 17163 .... 117 E2
Maunawili HI, 2040 .... 152 B3
Maupin OR, 418 .... 21 D2
Maurertown VA, 770 .... 102 C3

Matthews NC, 27198 .... 122 B1
Mattituck NY, 4219 .... 149 E3
Maury Co. TN, 80956 .... 109 E4
Maurice LA, 964 .... 133 F2
Mauriceville TX, 3252 .... 132 C2
Maury City TN, 687 .... 108 C4
Mauston WI, 4423 .... 74 A2
Mavisdale VA, 550 .... 111 E3
Max ND, 334 .... 18 B3
Max Meadows VA, 562 .... 112 A3
Maxwell CA, 1103 .... 36 B2
Maxwell IA, 920 .... 86 C1
Maxwell NM, 254 .... 49 E1
Maybee MI, 562 .... 90 C1
Maybeury WV, 234 .... 111 F1
Maybrook NY, 2958 .... 148 B3
Mayer AZ, 1497 .... 47 D4
Mayer MN, 1749 .... 66 C4
Mayersville MS, 547 .... 126 A1
Mayes Co. OK, 41259 .... 106 A3
Mayesville SC, 731 .... 122 B3
Mayfield KY, 10024 .... 108 C3
Mayfield NY, 832 .... 80 C4
Mayfield OH, 3460 .... 204 G1
Mayfield PA, 1807 .... 93 F2
Mayfield UT, 496 .... 39 E2
Mayfield Hts. OH, 19155 .... 91 E2
Mayflower AR, 2234 .... 117 E2
Maynard IA, 518 .... 73 E4
Maynard MA, 10106 .... 150 C1
Maynardville TN, 2413 .... 110 B3
Mayo FL, 1237 .... 137 F3
Mayo MD, 8298 .... 144 C3
Mayo SC, 1592 .... 121 F1
Mayodan NC, 2478 .... 112 B3
Maypearl TX, 934 .... 59 F3
Mays Landing NJ, 2135 .... 105 D3
Maysville GA, 1798 .... 121 D3
Maysville KY, 9011 .... 100 C3
Maysville MO, 1114 .... 96 B3
Maysville NC, 1019 .... 115 D4
Maysville OK, 1232 .... 51 E4
Maytown AL, 385 .... 195 D1
Mayville MI, 950 .... 76 C3
Mayville NY, 1711 .... 78 A4
Mayville ND, 1858 .... 19 D3
Mayville WI, 5154 .... 74 C3

McGregor IA, 871 .... 73 F3
McGregor TX, 4987 .... 59 F4
McHenry IL, 26992 .... 74 C4
McHenry KY, 388 .... 109 E1
McHenry Co. IL, 308760 .... 74 C4
McHenry Co. ND, 5395 .... 18 C2
McIntosh FL, 452 .... 138 C4
McIntosh MN, 625 .... 19 F3
McIntosh SD, 173 .... 26 B1
McIntosh Co. GA, 14333 .... 130 B4
McIntosh Co. ND, 2809 .... 27 D1
McIntosh Co. OK, 20252 .... 116 A1
McIntyre GA, 650 .... 129 E2
McKean Co. PA, 43450 .... 92 B1
McKee KY, 800 .... 110 B1
McKee City NJ, 2800 .... 147 F4
McKeesport PA, 19731 .... 92 A4
McKees Rocks PA, 6104 .... 250 B1
McKenna WA, 716 .... 12 C4
McKenney VA, 483 .... 113 E2
McKenzie AL, 530 .... 127 F4
McKenzie TN, 5310 .... 109 D4
McKenzie Co. ND, 6360 .... 17 F2
McKinley Co. NM, 71492 .... 48 A2
McKinleyville CA, 15177 .... 28 A4
McKinney TX, 131117 .... 59 F2
Mckownville NY, 2600 .... 188 D3
McLain MS, 441 .... 135 D1
McLaughlin SD, 663 .... 26 C1
McLean IL, 830 .... 88 B4
McLean TX, 778 .... 50 B3
McLean VA, 48115 .... 144 B3
McLean Co. IL, 169572 .... 88 C4
McLean Co. KY, 9531 .... 109 E1
McLean Co. ND, 8962 .... 18 B3
McLennan Co. TX, 234906 .... 59 F4
McLeod Co. MN, 36651 .... 66 C4
McLoud OK, 4044 .... 51 E3
McLouth KS, 880 .... 96 A2
McMechen WV, 1926 .... 101 F1
McMinn Co. TN, 52256 .... 120 C1
McMinnville OR, 32187 .... 20 B2
McMinnville TN, 13605 .... 110 A4
McMullen Co. TX, 707 .... 61 D4
McMurray PA, 4647 .... 92 A4
McNairy Co. TN, 26075 .... 119 D1
McNary AZ, 528 .... 47 F4
McNeil AR, 516 .... 125 D1
McPherson KS, 13155 .... 43 E3
McPherson Co. KS, 29180 .... 43 E3
McPherson Co. NE, 539 .... 34 B3
McPherson Co. SD, 2459 .... 27 D1
McQueeney TX, 2545 .... 61 D2
McRae AR, 682 .... 117 F1
McRae GA, 5942 .... 129 E3
McRoberts KY, 784 .... 111 E2
McSherrystown PA, 3038 .... 103 E1
McVeigh KY, 550 .... 111 E1
McVille ND, 349 .... 19 E3
Mead NE, 569 .... 35 F3
Mead WA, 7275 .... 14 A3
Meade KS, 1721 .... 42 C4
Meade Co. KS, 4575 .... 42 C4
Meade Co. KY, 28602 .... 99 F4
Meade Co. SD, 25434 .... 26 A3
Meadow TX, 593 .... 58 A1
Meadowlakes TX, 1777 .... 61 D1
Meadows Place TX, 4660 .... 132 A3
Meadow Vale KY, 736 .... 230 F1
Meadow Valley CA, 464 .... 36 C1
Meadowview VA, 967 .... 111 F2
Meadville MS, 449 .... 126 A4
Meadville PA, 13388 .... 92 A2
Meagher Co. MT, 1891 .... 15 F4
Mebane NC, 11393 .... 112 C4
Mecca CA, 8577 .... 53 E3
Mechanic Falls ME, 2237 .... 82 B2
Mechanicsburg OH, 1644 .... 90 C4
Mechanicsburg PA, 8981 .... 93 D4
Mechanicville IA, 1116 .... 87 F1
Mechanicsville VA, 36348 .... 113 E1
Mechanicville NY, 5196 .... 94 B1
Mecklenburg Co. NC, 919628 .... 122 B1
Mecklenburg Co. VA, 32727 .... 113 D2
Mecosta Co. MI, 42798 .... 75 F2
Medanales NM, 450 .... 48 C2
Medaryville IN, 614 .... 89 E3
Medfield MA, 6483 .... 151 D2
Medford MA, 56173 .... 151 D1
Medford MN, 1239 .... 73 D1
Medford NJ, 22858 .... 147 D3
Medford NY, 24142 .... 149 D4
Medford OK, 996 .... 51 E1
Medford OR, 74907 .... 28 B2
Medford WI, 4326 .... 68 B3
Medford Lakes NJ, 4146 .... 147 D3
Medary MN, 4892 .... 66 C3
Medina NY, 6065 .... 78 B3
Medina ND, 308 .... 19 D4
Medina OH, 26678 .... 91 D3
Medina TN, 3479 .... 108 C4
Medina WA, 2969 .... 262 B3
Medina Co. OH, 172332 .... 91 D3
Medina Co. TX, 46006 .... 60 C3

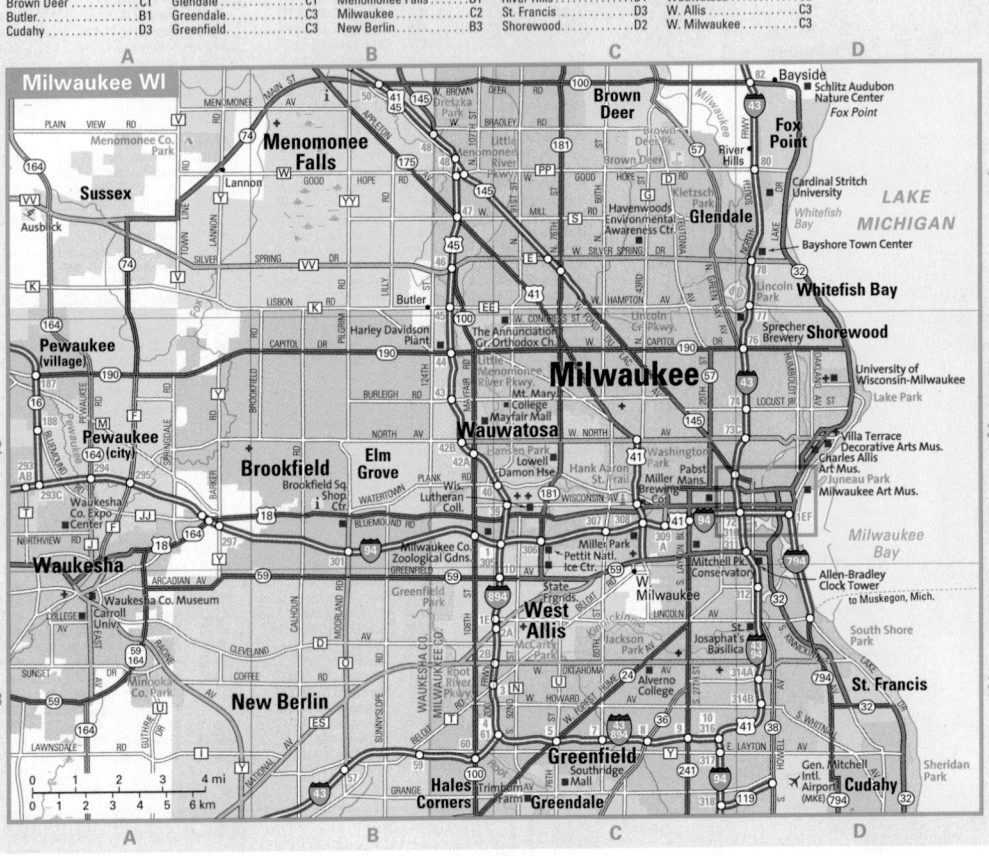

Bayside D1
Brookfield B2
Brown Deer B1
Butler B1
Cudahy D3

Elm Grove B2
Fox Pt. D1
Glendale C1
Greendale C3
Greenfield C3

Hales Corners B3
Lannon A1
Menomonee Falls B1
Milwaukee C2
New Berlin A3

Pewaukee (city) A2
Pewaukee (village) A2
River Hills D1
St. Francis D3
Shorewood D1

Sussex A1
Waukesha A2
Wauwatosa C2
W. Allis C3
W. Milwaukee C3

Whitefish Bay D1

Milwaukee WI

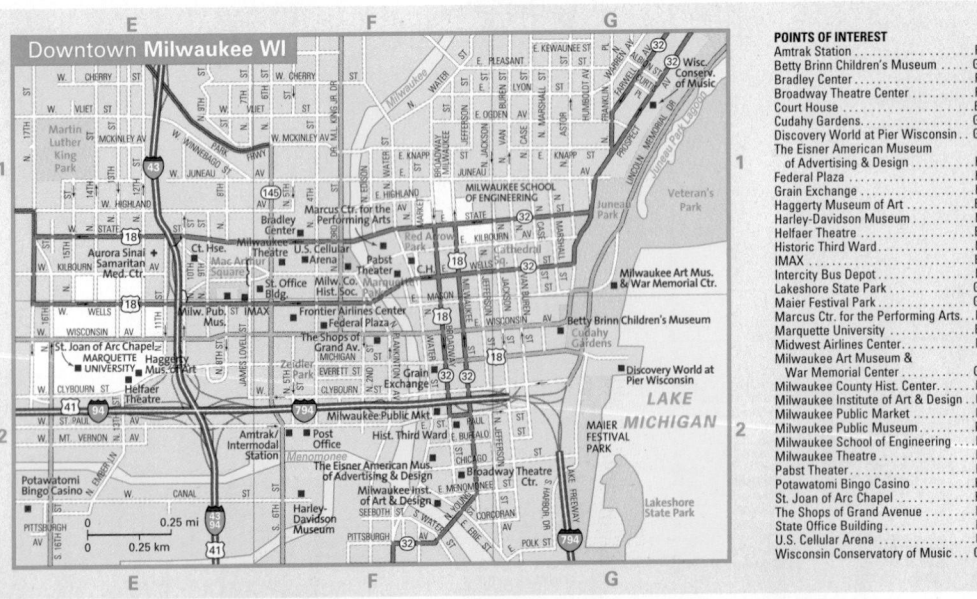

Downtown Milwaukee WI

POINTS OF INTEREST
Amtrak Station F2
Betty Brinn Children's Museum G2
Bradley Center F1
Broadway Theatre Center F2
Court House E1
Cudahy Gardens G2
Discovery World at Pier Wisconsin G2
The Eisner American Museum
  of Advertising & Design F2
Federal Plaza F2
Grain Exchange F2
Haggerty Museum of Art E2
Harley-Davidson Museum E3
Helfaer Theatre F2
Historic Third Ward F2
IMAX E1
Intercity Bus Depot F2
Lakeshore State Park G2
Maier Festival Park G2
Marcus Ctr. for the Performing Arts F1
Marquette University E2
Midwest Airlines Center F2
Milwaukee Art Museum &
  War Memorial Ctr. G1
Milwaukee County Hist. Center F1
Milwaukee Inst. of Art & Design F2
Milwaukee Public Library E2
Milwaukee Public Market F2
Milwaukee Public Museum F1
Milwaukee School of Engineering F1
Milwaukee Theatre F1
Pabst Theater F1
Potawatomi Bingo Casino E3
St. Joan of Arc Chapel E2
The Shops of Grand Avenue F2
State Office Building E1
U.S. Cellular Arena F1
Wisconsin Conservatory of Music G1

Entries in **bold black** indicate counties or parishes.
Entries in **bold color** indicate cities with detailed inset maps.

Minneapolis/St Paul MN

236

Mexia – Milbridge

Figures after entries indicate population, page number, and grid reference.

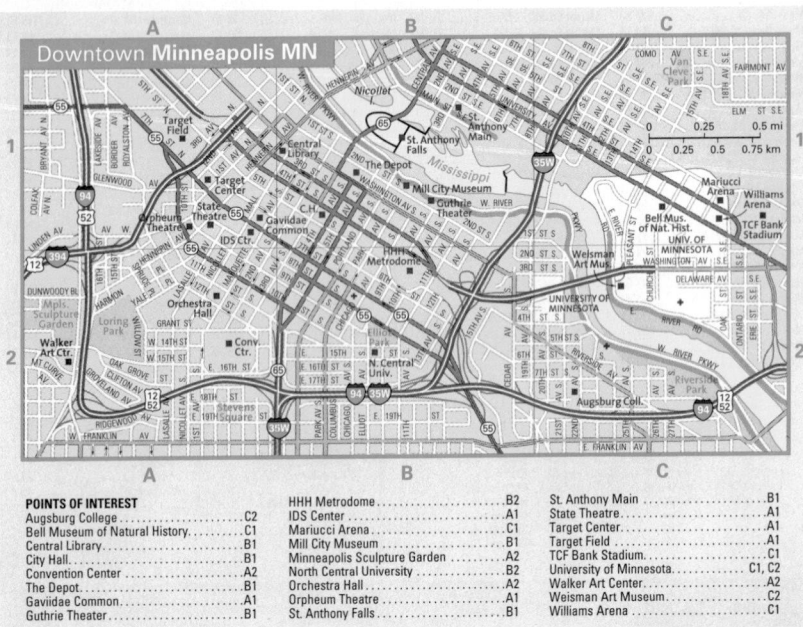

Downtown Minneapolis MN

POINTS OF INTEREST

Augsburg College................................C2	HHH Metrodome..........................B2
Bell Museum of Natural History.........C1	IDS Center.................................A1
Central Library................................B1	Mariucci Arena............................C1
City Hall...B1	Mill City Museum.........................B1
Convention Center..........................A2	Minneapolis Sculpture Garden.......A2
The Depot......................................C1	North Central University...............B2
Gaviidae Common...........................A1	Orchestra Hall.............................A2
Guthrie Theater..............................B1	Orpheum Theatre.........................A1
	St. Anthony Falls........................B1

St. Anthony Main.............................B1
State Theatre..................................A1
Target Center.................................A1
Target Field...................................A1
TCF Bank Stadium..........................C1
University of Minnesota................C1, C2
Walker Art Center..........................A2
Weisman Art Museum.....................C2
Williams Arena...............................C1

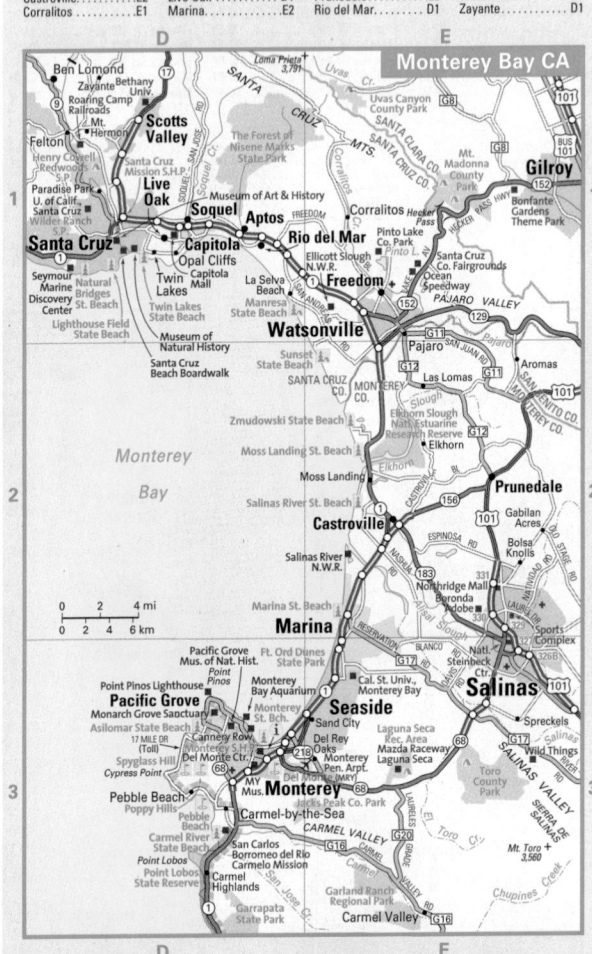

Monterey Bay CA

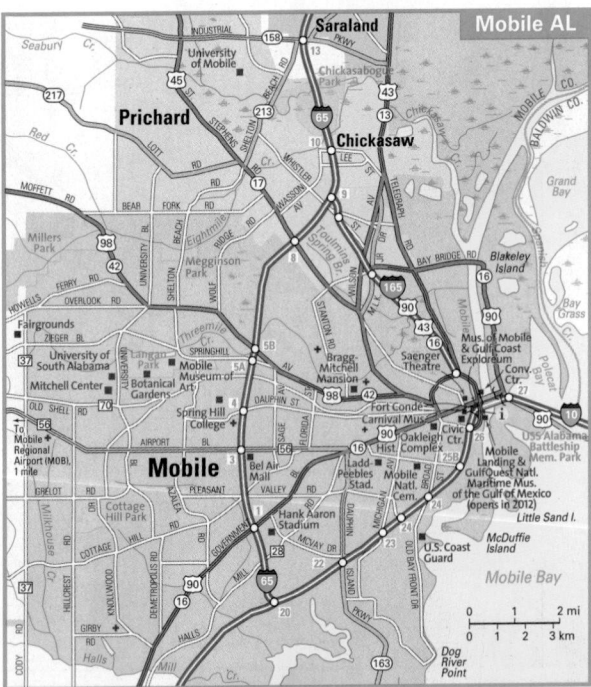

Missoula MT

Mobile AL

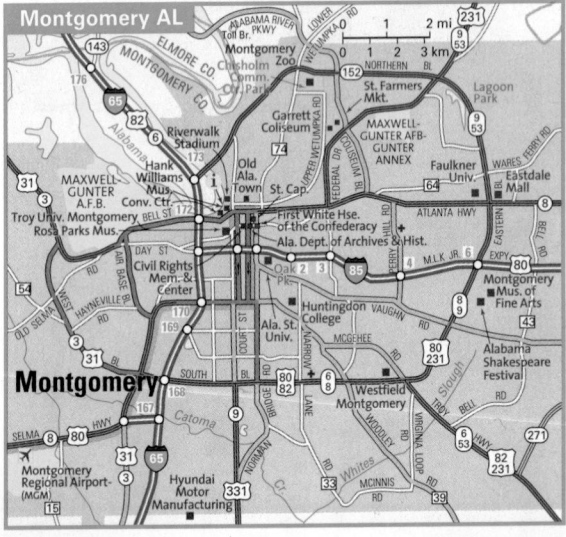

Montgomery AL

Entries in **bold black** indicate counties or parishes.
Entries in **bold color** indicate cities with detailed inset maps.

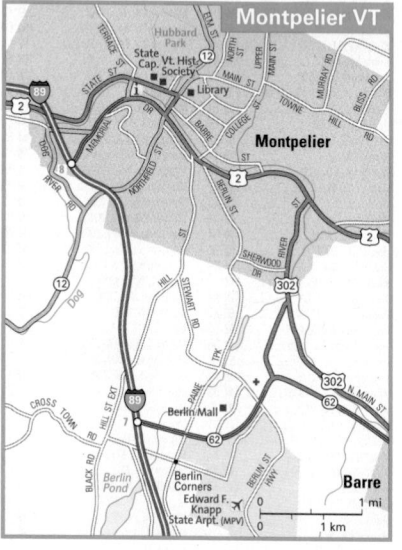

Montpelier VT

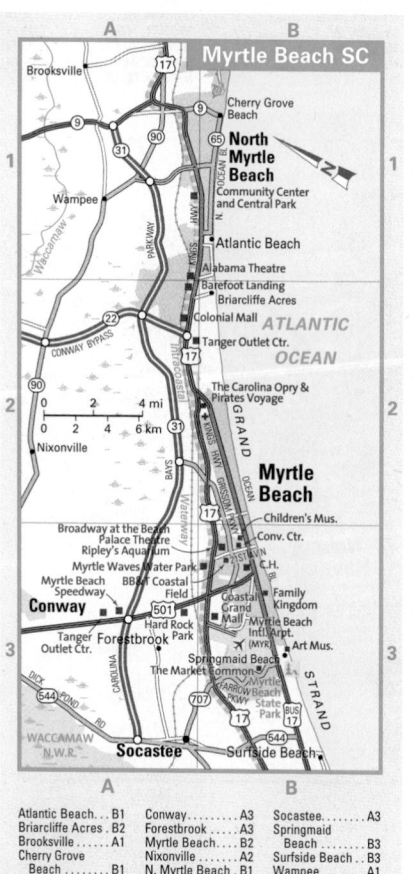

Myrtle Beach SC

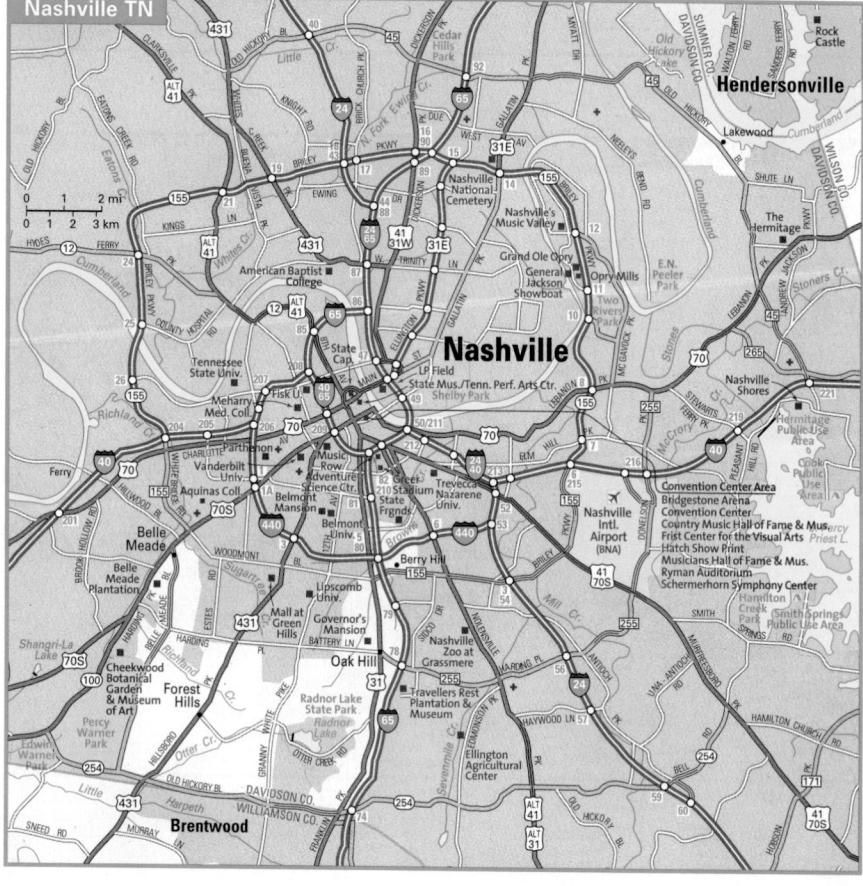

Nashville TN

238

Montello–Morris County

Figures after entries indicate population, page number, and grid reference.

Montello WI, *1495* **74** B2
Monterey CA, *27810* **44** B3
Monterey TN, *2850* **110** B4
Monterey VA, *147* **102** B3
Monterey Co. CA, *415057* **44** B3
Monterey Park CA, *60269* **228** D2
Monte Rio CA, *1152* **36** A3
Montesano WA, *3976* **12** B4
Montevallo AL, *6323* **127** F1
Montevideo MN, *5383* **66** A4
Monte Vista CO, *4444* **41** D4
Montezuma GA, *3460* **129** D2

Montezuma IN, *1022* **99** E1
Montezuma IA, *1462* **87** D2
Montezuma KS, *966* **42** C4
Montezuma Co. CO, *25535* **48** A1
Montezuma Creek UT, *335* **40** A4
Montfort WI, *718* **74** A3
Montgomery AL, *205764* **128** A2
Montgomery IL, *18438* **203** A5
Montgomery LA, *730* **125** D4
Montgomery MN, *2956* **72** C1
Montgomery NY, *3814* **148** A1
Montgomery OH, *10251* **204** C1

Montgomery PA, *1579* **93** D2
Montgomery WV, *1638* **101** F4
Montgomery City MO, *2834* **97** F2
Montgomery Co. AL, *229363* .. **128** A3
Montgomery Co. AR, *9487* **116** C3
Montgomery Co. GA, *9123* **129** F3
Montgomery Co. IL, *30104* **98** B2
Montgomery Co. IN, *38124* **89** E4
Montgomery Co. IA, *10740* **86** B3
Montgomery Co. KS, *35471* **106** A1
Montgomery Co. KY, *26499* **100** C4
Montgomery Co. MD, *971777* .. **144** B2

Montgomery Co. MS, *10925* ... **118** B4
Montgomery Co. MO, *12236* ... **97** F2
Montgomery Co. NY, *50219* ... **94** A1
Montgomery Co. NC, *27798* ... **122** C1
Montgomery Co. OH, *535153* .. **100** B1
Montgomery Co. PA, *799874* .. **146** B2
Montgomery Co. TN, *172331* .. **109** E3
Montgomery Co. TX, *455746* .. **132** A2
Montgomery Co. VA, *94392* ... **112** A2
Montgomery Vil. MD, *32032* ... **144** B2
Montgomeryville PA, *12624* ... **146** C2
Monticello AR, *9467* **117** F4

Monticello FL, *2506* **137** E2
Monticello GA, *2657* **129** D1
Monticello IL, *5548* **98** C1
Monticello IN, *5378* **89** E3
Monticello IA, *3796* **87** F1
Monticello KY, *6188* **110** B2
Monticello MN, *12759* **66** C3
Monticello MS, *1571* **126** B4
Monticello MO, *98* **87** E4
Monticello NY, *6726* **148** A1
Monticello UT, *1972* **40** A4
Monticello WI, *1217* **74** B4

Montmorency Co. MI, *9765* .. **70** C4
Montour Co. PA, *18267* **93** E3
Montour Falls NY, *1711* **79** D4
Montoursville PA, *4615* **93** D2
Montpelier ID, *2597* **31** F3
Montpelier IN, *1805* **90** A4
Montpelier OH, *4072* **90** B2
Montpelier VT, *7855* **81** E2
Montreal WI, *807* **65** E4
Montreat NC, *723* **111** E4
Montrose CA, *354* **125** F1
Montrose CO, *19132* **40** B3

Moraine OH, *6307* **100** B1
Moran KS, *558* **96** A4
Moravia IA, *665* **87** D3
Moravia NY, *1282* **79** D4
Moravian Falls NC, *1901* .. **111** F4
Moreauville LA, *929* **133** F1
Morehead KY, *6845* **100** C4
Morehead City NC, *8661* .. **115** E4
Morehouse Par. LA, *27979* .. **125** F1
Moreland KY, *550* **110** B1
Moreland Hills OH, *3320* .. **204** G2
Morenci AZ, *1489* **55** E2

Montrose IA, *898* **87** F4
Montrose MN, *2847* **66** C3
Montrose NY, *2731* **148** B2
Montrose OH, *5177* **188** A4
Montrose PA, *1617* **93** E1
Montrose SD, *472* **27** F4
Montrose VA, *384* **103** E4
Montvale NJ, *7844* **148** B3
Montverde FL, *1463* **140** C1
Mont Vernon NH, *2409* **95** D1
Montville NJ, *21150* **148** A3
Montz LA, *1918* **239** A1

Morenci MI, *2220* **90** B1
Moreno Valley CA, *193365* .. **53** D3
Morgan GA, *240* **128** C4
Morgan MN, *896* **72** B1
Morgan UT, *3687* **31** F3
Morgan Co. AL, *119490* ... **119** F3
Morgan Co. CO, *28159* **33** F4
Morgan Co. GA, *17868* **121** D4
Morgan Co. IL, *35547* **98** A1
Morgan Co. IN, *68894* **99** F2
Morgan Co. KY, *13923* **100** C4
Morgan Co. MO, *20565* **97** D3

Monument CO, *5530* **41** E2
Monument Beach MA, *2790* .. **151** E3
Moodus CT, *1413* **149** E1
Moody AL, *11726* **119** F4
Moody ME, *1000* **82** B4
Moody TX, *1371* **59** E4
Moody Co. SD, *6486* **27** F3
Moonachie NJ, *2708* **240** C2
Moorcroft WY, *1009* **25** E3
Moore ID, *189* **23** D4
Moore MT, *193* **16** B4
Moore OK, *55081* **51** E3

Morgan Co. OH, *15054* ... **101** E1
Morgan Co. TN, *21987* ... **110** B3
Morgan Co. UT, *9469* **31** F3
Morgan Co. WV, *17541* ... **102** C1
Morganfield KY, *3285* **109** D1
Morgan Hill CA, *37882* **44** B2
Morganton NC, *16918* **111** F4
Morgantown IN, *986* **99** F2
Morgantown KY, *2394* **109** F2
Morgantown PA, *826* **146** B2
Morgantown WV, *29660* .. **102** A1
Morganville NJ, *5040* **147** E1

Moore OK, *55081* **51** E3
Moore Co. NC, *88247* **122** C1
Moore Co. TN, *6362* **120** A1
Moore Co. TX, *21904* **50** A2
Moorefield WV, *2544* **102** C2
Moore Haven FL, *1680* **141** D4
Mooreland OK, *1190* **51** D1
Moores Hill IN, *597* **100** A2
Mooresville IN, *9326* **99** F1
Mooresville NC, *32711* **122** B1
Moorhead MN, *38065* **19** F4
Moorhead MS, *2405* **118** A4

Morganza LA, *610* **133** F1
Moriarty NM, *1910* **49** D3
Moriches NY, *2838* **149** D4
Morley MI, *493* **75** F2
Morley MO, *697* **108** B2
Morningdale MA, *2500* **275** D1
Morningside MD, *2015* **271** F4
Morning Sun IA, *836* **87** E3
Moro OR, *324* **21** D2
Morocco IN, *1129* **89** D3
Morongo Valley CA, *3552* .. **53** E4
Moroni UT, *1423* **39** E1

Mooringsport LA, *793* **124** C2
Moorland IA, *205* **86** B1
Moorland KY, *431* **230** F1
Moorpark CA, *34421* **52** B2
Moose Lake MN, *2751* **64** C4
Moosic PA, *5719* **261** D2
Moosup CT, *3231* **150** B3
Mora LA, *1918* **133** F1
Mora MN, *3571* **67** D2
Mora NM, *656* **49** D2
Mora Co. NM, *4881* **49** D2
Morada CA, *3828* **36** C3

Morrice MI, *927* **76** B3
Morrill NE, *921* **33** F2
Morrill Co. NE, *5042* **34** A2
Morrilton AR, *6767* **117** E1
Morris AL, *1859* **119** F4
Morris IL, *13636* **88** C2
Morris MN, *5286* **27** F1
Morris NY, *583* **79** E4
Morris OK, *1479* **116** A1
Morris Co. KS, *5923* **43** F3
Morris Co. NJ, *492276* ... **94** A4
Morris Co. TX, *12934* ... **124** B1

Moraga CA, *16016* **259** D1

Acushnet C1
Bliss Corner C2
Braleys C1
Coury Hts. C1
Eagleville A2

Fairhaven C2
Fall River B1
Faunce Corner C1
Head of Westport .. B2
Hixville B1

Idlewood C2
Island Park A2
Lakeside B2
Long Plain C1
New Bedford C2

N. Dartmouth C2
N. Fairhaven C2
N. Tiverton A2
Ocean Grove A1
Sherwood Forest .. C1

Somerset A1
S. Dartmouth C2
S. Swansea A1
Summit Grove B2
Swansea A1

The Hummocks A2
Tiverton A2
Westport Factory .. B2

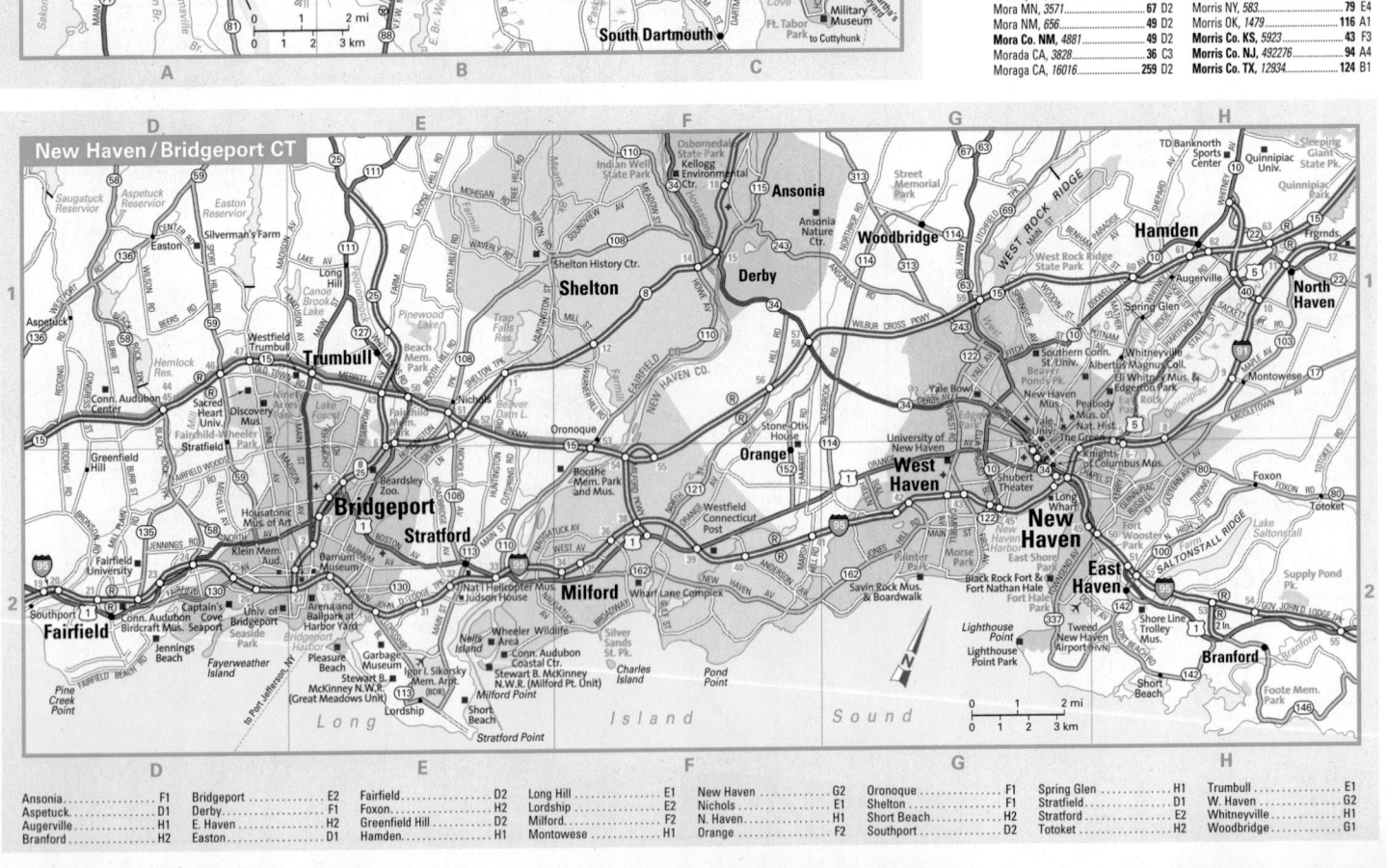

Entries in **bold black** indicate counties or parishes.
Entries in **bold color** indicate cities with detailed inset maps.

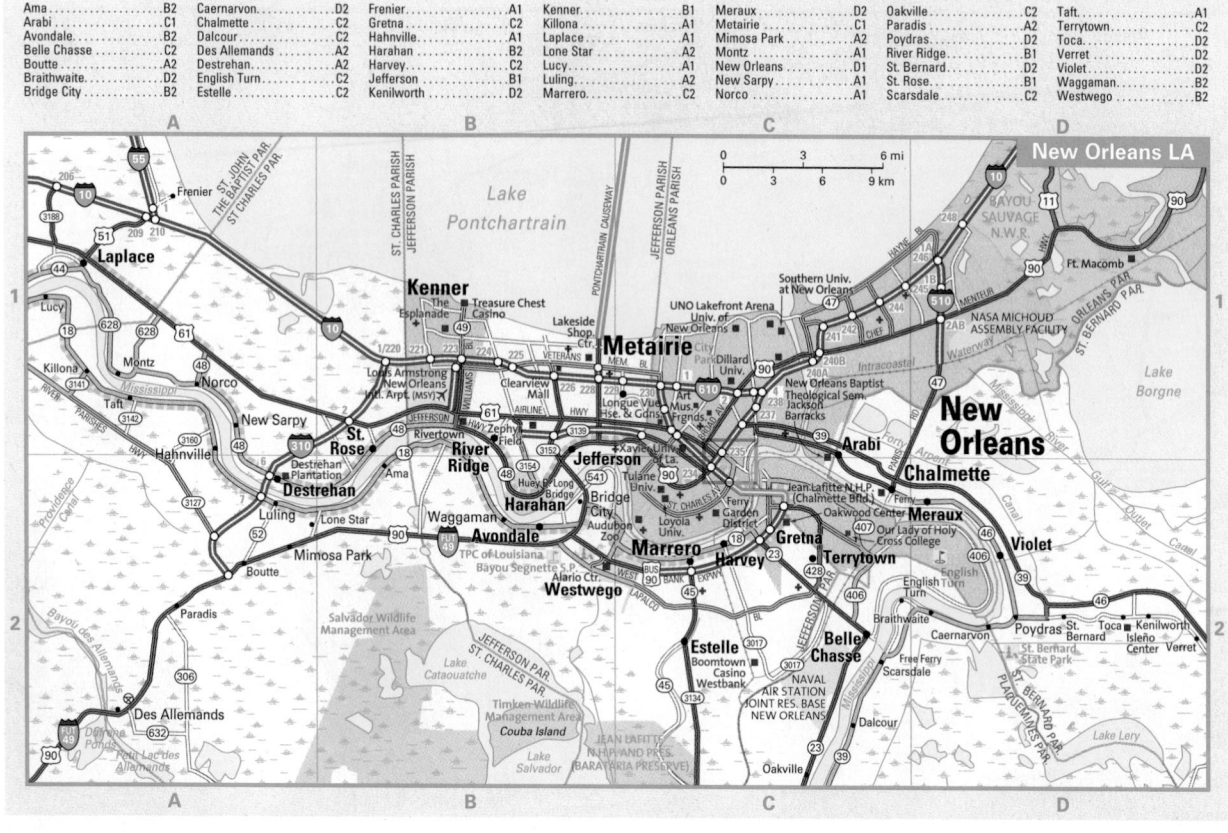

New Orleans LA

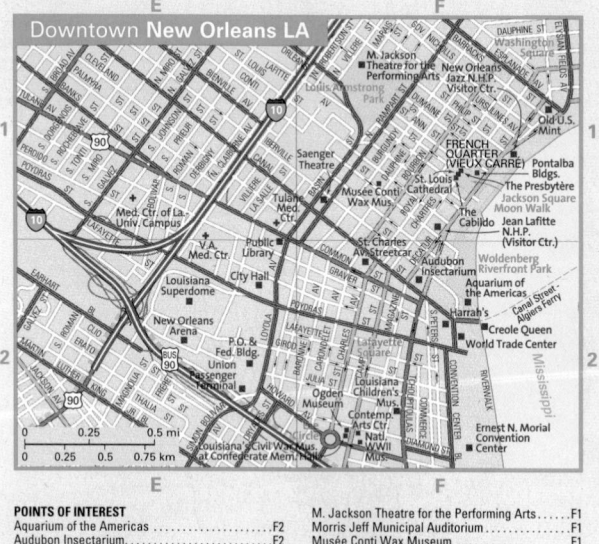

Downtown New Orleans LA

POINTS OF INTEREST

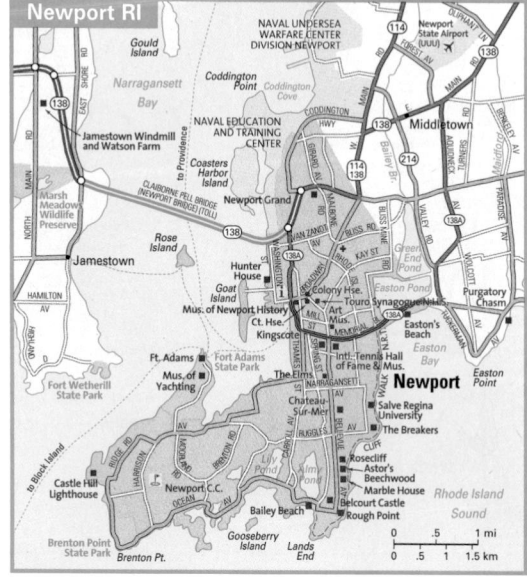

Newport RI

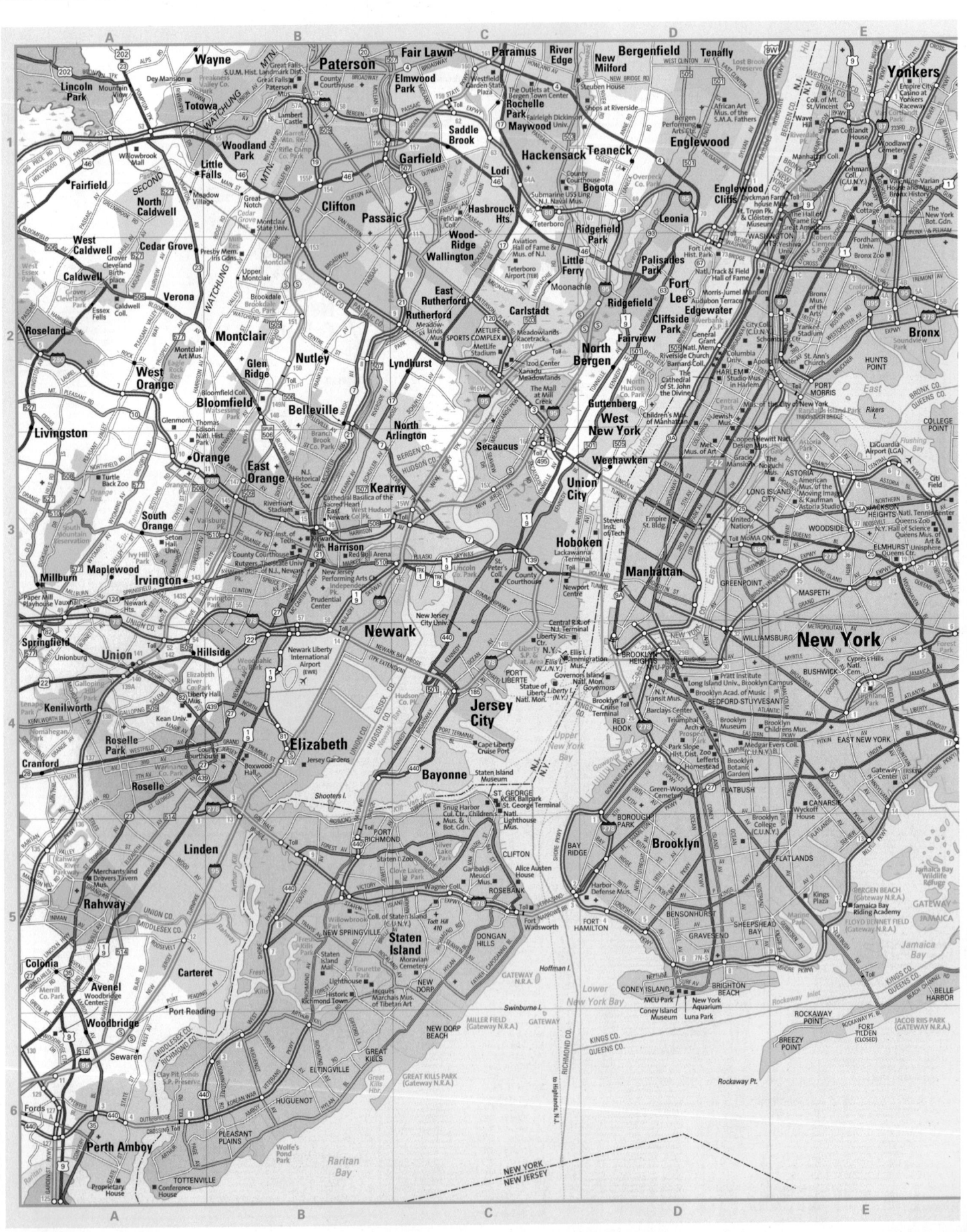

Entries in **bold black** indicate counties or parishes.
Entries in **bold color** indicate cities with detailed inset maps.

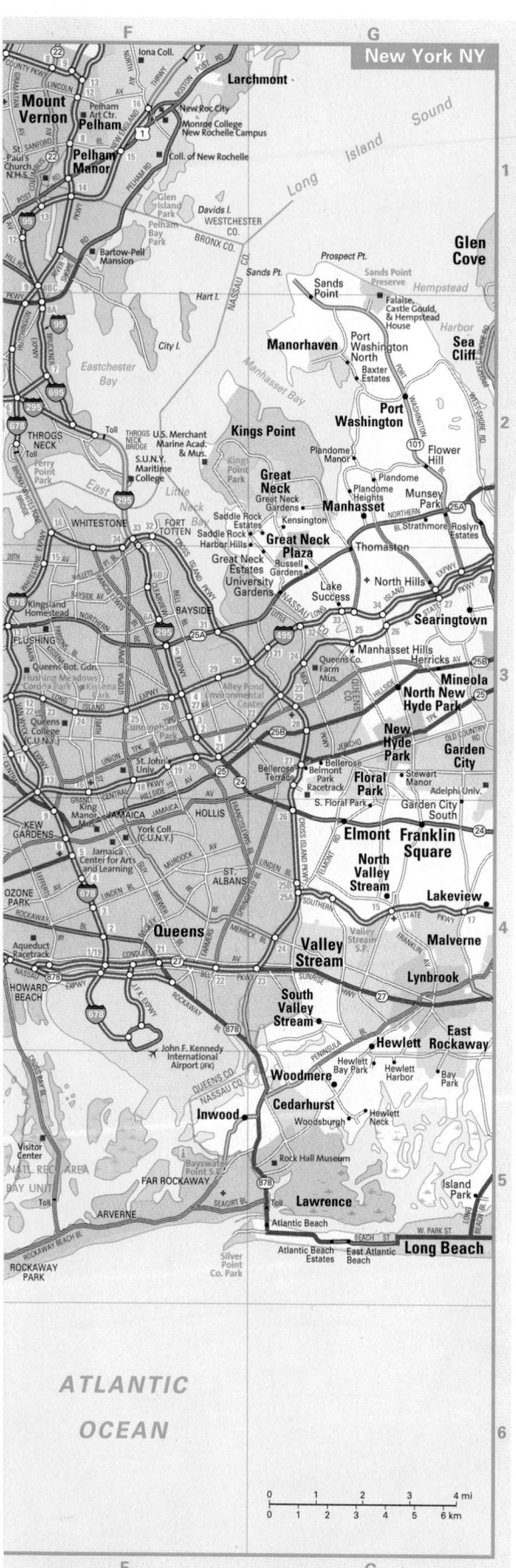

New York NY

242

New Castle–New Lenox

Figures after entries indicate population, page number, and grid reference.

POINTS OF INTEREST

Manhattan **New York NY**

Entries in **bold black** indicate counties or parishes.
Entries in **bold color** indicate cities with detailed inset maps.

Norfolk VA/Hampton Roads

Bartlett A3
Battery Park A2
Carrollton A3
Chesapeake B4
Grafton A1
Hampton C2
Hobson A3
Kiptopeke E1
Newport News B2
Norfolk C3
Poquoson B1
Portsmouth B3
Rescue A2
Suffolk A4
Tabb A1
Virginia Beach E3

244

North Acton–North Wilkesboro

Figures after entries indicate population, page number, and grid reference.

Oklahoma City OK

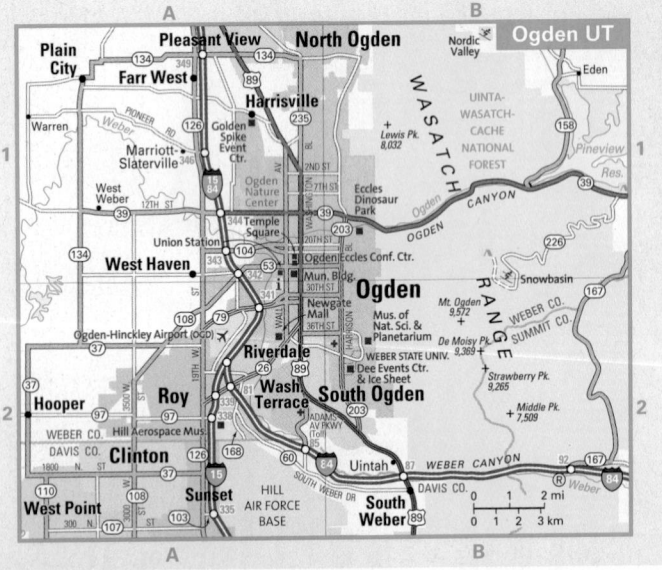

Ogden UT

Entries in **bold black** indicate counties or parishes.
Entries in **bold color** indicate cities with detailed inset maps.

Olympia WA

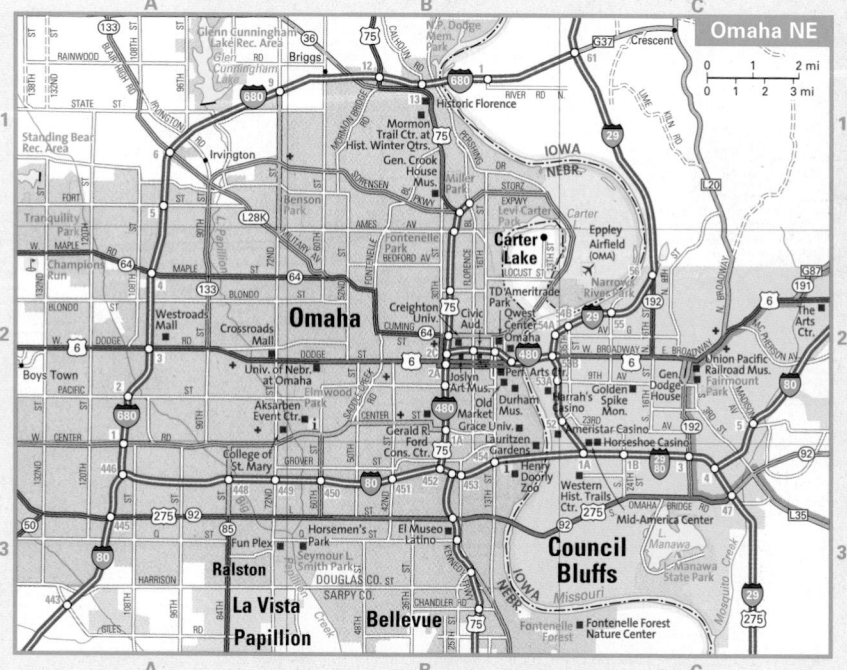

Omaha NE

246
Ossineke–Palm Springs

Figures after entries indicate population, page number, and grid reference.

Entries in **bold black** indicate counties or parishes.
Entries in **bold color** indicate cities with detailed inset maps.

Oxnard/Ventura CA

Palm Springs CA

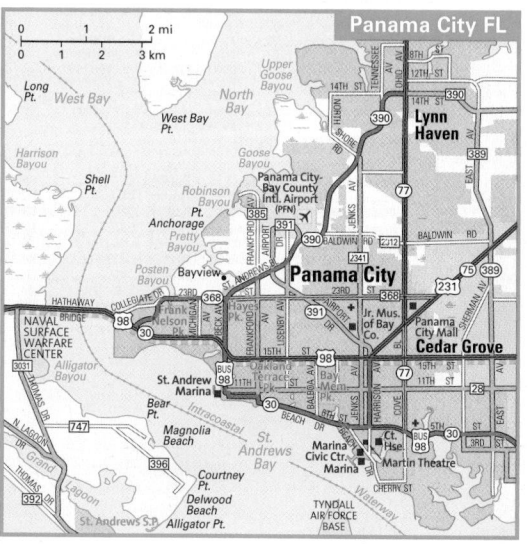

Panama City FL

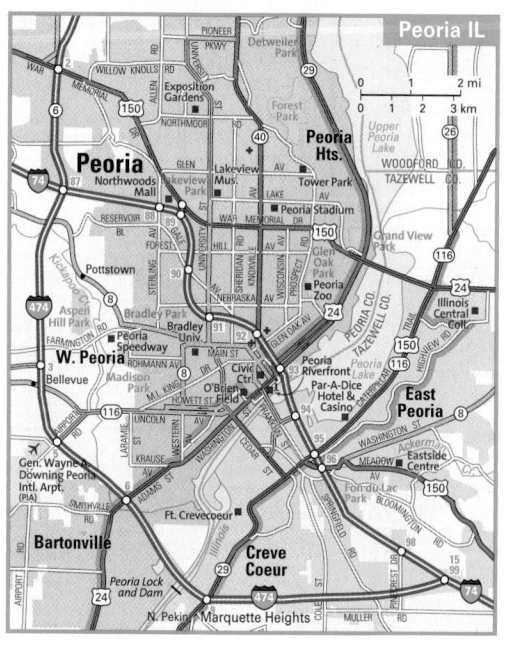

Pensacola FL

Peoria IL

248

Patterson Gardens–Pearl River

Figures after entries indicate population, page number, and grid reference.

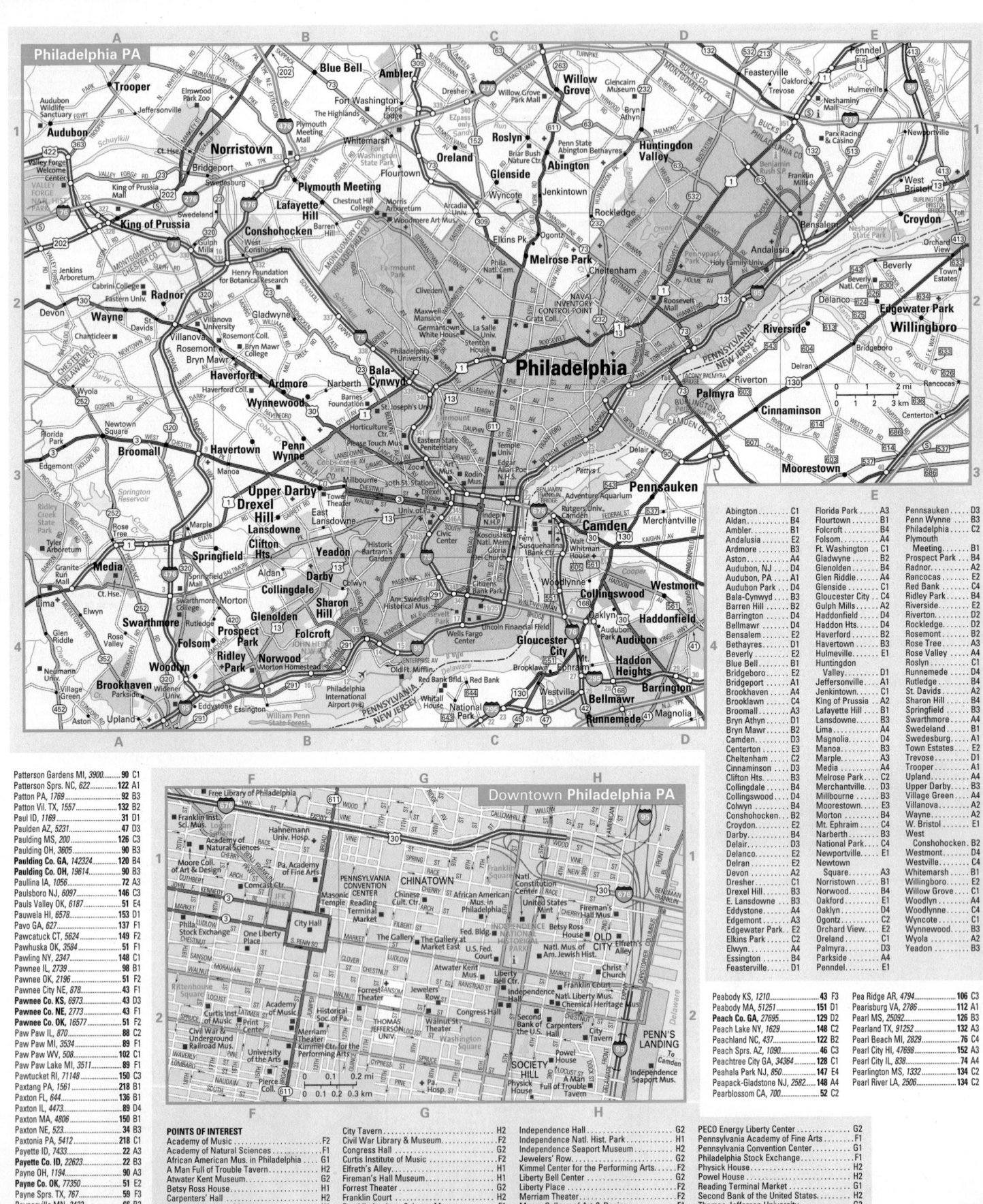

Philadelphia PA

Downtown Philadelphia PA

POINTS OF INTEREST

Entries in **bold black** indicate counties or parishes.
Entries in *bold color* indicate cities with detailed inset maps.

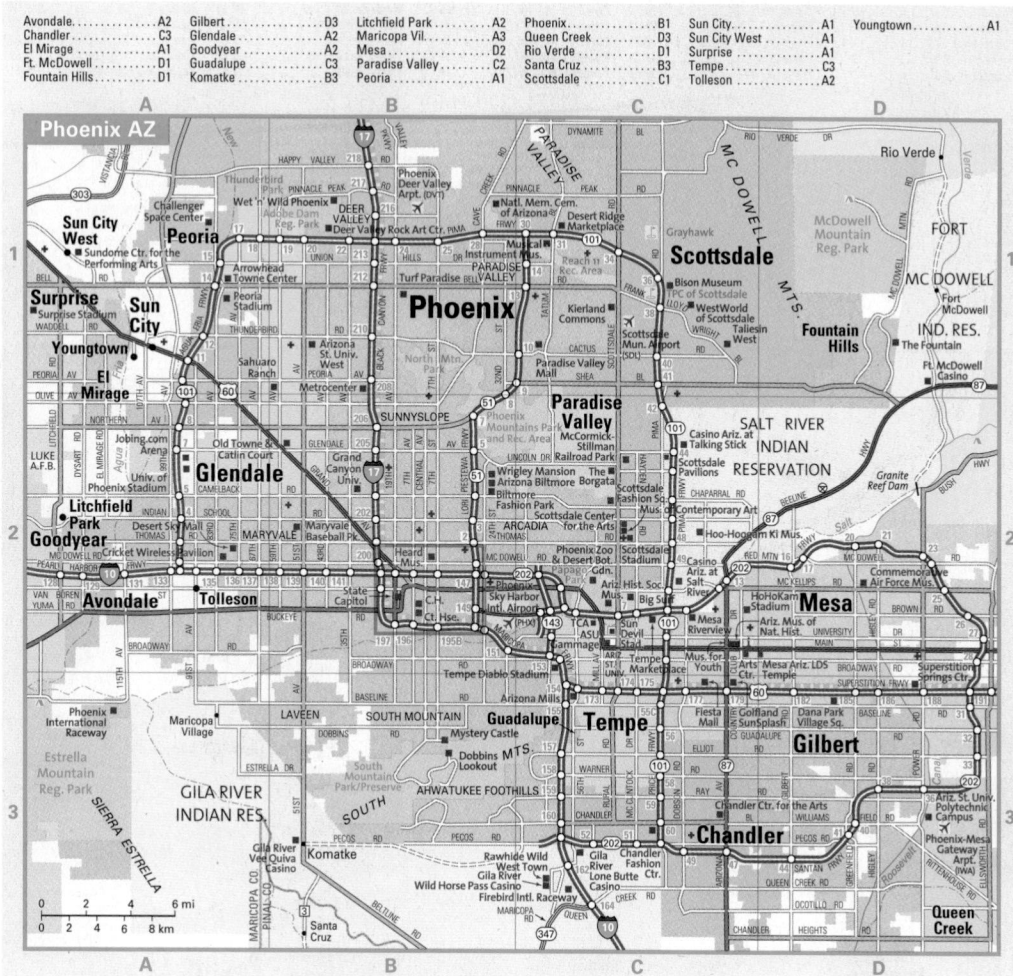

Phoenix AZ

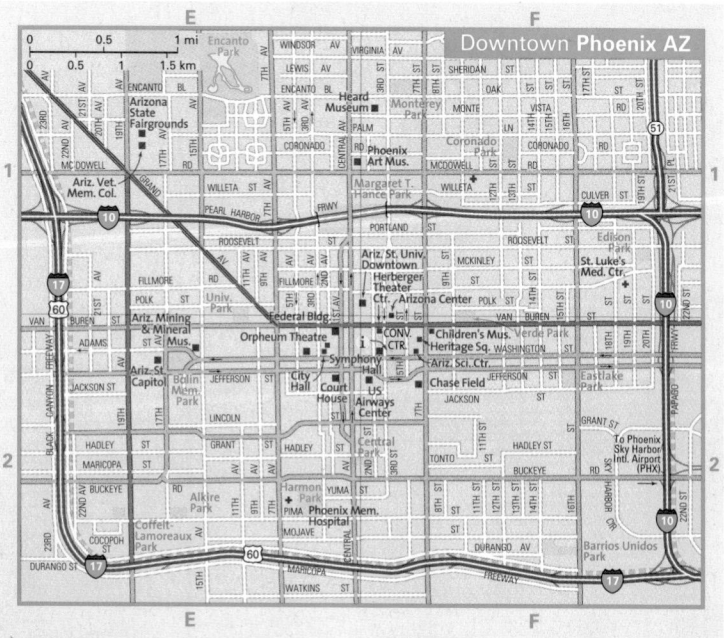

Downtown Phoenix AZ

POINTS OF INTEREST
Arizona Center F1
Arizona Mining & Mineral Museum E2
Arizona Science Center F2
Arizona State Capitol E2
Arizona State Fairgrounds E1
Arizona Veterans Memorial Coliseum E1
Chase Field F2
Children's Museum F2
City Hall E2
Convention Center F2
Dodge Theatre E2
Heard Museum F1
Herberger Theater Center F2
Heritage Square F2
Orpheum Theatre E2
Phoenix Art Museum E1
Phoenix Museum of History F2
Symphony Hall E2
US Airways Center E2

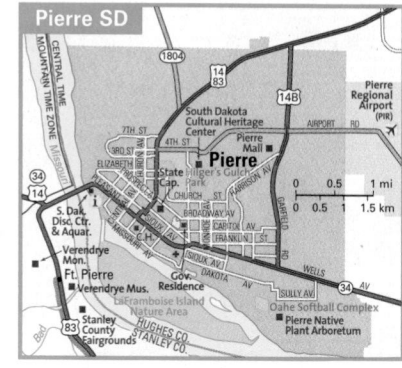

Pierre SD

Pierre

Figures after entries indicate population, page number, and grid reference.

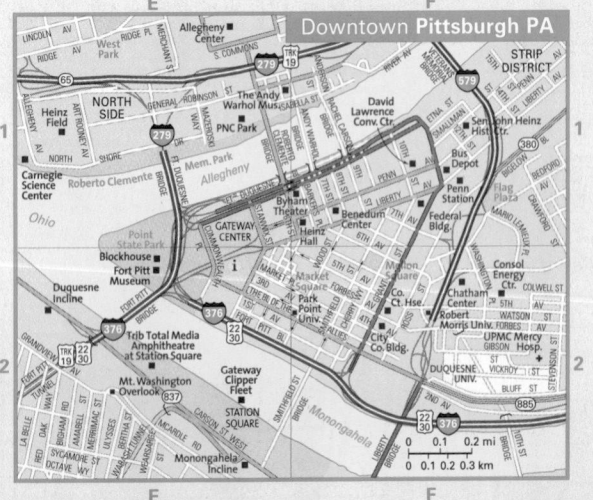

Pittsburgh PA

Downtown Pittsburgh PA

POINTS OF INTEREST

Allegheny Center E1
The Andy Warhol Museum E1
Benedum Center F1
Blockhouse E2
Bus Depot F1
Byham Theater F1
Carnegie Science Center E1
Chatham Center F2
Chevrolet Amphitheatre E1
City County Building F2
Consol Energy Center F2
County Court House F2
David Lawrence Convention Center F1
Duquesne Incline E2
Duquesne University F2
Federal Building F1
Fort Pitt Museum E2
Gateway Center E1
Gateway Clipper Fleet E2
Heinz Field E1
Heinz Hall F1
Monongahela Incline E2
Mt. Washington Overlook E2
Penn Station F1
PNC Park E1
Point Park University F2
Point State Park E1
Robert Morris University E1
Senator John Heinz Hist. Center F1
Station Square E2

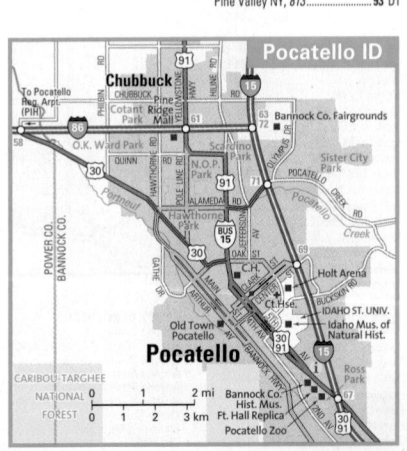

Pocatello ID

Entries in **bold black** indicate counties or parishes.
Entries in **bold color** indicate cities with detailed inset maps.

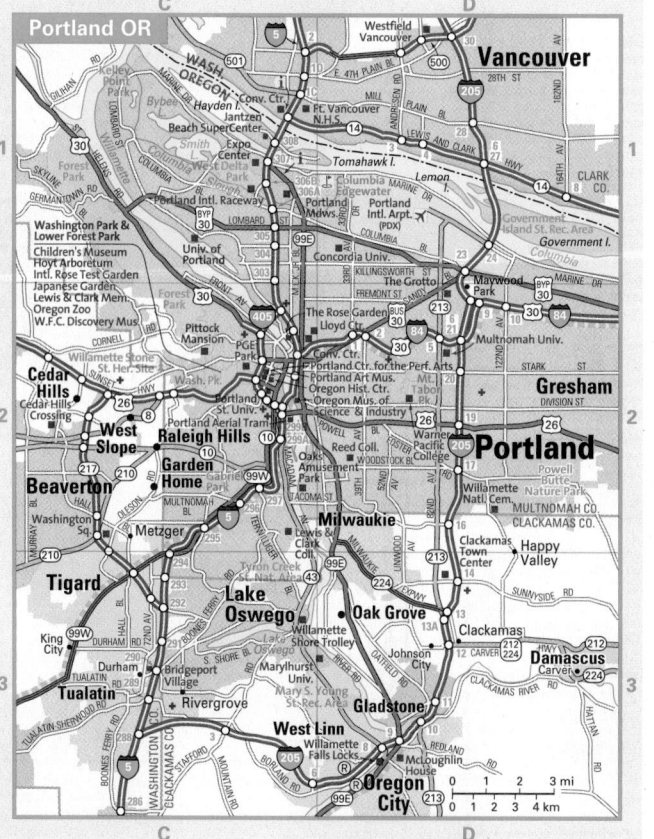

Portland ME

Providence RI

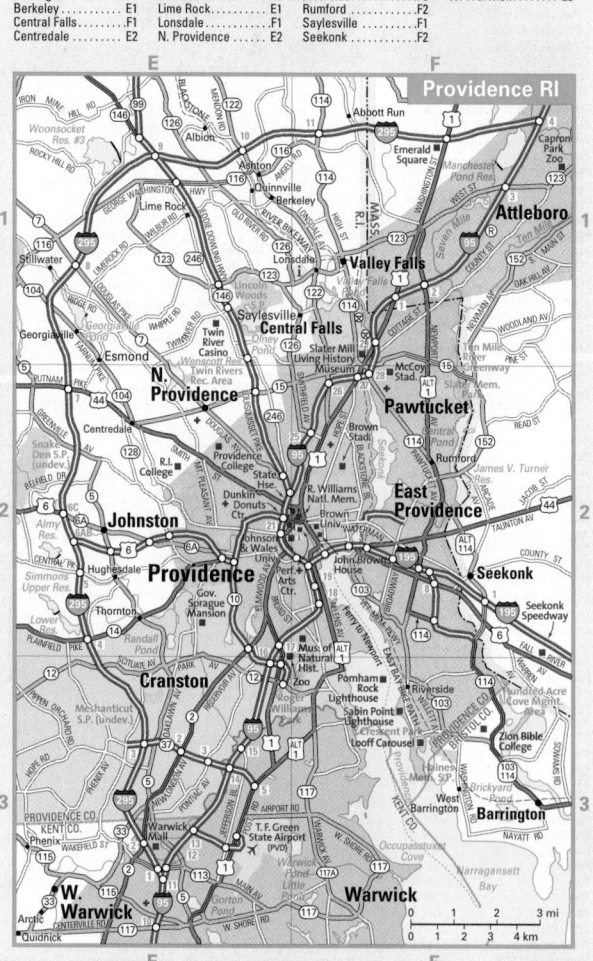

Portland OR

Figures after entries indicate population, page number, and grid reference.

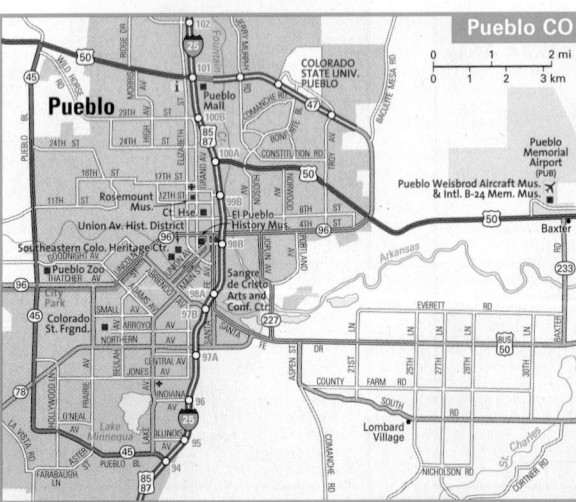

Provo UT

Pleasant Grove
Lindon
Orem
Provo
Springville

Pueblo CO

Pueblo
Baxter

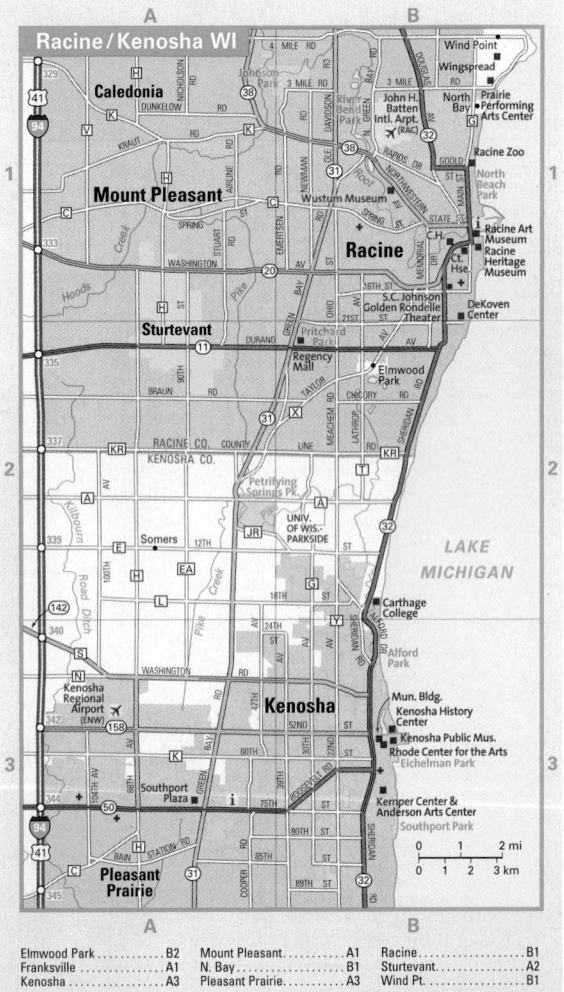

Racine/Kenosha WI

Caledonia
Mount Pleasant
Racine
Sturtevant
Kenosha
Pleasant Prairie

Entries in **bold black** indicate counties or parishes.
Entries in **bold color** indicate cities with detailed inset maps.

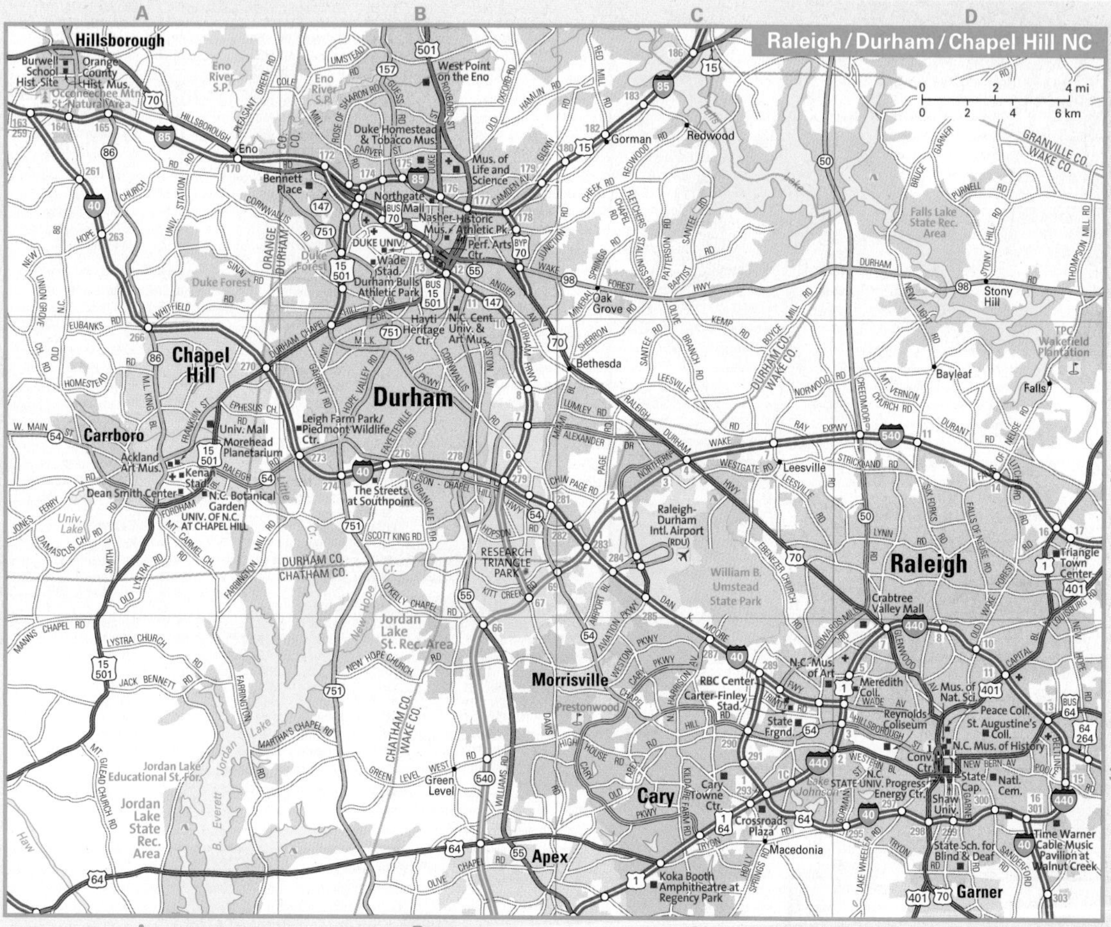

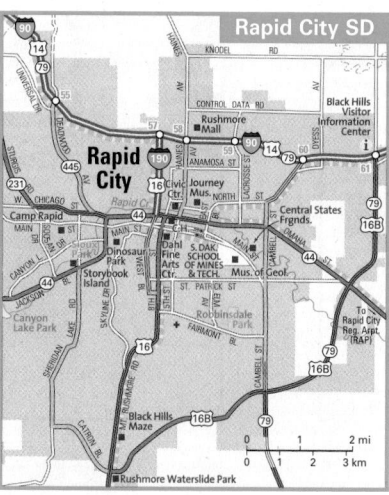

Raleigh/Durham/Chapel Hill NC

Rapid City SD

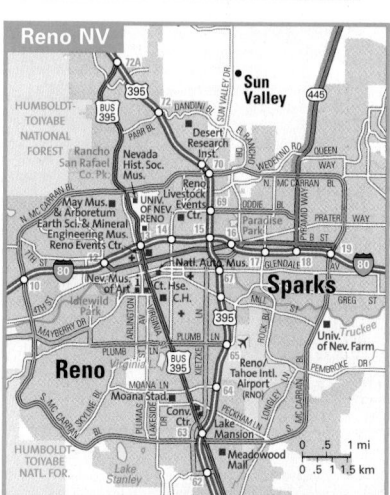

Reno NV

Figures after entries indicate population, page number, and grid reference.

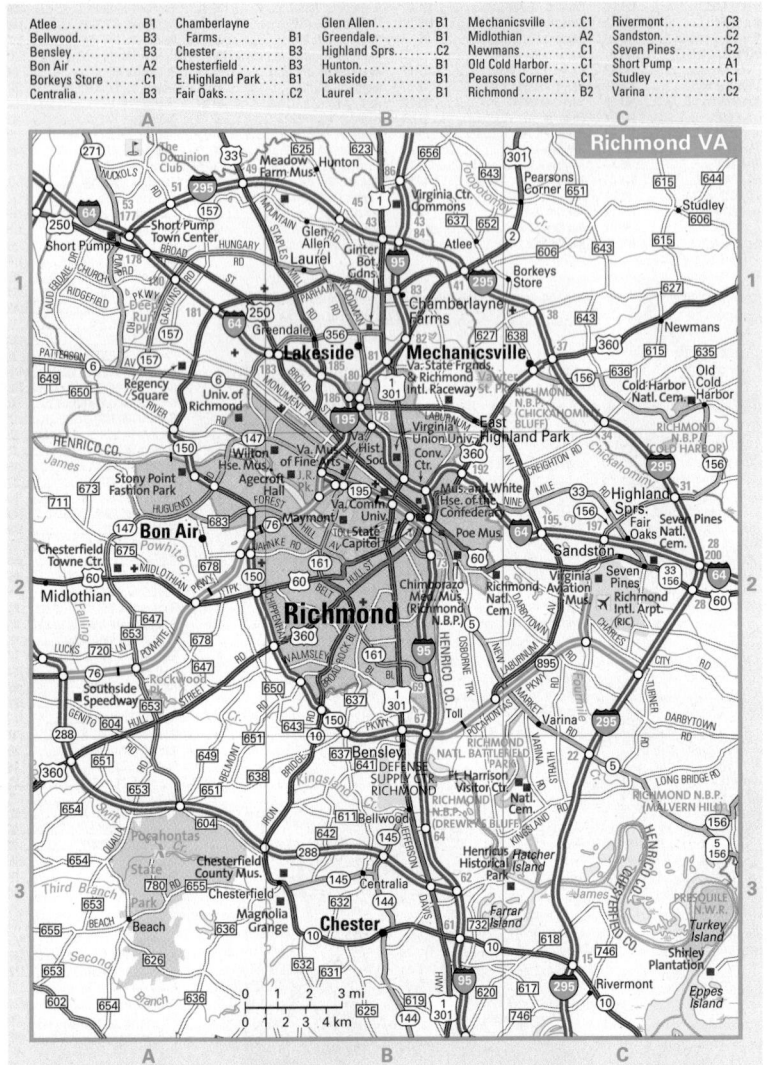

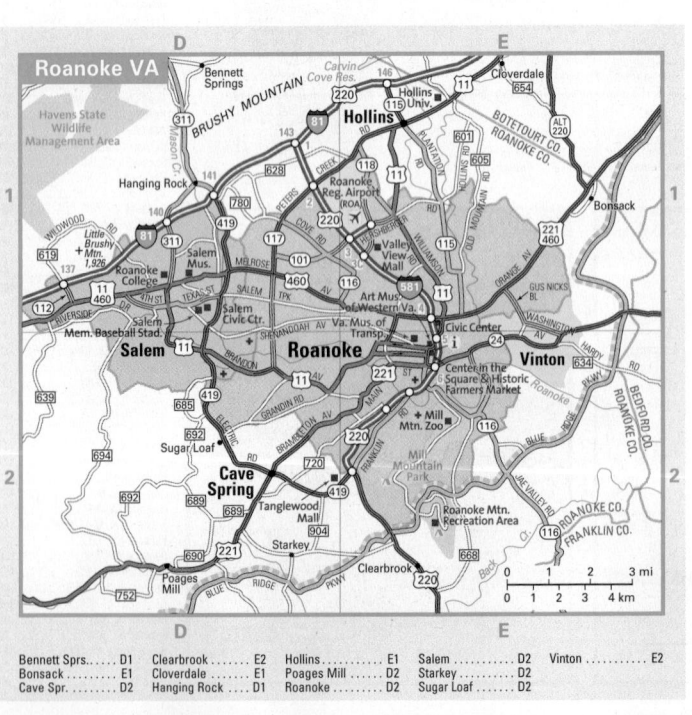

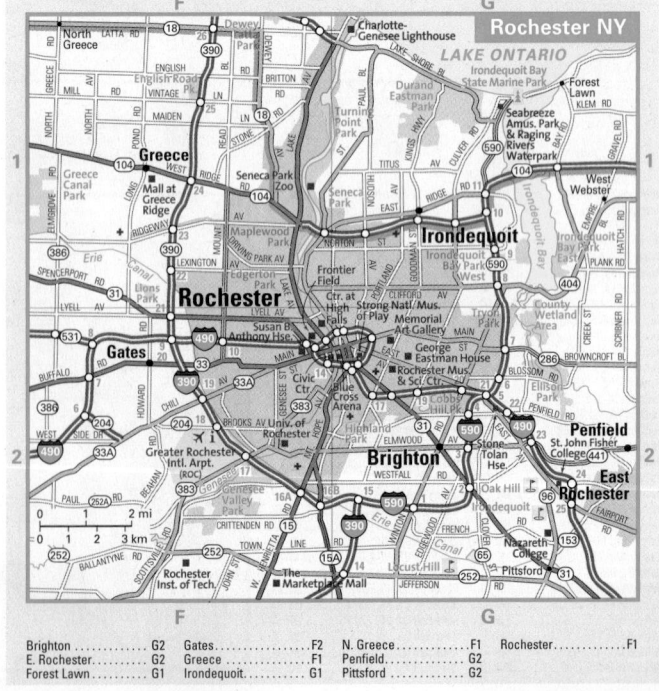

Entries in **bold black** indicate counties or parishes.
Entries in **bold color** indicate cities with detailed inset maps.

Rockford IL

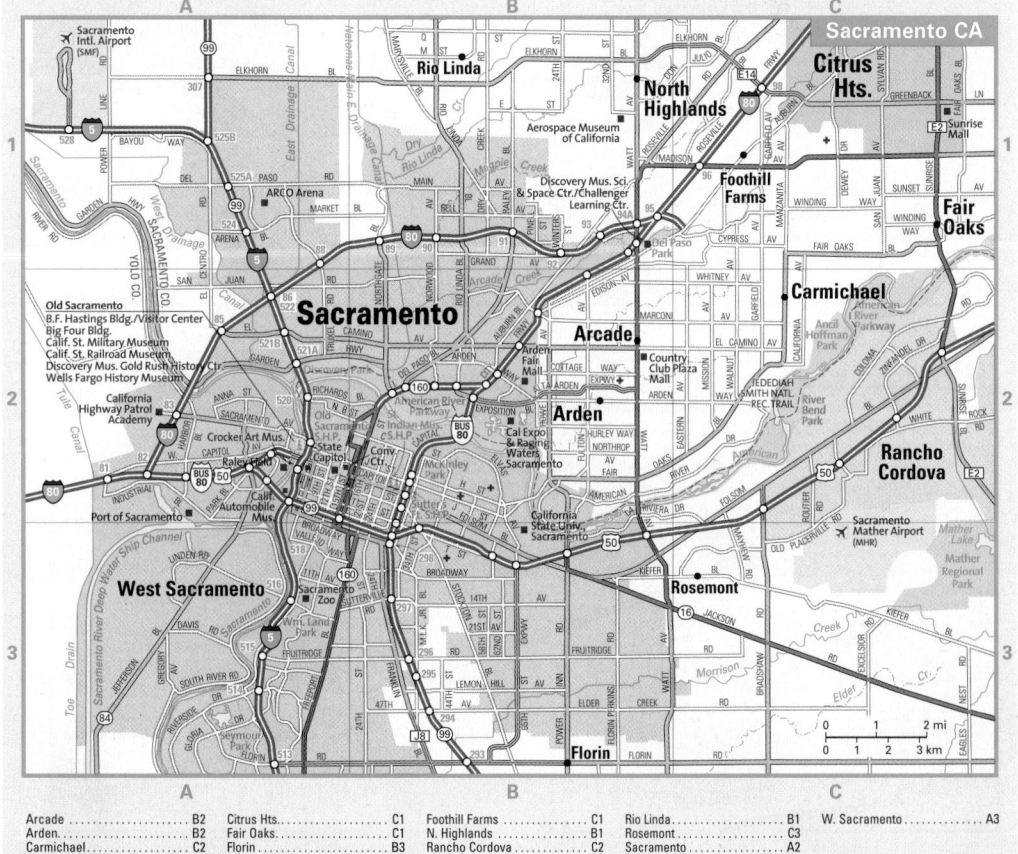

Sacramento CA

Figures after entries indicate population, page number, and grid reference.

Affton B3
Alorton C3
Ballwin A2
Bella Villa B3
Bellefontaine Neighbors C1
Bellerive B2
Belleville D3
Bel-Nor B2
Bel-Ridge B2
Benevolent Hts. D3
Berkeley B1
Beverly Hills B2
Black Jack B1
Breckenridge Hills B2
Brentwood B2
Bridgeton B1
Brooklyn C2
Cahokia C3
Calverton Park B1
Caseyville D2
Cedar Park D1
Centreville C3
Champ A1
Charlack B2
Chesterfield A2
Clayton B2
Collinsville D2
Columbia C3
Concord B3
Cool Valley B1
Country Club Hills B1
Country Life Acres A2
Crestwood B3
Creve Coeur A2
Crystal Lake Park B2
Dellwood B1
Des Peres A2
Dupo C3
E. Carondelet C3
E. St. Louis C2
Edmundson B1
Edwardsville D1
Ellisville A2
Fairmont City C2
Fairview Hts. D2
Fenton A3
Ferguson B1
Flordell Hills C1
Florissant B1
Forest Acres D2
Frontenac B2
Glasgow Vil. C1
Glen Carbon D1
Glendale B2
Granite City C1
Greendale B2
Green Park B3
Hanley Hills B2
Hartford D1
Hazelwood B1
Hillsdale B2
Hollywood Hts. D2
Huntleigh B2
Imbs C3
Jennings B1
Kinloch B1
Kirkwood B3
Ladue B2
Lakeshire B3
Lemay B3
Mackenzie B3
Madison C2
Manchester A3
Maplewood B2
Marlborough B3
Maryland Hts. A1
Maryville D1
Mattese B3
Mehlville B3
Mitchell D1
Moline Acres C1
Murphy A3
Normandy B2
N. Dupo C3
Northwoods B2
Oak Hills D2
Oakland B3
Oakville B3
Olivette B2
Overland B2
Pagedale B2
Parkdale A3
Peerless Park A3
Pine Lawn B2
Poag D1
Pontoon Beach D1
Richmond Hts. B2
Riverview C1
Robertson B1
Rock Hill B2
St. Ann B1
St. Charles A1
St. George B3
St. John B1
St. Louis C2
Sappington B3
Sauget C2
Shoveltown B1
Shrewsbury B3
Signal Hill D3
S. Roxana D1
Spanish Lake C1
Sunset Hills B3
Swansea D3
Town and Country A2
Twin Oaks A3
University City B2
Valley Park A3
Venice C2
Vinita Park B2
Warson Woods B2
Washington Park D2
Webster Groves B3
Wellston B2
Westwood A2
Wilbur Park B3
Winchester A2
Woodson Terrace B1

Rushville NY, *677* **78** C4
Rusk TX, *5551* **124** B3
Rusk Co. TX, *53330* **124** B3
Rusk Co. WI, *14755* **67** F3
Ruskin FL, *17208* **140** B3
Russell IA, *554* **87** D3
Russell KS, *4506* **43** D2
Russell KY, *3380* **101** D3
Russell MA, *786* **94** C2
Russell PA, *1408* **92** B1
Russell Co. AL, *52947* **128** C3
Russell Co. KS, *6970* **43** D2
Russell Co. KY, *17565* **110** B2
Russell Co. VA, *28897* **111** F2
Russell Gardens NY, *945* **241** G3
Russells Pt. OH, *1391* **90** B4
Russell Sprs. KY, *2441* **110** B2
Russellville AL, *9830* **119** E3
Russellville AR, *27920* **117** D1
Russellville KY, *6960* **109** E2
Russellville MO, *807* **97** E3
Russellville TN, *1000* **111** D3
Russiaville IN, *1094* **89** F4
Rustburg VA, *1431* **112** C2
Ruston LA, *21859* **125** E2
Ruston WA, *749* **262** A5
Ruth NV, *440* **38** B2
Rutherford NJ, *18061* **148** B3
Rutherford TN, *1151* **108** C4
Rutherford Co. NC, *67810* **121** F1
Rutherford Co. TN, *262604* **109** F4
Rutherford Hts. PA, *3859* **218** C1
Rutherfordton NC, *4213* **121** F1
Ruthven IA, *737* **72** B3
Rutland MA, *2111* **150** B1
Rutland ND, *163* **27** E1
Rutland VT, *16495* **81** D3
Rutland Co. VT, *61642* **81** D3
Rutledge AL, *467* **128** A4
Rutledge GA, *781* **121** D4
Rutledge PA, *784* **248** B4
Rutledge TN, *1122* **111** D3
Ryall Sprs. TN, *4600* **120** B2
Ryan OK, *816* **59** E1
Rye NH, *5298* **82** A4
Rye NY, *15720* **148** C3
Rye Beach NH, *750* **82** A4
Ryegate MT, *245* **16** B4
Ryland Hts. KY, *1022* **100** B2

S

Sabattus ME, *4486* **82** B2
Sabetha KS, *2571* **96** A1
Sabina OH, *2564* **100** C2
Sabinal TX, *1695* **60** C3
Sabine Co. TX, *10834* **124** C4
Sabine Par. LA, *24233* **125** D4
Sabula IA, *576* **88** A1
Sacaton AZ, *2672* **54** C2
Sac City IA, *2220* **72** B4
Sac Co. IA, *10350* **72** A4
Sachem Head CT, *600* **149** E2
Sachse TX, *20329* **207** E1
Sackets Harbor NY, *1450* **79** D1
Saco ME, *18482* **82** B4
Saco MT, *197* **17** D2
Sacramento CA, *466488* **36** C3
Sacramento KY, *468* **109** E1
Sacramento Co. CA, *1418788* **36** C3
Sacred Heart MN, *548* **66** B4
Saddle Brook NJ, *13929* **240** C1
Saddle River NJ, *3152* **148** B3
Saddle Rock NY, *830* **241** G2
Sadsburyville PA, *1800* **146** B3
Saegertown PA, *997* **92** A1
Safety Harbor FL, *16884* **140** B2
Safford AZ, *9566* **55** E2
Sagadahoc Co. ME, *35293* **82** B3
Sagamore MA, *3623* **151** E3

POINTS OF INTEREST

America's Center G1
Ballpark Village F2
Bowling Hall of Fame & Museum F2
Busch Stadium F2
Campbell House Museum F1
Casino Queen G1
City Hall F1
City Museum F1
Court House F1
Edward Jones Dome G1
Eugene Field House & Toy Museum F2
Federal Court House F1
Gateway Arch & Mus. of Westward Expansion G2
Gateway Geyser Fountain G2
Harris-Stowe State University E1
Jefferson Natl. Expansion Memorial G1
Laclede's Landing G1
Library F1
Lumière Place G1
Mississippi River Overlook G2
Old Cathedral G2
Old Court House G1
Post Office F1
President Casino on the Admiral G1
St. Louis Centre G1
St. Louis University E1
Samuel Cupples House E1
Scott Joplin House State Hist. Site F1
Scottrade Center F1
Soldiers' Memorial Military Museum F1
Union Station F1

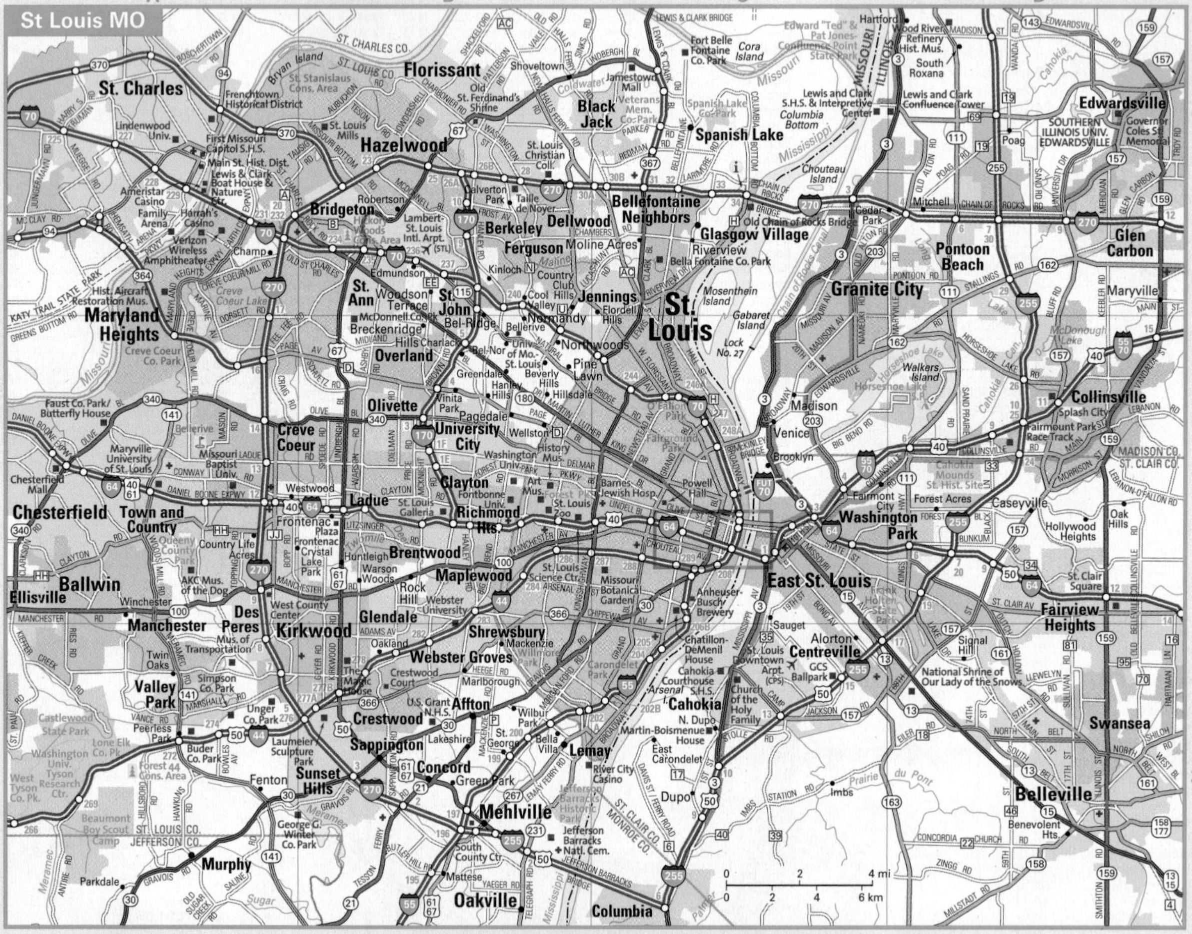

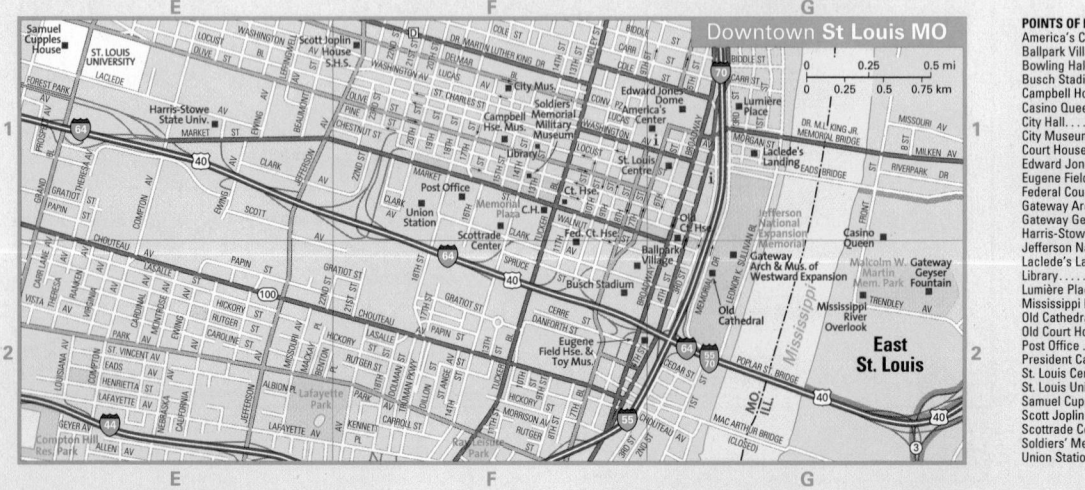

Entries in **bold black** indicate counties or parishes.
Entries in **bold color** indicate cities with detailed inset maps.

Salem OR

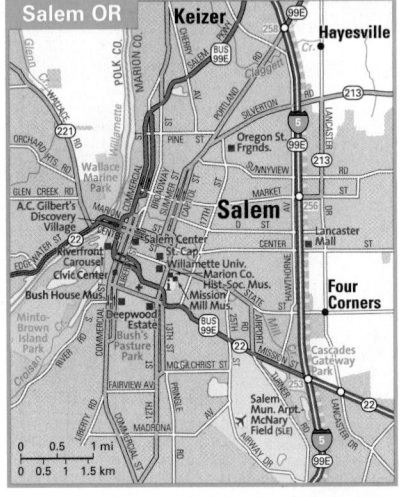

San Antonio TX

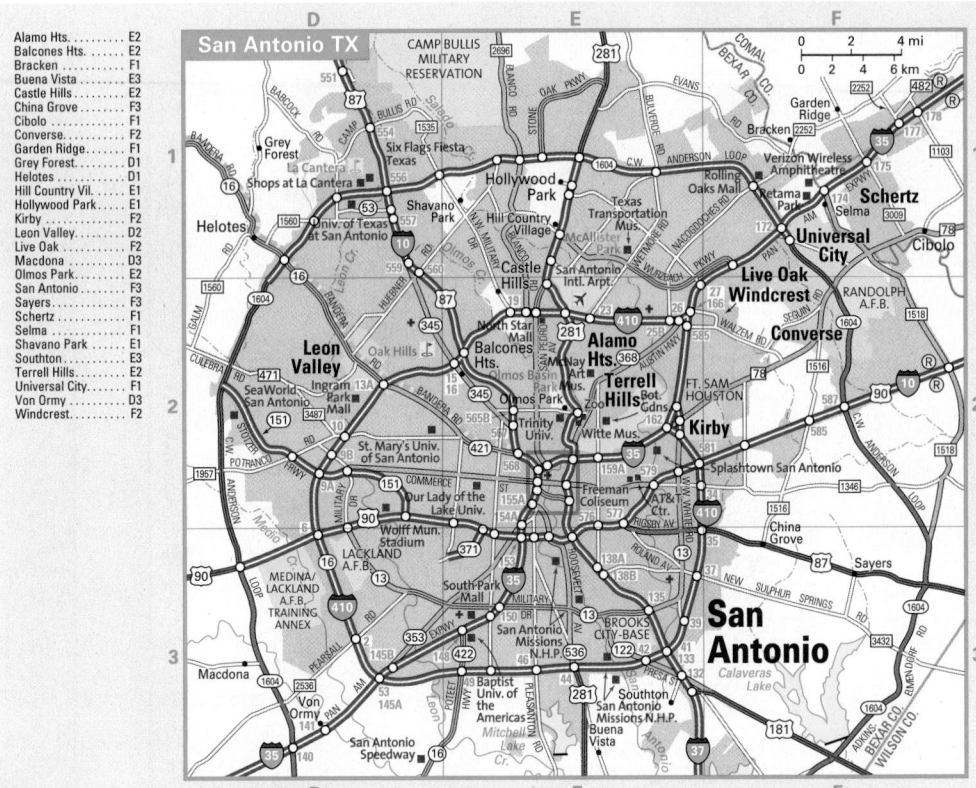

Salt Lake City UT

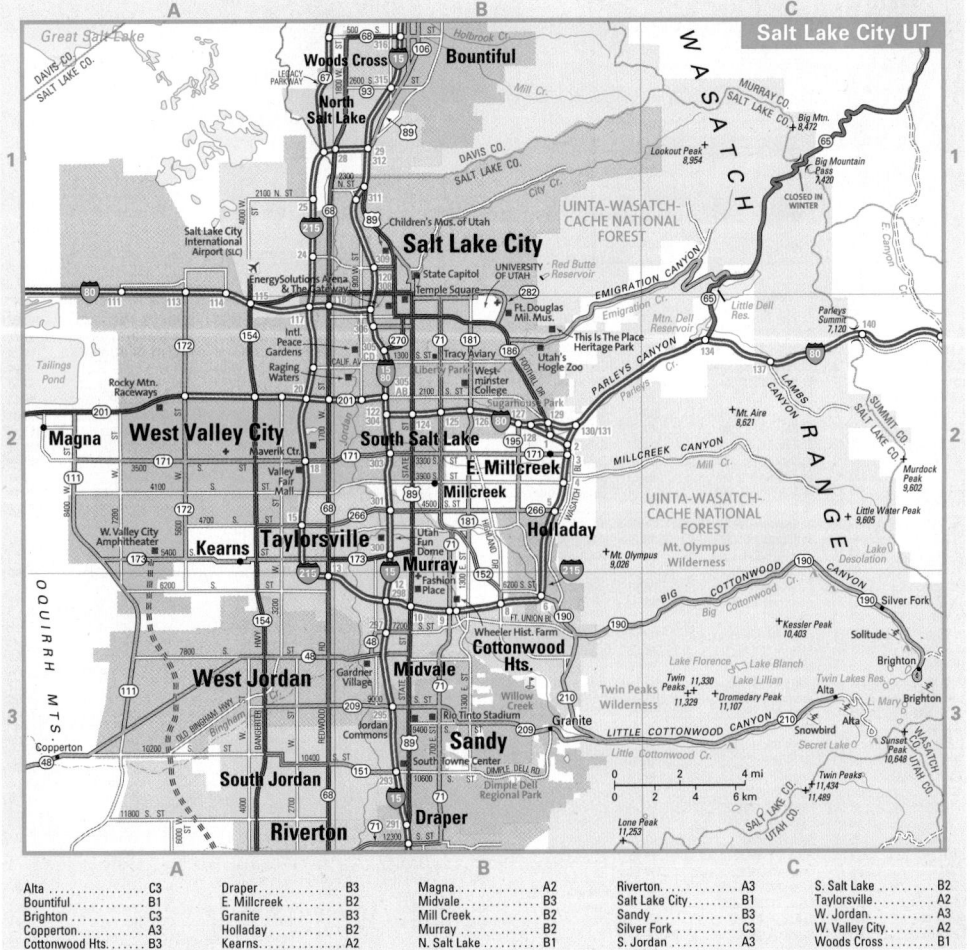

Downtown San Antonio TX

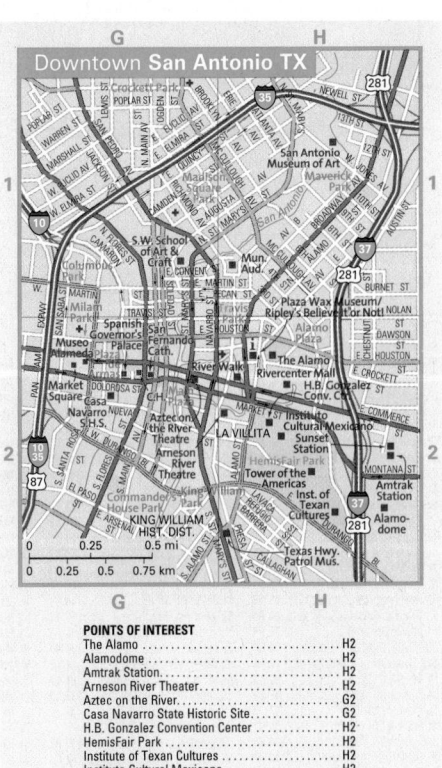

POINTS OF INTEREST

The Alamo	H2
Alamodome	H2
Amtrak Station	H2
Arneson River Theater	H2
Aztec on the River	G2
Casa Navarro State Historic Site.	G2
H.B. Gonzalez Convention Center	H2
HemisFair Park	H2
Institute of Texan Cultures	H2
Instituto Cultural Mexicano	G2
Market Square	G2
Municipal Auditorium	H1
Museo Alameda	G2
Plaza Wax Museum/Ripley's Believe It or Not! ..	H2
Rivercenter Mall	H2
River Walk	H2
San Antonio Museum of Art	H1
San Fernando Cathedral	G2
Spanish Governor's Palace	G2
Sunset Station	H2
Southwest School of Art & Craft	G1
Texas Highway Patrol Museum	H2
Tower of the Americas	H2

Figures after entries indicate population, page number, and grid reference.

San Diego CA

Downtown San Diego CA

San Francisco Bay CA

Figures after entries indicate population, page number, and grid reference.

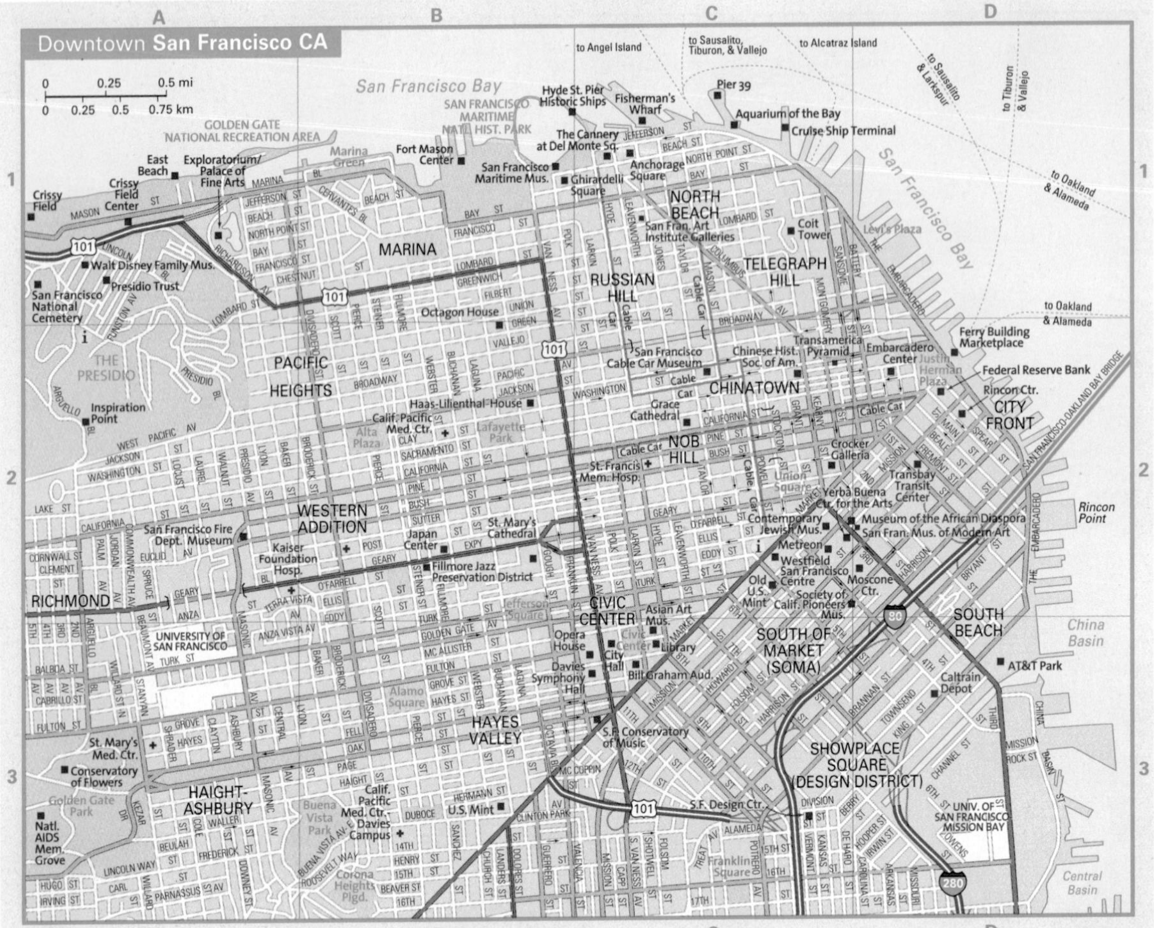

Downtown San Francisco CA

POINTS OF INTEREST

Anchorage Square C1
Ansel Adams Center
 for Photography D2
Aquarium of the Bay C1
Asian Art Museum C3
AT&T Park D3
Bill Graham Auditorium C3
Caltrain Depot D3
The Cannery
 at Del Monte Square C1
Chinese Historical
 Society of America C2
City Hall C3
Coit Tower C1
Conservatory of Flowers A3
Contemporary Jewish Mus. .. C2
Crissy Field A1
Crissy Field Center A1
Crocker Galleria C2
Cruise Ship Terminal C1
Davies Symphony Hall C3
East Beach A1
Embarcadero Center D2
Exploratorium/
 Palace of Fine Arts A1

Fillmore Jazz Preservation
 District B2
Ferry Building Marketplace ... D2
Fisherman's Wharf C1
Fort Mason Center B1
Ghirardelli Square B1
Golden Gate Natl. Rec. Area. A1
Golden Gate Park A3
Grace Cathedral C2
Haas-Lilienthal House B2
Hyde Street Pier Historic Ships. C1
Inspiration Point A2
Japan Center B2
Levi's Plaza D1
Library C3
Metreon C2
Moscone Center C2
Museum of the African
 Diaspora D2
National AIDS Memorial Grove. A3
Octagon House B2
Old U.S. Mint C2
Opera House C3
Pier 39 .... C1
The Presidio A2
Presidio Trust A1

Rincon Center D2
St. Mary's Cathedral B2
San Francisco Art Institute
 Galleries C1
San Francisco Cable Car Mus.. C2
San Francisco Cons. of Music. C3
San Francisco Design Center. C3
San Francisco Fire Dept. Mus.. A2
San Francisco Maritime Mus.. B1
San Francisco Maritime
 Natl. Hist. Park B1
San Francisco Museum of
 Modern Art D2
San Francisco Natl. Cemetery. A1
Soc. of Calif. Pioneers Mus... C2
Transamerica Pyramid C2
Transbay Terminal D2
U.S. Mint B3
Univ. of San Francisco A3
Univ. of San Francisco-
 Mission Bay D3
Walt Disney Family Mus. A1
Westfield San Francisco
 Centre C2
Yerba Buena
 Center for the Arts C2

Santa Barbara CA

Santa Fe NM

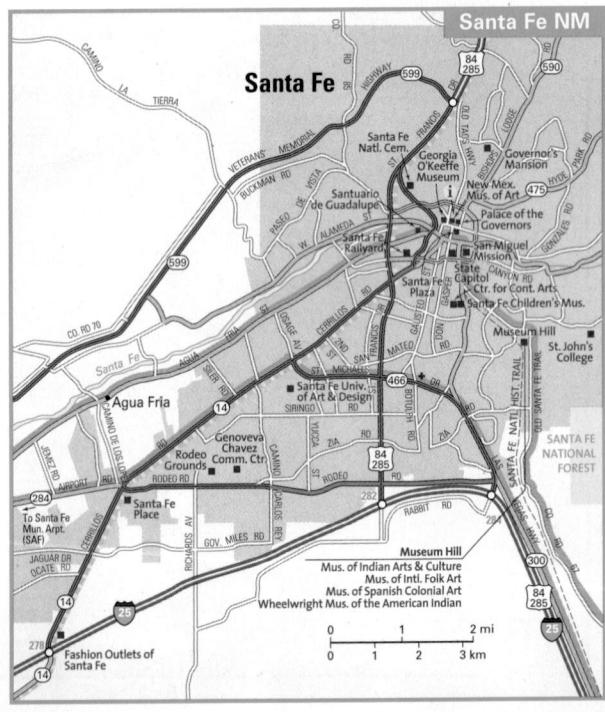

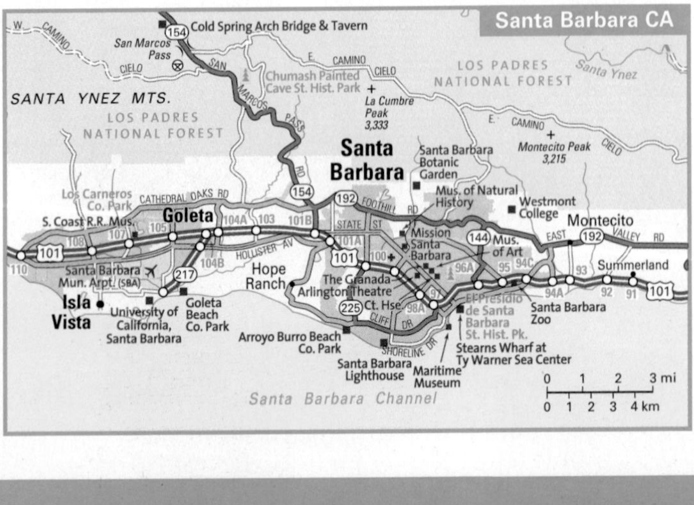

Entries in **bold black** indicate counties or parishes.
Entries in **bold color** indicate cities with detailed inset maps.

Savannah GA

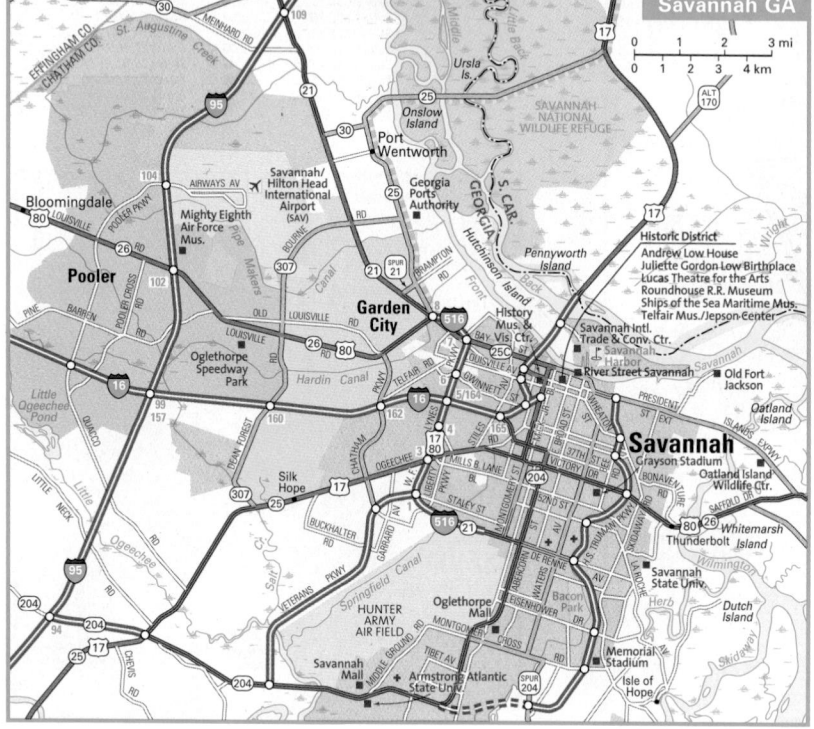

Scranton / Wilkes-Barre PA

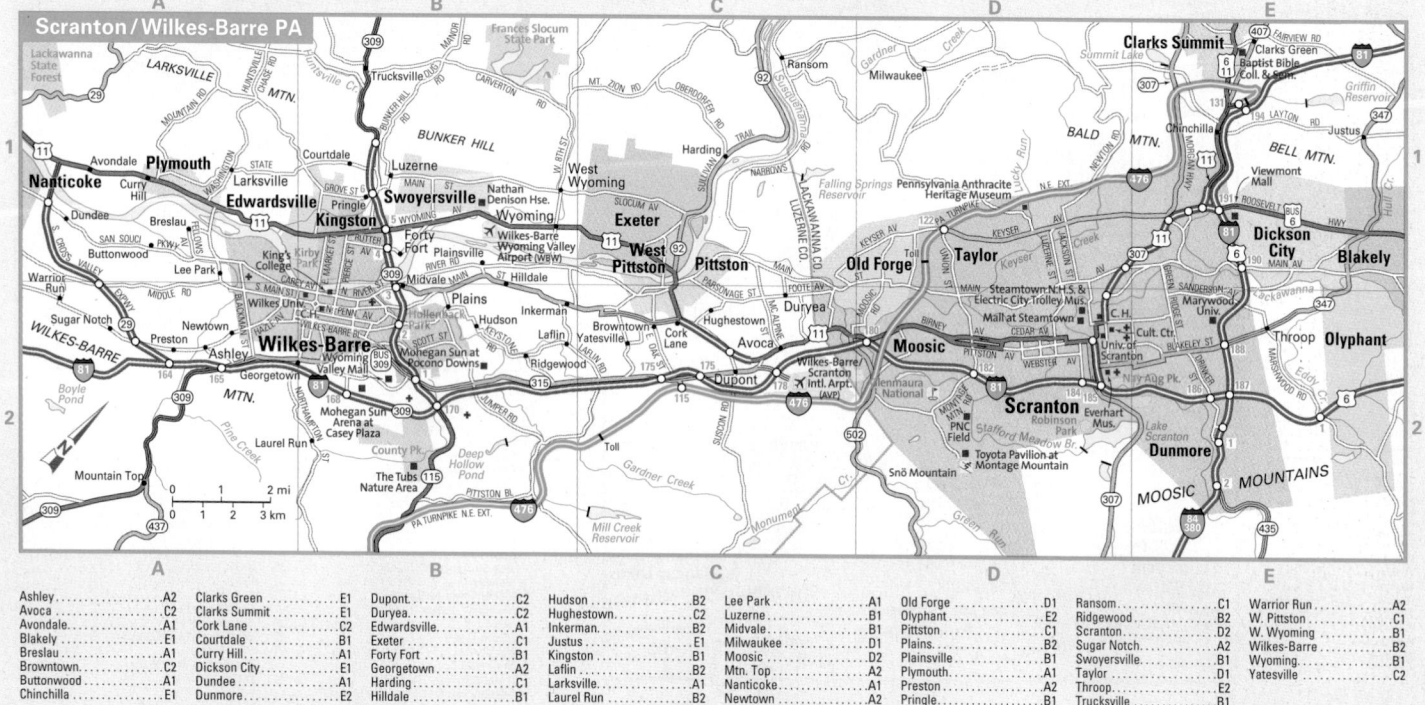

Figures after entries indicate population, page number, and grid reference.

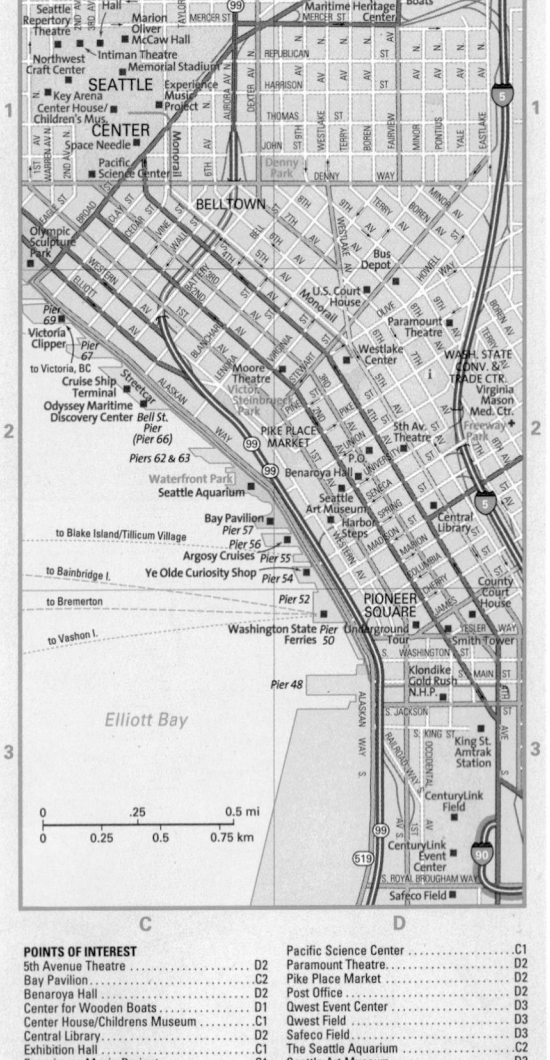

Seattle/Tacoma WA

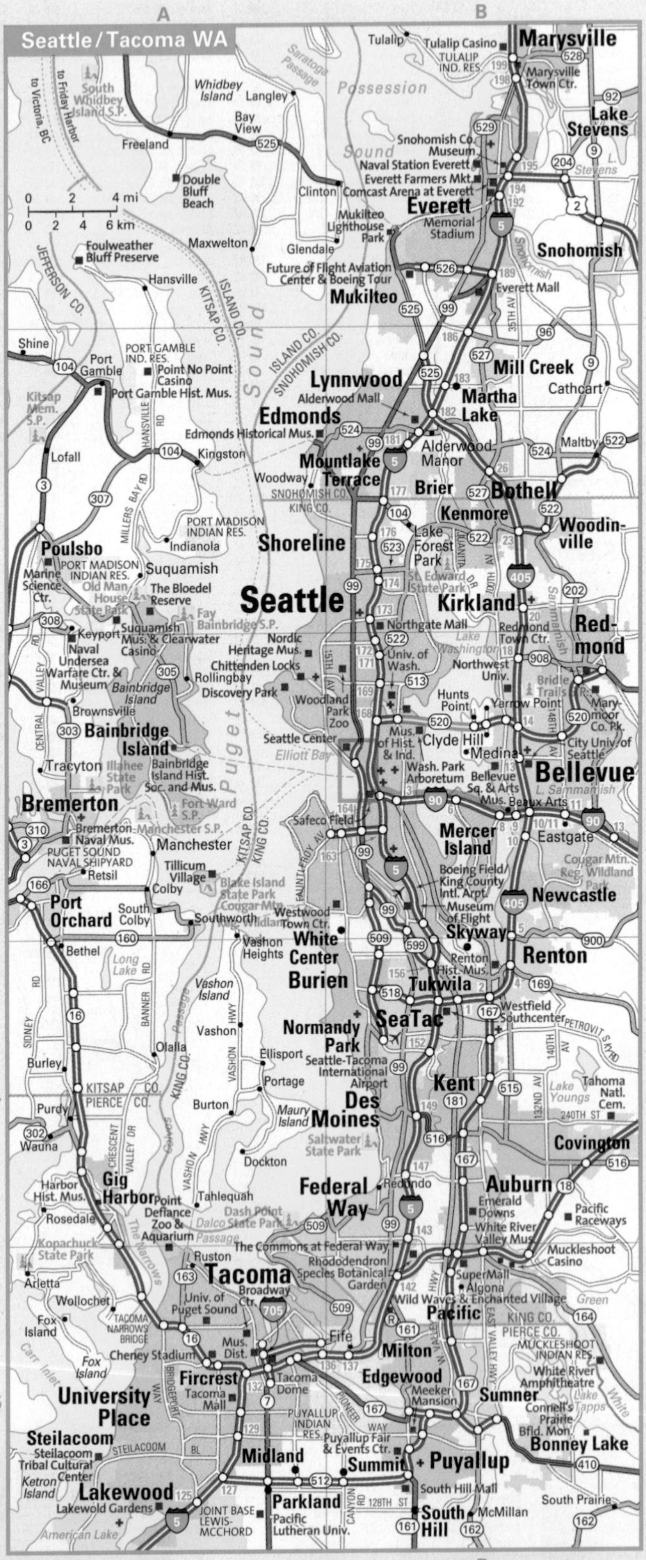

Downtown Seattle WA

Entries in **bold black** indicate counties or parishes.
Entries in **bold color** indicate cities with detailed inset maps.

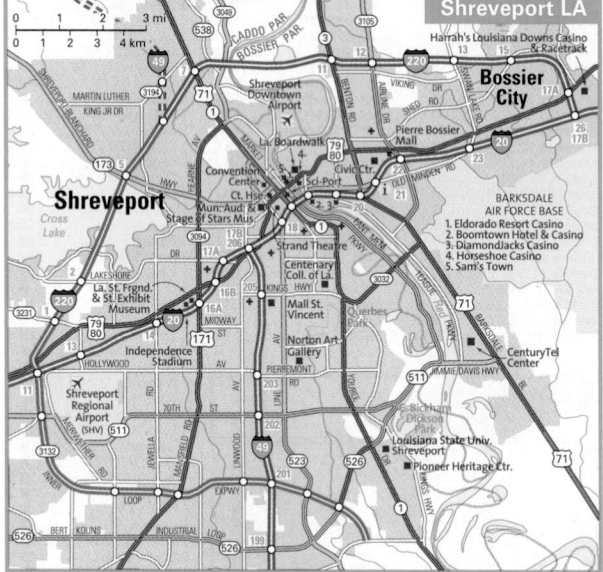

Shreveport LA

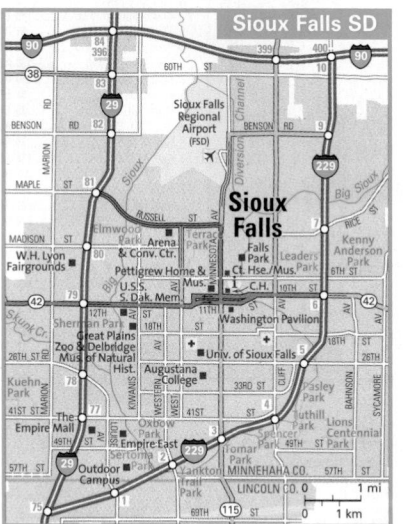

Sioux Falls SD

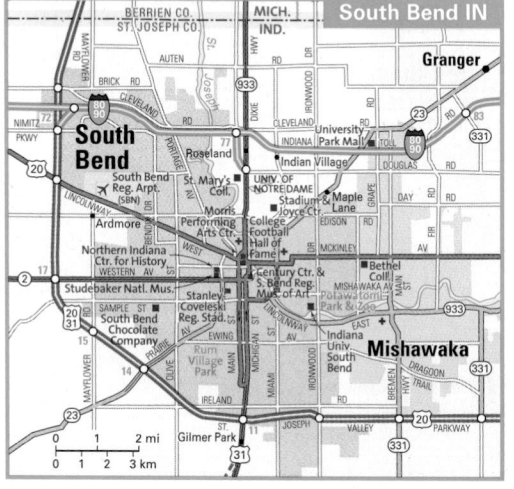

South Bend IN

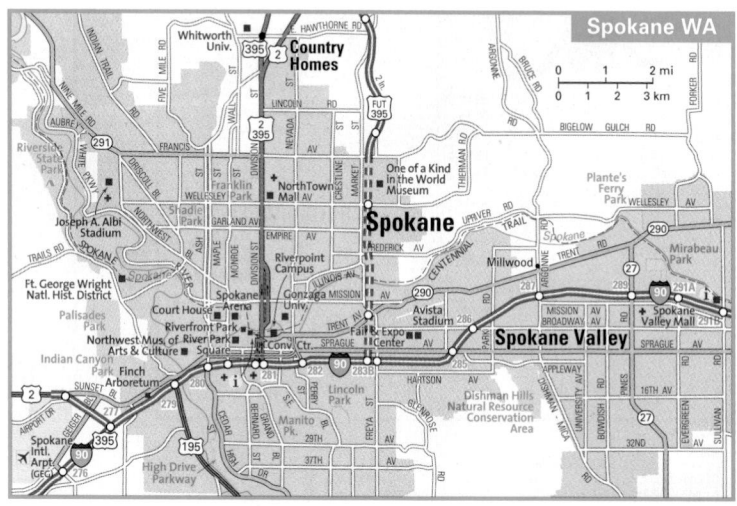

Spokane WA

Figures after entries indicate population, page number, and grid reference.

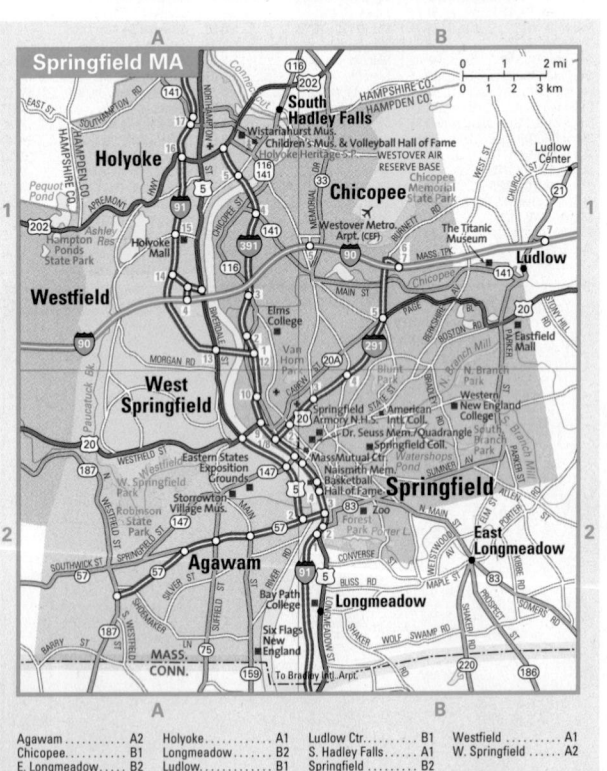

Springfield IL

Springfield MA

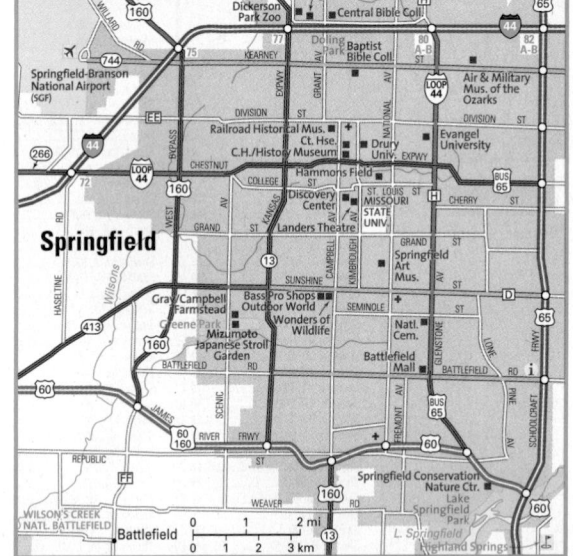

Springfield MO

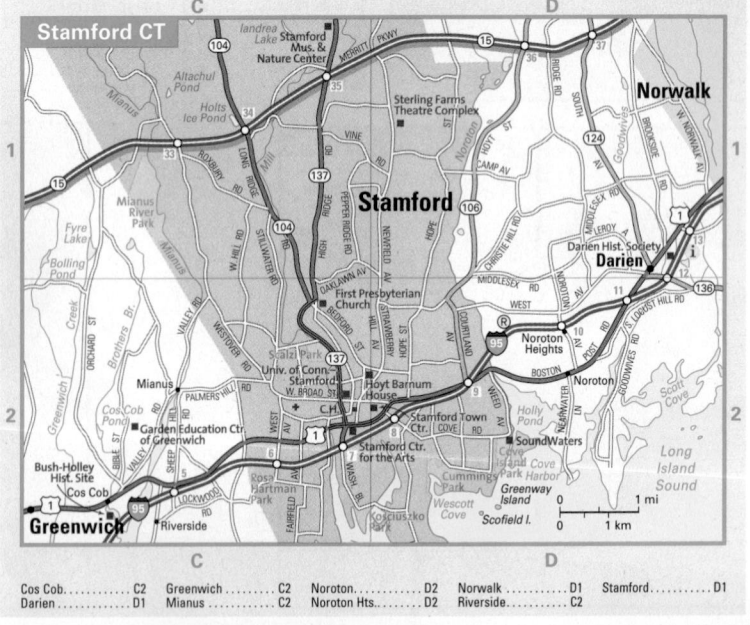

Stamford CT

Entries in **bold black** indicate counties or parishes.
Entries in **bold color** indicate cities with detailed inset maps.

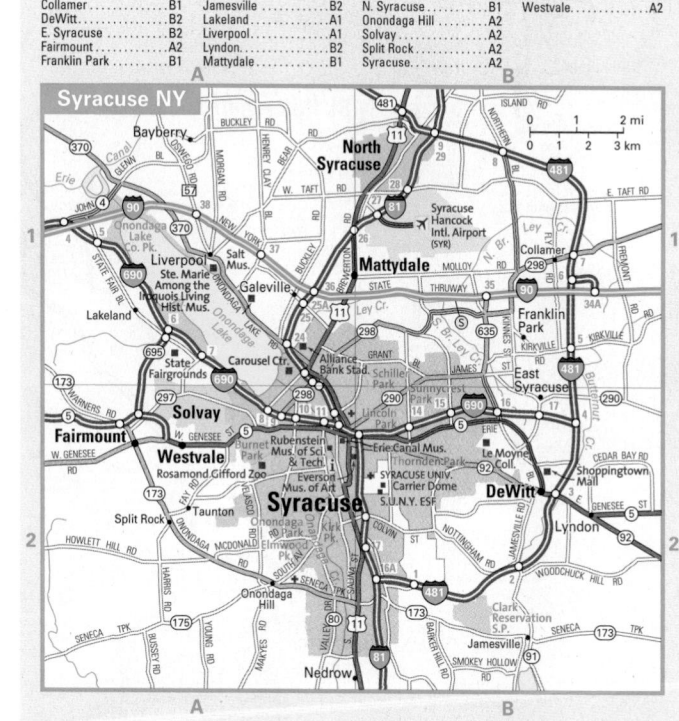

Syracuse NY

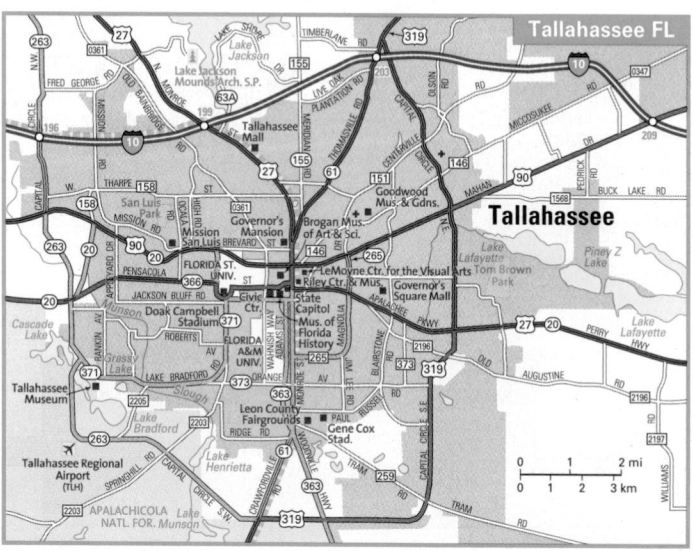

Stockton CA

Tallahassee FL

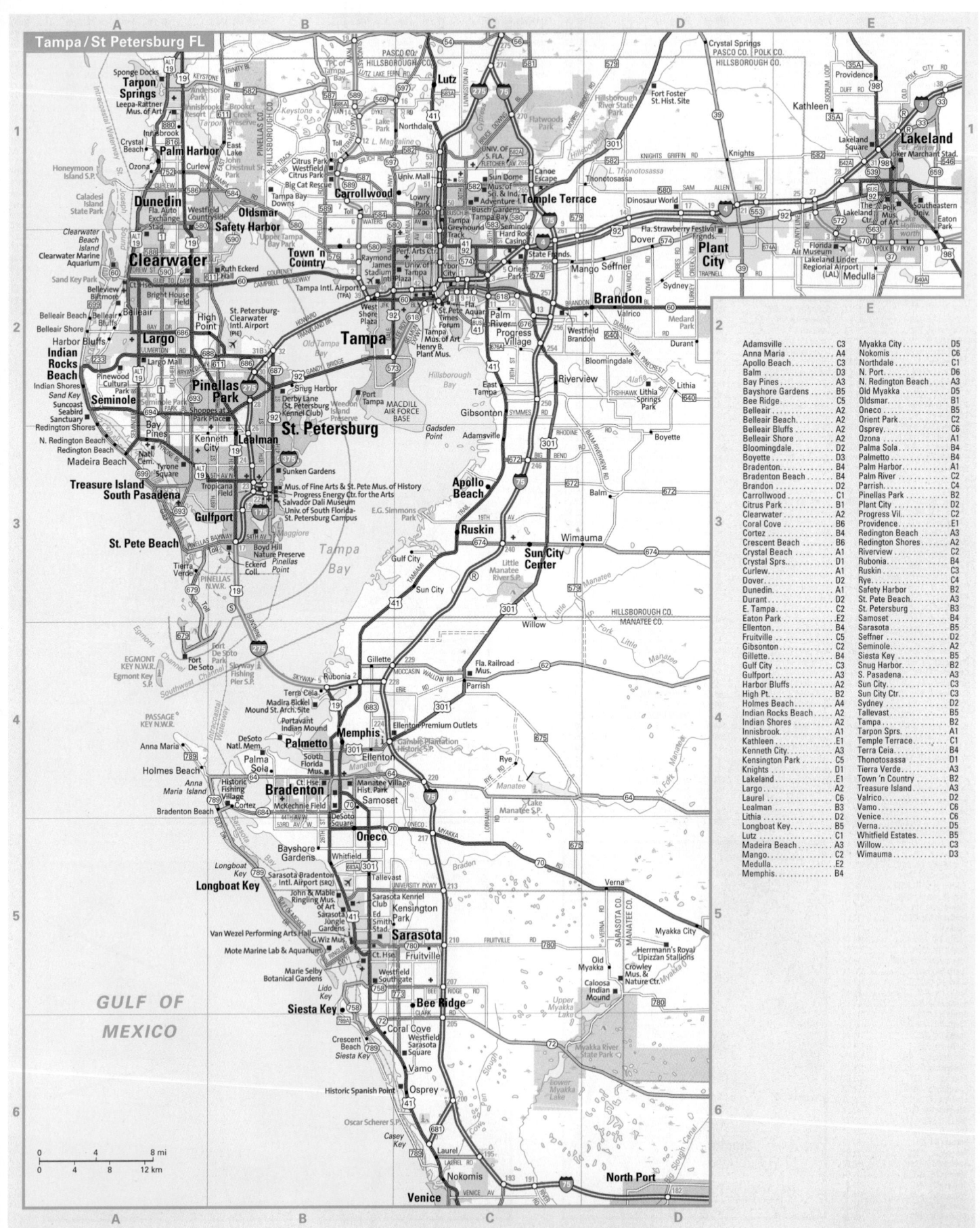

Tampa/St Petersburg FL

GULF OF MEXICO

267
Stillwater – Terre Haute

Entries in **bold black** indicate counties or parishes.
Entries in **bold color** indicate cities with detailed inset maps.

Stillwater ME, *1600* ... 83 D1
Stillwater MN, *18225* ... 67 D3
Stillwater NY, *1738* ... 94 B1
Stillwater OK, *45688* ... 51 F2
Stillwater Co. MT, *9117* ... 24 B1
Stilwell KS, *1200* ... 96 B3
Stilwell OK, *3949* ... 106 B4
Stimson Crossing WA, *773* ... 12 C2
Stinnett TX, *1881* ... 50 B2
Stinson Beach CA, *632* ... 259 A2
Stites ID, *221* ... 22 B1
Stockbridge GA, *25636* ... 120 C4
Stockbridge MA, *1947* ... 94 B2
Stockbridge MI, *1218* ... 76 B4
Stockbridge WI, *636* ... 74 C1
Stockdale TX, *1442* ... 61 E3
Stock Island FL, *3919* ... 142 C4
Stockton CA, *291707* ... 36 C3
Stockton IL, *1862* ... 74 A4
Stockton KS, *1329* ... 43 D2
Stockton MN, *697* ... 73 E1
Stockton MO, *1819* ... 106 C1
Stockton NJ, *538* ... 146 C1
Stockton UT, *616* ... 31 E4
Stockton Sprs. ME, *1481* ... 83 D2
Stockville NE, *25* ... 34 C4
Stoddard WI, *774* ... 73 F2
Stoddard Co. MO, *29968* ... 108 B2
Stokes Co. NC, *47401* ... 112 B3
Stokesdale NC, *5047* ... 112 B3
Stoneboro PA, *1051* ... 92 A2
Stone Co. AR, *12394* ... 107 E4
Stone Co. MS, *17786* ... 135 D1
Stone Co. MO, *32202* ... 107 D3
Stonega VA, *475* ... 111 D2
Stoneham MA, *21437* ... 151 D1
Stone Harbor NJ, *866* ... 104 C4
Stone Mtn. GA, *5802* ... 120 C4
Stone Park IL, *4946* ... 203 C4
Stone Ridge NY, *1173* ... 94 B3
Stoneville NC, *1056* ... 112 B3
Stonewall LA, *1814* ... 124 C3
Stonewall MS, *1088* ... 127 D3
Stonewall OK, *470* ... 51 F4
Stonewall Co. TX, *1490* ... 58 B2
Stonewood WV, *1806* ... 102 A2
Stoney Creek Mills PA, *5900* ... 146 B2
Stonington CT, *929* ... 149 F2
Stonington IL, *932* ... 98 C1
Stonington ME, *1152* ... 83 D2
Stony Brook NY, *13740* ... 149 D3
Stony Creek CT, *900* ... 149 E2
Stony Pt. NY, *12147* ... 148 B2
Stony Pt. NC, *1317* ... 112 A4
Storey Co. NV, *4010* ... 37 D2
Storm Lake IA, *10600* ... 72 A4
Stormstown PA, *2366* ... 92 C3
Storrs CT, *15344* ... 150 B3
Story WY, *828* ... 25 D3
Story City IA, *3431* ... 86 C1
Story Co. IA, *89542* ... 86 C1
Stottville NY, *1375* ... 94 B2
Stoughton MA, *26962* ... 151 D2
Stoughton WI, *12611* ... 74 B3
Stoutsville OH, *560* ... 101 D1
Stover MO, *1094* ... 97 D3
Stow OH, *34837* ... 91 E2
Stowe PA, *3695* ... 146 B2
Stowe VT, *495* ... 81 E2
Stowell TX, *1756* ... 132 C3
Strafford MO, *2358* ... 107 D2
Strafford Co. NH, *123143* ... 81 F4
Straitsville CT, *1000* ... 149 D1
Strasburg CO, *2447* ... 41 E1
Strasburg IL, *467* ... 98 C2
Strasburg ND, *409* ... 26 C1
Strasburg OH, *2608* ... 91 E4
Strasburg PA, *2809* ... 146 A3
Strasburg VA, *6398* ... 102 C2
Stratford CA, *1277* ... 44 C3
Stratford CT, *51384* ... 149 D2
Stratford IA, *743* ... 72 C4
Stratford NJ, *7040* ... 146 C3
Stratford OK, *1525* ... 51 F4
Stratford TX, *2017* ... 50 A2
Stratford WI, *1578* ... 68 A4
Stratham NH, *7255* ... 82 A4
Strathmoor Vil. KY, *648* ... 230 E2
Strathmore CA, *2819* ... 45 D3
Strathmore NJ, *7258* ... 147 E1
Stratmoor Hills CO, *6650* ... 205 D2
Stratton CO, *658* ... 42 A2
Stratton ME, *425* ... 82 B1
Stratton NE, *343* ... 42 B1
Strawberry AZ, *961* ... 47 E4
Strawberry Pt. IA, *1279* ... 73 E4
Strawn TX, *653* ... 59 D3
Streamwood IL, *39858* ... 203 B3
Streator IL, *14190* ... 88 C3
Streetsboro OH, *16028* ... 91 E2
Stroh IN, *700* ... 90 A2
Stromsburg NE, *1171* ... 35 E3
Strong AR, *558* ... 125 E1
Strong ME, *1259* ... 82 B1
Strong City KS, *485* ... 43 F3
Stronghurst IL, *883* ... 87 F3
Strongsville OH, *44750* ... 91 E2
Stroud OK, *2690* ... 51 F2
Stroudsburg PA, *5567* ... 93 F3
Strum WI, *1114* ... 67 F4
Struthers OH, *10713* ... 91 F3
Stryker OH, *1335* ... 90 B2
Stuart FL, *15593* ... 141 E4
Stuart IA, *1648* ... 86 B2
Stuart NE, *590* ... 35 D1
Stuart VA, *1408* ... 112 B3
Stuarts Draft VA, *9235* ... 102 C4
Sturbridge MA, *2253* ... 150 B2
Sturgeon MO, *872* ... 97 E2
Sturgeon Bay WI, *9144* ... 69 D4
Sturgis KY, *1898* ... 109 D1
Sturgis MI, *10994* ... 90 A1
Sturgis SD, *6627* ... 25 F3
Sturtevant WI, *6970* ... 74 C4
Stutsman Co. ND, *21100* ... 19 D3
Stuttgart AR, *9326* ... 117 F3
Suamico WI, *11346* ... 68 C4
Subiaco AR, *572* ... 116 C1
Sublette KS, *1453* ... 42 B4
Sublette Co. WY, *10247* ... 32 A1
Sublimity OR, *2681* ... 20 C2
Succasunna NJ, *9152* ... 148 A3
Sudan TX, *958* ... 57 F1
Sudbury MA, *17659* ... 150 C1
Suffern NY, *10723* ... 148 B2
Suffield CT, *14704* ... 150 A2
Suffolk VA, *84585* ... 113 F3
Suffolk Co. MA, *722023* ... 151 D1
Suffolk Co. NY, *1493350* ... 149 D3
Sugar City ID, *1514* ... 23 E4
Sugar Creek MO, *3345* ... 224 D3
Sugarcreek OH, *2220* ... 91 E4
Sugarcreek PA, *5294* ... 92 A2
Sugar Grove IL, *8997* ... 88 C1
Sugar Grove PA, *614* ... 92 B1
Sugar Grove VA, *758* ... 111 F2
Sugar Hill GA, *18522* ... 120 C3
Sugar Land TX, *78817* ... 132 A3
Sugarland Run VA, *11799* ... 144 A3
Sugar Loaf NY, *700* ... 148 A2
Sugar Notch PA, *989* ... 261 A2
Suisun City CA, *28111* ... 36 B3
Suitland MD, *25825* ... 144 B3
Sulligent AL, *1927* ... 119 D4
Sullivan IL, *4440* ... 98 C1
Sullivan IN, *4249* ... 99 E2
Sullivan MO, *7081* ... 97 F4
Sullivan WI, *669* ... 74 C3
Sullivan City TX, *4002* ... 63 E4
Sullivan Co. IN, *21475* ... 99 E2
Sullivan Co. MO, *6714* ... 87 D4
Sullivan Co. NH, *43742* ... 81 E4
Sullivan Co. NY, *77547* ... 94 A2
Sullivan Co. PA, *6428* ... 93 E2
Sullivan Co. TN, *156823* ... 111 E3
Sullivan's Island SC, *1791* ... 131 D2
Sully IA, *821* ... 87 D2
Sully Co. SD, *1373* ... 26 C3
Sulphur LA, *20410* ... 133 D2
Sulphur OK, *4929* ... 51 F4
Sulphur Rock AR, *456* ... 107 F4
Sulphur Sprs. AR, *1101* ... 106 B3
Sulphur Sprs. TX, *15449* ... 124 A1
Sultan WA, *4651* ... 12 C3
Sumas WA, *1307* ... 12 C1
Sumiton AL, *2520* ... 119 F4
Summerdale AL, *862* ... 135 E2
Summerfield NC, *10232* ... 112 B3
Summerland Key FL, *600* ... 143 D4
Summers Co. WV, *13927* ... 112 A1
Summerside OH, *5083* ... 204 C2
Summersville MO, *502* ... 107 F2
Summersville WV, *3572* ... 101 F4
Summerton SC, *1000* ... 122 B4
Summertown TN, *866* ... 119 E1
Summerville GA, *4534* ... 120 B3
Summerville SC, *43392* ... 131 D1
Summit AR, *604* ... 107 E3
Summit IL, *11054* ... 203 D5
Summit KY, *3400* ... 101 D3
Summit MS, *1705* ... 126 B4
Summit NJ, *21457* ... 148 A4
Summit SD, *288* ... 27 F2
Summit WA, *7985* ... 262 B5
Summit Co. CO, *27994* ... 41 D1
Summit Co. OH, *541781* ... 91 E3
Summit Co. UT, *36324* ... 31 F4
Summitville IN, *967* ... 89 F4
Sumner IL, *3174* ... 99 D3
Sumner IA, *2028* ... 73 E3
Sumner MS, *316* ... 118 B3
Sumner WA, *9451* ... 12 C3
Sumner Co. KS, *24132* ... 51 E1
Sumner Co. TN, *160645* ... 109 F3
Sumrall MS, *1421* ... 126 C4
Sumter SC, *40524* ... 122 B4
Sumter Co. AL, *13763* ... 127 E2
Sumter Co. FL, *93420* ... 140 C1
Sumter Co. GA, *32819* ... 129 D3
Sumter Co. SC, *107456* ... 122 B4
Sun LA, *470* ... 134 C1
Sunapee NH, *3365* ... 81 E4
Sunbright TN, *552* ... 110 B3
Sunburst MT, *375* ... 15 E1
Sunbury OH, *4389* ... 91 D4
Sunbury PA, *9905* ... 93 D3
Sun City AZ, *37499* ... 54 C1
Sun City Ctr. FL, *19258* ... 140 C3
Sun City West AZ, *24535* ... 249 A1
Suncook NH, *5379* ... 81 F4
Sundance WY, *1182* ... 25 F3
Sunderland MD, *1400* ... 144 C4
Sunderland MA, *3777* ... 150 A1
Sundown TX, *1397* ... 57 F1
Sunfield MI, *578* ... 76 A4
Sunfish Lake MN, *521* ... 235 D3
Sunflower MS, *1159* ... 118 A4
Sunflower Co. MS, *29450* ... 118 A4
Sun Lakes AZ, *13975* ... 54 C2
Sunland Park NM, *14106* ... 56 C4
Sunman IN, *1049* ... 100 A2
Sunnybrook MD, *2300* ... 144 C1
Sunny Isles Beach FL, *20832* ... 233 C3
Sunnyside UT, *377* ... 39 F1
Sunnyside WA, *15858* ... 13 E4
Sunnyvale CA, *140081* ... 36 B4
Sunol CA, *913* ... 259 E4
Sun Prairie WI, *29364* ... 74 B3
Sunray TX, *1926* ... 50 A2
Sunrise FL, *84439* ... 143 E1
Sunrise Beach Vil. TX, *713* ... 61 D1
Sunset LA, *2897* ... 133 F2
Sunset UT, *5122* ... 244 A2
Sunset Beach NC, *3572* ... 123 D4
Sunset Hills MO, *8496* ... 256 B3
Sun Valley ID, *1406* ... 22 C4
Superior AZ, *2837* ... 55 D2
Superior CO, *12483* ... 209 B1
Superior MT, *812* ... 14 C3
Superior NE, *1957* ... 43 E1
Superior WI, *27244* ... 64 C4
Superior WY, *336* ... 32 B2
Supreme LA, *1052* ... 134 A3
Suquamish WA, *4140* ... 262 A2
Surf City NJ, *1205* ... 147 E4
Surf City NC, *1853* ... 123 E3
Surfside FL, *5744* ... 233 C4
Surfside Beach SC, *3837* ... 123 D4
Surfside Beach TX, *482* ... 133 E4
Surgoinsville TN, *1801* ... 111 D3
Suring WI, *544* ... 68 C4
Surprise AZ, *117517* ... 54 C1
Surrey ND, *934* ... 18 B2
Surry VA, *262* ... 113 F2
Surry Co. NC, *73673* ... 112 A3
Surry Co. VA, *7058* ... 113 F2
Susan VA, *244* ... 113 F1
Susan Moore AL, *763* ... 119 F3
Susanville CA, *17947* ... 29 D4
Susquehanna PA, *1643* ... 93 F1
Susquehanna Co. PA, *43356* ... 93 E2
Sussex NJ, *2130* ... 148 A2
Sussex VA, *256* ... 113 E2
Sussex WI, *10518* ... 74 C3
Sussex Co. DE, *197145* ... 145 F4
Sussex Co. NJ, *149265* ... 148 A2
Sussex Co. VA, *12087* ... 113 E2
Sutcliffe NV, *253* ... 37 D1
Sutherland IA, *649* ... 72 A3
Sutherland NE, *1286* ... 34 B3
Sutherlin OR, *7810* ... 20 B4
Sutter CA, *2904* ... 36 B2
Sutter Co. CA, *94737* ... 36 B2
Sutter Creek CA, *2501* ... 36 C3
Sutton AK, *1447* ... 154 C3
Sutton MA, *8963* ... 150 C2
Sutton NE, *1502* ... 35 E4
Sutton WV, *994* ... 101 F3
Sutton Co. TX, *4128* ... 60 B1
Suttons Bay MI, *618* ... 69 F4
Suwanee GA, *15355* ... 120 C3
Suwannee Co. FL, *41551* ... 138 B2
Swain Co. NC, *13981* ... 121 D1
Swainsboro GA, *7277* ... 129 F2
Swampscott MA, *13787* ... 151 D1
Swannanoa NC, *4576* ... 121 E1
Swann Keys DE, *700* ... 145 F4
Swanquarter NC, *324* ... 115 E3
Swansboro NC, *2663* ... 115 D4
Swansea IL, *13430* ... 98 B3
Swansea SC, *827* ... 122 A4
Swanton OH, *3690* ... 90 B2
Swanton VT, *2386* ... 81 D1
Swan Valley ID, *204* ... 23 F4
Swarthmore PA, *6194* ... 146 C3
Swartz LA, *4536* ... 125 F2
Swartz Creek MI, *5758* ... 76 B3
Swayzee IN, *981* ... 89 F4
Swea City IA, *536* ... 72 B2
Swedesboro NJ, *2584* ... 146 C4
Sweeny TX, *3684* ... 132 A4
Sweet Briar VA, *750* ... 112 C1
Sweet Grass Co. MT, *3651* ... 24 A1
Sweet Home OR, *8925* ... 20 C3
Sweetser IN, *1229* ... 89 F3
Sweet Sprs. MO, *1484* ... 97 D3
Sweetwater FL, *13499* ... 143 E2
Sweetwater TN, *5764* ... 120 C1
Sweetwater TX, *10906* ... 58 B3
Sweetwater Co. WY, *43806* ... 32 B2
Swepsonville NC, *1154* ... 112 C4
Swift Co. MN, *9783* ... 66 A3
Swifton AR, *798* ... 107 F4
Swifts Beach MA, *2700* ... 151 E3
Swift Trail Jct. AZ, *2935* ... 55 E2
Swiftwater PA, *800* ... 93 F3
Swink CO, *617* ... 41 F3
Swisher IA, *879* ... 87 E1
Swisher Co. TX, *7854* ... 50 A4
Swissvale PA, *8983* ... 250 C2
Switzer WV, *595* ... 111 E1
Switzerland Co. IN, *10613* ... 100 B3
Swoyersville PA, *5062* ... 93 E2
Sycamore GA, *711* ... 129 D4
Sycamore IL, *17519* ... 88 C1
Sycamore OH, *861* ... 90 C3
Sycaway NY, *3000* ... 188 E2
Sykesville MD, *4436* ... 144 B1
Sykesville PA, *1157* ... 92 B3
Sylacauga AL, *12749* ... 128 A1
Sylva NC, *2588* ... 121 D1
Sylvan Beach NY, *897* ... 79 E3
Sylvania AL, *1837* ... 120 A2
Sylvania GA, *2956* ... 130 B2
Sylvania OH, *18965* ... 90 C2
Sylvan Lake MI, *1720* ... 210 B1
Sylvan Lake NY, *1200* ... 148 C1
Sylvan Shores FL, *2424* ... 141 D3
Sylvan Sprs. AL, *1542* ... 195 D2
Sylvester GA, *6188* ... 129 D4
Symsonia KY, *615* ... 109 D2
Syosset NY, *18829* ... 148 C3
Syracuse IN, *2810* ... 89 F2
Syracuse KS, *1812* ... 42 B3
Syracuse NE, *1942* ... 35 F4
Syracuse NY, *145170* ... 79 D3
Syracuse OH, *826* ... 101 E2
Syracuse UT, *24331* ... 31 E3

T

Tabor IA, *1040* ... 86 A3
Tabor SD, *423* ... 35 E1
Tabor City NC, *2511* ... 123 D3
Tacna AZ, *602* ... 54 A2
Tacoma WA, *198397* ... 12 C3
Taft CA, *9327* ... 52 B1
Taft FL, *2205* ... 246 C4
Taft TX, *3048* ... 61 E4
Tahlequah OK, *15753* ... 106 B4
Tahoe City CA, *1761* ... 37 D2
Tahoka TX, *2673* ... 58 A2
Taholah WA, *840* ... 12 A3
Takoma Park MD, *16715* ... 270 D2
Talbot Co. GA, *6865* ... 128 C2
Talbot Co. MD, *37782* ... 145 D3
Talbott TN, *1400* ... 111 D4
Talbotton GA, *970* ... 128 C2
Talco TX, *516* ... 124 B1
Talcottville CT, *4500* ... 150 A3
Talent OR, *6066* ... 28 B2
Taliaferro Co. GA, *1717* ... 121 E4
Talihina OK, *1114* ... 116 A2
Talkeetna AK, *876* ... 154 C3
Talladega AL, *15676* ... 120 A4
Talladega Co. AL, *82291* ... 128 A1
Tallahassee FL, *181376* ... 137 E2
Tallahatchie Co. MS, *15378* ... 118 B4
Tallapoosa GA, *3170* ... 120 B4
Tallapoosa Co. AL, *41616* ... 128 B1
Tallassee AL, *4819* ... 128 A2
Tallevast FL, *1100* ... 266 B5
Talleyville DE, *6300* ... 146 B3
Tallmadge OH, *17537* ... 91 E3
Tallula IL, *488* ... 98 B1
Tallulah LA, *7335* ... 126 A2
Talmage CA, *1130* ... 36 A2
Talmo GA, *180* ... 121 D3
Taloga OK, *299* ... 51 D2
Talty TX, *1535* ... 59 F2
Tama IA, *2877* ... 87 D1
Tama Co. IA, *17767* ... 87 D1
Tamalpais Valley CA, *10691* ... 259 A2
Tamaqua PA, *7107* ... 93 E3
Tamarac FL, *60427* ... 143 E1
Tamaroa IL, *638* ... 98 B4
Tamms IL, *632* ... 108 C2
Tampa FL, *335709* ... 140 B2
Tampico IL, *790* ... 88 B2
Taney Co. MO, *51675* ... 107 D3
Taneytown MD, *6728* ... 103 E1
Tangelo Park FL, *2231* ... 246 B3
Tangent OR, *1164* ... 20 B3
Tangier VA, *727* ... 114 B2
Tangipahoa LA, *748* ... 134 B1
Tangipahoa Par. LA, *121097* ... 134 B1
Tanner AL, *900* ... 119 F2
Tannersville PA, *1000* ... 93 F3
Tanque Verde AZ, *16901* ... 55 D3
Tantallon MD, *7900* ... 144 B4
Taos MO, *878* ... 97 E3
Taos NM, *5716* ... 49 D1
Taos Co. NM, *32937* ... 49 D1
Tappahannock VA, *2375* ... 103 E4
Tappan NY, *6613* ... 148 B3
Tappen ND, *197* ... 18 C4
Tara Hills CA, *5126* ... 259 B1
Tarboro NC, *11415* ... 113 E4
Tarentum PA, *4530* ... 92 A3
Tariffville CT, *1324* ... 150 A3
Tarkiln RI, *950* ... 150 C2
Tarkio MO, *1583* ... 86 A4
Tarpon Sprs. FL, *23484* ... 140 B2
Tarrant AL, *6397* ... 119 F4
Tarrant Co. TX, *1809034* ... 59 E2
Tarrytown NY, *11277* ... 148 B3
Tasso TN, *1300* ... 120 B1
Tatamy PA, *1203* ... 93 F3
Tate Co. MS, *28886* ... 118 B2
Tattnall Co. GA, *25520* ... 129 F3
Tatum NM, *798* ... 57 F2
Tatum TX, *1385* ... 124 B2
Taunton MA, *55874* ... 151 D3
Tavares FL, *13951* ... 140 C1
Tavernier FL, *2136* ... 143 E4
Tawas City MI, *1827* ... 76 B1
Taylor AL, *2375* ... 136 C1
Taylor AZ, *4112* ... 47 F4
Taylor AR, *566* ... 125 D1
Taylor MI, *63131* ... 90 C1
Taylor NE, *190* ... 35 D2
Taylor PA, *6263* ... 261 D1
Taylor TX, *15191* ... 61 E1
Taylor Co. FL, *22570* ... 137 F3
Taylor Co. GA, *8906* ... 129 D2
Taylor Co. IA, *6317* ... 86 B3
Taylor Co. KY, *24512* ... 110 B1
Taylor Co. TX, *131506* ... 58 C3
Taylor Co. WV, *16895* ... 102 A2
Taylor Co. WI, *20689* ... 67 F3
Taylor Creek FL, *4348* ... 141 E4
Taylor Lake Vil. TX, *3544* ... 132 B3
Taylor Mill KY, *6604* ... 204 B3
Taylors SC, *21617* ... 121 F2
Taylors Falls MN, *976* ... 67 D3
Taylor Sprs. IL, *583* ... 98 B2
Taylorsville IN, *919* ... 99 F2
Taylorsville KY, *763* ... 100 A4
Taylorsville MD, *900* ... 144 B1
Taylorsville MS, *1353* ... 126 C3
Taylorsville NC, *2098* ... 111 F4
Taylorsville UT, *58652* ... 257 A2
Taylortown NJ, *1200* ... 148 A3
Taylortown NC, *722* ... 122 C1
Taylorville IL, *11246* ... 98 B1
Tazewell TN, *2218* ... 111 D3
Tazewell VA, *4627* ... 111 F2
Tazewell Co. IL, *135394* ... 88 B4
Tazewell Co. VA, *45078* ... 111 F2
Tchula MS, *2096* ... 126 B1
Tea SD, *3806* ... 27 F4
Teague TX, *3560* ... 59 F4
Teaneck NJ, *38633* ... 148 B3
Teaticket MA, *1692* ... 151 E4
Teays Val. WV, *13175* ... 101 E3
Tecumseh MI, *8521* ... 90 B1
Tecumseh NE, *1677* ... 35 F4
Tecumseh OK, *6457* ... 51 F3
Teec Nos Pos AZ, *730* ... 48 A1
Tega Cay SC, *7620* ... 122 A2
Tehachapi CA, *14414* ... 52 C1
Tehama CA, *418* ... 36 B1
Tehama Co. CA, *63463* ... 36 B1
Tekamah NE, *1736* ... 35 F2
Tekoa WA, *778* ... 14 B3
Tekonsha MI, *717* ... 90 A1
Telfair Co. GA, *16500* ... 129 E3
Telford PA, *4872* ... 146 C2
Tell City IN, *7272* ... 99 E4
Teller Co. CO, *23350* ... 41 E2
Tellico Plains TN, *880* ... 120 C1
Telluride CO, *2325* ... 40 B3
Temecula CA, *100097* ... 53 D3
Tempe AZ, *161719* ... 54 C1
Temperance MI, *8517* ... 90 C1
Temple GA, *4228* ... 120 B4
Temple OK, *1002* ... 51 E4
Temple PA, *1877* ... 146 B1
Temple TX, *66102* ... 59 E4
Temple City CA, *35558* ... 228 E2
Temple Hills MD, *7852* ... 270 E5
Temple Terrace FL, *24541* ... 140 C2
Templeton CA, *7674* ... 44 C4
Templeton MA, *8013* ... 95 D1
Tenafly NJ, *14488* ... 148 B3
Tenaha TX, *1160* ... 124 C3
Tenants Harbor ME, *500* ... 82 C3
Tenino WA, *1695* ... 12 C4
Tennent NJ, *1100* ... 147 E2
Tennessee Ridge TN, *1368* ... 109 D3
Tennille GA, *1539* ... 129 E1
Tensas Par. LA, *5252* ... 125 F3
Ten Sleep WY, *260* ... 24 C3
Tequesta FL, *5629* ... 141 F4
Terra Alta WV, *1477* ... 102 B2
Terra Bella CA, *3310* ... 45 D4
Terrace Hts. WA, *6937* ... 13 D4
Terrace Park OH, *2251* ... 204 C2
Terrebonne OR, *1257* ... 21 D3
Terrebonne Par. LA, *111860* ... 134 A4
Terre Haute IN, *60785* ... 99 E2

Harbor View B1	Moline B2	Perrysburg A2	Toledo A1
Holland A2	Northwood B2	Rossford B2	Walbridge B2
Lime City B2	Oregon B1	Stony Ridge B2	
Maumee A2	Ottawa Hills A1	Sylvania A1	

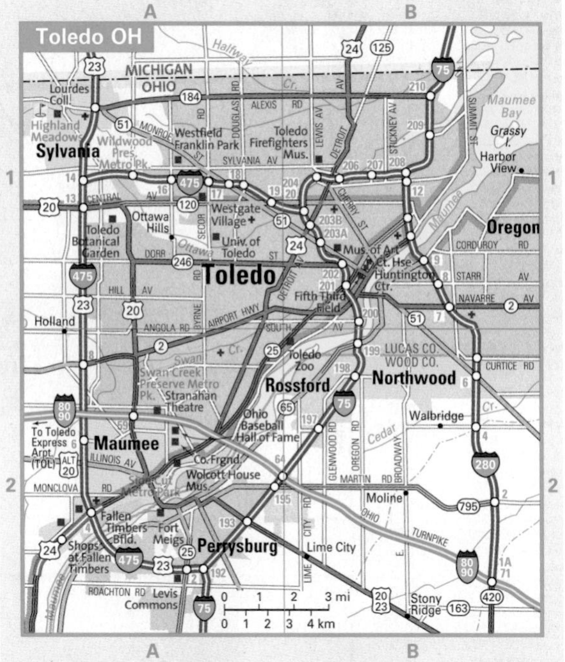
Toledo OH
A
B
1
2
MICHIGAN
OHIO
Lourdes Coll.
Sylvania
Westfield Franklin Park
Toledo Firefighters Mus.
Maumee Bay
Harbor View
Ottawa Hills
Westgate Village
Univ. of Toledo
Toledo Botanical Garden
Toledo
Mus. of Art
Ct. Hse.
Huntington Ctr.
Fifth Third Field
Oregon
Holland
Toledo Zoo
Swan Creek Preserve Metro Pk.
Stranahan Theatre
Rossford
Northwood
LUCAS CO.
WOOD CO.
Ohio Baseball Hall of Fame
Walbridge
Maumee
Co. Frgd.
Wolcott House Mus.
Moline
Fallen Timbers Btfld.
Fort Meigs
Perrysburg
Lime City
Shops at Fallen Timbers
Levis Commons
Stony Ridge
0 1 2 3 mi
0 1 2 3 4 km

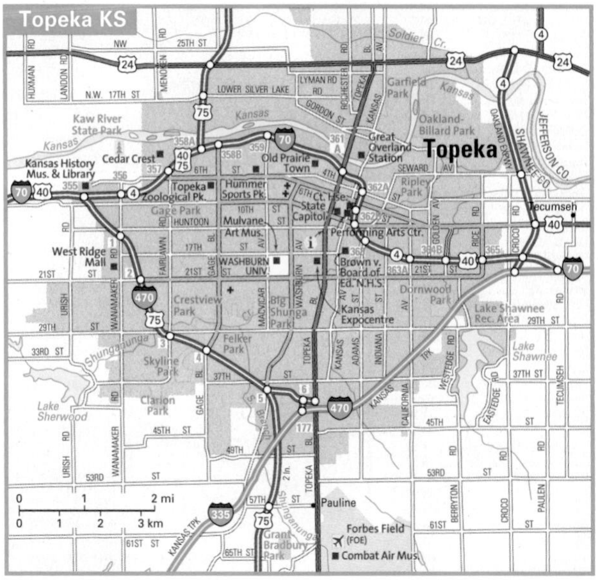
Topeka KS
Kaw River State Park
Kansas History Mus. & Library
Cedar Crest
Old Prairie Town
Topeka Zoological Pk.
Hummer Sports Pk.
Garfield Park
Oakland-Billard Park
Great Overland Station
Topeka
Ripley Park
Gage Park
State Capitol
Mulvane Art Mus.
Performing Arts Ctr.
West Ridge Mall
Washburn Univ.
Brown v. Board of Ed. N.H.S.
Dornwood Park
Crestview Park
Big Shunga Park
Kansas Expocentre
Lake Shawnee Rec. Area
Tecumseh
Felker Park
Skyline Park
Clarion Park
Lake Sherwood
Lake Shawnee
Pauline
Forbes Field (FOE)
Combat Air Mus.
0 1 2 mi
0 1 2 3 km

268

TERRE HILL–TROY

Figures after entries indicate population, page number, and grid reference.

Terre Hill PA, 1295.........146 A2
Terrell TX, 15816............59 F2
Terrell Co. GA, 9315......128 C4
Terrell Co. TX, 984.........60 A2
Terrell Hills TX, 4878.....257 E2
Terry MS, 1063.............126 B3
Terry MT, 605................17 E4
Terry Co. TX, 12651.......57 F2
Terrytown LA, 23319.......134 B3
Terrytown NE, 1198..........33 F2
Terryville CT, 5387........149 D1
Terryville NY, 11849.......149 D3
Tesuque NM, 925............49 D2
Teton ID, 735................23 F4
Teton Co. ID, 10170.......23 F4
Teton Co. MT, 6073........15 E3
Teton Co. WY, 21294.......24 A3
Tetonia ID, 269..............23 F4
Teutopolis IL, 1530.........98 C2
Tewksbury MA, 28961.......95 E1
Texarkana AR, 29919.......116 C4
Texarkana TX, 36411.......116 C4
Texas MA, 1300............150 B2
Texas City TX, 45099......132 B4
Texas Co. MO, 26008......107 E1
Texas Co. OK, 20640.......50 A1
Texhoma OK, 926............50 A1
Texico NM, 1130............49 F4
Thatcher AZ, 4865..........55 F3
Thaxton MS, 643...........118 C3
Thayer IL, 693..............98 B1
Thayer KS, 497............106 A1
Thayer MO, 2243...........107 F3
Thayer Co. NE, 5228.......35 E4
Thayne WY, 366.............31 F1
The Colony TX, 36328.......59 F2
The Dalles OR, 13620.......21 D2
Thedford NE, 188...........34 C2
The Hills TX, 2617..........61 E1
The Pinery CO, 10517......41 E1
The Plains OH, 3080.......101 E2
Theodore AL, 6130........135 E2
Theresa NY, 863.............79 E1
Theresa WI, 1262...........74 C2
Thermal CA, 2865...........53 E3
Thermalito CA, 6646........36 C1
Thermopolis WY, 3009......24 C4
The Village OH, 8929.......51 E3
The Vil. of Indian Hill OH, 5785...204 C2
The Woodlands TX, 93847...132 A2
Thibodaux LA, 14566......134 A3
Thief River Falls MN, 8573...19 F2
Thiells NY, 5032...........148 B2
Thiensville WI, 3235........74 C3
Thomas OK, 1181............51 D2
Thomas WV, 586...........102 B2
Thomasboro IL, 1188........88 C4
Thomas Co. GA, 44720....137 D5
Thomas Co. KS, 7900......42 B2
Thomas Co. NE, 647.......34 C2
Thomaston CT, 1910.......149 D1
Thomaston GA, 9170.......128 C1
Thomaston ME, 1875........82 C3
Thomaston NY, 2617........241 G3
Thomasville AL, 4209......127 E3
Thomasville GA, 18413....137 E1
Thomasville NC, 26757....112 B4
Thompson IA, 502...........72 C2
Thompson ND, 986..........19 E3
Thompson Falls MT, 1313...14 C3
Thompson's Sta. TN, 2194...109 F4
Thompsontown PA, 697.....93 D4
Thompsonville CT, 8577...150 A2
Thompsonville IL, 543......98 C4
Thompsonville MI, 441......69 E4
Thomson GA, 6778.........121 E4
Thomson IL, 590............88 A1
Thonotosassa FL, 13014...140 C2
Thoreau NM, 1865...........48 B3
Thorndale PA, 3407........146 B3
Thorndale TX, 1336.........61 E1
Thorne Bay AK, 471.......155 E4
Thornton AR, 407..........117 E4
Thornton CA, 1131..........36 C3
Thornton CO, 118772.......41 E1
Thornton TX, 526...........59 F4
Thorntown IN, 6291.........89 E4
Thornville OH, 991.........101 D1
Thornwood NY, 3759......148 B2
Thorofare NJ, 1500.......146 C3
Thorp WI, 1621.............67 F4
Thorsby AL, 1980..........127 F1
Thousand Oaks CA, 126683...52 B2
Thousand Palms CA, 7715...53 E3
Thrall TX, 839..............61 E1
Three Bridges NJ, 850....147 D1
Three Forks MT, 1869......23 F1
Three Oaks MI, 1622.......89 E1
Three Pts. AZ, 5581........55 D3
Three Rivers CA, 2182......45 D3
Three Rivers MA, 2939....150 A2
Three Rivers MI, 7811......89 F1
Three Rivers TX, 1848......61 D4
Three Way TN, 1709.......108 C4
Throckmorton TX, 828......59 D2
Throckmorton Co. TX, 1641...59 D2
Throop PA, 4088..........261 D2
Thurmont MD, 6170........144 A1
Thurston OH, 604..........101 D1
Thurston Co. NE, 6940.....35 F2
Thurston Co. WA, 252264...12 C4
Tiana NY, 2200............149 E3
Tiburon CA, 8962..........259 B2

Tice FL, 4470.............142 C1
Tickfaw LA, 694...........134 B2
Ticonderoga NY, 3382......81 D3
Tidioute PA, 688...........92 B2
Tierra Amarilla NM, 382....48 C1
Tierra Verde FL, 3721....266 A3
Tieton WA, 1191............13 D4
Tiffin IA, 1947..............87 E1
Tiffin OH, 17963............90 C3
Tift Co. GA, 40118.........129 E4
Tifton GA, 16350...........129 E4
Tigard OR, 48035...........20 C2
Tigerton WI, 741............68 B4
Tignall GA, 546............121 E4
Tiki Island TX, 968.......132 B4
Tilden IL, 934..............98 B4
Tilden NE, 953..............35 E2
Tilden TX, 261.............61 D4
Tilghman MD, 784.........145 D4
Tillamook OR, 4935.........20 B2
Tillamook Co. OR, 25250...20 B1
Tillman Co. OK, 7992.......51 D4
Tillmans Corner AL, 17398...135 E2
Tillson NY, 1586...........94 B3
Tilton IL, 2724..............89 D4
Tilton NH, 3567.............81 F4
Tiltonsville OH, 1372.......91 F4
Timber Lake SD, 443........26 C2
Timberlake VA, 12183.....112 C1
Timberon NM, 348..........57 D2
Timberville VA, 2522......102 C3

Timmonsville SC, 2320....122 C3
Timpson TX, 1155.........124 C3
Tinley Park IL, 56703......89 D2
Tinton Falls NJ, 17892....147 E2
Tioga LA, 1500............125 E4
Tioga ND, 1230.............18 A2
Tioga PA, 666..............93 D1
Tioga TX, 803..............59 F1
Tioga Co. NY, 51125.......93 E1
Tioga Co. PA, 41981........93 D1
Tionesta PA, 483............92 A2
Tippah Co. MS, 22232.....118 C2
Tipp City OH, 9689........100 B1
Tippecanoe Co. IN, 172780...89 E4
Tipton CA, 2543............45 D3
Tipton IN, 5106............89 F4

Tipton IA, 3221............87 F1
Tipton MO, 3262............97 D3
Tipton OK, 847.............51 D4
Tipton PA, 1083............92 C3
Tipton Co. IN, 15936......89 F4
Tipton Co. TN, 61081.....118 B1
Tiptonville TN, 4464......108 B3
Tishomingo OK, 3034.......51 F4
Tishomingo Co. MS, 19593...119 D2
Tiskilwa IL, 829............88 B2
Titonka IA, 476.............72 C3
Titus Co. TX, 32334......124 B1
Titusville FL, 43761......141 E1
Titusville NJ, 800.........147 D2
Titusville PA, 5601.........92 A2
Tivoli NY, 1118.............94 B2
Toano VA, 1400............113 F1
Toast NC, 1450............112 A3
Tobaccoville NC, 2441....112 A3
Toccoa GA, 8491..........121 D2
Todd Co. KY, 12460......109 E2
Todd Co. MN, 24895......66 B1
Todd Co. SD, 9612........34 C1
Togiak AK, 817............154 B3
Tohatchi NM, 808..........48 A2
Tok AK, 1258..............155 D2
Toksook Bay AK, 590......154 B3
Toledo IL, 1238.............99 D2
Toledo IA, 2341.............87 D1
Toledo OH, 287208.........90 C2
Toledo OR, 3465............20 B3
Toledo WA, 725............12 C4
Tolland CT, 1814..........150 A3
Tolland Co. CT, 152691...149 E1
Tolles CT, 650.............149 D1
Tolleson AZ, 6545.........249 A2
Tolono IL, 3447.............99 D1
Toluca IL, 1414.............88 B3
Tomah WI, 9093.............74 A1
Tomahawk WI, 3397........68 B3
Tomball TX, 10753.........132 A2
Tom Bean TX, 1045..........59 F1
Tombstone AZ, 1380.........55 E4
Tome NM, 1867..............48 C4
Tom Green Co. TX, 110224...58 C4
Tomkins Cove NY, 1400....148 B2
Tompkins Co. NY, 101564...79 D4
Tompkinsville KY, 2402...110 A1
Toms River NJ, 88791......147 E3
Tonalea AZ, 549............47 E2
Tonanawanda NY, 15130....78 A3
Tonganoxie KS, 4996.......96 B2
Tonica IL, 702..............88 B2
Tonkawa OK, 3216..........51 E1
Tonopah NV, 2478..........37 F3
Tontitown AR, 2460.......106 C4
Tooele UT, 31605............31 E4
Tooele Co. UT, 58218......31 D4
Tool TX, 2240...............59 F3
Toole Co. MT, 5324.........15 F1
Toombs Co. GA, 27223....129 F3
Toomsboro GA, 472.........129 E2
Topeka IN, 1153.............89 F2
Topeka KS, 127473.........96 A2
Toppenish WA, 8949........13 D4

Topsfield MA, 2717........151 F1
Topsham ME, 5931..........82 B3
Topton PA, 2069...........146 B1
Toquerville UT, 1370.......39 D4
Tornillo TX, 1568..........56 C4
Toronto OH, 5091...........91 F4
Toronto SD, 212.............27 F3
Torrance CA, 145438........52 C3
Torrance Co. NM, 16383....49 D4
Torreon NM, 326............48 B2
Torreon NM, 244............48 B2
Torrington CT, 36383.......94 C3
Torrington WY, 6501........33 F2
Totowa NJ, 10804..........148 A3
Toughkenamon PA, 1492...146 B3
Toulon IL, 1292.............88 B3
Towaco NJ, 2700...........148 A3
Towanda KS, 1450..........43 E4
Towanda PA, 2919..........93 E1
Towaoc CO, 1087............40 B4
Tower MN, 500..............64 C3
Tower City ND, 253.........19 E4
Tower City PA, 1346........93 E4
Tower Hill IL, 611...........98 C2
Tower Lakes IL, 1283......203 B1
Town and Country MO, 10815...256 A2
Town Creek AL, 1100.......119 E2
Towner ND, 533.............18 C2
Towner Co. ND, 2246.......19 D1
Town Line NY, 2367........78 B3
Town 'n Country FL, 78442...266 B2
Town of Pines IN, 708......89 E1
Towns Co. GA, 10471.....121 D2
Townsend DE, 2049........145 E1
Townsend MA, 1128.........95 D1
Townsend MT, 1878.........23 E1
Towson MD, 55197.........144 C1
Tracy CA, 82922.............36 C4
Tracy MN, 2163.............72 A1
Tracy City TN, 1481.......120 A1
Tracyton WA, 5233.........262 A3
Traer IA, 1703..............87 E1
Trafalgar IN, 1101.........99 E1
Trafford AL, 646...........119 F4
Trafford PA, 3174..........250 D3
Trail Creek IN, 2052.........89 E2
Traill Co. ND, 8121.........19 E3
Trainer PA, 1828..........146 C3
Tramway NC, 750..........122 C1
Tranquillity CA, 799........44 C3
Transylvania Co. NC, 33090...121 E1
Trappe MD, 1077...........145 D4
Trappe PA, 3509...........146 B2
Trapper Creek AK, 481...154 C3
Traskwood AR, 518.......117 E3
Travelers Rest SC, 4576...121 E2
Traver CA, 713.............45 D3
Traverse City MI, 14674....69 F4
Traverse Co. MN, 3558.....27 F1
Travis Co. TX, 1024266......61 E1
Treasure Co. MT, 718.......17 D4
Treasure Island FL, 6705...140 B3
Trego Co. KS, 3001.........42 C2
Tremont IL, 2236............88 B4
Tremont PA, 1752..........146 A1
Tremonton UT, 7647.........31 E3
Trempealeau WI, 1529......73 F1

Trempealeau Co. WI, 28816...67 F4
Trent SD, 232...............27 F4
Trenton FL, 1999...........138 C2
Trenton GA, 2301..........120 B2
Trenton IL, 2715............98 B3
Trenton KY, 384............109 E3
Trenton MI, 18853..........90 C1
Trenton MO, 6001...........86 C4
Trenton NE, 560.............42 M1
Trenton NJ, 84913.........147 D2
Trenton NC, 287............115 D3
Trenton OH, 11869.........100 B2
Trenton TN, 4264..........108 C4
Trenton UT, 464.............31 E2
Trent Woods NC, 4155....115 D3
Treutlen Co. GA, 6885....129 F2
Trevorton PA, 1834.........93 E3
Trevose PA, 3550..........146 C2
Trexlertown PA, 1988.....146 B1
Treynor IA, 919.............86 A2
Trezevant TN, 859.........108 C4
Triadelphia WV, 811........91 F4
Triana AL, 496.............119 F2
Triangle VA, 8188.........144 A4
Tribes Hill NY, 1003........94 A1
Trico KS, 741...............42 B3
Tri-City OR, 3931..........28 B1
Trigg Co. KY, 14339......109 D3
Tri-Lakes IN, 1421..........90 A2
Trilby FL, 419.............140 C1
Trimble CO, 650............40 B4
Trimble TN, 637...........108 C3
Trimble Co. KY, 8809.....100 A3
Trimont MN, 747............72 B2
Trinidad CA, 9096...........41 E4
Trinidad TX, 886............59 F3
Trinity AL, 2095...........119 F2
Trinity NC, 6614...........112 B4
Trinity TX, 2697...........132 A1
Trinity Co. CA, 13786.....28 B4
Trinity Co. TX, 14585.....132 B1
Trion GA, 1827............120 B2
Troup Co. GA, 67044.....128 C1
Trousdale Co. TN, 7870...109 F3
Trout Creek MT, 242.......14 C3
Troutdale OR, 15962........20 C2
Troutdale VA, 178.........111 F3
Trout Lake WA, 561........21 D1
Troutman NC, 2383........112 A4
Trout Valley IL, 537......203 A1
Trowbridge Park MI, 2176...69 D1
Troy AL, 18033............128 A3
Troy ID, 862................14 B4
Troy IL, 9888...............98 B3
Troy KS, 1010..............96 B1

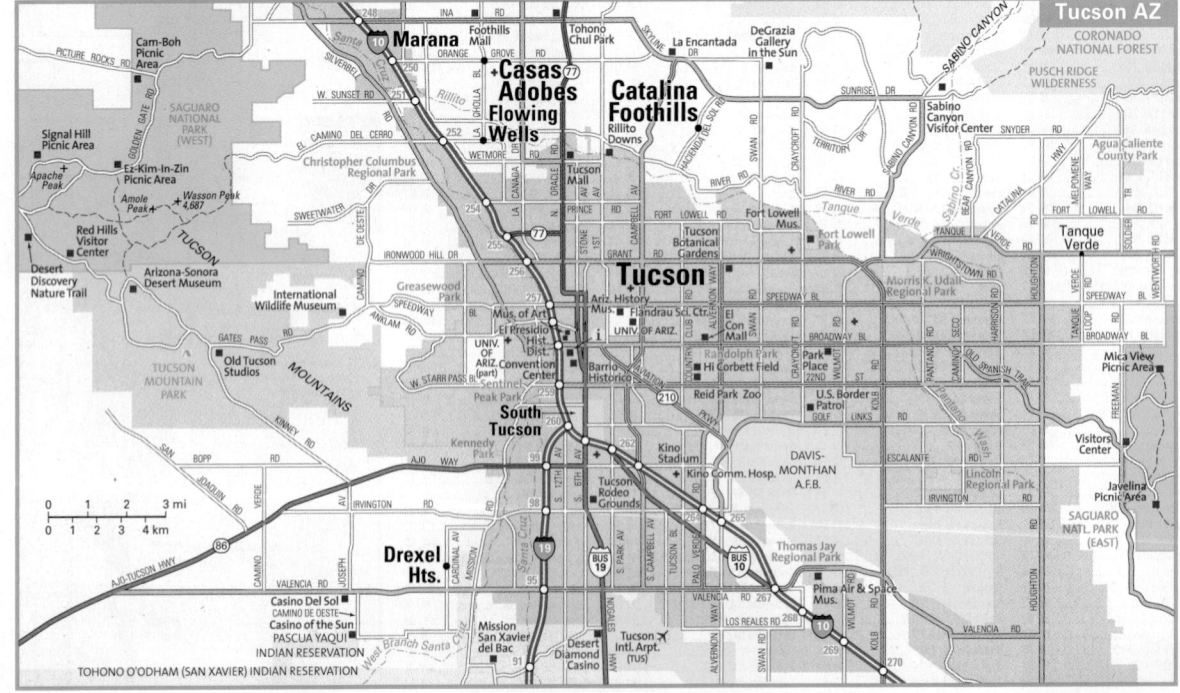

Trenton NJ

Tucson AZ

269
Troy – Vermillion County

Entries in **bold black** indicate counties or parishes.
Entries in **bold color** indicate cities with detailed inset maps.

Troy MI, 80980 76 C4
Troy MO, 10540 97 F2
Troy MT, 938 14 C2
Troy NH, 1221 95 D1
Troy NY, 50129 94 B1
Troy NC, 3189 122 C1
Troy OH, 25058 100 B1
Troy PA, 1354 93 D1
Troy TN, 1371 108 C3
Troy TX, 1645 59 E4
Troy VT, 243 81 E1
Truckee CA, 16180 37 D2
Truman MN, 1115 72 B2
Trumann AR, 7243 108 A4
Trumansburg NY, 1797 79 D4
Trumbauersville PA, 974 146 C1
Trumbull CT, 36018 149 D2
Trumbull Co. OH, 210312 91 F2
Trussville AL, 19933 119 F4
Truth or Consequences NM, 6475 56 B2
Tryon NE, 157 34 B3
Tryon NC, 1646 121 F1
Tryon OK, 491 51 F2
Tsaile AZ, 1205 48 A2
Tualatin OR, 26054 20 C2
Tubac AZ, 1191 55 D4
Tuba City AZ, 8611 47 E2
Tuckahoe NY, 1373 149 E3
Tucker MS, 662 126 C2
Tucker Co. WV, 7141 102 B2
Tuckerman AR, 1862 107 F4
Tuckerton NJ, 3347 147 E4
Tucson AZ, 520116 55 D3
Tucumcari NM, 5363 49 F3
Tukwila WA, 19107 262 B4
Tulalip WA, 1561 262 B1
Tulare CA, 59278 45 D3
Tulare SD, 207 27 E3
Tulare Co. CA, 442179 45 D3
Tularosa NM, 2842 56 C2
Tulelake CA, 1010 29 D2
Tulia TX, 4967 50 A4
Tullahoma TN, 18655 120 A1
Tullos LA, 385 125 E3
Tully NY, 873 79 E4
Tullytown PA, 1872 147 D2
Tulsa OK, 391906 51 F2
Tulsa Co. OK, 603403 106 A4
Tuluksak AK, 373 154 B3
Tumacacori AZ, 569 55 D4
Tunica MS, 1030 118 B2
Tunica Co. MS, 10778 118 B2
Tunkhannock PA, 1836 93 E2
Tunnel Hill GA, 856 120 B2
Tuolumne CA, 1779 37 D3
Tuolumne Co. CA, 55365 37 D3
Tupelo MS, 34546 119 D3
Tupper Lake NY, 3667 79 F1
Turbeville SC, 766 122 B4
Turbotville PA, 705 93 D3
Turley NM, 425 48 B1
Turley OK, 2756 51 F2
Turlock CA, 68549 36 C4
Turner ME, 4972 82 B2
Turner OR, 1854 20 B2
Turner Co. GA, 8930 129 D4
Turner Co. SD, 8347 27 F4
Turners Falls MA, 4470 94 C1
Turnersville NJ, 3742 146 C4
Turon KS, 387 43 D4
Turpin Hills OH, 5099 204 C3
Turrell AR, 615 118 B1
Turtle Creek PA, 5349 250 D2
Turtle Lake ND, 581 18 C3
Turtle Lake WI, 1050 67 E3
Tusayan AZ, 558 47 D2
Tuscaloosa AL, 90468 127 E1
Tuscaloosa Co. AL, 194656 119 E4
Tuscarawas OH, 1056 91 E4
Tuscarawas Co. OH, 92582 91 E4
Tuscarora PA, 980 93 E3
Tuscola IL, 4480 99 D1
Tuscola TX, 742 58 C3
Tuscola Co. MI, 55729 76 C2
Tusculum TN, 2663 111 E4
Tuscumbia AL, 8423 119 E2
Tuscumbia MO, 203 97 E4
Tuskegee AL, 9865 128 B2
Tustin CA, 75540 229 F5
Tuttle OK, 6019 51 E3
Tutwiler MS, 3550 118 A3
Tuxedo Park NY, 623 148 B2
Twain Harte CA, 2226 37 D3
Twentynine Palms CA, 25048 46 A4
Twiggs Co. GA, 9023 129 E2
Twin Bridges MT, 375 23 E2
Twin City GA, 1742 129 F2
Twin Falls ID, 44125 30 C1
Twin Falls Co. ID, 77230 30 C2
Twin Lake MI, 1720 75 E2
Twin Lakes CA, 4917 236 D1
Twin Lakes GA, 750 137 F1
Twin Lakes NM, 1052 48 A2
Twin Lakes WI, 5989 74 C4
Twin Rivers NJ, 7443 147 E2
Twinsburg OH, 18795 91 E2
Twin Valley MN, 821 19 F3
Twisp WA, 919 13 E2
Two Harbors MN, 3745 64 C4
Two Rivers WI, 11712 75 D1
Tybee Island GA, 2990 130 C3
Tye TX, 1242 58 C3
Tyler MN, 1143 27 F3
Tyler TX, 96900 124 A2
Tyler Co. TX, 21766 132 C1
Tyler Co. WV, 9208 101 F2
Tylersport PA, 950 146 C2
Tylertown MS, 1609 134 B1
Tyndall SD, 1067 35 E1
Tyrone GA, 6879 120 C4
Tyrone NM, 637 55 F2
Tyrone OK, 762 50 B1
Tyrone PA, 5477 92 C3
Tyronza AR, 762 118 B1
Tyrrell Co. NC, 4407 113 F4
Tysons Corner VA, 19627 270 A3
Ty Ty GA, 725 129 D4

U
Ubly MI, 858 76 C2
Ucon ID, 1108 23 E4
Udall KS, 746 43 F4
Uhrichsville OH, 5413 91 E4
Uinta Co. WY, 21118 31 F3
Uintah UT, 1322 244 B2
Uintah Co. UT, 32588 32 A4
Ukiah CA, 16075 36 A2
Ulah NC, 800 122 C1
Uledi PA, 1100 102 B1
Ulen MN, 547 19 F3
Ullin IL, 463 108 C2
Ulm MT, 738 15 F3
Ulster Co. NY, 182493 148 A1
Ulysses KS, 6161 42 B4
Ulysses PA, 621 92 C1
Umatilla FL, 3456 141 D1
Umatilla OR, 6906 21 E1
Umatilla Co. OR, 75889 21 E2
Unadilla GA, 3796 129 D3
Unadilla NY, 1128 79 E4
Unalakleet AK, 688 154 B2
Unalaska AK, 4376 154 A4
Uncasville CT, 1500 149 F1
Underhill VT, 2980 81 D2
Underwood IA, 917 86 A2
Underwood ND, 778 18 B3
Unicoi TN, 3632 111 E4
Unicoi Co. TN, 18313 111 E4
Union IL, 580 88 C1
Union KY, 5379 100 B3
Union ME, 2209 82 C2
Union MS, 1988 126 C2
Union MO, 10204 97 F3
Union NH, 204 81 F4
Union NJ, 56642 148 A4
Union OH, 6419 100 B1
Union OR, 2121 21 F2
Union SC, 8393 121 F2
Union WV, 565 112 A1
Union Beach NJ, 6245 147 E1
Union Bridge MD, 975 144 B1
Union City CA, 69516 259 D4
Union City GA, 19456 120 C4
Union City IN, 3584 90 A4
Union City MI, 1599 90 A1
Union City NJ, 66455 148 B4
Union City OH, 1666 90 A4
Union City OK, 1645 51 E3
Union City PA, 3320 92 A1
Union City TN, 10895 108 C3
Union Co. AR, 41639 125 E1
Union Co. FL, 15535 138 C3
Union Co. GA, 21356 120 C2
Union Co. IL, 17808 108 C1
Union Co. IN, 7516 100 B1
Union Co. IA, 12534 86 B3
Union Co. KY, 15007 109 D1
Union Co. MS, 27134 118 C3
Union Co. NJ, 536499 147 E1
Union Co. NM, 4549 49 F1
Union Co. NC, 201292 122 B2
Union Co. OH, 52300 90 C4
Union Co. OR, 25748 21 F2
Union Co. PA, 44947 93 D3
Union Co. SC, 28961 121 F2
Union Co. SD, 14399 35 F1
Union Co. TN, 19109 110 C3
Union Gap WA, 6047 13 D4
Union Grove WI, 4915 74 C4
Union Hall VA, 1138 112 B2
Union Lake MI, 2500 210 A1
Union Par. LA, 22721 125 E1
Union Park FL, 9765 246 D2
Union Pt. GA, 1617 121 E4
Union Sprs. AL, 3980 128 B3
Union Sprs. NY, 1197 79 D3
Uniontown AL, 1775 127 E2
Uniontown KY, 1002 109 D1
Uniontown OH, 3309 91 E3
Uniontown PA, 10372 102 B1
Unionville CT, 5100 94 C3
Unionville GA, 1845 129 E4
Unionville MI, 508 76 B2
Unionville MO, 1865 87 D4
Unionville NV, 250 29 F4
Unionville NY, 612 148 A2
Unionville NC, 5929 122 B1
Unionville PA, 962 146 B3
Unity ME, 469 82 C2
Universal City TX, 18530 61 D2
University City MO, 35371 256 B2
University Gardens NY, 4226 241 G3
University Hts. OH, 13539 204 G2
University Park IA, 487 87 D2
University Park MD, 2548 270 E2
University Park NM, 4192 56 C3
University Park TX, 23068 207 D2
University Place WA, 31144 12 C3
Upland CA, 73732 229 G2
Upland IN, 3845 89 F4
Upland PA, 3239 248 A4
Upper Arlington OH, 33771 101 D1
Upper Darby PA, 82795 248 B3
Upper Lake CA, 1052 36 A2
Upper Marlboro MD, 631 144 C3
Upper Saddle River NJ, 8208 148 B3
Upper Sandusky OH, 6596 90 C3
Upshur Co. TX, 39309 124 B2
Upshur Co. WV, 24254 102 A3
Upson Co. GA, 27153 129 D2
Upton KY, 683 110 A1
Upton MA, 3013 150 C2
Upton WY, 1100 25 F3
Upton Co. TX, 3355 58 A4
Urania LA, 1313 125 E3
Urbana IL, 41250 88 C4
Urbana IA, 1458 87 E1
Urbana OH, 11793 90 B4
Urbancrest OH, 960 206 A3
Urbandale IA, 39463 86 C2
Urbanna VA, 476 113 F1
Urich MO, 476 96 C3
Ursa IL, 626 87 F4
Usquepaug RI, 350 150 C4
Utah Co. UT, 516564 39 E1
Utica IN, 776 100 A4
Utica MI, 4757 210 C1
Utica MS, 820 126 A3
Utica NE, 861 35 E4
Utica NY, 62235 79 E3
Utica OH, 2132 91 D4
Utica SC, 1489 121 E2
Uvalda GA, 598 129 F3
Uvalde TX, 15751 60 C3
Uvalde Co. TX, 26405 60 C3
Uxbridge MA, 13457 150 C2

V
Vacaville CA, 92428 36 B3
Vader WA, 621 12 B4
Vadito NM, 270 49 D2
Vadnais Hts. MN, 12302 235 D1
Vado NM, 3194 56 C3
Vaiden MS, 734 126 C1
Vail AZ, 10208 55 D3
Vail CO, 5305 41 D1
Vails Gate NY, 3369 148 B1
Valatie NY, 1819 94 B2
Valders WI, 962 74 C1
Valdese NC, 4490 111 F4
Valdez AK, 3976 154 C3
Valdosta GA, 54518 137 F1
Vale OR, 1874 22 A4
Valencia NM, 2192 48 C4
Valencia Co. NM, 76569 48 C4
Valentine NE, 2737 34 C1
Valhalla NY, 3162 148 B3
Valier IL, 669 98 C4
Valier MT, 509 15 E2
Valinda CA, 22822 228 E2
Vallejo CA, 115942 36 B3
Vallersville MA, 2000 151 E3
Valley AL, 9524 128 B2
Valley NE, 1875 35 F3
Valley Brook OK, 765 244 E3
Valley Ctr. CA, 9277 53 D3
Valley Ctr. KS, 6822 43 E4
Valley City ND, 6585 19 E4
Valley Cottage NY, 9107 148 B2
Valley Co. ID, 9862 22 C2
Valley Co. MT, 7369 17 D2
Valley Co. NE, 4260 35 D3
Valley Falls KS, 1192 96 A2
Valley Falls RI, 11547 150 C3
Valley Farms AZ, 300 54 C2
Valley Forge PA, 1200 146 B2
Valley Grove WV, 378 91 F4
Valley Head AL, 558 120 A2
Valley Mills TX, 1203 59 E4
Valley Park MO, 6942 256 A3
Valley Sprs. CA, 3553 36 C3
Valley Sprs. SD, 759 27 F4
Valley Stream NY, 37511 148 C4
Valley View OH, 2034 204 F3
Valleyview OH, 620 206 A2
Valley View PA, 1683 93 E3
Valley View TX, 757 59 E1
Valliant OK, 754 116 B3
Valmeyer IL, 1263 98 A4
Valparaiso FL, 5036 136 B2
Valparaiso IN, 31730 89 E2
Valparaiso NE, 570 35 F3
Valrico FL, 35545 266 D2
Val Verde CA, 2468 52 C2
Val Verde Co. TX, 48879 60 B2
Vamo FL, 4727 140 B4
Van TX, 2632 124 A2
Van Alstyne TX, 3046 59 F1
Van Buren AR, 22791 116 C1
Van Buren IN, 864 89 F3
Van Buren ME, 1937 85 E1
Van Buren MO, 819 107 F2
Van Buren Co. AR, 17295 117 E1
Van Buren Co. IA, 7570 87 E3
Van Buren Co. MI, 76258 75 F4
Van Buren Co. TN, 5548 110 A4
Vance AL, 1529 127 F1
Vanceboro NC, 1005 115 D3
Vanceburg KY, 1518 100 C3
Vance Co. NC, 45422 113 D3
Vancleave MS, 5886 135 D2
Vancouver WA, 161791 20 C1
Vandalia IL, 7042 98 C3
Vandalia MO, 3899 97 F2
Vandalia OH, 15246 100 B1
Vandenberg Vil. CA, 6497 52 A1
Vander NC, 1146 123 D2
Vanderbilt MI, 562 70 C3
Vanderburgh Co. IN, 179703 99 D4
Vandercook Lake MI, 4721 90 B1
Vandergrift PA, 5205 92 A4
Vandling PA, 751 93 F2
Van Etten NY, 537 93 E1
Vanhiseville NJ, 700 147 E2
Van Horn TX, 2063 57 D4
Van Horne IA, 682 87 E1
Van Lear KY, 1100 111 E1
Vanlue OH, 359 90 C3
Van Meter IA, 1016 86 C2
Vansant VA, 470 111 E2
Van Vleck TX, 1844 132 A4
Van Wert OH, 10846 90 B3
Van Wert Co. OH, 28744 90 B3
Van Zandt Co. TX, 52579 124 A2
Vardaman MS, 1316 118 C4
Varnamtown NC, 541 123 E4
Varnell GA, 1744 120 B2
Varnville SC, 2162 130 B2
Vashon WA, 10624 262 A4
Vashon Hts. WA, 1100 262 A3
Vass NC, 720 122 C1
Vassalboro ME, 4047 82 C2
Vassar MI, 2697 76 B3
Vaughn MT, 658 15 F3
Vaughn NM, 446 49 D4
Veazie ME, 1744 83 D1
Veblen SD, 531 27 E1
Veedersburg IN, 2180 89 D4
Vega TX, 884 50 A3
Velma OK, 620 51 E4
Velva ND, 1084 18 B2
Venango Co. PA, 54984 92 A2
Veneta OR, 4561 20 B3
Venice FL, 20748 140 B4
Venice IL, 1890 256 C2
Venice LA, 202 134 C4
Venice Gardens FL, 7104 140 C4
Ventnor City NJ, 10650 147 F4
Ventura CA, 106433 52 B2
Ventura IA, 717 72 C3
Ventura Co. CA, 823318 52 B2
Venus TX, 2960 59 E3
Verden OK, 530 51 E3
Verdi NV, 1415 37 D1
Verdigre NE, 575 35 E1
Vergennes VT, 2588 81 D2
Vermilion OH, 10594 91 D2
Vermilion Co. IL, 81625 89 D4
Vermilion Par. LA, 57999 133 E3
Vermillion SD, 10571 35 F1
Vermillion Co. IN, 16212 99 E1

Bixby C3
Bowden A3
Broken Arrow C3
Catoosa C1
Jenks B3
Oakhurst A3
Sand Sprs. A2
Sapulpa A3
Tiger C1
Tulsa B2

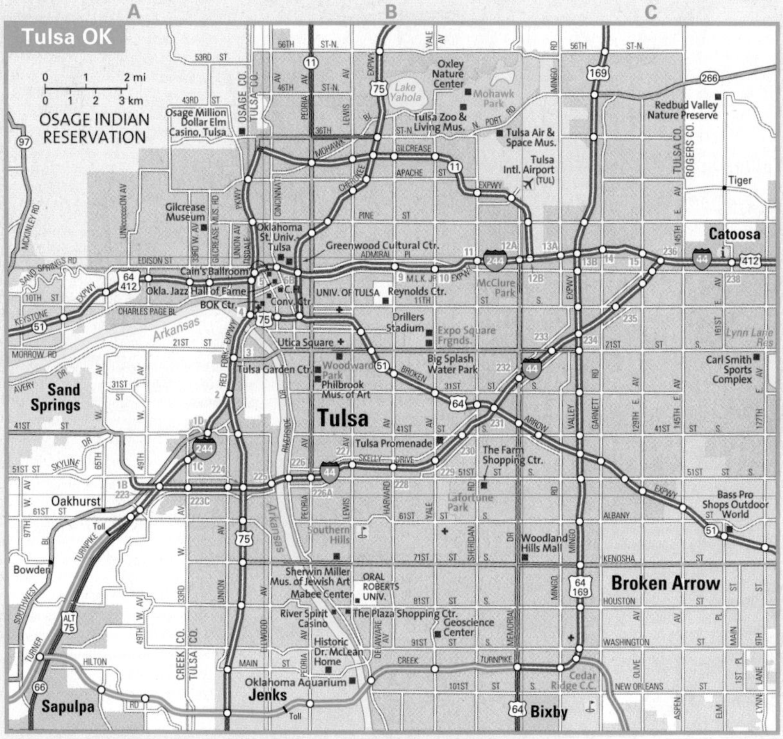
Tulsa OK
A
B
C
1
2
3
OSAGE INDIAN RESERVATION
Osage Million Dollar Elm Casino, Tulsa
Oxley Nature Center
Lake Yahola
Mohawk Park
Tulsa Zoo & Living Mus.
Redbud Valley Nature Preserve
Tulsa Air & Space Mus.
Tulsa Intl. Airport (TUL)
Tiger
Gilcrease Museum
Oklahoma St. Univ.-Tulsa
Greenwood Cultural Ctr.
Catoosa
Cain's Ballroom
Okla. Jazz Hall of Fame
BOK Ctr.
Conv. Ctr.
UNIV. OF TULSA
Reynolds Ctr.
McClure Park
Drillers Stadium
Expo Square Frgnds.
Arkansas
Utica Square
Woodward Park
Tulsa Garden Ctr.
Philbrook Mus. of Art
Big Splash Water Park
Carl Smith Sports Complex
Lynn Lane Res.
Sand Springs
Tulsa
Tulsa Promenade
The Farm Shopping Ctr.
Oakhurst
Bass Pro Shops Outdoor World
Southern Hills
Woodland Hills Mall
Bowden
Sherwin Miller Mus. of Jewish Art
Mabee Center
ORAL ROBERTS UNIV.
River Spirit Casino
The Plaza Shopping Ctr.
Geoscience Center
Broken Arrow
Historic Dr. McLean Home
Oklahoma Aquarium
Jenks
Sapulpa
Cedar Ridge C.C.
Bixby
Toll

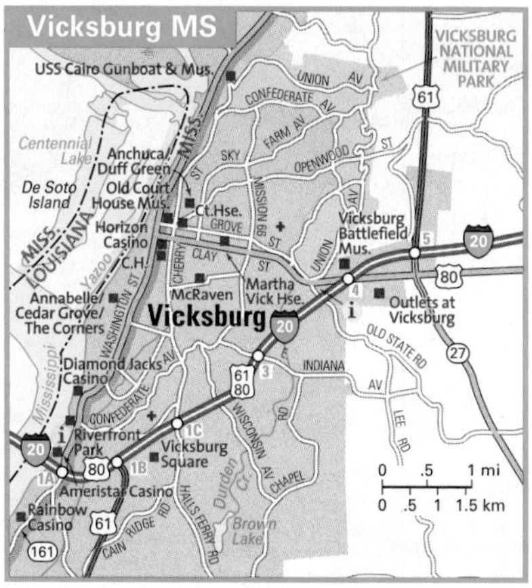
Vicksburg MS
USS Cairo Gunboat & Mus.
VICKSBURG NATIONAL MILITARY PARK
Centennial Lake
Anchuca
Duff Green
Old Court House Mus.
Ct.Hse.
De Soto Island
LOUISIANA
MISS.
Horizon Casino
C.H.
Vicksburg Battlefield Mus.
Annabelle
Cedar Grove/The Corners
McRaven
Martha Vick Hse.
Vicksburg
Outlets at Vicksburg
Diamond Jacks Casino
Riverfront Park
Vicksburg Square
Ameristar Casino
Rainbow Casino
Brown Lake
0 .5 1 mi
0 .5 1 1.5 km

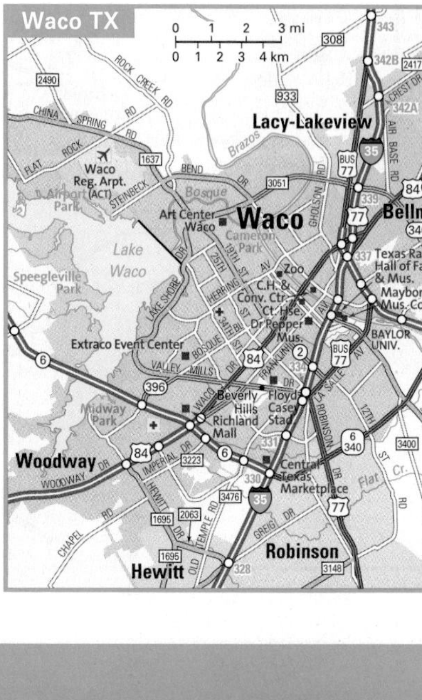
Waco TX
0 1 2 3 mi
0 1 2 3 4 km
Lacy-Lakeview
Waco Reg. Arpt. (ACT)
Airport Park
Bosque
Art Center Waco
Waco
Cameron Park
Bellmead
Lake Waco
Speegleville Park
Zoo
C.H. & Conv. Ctr.
Ct.Hse.
Texas Ranger Hall of Fame & Mus.
Mayborn Mus. Complex
Dr Pepper Mus.
BAYLOR UNIV.
Extraco Event Center
Beverly Hills
Floyd Casey Stad.
Richland Mall
Midway Park
Woodway
Central Texas Marketplace
Robinson
Hewitt

270

Figures after entries indicate population, page number, and grid reference.

Washington DC

Entries in **bold black** indicate counties or parishes.
Entries in **bold color** indicate cities with detailed inset maps.

Greenbelt

New Carrollton — Seabrook

Kentland

Palmer Park

Seat Pleasant — Largo

District Heights

Morningside

Forestville

JOINT BASE ANDREWS NAVAL AIR FACILITY

Woodyard

0 1 2 mi
0 1 2 3 km

272

Waynesboro–Wentzville

Figures after entries indicate population, page number, and grid reference.

POINTS OF INTEREST

Entries in **bold black** indicate counties or parishes.
Entries in **bold color** indicate cities with detailed inset maps.

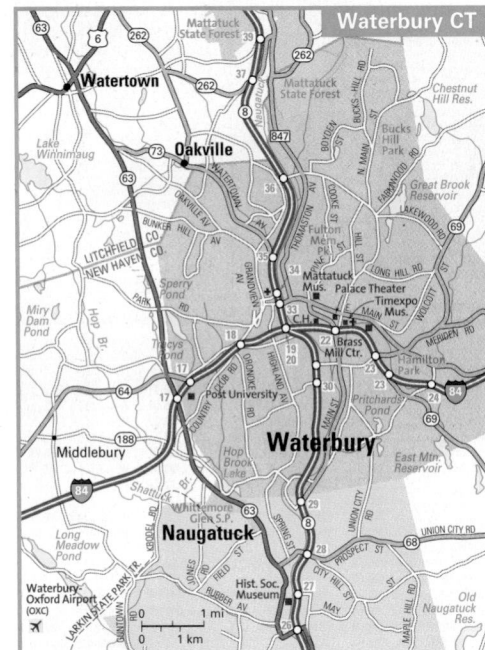

Waterbury CT

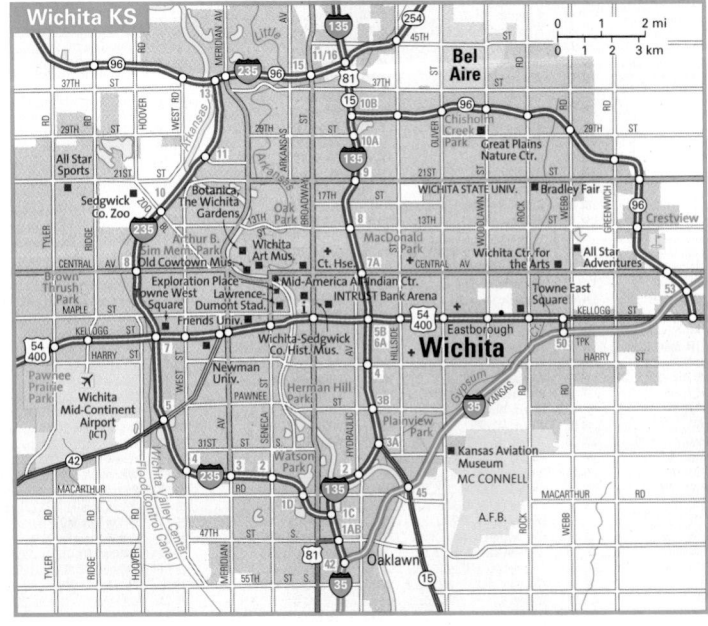

Wichita KS

Downtown Washington DC

Figures after entries indicate population, page number, and grid reference.

Wexford Co. MI, *32735* 69 F4	White Hall WV, *648* 102 A2	Whitsett NC, *590* 112 B4	Williamsburg IA, *3068* 87 E2	Wilmer TX, *3682* 207 E3	Wind Gap PA, *2720* 93 F3
Weyauwega WI, *1900* 74 B1	Whitehall WI, *1558* 73 F1	Whittemore IA, *504* 72 B3	Williamsburg KS, *397* 96 A3	Wilmerding PA, *2190* 250 D3	Windham CT, *23733* 149 F1
Weyers Cave VA, *2473* 102 C4	White Haven PA, *1097* 93 F3	Whittemore MI, *384* 76 B1	Williamsburg KY, *5245* 110 C3	Wilmette IL, *27087* 89 D1	Windham NH, *13592* 95 E1
Weymouth MA, *53743* 151 D2	White Horse NJ, *9494* 147 D2	Whittier CA, *85331* 52 C2	Williamsburg MA, *550* 150 A1	Wilmington DE, *70851* 146 B4	Windham OH, *2209* 91 F2
Wharton NJ, *6522* 148 A3	White Horse PA, *475* 146 A3	Whitwell TN, *1699* 120 B1	Williamsburg NM, *449* 56 B2	Wilmington IL, *142* 88 C2	Wind Lake WI, *5342* 74 C3
Wharton OH, *358* 90 C3	White Horse Beach MA, *2300* 151 E3	Why AZ, *167* 54 B3	Williamsburg OH, *2490* 100 C2	Wilmington NC, *106476* 123 E3	Wind Lake WI, *5342* 74 C3
Wharton TX, *8832* 61 F3	White House TN, *10255* 109 F3	Wibaux MT, *589* 17 F4	Williamsburg PA, *1254* 92 C4	Wilmington OH, *12520* 100 C2	Windom MN, *4646* 72 B2
Wharton Co. TX, *41280* 61 F3	White House Sta. NJ, *2089* 147 D1	**Wibaux Co. MT**, *1017* 17 F4	Williamsburg SC, *34423* 122 C4	Wilmington VT, *463* 94 C1	Window Rock AZ, *2712* 48 A2
What Cheer IA, *646* 87 E2	Whitehouse TX, *7660* 124 B3	**Wichita Co. KS**, *2234* 42 B3	**Williamsburg Co. SC**, *34423* 122 C4	Wilmington Island GA, *15138* 130 C3	Wind Pt. WI, *1723* 75 D4
Whatcom Co. WA, *201140* 12 C1	White Island Shores MA, *2106* 151 E3	**Wichita Co. TX**, *131500* 59 D1	**Williams Co. ND**, *22398* 17 F2	Wilmington Manor DE, *7889* 274 D3	**Windsor Co. VT**, *56670* 81 E3
Whately MA, *425* 150 A1	White Lake NY, *475* 94 A3	Wichita Falls TX, *104553* 59 D1	**Williams Creek IN**, *407* 221 C1	Wilmore KS, *3868* 100 B4	Windsor CO, *18644* 33 E4
Wheatfield IN, *853* 89 E2	White Lake NC, *802* 123 D2	Wickenburg AZ, *6363* 54 B1	Williamsfield IL, *578* 88 A3	Wilmot AR, *550* 125 F1	Windsor CT, *28778* 150 A3
Wheatland CA, *3456* 36 C2	White Lake SD, *372* 27 D4	Wickes AR, *754* 116 C3	Williamson NY, *2495* 78 C3	Wilmot SD, *492* 27 F2	Windsor IL, *1197* 98 C2
Wheatland IN, *480* 99 E3				Wilsall MT, *178* 23 F1	Windsor MO, *2901* 96 C3

					Windsor NY, *916* 93 F1

Five Forks . . . . A1 | Hayes . . . . C1 | Newport News . . . . C2 | Wicomico . . . . C1 | Yorktown C2
Gloucester Pt. . . . . C2 | Lackey . . . . C2 | Scotland . . . . A2 | Williamsburg A1

				Wilson AR, *903* 118 B1	Windsor NC, *3630* 113 D4
				Wilson KS, *781* 43 D2	Windsor VT, *2066* 81 E4
				Wilson LA, *595* 134 A1	Windsor VA, *2626* 113 F2
				Wilson NC, *49167* 113 D4	Windsor WI, *3573* 74 B3
				Wilson OK, *1724* 51 E4	**Windsor Co. VT**, *56670* 81 E3
				Wilson PA, *7896* 93 F3	Windsor Hts. WV, *423* 91 F4
				Wilson TX, *489* 58 A2	Windsor Hills CA, *10958* 228 C3
				Wilson WY, *1482* 23 F3	Windsor Locks CT, *12498* 150 A2
				Wilson Co. KS, *9409* 106 A1	Windthorst TX, *409* 59 D1
				Wilson Co. NC, *81234* 113 E4	Windy Hills KY, *2385* 230 E1
				Wilson Co. TN, *113993* 109 F3	Winfall NC, *594* 113 F3
				Wilson Co. TX, *42918* 61 E3	Winfield AL, *4717* 119 E4
				Wilson's Mills NC, *1277* 113 E3	Winfield IL, *9080* 203 B4

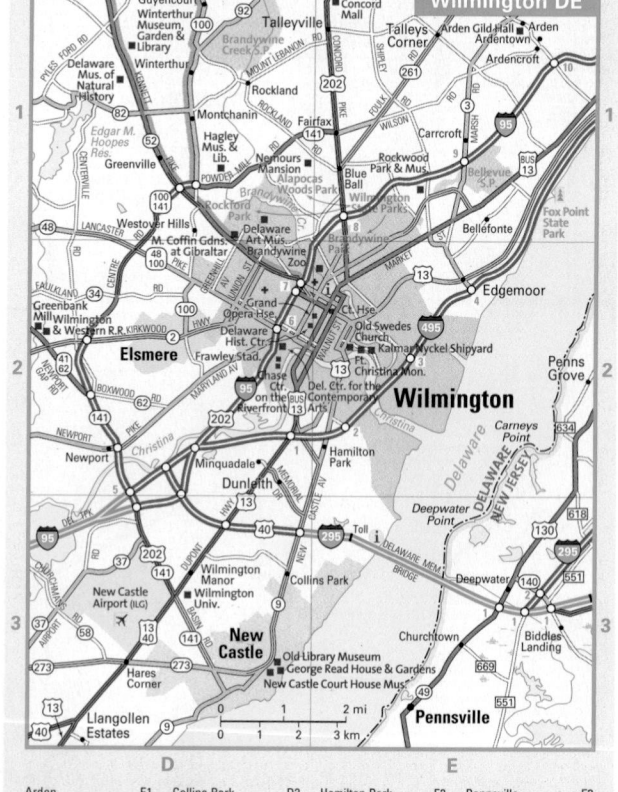

Williamsburg VA (map)
Williamsburg, Five Forks, Jamestown Settlement, Busch Gardens Europe, Newport News, Gloucester Point, Yorktown, Scotland, Kingsmill

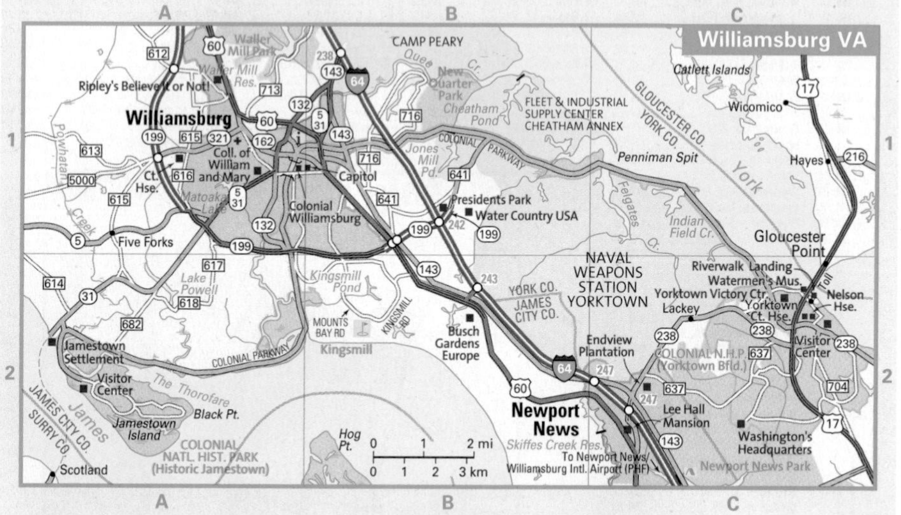

Wheatland IA, *764* 87 F1	Whiteland IN, *4169* 99 F1	Wickett TX, *498* 57 F4	Williamson WV, *3191* 111 E1	Wilmington Manor DE, *7889* 274 D3	Winfield IN, *4383* 89 D2
Wheatland WY, *3627* 33 E2	Whitelaw WI, *757* 75 D1	Wickford RI, *1900* 150 C4	**Williamson Co. IL**, *66357* 108 C1		Winfield IA, *1134* 87 F3
Wheatland Co. MT, *2168* 16 B4	White Marsh MD, *9513* 193 E2	Wickliffe KY, *688* 108 C2	**Williamson Co. TN**, *183182* 109 F4		Winfield KS, *12301* 43 F4
Wheatley AR, *355* 118 A2	White Marsh VA, *600* 113 F1	Wickliffe OH, *12750* 91 E2	**Williamson Co. TX**, *422679* 61 E1		Winfield MO, *1404* 98 A2
Wheaton IL, *52894* 89 D1	White Oak MD, *17403* 270 D1	Wicomico Church VA, *250* 113 F1	Williamsport IN, *1898* 89 D4		Winfield TN, *967* 110 C3
Wheaton MD, *48284* 144 B3	White Oak OH, *19167* 204 A2	**Wicomico Co. MD**, *98733* 114 C1	Williamsport MD, *2137* 103 D1		Winfield TX, *524* 124 B1
Wheaton MN, *1424* 27 F1	White Oak TX, *7862* 94 A4	Widefield CO, *29845* 205 D2	Williamsport OH, *1023* 101 D1		Winfield WV, *2301* 101 E3
Wheaton MO, *696* 106 C2	White Oak TX, *6469* 124 B2	Wiggins CO, *828* 33 F4	Williamsport PA, *29381* 93 D2		Wingate NC, *3491* 122 B2
Wheat Ridge CO, *30166* 209 B3	White Pigeon MI, *1522* 89 F1	Wiggins MS, *4390* 135 D1	Williamston MI, *3854* 76 A4		Wingo KY, *632* 108 C3
Wheeler MS, *300* 119 D2	White Pine MI, *474* 65 E4	Wilber NE, *1855* 35 F4	Williamston NC, *5511* 113 E4		Wink TX, *940* 57 F4
Wheeler OR, *414* 20 B1	White Pine TN, *2196* 111 D4	**Wilbarger Co. TX**, *13535* 58 C1	Williamston SC, *3934* 121 E2		**Winkler Co. TX**, *7110* 57 F3
Wheeler TX, *1592* 50 C3	**White Pine Co. NV**, *10030* 38 B1	Wilberforce OH, *2271* 100 C1	Williamstown KY, *3925* 100 B3		Winlock WA, *1339* 12 B4
Wheeler Co. GA, *7421* 129 D3	White Plains KY, *884* 109 E2	Wilbraham MA, *3915* 150 A2	Williamstown MA, *4325* 94 C1		Winnebago IL, *3101* 74 B4
Wheeler Co. NE, *818* 35 D2	White Plains MD, *3600* 144 B4	Wilbur WA, *884* 13 F3	Williamstown NJ, *15567* 146 C4		Winnebago MN, *1437* 72 C2
Wheeler Co. OR, *1441* 21 E3	White Plains NY, *56853* 148 B3	Wilbur Park MO, *471* 256 B3	Williamstown NY, *475* 79 E2		Winnebago NE, *774* 35 F2
Wheeler Co. TX, *5410* 50 C3	White Plains NC, *1074* 112 A3	Wilburton OK, *2843* 116 A2	Williamstown PA, *1387* 93 E4		**Winnebago Co. IL**, *295266* 74 B4
Wheelersburg OH, *6437* 101 D3	Whiteriver AZ, *4104* 55 E1	Wilcox NE, *356* 35 D4	Williamstown VT, *1162* 81 E2		**Winnebago Co. IA**, *10866* 72 C2
Wheeling IL, *37648* 89 D1	White River SD, *581* 26 C4	Wilcox PA, *383* 92 B2	Williamstown WV, *2908* 101 F2		**Winnebago Co. WI**, *166994* 74 C1
Wheeling WV, *28486* 91 F4	White River Jct. VT, *2286* 81 E3	**Wilcox Co. AL**, *11670* 127 F3	Williamsville DE, *350* 114 C1		Winneconne WI, *2383* 74 C1
Wheelwright KY, *1111* 111 E1	White Rock NM, *5725* 48 C2	**Wilcox Co. GA**, *9255* 129 E3	Williamsville IL, *1446* 98 B1		
Wheelwright MA, *425* 150 A1	Whiterocks UT, *289* 32 A4	Wilder ID, *1533* 22 A4	Williamsville MS, *400* 126 C1		
Whigham GA, *471* 137 E1	White Salmon WA, *2224* 21 D1	Wilder KY, *3005* 204 B3	Williamsville NY, *5300* 198 C2		
Whippany NJ, *3800* 148 A3	Whitesboro NY, *3772* 79 E3	Wilder VT, *1690* 81 E3	Willimantic CT, *17737* 150 B3		
Whispering Pines NC, *2928* 122 C1	Whitesboro TX, *3793* 59 F1	Wilderness VA, *300* 103 D4	Willingboro NJ, *36530* 147 D3		
Whitaker PA, *1271* 250 C2	Whitesburg GA, *588* 120 B4	Wildomar CA, *32176* 53 D3	Willis TX, *5662* 132 A2		
Whitakers NC, *744* 113 E4	Whitesburg KY, *2139* 111 D2	Wildorado TX, *190* 50 A4	Willisburg KY, *282* 110 B1		
White GA, *670* 120 C3	White Settlement TX, *16116* 207 A2	Wildwood FL, *6709* 140 C1	Williston FL, *2768* 138 C4		
White SD, *485* 27 F3	White Shield ND, *336* 18 B3	Wildwood MO, *35517* 98 A3	Williston ND, *14716* 17 F2		
White Bear Lake MN, *23797* 235 D1	**Whiteside Co. IL**, *58498* 88 A1	Wildwood NJ, *5325* 104 C4	Williston OH, *487* 90 C2		
White Bluff TN, *3206* 109 E4	White Sprs. FL, *777* 138 C2	Wildwood TX, *1235* 132 C2	Williston SC, *3139* 130 B1		
White Castle LA, *1883* 134 A2	White Stone VA, *352* 113 F1	Wildwood Crest NJ, *3270* 104 C4	Williston TN, *395* 118 C1		
White Ctr. WA, *13495* 262 B4	White Sulphur Sprs. MT, *939* 15 F4	Wiley CO, *405* 42 A3	Williston VT, *8698* 81 D2		
White City FL, *3719* 141 E3	White Sulphur Sprs. WV, *2444* 112 B1	Wilhoit AZ, *868* 47 D4	Willisville IL, *633* 98 B4		
White City KS, *618* 43 F2	Whitesville KY, *552* 109 F1	Wilkes-Barre PA, *41498* 93 E2	Willis Wharf VA, *475* 114 B3		
White City OR, *7975* 20 B2	Whitesville NY, *400* 92 C1	Wilkesboro NC, *3413* 111 F4	Willits CA, *4888* 36 A3		
White Cloud MI, *1408* 75 F2	Whitesville WV, *514* 101 F4	**Wilkes Co. GA**, *10593* 121 E4	Willmar MN, *19610* 66 B3		
White Co. AR, *77076* 117 F1	White Swan WA, *793* 13 D4	**Wilkes Co. NC**, *69340* 112 A3	Willoughby OH, *22268* 91 E2		
White Co. GA, *27144* 121 D1	Whiteville NC, *5394* 123 D3	Wilkeson WA, *477* 12 C3	Willoughby Hills OH, *9485* 204 G1		
White Co. IL, *14665* 99 D4	Whiteville TN, *4638* 118 C1	**Wilkin Co. MN**, *6576* 19 F4	Willow AK, *2102* 154 C3		
White Co. IN, *24643* 89 E3	Whitewater AZ, *843* 53 E3	Wilkinsburg PA, *15930* 250 C2	Willowbrook CA, *25983* 228 D3		
White Co. TN, *25841* 110 A4	Whitewater WI, *14390* 74 C3	**Wilkinson Co. GA**, *9563* 129 E2	Willowbrook IL, *8540* 203 C5		
White Deer TX, *1000* 50 B3	Whitewood SD, *927* 25 F3	**Wilkinson Co. MS**, *9878* 125 E4	Willow City ND, *163* 18 B2		
White Earth MN, *580* 19 F3	Whitfield FL, *2882* 140 B3	Willacoochee GA, *1381* 129 E4	Willow Creek CA, *1710* 28 B4		
Whiteface TX, *449* 57 F1	**Whitfield Co. GA**, *102599* 120 B2	**Willacy Co. TX**, *22134* 63 F3	Willow Creek MT, *210* 23 E1		
Whitefield NH, *1142* 81 F2	Whiting IN, *4997* 89 D2	Willamina OR, *2005* 20 B2	Willow Grove PA, *15726* 146 C2		
Whitefish MT, *6357* 15 D1	Whiting NJ, *762* 35 F2	Willard MO, *5288* 107 D2	Willow Lake SD, *263* 27 E2		
Whitefish Bay WI, *14110* 234 D1	Whiting NJ, *1800* 147 E3	Willard NM, *240* 49 D4	Willow Park TX, *3982* 59 E2		
Whiteford MD, *700* 146 A4	Whiting WI, *1724* 68 B4	Willard OH, *6236* 91 D3	Willows CA, *6166* 36 B1		
White Hall AL, *858* 127 F2	Whitley City KY, *1170* 110 C3	Willard UT, *1772* 31 E3	Willows MD, *900* 144 C4		
White Hall AR, *5526* 117 E3	**Whitley Co. IN**, *33292* 89 F3	Willards MD, *958* 114 C1	Willow Sprs. IL, *5524* 203 D5		
White Hall IL, *2520* 98 A2	**Whitley Co. KY**, *35637* 110 C2	Will Co. IL, *677560* 89 D2	Willow Sprs. MO, *2184* 107 E2		
Whitehall MT, *1038* 23 E1	Whitman MA, *13882* 151 D2	Willcox AZ, *3757* 55 E3	Willernie MN, *507* 235 E1		
Whitehall NY, *2614* 81 D3	**Whitman Co. WA**, *44776* 14 A4	Williams AZ, *3023* 47 D3	Wills Pt. TX, *7578* 146 A3		
Whitehall OH, *18062* 206 C2	Whitmer WV, *144* 121 F3	Williams CA, *5123* 36 B2	Willsboro NY, *753* 81 D2		
White Hall PA, *13944* 250 B3	Whitmire SC, *1441* 121 E2	Williams IA, *344* 72 C4	Wilshire OH, *397* 90 A3		
Whitehall WV, *250* 102 C4	Whitmore Vil. HI, *4499* 152 A2	Williams MN, *172* 28 B2	Wills Pt. TX, *3524* 59 F2		
White Hall VA, *300* 103 D2	Whitney TX, *2087* 59 E3	Williams Bay WI, *2564* 74 C4	Wilwood WY, *100* 24 B3		
	Whitney Pt. NY, *964* 79 E4	Williamsburg CO, *662* 41 E3	Wilmar AR, *511* 117 F4		
		Williamsburg FL, *7646* 246 B4	Wilmer AL, *500* 135 E1		

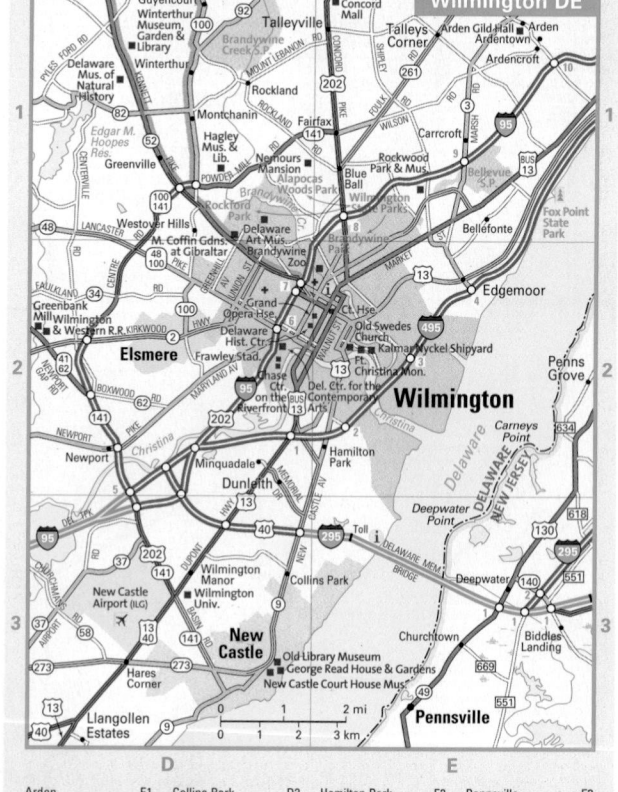

Wilmington DE (map)
Talleyville, Winterthur, Montchanin, Fairfax, Greenville, Westover Hills, Elsmere, Wilmington, Newport, Dunleith, New Castle, Minquadale, Llangollen Estates, Pennsville, Deepwater

Entries in **bold black** indicate counties or parishes.
Entries in **bold color** indicate cities with detailed inset maps.

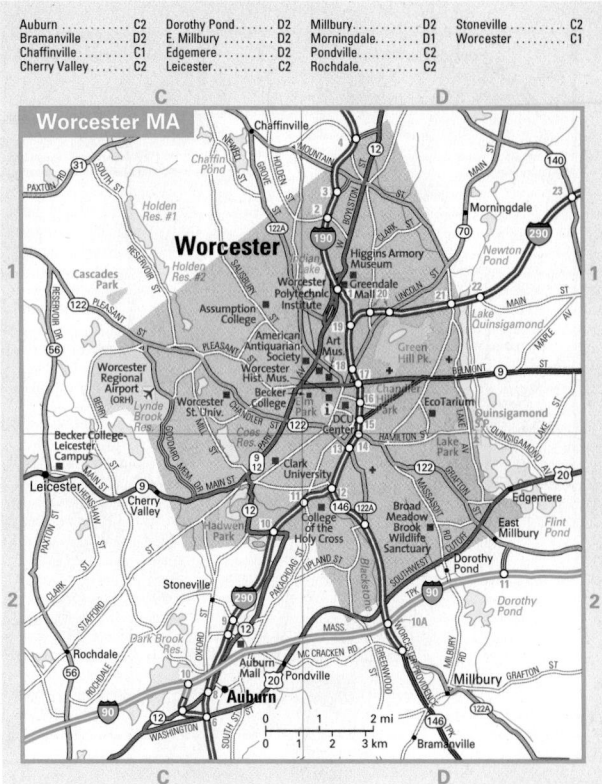

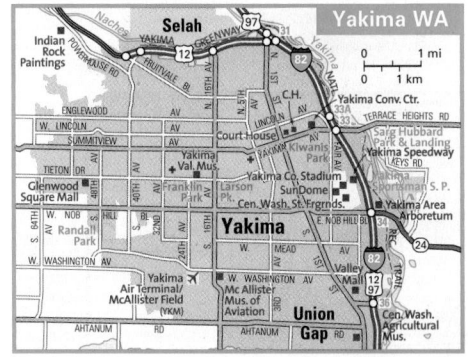

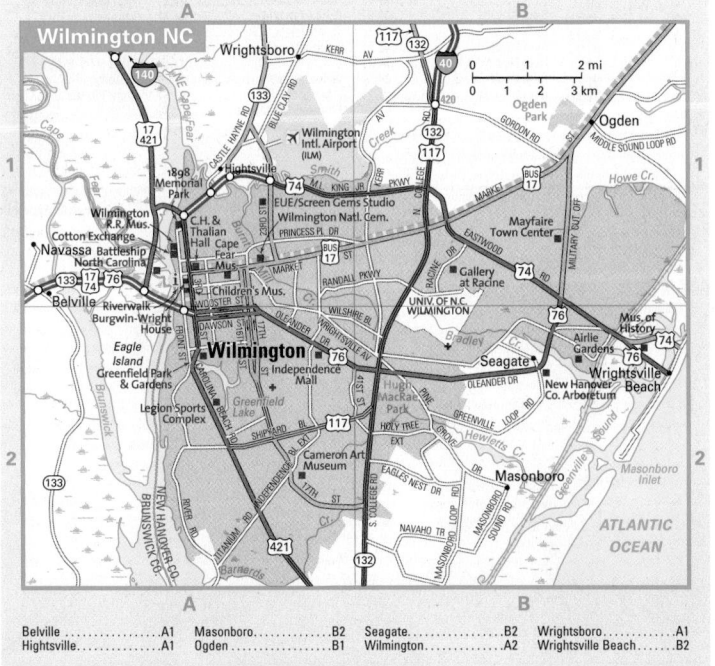

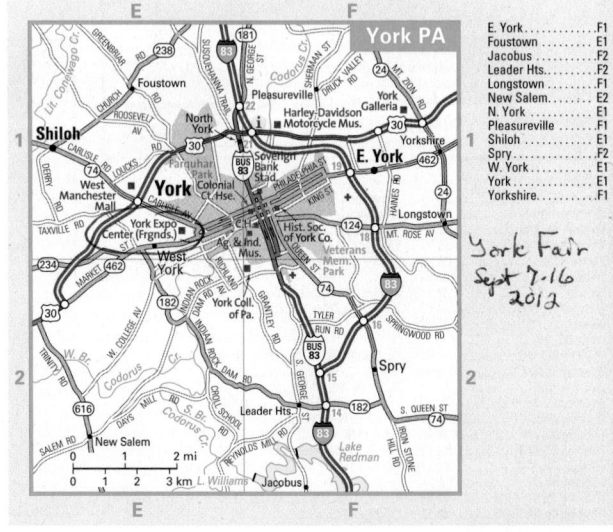

Figures after entries indicate population, page number, and grid reference.

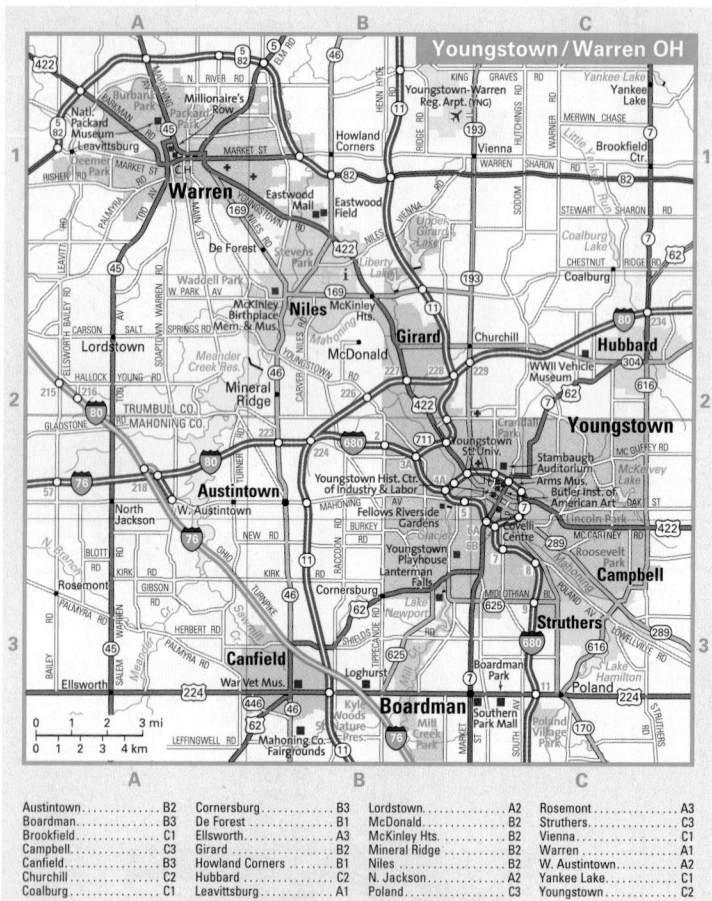

Youngstown/Warren OH

Austintown	B2	Cornersburg	B3	Lordstown	A2	Rosemont	A3
Boardman	B3	De Forest	B1	McDonald	B2	Struthers	C3
Brookfield	C1	Ellsworth	A3	McKinley Hts.	B2	Vienna	C1
Campbell	C3	Girard	B2	Mineral Ridge	B2	Warren	A1
Canfield	B3	Howland Corners	B1	Niles	B2	W. Austintown	A2
Churchill	C2	Hubbard	C1	N. Jackson	A2	Yankee Lake	C1
Coalburg	C1	Leavittsburg	A1	Poland	C2	Youngstown	C2

Yuma AZ

San Juan PR

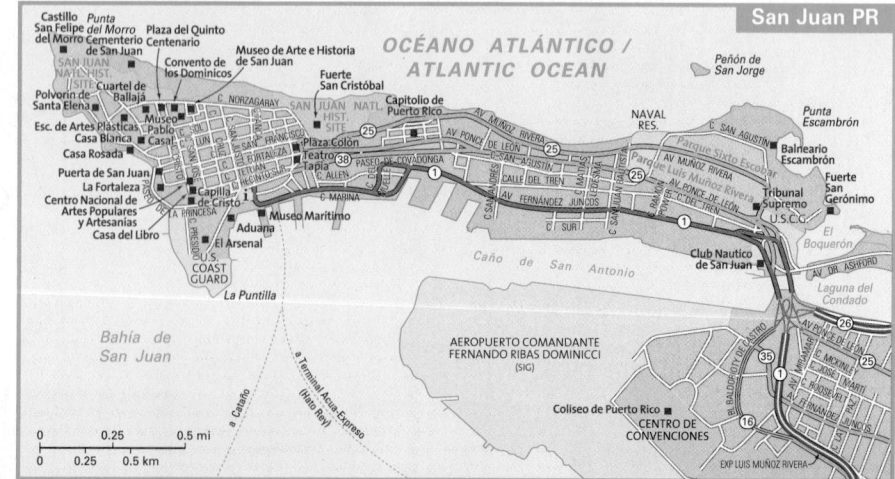

277
Abbotsford–Clinton

Entries in **bold color** indicate cities with detailed inset maps.

CANADA

Abbotsford BC, *115463* 163 D3
Aberdeen SK, *534* 165 F1
Acton ON, *7767* 172 C2
Acton Vale QC, *7299* 175 D3
Adstock QC, *1629* 175 E2
Airdrie AB, *20382* 164 C2
Air Ronge SK, *955* 160 B3
Ajax ON, *73753* 173 D2
Aklavik NT, *632* 155 D1
Alban ON, *1084* 170 C3
Albanel QC, *2455* 176 B3
Alberta Beach AB, *762* 158 C4
Alberton PE, *1115* 179 E3
Aldergrove BC, *11910* 163 D3
Alexandria ON, *3369* 174 B3
Alfred ON, *1348* 174 B3
Alix AB, *825* 164 C2
Allan SK, *679* 165 F2
Alliston ON, *9679* 172 C1
Alma QC, *25918* 176 C3
Almonte ON, *4659* 174 A3
Altona MB, *3434* 167 E4
Amherst NS, *9470* 180 C1
Amherstburg ON, *20339* 172 A4
Amos QC, *13044* 171 E1
Amqui QC, *6473* 178 B1
Ange-Gardien QC, *1994* 175 D3
Angus ON, *9722* 172 C1
Annapolis Royal NS, *550* 180 B3
Antigonish NS, *4754* 181 E1
Arborg MB, *959* 167 E3
Arcola SK, *532* 166 C4
Armagh QC, *1603* 175 F1
Armstrong BC, *4256* 164 A3
Arnold's Cove NL, *1024* 183 E4
Arnprior ON, *7192* 174 A3
Arthur ON, *2284* 172 C2
Asbestos QC, *6580* 175 E3
Ascot Corner QC, *2342* 175 E3
Ashcroft BC, *1788* 163 E1
Asquith SK, *574* 165 F2
Assiniboia SK, *2483* 166 A4
Athabasca AB, *2415* 159 D3
Athens ON, *1026* 174 A4
Atholville NB, *1381* 178 C2
Atikokan ON, *3560* 168 C4
Aurora ON, *40167* 173 D2
Austin QC, *1201* 175 D3
Avondale NL, *701* 183 E4
Ayer's Cliff QC, *1102* 175 D3
Aylesford NS, *807* 180 C2
Aylmer ON, *7126* 172 C3
Aylmer QC, *36085* 174 B3
Ayr ON, *3636* 172 C3
Baddeck NS, *907* 181 F1
Badger NL, *906* 183 D3
Baie-Comeau QC, *23079* 177 D2
Baie-du-Febvre QC, *1135* 175 D2
Baie-Ste-Anne NB, *1600* 179 D3
Baie-St-Paul QC, *7290* 176 C4
Baie Verte NL, *1492* 183 D2
Balcarres SK, *622* 166 B3
Balgonie SK, *1239* 166 B3
Balmoral NB, *1836* 178 C2
Bancroft ON, *4089* 171 E4
Banff AB, *7135* 164 B3
Barraute QC, *2010* 171 E2
Barrhead AB, *4213* 158 C3
Barrie ON, *103710* 173 D1
Barry's Bay ON, *1259* 171 E4
Bas-Caraquet NB, *1689* 179 D2
Bashaw AB, *825* 164 C1
Bassano AB, *1320* 165 D3
Bathurst NB, *12924* 179 D2
Battleford SK, *3820* 159 F4
Bay Bulls NL, *1014* 183 F4
Bayfield ON, *909* 172 B2
Bay Roberts NL, *5237* 183 E4
Beachburg ON, *870* 174 A3
Beamsville ON, *9047* 173 D3
Beauceville QC, *6261* 175 E2
Beauharnois QC, *6387* 174 C3
Beaumont AB, *7006* 159 D4
Beaumont QC, *2153* 175 E1
Beaupré QC, *2761* 175 E1
Beausejour MB, *2772* 167 F3
Beauval SK, *843* 159 F2
Beaverlodge AB, *2110* 157 F1
Beaverton ON, *3065* 173 D1
Bécancour QC, *11051* 175 D2
Bedford NS 181 D3
Bedford QC, *2667* 175 D4
Beechville NS, *2312* 181 D3
Beeton ON, *3822* 173 D2
Behchokǫ̀ NT, *1894* 155 F2
Beiseker AB, *838* 164 C2
Bella Bella BC, *1253* 156 C4
Belledune NB, *1923* 178 C2
Bellefeuille QC, *14066* 174 C3
Belleville ON, *45986* 173 E1
Belmont ON, *1819* 172 B3
Beloeil QC, *19053* 175 D3
Benito MB, *415* 166 C2
Bentley AB, *1035* 164 C2
Beresford NB, *4414* 179 D2
Berthierville QC, *3939* 175 D2
Bertrand NB, *1269* 179 D2
Berwick NS, *2282* 180 C2
Betsiamites QC, *1625* 178 A1
Bible Hill NS, *5741* 181 D2
Bienfait SK, *786* 166 C4
Biggar SK, *2243* 165 F2
Big River SK, *741* 159 F3
Binscarth MB, *445* 166 C3
Birch Hills SK, *957* 160 B4
Birchy Bay NL, *612* 183 E2
Birtle MB, *715* 167 D3
Bishop's Falls NL, *3688* 183 D3
Black Diamond AB, *1866* 164 C3
Blackfalds AB, *3042* 164 C2
Black Lake QC, *4109* 175 E2
Blacks Hbr. NB, *1082* 180 A2
Blackville NB, *1015* 178 C4
Blaine Lake SK, *508* 160 B4
Blainville QC, *36029* 174 C3
Blairmore AB, *1993* 164 C4
Blanc-Sablon QC, *1201* 183 D1
Blenheim ON, *4795* 172 B4
Blind Bay BC, *2464* 163 F1
Blind River ON, *3969* 170 B3
Blue Mts. ON, *6116* 172 C1
Bluewater ON, *6919* 172 B2
Blyth ON, *987* 172 B2
Bobcaygeon ON, *2854* 173 E1
Bois-Blanc NB, *857* 179 D2
Boischatel QC, *4303* 175 E1
Boissevain MB, *1495* 167 D4
Bolton ON, *20553* 173 D2
Bon Accord AB, *1532* 159 D4
Bonaventure QC, *2756* 179 D2
Bonavista NL, *4021* 183 E3
Bonnyville AB, *5709* 159 E3
Borden-Carleton PE, *798* 179 E4
Bothwell ON, *1002* 172 B3
Botwood NL, *3221* 183 D2
Bouctouche NB, *2426* 179 D4
Bourget ON, *1005* 174 B3
Bowden AB, *1174* 164 C2
Bowen Island BC, *2957* 163 D3
Bow Island AB, *1704* 165 D4
Bowmanville ON, *32556* 173 D2
Bowser BC, *1307* 162 C3
Bowsman MB, *320* 166 C2
Boyle AB, *836* 159 D3
Bracebridge ON, *13751* 171 D4
Bradford ON, *16978* 173 D2
Bradford-W. Gwillimbury ON, *22228* 173 D1
Bragg Creek AB, *678* 164 C3
Brampton ON, *325428* 173 D2
Brandon MB, *39716* 167 D4
Brant ON, *31669* 172 C3
Brantford ON, *86417* 172 C3
Brantville NB, *1153* 179 D3
Bridgenorth ON, *2279* 173 E1
Bridgetown NS, *1035* 180 B3
Bridgewater NS, *7621* 180 C3
Brigham QC, *2250* 175 D3
Brighton ON, *9449* 173 E2
Brigus NL, *784* 183 E4
Bristol NB, *719* 178 B4
Broadview SK, *669* 166 C3
Brochet MB, *226* 161 D1
Brockville ON, *21375* 174 B4
Bromont QC, *4808* 175 D3
Bromptonville QC, *5571* 175 E3
Brooklin ON, *5789* 173 D2
Brooklyn NS, *1078* 180 C4
Brooks AB, *11604* 165 D3
Brookside NS, *1286* 181 D3
Brownsburg-Chatham QC, *6770* 174 C3
Bruderheim AB, *1202* 159 D4
Bruno SK, *571* 166 B2
Brussels ON, *1143* 172 B2
Buchans NL, *877* 183 D3
Buckingham QC, *11668* 174 B3
Buffalo Creek BC, *701* 157 F4
Buffalo Lake AB, *722* 157 F1
Buffalo Narrows SK, *1137* 159 F2
Burford ON, *1841* 172 C3
Burgeo NL, *1782* 182 C4
Burin NL, *2470* 183 E4
Burk's Falls ON, *940* 171 D4
Burlington ON, *150836* 173 D3
Burnaby BC, *193954* 163 D3
Burns Lake BC, *1942* 157 D2
Burnt Islands NL, *801* 182 C4
Bury QC, *1171* 175 E3
Cabano QC, *3213* 178 A2
Cache Creek BC, *1056* 163 E1
Caledon ON, *50595* 172 C2
Caledon East ON, *1974* 172 C2
Caledonia ON, *8582* 172 C3
Caledon Vil. ON, *1651* 172 C2
Calgary AB, *878866* 164 C3
Calmar AB, *1902* 159 D4
Cambridge NS, *723* 180 C2
Cambridge ON, *110372* 172 C3
Cambridge-Narrows NB, *654* 180 B1
Campbellford ON, *3675* 173 E1
Campbell River BC, *28456* 162 B2
Campbellton NB, *7798* 178 C2
Camperville MB, *524* 167 D2
Camrose AB, *14854* 159 D4
Canal Flats BC, *709* 164 B3
Candle Lake SK, *503* 160 B4
Canmore AB, *10792* 164 B3
Canning NS, *811* 180 C2
Cannington ON, *2007* 173 D1
Canora SK, *2200* 166 C2
Canso NS, *992* 181 F2
Cantley QC, *5898* 174 B3
Cap-aux-Meules QC, *1659* 179 F3
Cap-Chat QC, *2913* 178 C1
Cap-de-la-Madeleine QC, *32534* 175 D2
Cape Breton Reg. Mun. NS, *105968* 181 F1
Cape St. George NL, *926* 182 C3
Caplan QC, *2010* 179 D2
Cap-Pele NB, *2266* 179 E4
Capreol ON, *3471* 170 C3
Cap-St-Ignace QC, *3204* 175 F1
Cap-Santé QC, *2571* 175 E1
Caraquet NB, *4442* 179 D2
Carberry MB, *1513* 167 D4
Carbonear NL, *4759* 183 E4
Cardigan PE, *382* 179 F4
Cardinal ON, *1739* 174 B4
Cardston AB, *3475* 164 C4
Carleton Place ON, *9083* 174 A3
Carleton-St-Omer QC, *4010* 178 C2
Carlisle ON, *2180* 172 C2
Carlyle SK, *1260* 166 C4
Carmacks YT, *431* 155 D3
Carman MB, *2831* 167 E4
Carmanville NL, *798* 183 E2
Carnduff SK, *1017* 166 C4
Caronport SK, *1040* 166 A3
Carrot River SK, *1017* 160 C4
Carseland AB, *662* 164 C3
Carstairs AB, *2254* 164 C2
Cartwright MB, *304* 167 D4
Cartwright NL, *629* 183 F1
Casselman ON, *2910* 174 B3
Cassidy BC, *978* 162 C3
Castlegar BC, *7002* 164 A4
Castor AB, *935* 165 D2
Catalina NL, *995* 183 E3
Causapscal QC, *2634* 178 B1
Cavendish PE, *267* 179 E4
Cawston BC, *1013* 163 F3
Cayuga ON, *1643* 172 C3
Cedar BC, *4440* 162 C3
Central Saanich BC, *15348* 163 D4
Centreville NS, *1047* 180 C2
Centreville-Wareham-Trinity NL, *1146* 183 E3
Chalk River ON, *975* 171 E3
Chambly QC, *20342* 175 D3
Chambord QC, *1693* 176 B3
Champlain QC, *1623* 175 D2
Chandler QC, *2817* 179 D1
Channel-Port aux-Basques NL, *4637* 182 C4
Chapais QC, *1795* 176 A2
Chapleau ON, *2832* 170 B2
Charlesbourg QC, *70310* 175 E1
Charlie Lake BC, *1727* 158 A2
Charlo NB, *1449* 178 C2
Charlottetown PE, *32245* 179 E4
Charny QC, *10507* 175 E1
Chase BC, *2460* 163 F1
Châteauguay QC, *41003* 174 C3
Château-Richer QC, *3442* 175 E1
Chatham ON, *44156* 172 B4
Chatham-Kent ON, *107341* 172 A4
Chemainus BC, *2706* 162 C3
Chertsey QC, *4112* 174 C2
Chesley ON, *1880* 172 B1
Chester NS, *1590* 180 C3
Chestermere AB, *3414* 164 C3
Chesterville ON, *1498* 174 B4
Chéticamp NS 181 E3
Chetwynd BC, *2591* 157 E1
Chibougamau QC, *7922* 176 A2
Chicoutimi QC, *60008* 176 C3
Chilliwack BC, *62927* 163 E3
Chipman NB, *1432* 178 C4
Christina Lake BC, *1035* 164 A4
Churchbridge SK, *796* 166 C3
Chute-aux-Outardes QC, *1968* 177 D2
Clair NB, *863* 178 A3
Clairmont AB, *1481* 157 F1
Clarence-Rockland ON, *19612* 174 B3
Clarenville NL, *5104* 183 E3
Claresholm AB, *3622* 164 C4
Clarington ON, *69834* 173 D2
Clarke's Beach NL, *1257* 183 E4
Clark's Hbr. NS, *944* 180 B4
Clermont QC, *3078* 176 C4
Clinton ON, *3117* 172 B2

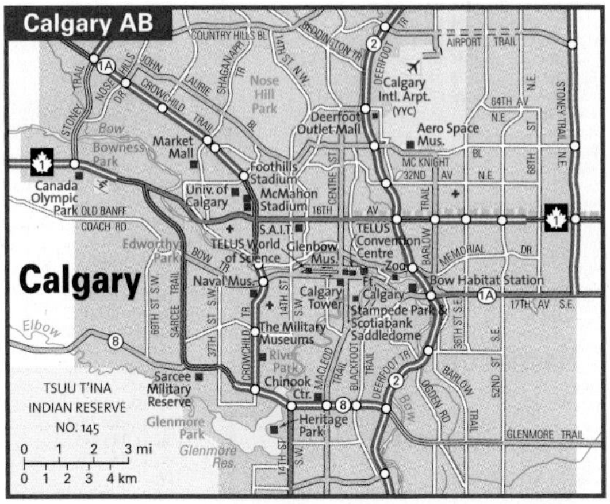
Calgary AB
Calgary
Calgary Intl. Arpt. (YYC)
Aero Space Mus.
Market Mall
Canada Olympic Park
Foothills Stadium
Univ. of Calgary
McMahon Stadium
Deerfoot Outlet Mall
TELUS World of Science
Glenbow Mus.
TELUS Convention Centre
Calgary Zoo
Bow Habitat Station
Naval Mus.
Calgary Tower
Ft. Calgary
Stampede Park & Scotiabank Saddledome
The Military Museums
Chinook Ctr.
Heritage Park
Sarcee Military Reserve
Glenmore Park
Glenmore Res.
TSUU T'INA INDIAN RESERVE NO. 145
0 1 2 3 mi
0 1 2 3 4 km

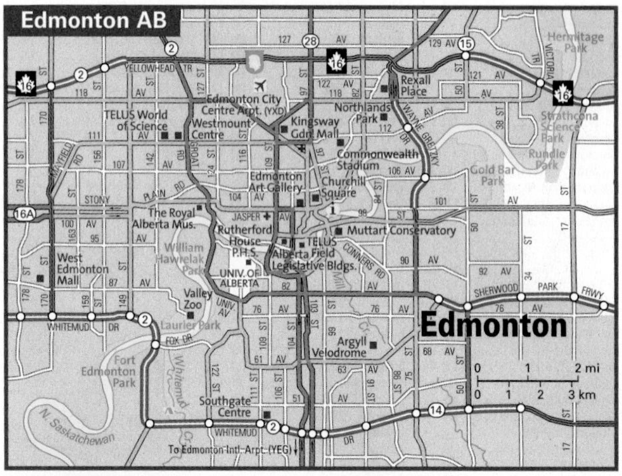
Edmonton AB
Edmonton
Edmonton City Centre Arpt. (YXD)
TELUS World of Science
Westmount Centre
Kingsway Gdn. Mall
Northlands Park
Rexall Place
Commonwealth Stadium
Edmonton Art Gallery
Churchill Square
The Royal Alberta Mus.
Muttart Conservatory
Rutherford House
TELUS Alberta Field
Legislative Bldgs.
UNIV. OF ALBERTA
West Edmonton Mall
Valley Zoo
Laurier Park
Fort Edmonton Park
Argyll Velodrome
Southgate Centre
Gold Bar Park
Hermitage Park
Strathcona Science Park
Rundle Park
N. Saskatchewan
To Edmonton Intl. Arpt. (YEG)
0 1 2 mi
0 1 2 3 km

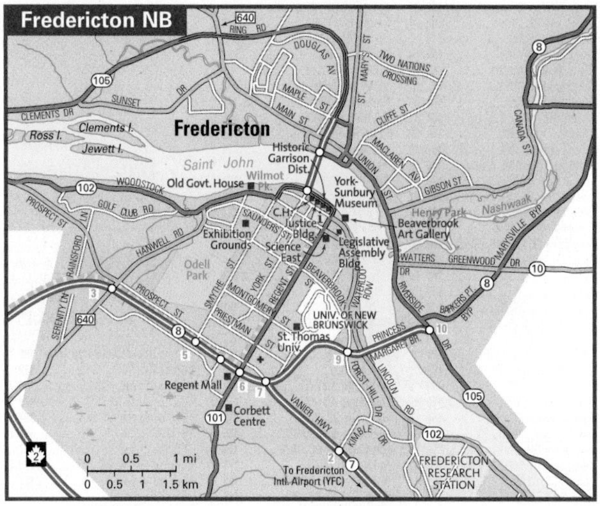
Fredericton NB
Fredericton
Saint John
Historic Garrison Dist.
Old Govt. House
York-Sunbury Museum
Beaverbrook Art Gallery
Legislative Assembly Bldg.
C.H.
Justice Bldg.
Science East
Exhibition Grounds
Odell Park
UNIV. OF NEW BRUNSWICK
St. Thomas Univ.
Regent Mall
Corbett Centre
Henry Park
Nashwaak
Ross I.
Clements I.
Jewett I.
To Fredericton Intl. Airport (YFC)
FREDERICTON RESEARCH STATION
0 0.5 1 mi
0 0.5 1 1.5 km

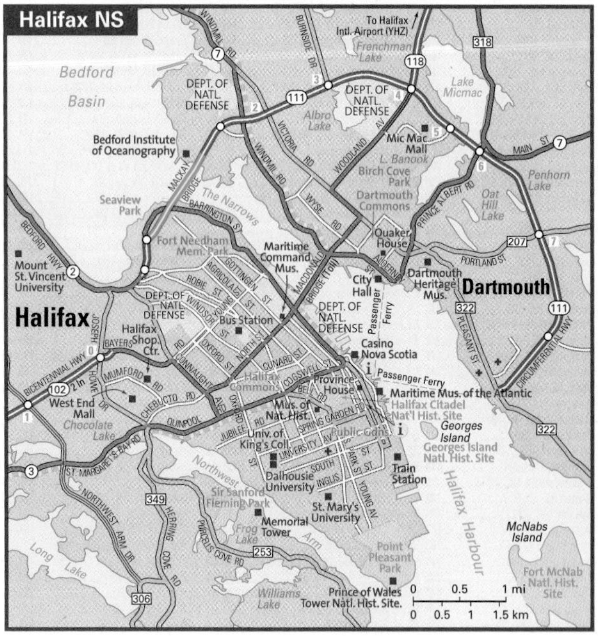
Halifax NS
Halifax
Dartmouth
Bedford Basin
To Halifax Intl. Airport (YHZ)
DEPT. OF NATL. DEFENSE
Bedford Institute of Oceanography
Seaview Park
Mic Mac Mall
Birch Cove Park
Dartmouth Commons
Fort Needham Mem. Park
Maritime Command Mus.
Quaker House
Dartmouth Heritage Mus.
Mount St. Vincent University
City Hall
Halifax Shop. Ctr.
Bus Station
Casino Nova Scotia
Province House
Maritime Mus. of the Atlantic
Halifax Citadel Nat'l Hist. Site
Halifax Common
West End Mall
Chocolate Lake
Mus. of Nat. Hist.
Univ. of King's Coll.
Dalhousie University
Georges Island Natl. Hist. Site
Train Station
Sir Sanford Fleming Park
Memorial Tower
St. Mary's University
Frog Lake
Long Lake
Point Pleasant Park
Prince of Wales Tower Natl. Hist. Site
McNabs Island
Fort McNab Natl. Hist. Site
Halifax Harbour
Northwest Arm
0 0.5 1 mi
0 0.5 1 1.5 km

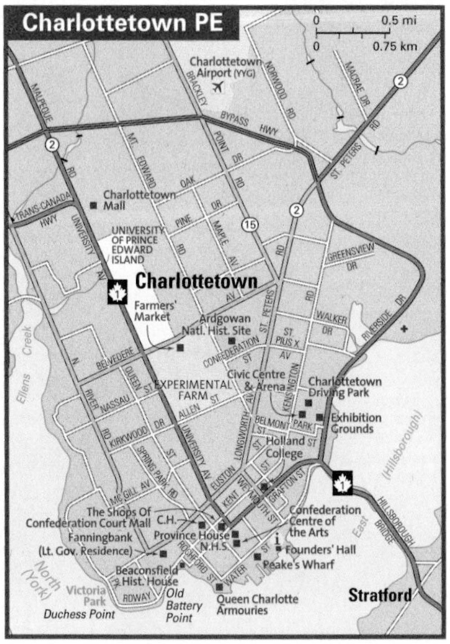
Charlottetown PE
Charlottetown
Charlottetown Airport (YYG)
Charlottetown Mall
UNIVERSITY OF PRINCE EDWARD ISLAND
Farmers' Market
Ardgowan Natl. Hist. Site
EXPERIMENTAL FARM
Civic Centre & Arena
Charlottetown Driving Park
Exhibition Grounds
Holland College
The Shops Of Confederation Court Mall
Fanningbank (Lt. Gov. Residence)
Province House N.H.S.
Confederation Centre of the Arts
Founders' Hall
Peake's Wharf
Beaconsfield Hist. House
Victoria Park
Old Battery Point
Queen Charlotte Armouries
Duchess Point
Stratford
0 0.5 mi
0 0.75 km

Figures after entries indicate population, page number, and grid reference.

Hamilton ON

London ON

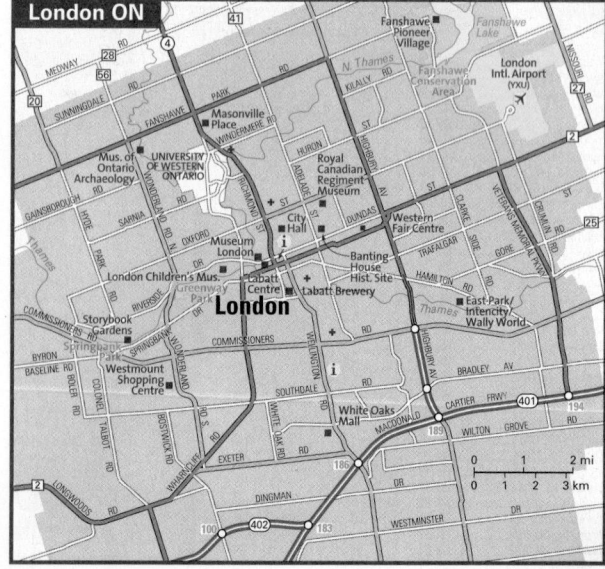

Entries in **bold color** indicate cities with detailed inset maps.

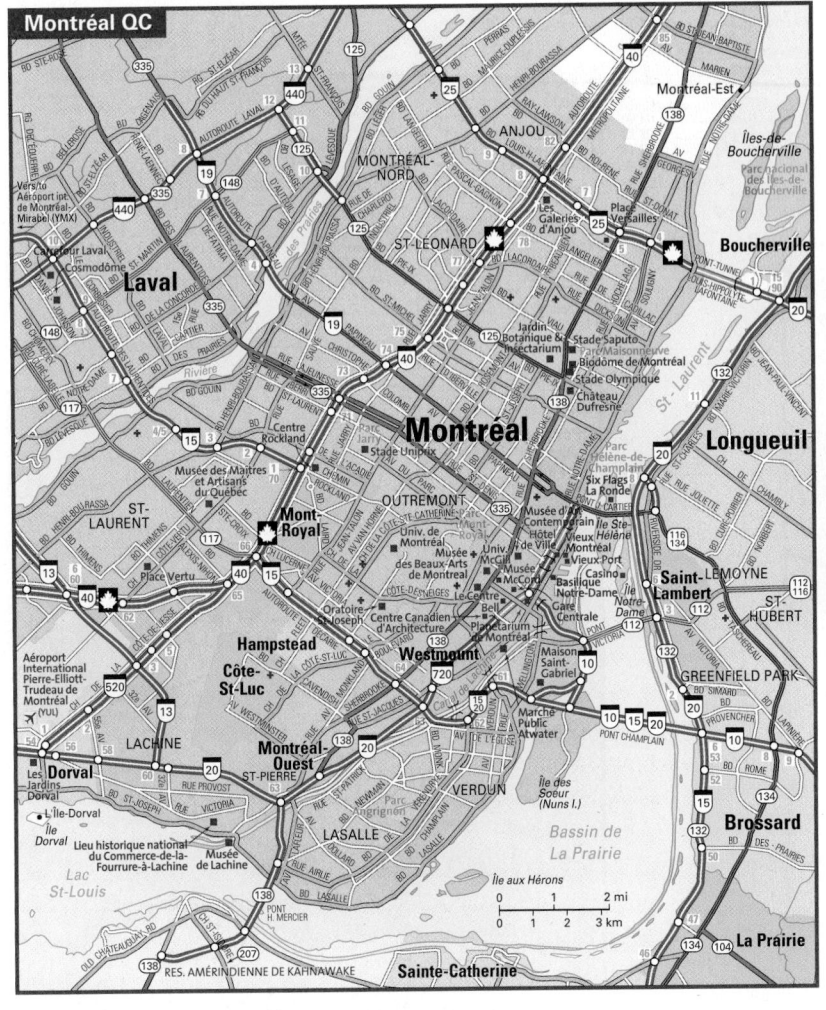

Montréal QC

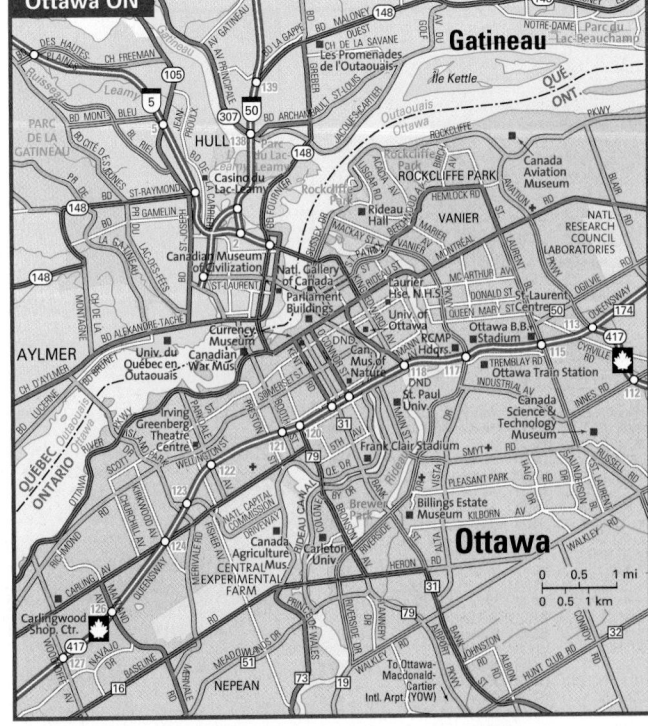

Ottawa ON

Figures after entries indicate population, page number, and grid reference.

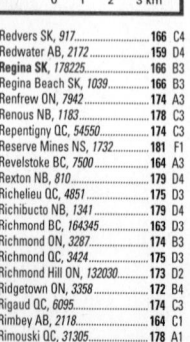
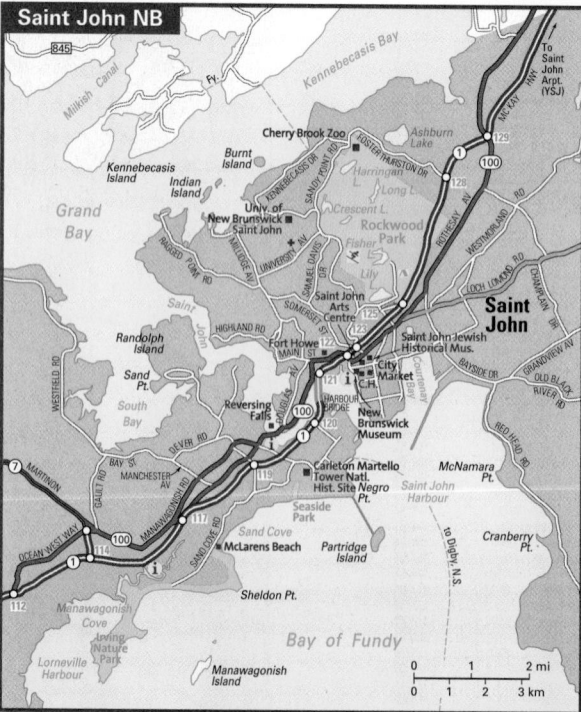

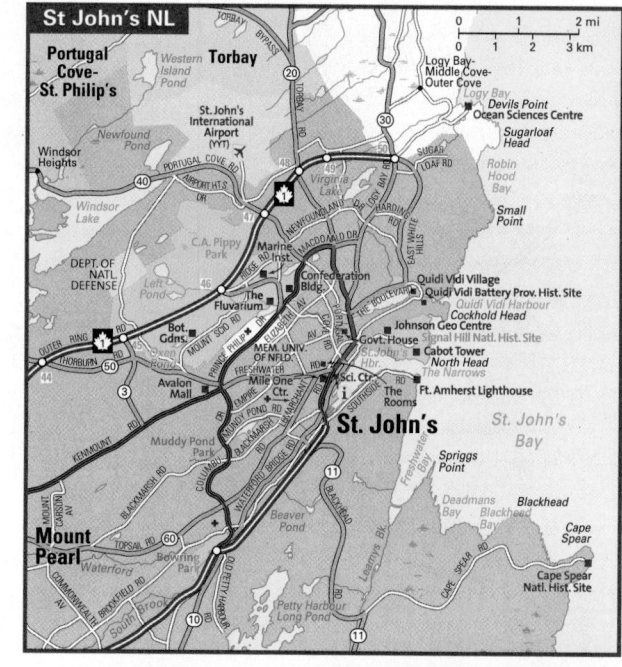

Entries in **bold color** indicate cities with detailed inset maps.

Toronto ON

Vaughan • Markham • SCARBOROUGH • NORTH YORK • YORK • EAST YORK • Toronto • ETOBICOKE • Mississauga • LAKE ONTARIO

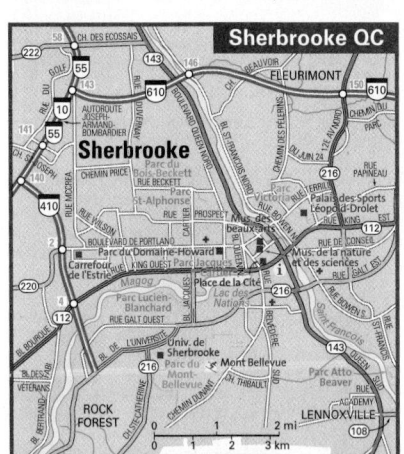

Sherbrooke QC

Sherbrooke • FLEURIMONT • ROCK FOREST • LENNOXVILLE

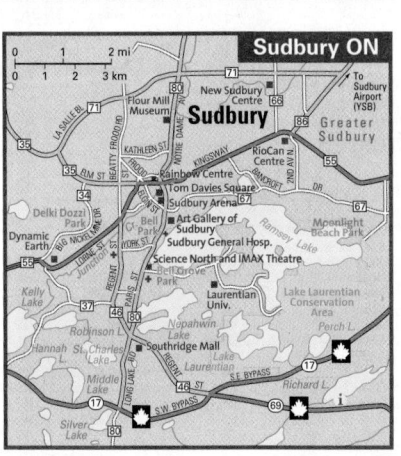

Sudbury ON

Sudbury • Greater Sudbury • New Sudbury Centre

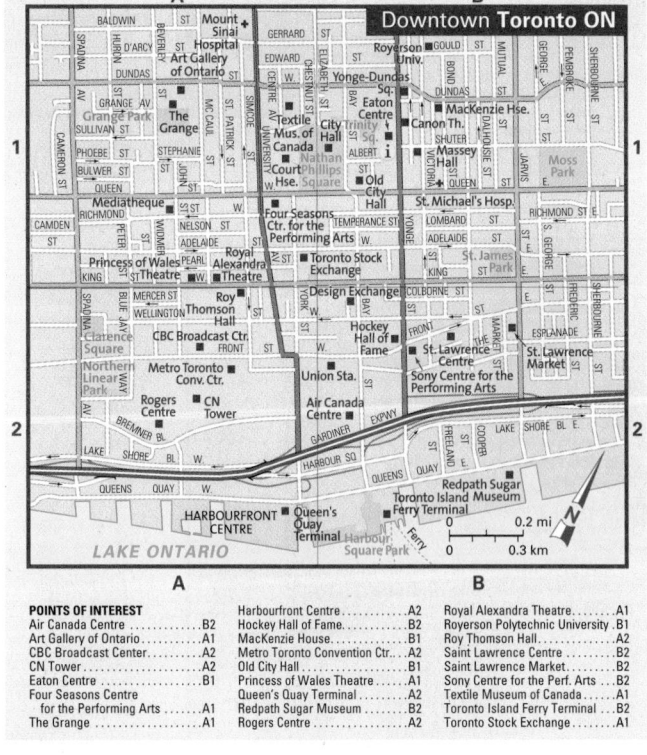

Downtown Toronto ON

LAKE ONTARIO

Figures after entries indicate population, page number, and grid reference.

Anmore ... D1
Belcarra ... D1
Burnaby ... D2
Coquitlam ... D2
New Westminster ... D2
N. Vancouver ... B1
N. Vancouver (DM) ... C1
Port Moody ... D1
Richmond ... C2
Surrey ... D2
Vancouver ... B2
W. Vancouver ... A1

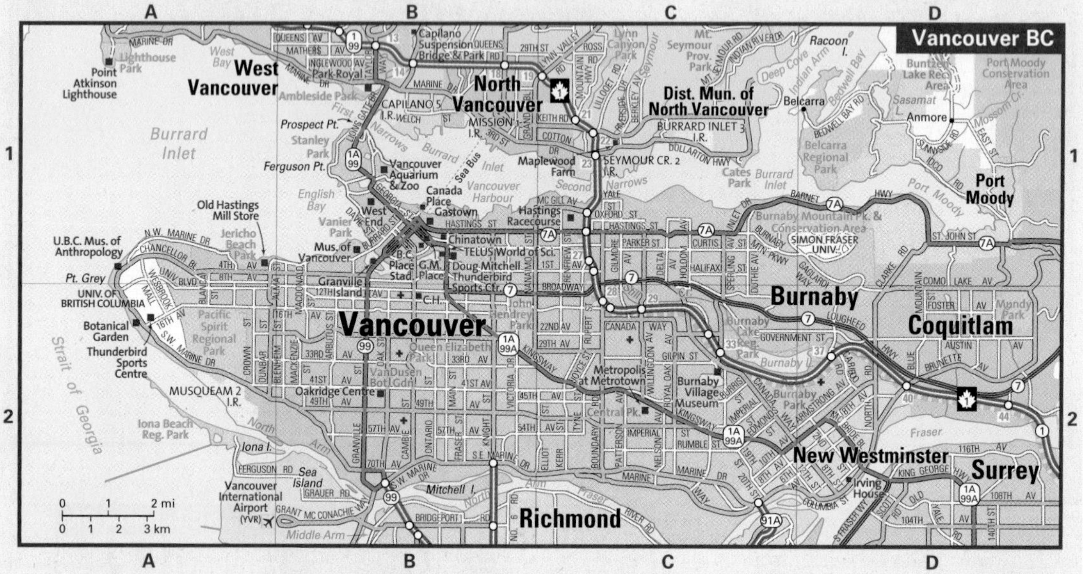

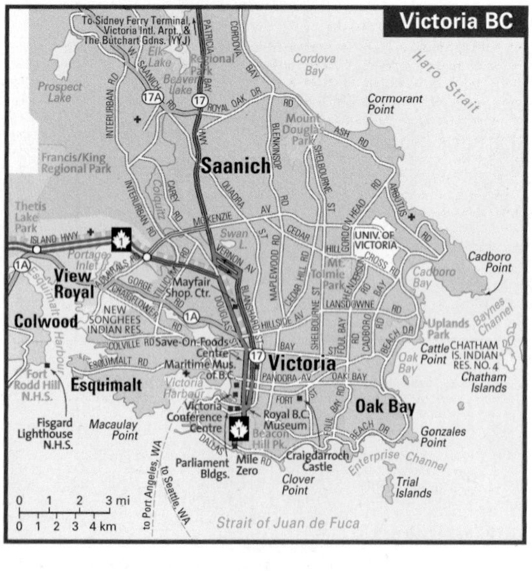

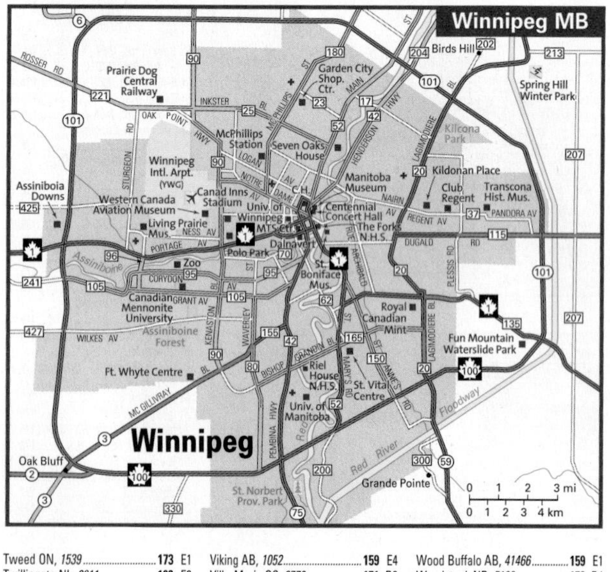

Vancouver BC

West Vancouver · North Vancouver · Dist. Mun. of North Vancouver · Port Moody · Vancouver · Burnaby · Coquitlam · New Westminster · Surrey · Richmond

Victoria BC

Saanich · View Royal · Colwood · Esquimalt · Victoria · Oak Bay

Winnipeg MB

Winnipeg

283
Acámbaro–Zumpango del Río

Entries in **bold color** indicate cities with detailed inset maps.

MEXICO

Acámbaro, *57972* **186** B3
Acaponeta, *17906* **186** A2
Acapulco, *673479* **186** B4
Acayucan, *50934* **187** D3
Actopan, *24097* **186** C2
Agua Dulce, *36079* **187** D3
Agua Prieta, *77254* **184** C1
Aguascalientes, *722250* **186** B2
Ajalpan, *28031* **186** C3
Álamo, *23281* **186** C2
Allende, *17753* **185** E2
Altamira, *59536* **186** C2
Alvarado, *23776* **187** D3
Apan, *26642* **186** C3
Apatzingán, *99010* **186** B3
Apizaco, *49506* **186** C3
Apodaca, *212118* **185** E3
Arcelia, *16609* **186** B3
Arriaga, *24447* **187** D4
Atlixco, *86690* **186** C3
Atoyac de Álvarez, *21407* **186** B4
Autlán de Navarro, *45382* **186** A2
Berriozábal, *16897* **187** D4
Caborca, *59922* **184** B1
Cabo San Lucas, *68463* **184** C4
Calvillo, *17966* **186** B2
Campeche, *220389* **187** E2
Cananea, *31560* **184** C1
Cancún, *628306* **187** F2
Cárdenas, *91558* **187** D3
Castaños, *19035* **185** E3
Catemaco, *27615* **187** D3
Celaya, *340387* **186** B2
Cerro Azul, *22268* **186** C2
Champotón, *30881* **187** E3
Chapala, *17998* **186** A2
Chetumal, *151243* **187** F3
Chiapa, *27654* **187** E4
Chihuahua, *809232* **185** D2
Chilpancingo, *187251* **186** C4
Cholula, *87897* **186** C3
Cintalapa, *42467* **187** D4
Cd. Acuña, *134233* **185** E2
Cd. Altamirano, *25168* **186** B3
Cd. Camargo, *37400* **185** D3
Cd. Constitución, *40935* **184** B4
Cd. del Carmen, *169466* **187** E3
Cd. Guzmán, *97750* **186** A3
Cd. Hidalgo, *60542* **186** B3
Cd. Ixtepec, *25381* **187** D4
Cd. Juárez, *1321004* **185** D1
Cd. Lerdo, *79669* **185** D4
Cd. Madero, *197216* **186** C2
Cd. Mante, *84787* **186** C1
Cd. Mendoza, *35641* **186** C3
Cd. Miguel Alemán, *16946* **185** F3
Cd. Obregón, *298625* **184** C3
Cd. Valles, *124644* **186** C2
Cd. Victoria, *305155* **185** F4
Coatepec, *53621* **186** C3
Coatzacoalcos, *235983* **187** D3
Colima, *137383* **186** A3
Comalcalco, *41458* **187** D3
Comitán de Domínguez, *97537* **187** E4
Comonfort, *23683* **186** B2
Córdoba, *140896* **186** C3
Cosamaloapan, *30577* **187** D3
Cosoleacaque, *22454* **187** D3
Costa Rica, *24874* **184** C4
Cozumel, *77236* **187** F2
Cuauhtémoc, *114007* **184** C2
Cuautla, *154358* **186** C3
Cuernavaca, *338650* **186** C3
Culiacán, *675773* **184** C4
Delicias, *118071* **185** D2
Dolores Hidalgo, *59240* **186** B2
Durango, *518709* **185** D4
Ébano, *24296* **186** C2
Emiliano Zapata, *16340* **187** E3
Empalme, *42516* **184** B2
Ensenada, *279765* **184** A1
Escárcega, *29477* **187** E3
Escuinapa de Hidalgo, *30790* **186** A1
Felipe Carrillo Puerto, *16427* **187** F3
Francisco I. Madero, *26201* **185** E3
Fresnillo, *120944* **185** E4
Frontera, *69462* **185** E3
Frontera, *69462* **187** E3
Garza García, *120868* **185** E3
Gómez Palacio, *257352* **185** D3
Guadalajara, *1495182* **186** A2
Guadalupe, *673616* **185** E3
Guadalupe, *673616* **186** B1
Guamúchil, *63743* **184** C4
Guanajuato, *72237* **186** B2
Guasave, *71196* **184** C3
Guaymas, *113082* **184** B2
Hermosillo, *715061* **184** B2
Hidalgo del Parral, *104836* **185** D3
Huajuapan de León, *53043* **186** C3
Huatabampo, *30475* **184** C3
Huatusco, *31305* **186** C3
Huauchinango, *56206* **186** C2
Huejutla de Reyes, *40015* **186** C2
Huetamo de Núñez, *21507* **186** B3
Huimanguillo, *27344* **187** D3
Huixtla, *32033* **187** E4
Hunucmá, *24910* **187** E2
Iguala, *118468* **186** C3
Irapuato, *380941* **186** B2
Ixmiquilpan, *34814* **186** C2
Ixtlán del Río, *21474* **186** A2
Izucar de Matamoros, *36531* **186** C3
Jacona, *56934* **186** B3
Jalostotitlán, *24423* **186** B2
Jáltipan de Morelos, *32778* **187** D3
Jérez de García Salinas, *43064* **186** A1
Jiménez, *34281* **185** D3
Jiutepec, *162427* **186** C3
Juchitán de Zaragoza, *74825* **187** D4
Kanasín, *77240* **187** F2
La Barca, *35219* **186** B2
Lagos de Moreno, *98206* **186** B2
La Paz, *215178* **184** B4
La Piedad de Cabadas, *83323* **186** B2
Las Choapas, *42693* **187** D3
Lázaro Cárdenas, *79200* **186** B3
León, *1238962* **186** B2
Linares, *63104* **185** F4
Loma Bonita, *31485* **187** D3
Loreto, *17714* **186** B2
Los Mochis, *256613* **184** C3
Los Reyes de Salgado, *39209* **186** B3
Macuspana, *32225* **187** E3
Magdalena de Kino, *19609* **184** B1
Manzanillo, *130035* **186** A3
Martínez de la Torre, *60074* **186** C2
Matamoros, *449815* **185** E4
Matamoros, *449815* **185** F3
Matehuala, *77328* **185** E4
Matías Romero, *20127* **187** D4
Mazatlán, *381583* **185** D4
Melchor Múzquiz, *35060* **185** E3
Meoqui, *22574* **185** D2
Mérida, *777615* **187** F2

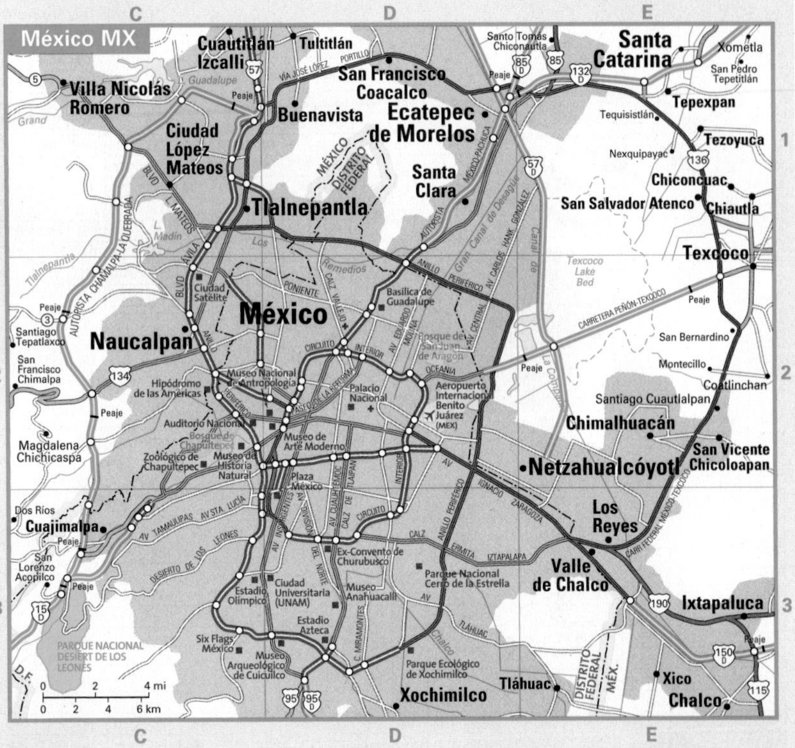
México MX
Cuautitlán Izcalli
Tultitlán
Villa Nicolás Romero
San Francisco Coacalco
Santa Catarina
Ciudad López Mateos
Buenavista
Ecatepec de Morelos
Tepexpan
Tezoyuca
Santa Clara
Tlalnepantla
Chiconcuac
San Salvador Atenco
Chiautla
Texcoco
México
Naucalpan
San Bernardino
Montecillo
Coatlinchan
Santiago Cuautlalpan
Chimalhuacán
Netzahualcóyotl
San Vicente Chicoloapan
Cuajimalpa
Los Reyes
Valle de Chalco
Ixtapaluca
Xico
Chalco
Xochimilco
Tláhuac
0 2 4 mi
0 2 4 6 km

Buenavista D1	Ecatepec de Morelos .. D1	Nexquipayac E1	San Vicente Chicoloapan E2	Texcoco E2
Chalco E3	Fuentes del Valle D1	Nicolás Romero C1	Santa Catarina E1	Tezoyuca E1
Chiautla E1	Ixtapaluca E3	San Bernardino E2	Santa Clara D1	Tláhuac E3
Chiconcuac E1	Los Reyes E3	San Francisco Chimalpa C2	Santo Tomás Chipiltepec E1	Tlalnepantla C1
Chimalhuacán E2	México D2	San Francisco Coacalco D1	Santiago Cuautlalpan ... E2	Tultitlán D1
Ciudad López Mateos .. C1	Magdalena Chichicaspa C2	San Lorenzo Acopilco . C3	Santiago Tepatlaxco .. C2	Valle de Chalco E3
Coatlinchan E2	Montecillo E2	San Pedro Tepetitlán ... E1	Tepexpan E1	Xico E3
Cuajimalpa C3	Naucalpan C2	San Salvador Atenco ... E1	Tequisistlán E1	Xochimilco D3
Cuautitlán Izcalli C1	Netzahualcóyotl E2			Xometla E1
Dos Rìos C3				

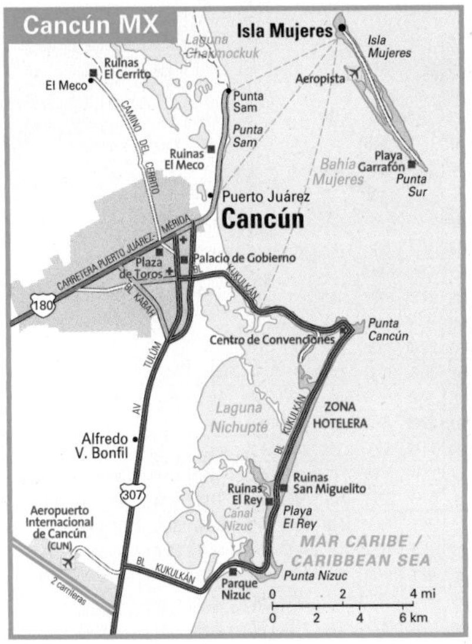
Cancún MX
Isla Mujeres
Ruinas El Cerrito
El Meco
Aeropista
Punta Sam
Ruinas El Meco
Playa Garrafón
Bahía Mujeres
Punta Sur
Puerto Juárez
Cancún
Palacio de Gobierno
Plaza de Toros
Centro de Convenciones
Punta Cancún
Laguna Nichupté
ZONA HOTELERA
Alfredo V. Bonfil
Ruinas San Miguelito
Ruinas El Rey
Playa El Rey
Aeropuerto Internacional de Cancún (CUN)
MAR CARIBE / CARIBBEAN SEA
Parque Nizuc
Punta Nizuc
0 2 4 mi
0 2 4 6 km

Mexicali, *689775* **184** A1
México, *8555272* **186** C3
Minatitlán, *112046* **187** D3
Misantla, *26827* **186** C3
Monclova, *215271* **185** E3
Montemorelos, *45108* **185** F4
Monterrey, *1135512* **185** E3
Morelia, *597511* **186** B3
Moroleón, *43200* **186** B2
Naranjos, *20073* **186** C2
Navojoa, *113836* **184** C3
Navolato, *29153* **184** C4
Netzahualcóyotl, *1104585* **186** C3
Nogales, *212533* **184** B1
Nueva Italia de Ruiz, *29598* **186** B3
Nueva Rosita, *38158* **185** E3
Nuevo Casas Grandes, *55553* **184** C2
Nuevo Laredo, *373725* **185** F3
Oaxaca, *255029* **186** C4
Ocotlán, *83769* **186** A2
Ocozocoautla, *39180* **187** D4
Orizaba, *120844* **186** C3
Pachuca, *256584* **186** C2
Pánuco, *40754* **186** C2
Papantla, *53546* **186** C2
Paraíso, *25186* **187** D3
Parras de la Fuente, *33817* **185** E4
Pátzcuaro, *55298* **186** B3
Perote, *37516* **186** C3
Petatlán, *21659* **186** B4
Piedras Negras, *150178* **185** E2
Playa del Carmen, *149923* **187** F2
Poza Rica, *185242* **186** C2
Progreso, *40005* **187** E2
Puebla, *1434062* **186** C3
Puerto Peñasco, *56756* **184** B1
Puerto Vallarta, *203342* **186** A2
Puruándiro, *30571* **186** B2
Querétaro, *626495* **186** B2
Reynosa, *589466* **185** F3
Rincón de Romos, *27988* **186** B2
Río Bravo, *95647* **185** F3
Río Grande, *32944* **185** E4
Río Verde, *53128* **186** B2
Sabinas Hidalgo, *29988* **185** E3
Sahuayo, *64431* **186** B2
Salamanca, *160169* **186** B2
Salina Cruz, *71464* **187** D4
Saltillo, *709671* **185** E4
Salvatierra, *37203* **186** B2
San Andrés Tuxtla, *61769* **187** D3
San Buenaventura, *17743* **185** E3
San Cristóbal de las Casas, *158027* **187** E4
San Felipe, *28452* **186** B2
San Fernando, *29665* **185** F4
San Francisco del Rincón, *71139* **186** B2
San José del Cabo, *69788* **184** C4
San Juan de los Lagos, *48684* **186** B2
San Juan del Río, *138878* **186** B2
San Luis de la Paz, *49914* **186** B2
San Luis Potosí, *722772* **186** B2
San Luis Río Colorado, *158089* **184** A1
San Miguel de Allende, *69811* **186** B2
San Nicolás de los Garza, *443273* **185** E3
San Pedro de las Colonias, *48746* **185** E3
Santa Catarina, *201233* **185** E3
Santiago, *36840* **185** E4
Santiago Papasquiaro, *26121* **185** D4
Sayula, *26789* **186** A3
Silao, *74242* **186** B2
Sombrerete, *17535* **185** D4
Tacámbaro de Codallos, *18742* **186** B3
Tala, *35396* **186** A2
Tamazunchale, *24562* **186** C2
Tampico, *297284* **186** C2
Tantoyuca, *30587* **186** C2
Tapachula, *202672* **187** E4
Taxco, *52217* **186** B3
Teapa, *26548* **187** E3
Tecamachalco, *28679* **186** C3
Tecate, *64764* **184** A1
Tecomán, *85689* **186** A3
Tehuacán, *248716* **186** C3
Tehuantepec, *36888* **187** D4
Tejupilco de Hidalgo, *17994* **186** B3
Teloloapan, *23549* **186** B3
Tenancingo, *25195* **186** B3
Tenosique, *32579* **187** E3
Teocaltiche, *23726* **186** B2
Tepatitlán, *91959* **186** B2
Tepeji de Ocampo, *29486* **186** C3
Tepic, *332863* **186** A2
Tequila, *29203* **186** A2
Tequisquiapan, *29799* **186** B2
Tequixquiac, *16789* **186** C3
Teziutlán, *58699* **186** C3
Ticul, *32796* **187** F2
Tierra Blanca, *47824* **186** C3
Tijuana, *1300983* **184** A1
Tizayuca, *43250* **186** C3
Tizimín, *46971* **187** F2
Tlapa de Comonfort, *46975* **186** C3
Tlapacoyan, *35338* **186** C3
Tlaxcala, *14692* **186** C3
Toluca, *489333* **186** B3
Tonalá, *408759* **186** A2
Tonalá, *29557* **187** D4
Torreón, *608836* **185** D3
Tres Valles, *18078* **187** D3
Tulancingo, *102406* **186** C2
Tuxpam, *84750* **186** C2
Tuxpan, *22481* **186** A2
Tuxpan, *27523* **186** A3
Tuxtepec, *101810* **187** D3
Tuxtla Gutiérrez, *537102* **187** E4
Umán, *39611* **187** E2
Uruapan, *264439* **186** B3
Valladolid, *48973* **187** F2
Valle de Santiago, *68058* **186** B2
Valle Hermoso, *48918* **185** F3
Veracruz, *428323* **187** D3
Víctor Rosales, *32721* **186** B1
Villa Flores, *28257* **187** D4
Villahermosa, *353577* **187** E3
Xalapa, *424755* **186** C3
Xicotepec de Juárez, *39803* **186** C2
Zacapu, *52806* **186** B3
Zacatecas, *129011* **186** B1
Zacatlán, *33736* **186** C2
Zamora de Hidalgo, *141627* **186** B3
Zapopan, *1142483* **186** A2
Zapotiltic, *22833* **186** A3
Zihuatanejo, *67408* **186** B3
Zitácuaro, *84307* **186** B3
Zumpango, *50742* **186** C3
Zumpango del Río, *18158* **186** B3

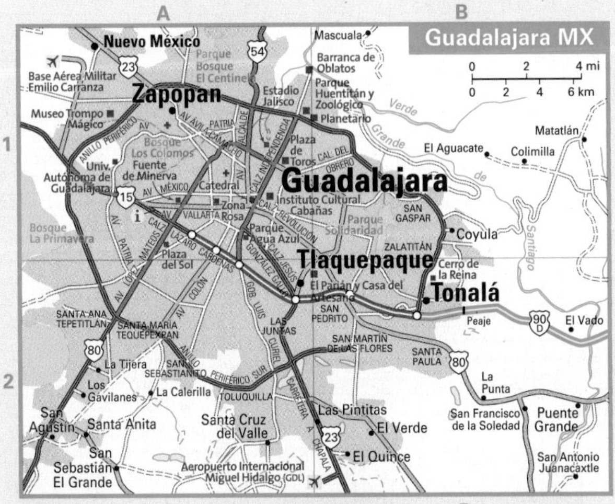
Guadalajara MX
Nuevo México
Mascuala
Barranca de Oblatos
Base Aérea Militar Emilio Carranza
Zapopan
Estadio Jalisco
Parque Huentitán y Zoológico
Planetario
Matatlán
El Aguacate
Colimilla
Guadalajara
Catedral
Instituto Cultural Cabañas
Coyula
Tlaquepaque
Tonalá
El Vado
La Tijera
La Calerilla
Los Gavilanes
La Punta
San Agustín
Santa Anita
Santa Cruz del Valle
Las Pintitas
El Verde
San Francisco de la Soledad
Puente Grande
El Quince
San Sebastián El Grande
Aeropuerto Internacional Miguel Hidalgo (GDL)
San Antonio Juanacaxtle
0 2 4 mi
0 2 4 6 km

Colimilla B1	La Calerilla A2	Nuevo México A1	San Sebastián El Grande A2
Coyula B1	La Punta B2	Puente Grande B2	Santa Anita A2
El Aguacate B1	La Tijera A2	San Antoni Juanacaxtle B2	Santa Cruz del Valle . A2
El Quince B2	Las Pintitas B2	San Francisco de la Soledad B2	Tlaquepaque A2
El Vado B2	Los Gavilanes A2	San Agustín A2	Tonalá B2
El Verde B2	Mascuala B1		Zapopan A1
Guadalajara A1	Matatlán B1		

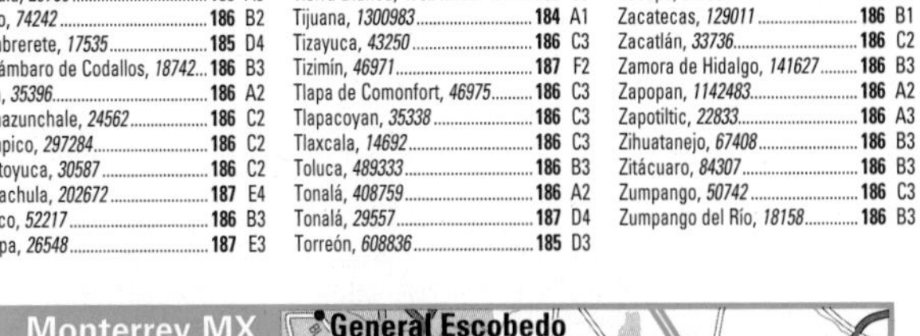
Monterrey MX
General Escobedo
Apodaca
San Nicolás de los Garza
Aeropuerto Internacional General Mariano Escobedo (MTY)
Universidad Autónoma de Nuevo León
Monterrey
Parque Niños Héroes
Plaza de Toros
Guadalupe
Parque Fundidora
San Pedro Garza García
Parque Zoológico La Pastora
Ciudad Benito Juárez
Jardines de la Silla
PARQUE NACIONAL CUMBRES DE MONTERREY
Parque Ecológico Chipinque
0 2 4 mi
0 2 4 6 km

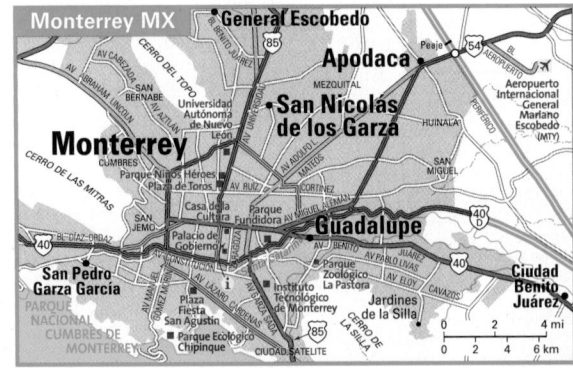

Miles

	Albany, NY	Albuquerque, NM	Amarillo, TX	Anchorage, AK	Atlanta, GA	Baltimore, MD	Billings, MT	Birmingham, AL	Bismarck, ND	Boise, ID	Boston, MA	Buffalo, NY	Calgary, AB	Charleston, SC	Charleston, WV	Charlotte, NC	Cheyenne, WY	Chicago, IL	Cincinnati, OH	Cleveland, OH	Columbus, OH	Dallas, TX	Denver, CO	Des Moines, IA	Detroit, MI	El Paso, TX	Halifax, NS	Houston, TX	Indianapolis, IN	Jackson, MS	Jacksonville, FL	Kansas City, MO	Las Vegas, NV	Little Rock, AR	Los Angeles, CA	Louisville, KY
Albany, NY		2095	1811	4421	1010	333	2083	1093	1675	2526	172	292	2512	913	634	771	1789	832	730	484	621	1680	1833	1155	571	2326	877	1768	795	1331	1094	1282	2586	1354	2859	832
Albuquerque, NM			286	3563	1490	1902	991	1274	1333	966	2240	1808	1498	1793	1568	1649	538	1352	1409	1619	1476	754	438	1091	1608	263	2945	994	1298	1157	1837	894	578	900	806	1320
Amarillo, TX				3734	1206	1618	988	991	1398	1266	1957	1524	1669	1510	1285	1365	534	1069	1126	1335	1192	470	434	808	1324	438	2662	711	1014	874	1517	610	864	617	1092	1036
Anchorage, AK					4304	4297	2601	4253	2724	2745	4592	4133	2065	4495	4093	4348	3056	3584	3890	3935	3946	4087	3300	3421	3872	4002	4821	4328	3771	4294	4652	3547	3356	3929	3403	3886
Atlanta, GA						679	1889	150	1559	2218	1100	910	2395	317	503	238	1482	717	476	726	577	792	1403	967	735	1437	1805	800	531	386	344	801	2067	528	2237	419
Baltimore, MD							1959	795	1551	2401	422	370	2388	583	352	441	1665	708	521	377	420	1399	1690	1031	532	2045	1128	1470	600	1032	763	1087	2445	1072	2705	602
Billings, MT								1839	413	626	2254	1796	536	2157	1755	2012	455	1246	1552	1597	1608	1433	554	1007	1534	1255	2806	1673	1432	1836	2237	1088	965	1530	1239	1547
Birmingham, AL									1509	2170	1215	909	2346	466	578	389	1434	667	475	725	576	647	1356	919	734	1292	1921	678	481	241	494	753	1852	381	2092	369
Bismarck, ND										1039	1846	1388	794	1749	1347	1604	594	838	1144	1189	1200	1342	693	675	1126	1597	2398	1582	1024	1548	1906	801	1378	1183	1702	1139
Boise, ID											2697	2239	735	2520	2182	2375	737	1708	1969	2040	2036	1711	833	1369	1977	1206	3249	1952	1852	2115	2566	1376	760	1808	1033	1933
Boston, MA												462	2683	1003	741	861	1961	1003	862	654	760	1819	2004	1326	741	2465	714	1890	940	1453	1184	1427	2757	1493	3046	964
Buffalo, NY													2224	899	431	695	1502	545	442	197	333	1393	1546	868	277	2039	1167	1513	508	1134	1080	995	2299	1066	2572	545
Calgary, AB														2586	2184	2441	991	1675	1981	2026	2037	2114	1234	1512	1963	1936	2912	2355	1862	2385	2743	1638	1291	2020	1565	1977
Charleston, SC															468	204	1783	907	622	724	637	1109	1705	1204	879	1754	1708	1110	721	703	238	1102	2371	900	2554	610
Charleston, WV																265	1445	506	209	255	168	1072	1367	802	410	1718	1446	1192	320	816	649	764	2122	745	2374	251
Charlotte, NC																	1637	761	476	520	433	1031	1559	1057	675	1677	1566	1041	575	625	385	956	2225	754	2453	464
Cheyenne, WY																		972	1233	1304	1300	979	100	633	1241	801	2513	1220	1115	1382	1829	640	843	1076	1116	1197
Chicago, IL																			302	346	359	936	1015	337	283	1543	1555	1108	184	750	1065	532	1768	662	2042	299
Cincinnati, OH																				253	105	958	1200	599	261	1605	1567	1079	116	700	803	597	1955	632	2215	106
Cleveland, OH																					144	1208	1347	669	171	1854	1359	1328	319	950	904	806	2100	882	2374	356
Columbus, OH																						1059	1266	665	192	1706	1465	1179	176	801	818	663	2021	733	2281	207
Dallas, TX																							887	752	1218	647	2524	241	913	406	1049	554	1331	327	1446	852
Denver, CO																								676	1284	701	2556	1127	1088	1290	1751	603	756	984	1029	1118
Des Moines, IA																									606	1283	1878	992	481	931	1315	194	1429	567	1703	595
Detroit, MI																										1799	1278	1338	318	960	1060	795	2037	891	2310	366
El Paso, TX																											3171	758	1489	1051	1642	1085	717	974	801	1499
Halifax, NS																												2595	1646	2158	1889	2133	3309	2198	3583	1669
Houston, TX																													839	445	884	795	1474	447	1558	972
Indianapolis, IN																														675	879	485	1843	587	2104	112
Jackson, MS																															598	747	1735	269	1851	594
Jacksonville, FL																																1148	2415	873	2441	766
Kansas City, MO																																	1358	382	1632	516
Las Vegas, NV																																		1478	274	1874
Little Rock, AR																																			1706	526
Los Angeles, CA																																				2126

Kilometers

	Albany, NY	Albuquerque, NM	Amarillo, TX	Anchorage, AK	Atlanta, GA	Baltimore, MD	Billings, MT	Birmingham, AL	Bismarck, ND	Boise, ID	Boston, MA	Buffalo, NY	Calgary, AB	Charleston, SC	Charleston, WV	Charlotte, NC	Cheyenne, WY	Chicago, IL	Cincinnati, OH	Cleveland, OH	Columbus, OH	Dallas, TX	Denver, CO	Des Moines, IA	Detroit, MI	El Paso, TX	Halifax, NS	Houston, TX	Indianapolis, IN	Jackson, MS	Jacksonville, FL	Kansas City, MO	Las Vegas, NV	Little Rock, AR	Los Angeles, CA	Louisville, KY
Albuquerque, NM	3371																																			
Amarillo, TX	2914	460																																		
Anchorage, AK	7113	5733	6008																																	
Atlanta, GA	1625	2397	1940	6925																																
Baltimore, MD	536	3060	2603	6914	1093																															
Billings, MT	3352	1595	1590	4185	3039	3152																														
Birmingham, AL	1759	2050	1595	6843	241	1279	2959																													
Bismarck, ND	2695	2145	2249	4383	2508	2496	665	2428																												
Boise, ID	4064	1554	2037	4417	3569	3863	1007	3492	1672																											
Boston, MA	277	3604	3149	7389	1770	679	3627	1955	2970	4339																										
Buffalo, NY	470	2909	2452	6650	1464	595	2890	1463	2233	3603	743																									
Calgary, AB	4042	2410	2685	3323	3854	3842	862	3775	1278	1183	4317	3578																								
Charleston, SC	1469	2885	2430	7232	510	938	3471	750	2814	4055	1614	1446	4161																							
Charleston, WV	1020	2523	2068	6586	809	566	2824	930	2167	3511	1192	693	3514	753																						
Charlotte, NC	1241	2653	2196	6996	383	710	3237	626	2581	3821	1385	1118	3928	328	426																					
Cheyenne, WY	2879	866	859	4917	2385	2679	732	2307	956	1186	3155	2417	1595	2869	2325	2634																				
Chicago, IL	1339	2175	1720	5767	1154	1139	2005	1073	1348	2748	1614	877	2695	1459	814	1224	1564																			
Cincinnati, OH	1175	2267	1812	6259	766	838	2497	764	1841	3168	1387	711	3187	1001	336	766	1984	486																		
Cleveland, OH	779	2605	2148	6331	1168	607	2570	1167	1913	3282	1052	317	3260	1165	410	837	2098	557	407																	
Columbus, OH	999	2375	1918	6349	928	676	2587	927	1931	3276	1223	536	3278	1025	270	697	2092	578	169	232																
Dallas, TX	2703	1213	756	6576	1274	2251	2306	1041	2159	2753	2927	2241	3401	1784	1725	1659	1575	1506	1541	1944	1704															
Denver, CO	2949	705	698	5310	2257	2719	891	2182	1115	1340	3224	2488	1986	2743	2200	2508	161	1633	1931	2167	2037	1427														
Des Moines, IA	1858	1755	1300	5504	1556	1659	1620	1479	1086	2203	2134	1397	2433	1937	1290	1701	1018	542	964	1076	1070	1210	1088													
Detroit, MI	919	2587	2130	6230	1183	856	2468	1181	1812	3181	1192	446	3158	1414	660	1086	1997	455	420	275	309	1960	2066	975												
El Paso, TX	3743	423	705	6439	2312	3290	2019	2079	2570	1940	3966	3281	3115	2822	2764	2698	1289	2483	2582	2983	2745	1041	1128	2064	2895											
Halifax, NS	1411	4739	4283	7757	2904	1815	4515	3091	3858	5228	1149	1878	4685	2748	2327	2520	4043	2502	2521	2187	2357	4061	4113	3022	2056	5102										
Houston, TX	2845	1599	1144	6964	1287	2365	2692	1091	2545	3141	3041	2434	3789	1786	1918	1675	1963	1783	1736	2137	1897	388	1813	1596	2153	1220	4175									
Indianapolis, IN	1279	2088	1632	6068	854	965	2304	774	1648	2980	1512	817	2996	1160	515	925	1794	296	187	513	283	1469	1751	774	512	2396	2648	1350								
Jackson, MS	2142	1862	1406	6909	621	1660	2954	388	2491	3403	2338	1825	3837	1131	1313	1006	2224	1207	1126	1529	1289	653	2076	1498	1545	1691	3472	716	1086							
Jacksonville, FL	1760	2956	2441	7485	553	1228	3599	795	3067	4129	1905	1738	4413	383	1044	619	2943	1714	1292	1455	1316	1688	2817	2116	1706	2642	3039	1422	1414	962						
Kansas City, MO	2063	1438	981	5707	1289	1749	1751	1212	1289	2214	2296	1601	2636	1773	1229	1538	1030	856	961	1297	1067	891	970	312	1279	1746	3432	1279	780	1202	1847					
Las Vegas, NV	4161	930	1390	5400	3326	3934	1553	2980	2217	1223	4436	3699	2077	3815	3414	3580	1356	2845	3146	3379	3252	2142	1216	2299	3278	1154	5324	2372	2965	2792	3886	2185				
Little Rock, AR	2179	1448	993	6322	850	1725	2462	613	1903	2909	2402	1715	3250	1448	1199	1213	1731	1065	1017	1419	1179	526	1583	912	1434	1567	3537	719	944	433	1405	615	2378			
Los Angeles, CA	4600	1297	1757	5475	3599	4352	1994	3366	2739	1662	4901	4138	2518	4109	3820	3947	1796	3286	3564	3820	3670	2327	1656	2740	3717	1289	5765	2507	3385	2978	3928	2626	441	2745		
Louisville, KY	1339	2124	1667	6253	674	969	2489	594	1833	3110	1551	877	3181	981	404	747	1926	481	171	573	333	1371	1799	957	589	2412	2685	1564	180	956	1232	830	3015	846	3421	
Memphis, TN	1953	1662	1207	6570	626	1501	2615	388	2151	3144	2177	1492	3498	1223	975	988	1958	867	793	1194	956	750	1796	1158	1210	1789	3311	943	747	339	1179	862	2592	225	2959	621
México, MX	4520	2352	2051	8061	2821	3899	3641	2624	3952	3985	4574	4058	4737	3319	3541	3208	2911	3421	3360	3760	3522	1815	2750	3002	3776	1926	5709	1535	3287	2249	2956	2684	2846	2344	2981	3187
Miami, FL	2315	3467	2951	7997	1064	1784	4109	1307	3578	4639	2460	2293	4925	938	1599	1175	3455	2224	1836	2011	1871	2200	3329	2626	2254	3152	3595	1932	1924	1472	555	2359	4397	1915	4439	1744
Milwaukee, WI	1495	2294	1837	5651	1308	1295	1891	1228	1234	2813	1770	1033	2579	1614	967	1379	1628	143	640	713	730	1625	1697	608	611	2602	2658	1920	449	1344	1866	922	2909	1202	3350	634
Minneapolis, MN	2003	2154	1697	5110	1817	1804	1350	1736	693	2357	2280	1541	2039	2122	1477	1887	1418	658	1149	1223	1241	1607	1487	396	1121	2462	3168	1995	959	1852	2376	710	2698	1310	3139	1144
Mobile, AL	2162	2162	1780	7258	534	1630	3249	415	2840	3704	2306	1874	4187	1033	1347	920	2526	1485	1176	1578	1339	1028	2378	1794	1595	1981	1981	761	1186	301	660	1496	3092	735	3268	1006
Montréal, QC	370	3495	3038	6607	1997	907	3368	2074	2711	4079	504	639	3535	1842	1323	1614	2895	1353	1311	946	1167	2851	2965	1874	907	3802	1150	3044	1403	2436	2132	2187	4177	2327	4616	1480
Nashville, TN	1614	2008	1553	6534	389	1152	2652	312	2116	3179	1828	1152	3463	874	636	639	1995	763	452	854	615	1096	1870	1167	870	2137	2962	1289	462	681	948	899	2938	571	3305	282
New Orleans, LA	2317	2053	1598	7207	761	1837	3146	565	2790	3595	2515	2018	4135	1260	1490	1147	2417	1504	1319	1722	1482	845	2267	1797	1736	1799	3649	579	1329	298	895	1500	2983	732	3084	1149
New York, NY	243	3242	2785	7062	1398	309	3297	1585	2640	4008	346	644	3990	1244	829	1015	2824	1282	1023	750	861	2557	2895	1804	1001	3596	1480	2671	1150	1968	1533	1934	4106	2031	4537	1189
Oklahoma City, OK	2492	879	422	6245	1519	2179	1974	1173	1828	2423	2726	2031	3070	2008	1644	1773	1244	1298	1389	1726	1496	336	1096	879	1709	1186	3862	722	1210	985	2077	560	1809	571	2175	1245
Omaha, NE	2079	1566	1168	5409	1591	1879	1455	1514	991	1986	2354	1617	2338	2076	1532	1841	800	763	1184	1297	1290	1076	870	219	1195	1989	3242	1464	994	1504	2150	302	2082	917	2521	1133
Orlando, FL	1987	3112	2595	7641	708	1455	3754	951	3223	4283	2130	1965	4570	610	1271	845	3099	1868	1480	1681	1541	1844	2972	2270	1899	2796	3266	1577	1569	1117	227	2003	4042	1559	4084	1389
Ottawa, ON	486	3392	2936	6455	1866	842	3265	1971	2608	3977	665	536	3384	1780	1221	1483	2793	1252	1208	845	1064	2748	2862	1772	805	3701	1324	2941	1302	2333	2069	2085	4074	2224	4515	1377
Philadelphia, PA	359	3144	2689	7010	1258	167	3249	1443	2592	3961	516	666	3939	1102	730	874	2776	1236	927	703	763	2415	2806	1755	953	3455	1651	2529	1054	1826	1393	1836	4023	1891	4441	1091
Phoenix, AZ	4121	750	1212	5776	3006	3807	1929	2772	2674	1598	4354	3659	2454	3514	3274	3390	1615	2927	3018	3355	3125	1733	1455	2507	3337	695	5490	1911	2838	2385	3334	2188	459	2200	594	2874
Pittsburgh, PA	780	2687	2230	6526	1088	396	2766	1228	2109	3477	953	349	3455	1033	349	705	2293	751	470	219	306	2005	2349	1273	470	3046	2087	2198	595	1590	1323	1379	3564	1480	3984	634
Portland, ME	434	3762	3305	7546	1926	837	3784	2113	3128	4497	172	901	4475	1772	1350	1543	3313	1772	1545	1208	1381	3084	3382	2291	1348	4124	872	3199	1670	2494	2061	2454	4594	2558	5059	1709
Portland, OR	4753	2245	2727	3902	4259	4553	1430	4182	2093	695	5030	4291	1371	4743	4199	4508	1876	3438	3858	3973	3965	3443	2029	2893	3870	2843	5918	3831	3669	4093	4817	2904	1911	3599	1562	3800
Québec, QC	582	3734	3279	6846	2209	1120	3607	2314	2951	4320	624	879	3775	2055	1564	1826	3136	1595	1564	1187	1406	3091	3205	2114	1147	4043	940	3284	1644	2676	2344	2428	4417	2566	4858	1720
Raleigh, NC	1028	2867	2412	7157	637	497	3395	880	2739	4014	1173	1033	4085	449	504	254	2829	1385	840	914	776	1913	2703	1862	1165	2951	2307	1928	1028	1260	740	1733	3797	1430	4164	907
Rapid City, SD	2816	1353	1347	4795	2431	2616	610	2354	515	1496	3091	2354	1472	2935	2288	2700	491	1469	1961	2034	2051	1733	650	1012	1932	1778	3979	2121	1772	2346	2991	1142	1665	1759	2106	1955
Reno, NV	4420	1641	2101	4843	3926	4220	1545	3849	2208	692	4697	3958	2069	4410	3866	4175	1543	3105	3525	3640	3632	3110	1696	2560	3537	2116	5585	3334	3335	3760	4484	2571	711	3266	835	3467
Richmond, VA	776	3018	2563	7065	848	245	3303	1091	2647	4016	920	780	3994	689	518	465	2832	1290	853	758	832	2106	2716	1812	1009	3146	2055	2140	1031	1471	980	1746	3932	1582	4315	920
St. Louis, MO	1667	1691	1234	6113	883	1353	2158	806	1694	2619	1900	1205	3041	1368	824	1133	1435	473	563	901	671	1022	1376	702	883	1998	3036	1389	385	813	1442	405	2590	669	2986	425
Salt Lake City, UT	3578	1004	1551	4729	3083	3379	882	3006	1545	550	3854	3115	1406	3569	3025	3334	702	2262	2682	2796	2790	2269	854	1717	2695	1390	4742	2655	2492	2917	3643	1728	671	2425	1112	2624
San Antonio, TX	3142	1316	825	6833	1609	2689	2414	1413	2573	2833	3366	2679	3511	2108	2162	1997	1683	2043	1981	2383	2143	436	1522	1623	2397	895	4500	322	1908	1036	1744	1307	2047	965	2182	1810
San Diego, CA	4697	1327	1788	5673	3485	4383	2095	3252	2840	1763	4932	4235	2619	3995	3850	3870	1897	3387	3595	3921	3701	2212	1757	2841	3818	1175	5866	2393	3414	2864	3813	2727	542	2740	200	3450
San Francisco, CA	4769	1788	2248	4940	4212	4570	1892	3977	2814	1039	5044	4307	2409	4721	4216	4439	1892	3453	3873	3987	3981	2940	2045	2907	3886	1900	5932	3118	3685	3591	4541	2919	925	3237	619	3817
Seattle, WA	4664	2354	2837	3623	4352	4465	1313	4275	1977	805	4940	4203	1093	4784	4137	4549	1986	3318	3810	3883	3900	3553	2138	2932	3781	3128	5828	3940	3619	4203	4911	3012	2021	3709	1847	3804
Tampa, FL	2076	3136	2619	7664	732	1545	3778	975	3247	4307	2220	2053	4592	698	1360	935	3123	1892	1504	1772	1667	1868	2996	2294	1921	2821	3355	1601	1593	1141	315	2026	4064	1583	4108	1413
Toronto, ON	644	2962	2505	6595	1541	909	2835	1541	2179	3546	917	171	3524	1619	864	1290	2362	821	779	488	708	2319	2433	1342	375	3269	1681	2512	870	1903	1910	1654	3644	1794	4084	948
Vancouver, BC	4878	2570	3052	3430	4566	4679	1527	4491	2191	1018	5155	4417	899	4998	4352	4763	2201	3533	4024	4098	4116	3768	2354	3147	3995	3358	6043	4156	3834	4418	5126	3229	2237	3924	2077	4018
Washington, DC	594	3051	2594	6903	1023	61	3142	1220	2486	3854	737	618	3831	867	557	639	2669	1128	832	595	669	2191	2713	1649	846	3231	1873	2306	959	1603	1158	1743	3928	1667	4348	959
Wichita, KS	2367	1138	681	5921	1591	2053	1717	1348	1503	2166	2600	1905	2814	2077	1533	1842	986	1171	1263	1601	1371	591	838	628	1583	1445	3736	978	1084	1241	2151	309	2053	747	2434	1134
Winnipeg, MB	2730	2587	2285	4385	2542	2531	1324	2463	668	2336	3006	2269	1313	2850	2203	2615	1821	1384	1876	1948	1966	2193	1892	1121	1847	3010	3361	2581	1685	2526	3102	1324	3012	1939	3453	1870

Milles

The table is a road-distance chart. The column headings run diagonally through the lower half of the grid; in reading order they are:

1. Memphis, TN — 2. México, MX — 3. Miami, FL — 4. Milwaukee, WI — 5. Minneapolis, MN — 6. Mobile, AL — 7. Montréal, QC — 8. Nashville, TN — 9. New Orleans, LA — 10. New York, NY — 11. Oklahoma City, OK — 12. Omaha, NE — 13. Orlando, FL — 14. Ottawa, ON — 15. Philadelphia, PA — 16. Phoenix, AZ — 17. Pittsburgh, PA — 18. Portland, ME — 19. Portland, OR — 20. Québec, QC — 21. Raleigh, NC — 22. Rapid City, SD — 23. Reno, NV — 24. Richmond, VA — 25. St. Louis, MO — 26. Salt Lake City, UT — 27. San Antonio, TX — 28. San Diego, CA — 29. San Francisco, CA — 30. Seattle, WA — 31. Tampa, FL — 32. Toronto, ON — 33. Vancouver, BC — 34. Washington, DC — 35. Wichita, KS — 36. Winnipeg, MB

Upper portion (distances in miles), row by row:

City	1	2	3	4	5	6	7	8	9	10	11	12	13	14	15	16	17	18	19	20	21	22	23	24	25	26	27	28	29	30	31	32	33	34	35	36
Albany, NY	1214	2809	1439	929	1245	1344	230	1003	1440	151	1549	1292	1235	302	223	2561	485	270	2954	362	639	1750	2747	482	1036	2224	1953	2919	2964	2899	1290	400	3032	369	1471	1697
Albuquerque, NM	1033	1462	2155	1426	1339	1344	2172	1248	1276	2015	546	973	1934	2108	1954	466	1670	2338	1395	2321	1782	841	1020	1786	1051	624	818	825	1111	1463	1949	1841	1596	1896	707	1608
Amarillo, TX	750	1275	1834	1142	1055	1106	1888	965	993	1731	262	726	1613	1825	1671	753	1386	2054	1695	2038	1499	837	1306	1593	767	964	513	1111	1397	1763	1628	1557	1897	1612	423	1420
Anchorage, AK	4083	5010	4970	3512	3176	4511	4106	4061	4479	4389	3881	3362	4749	4012	4357	3590	4056	4690	2425	4255	4448	2980	3010	4391	3799	2939	4247	3526	3070	2252	4763	4099	2132	4290	3680	2725
Atlanta, GA	389	1753	661	813	1129	332	1241	242	473	869	944	989	440	1160	782	1868	676	1197	2647	1373	396	1511	2440	527	549	1916	1000	2166	2618	2705	455	958	2838	636	989	1580
Baltimore, MD	933	2423	1109	805	1121	1013	564	716	1142	192	1354	1168	904	523	104	2366	246	520	2830	696	309	1626	2623	152	841	2100	1671	2724	2840	2575	960	565	2908	38	1573	1573
Billings, MT	1625	2263	2554	1175	839	2019	2093	1648	1955	2049	1227	904	2333	2029	2019	1199	1719	2352	889	2242	2110	379	960	2053	1341	548	1500	1302	1176	816	2348	1762	949	1953	1067	823
Birmingham, AL	241	1631	812	763	1079	258	1289	194	351	985	729	941	591	1225	897	1723	763	1313	2599	1438	547	1463	2392	678	501	1868	878	2021	2472	2657	606	958	2791	758	838	1531
Bismarck, ND	1337	2456	2224	767	431	1765	1685	1315	1734	1641	1136	616	2003	1621	1611	1662	1311	1944	1301	1834	1702	320	1372	1645	1053	960	1599	1765	1749	1229	2018	1354	1362	1545	934	415
Boise, ID	1954	2477	2883	1748	1465	2302	2535	1976	2234	2491	1506	1234	2662	2472	2462	993	2161	2795	432	2685	2495	930	430	2496	1628	342	1761	1096	646	500	2677	2204	633	2395	1346	1452
Boston, MA	1353	2843	1529	1100	1417	1433	313	1136	1563	215	1694	1463	1324	413	321	2706	592	107	3126	388	721	1921	2919	572	1219	2395	2092	3065	3135	3070	1380	570	3204	458	1616	1868
Buffalo, NY	927	2522	1425	642	958	1165	397	716	1254	400	1262	1005	1221	333	414	2274	217	560	2667	546	642	1463	2460	485	749	1936	1665	2632	2677	2612	1276	106	2745	384	1184	1410
Calgary, AB	2174	2944	3061	1603	1267	2602	2197	2152	2570	2480	1908	1453	2840	2103	2448	1525	2147	2781	852	2346	2539	915	1286	2482	1890	874	2182	1628	1497	679	2854	2190	559	2381	1749	816
Charleston, SC	760	2063	583	1003	1319	642	1145	543	783	773	1248	1290	379	1106	685	2184	642	1101	2948	1277	279	1824	2741	428	850	2218	1310	2483	2934	2973	434	1006	3106	539	1291	1771
Charleston, WV	606	2201	994	601	918	837	822	395	926	515	1022	952	790	759	454	2035	217	839	2610	972	522	1219	2407	322	512	1695	1344	2393	2620	2571	845	537	3070	346	953	1369
Charlotte, NC	614	1994	730	857	1173	572	1003	397	631	1102	1144	525	922	543	2107	438	959	2802	1135	158	1678	2405	289	704	2072	1241	2405	2759	2827	581	802	2960	371	1145	1625
Cheyenne, WY	1217	1809	2147	1012	881	1570	1799	1240	1502	1755	773	497	1926	1736	1725	1004	1425	2059	1166	1949	1758	305	959	1760	892	436	1046	1179	1176	1234	1941	1468	1368	1659	613	1132
Chicago, IL	539	2126	1382	89	409	923	841	474	935	797	807	474	1161	778	768	1819	467	1101	2137	991	861	913	1930	802	294	1406	1270	2105	2146	2062	1176	510	2196	701	728	860
Cincinnati, OH	493	2088	1141	398	714	731	815	281	820	636	863	736	920	751	576	1876	292	960	2398	972	522	1219	2191	530	360	1667	1231	2234	2407	2368	935	517	2547	785	1166	—
Cleveland, OH	742	2337	1250	443	760	981	588	531	1070	466	1073	800	1045	525	437	2085	136	751	2469	738	568	1264	2262	471	560	1738	1481	2437	2478	2413	1101	303	2547	370	995	1211
Columbus, OH	594	2189	1163	454	771	832	725	382	921	535	930	802	958	661	474	1942	190	858	2464	874	482	1275	2257	517	417	1734	1332	2300	2474	2424	1036	440	2558	416	852	1222
Dallas, TX	466	1128	1367	1010	999	639	1772	681	525	1589	209	669	1146	1708	1501	1077	1246	1917	2140	1921	1189	1077	1933	1309	635	1410	271	1375	1827	2208	1161	1441	2342	1362	367	1363
Denver, CO	1116	1709	2069	1055	924	1478	1843	1162	1409	1799	681	541	1847	1779	1744	904	1460	2102	1261	1992	1680	400	1054	1688	855	531	946	1092	1329	1862	1512	1463	1686	521	1176	1868
Des Moines, IA	720	1688	1632	378	246	1115	1165	725	1117	1121	546	136	1411	1101	1091	1558	791	1424	1798	1314	1157	621	1591	1126	436	1067	1009	1766	1807	1822	1426	834	1956	1035	390	697
Detroit, MI	752	2347	1401	380	697	991	564	541	1070	622	1062	743	1180	500	592	2074	292	838	2405	713	724	1201	2198	627	549	1675	1490	2373	2415	2350	1194	233	2483	526	984	1148
El Paso, TX	1112	1197	1959	1617	1530	1231	2363	1328	1118	2235	737	1236	1738	2300	2147	432	1893	2563	1767	2513	1834	1105	1315	1955	1242	864	556	730	1181	1944	1753	2032	2087	2008	898	1871
Halifax, NS	2058	3548	2234	1652	1969	1231	715	1841	2268	920	2400	2015	2030	823	1026	3412	1297	542	3678	584	1434	2473	3471	1277	1887	2947	2797	3646	3687	3622	2085	1045	3756	1164	2322	2089
Houston, TX	586	954	1201	1193	1240	473	1892	801	360	1660	449	910	980	1828	1572	1188	1366	2088	2381	2041	1198	1318	2072	1330	863	1650	200	1482	1933	2449	995	1561	2433	608	604	1604
Indianapolis, IN	464	2043	1196	279	596	737	872	287	826	715	752	618	975	809	655	1764	370	1038	2280	1022	639	1101	2073	641	239	1549	1186	2122	2290	2240	990	541	2383	596	674	1047
Jackson, MS	211	1398	915	835	1151	187	1514	423	185	1223	612	935	694	1450	1135	1482	988	1550	2544	1663	783	1458	2337	914	505	1813	644	1780	2232	2612	709	1183	2746	996	771	1570
Jacksonville, FL	733	1837	345	1160	1477	410	1325	589	556	953	1291	1336	141	1286	866	2072	822	1281	2994	1457	460	1859	2787	609	896	2264	1084	2370	2822	3052	196	1187	3186	720	1337	1928
Kansas City, MO	536	1668	1466	573	441	930	1359	559	932	1202	348	188	1245	1296	1141	1360	857	1505	1805	1509	1177	710	1598	1085	252	1172	1259	1028	1872	2007	1083	192	823	—	—	—
Las Vegas, NV	1611	1769	2733	1808	1677	1922	2596	1826	1854	2552	1124	1294	2512	2532	2500	285	2215	2855	1188	2745	2360	1035	442	2444	1610	417	1272	337	575	1226	2526	2265	1390	2441	1276	1872
Little Rock, AR	140	1457	1190	747	814	457	1446	355	455	1262	355	570	969	1382	1175	1367	920	1590	2237	1595	889	1093	2030	983	416	1507	600	1703	2012	2305	984	1115	2439	1036	464	1205
Los Angeles, CA	1839	1853	2759	2082	1951	2031	2869	2054	1917	2820	1352	1567	2538	2806	2760	369	2476	3144	971	3019	2588	1309	519	2682	1856	691	1356	124	385	1148	2553	2538	1291	2702	1513	2146
Louisville, KY	386	1981	1084	394	711	625	920	175	714	739	774	704	863	836	678	1786	394	1062	2362	1069	564	1125	2144	2372	2364	878	589	2497	596	705	1162	—	—	—	—	—

Lower portion — the diagonal header cities and their distance rows (miles to the right, kilometres to the lower left). Diagonal labels in order: Memphis, TN / México, MX / Miami, FL / Milwaukee, WI / Minneapolis, MN / Mobile, AL / Montréal, QC / Nashville, TN / New Orleans, LA / New York, NY / Oklahoma City, OK / Omaha, NE / Orlando, FL / Ottawa, ON / Philadelphia, PA / Phoenix, AZ / Pittsburgh, PA / Portland, ME / Portland, OR / Québec, QC / Raleigh, NC / Rapid City, SD / Reno, NV / Richmond, VA / St. Louis, MO / Salt Lake City, UT / San Antonio, TX / San Diego, CA / San Francisco, CA / Seattle, WA / Tampa, FL / Toronto, ON / Vancouver, BC / Washington, DC / Wichita, KS / Winnipeg, MB

TEMPERATURE CONVERSIONS

°F	°C	°C	°F
110	43.3	40	104
100	37.8	35	95
90	32.2	30	86
80	26.7	25	77
70	21.1	20	68
60	15.6	15	59
50	10.0	10	50
40	4.4	5	41
32	0	0	32
30	-1.1	-5	23
20	-6.7	-10	14
10	-12.2	-15	5
0	-17.8	-20	-4
-10	-23.3	-25	-13
-20	-28.9	-30	-22
-30	-34.4	-35	-31
-40	-40.0	-40	-40
-50	-45.6	-45	-49

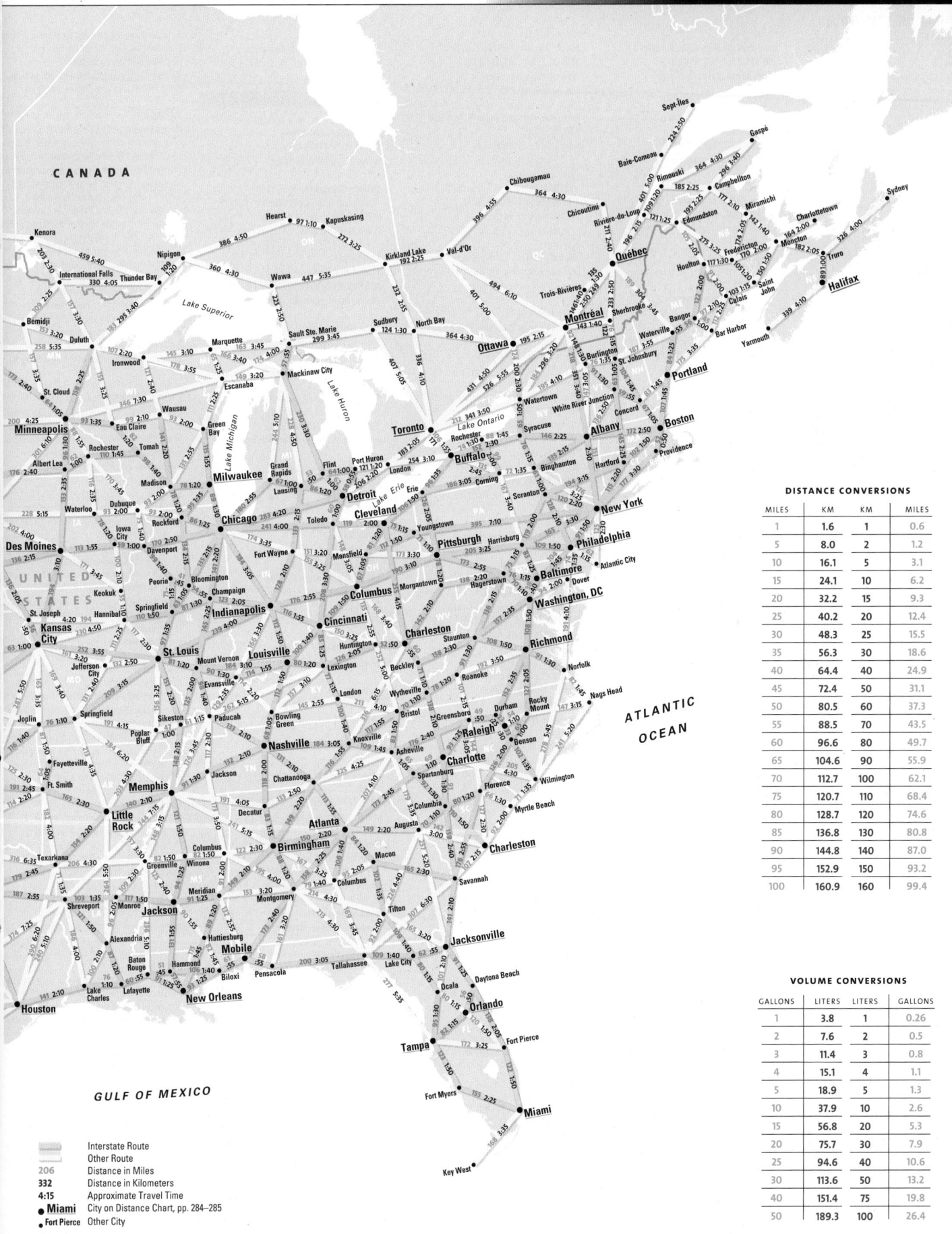

DISTANCE CONVERSIONS

MILES	KM	KM	MILES
1	1.6	1	0.6
5	8.0	2	1.2
10	16.1	5	3.1
15	24.1	10	6.2
20	32.2	15	9.3
25	40.2	20	12.4
30	48.3	25	15.5
35	56.3	30	18.6
40	64.4	40	24.9
45	72.4	50	31.1
50	80.5	60	37.3
55	88.5	70	43.5
60	96.6	80	49.7
65	104.6	90	55.9
70	112.7	100	62.1
75	120.7	110	68.4
80	128.7	120	74.6
85	136.8	130	80.8
90	144.8	140	87.0
95	152.9	150	93.2
100	160.9	160	99.4

VOLUME CONVERSIONS

GALLONS	LITERS	LITERS	GALLONS
1	3.8	1	0.26
2	7.6	2	0.5
3	11.4	3	0.8
4	15.1	4	1.1
5	18.9	5	1.3
10	37.9	10	2.6
15	56.8	20	5.3
20	75.7	30	7.9
25	94.6	40	10.6
30	113.6	50	13.2
40	151.4	75	19.8
50	189.3	100	26.4

Legend:

- Interstate Route
- Other Route
- 206 — Distance in Miles
- **332** — Distance in Kilometers
- 4:15 — Approximate Travel Time
- ● **Miami** — City on Distance Chart, pp. 284–285
- • Fort Pierce — Other City

Distances and driving times may vary depending on actual route traveled and driving conditions.

TOURISM INFORMATION

UNITED STATES

Alabama
Alabama Bureau of Tourism & Travel
800.252.2262, 334.242.4169
www.alabama.travel

Alaska
Alaska Travel Industry Association
800.327.9372, 907.929.2842
www.travelalaska.com

Arizona
Arizona Office of Tourism
866.275.5816, 602.364.3700
www.arizonaguide.com

Arkansas
Arkansas Dept. of Parks & Tourism
800.628.8725, 501.682.7777
www.arkansas.com

California
California Tourism
877.225.4367, 916.444.4429
www.visitcalifornia.com

Colorado
Colorado Tourism Office
800.265.6723, 303.892.3840
www.colorado.com

Connecticut
Connecticut Commission on
Culture & Tourism
888.288.4748, 860.256.2800
www.ctvisit.com

Delaware
Delaware Tourism Office
866.284.7483, 302.739.4271
www.visitdelaware.com

District of Columbia
Destination DC
800.422.8644, 202.789.7000
www.washington.org

Florida
Florida Tourism Industry
Marketing Corp.
850.488.5607, 866.972.5280
www.visitflorida.com

Georgia
Georgia Dept. of Economic Development
800.847.4842, 404.962.4000
www.exploregeorgia.org

Hawaii
Hawaii Visitors & Conv. Bureau
800.464.2924, 808.923.1811
www.gohawaii.com

Idaho
Idaho Div. of Tourism Development
800.847.4843, 208.334.2470
www.visitidaho.org

Illinois
Illinois Bureau of Tourism
800.226.6632, 312.814.4733
www.enjoyillinois.com

Indiana
Indiana Office of Tourism Development
800.677.9800
www.in.gov/visitindiana

Iowa
Iowa Div. of Economic Development
888.472.6035, 515.725.3083
www.traveliowa.com

Kansas
Kansas Travel & Tourism
785.296.2009
www.travelks.com

Kentucky
Kentucky Department of Travel
800.225.8747, 502.564.4930
www.kentuckytourism.com

Louisiana
Louisiana Dept. of Culture,
Recreation & Tourism
800.677.4082, 225.342.8119
www.louisianatravel.com

Maine
Maine Office of Tourism
888.624.6345
www.visitmaine.com

Maryland
Maryland Office of Tourism
866.639.3526
www.visitmaryland.org

Massachusetts
Mass. Office of Travel & Tourism
800.227.6277, 617.973.8500
www.massvacation.com

Michigan
Travel Michigan
888.784.7328
www.michigan.org

Minnesota
Explore Minnesota Tourism
888.868.7476, 651.296.5029
www.exploreminnesota.com

Mississippi
Mississippi Div. of Tourism Development
866.733.6477, 601.359.3297
www.visitmississippi.org

Missouri
Missouri Division of Tourism
800.519.2100, 573.751.4133
www.visitmo.com

Montana
Montana Office of Tourism
800.847.4868
www.visitmt.com

Nebraska
Nebraska Div. of Travel & Tourism
888.444.1867
www.visitnebraska.gov

Nevada
Nevada Commission on Tourism
800.638.2328, 775.687.4322
www.travelnevada.com

New Hampshire
New Hampshire Division of Travel &
Tourism Development
800.386.4664, 603.271.2665
www.visitnh.gov

New Jersey
New Jersey Div. of Travel & Tourism
800.847.4865, 609.292.2470
www.visitnj.org

New Mexico
New Mexico Tourism Department
800.733.6396, 505.827.7400
www.newmexico.org

New York
New York State Division of Tourism
800.225.5697, 518.474.4116
www.iloveny.com

North Carolina
North Carolina Division of Tourism,
Film & Sports Development
800.847.4862, 919.733.4171
www.visitnc.com

North Dakota
North Dakota Tourism Division
800.435.5663, 701.328.2525
www.ndtourism.com

Ohio
Ohio Division of Travel & Tourism
800.282.5393
www.discoverohio.com

Oklahoma
Oklahoma Tourism & Recreation Dept.
800.652.6552, 405.230.8400
www.travelok.com

Oregon
Oregon Tourism Commission
800.547.7842, 503.378.8850
www.traveloregon.com

Pennsylvania
Pennsylvania Tourism Office
800.847.4872, 717.787.5453
www.visitpa.com

Rhode Island
Rhode Island Tourism Division
800.250.7384
www.visitrhodeisland.com

South Carolina
S.C. Dept. of Parks, Rec. & Tourism
866.224.9339, 803.734.1700
www.discoversouthcarolina.com

South Dakota
South Dakota Department of Tourism
800.732.5682, 605.773.3301
www.travelsd.com

Tennessee
Tenn. Dept. of Tourist Development
800.462.8366, 615.741.2159
www.tnvacation.com

Texas
Office of the Governor,
Econ. Dev. & Tourism
800.888.8839
www.traveltex.com

Utah
Utah Office of Tourism
800.882.4386, 800.200.1160
www.utah.travel

Vermont
Vermont Dept. of Tourism & Marketing
800.837.6668, 802.828.3237
www.travel-vermont.com

Virginia
Virginia Tourism Corporation
800.847.4882, 804.545.5500
www.virginia.org

Washington
Washington State Tourism
800.544.1800, 360.725.4000
www.experiencewa.com

West Virginia
West Virginia Division of Commerce
800.225.5982, 304.558.2200
www.wvtourism.com

Wisconsin
Wisconsin Department of Tourism
800.432.8747, 608.266.2161
www.travelwisconsin.com

Wyoming
Wyoming Travel & Tourism
800.225.5996, 307.777.7777
www.wyomingtourism.org

Puerto Rico
Puerto Rico Tourism Company
800.866.7827
www.gotopuertorico.com

CANADA

Alberta
Travel Alberta Canada
800.252.3782, 780.427.4321
www.travelalberta.com

British Columbia
Tourism British Columbia
800.435.5622, 250.356.6363
www.hellobc.com

Manitoba
Travel Manitoba
800.665.0040, 204.927.7800
www.travelmanitoba.com

New Brunswick
New Brunswick Tourism
800.561.0123
www.tourismnewbrunswick.ca

Newfoundland & Labrador
Newfoundland & Labrador Tourism
800.563.6353, 709.729.2830
www.newfoundlandlabrador.com

Northwest Territories
Northwest Territories Tourism
800.661.0788, 867.873.7200
www.spectacularnwt.com

Nova Scotia
Nova Scotia Dept. of Tourism,
Culture & Heritage
800.565.0000, 902.425.5781
www.novascotia.com

Nunavut
Nunavut Tourism
866.686.2888
www.nunavuttourism.com

Ontario
Ontario Tourism Marketing
Partnership Corp.
800.668.2746
www.ontariotravel.net

Prince Edward Island
Tourism PEI
800.463.4734, 902.368.4444
www.tourismpei.com

Québec
Tourisme Québec
877.266.5687, 514.873.2015
www.bonjourquebec.com

Saskatchewan
Tourism Saskatchewan
877.237.2273, 306.787.9600
www.sasktourism.com

Yukon
Department of Tourism & Culture
800.661.0494
www.travelyukon.com

MEXICO

Mexico Tourism Board
800.446.3942
www.visitmexico.com

BORDER CROSSING INFORMATION

TRAVEL ADVISORY

All U.S. citizens are now required to present a passport, passport card, or WHTI (Western Hemisphere Travel Initiative)-compliant document when entering the United States by air, sea or land. U.S. citizens traveling directly to or from Puerto Rico and the U.S. Virgin Islands are not required to have a passport. For more detailed information and updated schedules, please see http://travel.state.gov.

CANADA

All persons entering Canada must carry both proof of citizenship and proof of identity. A valid U.S. passport, passport card or other WHTI-compliant document satisfies these requirements for U.S. citizens. U.S. citizens entering Canada from a third country must have a valid U.S. passport. A visa is not required for U.S. citizens to visit Canada for up to 180 days.

U.S. driver's licenses are valid in Canada; individual provinces and territories specify the length of time. Drivers should be prepared to present proof of their vehicle's registration, ownership, and insurance. International visitors to Canada who are not U.S. citizens must present a valid passport and visa (if required). Citizens of Mexico require a visa to enter Canada.

UNITED STATES (FROM CANADA)

Canadian driver's licenses are valid in the U.S.; lengths of time vary depending on state. Drivers should be prepared to present proof of their vehicle's registration, ownership, and insurance.

MEXICO

All persons entering Mexico must carry proof of citizenship, either a valid passport or their original birth certificate (U.S. citizens should bear in mind the requirements set by the U.S. government for re-entry to the U.S.). Visas are not required for stays of up to 180 days. Naturalized citizens and alien permanent residents should carry the appropriate official documentation. Individuals under the age of 18 traveling alone, with one parent, or with other adults must carry notarized parental/legal guardian authorization. All U.S. citizens visiting for up to 180 days must also procure a tourist permit, obtainable from Mexican consulates, tourism offices, border crossing points, and airlines serving Mexico. However, tourist cards are not needed for visits shorter than 72 hours to areas within the Border Zone (extending approximately 25 km into Mexico).

U.S. driver's licenses are valid in Mexico. Visitors who wish to drive beyond the Baja California Peninsula or the Border Zone must obtain a temporary import permit for their vehicles. To acquire a permit, one must submit evidence of citizenship and of the vehicle's title and registration, as well as a valid driver's license. A processing fee must be paid. Permits are available at border crossings or selected Mexican consulates. Mexican law also requires the posting of a refundable bond to guarantee the departure of the vehicle.

All visitors driving in Mexico should be aware that U.S. auto insurance policies are not valid and that full-coverage insurance from a Mexican insurance company is mandatory. Many U.S. insurance companies sell short-term tourist auto insurance for travel in Mexico.

IMPORTANT WEB SITES

U.S. State Department,
www.travel.state.gov
U.S. Customs and Border Protection,
www.cbp.gov
Canada Border Services Agency,
www.cbsa-asfc.gc.ca
Citizenship and Immigration Canada,
www.cic.gc.ca
Mexican Ministry of Foreign Affairs,
www.sre.gob.mx
Mexican National Institute of Migration,
www.inm.gob.mx

COMMON ABBREVIATIONS			
Arch.	Archaeological	N.H.S.	National Historic Site
Bfld.	Battlefield	N.H.P.	National Historical Park
Cons.	Conservation	N.M.P.	National Military Park
Ent.	Entrance	N.R.A.	National Recreation Area
Hist.	Historic(al)	Pk. Hqtrs.	Park Headquarters
Mem.	Memorial	Pres.	Preserve
Mon.	Monument	Prov.	Provincial
Mtn.	Mountain	Rec.	Recreation(al)
Mts.	Mountains	Res.	Reservation–Reserve
Mus.	Museum	S.H.S.	State Historic Site
Natl.	National	S.P.	State Park
Nat.	Natural	Sta.	Station
		Vis. Ctr.	Visitor Center

ALABAMA	PAGE	GRID	LATITUDE LONGITUDE
National Park & Rec. Areas			
Horseshoe Bend N.M.P.-Main Road	128	B1	32.977130 -85.739600
Horseshoe Bend N.M.P.-Vis. Ctr.	128	B1	32.977130 -85.739600
Russell Cave Natl. Mon.-Main Road	120	A2	34.980220 -85.809650
Russell Cave Natl. Mon.-Vis. Ctr.	120	A2	34.980400 -85.809800
Tuskegee Airmen N.H.S.	128	B2	32.424942 -85.691052
Tuskegee Airmen N.H.S.-Pk. Hqtrs.	128	B2	32.428600 -85.708500
Tuskegee Institute N.H.S.	128	B2	32.428751 -85.704120
Tuskegee Institute N.H.S.-Pk. Hqtrs.	128	B2	32.428600 -85.708500
State Park & Rec. Areas			
Bladon Springs S.P.	127	E4	31.730920 -88.195580
Blue Springs S.P.	128	B4	31.661990 -85.508150
Bucks Pocket S.P.	120	A3	34.469560 -86.049080
Cathedral Caverns S.P.	120	A2	34.572299 -86.221499
Cheaha S.P.	120	A4	33.474490 -85.807260
Chewacla S.P.	128	B2	32.554520 -85.481920
Desoto S.P.	120	A3	34.495460 -85.618860
Florala S.P.	136	B1	30.998590 -86.329980
Frank Jackson S.P.	128	A4	31.291400 -86.255900
Gulf S.P.	135	F2	30.270490 -87.582130
Joe Wheeler S.P.	119	E2	34.793020 -87.379950
Lake Guntersville S.P.	120	A3	34.367530 -86.222850
Lake Lurleen S.P.	127	E1	33.295880 -87.676870
Lakepoint Resort S.P.	128	C3	31.990320 -85.114970
Meaher S.P.	135	E1	30.669720 -87.936030
Monte Sano S.P.	119	F2	34.745220 -86.511650
Oak Mtn. S.P.	127	F1	33.324710 -86.758740
Paul M. Grist S.P.	127	F2	32.595380 -86.996080
Rickwood Caverns S.P.	119	F4	33.876870 -86.867230
Roland Cooper S.P.	127	F3	32.055350 -87.245330
Wind Creek S.P.	128	A1	32.856820 -85.946540

ALASKA	PAGE	GRID	LATITUDE LONGITUDE
National Park & Rec. Areas			
Admiralty Island Natl. Mon.	155	E4	57.618060 -134.161110
Aleutian WWII Natl. Hist. Area	154	A4	53.888889 -166.527222
Aniakchak Natl. Mon. & Pres.	154	B4	56.833333 -158.250556
Bering Land Bridge Natl. Pres.	154	B2	65.595320 -164.301800
Cape Krusenstern Natl. Mon.	154	B1	67.471630 -163.312300
Denali Natl. Park & Pres.-Denali Vis. Ctr.	154	C2	63.737000 -148.895000
Denali Natl. Park & Pres.-Eielson Vis. Ctr.	154	C2	63.440900 -150.239000
Gates of the Arctic Natl. Park & Pres.-Anaktuvuk Pass Ranger Sta.	154	C1	68.139900 -151.735400
Gates of the Arctic Natl. Park & Pres.-Arctic Interagency Vis. Ctr.	154	C1	67.253700 -150.187000
Gates of the Arctic Natl. Park & Pres.-Bettles Ranger Sta.	154	C1	66.912500 -151.667100
Gates of the Arctic Natl. Park & Pres.-Coldfoot Ranger Sta.	154	C1	67.253700 -150.187000
Glacier Bay Natl. Park & Pres.-Glacier Bay Lodge & Vis. Ctr.	155	D3	58.454900 -135.882600
Katmai Natl. Park & Pres.	154	C3	58.667030 -156.524600
Kenai Fjords Natl. Park-Vis. Ctr.	154	C3	60.105300 -149.435000
Klondike Gold Rush N.H.P.	155	D3	60.113550 -149.441342
Kobuk Valley Natl. Park	154	B1	67.073230 -159.839500
Lake Clark Natl. Park & Pres.	154	C3	60.471450 -154.576390
Misty Fiords Natl. Mon.	155	E4	55.472600 -130.429700
Noatak Natl. Pres.	154	C1	67.320740 -162.646370
White Mts. N.R.A.	154	C2	65.524300 -147.156400
Wrangell-Saint Elias Natl. Park & Pres.-Kennecott Vis. Ctr.	155	D3	61.485600 -142.881100
Wrangell-Saint Elias Natl. Park & Pres.-Wrangell-Saint Elias Vis. Ctr.	155	D3	61.964300 -145.317900
Yukon-Charley Rivers Natl. Pres.	155	D2	65.341680 -143.120650
State Park & Rec. Areas			
Afognak Island S.P.	154	C4	58.227100 -152.067300
Chilkat S.P.	155	D3	59.211111 -135.398056
Chugach S.P.	154	C3	61.037440 -149.780830
Denali S.P.	154	C3	62.734600 -150.199600
Point Bridget S.P.	155	E3	58.671225 -134.958801
Shuyak Island S.P.	154	C4	58.533100 -152.486100
Wood-Tikchik S.P.	154	B3	59.909600 -158.672000

ARIZONA	PAGE	GRID	LATITUDE LONGITUDE
National Park & Rec. Areas			
Agua Fria Natl. Mon.	47	D4	34.276490 -112.114350
Canyon de Chelly Natl. Mon.-Vis. Ctr.	48	A2	36.153200 -109.539000
Casa Grande Ruins Natl. Mon.-Ent. Sta.	54	C2	32.994700 -111.537000
Chiricahua Natl. Mon.-Main Road	55	E3	32.009250 -109.382290
Chiricahua Natl. Mon.-Ent. Sta.	55	E3	32.007500 -109.388900
Coronado Natl. Mem.-Vis. Ctr.	55	E4	31.346300 -110.254000
Fort Bowie N.H.S.-Vis. Ctr.	55	E3	32.146600 -109.435000
Glen Canyon N.R.A.-Ent. Sta.	47	E1	36.943300 -111.493600
Grand Canyon Natl. Park-East Ent.	47	D2	36.038800 -111.828000
Grand Canyon Natl. Park-North Ent.	47	D2	36.334900 -112.116000
Grand Canyon Natl. Park-South Ent.	47	D2	36.000100 -112.121600
Grand Canyon-Parashant Natl. Mon.	46	C2	36.452170 -113.724367
Ironwood Forest Natl. Mon.	54	C3	32.478380 -111.530220
Lake Mead N.R.A.-Boulder City Ent.	46	C2	36.020800 -114.796000
Lake Mead N.R.A.-Henderson Ent.	46	C2	36.105400 -114.901200
Lake Mead N.R.A.-Las Vegas–Rt 147 Ent.	46	C2	36.161000 -114.905100
Lake Mead N.R.A.-South Ent.	46	C2	35.225600 -114.551000
Montezuma Castle Natl. Mon.-Vis. Ctr.	47	D4	34.611600 -111.839000
Navajo Natl. Mon.-Betatakin Ruin	47	E1	36.683500 -110.541470
Navajo Natl. Mon.-Inscription House Ruin-Closed To Public	47	E1	36.661250 -110.775940
Navajo Natl. Mon.-Keet Seel Ruin	47	E1	36.683500 -110.541470
Navajo Natl. Mon.-Vis. Ctr.	47	E1	36.678200 -110.541000
Organ Pipe Cactus Natl. Mon.-Vis. Ctr.	54	B3	31.954800 -112.801000
Petrified Forest Natl. Park-North Ent.	47	F3	35.069600 -109.778000
Petrified Forest Natl. Park-South Ent.	47	F3	34.799600 -109.885000
Pipe Spring Natl. Mon.-Vis. Ctr.	47	D1	36.862500 -112.737000
Saguaro Natl. Park-East	55	D3	32.178430 -110.737990
Saguaro Natl. Park-Vis. Ctr.	55	D3	32.180200 -110.736000
Saguaro Natl. Park-West	55	D3	32.251660 -111.191660
Sonoran Desert Natl. Mon.	54	C2	33.001730 -112.421220
Sunset Crater Volcano Natl. Mon.-Vis. Ctr.	47	E3	35.368800 -111.543000
Tonto Natl. Mon.-Vis. Ctr.	55	D1	33.645200 -111.113000
Tumacácori N.H.P.-Vis. Ctr.	55	D4	31.567800 -111.051000
Tuzigoot Natl. Mon.-Pk. Hqtrs.	47	D4	34.561000 -111.853000
Vermilion Cliffs Natl. Mon.	47	D1	36.806389 -111.741111
Walnut Canyon Natl. Mon.-Walnut Canyon Vis. Ctr.	47	E3	35.171700 -111.509000
Wupatki Natl. Mon.-Vis. Ctr.	47	E3	35.520300 -111.372000
State Park & Rec. Areas			
Alamo Lake S.P.	46	C4	34.234270 -113.553220
Boyce Thmpson Arbrtum S.P.	55	D2	33.311150 -111.055790
Buckskin Mtn. S.P.	46	B4	34.255000 -114.134070
Catalina S.P.	55	D3	32.416760 -110.937500
Cattail Cove S.P.	46	B4	34.355075 -114.165877
Dead Horse Ranch S.P.	47	D4	34.748490 -112.022930
Homolovi Ruins S.P.	47	E3	35.023940 -110.630120
Kartchner Caverns S.P.	55	D3	31.840770 -110.342710
Lake Havasu S.P.	46	B4	34.473970 -114.345850
Lost Dutchman S.P.	54	C1	33.464920 -111.481350
Lyman Lake S.P.	48	A4	34.362870 -109.375370
Oracle S.P.	55	D2	32.610239 -110.740619
Patagonia Lake S.P.	55	D4	31.488970 -110.853790
Picacho Peak S.P.	54	C2	32.646340 -111.398090
Red Rock S.P.	47	D4	34.818920 -111.836700
Roper Lake S.P.	55	E2	32.758710 -109.709520
Slide Rock S.P.	47	D3	34.944340 -111.752810
Tonto Nat. Bridge S.P.	47	E4	34.323400 -111.449460

ARKANSAS	PAGE	GRID	LATITUDE LONGITUDE
National Park & Rec. Areas			
Fort Smith N.H.S.-Main Road	116	B1	35.387480 -94.429660
Fort Smith N.H.S.-Vis. Ctr.	116	B1	35.385800 -94.429800
Hot Springs Natl. Park-Main Road	117	D2	34.511660 -93.053980
Hot Springs Natl. Park-Vis. Ctr.	117	D2	34.513800 -93.053400
Pea Ridge N.M.P.-Main Road	106	C3	36.442600 -94.025980
Pea Ridge N.M.P.-Vis. Ctr.	106	C3	36.443800 -94.025900
State Park & Rec. Areas			
Bull Shoals-White River S.P.	107	E3	36.365590 -92.557490
Conway Cemetery S.P.	124	C1	33.101909 -93.683161
Crater of Diamonds S.P.	116	C3	34.038610 -93.667630
Crowley's Ridge S.P.	108	A4	36.044840 -90.666770
Degray Lake Resort S.P.-North Ent.	117	D3	34.248870 -93.116880
Degray Lake Resort S.P.-South Ent.	117	D3	34.217390 -93.085820
Hampson Arch. Mus. S.P.	118	B1	35.568990 -90.041060
Historic Washington S.P.	116	C4	33.774005 -93.683235
Hobbs S.P.-Cons. Area	106	C3	36.244880 -93.972640
Jacksonport S.P.	107	F4	35.641440 -91.305350
Jenkins' Ferry S.P.	117	E3	34.212070 -92.547490
Lake Charles S.P.	107	F4	36.066870 -91.132700
Lake Chicot S.P.	126	A1	33.373070 -91.194940
Lake Dardanelle S.P.	117	D1	35.251690 -93.213380
Lake Fort Smith S.P.	106	C4	35.654040 -94.150140
Lake Frierson S.P.	108	A4	35.988570 -90.717540
Lake Ouachita S.P.	117	D2	34.610990 -93.165520
Lake Poinsett S.P.	118	A1	35.535510 -90.688700
Louisiana Purchase S.P.	118	A2	35.150340 -90.734990
Lower White River Mus. S.P.	117	F2	34.977035 -91.495131
Mammoth Spring S.P.	107	F3	36.496010 -91.535960
Marks' Mills S.P.	117	E4	33.781085 -92.256427
Moro Bay S.P.	125	E1	33.298890 -92.348940
Mount Magazine S.P.	116	C1	35.149900 -93.563600
Mount Nebo S.P.	117	D1	35.224870 -93.229930
Ozark Folk Center S.P.	107	E4	35.883480 -92.116340
Parkin Arch. S.P.	118	A1	35.268607 -90.554809
Petit Jean S.P.	117	D1	35.128320 -92.898530
Poison Spring S.P.	117	D4	33.638340 -93.005250
Powhatan Hist. S.P.	107	F4	36.083234 -91.117858
Prairie Grove Bfld. S.P.	106	C4	35.983120 -94.305590
Toltec Mounds Arch. S.P.	117	E2	34.647370 -92.058510
Village Creek S.P.	118	A1	35.199650 -90.724540
White Oak Lake S.P.	117	D4	33.687490 -93.117240
Withrow Springs S.P.	106	C4	36.203800 -93.578200
Woolly Hollow S.P.	117	E1	35.286402 -92.285646

CALIFORNIA	PAGE	GRID	LATITUDE LONGITUDE
National Park & Rec. Areas			
Amboy Crater Natl. Nat. Landmark	53	E2	34.542196 -115.790920
Carrizo Plain Natl. Mon.	52	B1	35.191000 -119.792000
Channel Islands Natl. Park	52	B2	34.248500 -119.267000
Death Valley Natl. Park-Furnace Creek Vis. Ctr.	45	F3	36.461800 -116.867000
Devils Postpile Natl. Mon.	37	E4	37.630330 -119.084300
Giant Sequoia Natl. Mon.-North Unit	45	D2	36.705501 -118.824821
Giant Sequoia Natl. Mon.-South Unit	45	E3	36.062389 -118.317784
Golden Gate N.R.A.-Marin Headlands	36	B4	37.830900 -122.525000
Golden Gate N.R.A.-Mott Vis. Ctr.	36	B4	37.799800 -122.460000
Joshua Tree Natl. Park-Indian Cove	53	E3	34.120000 -116.156000
Joshua Tree Natl. Park-North Ent.	53	E3	34.078300 -116.037000
Joshua Tree Natl. Park-West Ent.	53	E3	34.093600 -116.266000
Kings Canyon Natl. Park-East Ent.	45	D2	36.715870 -118.940420
Kings Canyon Natl. Park-West Ent.	45	D2	36.723720 -118.956490
Lassen Volcanic Natl. Park-Ent.	29	D4	40.537900 -121.571000
Lava Beds Natl. Mon.-Vis. Ctr.	29	D2	41.713900 -121.509000
Manzanar N.H.S.	45	E3	36.732260 -118.148500
Pinnacles Natl. Mon.-East Ent.	44	B3	36.483200 -121.162000
Pinnacles Natl. Mon.-West Ent.	44	B3	36.473300 -121.224400
Point Reyes Natl. Seashore-Bear Valley Vis. Ctr.	36	A3	38.043100 -122.799000
Point Reyes Natl. Seashore-Kenneth C. Patrick Vis. Ctr.	36	A3	38.027800 -122.961000
Point Reyes Natl. Seashore-Vis. Ctr.	36	A3	37.996500 -123.021000
Redwood Natl. Park-Kuchel Vis. Ctr.	28	A3	41.286800 -124.090900
Redwood Natl. Park-Prairie Creek Vis. Ctr.	28	A3	41.365300 -124.022000
Santa Monica Mts. N.R.A.-Vis. Ctr.	52	B2	34.188600 -118.887000
Santa Rosa & San Jacinto Mts. Natl. Mon.	53	E3	33.755173 -116.729736
Sequoia Natl. Park-North Ent.	45	D3	36.647900 -118.826370
Sequoia Natl. Park-South Ent.	45	D3	36.487130 -118.836810
Shasta-Trinity N.R.A.	28	C4	40.633204 -122.601127
Trona Pinnacles Natl. Nature Landmark	45	F4	35.611944 -117.369444
Whiskeytown-N.R.A.	28	C4	40.751500 -122.320580
Yosemite Natl. Park-Arch Rock Ent.	37	D3	37.687500 -119.730000
Yosemite Natl. Park-Big Oak Flat Ent.	37	D3	37.800800 -119.874000
Yosemite Natl. Park-Hetch Hetchy Ent.	37	D3	37.893500 -119.842000
Yosemite Natl. Park-South Ent.	37	D3	37.507000 -119.632000
Yosemite Natl. Park-Tioga Pass Ent.	37	D3	37.910700 -119.258000
State Park & Rec. Areas			
Ahjumawi Lava Springs S.P.	29	D3	41.107140 -121.468600
Anza-Borrego Desert S.P.	53	E4	33.256550 -116.399340
Big Basin Redwoods S.P.	44	A2	37.168380 -122.221530
Bothe-Napa Valley S.P.	36	B3	38.553410 -122.525640
Butano S.P.	44	A2	37.200660 -122.344140
Carlsbad State Beach	53	D3	33.147530 -117.345280
Castle Crags S.P.	28	C3	41.149280 -122.317480
Caswell Mem. S.P.	36	C4	37.702660 -121.181770
China Camp S.P.	36	B3	38.003990 -122.466480
Clear Lake S.P.	36	B2	39.009780 -122.805400
Cuyamaca Rancho S.P.	53	D4	32.933790 -116.562560
Del Norte Coast Redwoods S.P.-North Ent.	28	A3	41.712860 -124.130310
Del Norte Coast Redwoods S.P.-South Ent.	28	A3	41.603280 -124.100130
Doheny State Beach	52	C3	33.463820 -117.688830
Donner Mem. S.P.	37	D2	39.323880 -120.228370
Ed Z'Berg-Sugar Pine Point S.P.	37	D2	39.056290 -120.119200
Emerald Bay S.P.	37	D2	38.956710 -120.108850
Fremont Peak S.P.	44	B3	36.760340 -121.502670
Garrapata S.P.	44	B3	36.475310 -121.936280
Gaviota S.P.	52	A2	34.475250 -120.228590
Grizzly Creek Redwoods S.P.	28	B4	40.486630 -123.903520
Grover Hot Springs S.P.	37	D3	38.695230 -119.836760
Henry Cowell Redwoods S.P.	44	A2	37.044020 -122.070990
Henry W. Coe S.P.	44	B2	37.085600 -121.467340
Humboldt Lagoons S.P.	28	A3	41.284330 -124.089720
Humboldt Redwoods S.P.	28	A4	40.284740 -124.056950
Jedediah Smith Redwoods S.P.	28	A2	41.798190 -124.084030
Julia Pfeiffer Burns S.P.	44	B3	36.160700 -121.668210
Limekiln S.P.	44	B3	36.013380 -121.526870
Little River State Beach	28	A3	41.013580 -124.109680
Los Osos Oaks State Rec.	52	A1	35.310200 -120.835300
Manchester S.P.	36	A2	38.980450 -123.703020
Marina State Beach	44	B3	36.683030 -121.809440
McGrath State Beach	52	B2	34.227270 -119.256460
Mendocino Headlands S.P.	36	A2	39.307570 -123.798910
Morro Bay S.P.	44	B4	35.354020 -120.843800
Morro Strand State Beach	44	B4	35.435390 -120.888060
Mount Diablo S.P.	36	B4	37.844210 -121.950200
Mount Tamalpais S.P.	36	B3	37.904290 -122.604040
Navarro River Redwoods S.P.	36	A2	39.175000 -123.676390

Pacheco S.P.	44	B2	37.055650 -121.016250
Palomar Mtn. S.P.	53	D3	33.325340 -116.893330
Patrick's Point S.P.	28	A3	41.135690 -124.150500
Pfeiffer Big Sur S.P.	44	B3	36.250930 -121.786550
Placerita Canyon S.P.	52	C2	34.377530 -118.470290
Plumas-Eureka S.P.	36	C1	39.758360 -120.695360
Point Dume State Beach	52	B2	34.003110 -118.807250
Point Sal State Beach	52	A1	34.897760 -120.642760
Prairie Creek Redwoods S.P.	28	A3	41.355490 -124.073670
Red Rock Canyon S.P.	52	C1	35.359734 -117.978351
Russian Gulch S.P.	36	A2	39.330990 -123.805050
Saddleback Butte S.P.	52	C2	34.689820 -117.824340
Samuel P. Taylor S.P.	36	B3	38.004660 -122.708400
San Gregorio State Beach	36	B4	37.321490 -122.401640
San Onofre State Beach	53	D3	33.383380 -117.580790
Sonoma Coast State Beach	36	A3	38.441060 -123.122970
Sunset State Beach	44	B2	36.897780 -121.835450
The Forest of Nisene Marks S.P.	44	B2	37.042024 -121.856231
Tolowa Dunes S.P.	28	A2	41.825800 -124.187500
Trinidad State Beach	28	A3	41.061090 -124.142290
Van Damme S.P.	36	A2	39.273990 -123.790490
Westport-Union Landing State Beach	36	A1	39.658350 -123.784930
Wilder Ranch S.P.	44	A2	36.962160 -122.080850
Zmudowski State Beach	44	B2	36.845580 -121.804300

COLORADO	PAGE	GRID	LATITUDE LONGITUDE
National Park & Rec. Areas			
Arapaho N.R.A.	41	D1	40.197870 -105.869440
Bent's Old Fort N.H.S.	41	F3	38.045980 -103.431440
Black Canyon-Gunnison Natl. Park-North Ent.	40	C3	38.586890 -107.695940
Black Canyon-Gunnison Natl. Park-South Ent.	40	C3	38.553980 -107.686390
Canyons of the Ancients Natl. Mon.	40	A4	37.587880 -108.916890
Colorado Natl. Mon.-Northwest Ent.	40	B2	39.117620 -108.730910
Colorado Natl. Mon.-Southeast Ent.	40	B2	39.032860 -108.631460
Colorado Natl. Mon.-South Ent.	40	B2	39.021100 -108.659540
Colorado Natl. Mon.-Southwest Ent.	40	B2	39.055070 -108.742500
Curecanti N.R.A.-East Ent.	40	C3	38.515010 -107.020560
Curecanti N.R.A.-North Ent.	40	C3	38.463380 -107.419580
Curecanti N.R.A.-South Ent.	40	C3	38.473160 -107.076450
Curecanti N.R.A.-West Ent.	40	C3	38.444680 -107.341980
Dinosaur Natl. Mon.-East Ent.	32	B4	40.443120 -108.517790
Dinosaur Natl. Mon.-South Ent.	32	B4	40.243920 -108.973750
Florissant Fossil Beds Natl. Mon.	41	E2	38.937440 -105.283400
Great Sand Dunes Natl. Park-Ent. Sta.	41	D4	37.725000 -105.519000
Hovenweep Natl. Mon.-Cutthroat	40	A4	37.413000 -108.720240
Hovenweep Natl. Mon.-Hackberry	40	A4	37.398890 -109.036680
Hovenweep Natl. Mon.-Holly	40	A4	37.398890 -109.036680
Hovenweep Natl. Mon.-Horseshoe	40	A4	37.464610 -108.974680
Mesa Verde Natl. Park-Ent. Sta.	40	B4	37.331100 -108.416000
Rocky Mtn. Natl. Park-Beaver Meadows Ent.	33	E4	40.367300 -105.578000
Rocky Mtn. Natl. Park-Fall River Ent.	33	E4	40.404000 -105.590000
Rocky Mtn. Natl. Park-Grand Lake Ent.	33	E4	40.267300 -105.833000
Rocky Mtn. Natl. Park-Wild Basin Ent.	33	E4	40.219000 -105.534000
Sand Creek Massacre N.H.S.	42	A3	38.541250 -102.505910
Yucca House Natl. Mon.	40	B4	37.251678 -108.684911
State Park & Rec. Areas			
Barr Lake S.P.	41	E1	39.938160 -104.733470
Bonny Lake S.P.	42	A1	39.601030 -102.245640
Boyd Lake S.P.	33	E4	40.428990 -105.045400
Castlewood Canyon S.P.	41	E2	39.325860 -104.737640
Crawford S.P.	40	C3	38.708000 -107.617550
Eleven Mile S.P.	41	D2	38.948570 -105.526450
Golden Gate Canyon S.P.	41	D1	39.875560 -105.453650
Harvey Gap S.P.	40	C1	39.606210 -107.659010
Highline Lake S.P.	40	B2	39.270910 -108.835930
Jackson Lake S.P.	33	F4	40.409110 -104.070130
James M. Robb-Colorado River S.P.-Corn Lake	40	B2	39.062709 -108.455110
James M. Robb-Colorado River S.P.-Island Acres	40	B2	39.165709 -108.300610
John Martin Reservoir S.P.	42	A3	38.065390 -102.927110
Lake Pueblo S.P.	41	E3	38.258130 -104.719160
Lathrop S.P.	41	E4	37.602830 -104.833740
Lone Mesa S.P.	40	B4	37.699890 -108.466750
Lory S.P.	33	E4	40.593143 -105.185413
Mancos S.P.	40	B4	37.399890 -108.266750
Mueller S.P.	41	E2	38.884940 -105.157710
Navajo S.P.	48	B1	37.067800 -107.407599
North Sterling S.P.	34	A4	40.787740 -103.264990
Paonia S.P.	40	C2	38.980440 -107.342900
Pearl Lake S.P.	33	D4	40.790160 -106.894610
Ridgway S.P.	40	B3	38.229710 -107.729410
Rifle Falls S.P.	40	B1	39.695290 -107.701090
Rifle Gap S.P.	40	B1	39.627460 -107.762520
Roxborough S.P.	41	E2	39.451300 -105.070200
San Luis S.P.	41	D4	37.663130 -105.734480
Spinney Mtn. S.P.	41	D2	39.014760 -105.625880
Stagecoach S.P.	33	D4	40.286100 -106.866920
Steamboat Lake S.P.	32	C4	40.805240 -106.943600
Sweitzer Lake S.P.	40	B2	38.712050 -108.042640
Sylvan Lake S.P.	40	C1	39.516710 -106.753170
Trinidad Lake S.P.	49	E1	37.149700 -104.563650
Vega S.P.	40	B2	39.226890 -107.810250
Yampa River S.P.	32	C4	40.533190 -107.444483

CONNECTICUT	PAGE	GRID	LATITUDE LONGITUDE
National Park & Rec. Areas			
Weir Farm N.H.S.	148	C2	41.255890 -73.455980
State Park & Rec. Areas			
Bigelow Hollow S.P.	150	B2	41.991600 -72.134840
Bluff Point S.P.	149	F2	41.335800 -72.033520
Chatfield Hollow S.P.	150	A4	41.361400 -72.580190
Day Pond S.P.	150	A4	41.553432 -72.418419
Devil's Hopyard S.P.	150	A4	41.486529 -72.342462
Gay City S.P.	150	A3	41.716100 -72.434470
Gillette Castle S.P.	150	A4	41.430670 -72.427990
Hammonasset Beach S.P.	149	E2	41.273640 -72.562350
Haystack Mtn. S.P.	94	C2	42.002010 -73.209960
Horse Guard S.P.	94	C3	41.807100 -72.848300
Hurd S.P.	150	A4	41.530650 -72.537650
John A. Minetto S.P.	94	C2	41.884020 -73.170280
Lake Waramaug S.P.	148	C1	41.706290 -73.382460
Mashamoquet Brook S.P.	150	B3	41.860320 -71.987230
Mount Riga S.P.	94	B2	42.028830 -73.428620
Putnam Mem. S.P.	148	C2	41.344200 -73.381500
Rocky Neck S.P.	149	F2	41.316920 -72.242690
Selden Neck S.P.	150	A4	41.287500 -72.331100
Silver Sands S.P.	149	D2	41.198410 -73.076180
Southford Falls S.P.	149	D1	41.455700 -73.166150
Squantz Pond S.P.	148	C1	41.508580 -73.471040
Stoddard Hill S.P.	150	B4	41.461900 -72.065500
Wadsworth Falls S.P.	150	A4	41.536080 -72.687380
West Rock Ridge S.P.	149	D2	41.347810 -72.968260

DELAWARE	PAGE	GRID	LATITUDE LONGITUDE
State Park & Rec. Areas			
Cape Henlopen S.P.	145	F3	38.782360 -75.103010
Delaware Seashore S.P.	145	F4	38.614420 -75.071540
Fenwick Island S.P.	145	F4	38.469740 -75.051550
Fort Delaware S.P.	145	E1	39.578700 -75.588320
Fort Dupont S.P.	145	E1	39.568930 -75.588590
Holts Landing S.P.	145	F4	38.584080 -75.128380
Killens Pond S.P.	145	E3	38.990320 -75.544920
Lums Pond S.P.	145	E1	39.570520 -75.733490
Trap Pond S.P.	145	E4	38.525860 -75.483170
White Clay Creek S.P.	146	B4	39.709810 -75.776560

FLORIDA	PAGE	GRID	LATITUDE LONGITUDE
National Park & Rec. Areas			
Biscayne Natl. Park-Dante Fascell Vis. Ctr.	143	F3	25.464400 -80.334900
Canaveral Natl. Seashore	141	E1	28.611410 -80.808390
Castillo de San Marcos Natl. Mon.	139	D3	29.897747 -81.311461
Dry Tortugas Natl. Park-Vis. Ctr.	142	B4	24.628500 -82.873400
Everglades Natl. Park-Ent.	143	E3	25.394400 -80.589300
Fort Matanzas Natl. Mon.	139	E3	29.715660 -81.234190
Gulf Islands Natl. Seashore	135	F2	30.362880 -87.139630
State Park & Rec. Areas			
Alafia River S.P.	140	C3	27.789920 -82.120830
Amelia Island S.P.	139	D2	30.543900 -81.449700
Anastasia S.P.	139	E3	29.874740 -81.285030
Anclote Key Pres. S.P.	140	B2	28.193070 -82.850660
Avalon S.P.	141	E3	27.542840 -80.318060
Bahia Honda S.P.	143	D4	24.659540 -81.277810
Bald Point S.P.	138	A3	29.902700 -84.408600
Big Lagoon S.P.	135	F2	30.322290 -87.401170
Big Shoals S.P.	138	C2	30.339115 -82.683182
Big Talbot Island S.P.	139	D2	30.460500 -81.421950
Blue Spring S.P.	141	D1	28.952270 -81.331300
Bulow Creek S.P.	139	E4	29.388000 -81.132399
Bulow Plantation Ruins Hist. S.P.	139	E4	29.433590 -81.144590
Caladesi Island S.P.	140	B2	28.059890 -82.813780
Cedar Key Mus. S.P.	138	B4	29.151172 -83.048299
Charlotte Harbor Pres. S.P.	140	C4	26.850691 -82.022026
Collier-Seminole S.P.	143	D2	25.991630 -81.591700
Crystal River Pres. S.P. & Arch. S.P.	140	B1	28.909530 -82.628680
Curry Hammock S.P.	143	E4	24.742640 -80.984793
Dade Bfld. Hist. S.P.	140	C1	28.654430 -82.124970
Deleon Springs S.P.	139	D4	29.131920 -81.360400
Delnor-Wiggins Pass S.P.	142	C1	26.272500 -81.826900
Dudley Farm Hist. S.P.	138	C3	29.649617 -82.630738
Eden Gardens S.P.	136	B2	30.361530 -86.125010
Egmont Key S.P.	140	B3	27.723490 -82.679390
Fakahatchee Strand Pres. S.P.	143	D2	25.961900 -81.364600
Faver-Dykes S.P.	139	E3	29.668050 -81.268030
Florida Caverns S.P.	137	D1	30.809160 -85.212270
Fort Clinch S.P.	139	D1	30.668010 -81.434300
Fort Cooper S.P.	140	C1	28.801300 -82.309200
Fort Pierce Inlet S.P.-East Ent.	141	E3	27.485160 -80.299430
Fort Pierce Inlet S.P.-West Ent.	141	E3	27.475930 -80.316980
Gasparilla Island S.P.	140	C4	26.718200 -82.261400
Grayton Beach S.P.	136	B2	30.328930 -86.155790
Henderson Beach S.P.	136	B2	30.387000 -86.447499
Highlands Hammock S.P.	141	D3	27.476554 -81.557148
Hontoon Island S.P.	141	D1	28.976680 -81.357690
Hugh Taylor Birch S.P.	143	F1	26.138220 -80.104450
Indian Key Hist. S.P.	143	E4	24.888056 -80.678056
John Gorrie Mus. S.P.	137	D3	29.725768 -84.983244
John Pennekamp Coral Reef S.P.	143	E3	25.127620 -80.409650
Jonathan Dickinson S.P.	141	F4	27.002920 -80.099980
Kissimmee Prairie Pres. S.P.	141	D3	27.538826 -81.022945
Lafayette Blue Springs S.P.	138	B2	30.115136 -83.229417
Lake Griffin S.P.	140	C1	28.857450 -81.902240
Lake Kissimmee S.P.	141	D2	27.971930 -81.380220
Lake Louisa S.P.	140	C1	28.460070 -81.751620
Lake Manatee S.P.	140	C3	27.475140 -82.336800
Little Talbot Island S.P.	139	D2	30.460500 -81.421950
Long Key S.P.	143	E4	24.821580 -80.819510
Lovers Key S.P.	142	C1	26.391000 -81.877800
Manatee Springs S.P.	138	B4	29.496230 -82.958630
Myakka River S.P.	140	C4	27.242670 -82.332240
Natural Bridge Bfld. Hist. S.P.	138	A2	30.284730 -84.152260
O'Leno S.P.	138	C3	29.809100 -82.550700
Olustee Bfld. Hist. S.P.	138	C2	30.214650 -82.428960
Oscar Scherer S.P.	140	B4	27.168840 -82.477360
Paynes Prairie Pres. S.P.	138	C3	29.520720 -82.300400
Perdido Key S.P.	135	F2	30.291480 -87.465360
Ponce De Leon Springs S.P.	136	C1	30.713260 -85.922490
Rainbow Springs S.P.	138	C4	29.103818 -82.438782
Ravine Gardens S.P.	139	D3	29.637490 -81.646830
River Rise Pres. S.P.	138	C3	29.859961 -82.605395
Saint Sebastian River Pres. S.P.	141	E3	27.815241 -80.513820
San Marcos de Apalache Hist. S.P.	138	A2	30.152890 -84.210030
Savannas Pres. S.P.	141	E3	27.245960 -80.250270
Sebastian Inlet S.P.	141	E2	27.870200 -80.453599
Silver River S.P.	139	D4	29.202550 -82.053610
Suwannee River S.P.	138	B2	30.389610 -83.157850
Three Rivers S.P.	137	D1	30.736800 -84.936500
Tomoka S.P.	139	E4	29.342210 -81.086200
Torreya S.P.	137	D2	30.553530 -84.946740
Troy Spring S.P.	138	B3	29.918000 -82.893300
Waccasassa Bay Pres. S.P.	138	B4	29.188100 -82.925500
Washington Oaks Gardens S.P.	139	E3	29.634670 -81.205500
Wekiwa Springs S.P.	141	D1	28.710490 -81.462810
Windley Key Fossil Reef Geological S.P.	143	E4	24.914100 -80.642800
Yulee Sugar Mill Ruins Hist. S.P.	140	B1	28.784730 -82.607370

GEORGIA	PAGE	GRID	LATITUDE LONGITUDE
National Park & Rec. Areas			
Chattahoochee River N.R.A.	120	C3	34.002910 -84.349180
Chickamauga & Chattanooga N.M.P.	120	B2	34.941430 -85.258790
Cumberland Island Natl. Seashore	139	D1	30.720300 -81.548760
Ed Jenkins N.R.A.	120	C2	34.682900 -84.198200
Fort Frederica Natl. Mon.	130	B4	31.219790 -81.386570
Fort Pulaski Natl. Mon.	130	C3	32.016520 -80.891680
Jimmy Carter N.H.S.	128	C3	32.034090 -84.401600
Kennesaw Mtn. Natl. Battlefied Park-Vis. Ctr.	120	C3	33.983000 -84.577900
Ocmulgee Natl. Mon.	129	D2	32.848560 -83.602140
State Park & Rec. Areas			
Amicalola Falls S.P.	120	C2	34.558940 -84.248890
Black Rock Mtn. S.P.	121	D2	34.918150 -83.400310
Bobby Brown State Outdoor Rec. Area	121	E3	33.979030 -82.588960
Cloudland Canyon S.P.	120	B2	34.830430 -85.482040
Crooked River S.P.	139	D1	30.844840 -81.559350
Elijah Clark S.P.	121	E4	33.854210 -82.391913
Florence Marina S.P.	128	C3	32.090988 -85.043263
Fort Mtn. S.P.	120	C2	34.763090 -84.689330
Fort Yargo S.P.	121	D4	33.984940 -83.733580
Franklin D. Roosevelt S.P.	128	C2	32.848670 -84.793230
General Coffee S.P.	129	E4	31.511490 -82.745360
George L. Smith S.P.	130	A2	32.570310 -82.103760
George T. Bagby S.P.	128	C4	31.739940 -85.074820
Georgia Veterans S.P.	129	D3	31.957951 -83.903787
Gordonia-Alatamaha S.P.	130	A3	32.081900 -82.123550
Hamburg S.P.	129	E1	33.208800 -82.774870
Hard Labor Creek S.P.	121	D4	33.677820 -83.593840
Hart State Outdoor Rec. Area	121	E3	34.376040 -82.910260
High Falls S.P.	129	D1	33.176590 -84.020280
Indian Springs S.P.	129	D1	33.247480 -83.921190
James H. "Sloppy" Floyd S.P.	120	B3	34.440260 -85.347580
John Tanner S.P.	120	B4	33.602750 -85.167070
Laura S. Walker S.P.	138	C1	31.143130 -82.212920
Little Ocmulgee S.P.	129	E3	32.100590 -82.886360
Magnolia Springs S.P.	130	A1	32.875760 -81.962560
Mistletoe S.P.	121	E4	33.638770 -82.390540
Moccasin Creek S.P.	121	D2	34.845160 -83.589140
Panola Mtn. S.P.	120	C4	33.622042 -84.173078
Providence Canyon State Outdoor Rec. Area	128	C3	32.068270 -84.929150
Red Top Mtn. S.P.	120	C3	34.145950 -84.720190
Reed Bingham S.P.	137	F1	31.161310 -83.538880
Richard B. Russell S.P.	121	E3	34.166778 -82.745691
Seminole S.P.	137	D1	30.811420 -84.873570
Skidaway Island S.P.	130	C3	31.947720 -81.052550
Sprewell Bluff State Outdoor Rec. Area	128	C2	32.857269 -84.482657
Stephen C. Foster S.P.	138	C1	30.827020 -82.361310

Tallulah Gorge S.P.	121	D2	34.736350 -83.391950
Tugaloo S.P.	121	E3	34.501940 -83.082320
Unicoi S.P.	121	D2	34.724620 -83.728170
Victoria Bryant S.P.	121	E3	34.299380 -83.158770
Vogel S.P.	121	D2	34.766190 -83.922000
Watson Mill Bridge S.P.	121	E3	34.041140 -83.126990

HAWAII	PAGE	GRID	LATITUDE LONGITUDE
National Park & Rec. Areas			
Haleakala Natl. Park-Main Road	153	D1	20.769130 -156.242850
Haleakala Natl. Park-Kipahulu Ent.	153	D1	20.662000 -156.045600
Haleakala Natl. Park-North Ent.	153	D1	20.769000 -156.243000
Hawaii Volcanoes Natl. Park-Ent.	153	F4	19.428700 -155.254500
Kalaupapa N.H.P.	152	C3	21.174110 -157.002830
State Park & Rec. Areas			
Ahupuaa O Kahana S.P.	152	A2	21.555210 -157.873260
Haena S.P.	152	B1	22.220930 -159.579600
Kaena Point S.P.	152	A2	21.551270 -158.244180
Kaumahina State Wayside Park	153	D1	20.871610 -156.170310
Kokee S.P.	152	B1	22.112580 -159.671050
Makena S.P.	153	D1	20.634030 -156.444180
Manuka State Wayside	153	E4	19.107990 -155.824610
Palaau S.P.	152	C3	21.174110 -157.002830
Polihale S.P.	152	B1	22.084480 -159.756700
Puaa Kaa State Wayside	153	D1	20.817560 -156.125800
Waianapanapa S.P.	153	E1	20.786230 -156.003010
Wailua River S.P.	152	B1	22.044180 -159.337250
Wailua Valley State Wayside	153	D1	20.840110 -156.139980
Wailuku River S.P.	153	F3	19.713340 -155.130490
Waimea Canyon S.P.	152	B1	22.031990 -159.671100

IDAHO	PAGE	GRID	LATITUDE LONGITUDE
National Park & Rec. Areas			
City of Rocks Natl. Res.	31	D2	42.078950 -113.677650
Craters of the Moon Natl. Mon. & Pres.	23	D4	43.462030 -113.559930
Hagerman Fossil Beds Natl. Mon.	30	C1	42.760980 -114.928220
Minidoka Natl. Hist. Site	31	D1	42.636944 -114.232222
Nez Perce N.H.P.-Clearwater Bfld.	22	B1	46.072600 -115.975400
Nez Perce N.H.P.-East Kamiah Site	22	B1	46.216600 -115.992400
Nez Perce N.H.P.-Vis. Ctr.	22	B1	46.446500 -116.817000
Nez Perce N.H.P.-White Bird Bfld.	22	B1	45.794000 -116.282000
Sawtooth N.R.A.	22	C3	44.211000 -114.946000
State Park & Rec. Areas			
Bear Lake S.P.	31	F2	42.026180 -111.257690
Bruneau Dunes S.P.	30	B1	42.910940 -115.713890
Castle Rocks S.P.	31	D2	42.135400 -113.670000
Dworshak S.P.	14	B4	46.577610 -116.327310
Eagle Island S.P.	22	B4	43.684510 -116.400300
Farragut S.P.	14	B2	47.952790 -116.602170
Harriman S.P.	23	F3	44.321000 -111.471200
Hells Gate S.P.	14	B4	46.380500 -117.044780
Henrys Lake S.P.	23	F3	44.620000 -111.373060
Heyburn S.P.	14	B3	47.353840 -116.748770
Lake Cascade S.P.	22	B3	44.520686 -116.046685
Lake Walcott S.P.	31	D1	42.674850 -113.482570
Land of the Yankee Fork S.P.	22	C3	44.475190 -114.208860
Lucky Peak S.P.	22	B4	43.530880 -116.055160
Massacre Rocks S.P.	31	D1	42.672200 -112.990800
McCroskey S.P.	14	B4	47.721080 -116.826310
Old Mission S.P.	14	B3	47.549420 -116.356940
Ponderosa S.P.	22	B2	44.926810 -116.083860
Priest Lake S.P.	14	B1	48.622082 -116.827798
Round Lake S.P.	14	B2	48.166110 -116.634230
Thousand Springs S.P.-Box Canyon	30	C1	42.709800 -114.791900
Thousand Springs S.P.-Malad Gorge	30	C1	42.864400 -114.854600
Thousand Springs S.P.-Niagara Springs	30	C1	42.662800 -114.672400
Three Island Crossing S.P.	30	C1	42.945280 -115.314850
Winchester Lake S.P.	22	B1	46.232280 -116.635570

ILLINOIS	PAGE	GRID	LATITUDE LONGITUDE
National Park & Rec. Areas			
Lincoln Home N.H.S.	98	B1	39.798120 -89.645150
Ronald Reagan Boyhood Home N.H.S.	88	B1	41.836700 -89.481100
State Park & Rec. Areas			
Apple River Canyon S.P.	74	A4	42.443990 -90.053280
Argyle Lake S.P.	87	F4	40.450680 -90.805080
Banner Marsh State Fish & Wildlife Area	88	B4	40.539600 -89.864500
Beall Woods S.P.	99	D4	38.351540 -87.836380
Beaver Dam S.P.	98	B2	39.214390 -89.959390
Big Bend State Fish & Wildlife Area	88	A2	41.634900 -90.044600
Buffalo Rock S.P.	88	C2	41.329720 -88.913090
Carlyle Lake State Fish & Wildlife Area	98	C3	38.768500 -89.193900
Castle Rock S.P.	88	B1	41.978230 -89.357040
Cave-In-Rock S.P.	109	D1	37.468010 -88.159950
Chain O'Lakes S.P.	74	C4	42.458390 -88.211950
Channahon S.P.	88	C2	41.415826 -88.223133
Coffeen Lake State Fish & Wildlife Area	98	B2	39.057000 -89.412400
Crawford County State Fish & Wildlife Area	99	D2	39.099800 -87.713100
Delabar S.P.	87	F3	40.957830 -90.939460
Des Plaines State Fish & Wildlife Area	88	C2	41.376600 -88.207400
Dixon Springs S.P.	108	C1	37.383600 -88.672830
Donnelley–Depue State Fish & Wildlife Area	88	B2	41.324000 -89.314100
Edward R. Madigan State Fish & Wildlife Area	88	B4	40.115280 -89.402240
Eldon Hazlet State Rec. Area	98	B3	38.667610 -89.327200
Ferne Clyffe S.P.	108	C1	37.532550 -88.966430
Fort Massac S.P.	108	C2	37.161720 -88.693850
Fox Ridge S.P.	99	D2	39.406020 -88.134810
Gebhard Woods S.P.	88	C2	41.357350 -88.440210
Giant City S.P.	108	C1	37.612250 -89.181790
Green River State Wildlife Area	88	B2	41.631600 -89.516500
Hamilton County State Fish & Wildlife Area	98	C4	38.065100 -88.404700
Hazel & Bill Rutherford Wildlife Prairie S.P.	88	B3	40.734180 -89.747270
Henderson County Cons. Area	87	F3	40.857505 -90.975005
Horseshoe Lake State Fish & Wildlife Area	108	C2	37.130465 -89.338505
Illini S.P.	88	C2	41.318770 -88.711070
Illinois Beach S.P.	75	D4	42.429920 -87.820150
Iroquois County State Wildlife Area	89	D3	40.994300 -87.598700
Jim Edgar Panther Creek State Fish & Wildlife Area	98	B1	40.011700 -90.177005
Johnson-Sauk Trail S.P.	88	A2	41.327510 -89.904850
Jubilee College S.P.	88	B3	40.844580 -89.827260
Kankakee River S.P.	89	D2	41.203400 -88.001880
Kaskaskia River State Fish & Wildlife Area	98	B4	38.229700 -89.879500
Kickapoo State Rec. Area	89	D4	40.138290 -87.737770
Lake Le Aqua-Na State Rec. Area	74	A4	42.422800 -89.823900
Lake Murphysboro S.P.	108	C1	37.771800 -89.382670
Lasalle Lake State Fish & Wildlife Area	88	C2	41.238400 -88.655500
Lincoln Trail S.P.	99	D2	39.346480 -87.696460
Lowden S.P.	88	B1	42.034860 -89.324950
Mackinaw River State Fish & Wildlife Area	88	B4	40.545801 -89.294301
Marshall State Fish & Wildlife Area	88	B3	41.007900 -89.410100
Matthiessen S.P.	88	C2	41.285010 -89.010050
Mautino State Fish & Wildlife Area	88	B2	41.323100 -89.718900
Middle Fork State Fish & Wildlife Area	89	D4	40.258300 -87.795900
Mississippi Palisades S.P.	88	A1	42.135820 -90.163300
Mississippi River State Fish & Wildlife Area	98	A2	38.991900 -90.542100
Morrison-Rockwood S.P.	88	A1	41.856350 -89.950120
Nauvoo S.P.	87	F4	40.543590 -91.386650
Newton Lake State Fish & Wildlife Area	99	D2	38.922400 -88.306700
Pere Marquette S.P.	98	A2	38.968110 -90.497430
Prophetstown S.P.	88	B2	41.672090 -89.920310
Pyramid S.P.	98	B4	38.004110 -89.425680
Ray Norbut State Fish & Wildlife Area	98	A1	39.685000 -90.648500
Red Hills S.P.	99	D3	38.728850 -87.838660
Rend Lake State Fish & Wildlife Area	98	C4	38.043800 -88.988900
Rice Lake State Fish & Wildlife Area	88	A4	40.476785 -89.949205
Saline County State Fish & Wildlife Area	109	D1	37.691300 -88.379100
Sam Dale Lake State Fish & Wildlife Area	98	C3	38.536005 -88.565605
Sam Parr State Fish & Wildlife Area	99	D2	39.011022 -88.126955
Sanganois State Fish & Wildlife Area	88	A4	40.091605 -90.283205
Sangchris Lake State Rec. Area	98	B1	39.656830 -89.487940
Shabbona Lake S.P.	88	C1	41.732250 -88.864930
Shelbyville State Fish & Wildlife Area	98	C2	39.566300 -88.566200
Siloam Springs S.P.	97	F1	39.899340 -90.955050
Silver Springs S.P.	88	C2	41.627500 -88.518550
Snakeden Hollow State Fish & Wildlife Area	88	A3	41.030200 -90.080100
South Shore S.P.	98	B3	38.610250 -89.314570
Starved Rock S.P.	88	C2	41.321750 -89.010850
Stephen A. Forbes State Rec. Area	98	C3	38.718140 -88.743250
Ten Mile Creek State Fish & Wildlife Area	98	C4	38.081200 -88.594200
Turkey Bluffs State Fish & Wildlife Area	98	B4	37.877200 -89.771100
Walnut Point S.P.	99	D1	39.705150 -88.030390
Wayne Fitzgerrell S.P.	98	C4	38.089250 -88.937010
Weinberg-King S.P.	87	F4	40.226830 -90.899700
Weldon Springs S.P.	88	C4	40.125080 -88.921400
White Pines Forest S.P.	88	B1	41.988730 -89.461590
Wolf Creek S.P.	98	C2	39.488310 -88.680370
Woodford State Fish & Wildlife Area	88	B3	40.878900 -89.444800

INDIANA	PAGE	GRID	LATITUDE LONGITUDE
National Park & Rec. Areas			
George Rodgers Clark N.H.P.	99	D3	38.677880 -87.535350
Indiana Dunes Natl. Lakeshore	89	D1	41.653160 -87.062630
Lincoln Boyhood Natl. Mem.	99	E4	38.116800 -86.997860
State Park & Rec. Areas			
Bass Lake State Beach	89	E2	41.220100 -86.580200
Brown County S.P.	99	F2	39.197170 -86.215830
Chain O' Lakes S.P.	90	A2	41.336000 -85.422950
Charlestown S.P.	100	A3	38.448300 -85.644700
Clifty Falls S.P.	100	A3	38.761220 -85.420720
Fort Harrison S.P.	99	F1	39.871921 -86.018859
Harmonie S.P.	99	D4	38.089210 -87.934080
Indiana Dunes S.P.	89	E2	41.651470 -87.062620
Lincoln S.P.	99	E4	38.118370 -86.980080
McCormick's Creek S.P.	99	E2	39.283340 -86.726680
O'Bannon Woods S.P.	99	F4	38.200600 -86.254678
Ouabache S.P.	90	A3	40.728090 -85.111060
Pokagon S.P.	90	A1	41.707960 -85.029320
Potato Creek S.P.	89	E2	41.534950 -86.360290
Prophetstown S.P.	89	E4	40.500211 -86.829548
Shades S.P.	99	E1	39.941630 -87.057670
Shakamak S.P.	99	E2	39.181800 -87.232200
Spring Mill S.P.	99	F3	38.723330 -86.418460
Summit Lake S.P.	100	A1	40.018680 -85.302720
Tippecanoe River S.P.	89	E3	41.117330 -86.602750
Turkey Run S.P.	99	E1	39.882010 -87.200550
Versailles S.P.	100	A2	39.063900 -85.205330
Whitewater Mem. S.P.	100	B1	39.611300 -84.942300

IOWA	PAGE	GRID	LATITUDE LONGITUDE
National Park & Rec. Areas			
Effigy Mounds Natl. Mon.	73	F3	43.089130 -91.192350
Herbert Hoover N.H.S.	87	F1	41.671390 -91.346640
State Park & Rec. Areas			
Ambrose A. Call S.P.	72	B3	43.049650 -94.243430
Backbone S.P.	73	E4	42.600730 -91.532700
Beed's Lake S.P.	73	D4	42.767209 -93.241705
Bellevue S.P.	88	A1	42.247870 -90.416920
Black Hawk S.P.	72	B4	42.302700 -95.048680
Bobwhite S.P.	86	C3	40.710200 -93.393850
Cold Springs S.P.	86	B2	41.289540 -95.083810
Crystal Lake S.P.	72	C3	43.224895 -93.792925
Echo Valley S.P.	73	E3	42.944040 -91.776880
Elk Rock S.P.	87	D2	41.400470 -93.063050
Fort Defiance S.P.	72	B2	43.393260 -94.851290
George Wyth Mem. S.P.	73	E4	42.536980 -92.394210
Green Valley S.P.	86	B3	41.114490 -94.377270
Heery Woods S.P.	73	D4	42.766450 -92.675250
Honey Creek S.P.	87	D3	40.863940 -92.939050
Lake Ahquabi S.P.	86	C2	41.286710 -93.572690
Lake Anita S.P.	86	B2	41.434150 -94.762470
Lake Icaria S.P.	86	B3	41.053380 -94.756990
Lake Keomah S.P.	87	D2	41.286570 -92.541660
Lake Macbride S.P.	87	F1	41.803090 -91.570950
Lake Wapello S.P.	87	D3	40.824890 -92.570530
Ledges S.P.	86	C1	41.998970 -93.896110
Maquoketa Caves S.P.	87	F1	42.119890 -90.770950
McIntosh Woods S.P.	72	C3	43.132580 -93.457580
Mini-Wakan S.P.	72	B2	43.498460 -95.102320
Nine Eagles S.P.	86	C3	40.591250 -93.765130
Oakland Mills S.P.	87	E3	40.935400 -91.619370
Palisades-Kepler S.P.	87	F1	41.916880 -91.497050
Pammel S.P.	86	C2	41.295590 -94.073150
Pikes Point S.P.	72	A2	43.415320 -95.162860
Pilot Knob S.P.	72	C3	43.255470 -93.574840
Prairie Rose S.P.	86	A2	41.601590 -95.210660
Preparation Canyon S.P.	86	A1	41.901570 -95.911670
Rice Lake S.P.	72	C2	43.401350 -93.502490
Rock Creek S.P.	87	D1	41.760580 -92.835410
Spring Lake S.P.	86	B1	42.070600 -94.291500
Stone S.P.	35	F1	42.555460 -96.476050
Trappers Bay S.P.	72	A2	43.453630 -95.335510
Twin Lakes S.P.	72	B4	42.480180 -94.629860
Viking Lake S.P.	86	B3	40.973170 -95.053710
Wanata S.P.	72	A3	42.911340 -95.338080
Waubonsie S.P.	86	A3	40.677770 -95.683680
Wildcat Den S.P.	87	F2	41.467700 -90.869330

KANSAS	PAGE	GRID	LATITUDE LONGITUDE
National Park & Rec. Areas			
Fort Larned N.H.S.	43	D3	38.188740 -99.220620
Fort Scott N.H.S.	106	B1	37.843350 -94.704840
Monument Rocks Natl. Landmark	42	B2	38.790569 -100.762366
Nicodemus N.H.S.	42	C2	39.390833 -99.617500
State Park & Rec. Areas			
Atchison State Fishing Lake	96	B1	39.639010 -95.171830
Black Kettle State Fishing Lake	43	E3	38.229240 -97.509390
Bourbon State Fishing Lake	106	B1	37.793450 -95.069690
Brown State Fishing Lake	96	A1	39.847030 -95.373860
Cedar Bluff S.P.	42	C2	38.798230 -99.715060
Chase State Fishing Lake	43	F3	38.368480 -96.588000
Cheney S.P.	43	E4	37.732700 -97.844350
Clark State Fishing Lake	42	C4	37.391670 -99.784720
Clinton S.P.	96	A3	38.941970 -95.353960
Cowley State Fishing Lake	51	F1	37.104040 -96.795000
Crawford S.P.	106	B1	37.634320 -94.809820
Cross Timbers S.P.	106	A1	37.774514 -95.943431
Douglas State Fishing Lake	96	B3	38.796030 -95.165150
Eisenhower S.P.	96	A3	38.535720 -95.744270
El Dorado S.P.	43	F4	37.861420 -96.749460
Elk City S.P.	106	A2	37.251130 -95.774090
Fallriver S.P.	43	F4	37.653550 -96.043600
Glen Elder S.P.	43	D1	39.512160 -98.339140
Hain State Fishing Lake	42	C4	37.854250 -99.858020
Hamilton State Fishing Lake	42	B3	38.039090 -101.816940
Hillsdale S.P.	96	B3	38.660700 -94.894000
Kanopolis S.P.	43	E3	38.600340 -97.979500
Kingman State Fishing Lake	43	E4	37.651390 -98.306940
Kiowa State Fishing Lake	43	D4	37.612570 -99.299000
Leavenworth State Fishing Lake	96	B2	39.126970 -95.141700
Logan State Fishing Lake	42	B2	38.940280 -101.236940
Lovewell S.P.	43	E1	39.903310 -98.043090
Lyon State Fishing Lake	43	F3	38.546520 -96.058190
McPherson State Fishing Lake	43	E3	38.478667 -97.468267
Meade S.P.	42	C4	37.172220 -100.450000

	PAGE	GRID	LATITUDE LONGITUDE
Miami State Fishing Lake	96	B3	38.422220 -94.785280
Milford S.P.	43	F2	39.104290 -96.895520
Mushroom Rock S.P.	43	E2	38.722222 -98.032222
Nebo State Fishing Lake	96	A2	39.447220 -95.595830
Neosho State Fishing Lake	106	B1	37.430570 -95.202550
Ottawa State Fishing Lake	43	E2	39.103040 -97.573060
Perry S.P.	96	A2	39.140210 -95.492480
Pomona S.P.	96	A3	38.652400 -95.600800
Pottawatomie State Fishing Lake No. 1	43	F1	39.470370 -96.407510
Pottawatomie State Fishing Lake No. 2	43	F2	39.228100 -96.533660
Prairie Dog S.P.	42	C1	39.811810 -99.963920
Prairie Spirit Trail S.P.	96	A4	38.280278 -95.242222
Rooks State Fishing Lake	43	D2	39.398290 -99.315020
Saline State Fishing Lake	43	E2	38.903159 -97.657510
Sand Hills S.P.	43	E3	38.116667 -97.833333
Scott S.P.	42	B2	38.684867 -100.922500
Shawnee State Fishing Lake	96	A2	39.206940 -95.804170
Tuttle Creek S.P.	43	F2	39.255560 -96.583330
Washington State Fishing Lake	43	E1	39.929780 -97.118830
Webster S.P.	43	D2	39.407840 -99.454550
Wilson State Fishing Lake	106	A1	38.910450 -98.497950
Wilson S.P.	43	D2	38.915000 -98.500000

KENTUCKY	PAGE	GRID	LATITUDE LONGITUDE
National Park & Rec. Areas			
Abraham Lincoln Birthplace N.H.S.	110	A1	37.532280 -85.733570
Land Between the Lakes N.R.A.	109	D2	36.776912 -88.059988
Mammoth Cave Natl. Park-Vis. Ctr.	109	F2	37.186800 -86.101300
State Park & Rec. Areas			
Barren River Lake State Resort Park	110	A2	36.853220 -86.053850
Ben Hawes S.P.	109	E1	37.797034 -87.188186
Blue Licks Bfld. State Resort Park	100	C3	38.434960 -83.991340
Buckhorn Lake State Resort Park	111	D1	37.312890 -83.423040
Carter Caves State Resort Park	101	D4	38.371470 -83.108510
Columbus-Belmont S.P.	108	C2	36.761990 -89.107000
Cumberland Falls State Resort Park	110	C2	36.834390 -84.350170
Fishtrap Lake S.P.	111	E1	37.432048 -82.417926
Fort Boonesborough S.P.	110	C1	37.899345 -84.270040
General Butler State Resort Park	100	A3	38.669950 -85.146050
Grayson Lake S.P.	101	D4	38.208630 -83.014910
Greenbo Lake State Resort Park	101	D3	38.479130 -82.867630
Green River Lake S.P.	110	A2	37.277440 -85.338730
Jenny Wiley State Resort Park-East Ent.	111	E1	37.730120 -82.740990
Jenny Wiley State Resort Park-South Ent.	111	E1	37.687680 -82.725690
Jenny Wiley State Resort Park-West Ent.	111	E1	37.727250 -82.745880
John James Audubon S.P.	99	D4	37.889250 -87.556510
Kentucky Dam Village State Resort Park	109	D2	36.996880 -88.285716
Kingdom Come S.P.	111	D2	36.981850 -82.982210
Lake Barkley State Resort Park	109	D2	36.809190 -87.928310
Lake Cumberland State Resort Park	110	B2	36.930320 -85.040960
Levi Jackson S.P.	110	C2	37.085250 -84.059250
Lincoln Homestead S.P.	110	B1	37.760080 -85.215930
My Old Kentucky Home S.P.	110	A1	37.808140 -85.458840
Natural Bridge State Resort Park	110	C1	37.777470 -83.676310
Nolin Lake S.P.	109	F1	37.297641 -86.212624
Old Fort Harrod S.P.	110	B1	37.762130 -84.845670
Pennyrile Forest State Resort Park	109	E2	37.057410 -87.649390
Pine Mtn. State Resort Park	110	C3	36.735270 -83.700790
Rough River State Resort Park	109	F1	37.615410 -86.504410
Taylorsville Lake S.P.	100	A4	37.993990 -85.227813
Yatesville Lake S.P.	101	D4	38.093300 -82.617800

LOUISIANA	PAGE	GRID	LATITUDE LONGITUDE
National Park & Rec. Areas			
Cane River Creole N.H.P.	125	D4	31.739690 -93.083080
Jean Lafitte N.H.P. & Pres.-Chalmette Vis. Ctr.	134	A3	29.942100 -89.994400
Jean Lafitte N.H.P. & Pres.-French Quarter Vis. Ctr.	134	A3	29.954600 -90.065100
Jean Lafitte N.H.P.-Wetlands Acadian Cultural Center	134	A3	29.795969 -90.824480
Poverty Point Natl. Mon. & S.H.S.	125	F2	32.633370 -91.403880
State Park & Rec. Areas			
Bayou Segnette S.P.	134	B3	29.902720 -90.153800
Chemin-A-Haut S.P.	125	F1	32.913460 -91.847550
Chicot S.P.	133	E1	30.829870 -92.276180
Cypremort Point S.P.	133	F3	29.731960 -91.840740
Fairview-Riverside S.P.	134	B2	30.408730 -90.140360
Fontainebleau S.P.	134	B2	30.345470 -90.022850
Grand Isle S.P.-Temp. Closed	134	B4	29.256640 -89.958480
Hodges Gardens S.P.	125	D4	31.369280 -93.424860
Jimmie Davis S.P.	125	E3	32.265000 -92.540300
Lake Bistineau S.P.	125	D2	32.440250 -93.395910
Lake Bruin S.P.	126	A3	31.955370 -91.198080
Lake Claiborne S.P.	125	D2	32.713000 -92.923360
Lake D'Arbonne S.P.	125	E2	32.784850 -92.490310
Lake Fausse Pointe S.P.	133	F3	30.067820 -91.615790
North Toledo Bend S.P.	124	C4	31.558910 -93.732060
Palmetto Island S.P.	133	F3	29.862877 -92.144165
Poverty Point Reservoir S.P.	125	F2	32.540446 -91.421356
Saint Bernard S.P.	134	C3	29.864460 -89.899190
South Toledo Bend S.P.	125	D4	31.213889 -93.575000
Tickfaw S.P.	134	B2	30.382180 -90.631150

MAINE	PAGE	GRID	LATITUDE LONGITUDE
National Park & Rec. Areas			
Acadia Natl. Park-Cadillac Mtn. Ent.	83	D2	44.384400 -68.229800
Acadia Natl. Park-Park Loop Road	83	D2	44.338700 -68.183200
Acadia Natl. Park-Sieur de Monts Ent.	83	D2	44.360000 -68.205200
Acadia Natl. Park-Stanley Brook Ent.	83	D2	44.296300 -68.242000
State Park & Rec. Areas			
Aroostook S.P.	85	E2	46.612720 -68.005840
Baxter S.P.	84	C3	45.950290 -69.049080
Camden Hills S.P.	82	C2	44.232050 -69.046530
Cobscook Bay S.P.	83	E1	44.855290 -67.171680
Damariscotta Lake S.P.	82	C2	44.200070 -69.452900
Ferry Beach S.P.	82	B4	43.482410 -70.391520
Lake Saint George S.P.	82	C2	44.398950 -69.345710
Lamoine S.P.	83	D2	44.456000 -68.298520
Mount Blue S.P.	82	B1	44.721780 -70.417080
Peaks-Kenny S.P.	84	C4	45.256680 -69.254600
Popham Beach S.P.	82	C3	43.738740 -69.795830
Rangeley Lake S.P.	82	B1	44.919550 -70.696950
Range Ponds S.P.	82	B3	44.033540 -70.345080
Roque Bluffs S.P.	83	E2	44.614680 -67.479300
Saint Croix Island International Hist. Site	83	E1	45.128333 -67.133333
Sebago Lake S.P.	82	B3	43.916590 -70.570190
Shackford Head S.P.	83	F1	44.906191 -66.989979
Swan Lake S.P.	82	C2	44.568860 -68.981070
Vaughan Woods S.P.	82	A4	43.212680 -70.809320
Warren Island S.P.	82	C2	44.260445 -68.952255
Wolfe's Neck Woods S.P.	82	B3	43.827190 -70.084460

MARYLAND	PAGE	GRID	LATITUDE LONGITUDE
National Park & Rec. Areas			
Assateague Island Natl. Seashore	114	C2	38.239580 -75.140410
Thomas Stone N.H.S.	144	B4	38.529700 -77.032370
State Park & Rec. Areas			
Assateague S.P.	114	C2	38.250170 -75.156270
Big Run S.P.	102	B1	39.545090 -79.137254
Catoctin Mtn. Park-Vis. Ctr.	144	A1	39.633100 -77.449700
Cunningham Falls S.P.	144	A1	39.625040 -77.458130
Deep Creek Lake S.P.	102	B1	39.512110 -79.300150
Elk Neck S.P.	145	D1	39.482890 -75.983630
Fort Frederick S.P.	103	D1	39.616050 -78.007060
Gambrill S.P.	144	A1	39.468330 -77.495730
Greenwell S.P.	103	E4	38.364930 -76.525260
Gunpowder Falls S.P.	144	C1	39.536710 -76.502800
Hart-Miller Island S.P.	144	C2	39.251219 -76.376903
Janes Island S.P.	103	F4	38.009810 -75.846380
Martinak S.P.	145	E3	38.862920 -75.837790
North Point S.P.	144	C2	39.221910 -76.431600
Patapsco Valley S.P.	144	B2	39.296580 -76.781500
Patuxent River S.P.	144	B2	39.280790 -77.129620
Pocomoke River S.P.	114	C2	38.135410 -75.494870
Point Lookout S.P.	103	F4	38.066190 -76.336550
Purse S.P.	103	E3	38.430540 -77.252030
Rocks S.P.	144	C1	39.630140 -76.418120
Rocky Gap S.P.	102	C1	39.698430 -78.651150
Rosaryville S.P.	144	C3	38.778450 -76.799260
Saint Clement's Island S.P.	103	E4	38.225200 -76.749690
Saint Mary's River S.P.	103	E4	38.262940 -76.525640
Sandy Point S.P.	144	C3	39.021750 -76.420280
Seneca Creek S.P.	144	A2	39.152200 -77.247710
Smallwood S.P.	144	B4	38.556509 -77.185257
South Mtn. S.P.	144	A1	39.540058 -77.607422
Susquehanna S.P.	145	D1	39.599840 -76.154590
Swallow Falls S.P.	102	B1	39.506550 -79.448750
Tuckahoe S.P.	145	D3	38.967120 -75.943410
Washington Mon. S.P.	144	A1	39.499810 -77.631890
Wye Oak S.P.	145	D3	38.939150 -76.080230

MASSACHUSETTS	PAGE	GRID	LATITUDE LONGITUDE
National Park & Rec. Areas			
Adams N.H.P.-Vis. Ctr.	151	D1	42.257000 -71.011200
Boston Harbor Island N.R.A.	151	D1	42.319705 -70.928555
Cape Cod Natl. Seashore	151	F2	41.835890 -69.973730
Lowell N.H.P.-Market Mills Vis. Ctr.	95	E1	42.644400 -71.312800
Minute Man N.H.P.-Minute Man Vis. Ctr.	151	D1	42.449000 -71.268700
Minute Man N.H.P.-North Bridge Vis. Ctr.	151	D1	42.470800 -71.352600
New Bedford Whaling N.H.P.	151	D4	41.635570 -70.924250
Salem Maritime N.H.S.	151	D1	42.521490 -70.886980
Saugus Iron Works N.H.S.	151	D1	42.468230 -71.009110
Waquoit Bay Natl. Estuarine Research Res.	151	E4	41.581300 -70.524800
State Park & Rec. Areas			
Ames-Nowell S.P.	151	D2	42.113140 -70.975230
Ashland S.P.	150	C2	42.246380 -71.475560
Blackstone River & Canal Heritage S.P.	150	C2	42.099500 -71.618780
Borderland S.P.	151	D2	42.058560 -71.166330
Bradley Palmer S.P.	151	F1	42.652180 -70.911000
Callahan S.P.	150	C1	42.315140 -71.367710
Demarest Lloyd S.P.	151	D4	41.525790 -70.990530
Dighton Rock S.P.	151	D3	41.811230 -71.098440
Halibut Point S.P.	151	F1	42.686100 -70.631070
Hampton Ponds S.P.	150	A2	42.178350 -72.690030
Holyoke Range S.P.	150	A1	42.297270 -72.530890
Joseph Sylvia State Beach	151	E4	41.424140 -70.553870
Lake Wyola S.P.-Carroll Holmes Rec. Area	150	A1	42.500366 -72.430642
Moore S.P.	150	B1	42.312354 -71.954269
Nickerson S.P.	151	F3	41.775550 -70.028290
Pilgrim Mem. (Plymouth Rock) S.P.	151	E2	41.958850 -70.662870
Red Bridge S.P.	150	A2	42.175500 -72.406600
Robinson S.P.	150	A2	42.081680 -72.658650
Rutland S.P.	150	B1	42.371470 -71.997680
Savoy Mtn. State Forest	94	C1	42.626540 -73.015580
Skinner S.P.	150	A1	42.304220 -72.598790
South Cape Beach S.P.	151	E4	41.554582 -70.508194
Wahconah Falls S.P.	94	C1	42.491430 -73.120790
Watson Pond S.P.	151	D2	41.956260 -71.116090
Wells S.P.	150	B2	42.142290 -72.042400
Whitehall S.P.	150	C2	42.227210 -71.584330
Wompatuck S.P.	151	D2	42.218770 -70.866600

MICHIGAN	PAGE	GRID	LATITUDE LONGITUDE
National Park & Rec. Areas			
Father Marquette Natl. Mem.	70	C2	45.853912 -84.728874
Grand Island N.R.A.	70	A1	46.500405 -86.657605
Isle Royale Natl. Park-Rock Harbor Vis. Ctr.	65	F2	48.145530 -88.482220
Isle Royale Natl. Park-Windigo Vis. Ctr.	65	F2	47.912700 -89.156990
Keweenaw N.H.P.	65	F3	47.242160 -88.448020
Pictured Rocks Natl. Lakeshore-East Ent.	70	A1	46.657450 -86.021160
Pictured Rocks Natl. Lakeshore-West Ent.	70	A1	46.474000 -86.553000
Sleeping Bear Dunes Natl. Lakeshore	70	A4	44.785210 -86.049690
State Park & Rec. Areas			
Albert E. Sleeper S.P.	76	C2	43.972880 -83.205530
Algonac S.P.	76	C4	42.654760 -82.514510
Aloha S.P.	70	C3	45.525850 -84.464390
Baraga S.P.	65	F4	46.762070 -88.499320
Bewabic S.P.	68	C2	46.094260 -88.422290
Brimley S.P.	70	C1	46.412970 -84.555040
Burt Lake S.P.	70	C3	45.401305 -84.619505
Cambridge Junction Hist. S.P.	90	B1	42.066990 -84.225550
Charles Mears S.P.	75	E2	43.781980 -86.439670
Cheboygan S.P.	70	C2	45.644860 -84.420440
Clear Lake S.P.	70	C3	45.127390 -84.173910
Coldwater Lake S.P.	90	A1	43.665975 -84.948703
Craig Lake S.P.	68	C1	46.538810 -88.127700
Duck Lake S.P.	75	E3	43.354880 -86.397560
F.J. Mclain S.P.	65	F3	47.239400 -88.587190
Fayette Hist. S.P.	70	A2	45.717200 -86.664600
Fisherman's Island S.P.	70	B3	45.307550 -85.301540
Fort Wilkins Hist. S.P.	65	F3	47.466780 -87.878240
Grand Haven S.P.	75	E3	43.056100 -86.245990
Grand Mere S.P.	89	E1	41.995190 -86.538790
Harrisville S.P.	71	D4	44.649800 -83.293920
Hart-Montague Trail S.P.	75	E2	43.688800 -86.371900
Hartwick Pines S.P.	70	C4	44.744180 -84.648340
Holland S.P.	75	E4	42.780310 -86.201410
Indian Lake S.P.	70	A2	45.960420 -86.364400
Interlochen S.P.	70	B4	44.631370 -85.766630
J.W. Wells S.P.	69	D3	45.389070 -87.371360
Kal-Haven Trail S.P.	75	E4	42.324698 -85.667739
Lake Gogebic S.P.	68	B1	46.459950 -89.573110
Lakelands Trail S.P.	76	B4	42.408249 -83.964043
Lakeport S.P.	76	C3	43.129120 -82.501820
Leelanau S.P.	70	B3	45.209320 -85.546220
Ludington S.P.	75	E1	44.031100 -86.505460
Mackinac Island S.P.	70	C2	45.849880 -84.617650
Muskallonge Lake S.P.	70	B1	46.677100 -85.625210
Muskegon S.P.	75	E3	43.247900 -86.341480
Negwegon S.P.	71	D4	44.855020 -83.329240
Newaygo S.P.	75	F2	43.500600 -85.582260
North Higgins Lake S.P.	70	C4	44.515030 -84.753980
Onaway S.P.	70	C3	45.430530 -84.229020
Orchard Beach S.P.	75	E1	44.278860 -86.314480
Otsego Lake S.P.	70	C4	44.927770 -84.688980
P.H. Hoeft S.P.	70	C3	45.463700 -83.883560
P.J. Hoffmaster S.P.	75	E3	43.132870 -86.265460
Palms Book S.P.	70	A2	46.003280 -86.385130
Petoskey S.P.	70	B3	45.407950 -84.902160
Porcupine Mts. Wilderness S.P.	65	E4	46.816070 -89.621850
Port Crescent S.P.	76	C1	44.007570 -83.051290
Sanilac Petroglyphs Hist. S.P.	76	C2	43.649367 -83.018016
Saugatuck Dunes S.P.	75	E4	42.695990 -86.186840
Seven Lakes S.P.	76	B3	42.816750 -83.648120
Silver Lake S.P.	75	E2	43.663650 -86.492660
Sleepy Hollow S.P.	76	A3	42.925020 -84.408620
South Higgins Lake S.P.	76	A1	44.432818 -84.670299
Sterling S.P.	90	C1	41.921490 -83.342680
Straits S.P.	70	C2	45.858090 -84.720200
Tahquamenon Falls S.P.-East Ent.	70	B1	46.598030 -85.147890
Tahquamenon Falls S.P.-West Ent.	70	B1	46.564190 -85.292530
Tawas Point S.P.	76	B1	44.255820 -83.443050
Thompson's Harbor S.P.	71	D3	45.346705 -83.567431
Traverse City S.P.	70	B4	44.748050 -85.553800
Twin Lakes S.P.	65	E4	46.892210 -88.856560
Van Buren S.P.	75	E4	42.333830 -86.304830

Van Buren Trail S.P.	89	F1	42.211405 -86.171105
Van Riper S.P.	68	C1	46.525260 -87.991150
Walter J. Hayes S.P.	90	B1	42.072830 -84.137820
Warren Dunes S.P.	89	E1	41.900980 -86.595260
Warren Woods S.P.	89	E1	41.840680 -86.631290
Wetzel Rec. Area	76	C4	42.596720 -82.825140
White Pine Trail S.P.	75	F2	44.222900 -85.426700
Wilderness S.P.-East Ent.	70	B2	45.748160 -84.853500
Wilderness S.P.-West Ent.	70	B2	45.679360 -84.964170
William Mitchell S.P.	75	F1	44.236880 -85.453990
Wilson S.P.	76	A1	44.029620 -84.806070
Young S.P.	70	B3	45.235240 -85.041450

MINNESOTA	PAGE	GRID	LATITUDE LONGITUDE
National Park & Rec. Areas			
Grand Portage Natl. Mon.	65	E2	47.996274 -89.734256
Pipestone Natl. Mon.	27	F3	44.013150 -96.325360
Voyageurs Natl. Park-Ash River Vis. Ctr.	64	C2	48.435600 -92.850300
Voyageurs Natl. Park-Kabetogama Lake Vis. Ctr.	64	C2	48.446100 -93.030100
Voyageurs Natl. Park-Rainy Lake Vis. Ctr.	64	C2	48.584400 -93.161500
State Park & Rec. Areas			
Afton S.P.	67	D4	44.847930 -92.791020
Banning S.P.	67	D2	46.179730 -92.855170
Bear Head Lake S.P.	64	C3	47.792720 -92.083720
Beaver Creek Valley S.P.	73	E2	43.636790 -91.573190
Blue Mounds S.P.	27	F4	43.714340 -96.183100
Buffalo River S.P.	19	F4	46.866260 -96.469980
Camden S.P.	27	F3	44.362880 -95.917480
Caribou Falls State Wayside	65	D3	47.463890 -91.030660
Carley S.P.	73	E1	44.116790 -92.169320
Cascade River S.P.	65	D3	47.712950 -90.497930
Charles A. Lindbergh S.P.	66	C2	45.959410 -94.387640
Cross River State Wayside	65	D3	47.543420 -90.897770
Crow Wing S.P.	66	C1	46.272630 -94.316400
Father Hennepin S.P.	66	C1	46.144520 -93.484260
Flandrau S.P.	72	B1	44.294360 -94.482020
Flood Bay State Wayside	64	C4	47.038500 -91.642540
Forestville Mystery Cave S.P.	73	E2	43.637520 -92.220270
Fort Ridgely S.P.	72	B1	44.454810 -94.718310
Franz Jevne S.P.	64	B2	48.641140 -94.058260
Frontenac S.P.	67	E4	44.525200 -92.338730
George H. Crosby Manitou S.P.	65	D3	47.478990 -91.123070
Glacial Lakes S.P.	66	A3	45.540550 -95.529600
Glendalough S.P.	19	F4	46.313314 -95.679290
Gooseberry Falls S.P.	65	D3	47.145430 -91.462380
Grand Portage S.P.	65	E2	47.999150 -89.598690
Great River Bluffs S.P.	73	E1	43.939100 -91.430050
Hayes Lake S.P.	19	F1	48.641070 -95.570600
Hill Annex Mine S.P.	64	B3	47.327490 -93.277520
Inspiration Peak State Wayside	66	A1	46.136880 -95.578650
Itasca S.P.	64	A3	47.194490 -95.166740
Jay Cooke S.P.	64	C4	46.658790 -92.349200
John A. Latsch S.P.	73	E1	44.164720 -91.823860
Joseph R. Brown State Wayside	66	B4	44.750328 -95.324425
Judge C.R. Magney S.P.	65	E3	47.818090 -90.051230
Kilen Woods S.P.	72	B2	43.732140 -95.072220
Kodonce River State Wayside	65	E3	47.793930 -90.154140
Lac Qui Parle S.P.	27	F2	45.024680 -95.896580
Lake Bemidji S.P.	64	A3	47.536890 -94.832320
Lake Bronson S.P.	19	F1	48.730940 -96.658720
Lake Carlos S.P.	66	B2	46.000540 -95.334430
Lake Louise S.P.	73	D2	43.532620 -92.509250
Lake Maria S.P.	66	C3	45.304810 -93.935570
Lake Shetek S.P.	72	A1	44.105740 -95.699730
Maplewood S.P.	19	F4	46.549910 -95.966720
McCarthy Beach S.P.	64	B3	47.674110 -93.027350
Mille Lacs Kathio S.P.	66	C2	46.160740 -93.758020
Minneopa S.P.	72	C1	44.162190 -94.110310
Monson Lake S.P.	66	B3	45.321300 -95.270470
Moose Lake S.P.	64	C4	46.436360 -92.743090
Myre-Big Island S.P.	73	D2	43.623847 -93.289096
Nerstrand Big Woods S.P.	73	D1	44.327040 -93.111210
Old Mill S.P.	19	F2	48.369790 -96.569420
Ray Berglund State Wayside	65	D3	47.608200 -90.771930
Rice Lake S.P.	73	D1	44.095380 -93.063940
Rush River State Wayside	66	C4	44.507240 -93.931409
Saint Croix S.P.	67	D2	45.960615 -92.611630
Sakatah Lake S.P.	72	C1	44.218000 -93.509970
Sam Brown Mem. State Wayside	27	F1	45.596160 -96.841410
Savanna Portage S.P.	64	B4	46.819130 -93.176040
Scenic S.P.	64	B3	47.702450 -93.564710
Schoolcraft S.P.	64	B3	47.223040 -93.805320
Sibley S.P.	66	B3	45.318990 -95.011930
Soudan Underground Mine S.P.	64	C2	47.818130 -92.246090
Split Rock Creek S.P.	27	F4	43.907240 -96.367970
Split Rock Lighthouse S.P.	65	D3	47.189800 -91.395010
Temperance River S.P.	65	D3	47.558780 -90.867930
Tettegouche S.P.	65	D3	47.337210 -91.200670
Upper Sioux Agency S.P.	66	B4	44.734540 -95.456460
Whitewater S.P.	73	E1	44.068880 -92.040100
Wild River S.P.	67	D3	45.524100 -92.754500
William O'Brien S.P.	67	D3	45.223900 -92.763500
Zippel Bay S.P.	64	A1	48.840630 -94.849950

MISSISSIPPI	PAGE	GRID	LATITUDE LONGITUDE
National Park & Rec. Areas			
Gulf Islands Natl. Seashore	135	D2	30.407200 -88.749220
Natchez N.H.P.-Vis. Reception Ctr.	125	F4	31.553900 -91.412400
State Park & Rec. Areas			
Bogue Homa State Fishing Lake	127	D4	31.703200 -89.026400
Calling Panther State Fishing Lake	126	B3	32.197100 -90.265100
Clarkco S.P.	127	D3	32.108500 -88.693970
Columbia State Fishing Lake	134	C1	31.183500 -89.738400
Florewood S.P.	118	B4	33.525120 -90.250362
George Payne Cossar S.P.	118	B3	34.122710 -89.882100
Golden Mem. S.P.	126	C2	32.568560 -89.407640
Great River Road S.P.	118	A4	33.851733 -91.027574
Hugh White S.P.	118	B4	33.796080 -89.743010
J.P. Coleman S.P.	119	D2	34.924254 -88.171706
Jeff Davis State Fishing Lake	126	B4	31.567700 -89.839800
Kemper County State Fishing Lake	127	D2	32.804167 -88.730556
Lake Lincoln S.P.	126	B4	31.684354 -90.337142
Legion S.P.	127	D1	33.148690 -89.042460
Leroy Percy S.P.	126	A1	33.160500 -90.938250
Mary Crawford State Fishing Lake	126	B4	31.574900 -90.154000
Monroe State Fishing Lake	119	D4	33.941500 -88.568700
Natchez S.P.	126	A4	31.589580 -91.220350
Neshoba County State Fishing Lake	126	C2	32.706200 -89.010500
Oktibbeha County State Fishing Lake	118	C4	33.505700 -88.933400
Paul B. Johnson S.P.	134	C1	31.133800 -89.233910
Percy Quin S.P.	134	B1	31.189020 -90.510660
Perry State Fishing Lake	135	D1	31.132400 -88.899800
Prentiss Walker State Fishing Lake	126	C3	31.833200 -89.589500
Roosevelt S.P.	126	C2	32.321920 -89.664980
Simpson County State Fishing Lake	126	C3	31.913500 -89.794500
Tippah County State Fishing Lake	118	C2	34.794290 -88.950660
Tishomingo S.P.	119	D2	34.615620 -88.183390
Tom Bailey State Fishing Lake	127	D2	32.425030 -88.523069
Tombigbee S.P.	119	D3	34.231870 -88.628870
Trace S.P.	118	C3	34.260020 -88.886560
Wall Doxey S.P.	118	C2	34.660270 -89.459290
Walthall State Fishing Lake	134	B1	31.059184 -90.133939

MISSOURI	PAGE	GRID	LATITUDE LONGITUDE
National Park & Rec. Areas			
George Washington Carver Natl. Mon.	106	C2	36.986160 -94.351890
Ozark Natl. Scenic Riverways	107	F2	37.281400 -91.408000
State Park & Rec. Areas			
Bennett Spring S.P.	107	D1	37.725440 -92.856390
Big Lake S.P.	86	A4	40.092090 -95.347300
Big Oak Tree S.P.	108	C3	36.641990 -89.290180
Big Sugar Creek S.P.	106	C3	36.584106 -93.819122
Crowder S.P.	86	C4	40.082140 -93.669310
Cuivre River S.P.	97	F2	39.062380 -90.938640
Elephant Rocks S.P.	108	A1	37.652150 -90.690810
Finger Lakes S.P.	97	E2	39.075400 -92.314750
Graham Cave S.P.	97	F3	38.908850 -91.576090
Grand Gulf S.P.	107	F3	36.544100 -91.636370
Ha Ha Tonka S.P.	97	D4	37.975410 -92.762230
Harry S. Truman S.P.	97	D4	38.274650 -93.442390
Hawn S.P.	108	B1	37.833660 -90.241610
Johnson's Shut-Ins S.P.	108	A1	37.547920 -90.853020
Katy Trail S.P.	97	E3	38.975190 -92.750160
Knob Noster S.P.	96	C3	38.753020 -93.577440
Lake of the Ozarks S.P.	97	E4	38.133990 -92.564260
Lake Wappapello S.P.	108	A2	36.942210 -90.344400
Lewis & Clark S.P.	96	B1	39.538900 -95.052900
Long Branch S.P.	97	E1	39.767610 -92.526480
Mark Twain S.P.	97	E2	39.485270 -91.795340
Meramec S.P.	97	F4	38.215350 -91.123070
Montauk S.P.	107	F1	37.454710 -91.690970
Morris S.P.	108	B3	36.554166 -90.043220
Onondaga Cave S.P.	97	F4	38.064310 -91.230140
Pershing S.P.	97	D1	39.776270 -93.211130
Pomme de Terre S.P.	107	D1	37.874380 -93.318700
Prairie S.P.	106	B1	37.518510 -94.571280
Roaring River S.P.	106	C3	36.590110 -93.834420
Robertsville S.P.	98	A3	38.429120 -90.818110
Rock Bridge Mem. S.P.	97	E3	38.883350 -92.331890
Saint Francois S.P.	98	A4	37.972900 -90.536210
Saint Joe S.P.	108	A1	37.824990 -90.537480
Sam A. Baker S.P.	108	A2	37.254530 -90.505080
Stockton S.P.	106	C1	37.622470 -93.753070
Table Rock S.P.	107	D3	36.583440 -93.309150
Taum Sauk Mtn. S.P.	108	A1	37.669500 -90.673400
Thousand Hills S.P.	87	D4	40.185160 -92.643070
Trail of Tears S.P.	108	B1	37.452880 -89.490760
Van Meter S.P.	97	D2	39.262590 -93.267210
Wakonda S.P.	97	F1	40.004250 -91.526060
Wallace S.P.	96	C1	39.660760 -94.213290
Washington S.P.	98	A4	38.085600 -90.685650
Watkins Mill S.P.	96	C2	39.383920 -94.265130
Weston Bend S.P.	96	B2	39.392960 -94.863430

MONTANA	PAGE	GRID	LATITUDE LONGITUDE
National Park & Rec. Areas			
Bighorn Canyon N.R.A.	24	C2	45.330090 -107.871650
Fort Benton Natl. Hist. Landmark	16	A2	47.823210 -110.661910
Glacier Natl. Park-Many Glacier Ent.	15	D1	48.827150 -113.551540
Glacier Natl. Park-St Mary Ent.	15	D1	48.747120 -113.439650
Glacier Natl. Park-Two Medicine Ent.	15	D1	48.494210 -113.262250
Glacier Natl. Park-West Ent.	15	D1	48.499890 -113.987190
Grant-Kohrs Ranch N.H.S.	15	E4	46.398900 -112.736680
Little Bighorn Bfld. Natl. Mon.	24	C1	45.570080 -107.434710
Natl. Bison Range	15	D3	47.371674 -114.262066
Rattlesnake N.R.A.	15	D4	47.040775 -113.933333
State Park & Rec. Areas			
Ackley Lake S.P.	16	B4	46.947220 -109.936110
Anaconda Smoke Stack S.P.	23	D1	46.111037 -112.969599
Bannack S.P.	23	D2	45.159170 -112.997780
Beaverhead Rock S.P.	23	E2	45.383330 -112.458330
Beavertail Hill S.P.	15	D4	46.721660 -113.576420
Big Arm S.P.	15	D3	47.815360 -114.307930
Black Sandy S.P.	15	E4	46.756940 -111.888890
Brush Lake S.P.	17	F1	48.603000 -104.113000
Chief Plenty Coups S.P.	24	B2	45.429700 -108.532500
Clark's Lookout S.P.	23	E2	45.236110 -112.630560
Cooney S.P.	24	B2	45.435050 -109.225330
Council Grove S.P.	15	D4	46.912500 -114.150000
Finley Point S.P.	15	D3	47.763830 -114.078723
First Peoples Buffalo Jump S.P.	16	A3	47.494887 -111.525201
Fort Owen S.P.	15	D4	46.519440 -114.095830
Frenchtown Pond S.P.	15	D3	47.039530 -114.259220
Granite Ghost Town S.P.	23	D1	46.319000 -113.257000
Greycliff Prairie Dog Town S.P.	24	B1	45.767600 -109.794180
Hell Creek S.P.	17	D3	47.620290 -106.884510
Lake Elmo S.P.	24	C1	45.845280 -108.481310
Lake Mary Ronan S.P.	15	D2	48.204020 -114.330340
Lewis & Clark Caverns S.P.	23	E1	45.821840 -111.848510
Logan S.P.	14	C2	48.204020 -114.330340
Lone Pine S.P.	15	D2	48.175580 -114.339560
Lost Creek S.P.	23	D1	46.203020 -112.993810
Madison Buffalo Jump S.P.	23	F1	45.665140 -111.062770
Makoshika S.P.	17	F4	47.090240 -104.709970
Medicine Rocks S.P.	25	F1	46.046460 -104.456740
Missouri Headwaters S.P.	23	F1	45.909129 -111.497411
Painted Rocks S.P.	22	C1	45.706650 -114.282530
Pictograph Cave S.P.	24	C1	45.737500 -108.430830
Pirogue Island S.P.	17	E4	46.440560 -105.816670
Placid Lake S.P.	15	D3	47.138040 -113.524960
Rosebud Bfld. S.P.	25	D2	45.208270 -106.944460
Salmon Lake S.P.	15	D4	47.042270 -113.390390
Sluice Boxes S.P.	16	A3	47.211400 -110.939660
Smith River S.P.	16	A4	46.721219 -111.173819
Spring Meadow Lake S.P.	15	E4	46.612220 -112.075000
Thompson Falls S.P.	14	C3	47.618060 -115.387500
Tongue River Reservoir S.P.	25	D2	45.093520 -106.804670
Tower Rock S.P.	15	E3	47.181000 -111.816000
Travelers' Rest S.P.	15	D4	46.751000 -114.089000
Wayfarers S.P.	15	D2	48.057400 -114.079550
West Shore S.P.	15	D2	47.948780 -114.189160
Whitefish Lake S.P.	15	D2	48.204020 -114.330340
Wild Horse Island S.P.	15	D3	47.844640 -114.279970
Yellow Bay S.P.	15	D2	47.874500 -114.027080

NEBRASKA	PAGE	GRID	LATITUDE LONGITUDE
National Park & Rec. Areas			
Agate Fossil Beds Natl. Mon.	33	F2	42.423860 -103.791120
Chimney Rock N.H.S.	33	F3	41.719650 -103.336070
Pine Ridge N.R.A.	33	F1	42.625880 -103.205570
Scotts Bluff Natl. Mon.	33	F2	41.832380 -103.717550
State Park & Rec. Areas			
Chadron S.P.	34	A1	42.711540 -103.008500
Eugene T. Mahoney S.P.	35	F3	41.026387 -96.314180
Fort Robinson S.P.	33	F1	42.654050 -103.492100
Indian Cave S.P.	86	A4	40.263280 -95.586630
Niobrara S.P.	35	E1	42.747450 -98.051850
Platte River S.P.	35	F3	40.986840 -96.219290
Ponca S.P.	35	F1	42.600360 -96.714940
Smith Falls S.P.	34	C1	42.891670 -100.316670

NEVADA	PAGE	GRID	LATITUDE LONGITUDE
National Park & Rec. Areas			
Devils Hole (Death Valley Natl. Park)	45	F3	36.423889 -116.305833
Great Basin Natl. Park-Vis. Ctr.	38	C2	39.005600 -114.220000
Lake Mead N.R.A.-North Ent.	46	B2	36.161180 -114.905200
Lake Mead N.R.A.-South Ent.	46	B2	36.021230 -114.796340
Lake Mead N.R.A.-West Ent.	46	B2	36.105980 -114.900940
Spring Mts. N.R.A.	46	A1	36.245200 -115.233910
State Park & Rec. Areas			
Beaver Dam S.P.	38	C4	37.529130 -114.107930
Berlin-Ichthyosaur S.P.	37	F2	38.880300 -117.607930
Big Bend of the Colorado State Rec. Area	53	F1	35.116730 -114.640820
Cathedral Gorge S.P.-North Ent.	38	C4	37.850890 -114.415120
Cathedral Gorge S.P.-South Ent.	38	C4	37.820280 -114.407890

Dayton S.P.-North Ent.	37	D2	39.253540 -119.587190
Dayton S.P.-South Ent.	37	D2	39.250650 -119.588020
Echo Canyon S.P.	38	C4	38.195000 -114.512900
Floyd Lamb S.P.	46	A2	36.321240 -115.269900
Kershaw-Ryan S.P.	38	C4	37.586380 -114.533260
Lake Tahoe-Nevada S.P.	37	D2	39.213670 -119.928300
Spring Mtn. Ranch S.P.	46	A2	36.073830 -115.443710
Spring Valley S.P.	38	C3	38.003920 -114.207570
Valley of Fire S.P.	46	B1	36.429710 -114.513590
Wild Horse State Rec. Area	30	B3	41.670739 -115.799805

NEW HAMPSHIRE	PAGE	GRID	LATITUDE LONGITUDE
National Park & Rec. Areas			
Saint-Gaudens N.H.S.	81	E4	43.501570 -72.362510
State Park & Rec. Areas			
Bear Brook S.P.	81	F4	43.133800 -71.366040
Cardigan S.P.	81	E3	43.647990 -71.949570
Crawford Notch S.P.	81	F2	44.181760 -71.398780
Echo Lake S.P.	81	F3	44.067430 -71.166000
Forest Lake S.P.	81	F2	44.354490 -71.673180
Hampton Beach S.P.	95	E1	42.898333 -70.812778
Kingston S.P.	95	E1	42.929020 -71.054680
Lake Tarleton S.P.	81	E3	43.975833 -71.963333
Miller S.P.	95	D1	42.861630 -71.878750
Monadnock S.P.	95	D1	42.845440 -72.086590
Mount Sunapee S.P.	81	E4	43.332120 -72.079800
Pawtuckaway S.P.	81	F4	43.082150 -71.152130
Pillsbury S.P.	81	E4	43.236860 -72.122830
Pisgah S.P.	94	C1	42.810310 -72.408340
Umbagog Lake S.P.	81	F1	44.712990 -71.072700
Wellington S.P.	81	F3	43.641280 -71.782980
Wentworth S.P.	81	F3	43.603056 -71.136389
White Lake S.P.	81	F3	43.830880 -71.218220
Winslow S.P.	81	E4	43.391730 -71.869540

NEW JERSEY	PAGE	GRID	LATITUDE LONGITUDE
National Park & Rec. Areas			
Delaware Water Gap N.R.A.	94	A4	40.970390 -75.128100
Gateway N.R.A.	147	F1	40.396420 -73.981160
Morristown N.H.P.	148	A4	40.744670 -74.565290
State Park & Rec. Areas			
Allaire S.P.	147	E2	40.153470 -74.111390
Allamuchy Mtn. S.P.	104	C1	40.921244 -74.782222
Barnegat Lighthouse S.P.	147	E4	39.762750 -74.107950
Cape May Point S.P.	104	C4	38.932950 -74.961010
Corson's Inlet S.P.	105	D4	39.216340 -74.647070
Delaware & Raritan Canal S.P.	147	D1	40.473230 -74.571100
Double Trouble S.P.	147	E3	39.900550 -74.225120
Farny S.P.	148	A3	40.997170 -74.459060
Forked River State Marina	147	E3	39.834886 -74.195019
Fortescue State Marina	145	F2	39.243178 -75.176636
Fort Mott S.P.	146	B4	39.612100 -75.543430
Hacklebarney S.P.	105	D1	40.751170 -74.736590
High Point S.P.	148	A2	41.304800 -74.669650
Hopatcong S.P.	148	A3	40.911780 -74.667000
Island Beach S.P.	147	E3	39.905240 -74.081510
Liberty S.P.	148	B4	40.697330 -74.063870
Long Pond Ironworks S.P.	148	A2	41.140986 -74.309228
Monmouth Bfld. S.P.	147	E2	40.269340 -74.302800
Parvin S.P.	146	C4	39.524490 -75.160460
Pigeon Swamp S.P.	147	E1	40.394420 -74.487150
Princeton Bfld. S.P.	147	D2	40.332490 -74.675650
Rancocas S.P.	147	D3	39.990420 -74.837480
Ringwood S.P.	148	A2	41.127600 -74.260130
Swartswood S.P.	94	A4	41.081680 -74.813620
Voorhees S.P.	104	C1	40.695060 -74.887030
Washington Crossing S.P.	147	D2	40.296920 -74.866420
Washington Rock S.P.	148	A4	40.613580 -74.472860
Wawayanda S.P.	148	A2	41.199240 -74.392440

NEW MEXICO	PAGE	GRID	LATITUDE LONGITUDE
National Park & Rec. Areas			
Aztec Ruins Natl. Mon.	48	B1	36.833920 -108.000570
Bandelier Natl. Mon.	48	C2	35.780130 -106.264830
Capulin Mtn. Natl. Mon.	49	E1	36.781990 -103.986110
Carlsbad Caverns Natl. Park-Vis. Ctr.	57	E3	32.175400 -104.444000
Chaco Culture N.H.P.	48	B2	36.016190 -107.924060
Datil Well N.R.A.	48	B4	34.154130 -107.852610
El Malpais Natl. Cons. Area	48	B4	35.059720 -107.876400
El Morro Natl. Mon.	48	B3	35.043480 -108.346250
Fort Union Natl. Mon.	49	D2	35.904230 -105.010740
Gila Cliff Dwellings Natl. Mon.	56	A2	33.229540 -108.264630
Kasha-Katuwe Tent Rocks Natl. Mon.	48	C2	35.663200 -106.410800
Pecos N.H.P.	49	D3	35.578750 -105.762400
Petroglyph Natl. Mon.	48	C3	35.139490 -106.709670
Salinas Pueblo Missions Natl. Mon.	48	C4	34.520370 -106.241250
Salinas Pueblo Missions Natl. Mon.-Gran Quivira	49	D4	34.260000 -106.091000
White Sands Natl. Mon.	56	C2	32.820130 -106.272980
State Park & Rec. Areas			
Bluewater Lake S.P.	48	B3	35.302730 -108.106930
Bottomless Lakes S.P.	57	E2	33.316630 -104.332880
Brantley Lake S.P.	57	E3	32.571390 -104.366210
Caballo Lake S.P.	56	B2	32.911370 -107.313580
Cimarron Canyon S.P.	49	D1	36.537600 -105.221130
City of Rocks S.P.	56	A2	32.594860 -107.973850
Clayton Lake S.P.	49	F1	36.573070 -103.300690
Conchas Lake S.P.	49	E3	35.394760 -104.181790
Coronado S.P.	48	C3	35.329130 -106.557870
Coyote Creek S.P.	49	D2	36.188020 -105.233260
Eagle Nest S.P.	49	D1	36.542100 -105.261300
Elephant Butte Res. S.P.-South Ent.	56	B1	33.176180 -107.207460
El Vado Lake S.P.	48	C1	36.593710 -106.735790
Fenton Lake S.P.	48	C2	35.887230 -106.723170
Heron Lake S.P.	48	C1	36.693840 -106.654230
Hyde Mem. S.P.	49	D2	35.737890 -105.836540
Leasburg Dam S.P.	56	B3	32.492680 -106.922380
Living Desert Zoo & Gardens S.P.	57	E3	32.449839 -104.286341
Manzano Mtn. S.P.	48	C4	34.603880 -106.360960
Morphy Lake S.P.	49	D2	35.968660 -105.366600
Navajo Lake S.P.	48	B1	36.831950 -107.586950
Oasis S.P.	49	F4	34.259740 -103.334280
Oliver Lee Mem. S.P.	56	C2	32.744640 -105.934520
Pancho Villa S.P.	56	B4	31.828050 -107.641200
Percha Dam S.P.	56	B2	32.873610 -107.308100
Red Rock S.P.	48	A3	35.537910 -108.605900
Rock Hound S.P.	56	B3	32.185550 -107.613090
Santa Rosa Lake S.P.	49	E3	34.987930 -104.658750
Smokey Bear Hist. S.P.	57	D1	33.545620 -105.573170
Spring Canyon Rec. Area-Rockhound S.P.	56	B3	32.125550 -107.589990
Storrie Lake S.P.	49	D2	35.655720 -105.231840
Sugarite Canyon S.P.	49	E1	36.944191 -104.381651
Sumner Lake S.P.	49	E4	34.607520 -104.389050
Ute Lake S.P.	49	F3	35.340630 -103.442500
Villanueva S.P.	49	D3	35.259530 -105.368970

NEW YORK	PAGE	GRID	LATITUDE LONGITUDE
National Park & Rec. Areas			
Eleanor Roosevelt N.H.S.	94	B3	41.763170 -73.902960
Fire Island Natl. Seashore	149	D4	40.735320 -72.866620
Fort Stanwix Natl. Mon.	79	E3	43.211930 -75.454740
Gateway N.R.A.	148	B4	40.581100 -73.887790
Home of F.D.R. N.H.S.	94	B3	41.767038 -73.938193
Sagamore Hill N.H.S.	148	C3	40.882480 -73.505550
Saratoga N.H.P.	81	D4	43.002690 -73.612110
Statue of Liberty Natl. Mon.	148	B4	40.689547 -74.044029
Thomas Cole N.H.S.	94	B2	42.225900 -73.861600
Van Buren N.H.S.	94	B2	42.370610 -73.701010
Vanderbilt Mansion N.H.S.	94	B3	41.796482 -73.942359
Women's Rights N.H.P.	79	D3	42.910580 -76.800260
State Park & Rec. Areas			
Adirondack Park	80	C2	43.455590 -73.695930
Allegany S.P.	92	B1	42.106480 -78.765940
Battle Island S.P.	79	D3	43.362780 -76.442150
Bear Mtn. S.P.	148	B2	41.278350 -73.970290
Beaver Island S.P.	78	A3	42.968170 -78.969560
Blauvelt S.P.	148	B3	41.069460 -73.949370
Bowman Lake S.P.	79	E4	42.516970 -75.670400
Buttermilk Falls S.P.	79	D4	42.347410 -76.489130
Caleb Smith S.P. Pres.	149	D3	40.854190 -73.221190
Canandaigua Lake State Marine Park	78	C3	42.875964 -77.275600
Captree S.P.	149	D4	40.636640 -73.263210
Catskill Park	94	A2	42.050290 -74.288840
Cedar Point S.P.	79	D1	44.200670 -76.191000
Chenango Valley S.P.	93	E1	42.215040 -75.818020
Chittenango Falls S.P.	79	E3	42.981520 -75.845030
Clarence Fahnestock S.P.	148	B1	41.423620 -73.799560
Cold Spring Harbor S.P.	148	C3	40.867450 -73.461900
Connetquot River S.P. Pres.	149	D4	40.748070 -73.153510
Cumberland Bay S.P.	81	D1	44.725090 -73.421450
Darien Lakes S.P.	78	B3	42.908460 -78.433300
Delta Lake S.P.	79	E3	43.290030 -75.414910
Evangola S.P.	78	A4	42.604460 -79.105610
Fair Haven Beach S.P.	79	D3	43.320570 -76.696210
Fort Niagara S.P.	78	A3	43.261790 -79.061460
Four Mile Creek S.P.	78	A3	43.272530 -78.996270
Golden Hill S.P.	78	B2	43.365250 -78.489310
Goosepond Mtn. S.P.	148	A2	41.354460 -74.254470
Gov. Alfred E. Smith/Sunken Meadow S.P.	149	D3	40.911970 -73.262940
Green Lakes S.P.	79	E3	43.060000 -75.969030
Hamlin Beach S.P.	78	C2	43.361130 -77.944460
Harriman S.P.	148	B2	41.293010 -74.026560
Heckscher S.P.	149	D4	40.712860 -73.168480
Highland Lakes S.P.	148	A1	41.489806 -74.325085
Hither Hills S.P.	149	F3	41.007700 -72.014500
Hudson Highlands S.P.	148	B2	41.428060 -73.966740
Hudson River Islands S.P.	94	B2	42.318574 -73.778343
Hunt's Pond S.P.	79	E4	42.594020 -75.378140
James Baird S.P.	148	B1	41.689100 -73.799390
Jones Beach S.P.	148	C4	40.595000 -73.521070
Keewaydin S.P.	79	E1	44.322390 -75.925740
Keuka Lake S.P.	78	C4	42.594280 -77.130360
Lake Erie S.P.	78	A4	42.419070 -79.434430
Lakeside Beach S.P.	78	B2	43.367090 -78.236040
Lake Superior S.P.	94	A3	41.658590 -74.869280
Letchworth S.P.	78	B4	42.693530 -77.961210
Lodi Point S.P.	79	D4	42.619210 -76.863980
Long Point S.P.	79	D1	44.026130 -76.219650
Mark Twain S.P.	93	D1	42.205200 -76.823799
Mary Island S.P.	79	E1	44.350460 -75.930400
Max V. Shaul S.P.	79	F4	42.546790 -74.410370
Mexico Point S.P.	79	D2	43.523050 -76.258733
Minnewaska S.P. Pres.	148	A1	41.745910 -74.268370
Montauk Point S.P.	149	F3	41.065020 -71.886700
Moreau Lake S.P.	80	C4	43.226370 -73.707710
Oquaga Creek S.P.	93	F1	42.172320 -75.442840
Orient Beach S.P.	149	F2	41.154580 -72.245600
Pinnacle S.P.	93	D1	42.098100 -77.220180
Pixley Falls S.P.	79	E2	43.401100 -75.345960
Point Au Roche S.P.	81	D1	44.779990 -73.411090
Robert Moses S.P.	148	C4	40.624930 -73.261900
Saratoga Spa S.P.	80	C4	43.056950 -73.801490
Selkirk Shores S.P.	79	D2	43.544300 -76.191510
Seneca Lake S.P.	79	D3	42.873410 -76.960940
Southwick Beach S.P.	79	D2	43.767270 -76.196230
Sterling Forest S.P.	148	A2	41.220200 -74.187210
Storm King S.P.	148	B2	41.432560 -73.987020
Taconic S.P.	94	B2	42.007680 -73.508400
Tallman Mtn. S.P.	148	B3	41.037270 -73.915920
Verona Beach S.P.	79	E3	43.179070 -75.725090
Waterson Point S.P.	79	E1	44.339030 -76.010580
Wellesley Island S.P.	79	E1	44.315970 -76.019480
Whetstone Gulf S.P.	79	E2	43.702310 -75.459120
Wildwood S.P.	149	D3	40.954230 -72.788470
Wilson-Tuscarora S.P.	78	B3	43.307080 -78.854500

NORTH CAROLINA	PAGE	GRID	LATITUDE LONGITUDE
National Park & Rec. Areas			
Cape Hatteras Natl. Seashore	115	F3	35.766700 -75.526640
Cape Lookout Natl. Seashore	115	E4	34.886110 -76.331220
Carl Sandburg Home N.H.S.	121	E1	35.270000 -82.450000
Fort Raleigh N.H.S.	115	F2	35.932360 -75.708500
Great Smoky Mts. Natl. Park-Cades Cove Vis. Ctr.	121	D1	35.585300 -83.842900
Great Smoky Mts. Natl. Park-Oconaluftee Vis. Ctr.	121	D1	35.515300 -83.305300
Great Smoky Mts. Natl. Park-Sugarlands Vis. Ctr.	121	D1	35.685600 -83.536700
State Park & Rec. Areas			
Carolina Beach S.P.	123	E3	34.045240 -77.903430
Cliffs of the Neuse S.P.	123	E1	35.232900 -77.898390
Crowders Mtn. S.P.	122	A1	35.212350 -81.292920
Dismal Swamp S.P.	113	F3	36.517470 -76.360720
Fort Macon S.P.	115	E4	34.697750 -76.699580
Goose Creek S.P.	123	F1	35.483140 -76.902290
Gorges S.P.	121	E1	35.108400 -82.943900
Hammocks Beach S.P.	123	F2	34.671810 -77.138720
Hanging Rock S.P.	112	B3	36.413030 -80.253950
Haw River S.P.	112	B3	36.249719 -79.755971
Jockey's Ridge S.P.	115	F2	35.961820 -75.626970
Jones Lake S.P.	123	D2	34.698900 -78.624990
Lake James S.P.	111	F4	35.728064 -81.901980
Lake Norman S.P.	112	A4	35.665780 -80.938410
Lake Waccamaw S.P.	123	D3	34.272650 -78.466040
Lumber River S.P.	123	D3	34.390831 -79.004145
Medoc Mtn. S.P.	113	D3	36.280410 -77.877820
Merchants Millpond S.P.	113	F3	36.450601 -76.692978
Morrow Mtn. S.P.	122	B1	35.370390 -80.102410
Mount Mitchell S.P.	111	E4	35.814600 -82.146100
Pettigrew S.P.	113	F4	35.789580 -76.406980
Pilot Mtn. S.P.	112	A3	36.345530 -80.478390
Raven Rock S.P.	123	D1	35.461520 -78.912660
Singletary Lake S.P.	123	D2	34.581570 -78.452070
South Mts. S.P.	121	F1	35.601190 -81.625700
Stone Mtn. S.P.	112	A3	36.374390 -81.018010

NORTH DAKOTA	PAGE	GRID	LATITUDE LONGITUDE
National Park & Rec. Areas			
Fort Union N.H.S.	17	F2	48.002390 -104.043560
Knife River N.H.S.	18	B3	47.336680 -101.387450
Theodore Roosevelt Natl. Park-Elkhorn Site	17	F3	47.226950 -103.622310
Theodore Roosevelt Natl. Park-North Unit	18	A3	47.600300 -103.261000
Theodore Roosevelt Natl. Park-South Unit	18	A4	46.915500 -103.527000
State Park & Rec. Areas			
Beaver Lake S.P.	18	C4	46.401260 -99.615860
Cross Ranch S.P.	18	B3	47.213530 -101.000180
Doyle Mem. S.P.	27	D1	46.204880 -99.482150
Fort Abercrombie S.P.	19	F4	46.444530 -96.718800
Fort Lincoln S.P.	18	B4	46.769420 -100.847860
Fort Ransom S.P.	19	E4	46.544100 -97.925570
Fort Stevenson S.P.	18	B3	47.596890 -101.420530
Grahams Island S.P.	19	D2	48.052500 -99.068300
Icelandic S.P.	19	E1	48.772620 -97.736990
Lake Metigoshe S.P.	18	C1	48.980640 -100.326710
Lake Sakakawea S.P.	18	B3	47.511020 -101.449350
Lewis & Clark S.P.	18	A2	48.115350 -103.241490
Little Missouri Bay S.P.	18	A3	47.550030 -102.738240

embina S.P.	19	E1	48.964720 -97.240500
urtle River S.P.	19	E2	47.931660 -97.505390
hitestone Bfld. S.P.	27	D1	46.169190 -98.857330

OHIO

ational Park & Rec. Areas

OHIO	PAGE	GRID	LATITUDE LONGITUDE
uyahoga Valley Natl. Park-Canal Vis. Ctr.	91	E2	41.372600 -81.613700
uyahoga Valley Natl. Park-Hunt Farm Vis. Info. Ctr.	91	E2	41.200900 -81.573100
opewell Culture N.H.P.	101	D2	39.298360 -82.917810
ames A. Garfield N.H.S.	91	E2	41.663600 -81.351260

tate Park & Rec. Areas

OHIO	PAGE	GRID	LATITUDE LONGITUDE
.W. Marion S.P.	101	D1	39.633730 -82.885720
dams Lake S.P.	100	C3	38.812900 -83.519400
um Creek S.P.	90	C4	40.226870 -82.981320
arkcamp S.P.	101	F1	40.047030 -81.031710
eaver Creek S.P.	91	F3	40.726220 -80.613590
ue Rock S.P.	101	E1	39.832780 -81.858370
uck Creek S.P.	100	C1	39.946410 -83.729550
uckeye Lake S.P.	101	D1	39.906540 -82.526270
urr Oak S.P.	101	E1	39.527740 -82.023260
aesar Creek S.P.	100	C1	39.515730 -84.041070
atawba Island S.P.	91	D2	41.573530 -82.855780
owan Lake S.P.	100	C2	39.387600 -83.882970
rane Creek S.P.	90	C2	41.603770 -83.192910
eer Creek S.P.	101	D1	39.649260 -83.246340
elaware S.P.	90	C4	40.377690 -83.071590
illon S.P.	101	E1	40.023600 -82.111910
ast Fork S.P.	100	C2	39.002050 -84.151210
ast Harbor S.P.	91	D2	41.540930 -82.820830
indley S.P.	91	D3	41.122990 -82.219390
orked Run S.P.	101	E2	39.085000 -81.770460
eneva S.P.	91	F1	41.852760 -80.963280
rand Lake Saint Marys S.P.	90	B4	40.549240 -84.436500
reat Seal S.P.	101	D2	39.401930 -82.946050
uilford Lake S.P.	91	F3	40.796100 -80.893760
arrison Lake S.P.	90	B2	41.637190 -84.361760
eadlands Beach S.P.	91	E1	41.752140 -81.294480
ocking Hills S.P.	101	D2	39.494180 -82.611910
ueston Woods S.P.	100	B1	39.573820 -84.715380
ndependence Dam S.P.	90	B2	41.282470 -84.313500
ndian Lake S.P.	90	B4	40.510360 -83.842980
ackson Lake S.P.	101	D3	38.902850 -82.596780
efferson Lake S.P.	91	F4	40.472050 -80.808930
ohn Bryan S.P.	100	C1	39.791020 -83.867790
elleys Island S.P.	91	D2	41.614080 -82.712110
iser Lake S.P.	90	B4	40.197650 -83.981740
ake Alma S.P.	101	D2	39.153450 -82.516810
ake Hope S.P.	101	E2	39.318500 -82.354920
ake Logan S.P.	101	D1	39.536400 -82.460590
ake Loramie S.P.	90	B4	40.359750 -84.359730
ake White S.P.	101	D2	39.109160 -83.040330
adison Lake S.P.	100	C1	39.866250 -83.374930
alabar Farm S.P.	91	D3	40.649590 -82.398390
ary Jane Thurston S.P.	90	B2	41.409630 -83.881320
aumee Bay S.P.	90	C2	41.678020 -83.353360
ohican S.P.	91	D4	40.609510 -82.257600
osquito Lake S.P.	91	F2	41.301940 -80.767990
ount Gilead S.P.	91	D4	40.547820 -82.816770
uskingum River S.P.	101	E1	40.044140 -81.978260
elson-Kennedy Ledges S.P.	91	F2	41.330090 -81.040190
aint Creek S.P.	100	C2	39.228360 -83.374450
ike Lake S.P.	101	D2	39.158270 -83.220950
ortage Lakes S.P.	91	E3	40.966260 -81.565190
underson S.P.	91	E2	41.461540 -81.219590
ymatuning S.P.	91	F2	41.580110 -80.541530
uail Hollow S.P.	91	E3	40.970200 -81.325100
ocky Fork S.P.	100	C2	39.188310 -83.529730
alt Fork S.P.	91	E4	40.081830 -81.460400
cioto Trail S.P.	101	D2	39.223620 -82.931210
hawnee S.P.	101	D3	38.747670 -83.211220
outh Bass Island S.P.	91	D2	41.644690 -82.835950
tonelick S.P.	100	C2	39.226160 -84.057210
trouds Run S.P.	101	E2	39.334320 -82.017690
ycamore S.P.	100	B1	39.803410 -84.373470
ar Hollow S.P.	101	D2	39.353790 -82.780200
inker's Creek S.P.	91	E2	41.276180 -81.368910
an Buren S.P.	90	C3	41.138290 -83.644940
Vest Branch S.P.	91	E3	41.133310 -81.189660
Volf Run S.P.	101	F1	39.789770 -81.540180

OKLAHOMA

National Park & Rec. Areas

OKLAHOMA	PAGE	GRID	LATITUDE LONGITUDE
hickasaw N.R.A.	51	F4	34.497390 -96.970110
Vinding Stair Mtn. N.R.A.	116	B2	34.749705 -94.793055

State Park & Rec. Areas

OKLAHOMA	PAGE	GRID	LATITUDE LONGITUDE
dair S.P.	106	B4	35.832230 -94.624100
labaster Caverns S.P.	51	D1	36.697490 -99.149430
rrowhead S.P.	116	A1	35.168240 -95.639970
eaver Dunes S.P.	50	B1	36.841129 -100.514988
ernice S.P.	106	B3	36.626670 -94.901670
lack Mesa S.P.	49	F1	36.855620 -102.885680
Boggy Depot S.P.	51	F4	34.321747 -96.311302
Boiling Springs S.P.	51	D1	36.452950 -99.298900
Brushy Lake S.P.	116	B1	35.543680 -94.817676
Cherokee Landing S.P.	106	B4	35.758890 -94.908610
Cherokee S.P.	106	B3	36.480280 -95.050560
Clayton Lake S.P.	116	A2	34.549420 -95.308330
Dripping Springs S.P.	51	F3	35.611437 -96.068911
Fort Cobb S.P.	51	D3	35.203720 -98.464990
Foss S.P.	51	D3	35.578510 -99.186830
Gloss Mtn. S.P.	51	D2	36.367190 -98.576460
Great Plains S.P.	51	D4	34.730340 -98.985690
Great Salt Plains S.P.	51	E1	36.753170 -98.149930
Greenleaf S.P.	106	A4	35.623260 -95.180950
Hochatown S.P.	116	B3	34.197390 -94.766300
Honey Creek S.P.	106	B3	36.574060 -94.784370
Hugo Lake S.P.	116	A3	34.016384 -95.375061
Keystone S.P.	51	F2	36.137440 -96.264340
Lake Eucha S.P.	106	B3	36.353930 -94.824000
Lake Eufaula S.P.	116	A1	35.427900 -95.546100
Lake Murray S.P.	51	F4	34.154880 -97.120950
Lake Texoma S.P.	59	F1	33.997590 -96.651310
Lake Thunderbird S.P.	51	E3	35.232320 -97.247550
Lake Wister S.P.	116	B2	34.948700 -94.710400
Little Blue-Disney S.P.	106	B3	36.480260 -95.009130
Little Sahara S.P.	51	D1	36.532900 -98.890870
McGee Creek S.P.	116	A3	34.302927 -95.875467
Natural Falls S.P.	106	B4	36.151900 -94.673300
Okmulgee S.P.	51	F2	35.621900 -96.067700
Osage Hills S.P.	51	F1	36.757360 -96.176220
Raymond Gary S.P.	116	A3	33.997580 -95.253860
Red Rock Canyon S.P.	51	D3	35.456350 -98.358310
Sequoyah Bay S.P.	106	A4	35.886000 -95.276000
Sequoyah S.P.	106	A4	35.932960 -95.230650
Snowdale S.P.	106	A3	36.307710 -95.199040
Spavinaw S.P.	106	B3	36.385890 -95.053290
Talimena S.P.	116	B2	34.788290 -94.950690
Tenkiller S.P.	116	B1	35.598000 -95.031100
Twin Bridges S.P.	106	B2	36.804320 -94.757920
Wah-Sha-She S.P.	51	F1	36.926000 -96.091000
Walnut Creek S.P.	51	F2	36.251210 -96.280130

OREGON

National Park & Rec. Areas

OREGON	PAGE	GRID	LATITUDE LONGITUDE
Cascade-Siskiyou Natl. Mon.	28	C2	42.068300 -122.399940
Crater Lake Natl. Park-Annie Spring Ent. Sta.	28	C1	42.868700 -122.169000
Crater Lake Natl. Park-North Ent. Sta.	28	C1	43.086900 -122.116000
Hells Canyon N.R.A.-East Ent.	22	B1	45.500680 -116.806560
Hells Canyon N.R.A.-South Ent.	22	B1	44.903300 -116.957080
Hells Canyon N.R.A.-West Ent.	22	B1	45.176360 -117.040740
John Day Fossil Beds Natl. Mon.-Clarno Unit	21	D2	44.911250 -120.431780
John Day Fossil Beds Natl. Mon.-Painted Hills Unit	21	D3	44.661170 -120.254750
John Day Fossil Beds Natl. Mon.-Sheep Rock Unit	21	E3	44.555480 -119.645010
Lewis & Clark N.H.P.-Fort Clatsop	20	B1	46.138260 -123.876670
Lewis & Clark N.H.P.-Salt Works	20	B1	46.134551 -123.880420
Lewis & Clark N.H.P.-Sunset Beach	20	B1	46.099430 -123.936390
Newberry Natl. Volcanic Mon.	21	D4	43.716800 -121.376960
Oregon Caves Natl. Mon.	28	B2	42.103910 -123.414300
Oregon Dunes N.R.A.-North Ent.	20	A4	43.885610 -124.120860
Oregon Dunes N.R.A.-South Ent.	20	A4	43.579470 -124.186490

State Park & Rec. Areas

OREGON	PAGE	GRID	LATITUDE LONGITUDE
Ainsworth S.P.	20	C2	45.595720 -122.052980
Alfred A. Loeb S.P.	28	A2	42.113180 -124.188520
Beverly Beach S.P.	20	B3	44.726250 -124.057290
Bullards Beach S.P.	28	A1	43.150990 -124.395480
Cape Arago S.P.	20	A4	43.326140 -124.381770
Cape Blanco S.P.	28	A1	42.826660 -124.524640
Cape Lookout S.P.	20	B2	45.367667 -123.961127
Carl G. Washburne Mem. S.P.	20	A3	44.141990 -124.117490
Cascadia S.P.	20	C3	44.397100 -122.477480
Catherine Creek S.P.	22	A2	45.148890 -117.733990
Collier Mem. S.P.	28	C1	42.641810 -121.880630
Ecola S.P.	20	B1	45.916550 -123.967430
Elijah Bristow S.P.	20	C4	43.935470 -122.844270
Fort Columbia S.P.	20	B1	46.252580 -123.921500
Fort Stevens S.P.	20	B1	46.183200 -123.959940
Harris Beach S.P.	28	A2	42.067930 -124.305860
Hat Rock S.P.	21	E1	45.908260 -119.164510
Hilgard Junction S.P.	21	F2	45.342060 -118.236470
Humbug Mtn. S.P.	28	A1	42.686870 -124.445970
Illinois River Forks S.P.	28	B2	42.154870 -123.649870
Jessie M. Honeyman Mem. S.P.	20	A4	43.933440 -124.106440
Lake Owyhee S.P.	22	A4	43.638380 -117.229090
Lapine S.P.	21	D4	43.768452 -121.513399
Maryhill S.P.	21	D1	45.683060 -120.825830
Mayer S.P.	21	D1	45.682780 -121.301080
Milo Mciver S.P.	20	C2	45.306110 -122.372220
Molalla River S.P.	20	C2	45.294840 -122.696400
Nehalem Bay S.P.	20	B1	45.710000 -123.931470
Ona Beach S.P.	20	B3	44.518060 -124.075960
Oswald West S.P.	20	B1	45.770000 -123.958610
Port Orford Heads S.P.	28	A1	42.739470 -124.509730
Prineville Reservoir S.P.	21	D3	44.144660 -120.737770
Robert Straub S.P.	20	B2	45.183160 -123.965116
Rooster Rock S.P.	20	C2	45.546320 -122.236500
Shore Acres S.P.	20	A4	43.329940 -124.376510
Silver Falls S.P.	20	C2	44.853752 -122.662258
Smith Rock S.P.	21	D3	44.360540 -121.138400
South Beach S.P.	20	B3	44.598450 -124.059350
Starvation Creek S.P.	20	C1	45.688550 -121.690180
Stub Stewart S.P.	20	B1	45.739050 -123.199461
Sunset Bay S.P.	20	A4	43.339010 -124.353990
The Cove Palisades S.P.	21	D3	44.557460 -121.262110
Tumalo S.P.	21	D3	44.086760 -121.308730
Umpqua Lighthouse S.P.	20	A4	43.669610 -124.182830
Valley of the Rogue S.P.	28	B1	42.410770 -123.129310
Viento S.P.	20	C1	45.697240 -121.668310
Wallowa Lake S.P.	22	A2	45.280690 -117.208230
White River Falls S.P.	21	D2	45.166870 -121.087420
Willamette Mission S.P.	20	B2	45.080740 -123.031510
William M. Tugman S.P.	20	A4	43.623640 -124.181910

PENNSYLVANIA

National Park & Rec. Areas

PENNSYLVANIA	PAGE	GRID	LATITUDE LONGITUDE
Allegheny N.R.A.	92	B1	41.943055 -78.867025
Allegheny Portage Railroad N.H.S.	92	B4	40.377020 -78.835870
Eisenhower N.H.S.	103	E1	39.818000 -77.232610
Flight 93 Natl. Mem.	92	B4	40.055200 -78.900900
Fort Necessity Natl. Bfld.	102	B1	39.816340 -79.584310
Friendship Hill N.H.S.	102	B1	39.777778 -79.929167
Gettysburg N.M.P.	103	E1	39.811600 -77.226100
Hopewell Furnace N.H.S.	146	B2	40.206760 -75.773570
Johnstown Flood Natl. Mem.	92	B4	40.350710 -78.772480
Valley Forge N.H.P.	146	C2	40.102240 -75.422960

State Park & Rec. Areas

PENNSYLVANIA	PAGE	GRID	LATITUDE LONGITUDE
Bald Eagle S.P.	92	C3	41.041960 -77.642780
Big Spring S.P.	92	C4	40.266850 -77.654410
Black Moshannon S.P.	92	C3	40.915190 -78.058570
Blue Knob S.P.	92	B4	40.265800 -78.584480
Buchanan's Birthplace S.P.	103	D1	39.872660 -77.953190
Caledonia S.P.	103	D1	39.905610 -77.478880
Canoe Creek S.P.	92	C4	40.475070 -78.277290
Chapman S.P.	92	B1	41.757850 -79.170350
Cherry Springs S.P.	92	C2	41.662778 -77.823056
Codorus S.P.	103	E1	39.783180 -76.908920
Colonel Denning S.P.	93	D4	40.281820 -77.416630
Colton Point S.P.	93	D2	41.711180 -77.465430
Cook Forest S.P.	92	B2	41.333790 -79.210440
Cowans Gap S.P.	103	D1	39.997980 -77.921530
Delaware Canal S.P.	146	C1	40.545565 -75.087831
Elk S.P.	92	B2	41.606100 -78.564780
Erie Bluffs S.P.	91	F1	42.008333 -80.410833
Evansburg S.P.	146	C2	40.197510 -75.407080
Frances Slocum S.P.	93	E2	41.347380 -75.893760
French Creek S.P.	146	B2	40.236580 -75.795660
Gouldsboro S.P.	93	F2	41.232250 -75.495730
Greenwood Furnace S.P.	92	C3	40.649610 -77.756090
Hickory Run S.P.	93	F3	41.035170 -75.736220
Hills Creek S.P.	93	D1	41.805190 -77.187600
Hyner Run S.P.	92	C2	41.359150 -77.623850
Kettle Creek S.P.	92	C2	41.377120 -77.930130
Keystone S.P.	92	A4	40.374250 -79.377830
Lackawanna S.P.	93	F2	41.575030 -75.711520
Laurel Hill S.P.	102	B1	39.984470 -79.234840
Laurel Mtn. S.P.	92	B4	40.179670 -79.131530
Laurel Ridge S.P.	92	B4	39.958400 -79.360160
Lehigh Gorge S.P.	93	F3	40.971900 -75.761840
Leonard Harrison S.P.	93	D2	41.698420 -77.450810
Little Buffalo S.P.	93	D4	40.454420 -77.169170
Little Pine S.P.	93	D2	41.371240 -77.360310
Lyman Run S.P.	92	C1	41.723650 -77.768470
Marsh Creek S.P.	146	B3	40.069360 -75.717320
Maurice K. Goddard S.P.	92	A2	41.428380 -80.145140
McConnells Mill S.P.	92	A3	40.963530 -80.168810
Memorial Lake S.P.	93	E4	40.424760 -76.590540
Mont Alto S.P.	103	D1	39.839130 -77.540630
Moraine S.P.	92	A3	40.940280 -80.098520
Nescopeck S.P.	93	E3	41.067100 -75.925300
Nockamixon S.P.	146	C1	40.463630 -75.242010
Ohiopyle S.P.	102	B1	39.865030 -79.504310
Oil Creek S.P.-East Ent.	92	A2	41.512130 -79.661810
Ole Bull S.P.	92	C2	41.543590 -77.709430
Parker Dam S.P.	92	C2	41.205140 -78.504310
Penn-Roosevelt S.P.	92	C3	40.726389 -77.702500
Pine Grove Furnace S.P.	103	D1	40.032910 -77.305070
Poe Paddy S.P.	93	D3	40.834150 -77.417380
Presque Isle S.P.	92	A1	42.114200 -80.153590
Prince Gallitzin S.P.	92	B3	40.669760 -78.575650
Promised Land S.P.	93	F2	41.313560 -75.210370
Pymatuning S.P.	91	F2	41.650440 -80.387840
Raccoon Creek S.P.	91	F4	40.503160 -80.424460
Ralph Stover S.P.	146	C1	40.440420 -75.106050

Raymond B. Winter S.P.	93	D3	40.992340 -77.200450
Ricketts Glen S.P.	93	E2	41.336190 -76.300420
Ryerson Station S.P.	102	A1	39.892310 -80.450030
S.B. Elliott S.P.	92	C3	41.112740 -78.526100
Salt Springs S.P.	93	E1	41.911090 -75.868720
Samuel S. Lewis S.P.	103	E1	39.996580 -76.550410
Shawnee S.P.	102	C1	40.038060 -78.645850
Shikellamy S.P.	93	D3	40.879390 -76.802950
Sinnemahoning S.P.	92	C2	41.450650 -78.055090
Susquehannock S.P.	146	A3	39.805770 -76.283410
Swatara S.P.	93	E4	40.481480 -76.551350
Tobyhanna S.P.	93	F2	41.214130 -75.384030
Trough Creek S.P.	92	C4	40.311620 -78.131820
Tyler S.P.	146	C2	40.233330 -74.951170
Upper Pine Bottom S.P.	93	D2	41.325071 -77.394699
Warriors Path S.P.	92	C4	40.193330 -78.249880
Whipple Dam S.P.	92	C3	40.682250 -77.868410
Worlds End S.P.	93	E2	41.471880 -76.587060
Yellow Creek S.P.	92	B4	40.575830 -79.004420

RHODE ISLAND	PAGE	GRID	LATITUDE LONGITUDE
State Park & Rec. Areas			
Beavertail S.P.	150	C4	41.457030 -71.396950
Block Island State Beach	95	D4	41.180850 -71.566460
Brenton Point S.P.	150	C4	41.450430 -71.355870
Burlingame S.P.	150	C4	41.361610 -71.701370
Casimir Pulaski Mem. S.P.	150	C3	41.950000 -71.766670
Colt S.P.	151	D3	41.684590 -71.288860
Diamond Hill S.P.	150	C2	42.009620 -71.431630
East Matunuck State Beach	150	C4	41.378350 -71.525630
Fishermen's Mem. S.P.	150	C4	41.380630 -71.488000
Fort Adams S.P.	150	C4	41.469150 -71.339990
Goddard Mem. S.P.	150	C3	41.651030 -71.442040
Haines Mem. S.P.	150	C3	41.752960 -71.348600
Misquamicut State Beach	95	D4	41.324510 -71.800670
R.W. Wheeler State Beach	150	C4	41.372620 -71.495530
Scarborough State Beach	150	C4	41.389770 -71.474260

SOUTH CAROLINA	PAGE	GRID	LATITUDE LONGITUDE
National Park & Rec. Areas			
Charles Pinckney N.H.S.	131	D2	32.847150 -79.824090
Congaree Natl. Park	122	A4	33.836100 -80.827660
Kings Mtn. N.M.P.	122	A1	35.140120 -81.386890
Ninety Six N.H.S.	121	F3	34.162740 -82.010980
State Park & Rec. Areas			
Andrew Jackson S.P.	122	B2	34.839560 -80.810110
Barnwell S.P.	130	B1	33.329250 -81.300400
Calhoun Falls S.P.	121	E3	34.106792 -82.604200
Cheraw S.P.	122	C2	34.642370 -79.927640
Colleton S.P.	130	C1	33.063520 -80.613440
Devils Fork S.P.	121	E2	34.952527 -82.946085
Edisto Beach S.P.	130	C2	32.505410 -80.310310
Givhans Ferry S.P.	130	C1	33.031640 -80.382150
Hickory Knob State Resort Park	121	E4	33.884250 -82.416010
Huntington Beach S.P.	123	D4	33.502650 -79.081200
Jones Gap S.P.	121	E1	35.126360 -82.558350
Kings Mtn. S.P.	122	A1	35.113030 -81.394040
Lake Warren S.P.	130	B2	32.844830 -81.165070
Little Pee Dee S.P.	122	C3	34.331020 -79.282170
Myrtle Beach S.P.	123	D4	33.649210 -78.938600
N.R. Goodale S.P.	122	B3	34.281580 -80.525150
Oconee S.P.	121	E2	34.867297 -83.106098
Paris Mtn. S.P.	121	E2	34.924970 -82.365540
Poinsett S.P.	122	B4	33.804360 -80.544920
Santee S.P.	122	B4	33.500200 -80.489820
Table Rock S.P.	121	E2	35.022050 -82.710700

SOUTH DAKOTA	PAGE	GRID	LATITUDE LONGITUDE
National Park & Rec. Areas			
Badlands Natl. Park-Interior Ent.	26	B4	43.741900 -101.957000
Badlands Natl. Park-Northeast Ent.	26	B4	43.792400 -101.906000
Badlands Natl. Park-Pinnacles Ent.	26	B4	43.885500 -102.238000
Jewel Cave Natl. Mon.	25	F4	43.736500 -103.819940
Minuteman Missile N.H.S.	26	B4	43.833931 -101.899685
Mount Rushmore Natl. Mem.	26	A4	43.886730 -103.440610
Wind Cave Natl. Park-Vis. Ctr.	26	A4	43.556100 -103.478000
State Park & Rec. Areas			
Bear Butte S.P.	26	A3	44.460580 -103.433750
Custer S.P.	26	A4	43.770310 -103.440130
Fisher Grove S.P.	27	E2	44.883340 -98.356640
Hartford Beach S.P.	27	F2	45.398870 -96.665260
Lake Herman S.P.	27	F4	43.993120 -97.159790
Newton Hills S.P.	35	F1	43.218860 -96.569700
Oakwood Lakes S.P.	27	F3	44.454310 -96.989490
Palisades S.P.	27	F4	43.687970 -96.511470
Roy Lake S.P.	27	E1	45.703360 -97.419650
Sica Hollow S.P.	27	E1	45.740690 -97.229150
Union Grove S.P.	35	F1	42.922630 -96.785530

TENNESSEE	PAGE	GRID	LATITUDE LONGITUDE
National Park & Rec. Areas			
Andrew Johnson N.H.S.	111	D4	36.157710 -82.836880
Big South Fork Natl. River & Rec. Area	110	B3	36.475400 -84.752100
State Park & Rec. Areas			
Big Hill Pond S.P.	119	D1	35.078890 -88.718860
Big Ridge S.P.	110	C3	36.241600 -83.929280
Bledsoe Creek S.P.	109	F3	36.378050 -86.356660
Cedars of Lebanon S.P. & Forest	109	F4	36.093930 -86.335620
Chickasaw S.P.	119	D1	35.393241 -88.772298
Cove Lake S.P.	110	C3	36.305830 -84.210750
Cumberland Mtn. S.P.	110	B4	35.898460 -84.995130
David Crockett S.P.	119	E1	35.242690 -87.354850
Davy Crockett Birthplace S.P.	111	E3	36.221980 -82.662770
Edgar Evins S.P.	110	A4	36.086050 -85.812460
Fall Creek Falls S.P.	120	B1	35.622200 -85.208000
Frozen Head S.P. & Nat. Area-North Ent.	110	B4	36.122550 -84.433320
Frozen Head S.P. & Nat. Area-South Ent.	110	B4	36.102180 -84.446970
Harpeth River S.P.	109	E4	36.079240 -86.956920
Harrison Bay S.P.	120	B1	35.175850 -85.115350
Henry Horton S.P.	119	F1	35.596510 -86.698690
Hiwassee–Ocoee Scenic Rivers S.P.	120	C1	35.224557 -84.504269
Indian Mtn. S.P.	110	C3	36.583050 -84.139900
Long Hunter S.P.	109	F4	36.094340 -86.557330
Meeman-Shelby Forest S.P.	118	B1	35.336800 -90.029010
Montgomery Bell S.P.	109	E4	36.106750 -87.268690
Mousetail Landing S.P.	109	D4	35.581900 -87.859100
Natchez Trace S.P.	109	D4	35.839580 -88.252820
Nathan Bedford Forrest S.P.	109	D4	36.087900 -87.979750
Norris Dam S.P.	110	C3	36.234560 -84.127020
Old Stone Fort State Arch. Park	120	A1	35.487270 -86.101330
Panther Creek S.P.	111	D3	36.212760 -83.412420
Paris Landing State Resort Park	109	D3	36.441760 -88.090180
Pickett S.P.	110	B3	36.537374 -84.802126
Pickwick Landing S.P.	119	D2	35.051790 -88.242650
Pinson Mounds State Arch. Park	119	D1	35.504130 -88.683020
Reelfoot Lake S.P.	108	B3	36.414410 -89.426880
Roan Mtn. S.P.	111	E4	36.161110 -82.097000
Rock Island S.P.	110	A4	35.810000 -85.641550
Standing Stone S.P.	110	A3	36.458910 -85.437690
T.O. Fuller S.P.	118	B2	35.057810 -90.113650
Tims Ford S.P.	120	A1	35.220999 -86.255889
Warriors Path S.P.	111	E5	36.504610 -82.481090

TEXAS	PAGE	GRID	LATITUDE LONGITUDE
National Park & Rec. Areas			
Alibates Flint Quarries Natl. Mon.	50	A3	35.571900 -101.633880
Amistad N.R.A.	60	B2	29.449920 -101.053170
Big Bend Natl. Park-North Ent.	62	C4	29.680900 -103.167000
Big Bend Natl. Park-West Ent.	62	C4	29.306600 -103.523000
Fort Davis N.H.S.	62	B2	30.604120 -103.886010
Guadalupe Mts. Natl. Park-Vis. Ctr.	57	D3	31.894300 -104.822000
Lyndon B. Johnson N.H.P.	61	D2	30.276020 -98.411990
Padre Island Natl. Seashore	63	F3	27.553470 -97.248370
Palo Alto Btfd. N.H.P.	63	F4	26.011630 -97.481570
State Park & Rec. Areas			
Abilene S.P.	58	C3	32.241360 -99.879230
Atlanta S.P.	124	C1	33.229500 -94.249300
Balmorhea S.P.	62	B2	30.946270 -103.784890
Bastrop S.P.	61	E2	30.098960 -97.229090
Bentsen-Rio Grande Valley S.P.	63	E4	26.182530 -98.382360
Big Bend Ranch S.P.	62	B4	29.265070 -103.791910
Big Spring S.P.	58	A3	32.229650 -101.483090
Blanco S.P.	61	D2	30.093240 -98.423420
Bonham S.P.	59	F1	33.543100 -96.149640
Brazos Bend S.P.	132	A4	29.371480 -95.631890
Buescher S.P.	61	E2	30.073570 -97.176140
Caddo Lake S.P.	124	C2	32.684230 -94.177070
Caprock Canyons S.P. & Trailway	50	B4	34.406440 -101.048830
Choke Canyon S.P.-Calliham Unit	61	D4	28.460970 -98.356380
Choke Canyon S.P.-South Shore Unit	61	D4	28.467610 -98.239550
Cleburne S.P.	59	E3	32.265180 -97.560680
Colorado Bend S.P.	61	D1	31.062510 -98.504250
Cooper Lake S.P.	124	A1	33.305282 -95.648346
Copper Breaks S.P.	50	C4	34.113660 -99.747800
Daingerfield S.P.	124	B1	33.028720 -94.714510
Davis Mts. S.P.	62	B2	30.599520 -103.929220
Dinosaur Valley S.P.	59	E3	32.250020 -97.814620
Eisenhower S.P.	59	F1	33.822670 -96.616120
Fairfield Lake S.P.	59	F3	31.765910 -96.076220
Falcon S.P.	63	D3	26.583500 -99.144790
Fort Boggy S.P.	124	A4	31.189627 -95.986069
Fort Griffin S.H.S.	58	C2	32.924690 -99.219370
Fort Parker S.P.	59	F4	31.592650 -96.524370
Fort Richardson S.P. & Hist. Site	59	D2	33.206060 -98.164810
Franklin Mts. S.P.	56	C3	31.912060 -106.517140
Galveston Island S.P.	132	B4	29.196240 -94.956210
Garner S.P.	60	C2	29.600900 -99.744220
Goliad S.P.	61	E4	28.655190 -97.383580
Goose Island S.P.	61	F4	28.134060 -96.984350
Guadalupe River S.P.	61	D2	29.849890 -98.509590
Huntsville S.P.	132	A2	30.638130 -95.511370
Inks Lake S.P.	61	D1	30.738290 -98.366450
Kerrville-Schreiner S.P.	60	C2	30.007930 -99.117640
Lake Arrowhead S.P.	59	D1	33.759300 -98.396610
Lake Bob Sandlin S.P.	124	B1	33.054090 -95.101250
Lake Brownwood S.P.	59	D3	31.857370 -99.021280
Lake Casa Blanca International S.P.	63	D2	27.536739 -99.432449
Lake Colorado City S.P.	58	B3	32.313460 -100.92480
Lake Corpus Christi S.P.	61	E4	28.060360 -97.867690
Lake Livingston S.P.	132	B1	30.671300 -95.008200
Lake Mineral Wells S.P.	59	E2	32.814570 -98.042270
Lake Somerville S.P. & Trailway	61	F1	30.315760 -96.625080
Lake Tawakoni S.P.	59	F2	32.841610 -95.990710
Lake Texana S.P.	61	F3	28.953610 -96.567190
Lake Whitney S.P.	59	E3	31.924780 -97.356280
Lockhart S.P.	61	E2	29.857610 -97.697400
Longhorn Cavern S.P.	61	D1	30.686610 -98.351380
Lyndon B. Johnson S.P. & Hist. Site-Ranch Unit	61	D2	30.235180 -98.629100
Martin Creek Lake S.P.	124	B3	32.283090 -94.583470
Martin Dies Junior S.P.	132	C1	30.848980 -94.164720
Meridian S.P.	59	E3	31.892440 -97.695670
Mission Tejas S.P.	124	A4	31.546110 -95.234720
Monahans Sandhills S.P.	57	F4	31.634940 -102.81485
Mother Neff S.P.	59	E4	31.319150 -97.474210
Mustang Island S.P.	63	F2	27.677020 -97.173730
Palmetto S.P.	61	E2	29.597280 -97.584640
Palo Duro Canyon S.P.	50	B3	34.985710 -101.70319
Pedernales Falls S.P.	61	D1	30.273110 -98.256830
Possum Kingdom S.P.	59	D2	32.878970 -98.561740
Purtis Creek S.P.	124	A2	32.373340 -95.974530
Ray Roberts Lake S.P.	59	F1	33.444050 -96.925860
Rusk–Palestine S.P.-East	124	B3	31.803560 -95.194880
Rusk–Palestine S.P.-West	124	A4	31.739260 -95.570450
Sabine Pass Battleground S.H.S.	132	C3	29.726520 -93.878280
San Angelo S.P.	58	B4	31.491919 -100.54714
Sea Rim S.P.	132	C3	29.677900 -94.039900
Seminole Canyon S.P. & Hist. Site	60	A2	29.709000 -101.29848
South Llano River S.P.	60	C1	30.445430 -99.804610
Stephen F. Austin S.P.	61	F2	29.812030 -96.108200
Tyler S.P.	124	A2	32.481750 -95.281760

UTAH	PAGE	GRID	LATITUDE LONGITUDE
National Park & Rec. Areas			
Arches Natl. Park	40	A2	38.615570 -109.61692
Bryce Canyon Natl. Park	39	E4	37.641700 -112.16800
Canyonlands Natl. Park-East Ent.	40	A3	38.168510 -109.75098
Canyonlands Natl. Park-Horseshoe Canyon Unit	39	F3	38.497740 -110.20596
Canyonlands Natl. Park-North Ent.	40	A3	38.490150 -109.80793
Canyonlands Natl. Park-West Ent.	40	A3	38.255440 -110.18005
Capitol Reef Natl. Park	39	E3	38.291020 -111.26141
Cedar Breaks Natl. Mon.-East Ent.	39	D4	37.655230 -112.81135
Cedar Breaks Natl. Mon.-North Ent.	39	D4	37.665730 -112.83813
Cedar Breaks Natl. Mon.-South Ent.	39	D4	37.598730 -112.85008
Glen Canyon N.R.A.	39	F4	38.255440 -110.18005
Golden Spike N.H.S.	31	E3	41.620482 -112.54747
Grand Staircase-Escalante Natl. Mon.	39	E4	37.420000 -111.55000
Natural Bridges Natl. Mon.	39	F4	37.608120 -109.96628
Rainbow Bridge Natl. Mon.	47	E1	37.110810 -110.40605
Zion Natl. Park-East Ent.	39	D4	37.235370 -112.86447
Zion Natl. Park-Main Ent.	39	D4	37.201970 -112.98838
State Park & Rec. Areas			
Anasazi S.P. Mus.	39	E3	37.922399 -111.42574
Antelope Island S.P.	31	E4	41.089290 -112.11649
Bear Lake (Rendezvous Beach) S.P.	31	F2	41.962200 -111.40032
Bear Lake S.P.	31	F2	41.965360 -111.39948
Camp Floyd– Stagecoach Inn S.P.	31	E4	40.258360 -112.09727
Coral Pink Sand Dunes S.P.-North Ent.	47	D1	37.065540 -112.70553
Coral Pink Sand Dunes S.P.-West Ent.	47	D1	37.034580 -112.74126
Dead Horse Point S.P.	40	A3	38.510220 -109.72946
Deer Creek S.P.	31	F4	40.452620 -111.47782
Edge of the Cedars S.P.	40	A4	37.629760 -109.49173
Escalante Petrified Forest S.P.	39	E4	37.783820 -111.63022
Fremont Indian S.P.	39	D3	38.579537 -112.31477
Goblin Valley S.P.	39	F3	38.580620 -110.71258
Goosenecks S.P.	40	A4	37.174730 -109.92695
Green River S.P.	39	F2	38.995500 -110.15691
Gunlock S.P.-North Ent.	38	C4	37.275970 -113.76878
Gunlock S.P.-South Ent.	38	C4	37.251490 -113.77282
Huntington S.P.	39	F2	39.315200 -110.97710
Hyrum S.P.	31	E3	41.626220 -111.87217
Iron Mission S.P.	39	D4	37.688349 -113.06189
Kodachrome Basin S.P.	39	E4	37.501670 -111.99361
Millsite S.P.	39	E2	39.099020 -111.18424
Otter Creek S.P.	39	E3	38.167430 -112.02157
Palisade S.P.	39	E2	39.195800 -111.69160
Piute S.P.	39	E3	38.322530 -112.20420
Quail Creek S.P.	39	D4	37.105000 -113.57660
Red Fleet S.P.	32	B4	40.553300 -109.51847
Rockport S.P.	31	F4	40.751890 -111.36741
Sand Hollow S.P.	46	C1	37.144830 -113.38213
Scofield S.P.	39	E1	39.708600 -110.92100
Snow Canyon S.P.-East Ent.	38	C4	37.212120 -113.63087
Snow Canyon S.P.-North Ent.	38	C4	37.256790 -113.63299
Snow Canyon S.P.-South Ent.	38	C4	37.183380 -113.64501
Starvation S.P.	32	A4	40.104100 -110.33090

Steinaker S.P.-North Ent.	32	A4	40.534870 -109.522440
Steinaker S.P.-South Ent.	32	A4	40.504850 -109.528870
Territorial Statehouse S.P.	39	D2	38.985880 -112.353530
Wasatch Mtn. S.P.	31	F4	40.477770 -111.519990
Willard Bay S.P.-North Ent.	31	E3	41.418810 -112.052390
Willard Bay S.P.-South Ent.	31	E3	41.350610 -112.069060
Yuba S.P.	39	E2	39.381240 -112.028360

VERMONT	PAGE	GRID	LATITUDE LONGITUDE
National Park & Rec. Areas			
Marsh-Billings-Rockefeller N.H.P.	81	E3	43.635833 -72.538333
State Park & Rec. Areas			
Allis S.P.	81	E3	44.051150 -72.626440
Branbury S.P.	81	D3	43.904250 -73.065370
Burton Island S.P.	81	D1	44.779660 -73.180050
Camp Plymouth S.P.	81	E4	43.475810 -72.694987
D.A.R. S.P.	81	D3	44.058850 -73.409210
Emerald Lake S.P.	81	D4	43.283790 -73.002250
Gifford Woods S.P.	81	D3	43.676500 -72.810860
Half Moon S.P.	81	D3	43.699720 -73.223220
Kingsland Bay S.P.	81	D2	44.226230 -73.277660
Lake Saint Catherine S.P.	81	D4	43.483000 -73.202580
Little River S.P.	81	D2	44.388940 -72.768360
Molly Stark S.P.	94	C1	42.854920 -72.813790
North Hero S.P.	81	D1	44.908210 -73.235110
Ricker Pond S.P.	81	E2	44.251467 -72.247550
Stillwater S.P.	81	E2	44.280200 -72.275060
Townshend S.P.	81	E4	43.041920 -72.691600
Underhill S.P.	81	D2	44.528880 -72.843920
Woodford S.P.	94	C1	42.894450 -73.037790
Woods Island S.P.	81	D1	44.802500 -73.209283

VIRGINIA	PAGE	GRID	LATITUDE LONGITUDE
National Park & Rec. Areas			
Appomattox Court House N.H.P.	112	C1	37.377367 -78.795290
Booker T. Washington Natl. Mon.	112	B2	37.120500 -79.733340
Cedar Creek & Belle Grove N.H.P.	102	C2	39.023500 -78.289000
Colonial N.H.P.	114	A4	37.211390 -76.776730
Cumberland Gap N.H.P.-Vis. Ctr.	111	D3	36.602600 -83.695400
Fredericksburg & Spotsylvania Co. Bflds. Mem. N.M.P.	103	D4	38.254300 -77.451890
George Washington Birthplace Natl. Mon.	114	A2	38.192353 -76.927192
Manassas Natl. Bfld. Park	144	A3	38.806030 -77.572810
Mount Rogers N.R.A.	111	F2	36.811360 -81.420130
Shenandoah Natl. Park-Front Royal North Ent.	102	C3	38.903300 -78.192400
Shenandoah Natl. Park-Rockfish Gap South Ent.	102	C3	38.033900 -78.858900
Shenandoah Natl. Park-Swift Run Gap Ent.	102	C3	38.359100 -78.546700
Shenandoah Natl. Park-Thornton Gap Ent.	102	C3	38.662300 -78.320600
State Park & Rec. Areas			
Bear Creek Lake S.P.	113	D1	37.532970 -78.274890
Belle Isle S.P.	114	B2	37.774526 -76.599222
Chippokes Plantation S.P.	114	A4	37.140400 -76.748590
Claytor Lake S.P.	112	A2	37.057620 -80.622140
Douthat S.P.	102	B4	37.914520 -79.796740
Fairy Stone S.P.	112	B2	36.791790 -80.117890
False Cape S.P.	115	F1	36.691370 -75.924410
First Landing S.P.	114	B4	36.915601 -76.057000
Grayson Highlands S.P.	111	F3	36.611920 -81.489900
Holliday Lake S.P.	113	D1	37.404610 -78.644920
Hungry Mother S.P.	111	F2	36.880860 -81.525750
James River S.P.	112	C1	37.540400 -78.839300
Kiptopeke S.P.	114	B4	37.169292 -75.982919
Lake Anna S.P.	103	D4	38.125850 -77.821690
Leesylvania S.P.	103	E3	38.591200 -77.248400
Mason Neck S.P.	103	E3	38.640740 -77.194400
Natural Tunnel S.P.	111	E3	36.707520 -82.744090
New River Trail S.P.	112	A2	36.870180 -80.868550
Occoneechee S.P.	113	D3	36.633330 -78.525420
Pocahontas S.P.	113	E1	37.366240 -77.573870
Sailor's Creek Bfld. Hist. S.P.	113	D1	37.298470 -78.229470
Sky Meadows S.P.	103	D2	38.988703 -77.968913
Smith Mtn. Lake S.P.	112	B2	37.091110 -79.592110
Twin Lakes S.P.	113	D2	37.336900 -77.934100
Westmoreland S.P.	103	E4	38.158690 -76.870120
Wilderness Road S.P.	111	D3	36.621300 -83.512900
York River S.P.	113	F1	37.414190 -76.713650

WASHINGTON	PAGE	GRID	LATITUDE LONGITUDE
National Park & Rec. Areas			
Columbia River Gorge Natl. Scenic Area	21	D1	45.715322 -121.818667
Fort Vancouver N.H.S.	20	C1	45.626940 -122.656310
Hanford Reach Natl. Mon.	13	E4	46.483333 -119.533333
Lake Chelan N.R.A.	13	D2	48.309080 -120.657730
Lake Roosevelt N.R.A.	13	F2	47.972680 -118.970580
Lewis & Clark N.H.P.-Discovery Trail	12	B4	46.370033 -124.053503
Lewis & Clark N.H.P.-Dismal Nitch	20	B1	46.249033 -123.862903
Lewis & Clark N.H.P.-Sta. Camp	20	B1	46.263111 -123.932571
Mount Baker N.R.A.	12	C1	48.714167 -121.805900
Mount Rainier Natl. Park-Carbon River Ent.	12	C6	46.994810 -121.918090
Mount Rainier Natl. Park-Nisqually Ent.	12	C5	46.741400 -121.919040
Mount Rainier Natl. Park-Stevens Can. Ent.	12	C7	46.754730 -121.557010
Mount Rainier Natl. Park-White River Ent.	12	C8	46.902040 -121.554340
Mount Saint Helens Natl. Mon.	12	C4	46.277590 -122.218820
North Cascades Natl. Park-Golden West	13	D1	48.308200 -120.655000
North Cascades Natl. Park-Northern Cascades Vis. Ctr.	13	D1	48.666100 -121.264000
Olympic Natl. Park-Vis. Ctr.	12	B2	48.096700 -123.428000
Olympic Natl. Park-Vis. Ctr.-Hoh Rain Forest	12	B2	47.860700 -123.935000
Olympic Natl. Park-Vis. Ctr.-Hurricane Ridge	12	B2	47.969200 -123.498000
Ross Lake N.R.A.	13	D1	48.674250 -121.244730
San Juan Island N.H.P.	12	B2	48.534580 -123.016250
Whitman Mission N.H.S.	21	F1	46.040910 -118.468110
State Park & Rec. Areas			
Alta Lake S.P.	13	E2	48.031990 -119.934710
Anderson Lake S.P.	12	C2	48.014590 -122.810680
Belfair S.P.	12	C3	47.430630 -122.881400
Birch Bay S.P.	12	C1	48.903210 -122.757880
Bogachiel S.P.	12	A2	47.894790 -124.362820
Brooks Mem. S.P.	21	D1	45.950590 -120.664200
Camano Island S.P.	12	C2	48.131680 -122.503240
Cape Disappointment S.P.	20	B1	46.294210 -124.053610
Columbia Hills S.P.	21	D1	45.643030 -121.106410
Crawford S.P.	14	A1	48.992070 -117.370370
Curlew Lake S.P.	13	F1	48.719280 -118.661740
Damon Point S.P.	12	B4	46.945300 -124.132100
Deception Pass S.P.	12	C2	48.390970 -122.646880
Dosewallips S.P.	12	C3	47.687570 -122.899860
Fields Spring S.P.	22	A1	46.087520 -117.173650
Flaming Geyser S.P.	12	C3	47.280230 -122.041870
Fort Casey S.P.	12	C2	48.159760 -122.672410
Fort Okanogan S.P.	13	E2	48.102370 -119.678720
Fort Simcoe S.P.	13	D4	46.345340 -120.823460
Fort Townsend S.P.	12	C2	48.078260 -122.805690
Ginkgo Petrified Forest S.P.	13	E4	46.949010 -119.997490
Goldendale Observatory S.P.	21	D1	45.837090 -120.815890
Griffiths-Priday S.P.	12	B3	47.125100 -124.179900
Ike Kinswa S.P.	12	C4	46.555780 -122.536570
Jarrell Cove S.P.	12	B3	47.285940 -122.881080
Joseph Whidbey S.P.	12	C2	48.308370 -122.713170
Kitsap Mem. S.P.	12	C3	47.816580 -122.646840
Lake Chelan S.P.	13	D2	47.869430 -120.191110
Lake Easton S.P.	13	D3	47.249380 -121.190920
Lake Wenatchee S.P.	13	D3	47.816340 -120.729780
Larrabee S.P.	12	C2	48.650620 -122.489810
Lewis & Clark S.P.	12	C4	46.525850 -122.817910
Lewis & Clark Trail S.P.	13	F4	46.287600 -118.073340
Lincoln Rock S.P.	13	D3	47.535490 -120.282280
Millersylvania S.P.	12	B4	46.909610 -122.905950
Moran S.P.	12	C1	48.657700 -122.859630
Mount Spokane S.P.	14	B2	47.899290 -117.124350
Nolte S.P.	12	C3	47.267320 -121.943420
Ocean City S.P.	12	B4	47.038520 -124.158130
Osoyoos S.P.	13	E1	48.950060 -119.434350
Pacific Beach S.P.	12	A3	47.205980 -124.202220
Pacific Pines S.P.	12	B4	46.507610 -124.049150
Palouse Falls S.P.	13	F4	46.664030 -118.228660
Peace Arch S.P.	12	C1	49.000980 -122.751580
Pearrygin Lake S.P.	13	E2	48.496720 -120.146950
Peshastin Pinnacles S.P.	13	D3	47.578810 -120.613860
Potholes S.P.	13	E4	46.970780 -119.351180
Potlatch S.P.	12	B3	47.363000 -123.158140
Rainbow Falls S.P.	12	B4	46.631010 -123.237350
Rockport S.P.	12	C2	48.487920 -121.601870
Sacajawea S.P.	21	F1	46.210140 -119.046050
Scenic Beach S.P.	12	C3	47.649250 -122.845470
Seaquest S.P.	12	C4	46.295880 -122.820860
Sequim Bay S.P.	12	B2	48.040750 -123.030920
Shine Tidelands S.P.	12	C2	47.867990 -122.638700
Steamboat Rock S.P.	13	E2	47.828650 -119.134340
Sun Lakes S.P.	13	E3	47.596540 -119.387760
Triton Cove S.P.	12	B3	47.609112 -122.986526
Twenty-Five Mile Creek S.P.	13	D2	47.992520 -120.263610
Twin Harbors S.P.	12	B4	46.858850 -124.104210
Wallace Falls S.P.	12	C2	47.865610 -121.680050
Wanapum S.P.	13	E4	46.924760 -119.991690
Westport Light S.P.	12	B4	46.891700 -124.111630

WEST VIRGINIA	PAGE	GRID	LATITUDE LONGITUDE
National Park & Rec. Areas			
Bluestone Natl. Scenic River	112	A1	37.584300 -80.957900
Gauley River N.R.A.	101	F4	38.191800 -81.001920
Harpers Ferry N.H.P.	103	D2	39.318820 -77.759060
New River Gorge Natl. River	101	F4	37.875670 -81.077598
Spruce Knob Seneca Rocks N.R.A.	102	B3	38.681180 -79.544480
State Park & Rec. Areas			
Audra S.P.	102	A2	39.041110 -80.067500
Beartown S.P.	102	A4	38.051750 -80.275420
Blennerhassett Island Hist. S.P.	101	E2	39.273300 -81.644800
Bluestone S.P.	112	A1	37.623050 -80.934710
Cacapon Resort S.P.	102	C1	39.502980 -78.291330
Camp Creek S.P.	111	F1	37.508173 -81.132873
Carnifex Ferry Bfld. S.P.	101	F4	38.211290 -80.941850
Cass Scenic Railroad S.P.	102	A3	38.396520 -79.914280
Cedar Creek S.P.	101	F3	38.880780 -80.849420
Droop Mtn. Bfld. S.P.	102	A4	38.113200 -80.271670
Holly River S.P.	102	A3	38.653140 -80.382620
Little Beaver S.P.	112	A1	37.756570 -81.079780
Moncove Lake S.P.	112	B1	37.616950 -80.354730
Pinnacle Rock S.P.	111	F1	37.308190 -81.291430
Prickett's Fort S.P.	102	A1	39.514090 -80.099960
Tomlinson Run S.P.	91	F4	40.550660 -80.595950
Tygart Lake S.P.	102	A2	39.248160 -80.021060
Valley Falls S.P.	102	A2	39.392900 -80.070480
Watoga S.P.	102	A4	38.122510 -80.155660
Watters Smith Mem. S.P.	102	A2	39.174520 -80.414260

WISCONSIN	PAGE	GRID	LATITUDE LONGITUDE
National Park & Rec. Areas			
Apostle Islands Natl. Lakeshore	65	D4	46.812210 -90.820780
Saint Croix Natl. Scenic Riverway	67	E2	45.415700 -92.646270
State Park & Rec. Areas			
Amnicon Falls S.P.	64	C4	46.608210 -91.887850
Aztalan S.P.	74	B3	43.068310 -88.863750
Belmont Mound S.P.	74	A4	42.768010 -90.349444
Big Bay S.P.	65	D4	46.811030 -90.696960
Big Foot Beach S.P.	74	C4	42.567330 -88.436790
Blue Mound S.P.	74	A3	43.026990 -89.840740
Brunet Island S.P.	67	F3	45.176220 -91.161610
Buckhorn S.P.	74	A1	43.948280 -90.002130
Copper Culture S.P.	68	C4	44.887440 -87.897940
Copper Falls S.P.	65	D4	46.351710 -90.643670
Council Grounds S.P.	68	A3	45.184840 -89.734290
Devil's Lake S.P.	74	A2	43.429010 -89.734900
Governor Dodge S.P.	74	A3	43.019560 -90.141950
Governor Thompson S.P.	68	C3	45.326309 -88.219205
Harrington Beach S.P.	75	D2	43.499430 -87.811890
Hartman Creek S.P.	74	B1	44.318070 -89.194320
High Cliff S.P.	74	C1	44.166680 -88.291760
Interstate S.P.	67	D3	45.396410 -92.636580
Kinnickinnic S.P.	67	D4	44.837280 -92.733190
Kohler-Andrae S.P.	75	D2	43.672740 -87.719320
Lake Kegonsa S.P.	74	B3	42.978005 -89.230300
Lake Wissota S.P.	67	F4	44.980950 -91.313740
Merrick S.P.	73	E1	44.152740 -91.744120
Mill Bluff S.P.	74	A1	43.961610 -90.317980
Mirror Lake S.P.	74	A2	43.568770 -89.834930
Natural Bridge S.P.	74	A2	43.344930 -89.928290
Nelson Dewey S.P.	73	F4	42.743740 -91.037860
New Glarus Woods S.P.	74	B4	42.786830 -89.631980
Newport S.P.	69	D3	45.241470 -86.998830
Pattison S.P.	64	C4	46.535290 -92.121410
Peninsula S.P.	69	D3	45.133080 -87.213280
Perrot S.P.	73	F1	44.016350 -91.479670
Potawatomi S.P.	69	D4	44.849990 -87.407640
Rib Mtn. S.P.	68	B4	44.915800 -89.669360
Roche-A-Cri S.P.	74	A1	43.996120 -89.812370
Rock Island S.P.	69	E3	45.398990 -86.855970
Rocky Arbor S.P.	74	A2	43.647890 -89.808240
Straight Lake S.P.	67	E2	45.597399 -92.406609
Tower Hill S.P.	74	A3	43.147090 -90.043750
Whitefish Dunes S.P.	69	D4	44.928910 -87.182150
Wildcat Mtn. S.P.	74	A2	43.688870 -90.566800
Willow River S.P.	67	D3	45.017610 -92.672610
Wyalusing S.P.	73	F3	42.978770 -91.118560
Yellowstone Lake S.P.	74	A4	42.777360 -89.993540

WYOMING	PAGE	GRID	LATITUDE LONGITUDE
National Park & Rec. Areas			
Devils Tower Natl. Mon.	25	E3	44.586870 -104.706710
Flaming Gorge N.R.A.	32	A3	41.254860 -109.611400
Fort Laramie N.H.S.	33	E2	42.202520 -104.558590
Fossil Butte Natl. Mon.	31	F2	41.855370 -110.782340
Grand Teton Natl. Park-Granite Canyon Ent.	23	F4	43.597990 -110.801640
Grand Teton Natl. Park-Moose Ent.	23	F4	43.655860 -110.718350
Grand Teton Natl. Park-Moran Ent.	23	F4	43.843640 -110.511950
John D. Rockefeller Jr. Mem. Parkway	24	A3	44.108800 -110.685508
Medicine Wheel Natl. Hist. Landmark	24	C2	44.826200 -107.921717
Yellowstone Natl. Park-East Ent.	23	F3	44.489540 -110.001560
Yellowstone Natl. Park-North East Ent.	23	F3	45.006120 -109.991550
Yellowstone Natl. Park-North Ent.	23	F3	45.030110 -110.705460
Yellowstone Natl. Park-South Ent.	23	F3	44.134730 -110.666170
Yellowstone Natl. Park-West Ent.	23	F3	44.658720 -111.098970
State Park & Rec. Areas			
Bear River S.P.	31	F3	41.267257 -110.938030
Boysen S.P.	32	C1	43.270160 -108.115260
Buffalo Bill S.P.	24	B3	44.505020 -109.249540
Curt Gowdy S.P.	33	E3	41.175380 -105.243640
Edness K. Wilkins S.P.	33	D1	42.857220 -106.177370
Glendo S.P.	33	E1	42.476060 -104.998910
Guernsey S.P.	33	E2	42.287400 -104.763460
Hot Springs S.P.	24	C4	43.653980 -108.201790
Keyhole S.P.	25	E3	44.356490 -104.825810
Seminoe S.P.	33	D2	42.150350 -106.905870
Sinks Canyon S.P.	32	B1	42.752600 -108.804770

CANADA

ALBERTA

ALBERTA	PAGE	GRID	LATITUDE LONGITUDE
National Park & Rec. Areas			
Banff Natl. Park-Banff Vis. Ctr.	164	B2	51.177400 -115.570900
Banff Natl. Park-Lake Louise Vis. Ctr.	164	B2	51.425200 -116.178400
Banff Park Mus. N.H.S.	164	B3	51.174300 -115.571100
Bar U Ranch N.H.S.	164	C3	50.420300 -114.244400
Cave and Basin N.H.S.	164	B3	51.168300 -115.591400
Elk Island Natl. Park	159	D4	53.572500 -112.841900
Jasper Natl. Park-Icefield Center	164	A1	52.233500 -117.234800
Jasper Natl. Park-Jasper Information Center	164	A1	52.877300 -118.080900
Rocky Mtn. House N.H.S.	164	C2	52.377590 -114.931237
Waterton Lakes Natl. Park-Waterton Vis. Ctr.	164	C4	49.051400 -113.906300
Wood Buffalo Natl. Park-Fort Chipewyan Vis. Ctr.	155	F2	48.714100 -111.154300
Provincial Park & Rec. Areas			
Aspen Beach Prov. Park	164	C2	52.454530 -113.975750
Beauvais Lake Prov. Park	164	C4	49.409500 -114.117000
Big Hill Springs Prov. Park	164	C3	51.251670 -114.386940
Big Knife Prov. Park	165	D2	52.489720 -112.210560
Birch Mts. Wildland Prov. Park	159	D1	57.509400 -112.957000
Bluerock Wildland Prov. Park	164	C3	50.642300 -114.654000
Bob Creek Wildland Prov. Park	164	C4	49.973700 -114.286000
Bow Valley Prov. Park	164	C3	51.040400 -115.077000
Bow Valley Wildland Prov. Park	164	B3	51.032600 -115.259000
Bragg Creek Prov. Park	164	C3	50.939170 -114.583330
Brown-Lowery Prov. Park	164	C3	50.813900 -114.430600
Calling Lake Prov. Park	159	D3	55.179720 -113.272500
Caribou Mts. Wildland Prov. Park	155	F3	59.205600 -114.897000
Carson-Pegasus Prov. Park	158	C3	54.295800 -115.645000
Chain Lakes Prov. Park	164	C3	50.200000 -114.183330
Chinchaga Wildland Prov. Park	158	B1	57.163400 -119.582000
Cold Lake Prov. Park	159	E3	54.602400 -110.072000
Cold Lake Prov. Park-North Shore	159	E3	54.644800 -110.103600
Crimson Lake Prov. Park	164	C2	52.466900 -115.048000
Cross Lake Prov. Park	159	D3	54.649300 -113.791000
Crow Lake Prov. Park	159	D2	55.800456 -112.152014
Dillberry Lake Prov. Park	165	E1	52.570200 -110.030000
Dinosaur Prov. Park	165	D3	50.770100 -111.480000
Don Getty Wildland Prov. Park	164	B2	50.893000 -114.993000
Dry Island Buffalo Jump Prov. Park	164	C2	51.929500 -112.975000
Dunvegan Prov. Park	158	B2	55.923600 -118.594400
Dunvegan West Wildland Prov. Park	158	B2	56.088900 -119.297000
Elbow Sheep Wildland Prov. Park	164	C3	50.703500 -114.939000
Fort Assiniboine Sandhills Wildland Prov. Park	158	C3	54.387100 -114.608000
Garner Lake Prov. Park	159	D3	54.183420 -111.741000
Gipsy Lake Wildland Prov. Park	159	E2	56.493500 -110.386000
Gooseberry Lake Prov. Park	165	D2	52.116940 -110.759170
Grand Rapids Wildland Prov. Park	159	D1	56.484200 -112.343000
Greene Valley Prov. Park	158	B2	56.140900 -117.242000
Gregoire Lake Prov. Park	159	E1	56.485000 -111.182780
Grizzly Ridge Wildland Prov. Park	158	C3	55.137700 -115.049000
Hay-Zama Lakes Wildland Prov. Park	155	F3	58.774100 -119.016000
Hilliard's Bay Prov. Park	158	C2	55.502900 -116.001000
Hubert Lake Wildland Prov. Park	158	C3	54.554100 -114.244000
Kakwa Wildland Prov. Park	158	A3	54.034600 -119.810000
Kinbrook Island Prov. Park	165	D3	50.437189 -111.910595
La Biche River Wildland Prov. Park	159	D3	54.987000 -112.626000
Lakeland Prov. Park	159	E3	54.759300 -111.557000
Lakeland Prov. Rec. Area	159	E3	54.721800 -111.398000
Lesser Slave Lake Prov. Park	158	C2	55.448000 -114.817000
Lesser Slave Lake Wildland Prov. Park	158	C2	55.497700 -115.567000
Little Bow Prov. Park	164	C3	50.227930 -112.926590
Little Fish Lake Prov. Park	165	D2	51.374246 -112.200944
Long Lake Prov. Park	159	D3	54.439986 -112.763465
Marguerite River Wildland Prov. Park	159	E1	57.638400 -110.266000
Midland Prov. Park	165	D2	51.478295 -112.771085
Miquelon Lake Prov. Park	159	D4	53.246900 -112.874000
Moonshine Lake Prov. Park	158	B2	55.883800 -119.216000
Moose Lake Prov. Park	159	E3	54.272986 -110.931143
Notikewin Prov. Park	158	C1	57.218300 -117.148000
Obed Lake Prov. Park	158	B4	53.558200 -117.101000
O'Brien Prov. Park	158	B3	55.065242 -118.822285
Otter-Orloff Lakes Wildland Prov. Park	159	D2	55.364200 -113.551000
Park Lake Prov. Park	164	C4	49.806621 -112.924681
Peace River Wildland Prov. Park	158	B2	55.983200 -117.765000
Pembina River Prov. Park	158	C4	53.611859 -114.985313
Peter Lougheed Prov. Park	164	B3	50.684100 -115.184000
Pigeon Lake Prov. Park	164	C1	53.029547 -114.150507
Police Outpost Prov. Park	164	C4	49.004503 -113.464980
Queen Elizabeth Prov. Park	158	B2	56.219128 -117.693540
Red Lodge Prov. Park	164	C2	51.947917 -114.243862
Rochon Sands Prov. Park	165	D2	52.461755 -112.892373
Rock Lake Solomon Creek Wildland Prov. Park	158	B4	53.413700 -118.118000
Saskatoon Island Prov. Park	158	B2	55.205201 -119.085401
Sheep River Prov. Park	164	C3	50.647300 -114.660000
Sir Winston Churchill Prov. Park	159	D3	54.832050 -111.976109
Spray Valley Prov. Park	164	B3	50.888700 -115.293000
Stony Mtn. Wildland Prov. Park	159	E2	56.211500 -111.244000
Sundance Prov. Park	158	B4	53.668700 -116.926000
Sylvan Lake Prov. Park	164	C2	52.315760 -114.092272
Thunder Lake Prov. Park	158	C3	54.131941 -114.725882
Tillebrook Prov. Park	165	D3	50.538593 -111.812268
Vermilion Prov. Park	159	E4	53.367679 -110.909771
Wabamun Lake Prov. Park	158	C4	53.565029 -114.441575
Whitehorse Wildland Prov. Park	164	B1	52.957900 -117.395000
Whitemud Falls Wildland Prov. Park	159	E1	56.703400 -110.084000
Whitney Lakes Prov. Park	159	E4	53.847100 -110.537000
William A. Switzer Prov. Park	158	B4	53.492000 -117.804000
Williamson Prov. Park	158	B3	55.081821 -117.560174
Willow Creek Prov. Park	164	C3	50.118067 -113.776021
Winagami Lake Prov. Park	158	C2	55.627500 -116.738000
Winagami Wildland Prov. Park	158	C2	55.611900 -116.635000
Woolford Prov. Park	164	C4	49.178498 -113.190438
Writing-On-Stone Prov. Park	165	D4	49.061400 -111.639000
Wyndham-Carseland Prov. Park	164	C3	50.827750 -113.436542
Young's Point Prov. Park	158	B3	55.148000 -117.572000

BRITISH COLUMBIA

BRITISH COLUMBIA	PAGE	GRID	LATITUDE LONGITUDE
National Park & Rec. Areas			
Chilkoot Trail N.H.S.	155	D3	59.756667 -134.960833
Fort Langley N.H.S.	163	D3	49.168056 -122.569167
Fort Saint James N.H.S.	157	D2	54.440278 -124.255556
Glacier Natl. Park-Eastern Welcome Sta.	164	A2	51.511700 -117.442000
Glacier Natl. Park-Rogers Pass Discovery Center	164	A2	51.300600 -117.521500
Gulf Islands Natl. Park Res.	163	D4	48.769400 -123.210000
Gulf of Georgia Cannery N.H.S.	163	D3	49.124722 -123.199722
Gwaii Haanas Natl. Park Res. & Haida Heritage Site	156	A3	52.349722 -131.433056
Kitwanga Fort N.H.S.	156	C1	55.119444 -128.018056
Kootenay Natl. Park-Radium Hot Springs Vis. Ctr.	164	B3	50.619500 -116.069800
Kootenay Natl. Park-Vermilion Crossing Vis. Ctr.	164	B3	51.000000 -115.966000
Mount Revelstoke Natl. Park-Western Welcome Sta.	164	A2	51.042000 -117.983900
Pacific Rim Natl. Park Res.-Broken Group Islands	162	B3	48.891100 -125.300800
Pacific Rim Natl. Park Res.-Pacific Rim Vis. Ctr.	162	B3	48.992000 -125.587200
Pacific Rim Natl. Park Res.-West Coast Trail	162	C4	48.704800 -124.866100
Pacific Rim Natl. Park Res.-Wickaninnish Interpretive Center	162	B3	49.012700 -125.674200
Yoho Natl. Park-Field Vis. Ctr.	164	B2	51.397800 -116.492000
Provincial Park & Rec. Areas			
Adams Lake Prov. Park	163	F1	50.983056 -119.733056
Akamina-Kishinena Prov. Park	164	C4	49.032700 -114.178000
Alexandra Bridge Prov. Park	163	E2	49.700000 -121.399722
Alice Lake Prov. Park	163	D2	49.783056 -123.116667
Allison Lake Prov. Park	163	F2	49.683056 -120.599722
Anstey Hunakwa Prov. Park	164	A2	51.140600 -118.924300
Arctic Pacific Lakes Prov. Park	157	E2	54.384400 -121.553000
Arrow Lakes Prov. Park	164	A3	49.883056 -118.065667
Arrowstone Prov. Park	163	E1	50.879900 -121.273000
Atlin Prov. Park	155	E3	59.165400 -133.914000
Babine Lake-Pendleton Bay Marine Prov. Park	157	D2	54.533000 -125.724800
Babine Lake-Smithers Landing Marine Prov. Park	156	C1	55.098400 -126.600000
Babine Mountains Prov. Park	156	C1	54.913100 -126.928000
Babine River Corridor Prov. Park	156	C1	55.577400 -127.032000
Barkerville Prov. Park	157	E3	53.088889 -121.510833
Bear Creek Prov. Park	163	F2	49.930556 -119.520556
Bearhole Lake Prov. Park	158	A3	55.043400 -120.568000
Beatton Prov. Park	158	A1	56.333056 -120.933056
Beaumont Prov. Park	157	D2	54.050000 -124.616667
Beaver Creek Prov. Park	164	A4	49.066667 -117.600000
Big Bar Lake Prov. Park	157	E4	51.316667 -121.816667
Big Bunsby Marine Prov. Park	162	A2	50.120800 -127.504200
Big Creek Prov. Park	157	E4	51.301500 -123.158000
Bijoux Falls Prov. Park	157	E1	55.300000 -122.666667
Birkenhead Lake Prov. Park	163	D1	50.577900 -122.737000
Bishop River Prov. Park	162	C1	50.912500 -124.038000
Blanket Creek Prov. Park	164	A3	50.833056 -118.083056
Bligh Island Marine Prov. Park	162	A2	49.633300 -126.553000
Bowron Lake Prov. Park	157	F3	53.174100 -121.012000
Boya Lake Prov. Park	155	E3	59.380500 -129.090000
Brandywine Falls Prov. Park	163	D2	50.033056 -123.116667
Bridal Veil Falls Prov. Park	163	E3	49.183056 -121.733056
Bridge Lake Prov. Park	157	F4	51.483056 -120.700000
Bromley Rock Prov. Park	163	F3	49.416667 -120.258056
Brooks Peninsula Prov. Park	162	A2	50.180300 -127.657000
Broughton Archipelago Marine Prov. Park	162	A1	50.687100 -126.663000
Bugaboo Prov. Park	164	B3	50.794700 -116.808000
Callaghan Lake Prov. Park	163	D2	50.206900 -123.189000
Bull Canyon Prov. Park	157	E4	52.091667 -123.374722
Canal Flats Prov. Park	164	B3	50.183056 -115.816667
Canim Beach Prov. Park	157	F4	51.816667 -120.872667
Cape Scott Prov. Park	162	A1	50.765900 -128.246000
Cariboo Mts. Prov. Park	157	F3	52.852600 -120.538000
Cariboo River Prov. Park	157	F3	52.873600 -121.222000
Carmanah Walbran Prov. Park	162	C4	48.654500 -124.628000
Carp Lake Prov. Park	157	E2	54.769400 -123.387000
Catala Island Marine Prov. Park	162	A2	49.835833 -127.054167
Cathedral Prov. Park	163	F3	49.069800 -120.174000
Champion Lakes Prov. Park	164	A4	49.184100 -117.624000
Charlie Lake Prov. Park	158	A1	56.316667 -120.999722
Chasm Prov. Park	157	F4	51.178900 -121.438000
Chilliwack Lake Prov. Park	163	E3	49.072200 -121.436000
Clayoquot Arm Prov. Park	162	B3	49.172800 -125.560000
Clayoquot Plateau Prov. Park	162	B3	49.225100 -125.428000
Clendinning Prov. Park	162	C1	50.429700 -123.733000
Codville Lagoon Marine Prov. Park	156	C4	52.060833 -127.855556
Conkle Lake Prov. Park	164	A4	49.166667 -119.100000
Coquihalla Canyon Prov. Park	163	E3	49.371944 -121.366667
Cormorant Channel Marine Prov. Park	162	A1	50.593500 -126.850900
Cowichan River Prov. Park	162	C4	48.780800 -123.920000
Crooked River Prov. Park	157	E2	54.466667 -122.666667
Crowsnest Prov. Park	164	C4	49.649722 -114.699722
Cummins Lakes Prov. Park	164	A2	52.104100 -118.066000
Cypress Prov. Park	163	D3	49.425800 -123.209000
Dahl Lake Prov. Park	157	E2	53.769900 -123.293000
Desolation Sound Marine Prov. Park	162	C2	50.101100 -124.710000
Diana Lake Prov. Park	156	B2	54.216667 -130.166667
Downing Prov. Park	163	E1	51.000000 -121.783056
Dry Gulch Prov. Park	164	B3	50.583056 -116.033056
Duffey Lake Prov. Park	163	D1	50.407500 -122.337000
Dune Za Keyih Prov. Park	155	E3	58.323000 -126.355000
Echo Lake Prov. Park	164	A3	50.199722 -118.700000
Edge Hills Prov. Park	163	E1	51.035900 -121.871000
Elk Falls Prov. Park	162	B2	50.041000 -125.324000
Elk Lakes Prov. Park	164	C3	50.480800 -115.088000
Ellison Prov. Park	164	A3	50.173333 -119.433056
Emory Creek Prov. Park	163	E3	49.516667 -121.416667
Eneas Lakes Prov. Park	163	F2	49.752400 -119.936000
Entiako Prov. Park	157	D3	53.221500 -125.443000
Epper Passage Prov. Park	162	B3	49.219167 -125.949722
Eskers Prov. Park	157	E2	54.081300 -123.205000
Ethel F. Wilson Mem. Prov. Park	157	D2	54.416667 -125.683056
Fillongley Prov. Park	162	C3	49.534100 -124.755200
Finger-Tatuk Prov. Park	157	D2	53.515600 -124.226000
Flat Lake Prov. Park	157	F4	51.499400 -121.521000
Flores Island Prov. Park	162	B3	49.291000 -126.173000
Francois Lake Prov. Park	157	D2	53.966667 -125.166667
French Beach Prov. Park	162	C4	48.383056 -123.933056
Garibaldi Prov. Park	163	D2	49.943200 -122.751000
Gibson Marine Prov. Park	162	B3	49.266667 -126.066667
Gitnadoiks River Prov. Park	156	B2	54.161700 -129.162000
Gladstone Prov. Park	164	A4	49.268900 -118.269000
God's Pocket Marine Prov. Park	162	A1	50.837200 -127.562000
Goldpan Prov. Park	163	E2	50.350000 -121.383056
Gordon Bay Prov. Park	162	C4	48.833056 -124.199722
Graham-Laurier Prov. Park	155	F4	56.594900 -123.466000
Graystokes Prov. Park	164	A3	49.986200 -118.850000
Green Inlet Marine Prov. Park	156	C3	52.918167 -128.485944
Green Lake Prov. Park	157	F4	51.400000 -121.199722
Hamber Prov. Park	164	A2	52.380300 -117.882000
Harmony Islands Marine Prov. Park	162	C2	49.862222 -124.012222
Ha'thayim Marine Prov. Park	162	C2	50.169400 -124.955000
Heather-Dina Lakes Prov. Park	157	E1	55.508300 -123.285000
Height of the Rockies Prov. Park	164	B3	50.488900 -115.228000
Herald Prov. Park	164	A3	50.788056 -119.201000
Hesquiat Lake Prov. Park	162	B3	49.500000 -126.385833
Hitchie Creek Prov. Park	162	C4	48.795556 -124.737500
Horne Lake Caves Prov. Park	162	C3	49.344167 -124.755556
Horsefly Lake Prov. Park	157	F3	52.383056 -121.300000
Inkaneep Prov. Park	163	F3	49.233056 -119.533056
Inland Lake Prov. Park	162	C2	49.953800 -124.481000
Itcha Ilgachuz Prov. Park	157	D3	52.711500 -124.974000
Jackman Flats Prov. Park	164	A1	52.950000 -119.416667
Jedediah Island Marine Prov. Park	162	C3	49.500000 -124.199722
Jewel Lake Prov. Park	164	A4	49.183056 -118.599722
Jimsmith Lake Prov. Park	164	B4	49.483056 -115.833056
Joffre Lakes Prov. Park	163	D2	50.344100 -122.477000
Johnstone Creek Prov. Park	164	A4	49.050000 -119.049722
Juan De Fuca Prov. Park	162	C4	48.489800 -124.290000
Junction Sheep Range Prov. Park	157	E4	51.801000 -122.435000
Juniper Beach Prov. Park	163	E1	50.785833 -121.083056
Kakwa Prov. Park & Protected Area	158	A3	54.057200 -120.296000
Kekuli Bay Prov. Park	164	A3	50.183056 -119.340278
Kentucky-Alleyne Prov. Park	163	F2	49.916667 -120.566667
Kianuko Prov. Park	164	B4	49.421600 -116.456000
Kikomun Creek Prov. Park	164	B4	49.233056 -115.250000
Kilby Prov. Park	163	E3	49.237500 -121.960833
Kinaskan Lake Prov. Park	155	E4	57.496100 -130.234000
Kiskatinaw Prov. Park	158	A2	55.950000 -120.566667
Kleanza Creek Prov. Park	156	C2	54.599722 -128.399722
Klewnuggit Inlet Marine Prov. Park	156	B2	53.688500 -129.697000
Kluskoil Lake Prov. Park	157	D3	53.202900 -123.892000
Kokanee Creek Prov. Park	164	B4	49.605722 -117.133056
Kokanee Glacier Prov. Park	164	B4	49.781800 -117.136000
Kootenay Lake Prov. Park	164	B3	50.085000 -116.931189

Kwadacha Wilderness Prov. Park	155	E3	57.820400 -125.058000
Lac Le Jeune Prov. Park	163	F1	50.483056 -120.485056
Lakelse Lake Prov. Park	156	C2	54.398900 -128.533000
Lawn Point Prov. Park	162	A1	50.333056 -127.966667
Lockhart Beach Prov. Park	164	B4	49.516667 -116.783056
Lockhart Creek Prov. Park	164	B4	49.497300 -116.705000
Loveland Bay Prov. Park	162	B2	50.049722 -125.450000
Lowe Inlet Marine Prov. Park	156	B2	53.555556 -129.580278
MacMillan Prov. Park	162	C3	49.283056 -124.666667
Main Lake Prov. Park	162	B2	50.210000 -125.215000
Mansons Landing Prov. Park	162	C2	50.121500 -124.928300
Maquinna Marine Prov. Park	162	B3	49.390500 -126.342000
Marble River Prov. Park	162	A1	50.544300 -127.526000
Martha Creek Prov. Park	164	A3	51.141667 -118.198122
McConnell Lake Prov. Park	163	F1	50.521944 -120.456667
McDonald Creek Prov. Park	164	A3	50.131056 -117.813667
Mehatl Creek Prov. Park	163	E2	50.036100 -122.054000
Moberly Lake Prov. Park	158	A2	55.800000 -121.700000
Momich Lakes Prov. Park	164	A2	51.327200 -119.353000
Monck Prov. Park	163	F2	50.178667 -120.533056
Moose Valley Prov. Park	157	E4	51.649800 -121.648000
Morton Lake Prov. Park	162	B2	50.116667 -125.483056
Mount Assiniboine Prov. Park	164	B3	50.937400 -115.761000
Mount Blanchet Prov. Park	157	D1	55.275500 -125.863000
Mount Fernie Prov. Park	164	C4	49.483056 -115.099722
Mount Pope Prov. Park	157	D2	54.490700 -124.331000
Mount Robson Prov. Park	164	A1	52.927000 -118.831000
Mount Seymour Prov. Park	163	D3	49.392400 -122.926000
Mount Terry Fox Prov. Park	164	A1	52.940800 -119.254000
Moyie Lake Prov. Park	164	B4	49.373333 -115.837222
Myra-Bellevue Prov. Park	164	A4	49.752100 -119.374000
Nahatlatch Prov. Park	163	E2	49.980200 -121.780000
Naikoon Prov. Park	156	A2	53.863400 -131.889000
Nairn Falls Prov. Park	163	D2	50.283056 -122.833056
Nancy Greene Prov. Park	164	A4	49.250000 -117.933056
Nickel Plate Prov. Park	163	F3	49.399722 -119.949722
Nicolum River Prov. Park	163	E3	49.366667 -121.341667
Nimpkish Lake Prov. Park	162	A2	50.337700 -127.005000
Niskonlith Lake Prov. Park	163	F1	50.795556 -119.777778
Norbury Lake Prov. Park	164	B4	49.533056 -115.483056
Nuchatlitz Prov. Park	162	A2	49.815700 -126.981000
Octopus Island Marine Prov. Park	162	B2	50.278400 -125.242100
Okanagan Lake Prov. Park	163	F2	49.683056 -119.719867
Okanagan Mtn. Prov. Park	163	F2	49.724600 -119.629000
Okeover Arm Prov. Park	162	C2	49.999722 -124.726667
One Island Lake Prov. Park	158	A2	55.300000 -120.266667
Paarens Beach Prov. Park	157	D2	54.416667 -124.399722
Paul Lake Prov. Park	163	F1	50.741667 -120.120556
Pinecone Burke Prov. Park	163	D3	49.526200 -122.721000
Porpoise Bay Prov. Park	162	C3	49.516667 -123.749722
Porteau Cove Prov. Park	163	D3	49.549722 -123.233056
Premier Lake Prov. Park	164	B4	49.900000 -115.650000
Princess Louisa Marine Prov. Park	162	C2	50.203722 -123.766667
Ptarmigan Creek Prov. Park	157	F2	53.487600 -120.880000
Puntchesakut Lake Prov. Park	157	E3	52.983056 -122.933056
Purden Lake Prov. Park	157	E2	53.928000 -121.912000
Quatsino Prov. Park	162	A1	50.491667 -127.816667
Rearguard Falls Prov. Park	157	F3	52.973333 -119.366667
Redfern-Keily Prov. Park	155	F3	57.405600 -123.878000
Roberts Creek Prov. Park	162	C3	49.433056 -123.666667
Rolley Lake Prov. Park	163	D3	49.250000 -122.400000
Rosebery Prov. Park	164	B3	50.033056 -117.400000
Rubyrock Lake Prov. Park	157	D2	54.677100 -125.348000
Ruckle Prov. Park	163	D4	48.766667 -123.383056
Rugged Point Marine Prov. Park	162	A2	49.963889 -127.238889
Saint Mary's Alpine Prov. Park	164	B4	49.877000 -116.348000
Sandy Island Marine Prov. Park	162	C3	49.616667 -124.849722
Schoen Lake Prov. Park	162	B2	50.176500 -126.245000
Schoolhouse Lake Prov. Park	157	F4	51.883600 -120.993000
Seeley Lake Prov. Park	156	C1	55.199722 -127.683056
Seven Sisters Prov. Park	156	C1	54.946900 -128.150000
Silver Beach Prov. Park	164	A2	51.240278 -118.955556
Silver Lake Prov. Park	163	E3	49.316667 -121.399722
Silver Star Prov. Park	164	A3	50.376900 -119.082000
Simson Prov. Park	162	C3	49.479700 -123.962900
Skihist Prov. Park	163	E2	50.249722 -121.500000
Skookumchuck Narrows Prov. Park	162	C2	49.744700 -123.915500
Smelt Bay Prov. Park	162	C2	50.033056 -124.983056
Sowchea Bay Prov. Park	157	D2	54.419167 -124.448333
Sproat Lake Prov. Park	162	C3	49.300000 -124.916667
Squitty Bay Prov. Park	162	C3	49.454167 -124.166667
Stagleap Prov. Park	164	B4	49.058700 -117.048000
Steelhead Prov. Park	163	E1	50.752778 -120.868056
Stemwinder Prov. Park	163	F3	49.366667 -120.133056
Stone Mtn. Prov. Park	155	E3	58.588600 -124.757000
Strathcona Prov. Park	162	B2	49.629300 -125.710000
Stuart Lake Marine Prov. Park	157	D2	54.650000 -125.000000
Sugarbowl Prov. Park	157	E2	53.801200 -121.589000
Sukunka Falls Prov. Park	157	E1	55.316667 -121.700000
Sulphur Passage Prov. Park	162	B3	49.412000 -126.094000
Summit Lake Prov. Park	164	A3	50.150000 -117.666667
Surge Narrows Prov. Park	162	B2	50.233056 -125.149722
Sutherland River Prov. Park	157	D2	54.338300 -124.818000
Sydney Inlet Prov. Park	162	B3	49.480000 -126.283000
Syringa Prov. Park	164	A4	49.378000 -117.906000
Tahsish-Kwois Prov. Park	162	A2	50.189100 -127.161000
Tatlatui Prov. Park	155	E4	56.996200 -127.386000
Tatshenshini-Alsek Prov. Park	155	D3	59.595900 -137.443000
Taylor Arm Prov. Park	162	B3	49.283056 -125.049722
Ten Mile Lake Prov. Park	157	E3	53.066667 -122.450000
Thurston Bay Marine Prov. Park	162	B2	50.383056 -125.316667
Ts'il-os Prov. Park	157	D4	51.191700 -123.971000
Tudyah Lake Prov. Park	157	E1	55.066667 -123.033056
Tunkwa Prov. Park	163	E1	50.615200 -120.887000
Tyhee Lake Prov. Park	156	C2	54.700000 -127.033056
Union Passage Marine Prov. Park	156	B3	53.410900 -129.436000
Upper Adams River Prov. Park	164	A2	51.682700 -119.228000
Valhalla Prov. Park	164	A4	49.873700 -117.567000
Vargas Island Prov. Park	162	B3	49.174000 -126.031000
Vaseux Lake Prov. Park	164	A4	49.268200 -119.474000
Walsh Cove Prov. Park	162	C2	50.268056 -124.800000
Wasa Lake Prov. Park	164	B4	49.793056 -115.738056
West Arm Prov. Park	164	B4	49.507000 -117.118000
West Lake Prov. Park	157	E2	53.733056 -122.866667
Whiskers Point Prov. Park	157	E1	54.900000 -122.933056
White Pelican Prov. Park	157	E3	52.284000 -123.031000
Whiteswan Lake Prov. Park	164	B3	50.145300 -115.487000
Woss Lake Prov. Park	162	A2	50.060400 -126.626000
Yahk Provincial Park	164	B4	49.083056 -116.083056
Yard Creek Prov. Park	164	A3	50.899722 -118.799722

MANITOBA	PAGE	GRID	LATITUDE LONGITUDE
National Park & Rec. Areas			
Lower Fort Garry N.H.S.	167	E3	50.136850 -96.940569
Riding Mtn. Natl. Park-Deep Lake Ranger Sta.	167	D3	50.860300 -100.836600
Riding Mtn. Natl. Park-Lake Audy Ranger Sta.	167	D3	50.712900 -100.230600
Riding Mtn. Natl. Park-McKinnon Creek Ranger Sta.	167	D3	50.787100 -99.579500
Riding Mtn. Natl. Park-Moon Lake Ranger Sta.	167	D3	50.995900 -100.067200
Riding Mtn. Natl. Park-South Lake Ranger Sta.	167	D3	50.655200 -100.061600
Riding Mtn. Natl. Park-Sugarloaf Ranger Sta.	167	D3	50.985300 -100.742100
Riding Mtn. Natl. Park-Whirlpool Ranger Sta.	167	D3	50.683300 -99.553500
Provincial Park & Rec. Areas			
Asessippi Prov. Park	166	C3	50.966400 -101.379700
Atikaki Prov. Wilderness Park	167	F2	51.532200 -95.547000
Bakers Narrows Prov. Park	161	D3	54.671100 -101.675000
Beaudry Prov. Park	167	E4	49.853900 -97.473300
Bell Lake Prov. Park	166	C1	52.541700 -101.241400
Birds Hill Prov. Park	167	E3	50.028800 -96.893200
Camp Morton Prov. Park	167	E3	50.710000 -96.990300
Clearwater Lake Prov. Park	161	D3	54.096200 -101.162000
Criddle–Vane Homestead Prov. Park	167	D4	49.707600 -99.596600
Duck Mtn. Prov. Park	167	D2	51.715600 -101.112000
Elk Island Prov. Park	167	E3	50.758300 -96.536500
Grand Beach Prov. Park	167	E3	50.567900 -96.554900
Grass River Prov. Park	161	D3	54.655500 -101.092000
Hecla–Grindstone Prov. Park	167	E2	51.198300 -96.660200
Hnausa Beach Prov. Park	167	E3	50.900300 -96.992200
Kettle Stones Prov. Park	167	D2	52.359200 -100.595300
Lake Saint George Prov. Park	167	E2	51.719703 -97.406772
Lundar Beach Prov. Park	167	E3	50.724000 -98.273000
Manipogo Prov. Park	167	D2	51.517000 -99.550000
Nopiming Prov. Park	167	F3	50.665200 -95.305600
North Steeprock Lake Prov. Park	166	C1	52.611800 -101.380000
Paint Lake Prov. Park	161	E2	55.492100 -98.018000
Patricia Beach Prov. Park	167	E3	50.467300 -96.575300
Pembina Valley Prov. Park	167	E4	49.038500 -98.296400
Pinawa Dam Prov. Park	167	F3	50.145200 -95.945700
Rainbow Beach Prov. Park	167	D3	51.099400 -99.718400
Saint Ambroise Beach Prov. Park	167	E3	50.275500 -98.074300
Saint Malo Prov. Park	167	E4	49.321400 -96.930490
South Atikaki Prov. Park	167	F3	51.041400 -95.417600
Spruce Woods Prov. Park	167	D4	49.703100 -99.141900
Stephenfield Prov. Park	167	E4	49.523400 -98.300500
Turtle Mtn. Prov. Park	167	D4	49.041500 -100.216000
Watchorn Prov. Park	167	E2	51.293100 -98.598500
Whitefish Lake Prov. Park	166	C2	52.333900 -101.587100
Whiteshell Prov. Park	167	F3	50.140900 -95.584400
William Lake Prov. Park	167	D4	49.055000 -100.038800
Winnipeg Beach Prov. Park	167	E3	50.512300 -96.967000

NEW BRUNSWICK	PAGE	GRID	LATITUDE LONGITUDE
National Park & Rec. Areas			
Beaubears Island N.H.S.	179	D3	46.972778 -65.569444
Fort Beauséjour N.H.S.	180	C1	45.865278 -64.290278
Fort Gaspareaux N.H.S.	180	C1	46.040833 -64.072778
Fundy Natl. Park-Vis. Ctr.	180	C1	45.659500 -65.132600
Kouchibouguac Natl. Park-Vis. Ctr.	179	D3	46.773200 -65.004900
Monument Lefebvre N.H.S.	180	C1	45.979167 -64.567222
Roosevelt Campobello International Park	180	A2	44.849722 -66.949722
Saint Andrews Blockhouse N.H.S.	180	A2	45.076389 -67.063889
Saint Croix Island International Hist. Site	180	A2	45.127778 -67.133333
Provincial Park & Rec. Areas			
De la République Prov. Park	178	B3	47.442778 -68.395556
Herring Cove Prov. Park	180	A2	44.866667 -66.933056
Mactaquac Prov. Park	180	A1	45.959025 -66.892556
Mount Carleton Prov. Park	178	C3	47.392300 -66.835500
Murray Beach Prov. Park	180	C1	46.016667 -63.983056
New River Beach Prov. Park	180	A2	45.133056 -66.533056
Parlee Beach Prov. Park	180	C1	46.233056 -64.499722
Sugarloaf Prov. Park	178	C2	47.974000 -66.671900
The Anchorage Prov. Park	180	A3	44.649722 -66.800000

NEWFOUNDLAND & LABRADOR	PAGE	GRID	LATITUDE LONGITUDE
National Park & Rec. Areas			
Castle Hill N.H.S.	183	E4	47.251389 -53.971111
Gros Morne Natl. Park-Vis. Ctr.	182	C2	49.571500 -57.877900
Hawthorne Cottage N.H.S.	183	E4	47.543333 -53.210833
L'Anse aux Meadows N.H.S.	183	F1	51.595000 -55.532778
Port au Choix N.H.S.	182	C1	50.712222 -57.375278
Red Bay N.H.S.	183	F1	51.733056 -56.415556
Ryan Premises N.H.S.	183	E3	48.648056 -53.112500
Terra Nova Natl. Park-Information Center	183	E3	48.394900 -54.204000
Terra Nova Natl. Park-Saltons Vis. Ctr.	183	E3	48.580600 -53.958900
Provincial Park & Rec. Areas			
Barachois Pond Prov. Park	182	C3	48.477100 -58.256600
Blow Me Down Prov. Park	182	C2	49.090833 -58.364444
Butter Pot Prov. Park	183	F4	47.390900 -53.071300
Chance Cove Prov. Park	183	F4	46.776900 -53.045400
Codroy Valley Prov. Park	182	C4	47.833333 -59.337778
Deadman's Bay Prov. Park	183	E2	49.331389 -53.692500
Dildo Run Prov. Park	183	E2	49.535556 -54.721667
Dungeon Prov. Park	183	E3	48.666667 -53.083611
Frenchman's Cove Prov. Park	183	D4	47.209444 -55.401667
Gooseberry Cove Prov. Park	183	E4	47.068056 -54.087778
J.T. Cheeseman Prov. Park	182	C4	47.631111 -59.249444
La Manche Prov. Park	183	F4	47.175200 -52.901200
Lockston Path Prov. Park	183	E3	48.437778 -53.379722
Notre Dame Prov. Park	183	E2	49.115833 -55.086389
Pinware River Prov. Park	183	F1	51.631667 -56.704167
Sandbanks Prov. Park	182	C4	47.607222 -57.646944
Sir Richard Squires Mem. Prov. Park	183	D2	49.354000 -57.213400
The Arches Prov. Park	182	C2	50.113333 -57.663056

NORTHWEST TERRITORIES	PAGE	GRID	LATITUDE LONGITUDE
National Park & Rec. Areas			
Nahanni Natl. Park Res.	155	E2	61.083333 -123.600000
Tuktut Nogait Natl. Park	155	E1	69.283333 -123.016667

NOVA SCOTIA	PAGE	GRID	LATITUDE LONGITUDE
National Park & Rec. Areas			
Alexander Graham Bell N.H.S.	181	F1	46.102778 -60.745556
Cape Breton Highlands Natl. Park-East Ent.	182	B4	46.642800 -60.404200
Cape Breton Highlands Natl. Park-West Ent.	182	B4	46.647300 -60.950200
Fort Anne N.H.S.	180	B3	44.741667 -65.519167
Fort Edward N.H.S.	180	C2	44.995556 -64.135278
Fortress of Louisbourg N.H.S.	181	F1	45.900300 -59.995100
Grand-Pré N.H.S.	180	C2	45.108889 -64.311944
Grassy Island N.H.S.	181	F2	45.336667 -60.973611
Kejimkujik Natl. Park (Seaside Adjunct)	180	C4	43.865800 -64.836900
Kejimkujik Natl. Park and N.H.S.	180	B3	44.336700 -65.268200
Marconi N.H.S.	181	F4	46.211111 -59.952778
Port-Royal N.H.S.	180	B3	44.712500 -65.610556
Saint Peters Canal N.H.S.	181	F1	45.655556 -60.870556
York Redoubt N.H.S.	181	D3	44.596583 -63.552439
Provincial Park & Rec. Areas			
Amherst Shore Prov. Park	180	C1	45.961181 -63.879025
Battery Prov. Park	181	F1	45.657022 -60.866764
Beaver Mtn. Prov. Park	181	E2	45.567556 -62.153583
Blomidon Prov. Park	180	C2	45.255869 -64.352056
Boylston Prov. Park	181	E2	45.426839 -61.510603
Cape Chignecto Prov. Park	180	C2	45.375800 -64.891300
Caribou–Munroes Island Prov. Park	181	D1	45.721800 -62.656914
Clam Harbour Beach Prov. Park	181	D3	44.731390 -62.891110
Ellenwood Lake Prov. Park	180	B4	43.929481 -66.005700
Five Islands Prov. Park	180	C2	45.407781 -64.021500
Graves Island Prov. Park	180	C3	44.565550 -64.218642
Laurie Prov. Park	181	D2	44.878175 -63.602194
Martinique Beach Prov. Park	181	D3	44.689911 -63.147567
Mira River Prov. Park	181	F1	46.026006 -60.037433
Porters Prov. Park	181	D3	44.691106 -63.308892
Rissers Beach Prov. Park	180	C3	44.232397 -64.423919
Salsman Prov. Park	181	E2	45.236856 -61.767150
Salt Springs Prov. Park	181	D2	45.545280 -62.878890
Shubenacadie Prov. Wildlife Park	181	D2	45.087222 -63.387500
Smileys Prov. Park	180	C2	45.013925 -63.961247
The Islands Prov. Park	180	B4	43.765503 -65.340347
Thomas Raddall Prov. Park	180	C4	43.844783 -64.919694
Valleyview Prov. Park	180	B2	44.875200 -65.316064
Wentworth Prov. Park	181	D2	45.627222 -63.552222
Whycocomagh Prov. Park	181	F1	45.968094 -61.109908

ONTARIO	PAGE	GRID	LATITUDE LONGITUDE
National Park & Rec. Areas			
Battle of the Windmill N.H.S.	174	B4	44.722778 -75.486944
Bellevue House N.H.S.	173	F1	44.220556 -76.506667
Bruce Peninsula Natl. Park	170	C4	45.189100 -81.485500
Fathom Five Natl. Marine Park	170	C4	45.304800 -81.727600
Fort George N.H.S.	173	D3	43.252778 -79.051111
Fort Henry N.H.S.	173	F1	44.230833 -76.459444
Fort Malden N.H.S.	172	A4	42.108056 -83.113889
Fort Mississauga N.H.S.	173	D3	43.260833 -79.076667
Fort Saint Joseph N.H.S.	170	B3	46.063889 -83.944167
Fort Wellington N.H.S.	174	B4	44.713889 -75.510833
Georgian Bay Islands Natl. Park-Welcome Center	171	D4	44.803900 -79.720400
Glengarry Cairn N.H.S.	174	C3	45.121667 -74.490278
Merrickville Blockhouse N.H.S.	174	B4	44.916667 -75.837500
Peterborough Lift Lock N.H.S.	173	E1	44.308056 -78.300556
Point Clark Lighthouse N.H.S.	172	B2	44.073056 -81.756667
Point Pelee Natl. Park-Park Ent. Kiosk	172	A4	41.987700 -82.549900
Point Pelee Natl. Park-Vis. Ctr.	172	A4	41.931700 -82.513500
Pukaskwa Natl. Park-Information Center	170	A2	48.700400 -86.197200
Queenston Heights N.H.S.	173	D3	43.158056 -79.052778
Saint Lawrence Islands Natl. Park-Vis. Ctr.	174	A4	44.452300 -75.860300
Sault Ste. Marie Canal N.H.S.	170	B3	46.511667 -84.355556
Sir John Johnson House N.H.S.	174	C4	45.144444 -74.580000
Southwold Earthworks N.H.S.	172	B3	42.677778 -81.351389
Trent-Severn Waterway N.H.S.	173	E1	44.137500 -77.590100
Woodside N.H.S.	172	C2	43.466667 -80.499722
Provincial Park & Rec. Areas			
Aaron Prov. Park	168	C3	49.758390 -92.653440
Abitibi-De-Troyes Prov. Park	171	D1	48.786500 -80.066300
Albany River Prov. Park	169	E1	51.358200 -88.134000
Algonquin Prov. Park	171	E4	45.605300 -78.323900
Arrowhead Prov. Park	171	D4	45.391700 -79.197200
Awenda Prov. Park	172	C1	44.854400 -79.989800
Balsam Lake Prov. Park	173	D1	44.642000 -78.864000
Bass Lake Prov. Park	173	D1	44.602000 -79.475000
Batchawana Prov. Park	170	B3	46.941900 -84.587010
Blue Lake Prov. Park	168	B3	49.904200 -93.525600
Bon Echo Prov. Park	171	E4	44.905600 -77.246600
Bonnechere Prov. Park	171	E4	45.658400 -77.570800
Bonnechere River Prov. Park	171	E4	45.674400 -77.661500
Brightsand River Prov. Park	169	D3	49.936700 -90.265400
Bronte Creek Prov. Park	173	D2	43.410490 -79.767830
Caliper Lake Prov. Park	168	B3	49.061670 -93.912780
Carson Lake Prov. Park	171	E4	45.502780 -77.746390
Chapleau-Nemegosenda River Prov. Park	170	B2	48.262300 -83.035300
Charleston Lake Prov. Park	174	A4	44.515400 -76.013600
Chutes Prov. Park	170	C3	46.219510 -82.071480
Craigleith Prov. Park	172	C1	44.535000 -80.367000
Darlington Prov. Park	173	D2	43.875480 -78.778300
Devil's Glen Prov. Park	172	C1	44.361000 -80.207800
Driftwood Prov. Park	171	E3	46.179000 -77.843000
Earl Rowe Prov. Park	172	C1	44.150000 -79.898000
Emily Prov. Park	173	D1	44.340530 -78.532860
Esker Lakes Prov. Park	171	D2	48.290100 -79.906100
Fairbank Prov. Park	170	C3	46.468070 -81.440410
Ferris Prov. Park	173	E1	44.293000 -77.788000
Finlayson Point Prov. Park	171	D3	47.055000 -79.797000
Fitzroy Prov. Park	174	A3	45.482680 -76.209400
French River Prov. Park	171	D3	46.008600 -80.620900
Frontenac Prov. Park	174	A4	44.540500 -76.512700
Fushimi Lake Prov. Park	169	F3	49.824800 -83.913800
Greenwater Prov. Park	170	C1	49.215900 -81.291000
Grundy Lake Prov. Park	171	D4	45.939800 -80.530400
Halfway Lake Prov. Park	170	C3	46.905700 -81.650500
Inverhuron Prov. Park	172	B1	44.298000 -81.580000
Ivanhoe Lake Prov. Park	170	C2	47.957600 -82.742600
John E. Pearce Prov. Park	172	B4	42.617000 -81.444000
Kakabeka Falls Prov. Park	169	D4	48.403290 -89.624130
Kap-Kig-Iwan Prov. Park	171	D2	47.789960 -79.884990
Kettle Lakes Prov. Park	170	C1	48.569400 -80.865400
Killarney Prov. Park	170	C3	46.099400 -81.386900
Killbear Prov. Park	171	D4	45.346200 -80.191200
Kopka River Prov. Park	169	D2	50.006300 -89.493000
Lady Evelyn-Smoothwater Prov. Park	171	D2	47.368500 -80.489300
Lake of the Woods Prov. Park	168	B3	49.221200 -94.606000
Lake on the Mtn. Prov. Park	173	F1	44.039940 -77.056080
Lake Saint Peter Prov. Park	171	E4	45.322000 -78.024000
Lake Superior Prov. Park	170	A2	47.595200 -84.756500
Larder River Prov. Park	171	D2	47.936300 -79.642800
La Verendrye Prov. Park	169	D4	48.138300 -90.431300
Little Abitibi Prov. Park	170	C1	49.637900 -80.922900
Little Current River Prov. Park	169	E2	50.724100 -86.211000
Long Point Prov. Park	172	C4	42.565000 -80.306000
Lower Madawaska River Prov. Park	171	E4	45.236200 -77.289300
MacGregor Point Prov. Park	172	B1	44.403700 -81.465600
Macleod Prov. Park	169	E3	49.676190 -86.931000
Makobe-Grays River Prov. Park	171	D2	47.617200 -80.376300
Mara Prov. Park	173	D1	44.589000 -79.349000
Mark S. Burnham Prov. Park	173	E1	44.299900 -78.257000
Marten River Prov. Park	171	D3	46.729000 -79.807000
Mattawa River Prov. Park	171	D3	46.315000 -79.108400
McRae Point Prov. Park	173	D1	44.569000 -79.320000
Mikisew Prov. Park	171	D4	45.820000 -79.512000
Missinaibi River Prov. Park	170	B1	49.101400 -83.234700
Mississagi Prov. Park	170	C3	46.596500 -82.682500
Mississagi River Prov. Park	170	C3	47.012600 -82.632700
Murphys Point Prov. Park	174	A4	44.774300 -76.240700
Nagagamisis Prov. Park	169	F3	49.475700 -84.771000
Neys Prov. Park	169	E4	48.750500 -86.591900
North Beach Prov. Park	173	E2	43.951050 -77.522660
Oastler Lake Prov. Park	171	D4	45.309000 -79.964800
Obabika River Prov. Park	171	D3	47.221200 -80.262600
Obatanga Prov. Park	170	A2	48.323000 -85.093700
Ojibway Prov. Park	168	C3	49.990900 -92.144400
Opeongo River Prov. Park	171	E4	45.576256 -77.887363
Otoskwin-Attawapiskat River Prov. Park	169	D1	52.235700 -87.491300
Ottawa River Prov. Park	174	A3	45.741700 -76.779800
Ouimet Canyon Prov. Park	169	D4	48.773350 -88.667400
Oxtongue River-Ragged Falls Prov. Park	171	D4	45.366900 -78.914100
Pakwash Prov. Park	168	B2	50.749800 -93.551400
Pancake Bay Prov. Park	170	B3	46.967200 -84.661100
Petroglyphs Prov. Park	173	E1	44.618300 -78.041700
Pigeon River Prov. Park	169	D4	48.025041 -89.572294
Pipestone River Prov. Park	169	D1	52.244300 -90.313500
Point Farms Prov. Park	172	B2	43.804000 -81.700000
Port Bruce Prov. Park	172	B3	42.664000 -81.027000
Port Burwell Prov. Park	172	C3	42.646000 -80.816000
Potholes Prov. Park	170	B2	47.958700 -84.294020
Presqu'Ile Prov. Park	173	E2	44.007000 -77.735000
Quetico Prov. Park	168	C4	48.404500 -91.498700
Rainbow Falls Prov. Park	169	E4	48.830090 -87.389580
Renè Brunelle Prov. Park	170	C1	49.453700 -82.147900
Restoule Prov. Park	171	D3	46.080400 -79.839800
Rideau River Prov. Park	174	B4	45.060000 -75.672000
Rock Point Prov. Park	173	D3	42.854000 -79.552000
Rondeau Prov. Park	172	B4	42.278200 -81.865100
Rushing River Prov. Park	168	B3	49.681850 -94.234890
Samuel de Champlain Prov. Park	171	D3	46.301900 -78.864100
Sandbanks Prov. Park	173	F2	43.910200 -77.267200
Sandbar Lake Prov. Park	168	C3	49.491000 -91.555700
Sauble Falls Prov. Park	172	B1	44.673170 -81.257350
Selkirk Prov. Park	172	C3	42.824000 -79.961000
Sharbot Lake Prov. Park	174	A4	44.775500 -76.724600
Sibbald Point Prov. Park	173	D1	44.322160 -79.325570
Silent Lake Prov. Park	171	E4	44.907500 -78.047200
Silver Lake Prov. Park	174	A4	44.829770 -76.574680
Sioux Narrows Prov. Park	168	B3	49.429570 -94.037260
Six Mile Lake Prov. Park	171	D4	44.819500 -79.733500
Sleeping Giant Prov. Park	169	D4	48.419300 -88.795500
Solace Prov. Park	170	C3	47.189200 -80.683500
Springwater Prov. Park	173	D1	44.443500 -79.748500
Steel River Prov. Park	169	E3	49.161900 -86.812600
Sturgeon Bay Prov. Park	171	D4	45.623400 -80.414100
Sturgeon River Prov. Park	170	C3	46.949800 -80.523900
The Massasauga Prov. Park	171	D4	45.203400 -80.044300
The Pinery Prov. Park	172	B3	43.257200 -81.834000
The Shoals Prov. Park	170	B2	47.884800 -83.808000
Turkey Point Prov. Park	172	C3	42.694000 -80.333150
Turtle River-White Otter Lake Prov. Park	168	C3	49.129700 -92.042300
Upper Madawaska River Prov. Park	171	E4	45.513700 -78.078700
Wabakimi Prov. Park	169	D2	50.719100 -89.448500
Wakami Lake Prov. Park	170	C2	47.489700 -82.842000
Wasaga Beach Prov. Park	172	C1	44.494000 -80.027100
Wheatley Prov. Park	172	A4	42.098000 -82.448800
White Lake Prov. Park	170	A1	48.603500 -85.880900
Windy Lake Prov. Park	170	C3	46.619820 -81.455980
Woodland Caribou Prov. Park	168	B2	51.096900 -94.744900

PRINCE EDWARD ISLAND	PAGE	GRID	LATITUDE LONGITUDE
National Park & Rec. Areas			
Port-la-Joye–Fort Amherst N.H.S.	179	E4	46.195278 -63.133611
Prince Edward Island Natl. Park-Brackley Vis. Ctr.	179	E4	46.406200 -63.196600
Prince Edward Island Natl. Park-Cavendish Vis. Ctr.	179	E4	46.492300 -63.379700
Provincial Park & Rec. Areas			
Brudenell River Prov. Park	179	F4	46.209583 -62.588556
Buffaloland Prov. Park	179	F4	46.092500 -62.617778
Cabot Beach Prov. Park	179	E4	46.557250 -63.704250
Cedar Dunes Prov. Park	177	F4	46.622222 -64.381944
Chelton Beach Prov. Park	179	E4	46.303944 -63.747167
Green Park Prov. Park	177	F4	46.590972 -63.890333
Jacques Cartier Prov. Park	177	F4	46.851222 -64.013000
Kings Castle Prov. Park	179	F4	46.019167 -62.567389
Linkletter Prov. Park	179	E4	46.402694 -63.850361
Lord Selkirk Prov. Park	179	F4	46.091889 -62.906000
Mill River Prov. Park	177	F4	46.749722 -64.166667
Northumberland Prov. Park	179	F4	45.966667 -62.716667
Panmure Island Prov. Park	179	F4	46.133056 -62.466667
Red Point Prov. Park	179	F4	46.366667 -62.133056
Wood Islands Prov. Park	181	D1	45.949722 -62.749722

QUÉBEC	PAGE	GRID	LATITUDE LONGITUDE
National Park & Rec. Areas			
Lieu Historique Natl. du Fort-Lennox	175	D4	45.120556 -73.268056
Lieu Historique Natl. du Fort-Témiscamingue	171	D2	47.295000 -79.456667
Parc Natl. de Forillon-North Ent.	179	D1	48.960100 -64.339000
Parc Natl. de Forillon-South Ent.	179	D1	48.854300 -64.396300
Parc Natl. de la Mauricie-East Ent.	175	D1	46.752600 -72.792600
Parc Natl. de la Mauricie-South Ent.	175	D1	46.650000 -72.969200
Réserve de Parc Natl. de l'Archipel-de-Mingan	177	F1	50.237100 -63.606900
Provincial Park & Rec. Areas			
Parc d'Aiguebelle	171	D1	48.510300 -78.745800
Parc d'Anticosti	182	A2	49.463200 -62.819000
Parc de Frontenac	175	E3	45.848600 -71.184600
Parc de la Gaspésie	178	C1	48.941500 -66.214400
Parc de la Gatineau	174	A3	45.566667 -75.949722
Parc de la Jacques-Cartier	175	E1	47.317300 -71.347000
Parc de la Pointe-Taillon	176	C3	48.717300 -71.993600
Parc de la Yamaska	175	D3	45.429400 -72.601800
Parc de l'Île-Bonaventure-et-du-Rocher-Percé	179	E1	48.496389 -64.161944
Parc de Miguasha	178	C2	48.110556 -66.369444
Parc de Plaisance	174	B3	45.597900 -75.123600
Parc de Récréation du Mont-Orford	175	D3	45.344700 -72.212900
Parc des Grands-Jardins	176	C4	47.681300 -70.836900
Parc des Hautes-Gorges-de-la-Rivière-Malbaie	176	C3	47.918700 -70.498700
Parc des Monts-Valin	176	C3	48.598600 -70.825300
Parc du Bic	178	A1	48.355300 -68.797600
Parc du Mont-Mégantic	175	E3	45.450700 -71.167300
Parc du Mont-Saint-Bruno	175	D3	45.555278 -73.309722
Parc du Mont-Tremblant	174	C2	46.443000 -74.344600
Parc du Saguenay	176	C3	48.289900 -70.243400
Parc Marin du Saguenay-Saint-Laurent	178	A2	48.133056 -69.733056
Parc Régional du Massif du Sud	175	F2	46.581389 -70.467778

SASKATCHEWAN	PAGE	GRID	LATITUDE LONGITUDE
National Park & Rec. Areas			
Batoche N.H.S.	165	F1	52.752800 -106.116700
Battle of Fish Creek N.H.S.	165	F1	52.550000 -106.180300
Fort Battleford N.H.S.	165	E1	52.713800 -108.259600
Fort Espèrance N.H.S.	166	C3	50.451400 -101.712800
Fort Livingstone N.H.S.	166	C2	51.903880 -101.960620
Fort Pelly N.H.S.	166	C2	51.795900 -101.951800
Fort Walsh N.H.S.	165	E4	49.559100 -109.901700
Grasslands Natl. Park-East Block Vis. Ctr.	166	A4	49.370800 -106.384800
Grasslands Natl. Park-West Block Vis. Reception Ctr.	166	A4	49.203800 -107.732700
Prince Albert Natl. Park-Waskesiu Vis. Ctr.	160	B3	53.922500 -106.081800
Provincial Park & Rec. Areas			
Blackstrap Prov. Park	166	A2	51.755600 -106.458300
Buffalo Pound Prov. Park	166	B3	50.576200 -105.361000
Candle Lake Prov. Park	160	B4	53.845000 -105.252000
Cannington Manor Prov. Hist. Park	166	C4	49.712900 -102.027300
Clearwater River Prov. Park	159	E1	56.929300 -109.043000
Crooked Lake Prov. Park	166	C3	50.592200 -102.741400
Cumberland House Prov. Hist. Park	160	C4	53.948000 -102.421400
Cypress Hills Interprovincial Park	165	E4	49.632400 -109.809000
Danielson Prov. Park	166	A2	51.252200 -106.866000
Douglas Prov. Park	166	A3	51.025300 -106.480000
Echo Valley Prov. Park	166	B3	50.808500 -103.891900
Fort Carlton Prov. Park	166	A1	52.867100 -106.542700
Fort Pitt Prov. Park	165	E1	53.577000 -109.806300
Good Spirit Lake Prov. Park	166	C2	51.543500 -102.707000
Greenwater Lake Prov. Park	166	C1	52.532000 -103.448000
Katepwa Point Prov. Park	166	B3	50.693165 -103.626025
Lac La Ronge Prov. Park	160	C3	55.249200 -104.769000
Last Mtn. House Prov. Park	166	B3	50.722800 -104.823300
Makwa Lake Prov. Park	159	E3	54.016800 -109.234000
Meadow Lake Prov. Park	159	E3	54.501400 -109.076000
Moose Mtn. Prov. Park	166	C4	49.821300 -102.424000
Narrow Hills Prov. Park	160	C3	54.091300 -104.643000
Pike Lake Prov. Park	166	A2	51.893200 -106.819000
Rowan's Ravine Prov. Park	166	B3	50.995600 -105.179700
Saint Victor Prov. Park	166	A4	49.395300 -105.873200
Saskatchewan Landing Prov. Park	165	F3	50.664600 -107.997000
Steele Narrows Prov. Park	159	E3	54.025900 -109.318400
The Battlefords Prov. Park	165	E1	53.132500 -108.381300
Touchwood Hills Prov. Park	166	B2	51.306400 -104.014100
Wildcat Hill Prov. Park	166	C1	53.273946 -102.492828
Wood Mtn. Post Prov. Hist. Park	166	A4	49.320833 -106.379167

YUKON	PAGE	GRID	LATITUDE LONGITUDE
National Park & Rec. Areas			
Dawson Hist. Complex N.H.S.	155	D2	64.050000 -139.433330
Ivvavik Natl. Park	155	D1	69.519722 -139.525000
Kluane Natl. Park and Res.-North Vis. Ctr.	155	D3	60.991800 -138.520800
Kluane Natl. Park and Res.-South Vis. Ctr.	155	D3	60.752900 -137.510100
Vuntut Natl. Park	155	D1	68.306944 -140.047500
Provincial Park & Rec. Areas			
Herschel Island-Qikiqtaruk Territorial Park	155	D1	69.592100 -139.092400

Continued from page 11.

THE WHITE MOUNTAINS★★★

127 miles/204 kilometers   *Map 81*

From the all-season resort of **Conway**, drive N on Rte. 16 to **North Conway**★. Continue N on US-302/Rte. 16 through **Glen**, passing **Glen Ellis Falls**★ and **Pinkham Notch**★★ en route to Glen House. There, drive the **Auto Road** to the top of **Mount Washington**★★★ (or take a guided van tour). Head N on Rte. 16 to Gorham, near the Androscoggin River, then W on US-2 to Jefferson Highlands. Travel SW on Rte. 115 to Carroll, then S on US-3 to Twin Mountain. Go SW on US-3 to join I-93. Head S on I-93/Rte. 3, passing scenic **Franconia Notch**★★★ and **Lonesome Lake**★. Bear E on Rte. 3 where it separates from the interstate to visit **Flume Gorge**★★, a natural gorge 90ft deep. Rejoin I-93S to the intersection with Rte. 112. Head E on Rte. 112 through **Lincoln** on the **Kancamagus Highway**★★★ until it joins Rte. 16 back to Conway.

🚗 SOUTHEAST DRIVING TOURS

BLUE RIDGE PARKWAY★★

574 miles/924 kilometers   *Maps 102, 112, 111, 190, 121*

♿ *Note: Sections of Skyline Drive and the Blue Ridge Parkway may be closed in winter due to weather conditions. For updated Blue Ridge Parkway road closures, check www.nps.gov/blri/planyourvisit/roadclosures.htm or call 828-298-0398.*

From **Front Royal**, take US-340 S to begin **Skyline Drive**★★, the best-known feature of **Shenandoah NP**★★. The drive follows former Indian trails along the **Blue Ridge Parkway**★★. **Marys Rock Tunnel to Rockfish Gap Entrance Station**★★ passes the oldest rock in the park and **Big Meadows**★. The Drive ends at **Rockfish Gap** at I-64, but continue S on the **Blue Ridge Parkway**★★. From Terrapin Hill Overlook, detour 16mi W on Rte. 130 to see **Natural Bridge**★★. Enter NC at **Cumberland Knob**, then pass **Blowing Rock**★, **Grandfather Mountain**★★ and **Linville Falls**★★. Detour 4.8mi to **Mount Mitchell SP**★ to drive to the top of the tallest mountain (6,684ft) E of the Mississippi. At mile 382, the **Folk Art Center** stocks high-quality regional crafts. Popular **Biltmore Estate**★★ in **Asheville**★ (North Exit of US-25, then 4mi N) includes formal **gardens**★★. The stretch from **French Broad River to Cherokee** courses 17 tunnels within two national forests. **Looking Glass Rock**★★ is breathtaking. The Parkway ends at **Cherokee**, gateway to **Great Smoky Mountains NP**★★★.

Everglades National Park

©Tomasz Szymanski/iStockphoto.com

CENTRAL KENTUCKY★★

379 miles/610 kilometers   *Maps 230, 100, 214, 227, 110*

From **Louisville**★★, home of the **Kentucky Derby**★★★, take I-64 E to **Frankfort**★★, the state capital. Continue E to **Lexington**★★, heart of **Bluegrass Country**★★ with its rolling meadows and white-fenced horse farms. Stop at the **Kentucky Horse Park**★★★ (4089 Iron Works Pkwy.) for the twice-daily **Parade of Breeds**. Then head S on I-75 through Richmond to the craft center/college town of **Berea**★. Return to Lexington and from US-60 follow the Blue Grass Parkway SW to Exit 25. There, US-150 W leads to Bardstown, site of **My Old Kentucky Home SP**★★, immortalized by **Stephen Foster** in what is now the state song. Drive S from Bardstown on US-31E past **Abraham Lincoln Birthplace NHS**★. Turn right onto Rte. 70 to Cave City; then take US-31W to Park City, gateway to **Mammoth Cave NP**★★★, which features the world's longest cave system. Return to Louisville via I-65 to end the tour.

SOUTHERN EVERGLADES★★★

78 miles/126 kilometers   *Map 143*

From **Miami**★★★, travel W to Florida's Turnpike and S to Florida City. Turn right on Rte. 1, S to Palm Drive. Follow Rte. 9336 to 192nd Ave. Continue to 376th Street SW and turn right to follow the road to the **Everglades NP**★★★ entrance. Stop at the **Ernest F. Coe VC** for park information before heading back along Rte. 9336 to the **Royal Palm VC**. Choose from the half-mile **Anhinga Trail**★★ or the **Gumbo Limbo Trail**★ for a glimpse at local flora and fauna. Returning to Rte. 9336, continue to the turn-off for **Pa-hay-okee Overlook**★★,with a sweeping **view**★★ of the saw grass prairie. To the S 18mi, visit the mangrove swam at **West Lake Trail**★. Continue on to **Mrazke Pond** at dusk to watch the pond fill with herons, egrets, ibis, roseate spoonbills and other water birds. The road ends at **Flamingo**,

where a variety of **cruises**★★ offer tours of the backcountry canals and open waters of Florida Bay.

FLORIDA KEYS★★

168 miles/270 kilometers   *Maps 143, 142*

*Note: Green **mile-marker** (MM) posts, sometimes difficult to see, line US-1 (Overseas Hwy.), showing distances from Key West (MM 0). Much of the route is two-lane, and traffic can be heavy from December to April and on weekends. Allow 3hrs for the drive. Crossing 43 bridges and causeways (only one over land), the highway offers fine views of the Atlantic Ocean (E) and Florida Bay (W).* Drive S from **Miami**★★★ on US-1. Near **Key Largo**★, **John Pennekamp Coral Reef SP**★★ harbors tropical fish, coral and fine snorkeling waters. To the SW, **Islamorada** is known for **charter fishing**. At **Marathon** (MM 50), explore 63 acres of tropical forest at **Tropical Crane Point Hammock**★. S of **Seven-Mile Bridge**★, **Bahia Honda SP** (MM 36.8) is considered the best **beach**★★ in the Keys. Pass **National Key Deer Refuge**★ (MM 30.5), haven to the 2ft-tall deer unique to the lower Keys. End at **Key West**★★★ to join the **sunset**★★ gathering at **Mallory Square Dock**.

THE OZARKS★

343 miles/552 kilometers   *Maps 227, 117, 219, 107, 106*

From the state capital of **Little Rock**, take I-30 SW to Exit 111, then US-70 W to Hot Springs. Drive N on Rte. 7/ Central Ave. to **Hot Springs NP**★★ to enjoy the therapeutic waters. Travel N on Rte. 7 across the Arkansas River to Russellville. Continue on **Scenic Highway 7**★ N through **Ozark National Forest** and across the **Buffalo National River** to Harrison. Take US-62/65 NW to Bear Creek Springs, continuing W on US-62 through **Eureka Springs**★, with its **historic district**. Return E on US-62 to the junction of Rte. 21 at Berryville. Travel N on Rte. 21 to Blue Eye, taking Rte. 86 E to US-65, which leads

N to the entertainment hub of **Branson**, Missouri, to end the tour.

RIVER ROAD PLANTATIONS★★

200 miles/323 kilometers   *Maps 239, 134, 194*
From **New Orleans**★★★, take US-90 W to Rte. 48 along the Mississippi River to Destrehan. At no. 13034, **Destrehan**★★ is considered the oldest plantation house in the lower Mississippi Valley. Continue NW on Rte. 48 to US-61 to Laplace to connect to Rte. 44. Head N past **San Francisco Plantation**★, built in 1856. At Burnside, take Rte. 75 N to St. Gabriel. En route, watch for **Houmas House**★ (40136 Hwy. 942). Take Rte. 30 to **Baton Rouge**★, the state capital. Cross the Mississippi River bridge (I-10) and take Rte. 1 S along the **West Bank** to White Castle, site of **Nottoway**★, the largest plantation home in the South. Continue to Donaldsonville, then turn onto Rte. 18. Travel E to Gretna, passing **Oak Alley**★ (no. 3645) and **Laura Plantation**★★ (no. 2247) along the way. From Gretna, take US-90 to New Orleans, where the tour ends.

🚗 CANADA DRIVING TOURS

GASPÉSIE, QUÉBEC★★★

933 kilometers/578 miles   *Maps 178, 179*
Leave **Sainte-Flavie** via Rte. 132 NE, stopping to visit **Reford Gardens**★★ en route to **Matane**. After **Cap-Chat**, take Rte. 299 S to **Gaspésie Park**★ for expansive **views**★★. Back on Rte. 132, follow the **Scenic Route from La Martre to Rivière-au-Renard**★★. Continue to **Cap-des-Rosiers**, entrance to majestic **Forillon NP**★★. Follow Rte. 132 along the coast through **Gaspé**★, the administrative center of the peninsula, to **Percé**★★★, a coastal village known for **Percé Rock**★★, a mammoth offshore rock wall. Drive SW on Rt. 132 through **Paspébiac** to **Carleton**, which offers a **panorama**★★ from the summit of **Mont Saint-Joseph**. Farther SW, detour 6km/4mi S to see an array of fossils at **Parc National de Miguasha**★. Back on Rte. 132, travel W to Matapédia, then follow Rte. 132 N, passing **Causapscal**—a departure point for salmon fishing expeditions— to end the tour at Sainte-Flavie.

NORTH SHORE LAKE SUPERIOR★★

275 kilometers/171 miles   *Map 169*
From the port city of **Thunder Bay**★★—and nearby **Fort William Historical Park**★★—drive the Trans-Canada Hwy. (Rte. 11/17) E to Rte. 587. Detour to **Sleeping Giant PP**★, which offers fine **views**★ of the lake. Back along the Trans-Canada Hwy., **Amethyst Mine** (take E. Loon Rd.) is a rock hound's delight (fee). Far-

ther NE, located 12km/8mi off the highway, **Ouimet Canyon**★★ is a startling environment for the area. Just after the highway's Red Rock turnoff, watch for **Red Rock Cuesta**, a natural formation 210m/690ft high. Cross the Nipigon River and continue along **Nipigon Bay**★★, enjoying **views**★★ of the rocky, conifer-covered islands. The **view**★★ of Kama Bay through Kama Rock Cut is striking. Continue to Schreiber to end the tour.

NOVA SCOTIA'S CABOT TRAIL★★

338 kilometers/210 miles   *Map 181*
From **Baddeck**★, follow Hwy. 105 S to the junction with Rte. 19 to **North East Margaree** in salmon-fishing country. Take this road NW to Margaree Harbour, then N to **Chéticamp**, an enclave of Acadian culture. Heading inland, the route enters **Cape Breton Highlands NP**★★, combining seashore and mountains. At Cape North, detour N around Aspy Bay to **Bay St. Lawrence**★★. Then head W to tiny **Capstick** for shoreline **views**★. Return S to Cape North, then drive E to South Harbour. Take White Pointe Rd. along the coast, traveling S through the fishing villages of **New Haven** and **Neils Harbour**★. Rejoin Cabot Trail S, passing the resort area of **The Ingonishs**. Take the right fork after Indian Brook to reach St. Ann's, home of **Gaelic College**★, specializing in bagpipe and Highland dance classes. Rejoin Hwy. 105 to return to Baddeck.

CANADIAN ROCKIES★★★

467 kilometers/290 miles   *Map 164*
Leave **Banff**★★ by Hwy. 1, traveling W. After 5.5km/3.5mi, take **Bow Valley Parkway**★ (Hwy. 1A) NW within **Banff NP**★★★. At **Lake Louise Village**, detour W to find **Lake Louise**★★★. Back on Hwy. 1, head N to the junction of Hwy. 93, turn W and follow Hwy. 1 past **Kicking Horse Pass** into **Yoho NP**★★. Continue through **Field**, and turn right onto the road N to **Emerald Lake**★★★. Return to the junction of Rte. 93 and Hwy. 1, heading N on Rte. 93 along the **Icefields Parkway**★★★. Pass **Crowfoot Glacier**★★ and **Bow Lake**★★ on the left. **Peyto Lake**★★★ is reached by spur road. After **Parker Ridge**★★, massive **Athabasca Glacier**★★★ looms on the left. Continue to **Jasper**★ and **Jasper NP**★★★. From Jasper, turn left onto Hwy. 16 and head into **Mount Robson PP**★★, home to **Mount Robson**★★★ (3,954m/12,972ft.). End the tour at Tête Jaune Cache.

VANCOUVER ISLAND★★★

337 kilometers/209 miles   *Maps 282, 163, 162*
To enjoy a scenic drive that begins 11mi N of **Victoria**★★★, take Douglas St. N from Victoria to the Trans-Canada Highway (Hwy. 1) and follow **Malahat**

Tofino Harbour, British Columbia   ©Eric P. Lucas/Michelin

Drive★ (between Goldstream PP and Mill Bay Rd.) for 12mi. Continue N on Hwy. 1 past Duncan, **Chemainus**— known for its murals—and Nanaimo. From there take Hwy. 19A, then Hwy. 19 NW to Parksville. Take winding Rte. 4 W (Pacific Rim Hwy.) passing **Englishman River Falls PP**★ and **Cameron Lake**. Just beyond the lake, **Cathedral Grove**★★ holds 800-year-old Douglas firs. The road descends to **Port Alberni**★, departure point for cruises on Barkley Sound, and follows Sproat Lake before climbing Klitsa Mountain. The route leads to the Pacific along the Kennedy River. At the coast, turn left and drive SE to Ucluelet. Then head N to enter **Pacific Rim NPR**★★★. Continue to the road's end at **Tofino**★★ to end the tour.

YUKON CIRCUIT★★

1,485 kilometers/921 miles   *Map 155*
🅐 *Note: Rte. 9 and Rte. 5 are unpaved in places; proceed with caution. Both roads are closed in winter.*
From **Whitehorse**★, capital of Yukon Territory, drive N on the **Klondike Hwy.** (Rte. 2), crossing the Yukon River at **Carmacks**. After 196km/122mi, small islands divide the river into fast-flowing channels at **Five Finger Rapids**★. From Stewart Crossing, continue NW on Rte. 2 to **Dawson City**★★, a historic frontier town. Ferry across the river and drive the **Top of the World Hwy.** ★★ (Rte. 9), with extensive **views**★★★, to the Alaska border. Rte. 9 joins Rte. 5, passing tiny **Chicken**, Alaska. At **Tetlin Junction**, head SE on Rte. 2, paralleling **Tetlin NWR**. Enter Canada and follow the **Alaska Highway**★★ (Rte. 1) SE along **Kluane Lake**★★ to **Haines Junction**, gateway to **Kluane NPR**★★, home of **Mount Logan**, Canada's highest peak (5,959m/19,550ft). Continue E to Rte. 2 to return to Whitehorse.

Notes

_____

_____

_____

_____

_____

_____

_____

_____

_____

_____

_____

_____

_____

_____

_____

_____

_____

_____

_____

MICHELIN NORTH AMERICA, INC.
Michelin Travel & Lifestyle North America
One Parkway South
Greenville, SC 29615 U.S.A.

www.michelintravel.com
Find us on Facebook.com/michelinguides

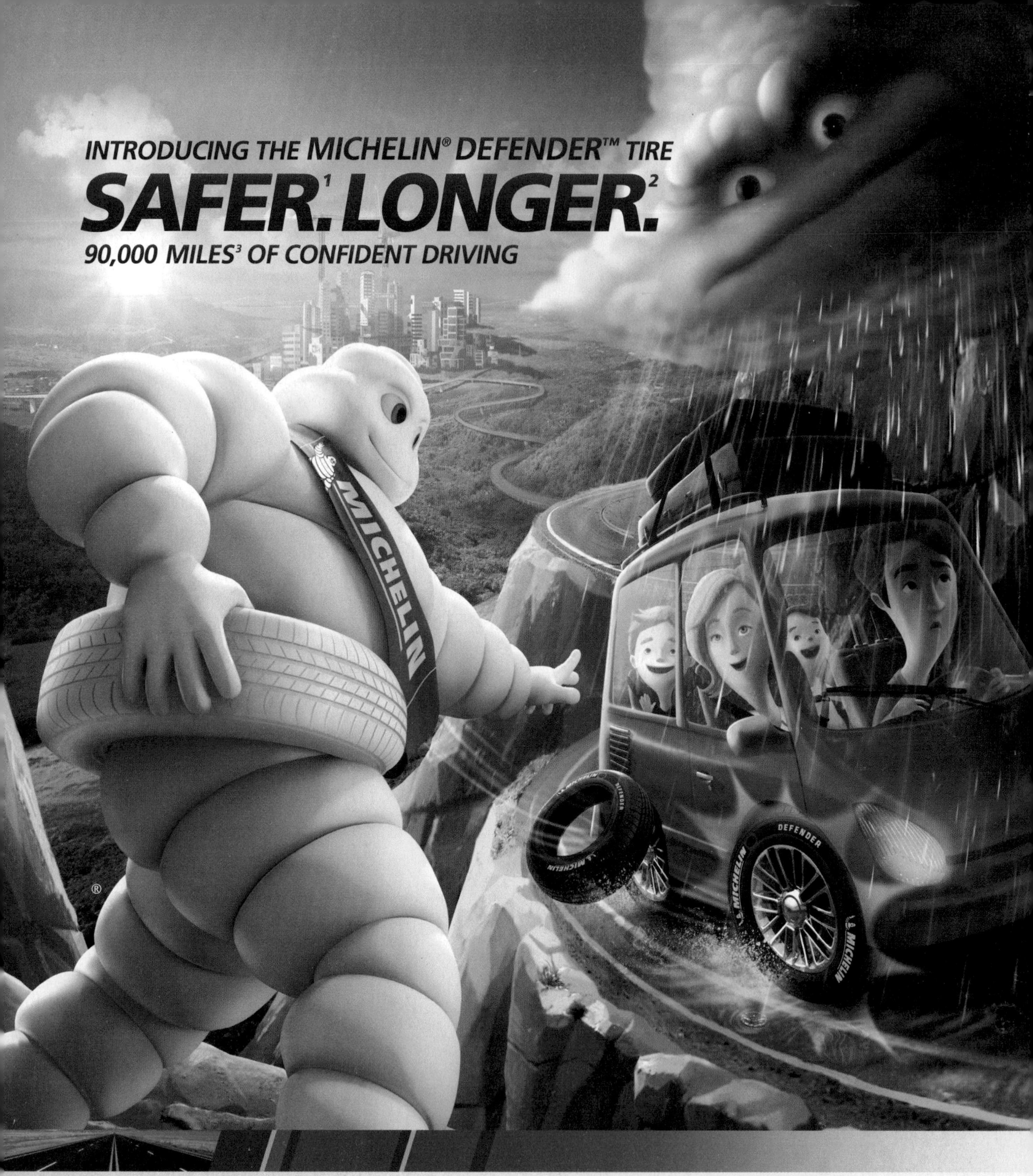